PROTECTION OFFICER TRAINING MANUAL

PROTECTION OFFICER TRAINING MANUAL

Sixth Edition

International Foundation for Protection Officers

Bellingham Business Park, #200, 4200 Meridian, Bellingham, WA 98226

Butterworth-Heinemann

Boston   Oxford   Johannesburg   Melbourne   New Delhi   Singapore

Butterworth–Heinemann is an imprint of Elsevier Science.

 Recognizing the importance of preserving what has been written, Elsevier Science prints its books on acid-free paper whenever possible.

Library of Congress Cataloging-in-Publication Data

Protection officer training manual / International Foundation for Protection
    Officers. — 6th ed.
        p.   cm.
    Includes bibliographical references and index.
    ISBN 0-7506-9934-5 (alk. paper)
    1. Police, Private—Training of—United States—Handbooks, manuals, etc.
2. Private security services—United States—Handbooks, manuals, etc.
I. International Foundation for Protection Officers.
HV8291.U6P76   1997
363.28'9'0683—dc21   97-18306
                                                                     CIP

British Library Cataloguing-in-Publication Data

A catalogue for this book is available from the British Library.

The publisher offers special discounts on bulk orders of this book.
For information, please contact:
Manager of Special Sales
Elsevier Science
200 Wheeler Road, 6th Floor
Burlington, MA 01803
Tel: 781-313-4700
Fax: 781-313-4882

For information on all Butterworth–Heinemann publications available, contact our World Wide Web homepage at: http://www.bh.com.

10 9 8 7

Printed in the United States of America

CONTENTS

Unit 4

Unit 5

Unit 6

Unit 9

Florence J. Slomp, MSc
Debbie Y. Minion, BA

Unit 10

Barry D. Panrucker, EMT (A)
Reviewed by Robert Wilson

Unit 11

Charles T. Thibodeau, M.Ed, CPP, CSS
Christopher A. Hertig, CPP, CPO

Unit 12

Introduction

Writers' Gallery
Code of Ethics
Content Summary Review
Learning Skills – Study Habits

PROTECTION OFFICER TRAINING MANUAL

INTRODUCTION

By Ronald R. Minion, CPP, CPO
Sandi J. Davies

Purpose: To provide a current, useful, consolidated Security Officer Training Manual which provides "need-to-know" information for Protection Officers throughout the Security Industry. This manual serves as the course text for the Certified Protection Officer (CPO) Program.

General Information

The previous five editions of the Protection Officer Training Manual have had a positive impact on the Security Industry in the United States and Canada. With each subsequent edition, new writers have contributed a wealth of information which has enabled readers to keep pace with an ever changing security industry.

Since edition number one, published in 1988, readers have generously provided us with constructive feed-back, which has been extremely helpful in the development of each ensuing edition.

A special thanks is extended to the many students enrolled in security programs at well known private and public post secondary education institutions. These students have studied the manual during their courses of study. They have voiced their opinions. They did not always say what we wanted to hear, but their comments/opinions have been heard. It is this kind of feed-back that has been helpful to us in our continuing efforts to keep this manual current and meaningful.

Certified Protection Officer (CPO) program graduates, from professional inhouse and contract security organizations throughout North America, have also extended to us their opinions about the Protection Officer Training Manual, and how it can be improved and expanded. They spoke, we listened, we acted.

Ongoing dialogue with security managers, supervisors, consultants, authors, educators and protection officers is a fundamental process in the sustainment of a training manual which will serve the future learning needs of line security officers and supervisors in all security work environments.

The authors, profiled in the writers' gallery of the Protection Officer Training Manual, are security professionals who have made outstanding contributions to the development of this manual. They are recognized by their colleagues and the security community for their unselfish commitment to security service professionalism. They have disseminated information which is vital to each protection officer, who is responsible to enhance life safety and asset security within public and private facilities.

Expanded Protection Roles

In the past decade, a kind of Private Justice has emerged to facilitate Private/Public Corporate Protection. For a number of reasons, not the least of which is a burdensome public justice system and declining police availability to protect business and industry, management has undertaken to develop and maintain a "self protection" posture.

Corporations that once required limited security measures have now placed personnel and asset protection as organizational priorities to sustain a safe and productive work environment.

An integral part of this overall protection process is the professional security manager and supervisor, complemented with a security staff capable of attending to ongoing protection needs. While public law enforcement and private protection roles have many similarities, asset protection is becoming a paramount concern for every public organization.

Who will assume the responsibility to protect private and government organizations?

We suggest that a new, effective, enlightened protection officer is essential to assist management with the responsibilities of personnel, asset and information security. Public law enforcement organizations lack the human and financial resources required to enhance organizational safety and security.

Police organizations will continue to maintain a reactive posture, while protection groups must undertake to develop even more effective integrated security systems. There must be better communication and role appreciation developed among public police and private security organizations. This is a difficult task that requires a creative approach initiated by security and police administrators.

There should be cooperation, resulting from mutual understanding and a "joint venture" approach to crime prevention. When we consider that there are more than two, and soon to be three, private security employees to every one civil law enforcement officer, there have to be cost-effective benefits available to governments and free enterprise who recognize the important role of private security in our modern society.

INTERNATIONAL FOUNDATION FOR PROTECTION OFFICERS

UNITED STATES
#200, 4200 Meridian
Bellingham, WA 98226
Telephone: (360) 733-1571
Fax: (360) 671-4329

CANADA
#1015, 105-150 Crowfoot Cres. N.W.
Calgary, AB T3G 3T2
Telephone: (403) 932-7785
Fax: (403) 932-9521

http://www.ifpo.com

Manual Format

The contents of this manual are sometimes quite basic. However, every security Supervisor and Manager should fully understand all of the information contained so as to provide better leadership and interpretation of officer responsibilities.

This edition is divided into twelve (12) units. The material contained in each unit is arranged so as to provide the reader with a smooth flow of related security information. The final part of the manual is a Miscellaneous Section containing a variety of material that is either too short to constitute a complete chapter, or is not relevant to any other part of the manual.

At the conclusion of each chapter there are 10 questions of the fill-in-the-word, multiple choice, and true/false variety. Before the reader proceeds to the next chapter, it is vitally important to be able to answer each question correctly.

Certified Protection Officer (CPO) Program

The Protection Officer Training Manual is the course text for the Certified Protection Officer (CPO) program.

The CPO designation is a professional accreditation which can be earned by completing a self-pacing course based on this manual.

Briefly, a candidate must complete the following stages of progression to earn the CPO designation:
- Submit application for enrollment
- Successfully complete a midterm examination
- Successfully complete a supervised final examination (Proctor may be located within the candidate's organization or community)

(Both examinations are based on the contents of this manual).

Certified Protection Officer (CPO) Final Challenge Program

The CPO Final Challenge concept reduces the time of study required, in that the midterm examination process has been eliminated. The only requirement in this program is to write the CPO final examination. A suitable proctor must be identified to supervise this portion of the program.

The CPO program is an internationally recognized certification for Protection Officers.

Contact the International Foundation for Protection Officers (IFPO) for more information regarding the Certified Protection Officer and/or other programs.

Conclusion

The term Protection Officer frequently appears in this manual. What is a Protection Officer? A Protection Officer is the individual who this manual is intended to serve, such as:
- A non-police person employed in private or public security.
- An individual committed to fulfilling a functional role in the modern security community.
- An individual who provides security from a fixed location or in the capacity of a patrol officer.

Indeed, the manual is a useful tool for Security Supervisors and Managers, but the primary beneficiary is the Protection Officer.

The editors of the Protection Officer Training Manual are honored to have worked with Christopher A. Hertig, CPP, CPO since the planning stages of the first edition. Chris is a talented, dedicated security professional. He has worked tirelessly in supporting, promoting, and contributing to the International Foundation for Protection Officers, the Certified Protection Officer, and Certified Security Supervisor Programs.

"Chris, we could not have done it without you!"

**RONALD R. MINION
CPP CPO**

Ronald R. Minion, CPP, CPO

Founding Director, International Foundation for Protection Officers. Mr. Minion is a former member of the Royal Canadian Mounted Police, and Founder of one of Canada's largest Security Service Companies. He is a graduate of Mount Royal College and Columbia Pacific University, and is a long time member of the American Society for Industrial Security (ASIS). He is a past ASIS Chapter Chairman and Regional Vice President, and was named International Regional Vice President of the Year. He was the recipient of the ASIS President's Certificate of Merit, and was the first examined Certified Protection Professional (CPP) in Canada. Ron is best known for his continuing efforts to develop professional growth opportunities for Private and Public Security Personnel.

Sandi J. Davies

Executive Director, International Foundation for Protection Officers. Ms. Davies began her career in contract security in 1980, with a primary focus on personnel administration. She became deeply involved in training, and was instrumental in developing Security Officer training programs for a major national guard company. Her interest in security training grew, and in 1988 she joined the newly founded IFPO as an administrative assistant. In 1991 she was named executive director of the IFPO, and has been a driving force in Foundation program development and administration. Sandi is a long-time member of the American Society for Industrial Security (ASIS), having served in various executive positions at the chapter level.

SANDI J. DAVIES

WRITERS' GALLERY

PATRICK C. (PAT) BISHOP

Patrick C. (Pat) Bishop
Pat holds the position of Director of Operations, Metropol Base-Fort Security Group. In his present position he manages 500 contract security officers and is instrumental in developing operational procedures and policies. Prior to his present employment, he served with the Canadian Forces as a Military Policeman for a term of 13 years. Pat has been instrumental in the development of Edmonton/Northern Alberta Chapter 156 of the American Society for Industrial Security. He has served two years as Chapter Vice-Chairman and was the Chapter Chairman (1986).

Dr. Norman R. Bottom Jr. CPP, CST, CPO
Norman is presently Loss Control Consultant in which capacity he is frequently called upon to testify as an expert witness in security negligence suits. He has a wide and diversified background in law enforcement, intelligence and loss control. He is the author of three books: "Security and Loss Control" (McMillan), "Industrial Espionage" (Butterworth's), and "Security/Loss Control Negligence" (Hanrow Press). He is the editor of the Journal of Security Administration. Dr. Bottom was the first chairman of the International Foundation for Protection Officers and is a permanent writer for Protection Officer Magazine.

DR. NORMAN R. BOTTOM Jr. CPP, CST, CPO

R. LORNE BRENNAN CPO

R. Lorne Brennan CPO
Lorne is a Health Care Security Supervisor for Peter Lougheed Hospital in Calgary. He is actively involved with such programs as Fire Suppression and Protection Training, and Environmental Awareness for Hospital Administration. He has instructed at Alberta Vocational Centre in its Security Officer's Training Course. Lorne was one of the first Certified Protection Officers to earn the designation CPO. He has also been the editor of the Foothills Hospital Security Newsletter, "ROLECALL", and is actively involved with Health Care Security Awareness programs for hospital employees.

John H. Christman CPP
John is the Vice-President and Director of Security for Macy's California. He has worked for 25 years in security, law enforcement and intelligence areas. He is a graduate of Muhlenberg College and the Los Angeles County Sheriff's Academy. Mr. Christman serves on numerous security advisor's boards and is the past Chairman of the California Retailers Association Security Committee. He is a member of the Board of Directors of the NRCA Security Group and a former member of the Marin County Criminal Justice Commission. John is a noted authority on the history of Private Security. He is a Certified Protection Professional.

JOHN H. CHRISTMAN CPP

DAVID J. DeLONG CPP

David J. Delong CPP

Dave is the Security Supervisor at Fording Coal in Elkford, British Columbia. His responsibilities include the development and maintenance of security policies, procedures and programs for the mining facility. Prior to assuming that position, he was the Head of Security & Safety at Mount Royal College in Calgary. Dave is a graduate of Memorial University in St. John's, Newfoundland and is currently enrolled in Ohio University, working toward his degree in Security & Safety Technology. Dave is a permanent writer for Protection Officer Magazine and is a Certified Protection Professional.

Thomas A. Dobbie CPO

Tom is presently the Security Co-ordinator for Syncrude Canada Ltd. at Fort McMurray, Alberta. He is responsible for the implementation and direction of Security procedures and is responsible for the activities of a large force of In-House and Contract Security personnel. Prior to joining Syncrude in July of 1980, he served with the Royal Canadian Mounted Police for 24 years working in Manitoba, Northwest Territories and Alberta. Prior to retiring from the Force, he was in charge of Fort McMurray Detachment holding the rank of Staff-Sergeant. Mr. Dobbie is a Certified Protection Officer.

THOMAS A. DOBBIE CPO

MARTIN A. FAWCETT CPO

Martin A. Fawcett CPO

Martin is the Training Co-ordinator for Metropol Base-Fort Security Group responsible for developing and maintaining effective security training programs on a national basis. He is instrumental in lesson plan development and co-ordinates classroom and on-the-job training projects. Martin completed the Calgary Police service training course prior to joining the Port Moody Police Department where he served in a number of general law enforcement capacities. He also attended the Justice Institute of British Columbia prior to taking his position with Metropol. He is a Certified Protection Officer.

Dr. Robert C. Harris

Bob is currently a faculty member of the Criminology Department of Mount Royal College. He maintains a private practice in clinical psychology, specializing in stress-related therapy. Dr. Harris completed his graduate work at the Universities of Toronto and McGill, and was an Associate Professor to the Department of Psychiatry at both the University of Toronto and the University of Calgary. Dr. Harris has been a popular speaker at Law Enforcement, Correctional & Security oriented seminars. He is a recognized authority in the social/psychological aspects of criminology.

DR. ROBERT C. HARRIS

PAUL J. HAWTHORN

Paul J. Hawthorn

Paul received his training/experience with explosives and ordinance from the United States Army, as well as with local law enforcement agencies. He presents his program called "B.A.N.G." (Bombs and Nasty Gadgets) to students and managers in the Public Safety fields. The program centers on the identification of hazardous devices and bomb/threat search and procedures. He is a Pennsylvania State Certified Lethal Weapons instructor and serves as an Associate Lecturer at Harrisburg Area Community College. He holds A.A. degrees in Police Administration, Education and Liberal Studies. Paul is a regular writer for Protection Officer Magazine.

Christopher A. Hertig, CPP, CPO
Chris is a member of the Behavioral Sciences Department at York College of Pennsylvania, where he teaches Security, Criminal Investigation, and Ethics courses. He holds degrees from Indiana University of Pennsylvania (M.A., Criminology), Bloomsburg University of Pennsylvania (B.A., Sociology), and Harrisburg Area Community College (AA, Commercial Security). He is both a Certified Protection Professional, and a Certified Protection Officer. Mr. Hertig also holds instructor credentials in various Defensive Tactics related areas, and is a Master Level Instructor in Nonviolent Crisis Intervention. Mr. Hertig has been published widely on such topics as Report Writing, Officer Survival, Civil Liability, and various issues relating to the professionalism of Protection Officers.

CHRISTOPHER A. HERTIG CPP CPO

ROONEY H. HODGINS

Rooney Hodgins
Rooney is a Policy Development Officer for the National Museums of Canada (NMC) Protective Services. He joined N.M.C. Protection/Security division in 1975, beginning as a mobile patrol officer. He has since worked as a Security Investigator in addition to his work in policy development. Mr. Hodgins is actively engaged as a Protection Officer instructor, teaching general security subjects, first aid and defensive driving. He is a sessional instructor in the basic security program at Algonquin College, Ottawa, Canada, and has earned a diploma in Law and Security from Algonquin.

Dr. Kenneth C. Hollington
Ken is the Chairman of the Criminology Department at Mount Royal College in Calgary, Alberta, Canada. He served with the Royal Canadian Mounted Police for 15 years, where he worked in various general law enforcement roles, and spent the last five years of his service in the Management Training Unit, prior to assuming his present position. He earned his Master's degree at Carlton University, and his Doctorate in Education Administration at Brigham Young University. Ken has developed numerous training courses for members of the justice administration system, and works extensively with the Solicitor General of Alberta (Corrections).

DR. KENNETH C. HOLLINGTON

ARTHUR A. HOLM CPO

Arthur A. Holm, CPO
Art is a Security Supervisor at Calgary Municipal Airport and a Sessional Instructor at the International Foundation for Protection Officers. He is responsible for lecturing in areas of Traffic and Crowd Control, as well as organizing job orientation exercises. Prior to assuming his role in Airport Security, he was a Field Superintendent for a large industrial company, and completed a number of advanced supervisory courses. He has been the Commanding Officer at the First Provost Cadet Corps in Canada. Prior to assuming the post of Commanding Officer, he was the Corps Training Officer. Art is a Certified Protection Officer.

MICHAEL KRIKORIAN CPP

Michael Krikorian CPP

Mike is currently the President of Diversified Protection Resources, Inc., a management consulting firm providing consultative services in Safety, Security and Executive Protection. Prior to assuming his present position, he was Corporate Manager - Safety, Occupational Health and Security for Brunswick Corporation, a post he held for 15 years. Mike was among the first 50 to become Certified Safety Professionals and is the National Past President of the American Society of Safety Engineers. He is the author of two books and has written numerous articles for a variety of publications. He is a Certified Protection Professional.

Debbie Y. Minion B.A.

Debbie is employed with Ocean Sport of Edmonton where she specializes in Scuba Diving, Windsurfing and Water Skiing. She is a recent graduate of the University of Alberta where she earned her Bachelor's degree in Physical Education, majoring in Sports Medicine. While attending university, she was employed as a Fitness Consultant for the University Fitness Testing Unit and became deeply involved in fitness testing of faculty members, students and the general public. She was a member of the well-known University Pandas Field Hockey team and is active in cycling and backpacking.

DEBBIE Y. MINION B.A.

JOAN MULDER M.A.

Joan Mulder M.A.

Joan is currently the Coordinator of Program Development at Alberta Vocational Centre (AVC). This post-secondary institute currently enrolls approximately 13,000 continuing-education students, and 7,500 full-time adult students. One of Joan's most recent achievements was the development of an entry level Security Officer training course. Prior to taking on her current responsibilities, she coordinated the establishment of AVC's Learning Assistance Centre. She is a graduate of the University of Calgary, specializing in adult reading and writing skills and is currently enrolled in a Ph.D. program in Education Management.

Charles F. Nash

Chuck is employed with Syncrude Canada Ltd. with Process Safety & Standards Fire Protection Unit. Prior to that position, he served for six years with the Syncrude In-House Fire Department. Chuck began his security career with Metropolitan Security Services Ltd. and was a Shift Commander at Thompson, Manitoba. He later worked for three years with Base-Fort Security Services Ltd. and was an inspector in charge of northern operations. Prior to assuming that position, he was employed with the Calgary Police Service. Chuck is an active member of the National Fire Prevention Association.

CHARLES F. NASH

DENIS A. O'SULLIVAN CPP, CPO

Denis A. O'Sullivan CPP

Denis, formerly a Special Branch Detective with the Irish Police, is currently a Corporate Security Advisor with the City of Edmonton, Risk Management and Security Branch. He has authored several published articles on security, and currently instructs two Security Management courses at the University of Alberta. He also instructs a Security course at Grant McEwan College. Denis has been actively involved in the development of the American Society for Industrial Security (ASIS) in Canada. He is a past A.S.I.S. Chapter Chairman, Regional Vice-President, and member of the Board of Directors 1988/89.

**BARRY D.
PANRUCKER EMT(A)**

Barry D. Panrucker EMT (A)
Barry is the President of Emergency Training Services (ETS), a firm that provides consulting to the Petro-Chemical and other types of industrial corporations. He specializes in Occupational Health and Safety First-Aid, Cardiopulmonary Resuscitation (CPR), Hydrogen Sulfide Alert, and Fire Suppression Training. Barry is a sessional instructor at the Protection Officer Training Academy, and a permanent writer for Protection Officer Magazine. Prior to establishing his own firm, he was an Emergency Response Coordinator with Gulf Canada Products Ltd. He is a registered Emergency Medical Technician EMT (A).

**CHARLES T.
THIBODEAU M.ED CPP CSS**

Charles. T. Thibodeau, M.Ed., CPP, CSS
Chuck is a prominent Minnesota Consultant and College Instructor. He is the owner and senior consultant of Q/A Systems and Consultants in Minneapolis, Minnesota. He is currently the lead instructor and coordinator of the Security Management AAS Degree program at Pine Technical College. Chuck has a Masters of Education Degree from the University of Minnesota, an AAS Degree in Electronic Technology. He is also a Certified Protection Professional and a Certified Security Supervisor. Mr. Thibodeau is a Member of the Board of Directors for the International Foundation for Protection Officers.

David L. Ray LL.B
Dave is currently the Security Manager for Shell Canada, responsible for Corporate Security throughout Canada. He is a former member of the Royal Canadian Mounted Police, where he served for 14 years. The last seven years of his service was with the Commercial Crime Section. He is a graduate of York University where he earned his Bachelor's degree. He went on to Osgoode Hall Law School, where he gained his degree in Law, and was admitted to the British Columbia Bar in 1982. He is the President of the Canadian Society for Industrial Security, and has made significant contributions to private and corporate security.

**DAVID L.
RAY LL.B.**

**CHARLES A.
SENNEWALD CPP**

Charles A. Sennewald, CPP
Chuck is the President of Sennewald and Associates, Management Consultants. He has a very interesting employment history including Military Police Service in Korea, Los Angeles Sheriff's Vice Squad, and Chief of Campus Police at Clairmont College. He became internationally recognized as an innovator of Participative Security Management, and pace-setting security awareness programs during his tenure as Security Director for Broadway Stores. He is the author of two books, and is the founder and first President of the International Association of Professional Consultants. Chuck is a Certified Protection Professional.

FLORENCE (FLO) SLOMP M.Sc.

Florence (Flo) Slomp M.Sc.

Flo completed her Bachelor's degree in Physical Education and Biology at Calvin College in Grande Rapids, Michigan in 1982. She pursued her Master's degree in Science and Exercise Physiology at the University of Alberta and completed her degree in 1985. She has been active in fitness testing for Elite Athletes and is deeply involved in areas of fitness and health promotion. Flo is currently employed as an Isokinetic Specialist at the Workers Compensation Board Rehabilitation Centre in Edmonton, Alberta. During her educational experience at the University of Edmonton, she participated in numerous individual and campus team sports.

Professor George E. Strouse

Professor Strouse teaches computer programming, networking and telecommunications, management of information systems and other computer related courses at York College of Pennsylvania. He is the senior associate of Strouse and Associates, a data processing consulting firm, specializing in management analysis of information systems and the design and implementation of systems, databases, telecommunications and networks. Professor Strouse has worked with specialized computer systems using barcoding, voice input/output, text scanning, sonic sensing and other forms of source data automation. He has implemented computer related applications for the U.S. Government, hospitals, and large corporations.

PROFESSOR GEORGE E. STROUSE

WILFRED S. (BUD) THOMPSON

Wilfred S. (Bud) Thompson CPO

As of this writing, Bud said he joined the Royal Canadian Mounted Police exactly 40 years ago. He has spent the last 30 years in private security and is considered one of the industry's seniors in terms of knowledge and service. His first work in private security involved the founding of Western Investigation Bureau, a company that grew to become one of Alberta's largest Private Security firms. Bud was well known for his awareness of employee needs during his term as President of Western. He is also recognized for his expertise in the Alarm industry. Bud was the Chairman of Calgary/Southern Alberta Chapter of ASIS (1986).

Jeff B. Wilt CPP, CPO

Jeff is currently a Section Supervisor in Operations, Protective Services Division of the Salt River Project in Tempe, Arizona. Mr. Wilt was previously employed in Retail Security and worked as a Security Officer before being promoted into a Security Management position. Mr. Wilt's career now focuses on Industrial Security and he has served in numerous positions in both contract and proprietary organizations. He has an Associate of Applied Science in Administration of Justice and is now concentrating on earning his Bachelor's degree in Criminal Justice. Jeff is a Certified Protection Professional.

JEFF B. WILT CPP, CPO

**JOHNNY R. MAY
CPP CPO**

Johnny R. May, CPP, CPO
Johnny is currently employed by Henry Ford Community College (Dearborn, Michigan), where he serves as a security supervisor/crime prevention specialist with the college's campus safety department, and as the Program Coordinator for HFCC's Security and Private Investigations Program. He is also a licensed private investigator, and adjunct professor at the University of Detroit-Mercy, where he teaches graduate level Security Administration courses. Johnny has had articles published in various security publications. He is a graduate of the University of Detroit-Mercy, where he earned his B.S. in Criminal Justise, and his M.S. in Security Administration.

Christopher L. Vail
Chris is President of Law Enforcement Development, a firm specializing in training security and law enforcement personnel in such topics as, First Line Supervision, Testifying in Court, and Investigative Techniques. Mr. Vail began his career as a Military Policeman with the United States Marine Corp. His security experience includes being in charge of security for a high profile Congressional Committee. He has also served as Director of Security on a college campus. Mr. Vail has served as President of the Georgia Criminal Justice Educator's Association.

**CHRISTOPHER
L. VAIL**

FRANK ELLIOTT

Francis J. Elliott, CPP
Frank is the founder and president of the National Drug Institute, and National Security Protective Services, Inc. of Lowell, MA. His firms provide consultation on security and substance abuse related issues. He has developed an award winning substance abuse prevention program for private industry and has authored several articles on drugs in the workplace. Frank is a former Special Agent of the U.S. Department of Justice, Drug Enforcement Administration. He earned both a Bachelor and Masters degree in Criminal Justice Administration and Planning from Northeastern University. Frank has hosted his own radio talk show on substance abuse issues. He is a Certified Protection Professional.

George Barnett, CPO
George is Coordinator of Safety and Security at York Hospital, a community teaching hospital with over 4,300 employees. He has 14 years of experience in health care security and 3 years in contract security. A former member of the United States Marine Corps, George was the first Certified Protection Officer in York, Pennsylvania. George has also been through the Basic Level certification process of the International Association of Healthcare Safety and Security.

**GEORGE A. BARNETT
CPO**

ROBERT WILSON

Robert Wilson
Robert has a combined 17 years of experience in Emergency Services, Law Enforcement, and Fire Fighting. Robert graduated from the Criminal Justice program at Mount Royal College in Calgary, Alberta, Canada. He then went on to serve 8 years as a Patrol Officer with Alberta Highway Patrol. Following that, Robert became a member of the City of Calgary, Fire Department. He is also a Captain with the Cochrane Fire Department.

**THOMAS E. KOLL
CPP**

Thomas E. Koll, CPP

Tom is a safety and Security Specialist for Panduit Corp., an international electrical products manufacturer. He oversees hazardous material and fire safety training for a multifacility emergency response brigade. He takes every opportunity to research hazardous materials and safety practices and frequently lectures employee groups from within and outside of Panduit. He is an active member of the American Society for Industrial Security and several safety organizations. Tom is a 12-year veteran in safety and security and in addition to his ongoing research he takes an active role in various line officer safety training programs. He is a Certified Protection Professional (CPP).

**MICHAEL A. HANNIGAN
CPO, EMT**

Michael A. Hannigan, CPO, EMT

Mike is the Security Supervisor and Training Coordinator at St. Luke's Hospital in Newburgh, New York. Prior to assuming his present role in hospital security he was engaged in nuclear security at the Indian Point Nuclear Plant. Mr. Hannigan enjoys instructing in hospital loss control procedures as well as crisis intervention techniques. He also holds a part time position as a practising Emergency Medical Technician with the City of Newburgh Ambulance Service. Mike is a member of the International Association for Hospital Security & Safety. He is a Certified Protection Officer (CPO).

PROTECTION OFFICER CODE OF ETHICS

The Protection Officer Shall

I   Respond to employer's professional needs

II   Exhibit exemplary conduct

III   Protect confidential information

IV   Maintain a safe & secure workplace

V   Dress to create professionalism

VI   Enforce all lawful rules & regulations

VII   Encourage liaison with public officers

VIII   Develop good rapport within the profession

IX   Strive to attain professional competence

X   Encourage high standards of officer ethics

Protection Officer Code of Ethics

Today business and the public expect a great deal from the uniformed security officer. In the past there has been far too little attention paid to the ethical aspects of the profession. There has to be solid guide lines that each officer knows and understands. More importantly, it is essential that each manager and supervisor perform his or her duties in a manner that will reflect honesty, integrity and professionalism.

Every training program should address the need for professional conduct on and off duty. Line officers must exhibit a willingness to gain professional competency and adhere to a strict code of ethics that must include:

Loyalty:

To the employer, the client and the public. The Officer must have a complete and thorough understanding of all of the regulations and procedures that are necessary to protect people and assets on or in relation to the facility assigned to protect.

Exemplary Conduct:

The officer is under constant scrutiny by everyone in work and public places. Hence it is essential that he/she exhibit exemplary conduct at all times. Maturity and professionalism are the key words to guide all officers.

Confidentiality:

Each officer is charged with the responsibility of working in the interests of his/her employer. Providing protection means that the officer will encounter confidential information which must be carefully guarded and never compromised.

Safety & Security:

The foremost responsibility of all officers is to ensure that the facility that must be protected is safe and secure for all persons with lawful access. The officer must fully understand all necessary procedures to eliminate or control security and safety risks.

Deportment:

Each officer must dress in an immaculate manner. Crisp, sharp, clean and polished are the indicators that point to a professional officer that will execute his/her protection obligations in a proficient manner and will be a credit to the profession.

Law Enforcement Liaison:

It is the responsibility of each officer to make every effort to encourage and enhance positive relations with members of public law enforcement. Seek assistance when a genuine need exists and offer assistance whenever possible.

Strive to Learn:

To become professionally competent, each officer must constantly strive to be knowledgeable about all his/her chosen career. How to protect people, assets and information must always be a learning priority for every officer.

Develop Rapport:

It is necessary to be constantly aware of the image that our profession projects. All officers can enhance the image of the industry, their employer and themselves. Recognize and respect peers and security leaders throughout the industry.

Honesty:

By virtue of the duties and responsibilities of all officers, honest behavior is absolutely essential at all times. Each officer occupies a position of trust that must not be violated. Dishonesty can never be tolerated by the security profession.

Prejudice:

The job of protecting means that the officer must impose restrictions upon people that frequent the security workplace. All human beings must be treated equally; with dignity and respect, regardless of color, race, religion or political beliefs.

Self Discipline:

With the position of trust comes the responsibility to diligently protect life and property. These duties can only be discharged effectively when the officer understands the gravity of his/her position. Self discipline means trying harder and caring more.

Conclusion:

The job of protecting life and property focuses much attention on the individual Security Officer. Hence, it is essential to be aware of the need for professional conduct at all times. By strictly adhering to each section in this code of ethics, it may be expected that we as individuals and the industry as a whole will enjoy a good reputation and gain even more acceptance from the public as well as private and government corporations. You as the individual officer must be a principle in this process.

CONTENT SUMMARY REVIEW

PURPOSE AND SCOPE

For the convenience of readers of this manual, each unit and chapter have been summarized. An abbreviated narrative of the contents is set forth in a manner that offers a quick and concise reference to the core material.

There are 12 units, containing 34 regular chapters and one separate Miscellaneous Section. Pages are numbered by unit, chapter and page, i.e. Unit V, Chapter 2, Page 7 would appear:

PROTECTION OFFICER TRAINING MANUAL: Unit V-2-7

The chapter on Learning Skills and Study Habits is essential for candidates wishing for maximum utilization of this manual as the CPO Course Text.

Protection Officer Ethics

The Security Industry has not developed a recognized code of ethics or standard of conduct for Security Personnel. Senior Management in large corporations, both private and public, have often been remiss for failing to develop a code of ethics for all employees, to be used as a guide to encourage integrity-based behavior.

Leaders must not only produce a code of ethics, but demonstrate by exemplary personal and business conduct that rules are for everyone in the organization. Because of the nature of the duties performed by protection officers, it is imperative that a code of ethics be readily available for constant reference, and application to duties performed.

The matter of professional ethics for protection officers is a topic that is seldom discussed, but is of vital importance to the entire profession. These ethics provide not only a guide to the officer, but also for the various levels of security management, and the user of security services.

Learning Skills and Study Habits

This chapter has been prepared by a professional educator with a view to enhance the opportunity for readers to better understand the contents of each section. While the Manual is primarily designed for the Certified Protection Officer (CPO) program, every member of the security community that reads this manual may improve their ability to retain information.

Educators have determined that by purely reading straight script, the retention rate varies. It can, however, be improved by applying a number of the effective learning techniques that are discussed in this chapter. Some effective study habits and methods of retaining the core information in each chapter are presented, in order to assist the reader in gaining more of the valuable contents of this professional manual. Timely illustrations, charts, photos, and other descriptive graphics and comparisons, make this manual easy to read and understand.

UNIT I

History of Private Security

To fully understand the state of the Security Industry, one must examine the history of security. This chapter begins by dealing with the security methods employed by tribal chiefs to enhance protection among members of the tribe, and will take the reader through the days of the Emperor of Rome, through the middle ages, and will finally examine the present state of the industry.

Statistics are made available from the Hallcrest Report, prepared for the National Institute of Justice. This is a thoroughly researched chapter developed to provide a better understanding of the present state of the security industry, and how public law enforcement and justice administration interface with Private and Corporate Security.

A number of important trends are surfacing in the security community, such as the need for law enforcement to better utilize the resources available, by involving security in crime prevention practices. Enhanced roles, and more responsibility for security organizations in the overall protection process, are anticipated.

Field Notes - Report Writing

This chapter begins by stressing the importance of the written word, particularly as it relates to the role of the protection officer. The notebook is described as a "tool of the trade". The reader is given guidance in selection of a suitable notebook, proper note-taking, notebook maintenance, notes for future reference, and utilizing the notebook as an aid in giving evidence.

The best methods of transferring information from the notebook to the report format are discussed in detail. The importance of a well-written report is underscored as the most effective means by which the work of the protection officer may be evaluated by fellow officers, supervisors, the courts, and other departments and organizations, both private and public.

The chapter discusses the various kinds of reports that may be encountered by the protection officer, and how these reports form an integral part of the security organization's administration process. Finally, the chapter spells out how the written report conveys to the reader how competent the officer really is, in terms of effective task completion.

Memory and Observations

The modern Protection Officer must improve memory skills, as do Security Supervisors and Managers. This is a popular and useful chapter for all security personnel. What one professional protection officer might observe during a normal tour of duty after studying this chapter, and what one who has not, is quite different.

By using the methods of observation suggested in this chapter, readers will discover that there is an opportunity to detect, observe, and report more information, than was previously thought possible.

This chapter will enhance the opportunity for the protection officer to be more resourceful, observant, and provide more in-depth and meaningful reports. By combining learning skills, study habits, and memory and observation techniques, a much higher level of information retention will result, as well as improved performance.

Preventive Security
The role of the modern Protection Officer is one of prevention. Prevention and security awareness are topics that are constantly referred to in this manual. Good prevention equals effective security and loss control. Security personnel must be ever-conscientious of the need for preventive security in the performance of security duties.

Generally, the police role is one of detection and apprehension, although law enforcement organizations make every effort to prevent crime. On the contrary, security officers must be aware of methods to prevent acts or omissions, that will endanger the safety and security of people, assets, and information of the organization that is protected.

Preventive security is an excellent lead-in chapter for readers to consider, as reference is made to the many complex aspects of security work. This chapter provides an overview of preventive security philosophies, and discusses management expectations in developing and maintaining sound security measures.

UNIT II

Patrol Techniques
The patrol function can be significantly improved by applying some of the awareness, observation, memory, and preventive skills covered in Unit One of this manual. This is one of the most important functions of the modern protection officer.

Results of effective patrolling can enhance the overall protection of personnel, assets and information. Protection officers are advised as to the kind of facility violations to be expected, a description of potential perpetrators, and the danger signals that can alert the officer.

This chapter gives the reader information on patrol preparation, execution, and reporting. It clearly illustrates the most effective methods of patrolling, and provides excellent cautionary guidelines to promote officer safety. The importance of the connection between the patrol, field notes, and the finished report, is reiterated in this chapter.

Security - Safety Considerations
There has always been a close link between safety and security. For example, the title "Public Safety Officer" frequently replaces a more traditional security-oriented rank description. And some organizations have attempted to incorporate a total "Loss Control concept" by including safety, security, and fire protection, into one organizational job description.

The Protection Officer is in an ideal position to combine safety responsibilities, with regular security duties. This chapter gives the reader a clear picture of the overall organizational safety structure, individual responsibilities, and how the protection officer can bring safety hazards to light. By close scrutiny of potential safety risks, and effective reporting, the protection officer can make beneficial contributions to organizational safety.

Traffic Control
Vehicular movement, at every location that is protected by security, becomes a responsibility of the Protection Officer. This chapter first discusses the need for proper preparation for duty, by describing the physical items required to get the job done. The importance of "good attitude" `is explained, and the need for full officer attention to safety is emphasized.

Signs and automatic signals are discussed, as well as a careful description of hand gestures, and the officer's position when directing traffic. The use of the whistle can maximize effective traffic movement and control. Reference is made to pedestrian traffic, handicapped persons, emergency vehicles, and how the traffic officer can assist police in the execution of this important security function.

The chapter concludes by providing some useful tips on traffic control, and site locations from which the protection officer may be expected to perform traffic control duties.

Crowd Management
The effective management of large groups of people is becoming a major role of the Protection Officer. Failure to understand or execute correct procedures can lead to disastrous consequences. Effective crowd control is the difference between a smooth flow of pedestrian traffic, and a hysterical mob of uncontrollable individuals who can cause serious injury or death to innocent people, and countless amounts of property damage.

This chapter describes the kind of gatherings of people that can be defined as a crowd, demonstration, riot, or a disaster. The reader is made to understand the causes of crowd formation, such as casual, social, political or economic. It discusses countermeasures that can be employed to neutralize a crowd that is becoming unruly.

Manpower considerations are covered as well as liaison with local law enforcement personnel. Additional methods of crowd management such as isolating individuals, removing leaders, diverting attention, and other effective tactics, are covered in detail. The chapter concludes with a crowd control planning checklist, and shows some illustrations that indicate effective personnel deployment.

Crime Scene, Evidence Preservation
How successfully the Protection Officer is able to protect the crime scene and preserve evidence has considerable impact on the outcome of a criminal investigation, either by the police or senior members of the security organization.

The protection officer who encounters a crime scene must first take measures that will afford officer safety. Criminal apprehension is less important than reducing the chance of injury or death to protection personnel.

Once it has been established that a crime has taken place and in fact a crime scene does exist, the officer must then seek backup personnel. The boundaries of the crime scene must be determined, and declared a sterile area. No one without authorization from the senior security or police officials may be allowed into the restricted area.

The protection officer has specific responsibilities, foremost of which is properly preparing notes that may later be helpful in crime detection activities. This chapter explains what the protection officer might expect to find at a crime scene. It also provides information as to how the protection officer can best render assistance to investigating officers on the scene. The chapter concludes with a caution to the protection officer: "Don't touch - preserve and protect".

UNIT III

Physical Security

This facet of security is vitally important to the Protection Officer. Every facility requires various forms of physical security, from a simple access control system such as key control, to the various sophisticated, integrated control access methods, ranging from magnetic strip cards, voice prints, laser readers, and new technology such as retina scan (eye readers), advanced hi-tech access control systems, Closed Circuit T.V., robots, alarms systems that monitor unauthorized and authorized movement of personnel, as well as the environment, are becoming common methods designed to improve physical security.

At the top of the list of physical security measures is the trained protection officer. Adding integrated security systems to any facility means more effective deployment of security personnel. Personnel, hardware, and software, are all part of the protection link.

This chapter discusses physical security in-depth and it is essential that officers fully understand the connection between the human and technical aspects of physical security. This chapter discusses the five steps that are involved with physical security, namely:

Identification of Assets: Asset protection includes safeguarding personnel, information, and all corporate possessions that can be classified and protected. Corporate Assets must be accurately inventoried, so that effective measures of protection can be implemented to preserve these assets. Failure to develop and maintain productive asset protection can most certainly result in business failure.

Loss Events: Threats to organizational assets must be identified. Considering the potential consequences of the threat, the likelihood of the loss event actually occurring and the effects that such a loss event would have on the organization is a vital exercise in physical security planning. The protection officer can be an integral part of the system that monitors the effectiveness of physical security measures.

Occurrence Probability: There are a number of methods that will assist in determining with reasonable accuracy, the likelihood of a loss event actually occurring. This condition has significant bearing on the level of physical security that must be placed upon assets that are affected. Gathering intelligence from past, present, and anticipated events, is a function that can be enhanced by effective officer observations and reports.

Impact of Occurrence: The effects that a loss event may have on an organization are critical in the overall loss control planning process. For example, a disaster, man-made or by act of God, could require numerous contingency plans, ranging from auxiliary power, to such considerations as mutual aid from other corporations. When a loss event occurs, the protection officer is often first on the scene, and must take immediate remedial action.

Countermeasures: There are a wide range of countermeasures that must be considered in the physical security planning process. Asset identification, potential loss events, the probability of an occurrence, and the impact this occurrence (event) would have on the organization, are all factors that influence the level of physical security. Readers should relate Emergency, Disaster Planning Techniques covered separately in Unit four of this manual when considering physical security countermeasures.

General Physical Security Considerations

This chapter goes on to explain the various lines of defence that are incorporated into the physical security process. The first line of defence is the property boundary that requires a varying degree of security, and is based on many factors such as location, natural barriers, assets protected, and the kind of pedestrian or vehicular traffic expected.

The second line of defence is the exterior of the building, that can be secured in a number of effective manners. If physical security planning is incorporated into building design, less add-on measures are required. However, older buildings require special measures applied to the walls, doors, windows, skylights, and other areas of possible access.

The final line of defence is the interior of the building. Security to areas such as the computer centre, boardroom, safes, vaults and other offices must be considered, as well as the location and role of employees, the value of assets, and the classification of proprietary information.

There are a number of vital considerations in security that are discussed in detail. The chapter goes on to discuss lighting, glazing, intrusion detection, and devices, sensors, control systems, security monitoring, card access, locating hardware, CCTV, safes and vaults, fire-resistant containers, and fencing.

With the advent of high technology in the administration of physical security, we sometimes tend to lose sight of the "old lock and key". There is a danger that in planning for effective security controls, we have a tendency to sometimes "over-kill" in the implementation of security control systems.

The old theory that identifies what is critical to the survival of the organization and how vulnerable to compromise these assets may be, is still a prime consideration in physical security planning. We must not lose sight of the human aspect of hi-tech security. For without well-trained, alert officers providing back-up and support to security systems, they become virtually useless. Personnel is a key component to any integrated security system.

UNIT IV

Explosive Devices, Bomb Threat and Search Procedure

This chapter begins by pointing out that explosives are not that difficult to obtain, and are commonly used by the construction industry and certain other professions. The use of bombs and other explosive devices is not exclusive to terrorists, and threats are often received from disgruntled employees, individuals with political motives, and even pranksters. Explosives can be acquired by theft, legal purchase, mail order in some instances, and of course, there are home mixtures. Numerous publications are available that provide explicit instruction on the production and use of explosive devices.

Because of the mounting threat of terrorism in our society, the countless incidents of bombings and threats, the Protection Officer must be conversant with this ever-increasing problem. This chapter provides excellent information that will assist the protection officer by understanding relevant terminology, and the use and deployment of explosive devices. The following topics are covered, supported by excellent graphics:

-   Bombs
-   Bomb Threats
-   Explosives
-   Bomb Incident Plans
-   Blasting Caps
-   Pyrotechnics

- Explosive Ordinance Disposal
- Bombers

Explosive firing systems are described. The explosion results from a chain reaction of specific elements in an explosive fire system. There are two types: electric and non-electric. Basic components of the firing system are illustrated throughout this chapter. However, protection officers should take every possible step to expand their knowledge of the items used in a firing system. There are several different types of activating sources, firing lines, detonators, and explosives.

A bomb is basically an explosive firing system in a box or other container. While this seems like a simple description, readers are cautioned that there is no such thing as a simple bomb.

Bombs can be found concealed in such conveyances as shoe boxes, briefcases, backpacks and such items as appliances, lunch boxes, thermos bottles, or books. Even ink pens can be converted into hazardous devices. These are sometimes referred to as booby-traps. Bombs are activated in many ways such as:
- by Chemical Reaction
- by Motion
- Mechanically
- Frictionally
- Electrically

This chapter cites a number of Do's and Don'ts such as Don't cut wires, and Do report, evacuate, and isolate area, etc. And, if time permits, attend to such details as opening doors, and windows, and remove flammables from the immediate area.

The chapter provides detail with respect to the actions of the first officer on the scene that are necessary for effective execution of bomb threat procedures. The chapter goes on to describe hazardous devices, domestic explosives, and other items termed "nasty devices". Preventive measures are discussed in detail.

The chapter goes into considerable detail discussing bomb threats. A sample report is provided and useful search procedures are discussed. Drawings support the written instruction, that provide the reader with direction in conducting searches. The chapter concludes by explaining the components of a bomb incident plan, and cautions protection officers as to the inherent dangers which can result from bomb threats and bombings. Nearly 10% of the threats are real.

Basic Alarm Systems

Today more than ever in the history of security, Protection Officers have had the opportunity to work with electronics and alarms. A non-technical person can easily be intimidated by the term 'electronic'. This chapter will dispel many fears an officer may have in terms of working with modern alarms. The popular term 'user friendly' is a prime consideration for developers of advanced alarm technology.

Alarms are activated for number of reasons, least of which is when an actual intruder is on the premises. This fact is extremely important, and must affect officer attitude and performance in terms of personal safety.

Malfunctions are the second most common cause of alarm activation, and human error is by far the most common reason for alarm activation. For this reason, officers frequently tend to become complacent, and seldom take adequate precautions when responding to an alarm.

The chapter goes on to explain alarm function in simple terminology, beginning with perimeter protection, and then describing interior protection systems and devices. Monitoring systems, and local and central alarm stations, are discussed as well as the role of response personnel. Alarm activation, supervision, monitoring, and responding, are also discussed in this chapter.

Suffice to again emphasize the inherent dangers that may confront the protection officer who does not take alarm responses seriously. Based on 1,796 reported alarms, only 21 were a result of violations of a facility. While this may seem like a small number of incidents, it is vitally important that the officer assumes that each alarm has been activated by an illegal act, or initiated by an unauthorized person. The officer must employ extreme caution in dealing with each and every alarm response.

Fire Prevention and Detection

Of all the disasters that face industry (in both the past and the present), fires are by far the most devastating. Fire Prevention and Detection has always been a major concern for security organizations. In each case when a fire occurs, the protection officer has a very important role. Selecting the correct fire extinguisher, preliminary fire-fighting, activating an alarm, directing professional fire-fighting units, evacuating personnel, and maintaining security conditions during and after a fire, are all protection officer responsibilities.

Protection Officers are usually the first officers on the scene. In terms of fire prevention and detection, the officer must make judgement calls that could affect the survival of the entire organization. This chapter gives the reader information that will assist in the identification of a fire hazard, and how this hazard can be eliminated. The effects that Air, Heat and Fuel have on fire is discussed in detail.

Much of this chapter deals with prevention, which means that the protection officer should be able to recognize a fire hazard, and take appropriate action. Approximately 10 of the most common fire hazards are identified, and examples of each are cited. Of the list of hazards, carelessness by employees, visitors, and the public, leads the list. Good fire prevention practises can be related to effective security, because fire prevention patrols can enhance general facility, security, and safety.

The chapter goes into considerable detail discussing the various kinds of fire extinguishers and their application to fire-fighting and control. Instructions are provided in the use of fire extinguishers, and the classifications of fires each extinguisher is designed to combat.

Sprinkler systems, stand-pipes, fire doors, and escape routes are discussed. Employee roles in the development of a fire control contingency plan is covered, along with the action that would be taken by off-site fire-fighting units.

Hazardous Materials

Considerably more attention has been focused on the topic of Hazardous Materials in recent years. The day to day and long term management of these kind of materials is becoming a part of everyday life, particularly in the industrial world. The Protection Officer is now called upon not only to have a good understanding of what constitutes a hazardous material, but what has to be done to ensure that the same substance does not pose a risk to employees and the public. While the types of materials are not discussed in detail, there are numerous suggestions as to how these materials can be identified.

People play a key role in the misuse and abuse of hazardous materials. The Protection Officer plays a key role in enforcing the rules and procedures that are designed to safeguard a contaminated area. Numerous locations and facilities, both public and private, industrial, commercial, and recreational, may be adversely affected by improperly stored, handled or transported hazardous materials. By developing a broad knowledge base about this topic, the Protection Officer can do a great deal to protect people and the environment.

This chapter begins by discussing the response methods to deal with the uncontrolled release of hazardous material. The statement "'dilution was the solution to pollution" does not necessarily hold true today. Diluted hazardous solutions can have long term devastating effects on the environment. In years past, the job of dealing with these situations was primarily a fire department responsibility. Today specialized hazardous material (HazMat) response teams have been developed to respond to uncontrolled releases of hazardous substances. This chapter deals with the necessary response needed to deal with the risk of uncontrolled hazardous materials which includes:

- Activate the Contingency Plan
- Identify the substance released
- Determine the quantity of the released substance
- Determine the extent of the damage
- Perform "Site Security"

This chapter provides details of each of the necessary steps to manage uncontrolled hazardous materials that pose an immediate threat to life and property.

While each of the five steps is of vital importance, the final step, "site security", is of primary importance to the Protection Officer. This relates to keeping onlookers and bystanders out of the contaminated area. Co-workers, the public, and even the media, can all pose serious security problems. They must be kept clear of the affected area for their own safety. The HazMat response team has a big job to do, and can't be burdened with the task of dealing with unwanted onlookers.

An excellent illustration depicts how the security function can be implemented. It describes the three critical zones: Hot, Warm, and Cold. All non-essential personnel must be kept clear of the contaminated area, and restricted to the cold zone area, where the Command Post is established, and controlled by the Incident Commander.

Once the contamination has been cleaned up or safely controlled (decontaminated or DECONed), the Incident Commander will make a decision about further security measures. Only once the area has been classified as safe, will the strict security procedures be relaxed.

UNIT V

Security and Labor Relations

Wild-cat strikes, lawful strikes, and lock-outs are frequent occurrences on the labor scene. When any of these conditions are anticipated by management, extensive contingency plans are developed with a view to protecting non-striking employees, and the physical aspects of the struck facility. The roles of the Protection Officer in labor disputes include but are not limited to:

- Access Control
- Escorts
- Chain of Command (Security)
- Police Liaison
- Communication
- Pre-strike Vandalism
- Fire Safety
- Building Security
- Security Lighting
- Supply Acquisitions
- Threatening Phone Calls
- Crossing Picket Lines
- Picket Line Surveillance

Other strike conditions that are discussed in this chapter are searches, employee misconduct and dishonesty, employee discipline, types of discipline, arbitration, and interviews. It must be remembered that the protection officer's role in matters of labor unrest is one of neutrality. It is important that strikers do not perceive security as an extension of management.

By maintaining a friendly, cooperative attitude, it is possible to reduce much of the friction that is normally present during strike or lock-out conditions. However, disgruntled strikers will resort to numerous tactics designed to intimidate non-striking employees and cause management hardships.

While maintaining good relations is very important, sometimes it is necessary to compel strikers to adhere to company strike policy. In the absence of court injunctions, the employee has all of the legal powers necessary to protect the property, and the people having legal access to the facility.

Emergency Planning and Disaster Control

Advanced planning is the key to controlling emergencies and disasters in any workplace. For this reason, such a plan should be a basic part of every safety and accident prevention program.

This chapter presents general guidelines to follow in setting up a disaster control plan, and then provides a step-by-step outline of specific actions to be taken, including an organizational chart showing how to assign individual responsibilities for each step of the plan. Prominent in the emergency plan is the protection officer, who once again is often the first officer available to take action.

Some of the man-made or act-of-God disasters discussed in this chapter are:

- Fire
- Explosion
- Civil disturbance
- Hazardous chemical or gas leaks, and spills
- Earthquake
- Building collapse
- Hurricane
- Tornado
- Flood
- Nuclear holocaust, radiation accident

Once the type of disaster has been identified, it is essential that the correct group(s) or individuals be identified and located to render all possible and necessary assistance. Protection officers must be aware of the signs and effects that will assist in determining the kind of disaster that has occurred.

The next step is to have available a list of personnel and organizations that have been designated to cope with the disaster. Home telephone numbers, as well as alternately designated personnel who are trained to deal with disasters, must be known to the officer, so as to limit the time consumed in summoning assistance. Other considerations that involve security personnel are:

- Plant warning and communication systems
- Transportation
- Medical services
- Employee training - first aid, fire fighting and rescue
- Emergency power sources
- Mutual aid programs
- Availability of facility plans, maps and diagrams

Security personnel must assume a major responsibility in such crisis conditions. It is essential that each officer carefully studies the Emergency-Disaster plan, and understands how his/her responsibilities interface with other designated employees named in the plan. Protecting life and property is a major concern of the protection officer, and it is important to restore full security as quickly as possible. This means gaining control of access points, providing direction to emergency response units and encouraging an atmosphere that will reduce panic.

Terrorism, VIP Protection, Hostage Conditions

This chapter begins by explaining the current state of terrorism. Terrorism is a strategy employing the use, or threat of force to achieve political or social objectives. It is a form of coercion designed to manipulate an opponent (government or private organization). The chapter describes a terrorist as:

- 21 to 40 years old
- Often female
- Having no criminal record
- Well-educated
- Skilled in military techniques
- Dedicated to a cause

This chapter explains the structure of terrorist groups by geographical location, and provides details on the methods of operation employed by the various terrorist groups. Counter-terrorist security personnel are given excellent information as to the tactics that are employed by terrorists. Foremost in terrorist groups is advanced intelligence and careful planning. They will only attempt a mission if they believe that it has an excellent opportunity to succeed.

Terrorist plans include the manipulation of existing security systems, including the recruitment of personnel from within the organization. They most frequently have inside sources of information that provide them with the ability to strike at a time and a place when they are least expected. Frequently, they will kidnap an employee or employee's family prior to an attack, or they will seize a hostage during the attack.

Prior to the attack, they will embark upon such measures as isolating the facility by eliminating power or communication. They are either experts at detonating explosive devices, or they recruit sympathetic groups or individuals to assist in the deployment of explosives. They will rehearse their plan at length and usually implement an attack under adverse weather conditions.

The thrust of this chapter is to point out that effective physical security measures are frequently one of the best means of countering terrorism. The chapter lists more than 25 tactical procedures that can reduce the threat of terrorism.

The author suggests that a well-trained security force, conversant with terrorist tactics, and trained in all security areas ranging from physical fitness to recognizing ploys that are utilized by terrorists, is necessary to protect against terrorism.

This chapter also offers readers excellent information on current strategies that may be employed to enhance VIP protection. The matter of hostage-taking is discussed at length, and techniques that are essential to improve the chance of hostage survival are dealt with in considerable detail. Hostage negotiation and release measures are also integral parts of this excellent guide to life-threatening facets of crisis management.

UNIT VI

Human Relations

Understanding human behavior is very necessary for the Protection Officer, as duties and responsibilities usually entail ongoing dialogue with fellow employees, client employees, visitors, customers, and the public. By applying basic techniques in communication skills, it can be expected that the officer will enjoy a much higher ratio of on-the-job success.

The ability to utilize basic public relation training is not necessarily sufficient. Today's officer has to have a better understanding of a human behavior. This chapter attempts to explain the underlying causes for certain kinds of behavior. Having the skills to identify the behavioral traits exhibited by individuals, gives the officer a much better opportunity to control a situation involving conflict or emotional behavior.

This chapter divides individual behavior into three categories: parent, adult and child (P.A.C.). These characteristics are described as an ego status that describes individual behavior that is visible and easy to identify.

People function in one of these three ego states at all times and it is possible to determine which of the three ego positions an individual occupies at any point in time. So, by identifying if the person is behaving like a parent, adult or child, it makes it much easier for the officer to deal with the situation.

For example, "parent" behavior is derived from the parent or a person in authority. A typical parent response might be, "You will have to be more careful; try to remember your manners". Adult behavior makes the job of protection much easier. Adult responses are practical, impassionate and predictable. A typical adult response might be, "That seems to be a logical solution; why don't we try to make it work?". Child behavior is easy to identify; it is basically childish, so you might expect a comment like: "I'm not going to sign that dumb book; leave me alone".

For those officers who would like to make a study of human behavior, you could for example role play to accommodate the behavior of another person and very likely take charge of a situation. For example, the childish response likely is coming from an immature person requiring the take-charge 'parental' reply.

The safe approach in dealing with people, however, is to attempt to bring each individual to the adult ego status. Countering one type of behavior by utilizing another gets tricky, and this chapter is not intended to explore human behavior to such depth. It does, however, give some fresh ideas about interpersonal skills and how the astute officer can benefit from a fresh approach in the day-to-day dealings with people.

Interviewing Techniques

The Protection Officer has been described a number of times in this manual as the 'first officer' on the scene. First officer at a fire, emergency, accident, crime scene, alarm response, a labor dispute - you name it, the officer must be there. Interviewing is no exception.

The officer must carefully record initial remarks made by witnesses or suspects, record what occurred at a crime or accident scene, and take statements given under conditions of distress. This is not an easy task because how well this information is obtained and recorded, will frequently have a major impact on the action taken by affected parties and individuals.

Readers should review the Field Note and Report Writing chapter in conjunction with this part of the manual.

The basic difference between note taking and interviewing is that the interviewer must take charge of the situation. There are a number of proven methods that will assist the officer in assuming the command position in these circumstances. There are several stages that should be followed when interviewing, which are:

- Getting acquainted
- Developing rapport
- Motivating the subject
- Keeping the subject talking
- Listening to what is said

Many times it is not possible to conduct a structured interview, so it is doubly important to carefully record all information that is seen or heard. If the formal interview is conducted by a senior member of the guard force, the preliminary information obtained by the field officer will prove invaluable to the supervisor.

This chapter discusses obstacles that can be encountered in an interview, and gives the interviewer helpful tips to avoid losing the lead role. Such tactics as 'Initially avoiding specific questions', 'Avoiding yes or no answers', 'Not using leading questions', 'Avoiding rapid-fire questions', 'Not using open-ended questions', 'Allowing a long pause if necessary', 'Not taking the non-direct approach'; are all useful interviewing techniques. The

chapter concludes with helpful suggestions on how to successfully conclude the interview.

Stress Management

Stress is not limited to the chief executive officer, the
senior vice-president, or the corporate security director. Stress
effects everyone to varying degrees. It is said that a certain
amount of stress is healthy and provides stimulation.

However, stress that is not recognized and managed can
have devastating effects - reducing productivity, lowering
resistance, causing physical disorders which could lead to drugs,
alcohol, or even suicide. To lead a healthy professional and
personal life, we must have the ability to recognize situations
that are personally stressful, and master the skills to cope.

This chapter points out that most of our stress is caused
by boredom. We have the ability to be extremely productive,
but this ability is retarded if we are hampered by the effects
and causes of stress. It is not always possible to alter our
professional and personal lives.

If for example, the protection officer is bored on the job,
there are a number of remedies to this condition. It is possible
to create new challenges, and enrich one's role in security.

"Job Enlargement" does not mean job enrichment. In
protection, the challenge to be professional is a significant one.
This chapter tells us the cause, effects and how to cope with
the stress. It is then up to the individual to create an interesting
work environment in an effort to gain more fulfillment from
the job. A good supervisor (boss) can often be helpful in
making work more interesting, challenging and rewarding.

This chapter describes the characteristics of a healthy per-
sonality as:
- A high level of self-esteem
- Action-orientated behavior
- A high level of internal control
- The capability of establishing priorities

To survive happily in a world of hassles and ensuing
stress, the individual must develop coping mechanisms. One
needs to start with a healthy personal lifestyle, based on values
and attitudes that lead to the appropriate use of time management, exercise, sleep, vacations, intimacy, and family life.

Relaxation techniques can release endorphin, a powerful
natural tranquilizer that can turn off the mechanism that causes
stress. We must all recognize that we have limitations, and
should not set unrealistic goals that are impractical and often
impossible to fulfill. We should not actively seek happiness,
because we may well have already found happiness and don't
realize it.

This chapter is one that is thought-provoking and affords
readers the opportunity to better understand the complex topic
of stress and burn-out. There are a number of intriguing and
useful living lessons to be learned and one must read this work
very carefully to fully understand how we can benefit from the
ability to manage stress, the silent killer.

Crisis Intervention

The personal safety of Protection Officers has to be of
paramount importance because each officer working in security
today is frequently exposed to conflict oriented situations.
Crisis Intervention/Management is a technique of communicating in a non-threatening manner with individual(s) that are
behaving in a disruptive or violent manner.

This chapter deals with the causes that lead to disruptive
behavior such as illness, injury, emotional problems, substance
abuse, stress, or anger. To cope with individuals exhibiting
these kinds of characteristics, the Protection Officer must
develop a plan of action that is designed to reduce the risk,
not only to the distraught individual, but also to employees,
and of course, the officer.

Each situation must be evaluated. That is to say, "what
is going on here". Once it has been determined what is actually
happening, there has to be a plan of action. This deals with
ensuring that necessary personnel and other resources are available
to manage the situation. The next step is to implement the plan.
The action taken must be appropriate and designed to sustain the
safety of the officer(s) and subject(s). After the appropriate action
has been taken, it is necessary to carefully document the entire
crisis situation. Finally a review process must take place that
includes all of the personnel involved. This gives everyone the
opportunity to openly discuss what happened. It is a positive
critiquing exercise.

The writer of this chapter encourages effective listening
techniques. Listening in an empathetic manner tends to reduce
anxiety on the part of the subject. By projecting a caring attitude
there is a greater opportunity to gain the confidence of the
individual. Past prejudices and biases must be put aside, and the
Protection Officer has to be objective. A person suffering from
distress, frustration, anger, or dismay, can easily detect insincerity.
Be genuine and never ignore the principal of the conflict. Listen
carefully to clarify any messages. Reinforce in the subject's mind
what has been said so that he/she knows that you really do
understand.

The chapter also deals in some length with non-verbal
communications. Almost 85% of messages are conveyed without
words, hence it is vitally important to watch for body language
that will give clues as to the emotional state of a principal(s) to
a conflict. Honor the personal space of the subject and be aware
of posture that may be interpreted as threatening. Maintain a
position/stance that is non-threatening while rendering maximum
personal safety.

The "team approach" is suggested in dealing with crisis
situations. It offers more personal safety to other team members,
while maintaining a stronger deterrent. Team members do not
feel that aggression is directed at them personally, rather at the
team. A team should remain small and back-up personnel should
avoid the scene unless the situation requires support personnel.
Avoid a mass convergency. Pre-incident training is extremely
important. Team drills are performed to ensure that each player
fully understands his/her role.

In extreme situations of emotional turmoil that has been
initiated by an individual(s) that is suffering from severe stress
or behaving in a violent manner, the action taken by the first officer
on the scene is critical to successfully resolve the situation. By
carefully analyzing the threat, keeping calm, being objective and
listening in an empathetic manner, the potentially violent situation
can usually be diffused. The author cautions all officers to first
ensure that there is sufficient back-up personnel before taking a
corrective action.

UNIT VII

Security Awareness

This chapter begins by giving the definition of awareness
from the Webster Dictionary: "watchful, wary and having or
showing realization, perception or knowledge". The challenge is
to create awareness or watchfulness in the minds of potential law
breakers, and a realization that security does exist in the minds
of employees and those with lawful access to the facility.

An eight-story building is described as (1) with virtually
no security and (2) with a maximum level of security, such as
adequate fencing, entrance with security officer, CCTV mounted
on four corners of the building, security check upon entering the
building, signing in and being issued a badge, the party being
visited is contacted to verify the visitor, the visitor is escorted to
and from the office in question, and the attache case is inspected

upon departure.

In the first scenario there is 'no presence' of security, but in the second instance there is a 'real presence' of security.

The point is that security awareness must be real. It can't be counterfeit, because false security will be discovered and the awareness becomes a negative factor. Effective security awareness must be created through education, and the presence of effective security measures that are not only apparent, but capable of deterring illegal acts.

This chapter gives numerous methods of making employees aware of security through a well-prepared and structured education program introduced to the work environment, and carefully maintained on a continuous basis. To create a real security environment that is not only effective but serves as an ongoing deterrent, management must attend to the following security procedures:

- Background checks
- New employee orientation
- Security signs and posters
- Paycheck messages
- Communicating security news events
- Videos and films
- Employee information sessions

The chapter describes how these kind of security awareness programs can be communicated to employees through the written and spoken word. Employee involvement in security awareness programs is desirable and can be achieved through the formation of a security committee. Input is needed from employees at all levels of the organization. Soliciting the cooperation of employees is the best way to achieve effective security.

Security Investigations

Most Protection Officers are of the opinion that investigations relate to white-collar crime, involve the mafia with a blonde, trenchcoat and flashy car thrown in for good measure. As the protection officer is an adjunct member of the management team, it is his/her duty to provide management with information.

The officer reports this information after conducting some basic types of investigative activity such as searching, interviews, attending an accident or crime scene, intervening in a conflict situation, or any number of the routine occurrences that involve security on a regular basis.

Generally, the protection officer becomes involved in the preliminary investigation. This is an important facet of the entire investigation process as initial information must be factual, and accurately recorded. Initial investigation steps include:

- Attending to injured persons
- Detaining suspects known to have committed a crime
- Finding and questioning witnesses
- Preserving the crime/accident scene
- Forwarding information to dispatch
- Completing a preliminary report

The chapter goes on to discuss follow up investigations, auditing, interviews, interrogations, informants, undercover investigations, and testifying in court. The role of the protection officer is often limited to the preliminary investigation, but officers should have an overall understanding of the entire investigative process.

With fewer law enforcement personnel available to private and government organizations, and more crime, corporations are becoming more dependent upon professional security personnel to provide organizational protection. An informed officer who understands the entire investigative process is a valuable asset to any security organization.

Employee Dishonesty

Employee theft is not uncommon. In fact, it has been said that the level of controls and the threat of punishment are directly linked to the amount of dishonest behavior that can be expected in an organization.

Preventive security and security awareness programs, have a definite relationship with increased loss control resulting from dishonesty in the workplace.

This chapter discusses the WAECUP acronym which is pronounced 'Wake-Up'. The key terms that relate to employee theft in the WAECUP program are:

W	-	**Waste**
A	-	**Accident**
E	-	**Error**
C	-	**Crime**
UP	-	**Unethical Practices**

Each term in this model is discussed, and shows the connection between each portion of the acronym as it relates to losses resulting from a criminal act committed within the organization.

Not all internal (employee) theft is preventable. We will learn in this chapter some ways in which to minimize, moderate, and control criminal activity. This will enhance our ability to be effective Protection Officers. The protection officer can have a significant impact on theft prevention. They can deter and displace theft. When security is tight, thieves look for another place to steal.

Employees will recognize that effective professional security is in place, and generally avoid the risk of detection that would precede an illegal act directed against the organization.

This chapter gives tips on observation techniques that enhance effective theft prevention. It explains the importance of effective reports, and the correlation between information related to management and increased security. It will provide a number of suggested actions in theft prevention. It also provides the officer with cautionary practises that if followed, will reduce the opportunity for unfavorable publicity or even possible lawsuits, for acts or omissions on the part of the officer(s). It is essential to understand the protection officer's authority to search and seize. It is also necessary to fully understand company policy and the organization's expectations of security.

Substance Abuse

Substance abuse is one of the leading social problems of our time. It adversely effects the health and creative potential of individual abusers, and therefore deteriorates the stability of institutions under individual control. One such institution is the workplace.

Throughout this chapter the Protection Officer will develop an awareness for the issues related to an individual's motives to abuse drugs; why they continue using drugs in spite of deteriorating physical and mental health, and how they become dependent. Also, the Protection Officer will become familiar with the meaning of substance abuse, and a variety of terms associated with the prevention and treatment of the problem.

Specific workplace issues are discussed and the cost associated with substance abuse are identified. To effectively address substance abuse in the workplace, requires a comprehensive Drug-Free Workplace Program. Such a program consists of several components. These components, including the security function, will be reviewed.

The security response is a critical component of any Drug-Free Workplace Program. As such, the Protection Officer is presented with information about the various techniques available to respond to criminality and major policy violations.

Finally, this chapter reviews the most prevalent drugs of abuse and their signs and symptoms. A chart graphically displaying this information and more is presented

By carefully reviewing this chapter the Protection Officer will gain sufficient insight into the general nature of substance abuse and drug dependence and a specific awareness regarding workplace issues, the security response, and the officer's responsibility.

UNIT VIII

Legal Aspects in Security

Protection Officer discretion is the fundamental message that should be derived from this chapter. The law is a complex and changing field, and the members of the Security community cannot be expected to be totally conversant with all facets of the administration of justice. It is, however, of vital importance to understand the rights and duties that are exercised in the everyday security role.

This section will examine what law is, the sources of our laws, and the differences between some of the more important parts of the legal framework. The powers of the protection officer are examined, including arrest and search. When the term 'arrest' is mentioned, it is essential that cautionary remarks accompany any reference to this aspect of security and the law.

Two types of arrest are covered in his chapter: "Arrest with a Warrant" and "Arrest without a Warrant". Arrests with a warrant are generally a matter for police authorities, and the only involvement on the part of security personnel would be a supportive role.

To arrest a person without a warrant is a very serious undertaking, which could have far-reaching civil and criminal legal repercussions if complete adherence to the law is not observed. A protection officer who is in lawful possession of real property, may arrest a person, without a warrant, found committing a criminal offence on or in relation to the property that is being protected.

If it is essential to execute an arrest, there must be absolutely no doubt in the mind of the protection officer that the offence was committed. The officer protecting the property must have found the offence being committed.

Prior to effecting an arrest, every other possible means of detaining the person should be explored. It is inherently dangerous to take away the liberties of a person. Every possible effort should be made to detain the individual on a voluntary basis. An arrest should only be made if there are no other courses of action available and there is a serious threat to life or property.

If every other course of action has been explored and an arrest must be effected, support personnel is the prime consideration. Officer safety and the safety of others is essential.

If a person responsible for committing a criminal offence is arrested, there are several important procedures that are followed. The arrested person(s) must be advised:

- As to the reason for the arrest
- The right to legal counsel
- That the person under arrest is not required to say anything

Once arrested, the protection officer is responsible for the safety of the individual(s). The protection officer has a legal responsibility to deliver the arrested person(s) to a police officer as soon as practically possible.

This chapter provides readers with general information on Common law, Criminal and Civil law, Search authority, Use of force, Evidence, Confessions, and gives the reader an overview of legal aspects in security.

The objective of the section is to help members of the Security community to understand the authority that is available to them, and how it can be applied to the protection of life and property. The protection officer who understands the nature and extent of their personal authority, does the best job for his/her employer without unnecessary exposure to liability.

Court actions for false arrest and illegal searches can be costly in terms of legal fees and damages, if the case is lost. It is the duty of every protection officer to keep current, and understand the administration of justice as it relates to security in the particular jurisdiction concerned.

UNIT IX

Health, Fitness and Exercise Prescription

In the preceding units of this manual, it would seem that the Protection Officer is frequently first on the scene. The situations that have been described are very often emergency conditions, requiring quick, effective action on the part of the officer. Examine if you will, an officer who has given no thought to personal fitness for many years, and is called upon to react under crisis conditions. The officer will most certainly lack the mental and physical endurance to cope with the emergency. This leads to mistakes and poor judgement, which will most certainly compound the problem.

Examine if you will, an officer who pays attention to correct diet and keeps physically fit. When this officer is first on the scene, you can expect better performance as a direct result of better physical condition. Good physical condition creates endurance, confidence, self-respect and the ability to make sound judgement calls. There is no professional that should be more concerned about fitness. Why? Simply because security is protection, and to adequately protect life and property, one must be physically capable of performing under adverse conditions.

This does not mean that a protection officer should be skilled in the art of hand-to-hand combat or martial arts, it merely means that the officer must be adequately fit to do the job. This chapter can get the unfit officer on the right track and keep the fit officer on track.

The first step is to eat sensibly; the next step is to get on a fitness program that can work. Fitness may be nothing more than walking briskly about the facility that the officer is employed to protect, or it may mean joining a team of some sort, and getting proper exercise. The important thing is to get involved with a fitness/exercise program that is right for you. Know your limitations, and make an attempt to find a fitness program that can be fun or even incorporated with work and family life.

This chapter provides a simple fitness model that is self-explanatory:

F	**freqency**
I	**intensity**
T	**time**
T	**type**

In terms of frequency, don't get involved in a program that you can't manage because it conflicts with personal and business life. However, the program selected must be continued on a regular basis, at least three times a week for not less than 20 minutes.

Intensity means just that - don't go beyond your realm of capability. Increase intensity over a long period of time. Time must be made for exercise, this is the part that knocks most new entrants into fitness out of the program. Don't procrastinate - make time. Type is the kind of exercise you choose. It doesn't mean you should necessarily 'pump iron'. Do something you enjoy.

This chapter illustrates some myths about fitness, such as:
- No pain, no gain.
- Go for the burn
- Exercise turns fat to muscle
- You need extra vitamins when exercising
- Exercise will increase appetite
- Weight lifting makes you muscle-bound

- Protein supplement is needed to build muscles
- Massagers and vibrators get rid of fat

These folklores of exercise are explained in detail, along with all of the facets of fitness that will lead to a healthier, happier life for those who care about themselves. If protection is your career, go for it, what do you have to lose? A fit body relates to a fit mind.

UNIT X

First Aid and C.P.R.

The purpose of first aid is to provide temporary care for the injured with a view to obtaining medical assistance as quickly as possible. The term 'first actions' relates to the following steps that must be taken immediately to increase the life sustainment of the injured party:

- Safety at the Scene
- Triage (identify who requires assistance)
- Responsiveness (level of consciousness)
- Airway
- Respiratory system
- Circulatory system
- Cardiopulmonary Resuscitation (CPR)

Once the life-threatening 'first action' steps have been taken, additional injuries must be dealt with. Second action steps that must be taken are:

- Monitoring Vital Signs
- Treatment of Shock
- Treatment of Wounds

The chapter gives the reader the opportunity to follow a pattern of sequence of actions that are designed to render all possible assistance to the injured person. Monitoring signs is extremely important, and the first aid administered should pay close attention to breathing, pulse, skin color, skin temperature, eyes and level of consciousness. Any change in the general condition of the victim can usually be determined by paying close attention to these vital signs.

The qualified first aider (Protection Officer) must take charge of the situation, and portray the image of a professional person capable of attending to all of the needs of the injured person(s). Proper training to a standard is essential, and the first aider must remember that it is imperative to keep up-to-date in first aid and CPR training.

How the public, employees, and other affected parties perceive the protection officer administering the first aid is very important. A competent officer who effectively attends to all details, has a major impact on reducing panic, and restoring a calm and stable environment.

The protection officer must understand what conditions need immediate attention. By doing first things first, the officer will minimize life-threatening conditions. The experienced protection officer is accustomed to being the first person on the scene, and first aid is certainly no exception. Taking charge of the situation is imperative. This can best be achieved by delegating responsibilities, such as seeking the assistance of bystanders who can be instructed to attend to such activities as directing traffic, moving curious bystanders, summoning medical assistance, and the protection of the injured.

This chapter provides the first aider with a sequence of events that are to be followed in the event of an emergency. Briefly, the following steps should be taken:

- Assess the situation
- Control the scene
- Gain access to the injured
- Assess the injuries and treat as required
- Ensure transportation is arranged
- Pertinent details should be recorded

Prepare any special reports relating to industrial accidents

For the professional Protection Officer, reference should be made to the chapter on "Field Notes and Report Writing". The best action that can be initiated to prevent post-accident legal matters is to properly document as much detail as possible. It is extremely important to solicit information/statements from witnesses. A well-written report will prove very valuable to all parties concerned.

UNIT XI

Use of Force

In this chapter the use of force is thoroughly discussed, particularly with respect to its legal implications for the security officer. Ultimately, the use of force should be considered as an absolutely last resort. Rather, the security officer is encouraged to develop his/her abilities in the use of verbal de-escalation techniques, such as slowing down the action of, and actively listening to, the perpetrator, and asking the perpetrator's friends and/or relatives to assist in the negotiation, by speaking directly to the perpetrator.

The key to effecting calmness in a potentially aggressive situation, is for the security officer to maintain self control at all times. The formula for self-control is presented: control = I/E, where I and E represent intellect and emotion, respectively. While fear/stress may have the effect of altering the officer's physical state, such as inducing sweating, rapid heartbeat, and shortness of breath, and ultimately lowering his/her capacity for self-control, intensive professional training will allow the officer to quickly regain his/her confidence and self-control in these threatening situations.

Recognizing potentially dangerous situations before they start, is a very important skill for the security guard to master. Several indicators, or "red flags", are discussed, such as the posture and hand movements of the subject.

Finally, the writing of reports is considered, with specific reference to a use of force incident. The goal of the report is to clearly show that, under identical circumstances, anyone would have done exactly the same things as the attending officer. However, because of the potential legal and social hazards associated with the use of force, it is portrayed throughout this chapter as something to be avoided, with verbal de-escalation the much more favoured method of dealing with potentially violent situations. Successful verbal de-escalation depends upon impeccable self-control, which is considered to be one of the primary goals of every security professional.

UNIT XII

Public Relations

The security officer is often the first person that a member of the public will encounter, when approaching a particular private company or institution. As such, the security professional must be well versed in the "art" of maintaining good public relations. This is because the security officer is the direct, out-front representative of his/her company, and by maintaining favorable relationships with the public and the community as a whole, the criminal element may be subdued. Good public relations are, in effect, good loss control tactics.

Security professionals should consider themselves to be "sales-people". They should always present a professional image to the public by dress code, posture, demeanor, and by their eagerness to genuinely volunteer assistance to anyone who approaches them.

Special emphasis is given to the methods by which good public relations may be maintained with respect to the media. Again the emphasis is always on the attending security officer being as helpful and courteous as possible, without volunteering specific information. That job is always handled by the public information officer (PIO). The skill with which a security professional can guide the interests of the media to the PIO is an invaluable asset to his/her company.

Finally, specific tactics regarding public relations and the occurrence of an emergency within the parent organization are discussed. Two strategies: creating a plant emergency organization; and contacting an external security contingent, are outlined. The "bottom line" is that the security professional must become skilled at managing situations so that good public and media relations are maintained at all times.

Security and Police Liaison

This chapter takes an in depth look at some of the past and present problems that have hampered the relationship between law enforcement and private security personnel. It also discusses some of the findings of various studies that have been conducted on the relationship between the two professions (Hallcrest I and II).

Later sections of the chapter discuss the differences between the two professions and the common ground that the two professions share (personal protection, crime prevention, and order maintenance). Growth trends of industry, and privatization are also discussed.

The chapter closes by giving some general recommendations for improving relationships between police and security personnel. The following recommendations are discussed:

- Establishing credibility with local law enforcement
- Establishing and/or following a code of ethics
- Maintaining the highest levels of professionalism
- Increasing police knowledge of private security
- Establishing mutual agreements between security and law enforcement personnel
- Developing cooperative programs
- Nurturing professional growth and development

Ethics and Professionalism

Private security is rapidly becoming a profession in its own right. As such it is necessary for security officers to abide by a code of ethics, and present themselves in professional ways. Ten items are presented and discussed as the International Foundation for Protection Officers, Code of Ethics. These include: Exhibiting exemplary conduct; encouraging liaison with public officers; and, maintaining a safe and secure workplace.

Continued education and training are key issues to obtaining and maintaining professional status. Several acronyms are presented in order to more clearly illustrate the important points about portraying a professional image, such as, P for precise, exact, detailed, and F for factual in all reporting processes, honest, for example. The personal deportment of individual officers is also discussed with the use of the acronym, placing particular emphasis on a dress code, professionalism and high self-esteem.

Understanding why unethical behavior occurs is presented as an important skill for the security officer to obtain, as it relates to controlling losses for the organization with which he/she is employed. Only when ethical behavior is truly understood and adopted as the required norm for the security professional, can unethical behavior be clearly recognized for its potential dangers to the companies and institutions which will be hiring professional protection officers.

LEARNING SKILLS - STUDY HABITS

By Joan Mulder M.A.

To everything there is a season.
And a time for every purpose under heaven:
A time to be born, and a time to die;
A time to plant and a time to reap ...

Ecclesiastes 3:1-8

The idea expressed in these lines has endured for centuries. The words originated in the Book of Ecclesiastes, were popularized in the 1960s by Pete Seeger's folk song "Turn! Turn! Turn!", have been read at funerals and weddings, and used as titles of books on various subjects.

The thoughts and feelings of "to everything there is a season" are also appropriate when applied to the experience you are embarking upon as an adult learner — it is again a "time to learn", but at a different level of intensity and purpose than when you were in high school or college.

As you know, learning does not simply occur by magic nor by spending time with textbooks. Learning requires your specific organized effort and your investment of time and energy.

The purpose of this chapter is to provide you with strategies in the 'art' of learning. Three specific areas are targeted:

1. How to be effective as an independent learner;
2. How to read efficiently and effectively study this manual;
3. And how to score higher on the objective tests required for your certification.

While this chapter will not provide you with the 'perfect' way to study and learn, because no two people are exactly the same in their learning styles, it will give you many study and learning skills, suggestions and techniques. Try them out, modify and adapt them to your personal way of learning and your individual situation.

A listing of additional readings is included as reference for a more in-depth look at the areas presented, and for other academic skills not elaborated in this chapter (such as writing essay exams, writing reports and research papers, taking notes from the lecturer ...).

First, though, do you know how you compare with other adult learners? To begin your 'time to learn', try this short quiz to find out how you rank in the range of efficient, effective adult students.

Study Skills Quiz

Answer the following questions by placing a check mark in the box that best describes when you do the stated activities. The choices in the boxes are:

Almost Always	More than half of	About half of	Less than half of	Almost never
4	3 the time	the time 2	1 the time	0

Being an Independent Learner:

1. Do you have a study schedule in which you set aside time each day for studying?

2. Do you estimate how long it will take you to read an assignment and plan your study time in accordance with this?

3. Do you reward yourself when you complete a set amount of studying?

Being an Efficient, Effective Reader and Learner:

4. Before studying a chapter in detail, do you make use of any of the clues in the book such as headings, illustrations and chapter summaries?

5. Do you spend at least 50% of your study time reciting (testing yourself)?

6. Do you read with a pencil in hand in order to underline or make notes?

7. Do you know your best time of day for studying?

8. Do you vary your reading speed according to the type of material that you're reading?

9. Do you read without daydreaming?

Being a 'Smart Test Taker'

10. At the start of an examination, do you make plans for suitably distributing your time among the questions?

11. Can you write an exam without feeling overly nervous or anxious?

12. Do you plan to answer all easy questions first, leaving the more difficult ones until the end?

How did you score?

- If you got 40 or above, you are using many of the right techniques in your learning already.
- If you scored between 30 and 40, you need to apply some specific strategies in order to be an efficient student.

Below 30 means that you are probably spending too much time on your studying, probably with negligible results.

What strategies and techniques can you apply? Over the years, adults returning to school have discussed their concerns and their study methods. I've made note of the most interesting comments and the most common concerns that these people have expressed.

Following are the eight most often heard comments (along with one comment about memory that I've only heard once!). The discussion following each is based, for the most part, on research in human learning. Practical ideas for applying this research to your daily study habits are suggested.

You will note that there is an overlap among some of the concerns and suggestions. I urge you to integrate, modify, personalize, and transfer the suggestions to various areas of your learning — by doing so, you will be more efficient and effective in your "time to learn".

Comment 1: How many times have I heard this one!?

"I'm 40 years old — I can't remember as well as I could when I was younger. Because I'm older, it is more difficult for me to learn."

As an adult, you bring to any learning situation many years of experience. Research has shown that your ability to learn **does not** decrease with age. Apps, in his book "Study Skills for Those Adults Returning to School" states that "... the accumulated experiences of learning are a considerable asset to you as an adult learner. As you face new experiences, you can often relate parts or all of the new experiences to something you have experienced previously." (Apps, page 10)

In fact, studies have shown that older students in colleges and universities consistently earn higher grades than their younger classmates. A number of years ago, a group of 50-year-olds were given the same intelligence test that they had taken when they were 19. They consistently made higher scores on all but one section of the test.

Tony Buzan, in his book "Use Your Head", talks about age and human mental performance. He concludes that older people who have remained "active and explorative" have the ability to understand and learn new areas of knowledge far surpassing that of "equally enthusiastic but younger and less experienced minds". (Buzan, page 63)

Comment 2: This is the concern expressed by 90% of adult students who enroll in non-traditional programs or courses.

"With independent study courses, I find it difficult to get started. There is no instructor telling me to read Chapter 2 for next week, and there are no set dates for exams — it is all up to me! I tend to procrastinate for the first month, and then I have to hussle to finish the course. I could have done a lot better if I had started the first day I got the book."

Procrastination is a basic trait that we all possess. Some of us are worse than others — only doing our work when the deadline is the next day. A proven technique to break the procrastination habit involves time management. Use these weekly and monthly schedules to keep track of where you are and where you are going. The forms are presented as examples. Remember to try out the various formats and use the system and forms that will work for your unique situation.

Tips for schedule planning:

1   The first day you begin your program, sit down with a schedule sheet (see examples) and a list of the required readings. Plan when you will complete each section. Treat the self-quiz at the end of each chapter as a real "test". Keep track of your scores.

2   On all schedules, it is often easy to get started by writing in all the things that you cannot change, e.g. appointments, work times, community responsibilities, children's activities, and things that involve other people in your life. Now you can see when your free time is and how much free time you have. Remember to schedule some recreation time for yourself.

3   Many study-skills experts recommend that you do not open a book for one day of the week — maybe a Saturday, a Sunday or a Friday night. Their idea is that you will be "fresher" that way and will be able to concentrate more effectively during the five or six "study days". See if that works for you.

4   Plan as far ahead as possible — note your final test date and work toward that. At the beginning of each month or week, fill in details (times, pages and rewards). Be as specific as possible — set hours, number of pages, type of reward.

Comment 3:

"I sit and read this chapter from beginning to end, over and over. I guess I can't concentrate. Last night I sat for two hours reading Chapter 5, but halfway through I caught myself daydreaming about that great party we had last weekend."

You should have a basic time planning schedule(s) in place. Look at your use of time within the schedules. You need to get off the 'procrastination trip' and on with some high-speed learning.

1   First, decide when your "best" time of day is — in terms of being energetic, productive, active and ready to learn. If you don't know, try out some times. Wake up at 5:30 a.m. and after a quick shower, get a coffee and study for an hour when the house is quiet. Maybe you didn't know that you were a "morning person". One student I know works best during the hours of 10 p.m. to 2 a.m. He knows his best body time — his peak time for productivity — and he capitalizes on it.

2   How long can you expect yourself to sit in one place and be productive in your studying? Research has shown that the average student needs a break after 40-60 minutes of reading or studying.

I recently heard a speaker state that after 40 minutes of listening, people tend to shuffle in their seats and look through the program to see what is coming next. After 45 minutes, people begin to think about their financial problems. After 60 minutes, they tend to have wild sexual fantasies.

With that in mind, you should plan your 2-hour study session in terms of:

- 40 minutes of study and 10 minutes break;
- 40 minutes study and 10 minutes break; then
- 20 minutes review.

Other combinations may work better for you:

- 60 minutes study and 20 minutes break;
- 40 minutes study with 10 minutes review.

Be sure to experiment with various time frames. At your peak times or when you are reading about a particular subject, you may be able to concentrate longer.

Comment 4:

"When I get a new text book, I sit down and begin reading at page one."

Never treat a text book like a mystery novel. Authors of text books, or manuals such as this, use many aids to help you prepare to read, to help you organize as you read and to help you review.

First, let's look at the total book. Plan to spend about 45 minutes at previewing or surveying the total book. Think of previewing as you're planning for a car trip to visit Aunt Hilda in New York City. In the initial planning stages, you get an AMA road map of North America and plan the best route — "best" in terms of shortness, scenery and good highways. You plan an estimated day and time of departure and arrival, what you will see there, as well as along the way.

The analogy holds for your study "trip" as well — you do some organizational work (study schedules), but you also plan your way through the book by doing the following:

1   Look at both front and back covers (book jacket flaps as well). Read the preface and/or the introduction. From all of this, you will get important background on why the author or editor wrote or compiled the book, for whom the book is intended, and the credentials of the author(s). Note where the book was printed and in what year. (It may have U.S. examples; it may not be up-to-date.)

2   Go through the table of contents and, if it has one, the index in the back. This gives you an overview of the book's contents.

3   Leaf through, noting the visual aids (research substantiates the fact that "a picture is worth a thousand words"). We tend to remember better when visual aids such as pictures, graphs, charts and cartoons are used. More on that later.

4   Check to see if other 'goodies' are provided; reading lists, a glossary of specialized words with their meaning. (The glossary can save you many trips to your dictionary).

5   Spend time reading over the summaries. This gives you a good idea of what the book covers and gives you a sense of direction — a 'map' of the total book.

Comment 5:

"I try to be really "neat" when I take notes. By this I mean I keep the text book spotless — no writing in the margins or underlining. In my notebook, I write in complete sentences, but I often have about one page of notes for every page of text book."

Notes should **never** be particularly neat. They should **never** be in complete sentences. You spend valuable time writing when you really should be "reciting" or asking yourself questions. Your notes should have lots of diagrams or little charts — remember the old Chinese proverb that "a picture is worth 1,000 words".

What is the most efficient and effective way of taking notes? Following are proven "tips".

1. Survey

   The 10 minutes that you spend at surveying the chapter is perhaps the most valuable time (along with the 10 or 15 minutes you spend reviewing at the end).

   ● Read the chapter **title** for a general idea of what the author is discussing. With colored pen or highlighter in hand, go through the chapter, checking for the **organization**, using the headings and subheadings. For example, on the "History of Security" chapter, note that there are five (number them) identified periods. Note how the author is organizing his subject' in his case, chronologically from Ancient and Biblical times to the future.

   ● Note the typeset. The important five periods are set in bold type and in capitals.

   ● Glance through any **pictures**, and **diagrams** — read the captions. If you know anything about the subject from past experiences (you've worked in The Bay and know their alarm system), these key words and diagrams or charts will trigger what you have stored in your memory about these past experiences, and bring them up from you subconscious mind.

   ● Read through the **summary**, noting the specific 'areas'. When you go back to read the chapter, you will know what the author thinks is important and thus you can pay more attention to those areas.

2. Now for the actual **notetaking**. Many methods are detailed in the books listed in the "additional readings". Following is one way that has worked for the majority of my adult students.

   ● Take one sheet of paper, **only one**, and outline out the chapter in order to get the 'big picture' or the total 'map' of the chapter. You know that you must get **all** the notes for the chapter on **one** page. This system discourages too much writing. You save your valuable time for "reciting" or learning the material, not writing it down. Following is an example from the "History" chapter.

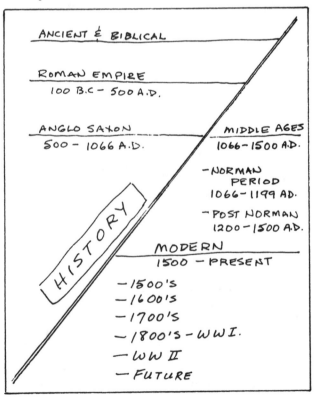

● Develop your own shorthand system. For example, use H_2O for "water", "exting" for "extinguisher", etc. Give yourself credit for being able mentally to fill in words in your notes. The example on the review cards makes use of only "key" words.

● As you come to the 40 minute mark of your study session, you need to take four or five minutes to test yourself on the review cards. You need to set aside the ones that you need more practice on, for a second review.

● Your 'learning schedule' could be outlined as:

a) survey chapter and do 'map' sheet	10 min.
b) read each section, make notes.	40 min.
c) review	5 min.
d) before sleep; review.	5 min.
e) next day (lunchtime), review	5 min.
f) end of week - review	5 min.
g) end of month - review	5 min.

Remember, by the week and month-end, you will have a number of chapters to review.

Comment 6:

   "Usually I try to do my studying in the evenings at the kitchen table. The kids sometimes bother me, I get a few phone calls, and the T.V. is noisy, even though the door is closed."

1   The **physical environment** for studying effectively is extremely important. Research indicates that instrumental music — particularly with head sets — provides a "cover" for distracting noises. The ideal situation is to have a room set aside as your study (preferably off the traffic pattern for the rest of the family). Equip it with a desk, good lighting, a firm chair, a clock, a dictionary, pencils, pens — everything you need (and lock the door so your 10-year-old doesn't take off with the ruler, pencils and your walk-man!).

2   Make it a habit to begin studying as soon as your bottom hits the chair in that room. Psychologists have long told us that certain **behaviors** are "habits" in certain places. For example, when people go to a football stadium, yelling and cheering behavior is automatic. Likewise, certain behaviors are habitual in church. Never let yourself sit and daydream or read the newspaper in your study — it is too easy to fall into an avoidance-behavior pattern.

3   Remember to inform your family of your schedule
and then stick to it. **Post a schedule** on the study door
indicating that you are not to be disturbed from 8:00 -
8:45; you will then have a 15-minute break when you
can deal with any phone calls, concerns, etc.; go
back in from 9:00 - 9:45. It is amazing how people
will cooperate when they know the rules and know
that you are adamant about enforcing them. (A
woman I know has cautioned her children that unless
one of them is gushing blood or smoke is rising, they
are not to disturb her until the posted time. She plugs
in her special study music, and after 45 minutes,
comes out for some "quality" time with her
children).

Comment 7:

"My memory is like the muscles in my body, and I'm
working at expanding my brain power. When I jog, I do
mental exercises. I memorize the number of houses on
my route, the names of all the streets I cross, and the
number of poplar trees that I pass. The more I exercise
my 'memory muscle', the stronger it will be, just as the
more I work out on my weight machine, the stronger
my body muscles will be."

Memory Pre-Test

Before you read the response to the above comment, try
this little pre-test:

1. Copy the following words on a sheet of paper.
2. Have someone time you exactly one minute as you study
   the list.
3. After one minute, turn your study sheet over; and in the
   correct sequence, write all ten words from memory.
4. Score one point for every word in the correct sequence.

man   table   pop   counter   brush

tree   swing   flower   dress   tap

We have tried this little test with adult
learners and found that the average score is 7.
The average score on a similar test by
University of Minnesota students was 6.5
(Ragor, p.130).

What is the best way to memorize? Is it "strengthening
your memory muscle"? A study done by Professor Woodrow
at Michigan State was designed to answer this. He pre-tested
a group of students and randomly divided them into two
groups. The memory muscle group spent three hours

memorizing poetry and nonsense syllables — drilling
themselves over and over. The other group learned techniques for remembering and did limited practice. The results
from the post-test? The memory muscle group made a 4.5 per
cent improvement; the technique group a 36.0 per cent improvement. (Ragor, p.132-133)

What are some of the techniques that Woodrow taught his
students?

1   First, **select** what you want to remember. This is probably the most difficult part of the whole process.
You can get a good idea from the summary and the
practice tests. By reading, underlining and making
notes (on review cards) on each chapter, you focus
yourself on what is to be remembered.

2   **Visualize** - Build a mental picture (remember, a picture is worth a thousand words!) Dream up a vivid,
even outrageous picture of a pot-bellied **man**, standing on a little wooden **table**, balancing a can of **pop**
as he tries to reach across to the kitchen **counter** to
get a **brush**.

3   **Group** - It's easier to remember two groups of five
things than ten separate things. Build some type of
organizational 'tree'. This also makes use of the 'picture' idea; for example:

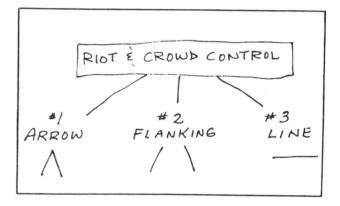

4   **Number** - If you know that you must remember ten
items at Safeway or have three methods of crowd
control, your mind will tend to work toward
remembering that number.

5   **Use Color** - Another wonderful property of the brain
is that it tends to remember best when a color is involved. Somehow when you're sitting in the test
room, you visualize the seven types of communication systems circled with red ink.

6   **Use memory formulas or association** - You may want
to use mnemonic (pronounced "nee-mon-ic") devices
to help you recall such things as items on a list, steps
to a procedure, or the nine types of alarm systems.
Remember how to spell "arithmetic" — a red Indian thought he might eat turnips in church.

Remember that nothing engages the senses as well as the
real thing. As you walk by a fire extinguisher, check it out. If
it says "soda acid", you would immediately recall "Type A
fires, and small type 'B', has a little bottle of sulfuric acid in
the neck which, when inverted, mixes with the soda and
water to form CO_2 which forces water out." You may even
pull the review card out of your pocket to confirm your
knowledge.

The human brain seems to have an almost infinite capacity
for memory. Some scientists have speculated that an
average brain:

can store up to 199 billion different bits of information;

- has 10 billion individual neurons or nerve cells, and
- could have about a million different chemical reactions taking place every minute.

The human brain is indeed complex. Dr. Houston states: "We are just beginning to discover the virtually limitless capacities of the mind ...(Superlearning, p.3)

Superlearning and **Use Your Head** discuss, among other things, the concept of discovering the enormous potential of the human brain. Both books suggest excellent systems and techniques in "learning how to learn".

However, very simplistically, the brain may be said to have three areas of memory:

Short Term

Middle Term

Long Term

- **Short term** - all kinds of information hits here and bounces right back out again unless you **select** that information as worth remembering and then do something in order to force the information into the:

- **Middle term** area where a lot of it stays for a few weeks or months before fading.

- **Long term** memory is reserved for such details as your name, the ages of your children and your telephone number.

Now you know some techniques, try a post-test; same format as the pre-test:
1. Copy the words.
2. Memorize for one minute.
3. Turn your page over and write from memory, scoring one point for each word in the correct sequence.

beer	dog	grass	book	jar
floor	sky	stove	lady	deer

In our study skills workshops, 90 per cent of the students score 100 per cent on the post-test.

It's now Up to You!

By knowing the principles and the "best" techniques for learning, you need to develop your personal study and learning system.

Don't be hesitant in experimenting — in growing by challenging yourself. This is your time to achieve excellence in your personal and academic life — "your time to learn".

And, remember to keep it all in perspective.

If you have comments, queries or would like to share a favorite "learning to learn" tactic, write to Joan Mulder at Alberta Vocational Centre, 332 - 6 Ave. S.E., Calgary, Alberta T2G 4S6.

Additional Readings

Adams, W. Royce. "Reading Skills: A Guide for Better Reading". Toronto: John Wiley & Sons, 1974. A programmed format with lots of exercises to provide practice in all kinds of reading activities such as skimming, scanning, vocabulary development, study reading procedures.

Alberta Manpower, Career Services Branch. "The Adult Back-to-School Book", 1985. (free copy from Career Services Branch, Alberta Manpower, 201 Sun Building, 10363 - 108 St., Edmonton, Alberta T5J 1L8).

Apps, Jerold W. "Study Skills for those Adults Returning to School". New York: McGraw Hill, 1978.

Buzan, Tony. "Use Your Head", London: British Broadcasting Corporation, 1982. A terrific little pocketbook that talks about how to use your mind to the best advantage in reading, studying, memorizing. Includes practice exercises.

Carman, R.A. & W. Royce Adams. "Study Skills, A Student's Guide for Survival", Toronto: John Wiley & Sons, 1972. (If I could buy one book, it would be this one! It is organized in a programmed format and written in a humourous style with lots of diagrams and exercises. Probably not to be used in its entirety; it contains excellent ideas for you to become a more effective, efficient adult learner (and it's fun to read!)

Gilbert, Sara. "How to Take Tests" New York: William Morrow & Co., 1983.

Grassick, Patrick. "Making the Grade" Toronto: MacMillan of Canada, 1983. Grassick has tested out his ideas with University of Calgary students who have participated in his Exam Skills Workshops. Good sections on the 'Global Map' approach to notetaking, and on a step-by-step approach for reducing test anxiety.

Kasselman-Turkel, Judi & Franklyn Peterson. "Study Smarts: How to Learn More in Less Time." Chicago: Contemporary Books, Inc., 1981.

Ostrander, Sheila and Lynn Schroeder, "Super Learning" New York: Dell Publishing, 1979. Based on Dr. Lazanov's research on learning systems, this pocketbook talks about a relaxed method of accelerated learning.

Raygor, Alton L. and David M. Wark. "Systems for Study" Toronto: McGraw-Hill, 1970. Designed for the college student; contains interesting implications of what has been learned from research for students' study behaviors.

And last, a good little booklet designed to help you improve your child's study and homework behavior (with a few tips for you as well):

Zifferblatt, Steven. "Improving Study and Homework Behaviors" Champaign, Illinois: Research Press, 1970.

Music Cassettes available from the Lind Institute, P.O. Box 14487, San Francisco, California 94114 USA

Unit 1

History of Security
Field Notes – Report Writing
Memory and Observations

HISTORY OF PRIVATE SECURITY

By John. H. Christman CPP

Figure 1

Contrary to popular belief, private security, particularly as a profession, is not a relatively modern development. A study of history from the beginnings of mankind shows that the protection of life and property is one of the oldest tasks both faced and undertaken by man.

Thus, what today is a multi-faceted and broad-based business and profession with specialties and sub-specialties, employing more people than public law enforcement, and financially representing over one per cent of the entire gross national product of the United States with projections of continued growth, private security has had an evolutionary growth — with its roots buried deep in history and extending back to antiquity.

Because private security as we know it today has developed as the result of a multitude of ideas, concepts, historical events and identifiable individuals and personalities, and because private security has become an essential and necessary ingredient of modern business, industry and society; some knowledge of how it developed is not only interesting but also helpful in understanding this emerging profession and its future.

Ancient and Biblical Periods

Archaeological digs and historical evidence indicate that the most primitive of man was concerned with security and developed rudimentary security techniques. Cave drawings and other evidence clearly demonstrate that protection and enforcement of social codes was of concern to earliest man. Meeting these needs, from then until now, resulted in the development of modern day public law enforcement and private security — and that the development of these two now distinct and separate functions were in the past often interwoven and indistinguishable.

In tribal society, needs were basic; security probably did not extend beyond keeping marauding animals from devouring others in the tribe while they slept. While 'laws' as such did not yet exist, we do know that tribal customs were followed, and that some means of identifying and bringing violators of these customs before the tribal chief for punishment existed.

Because private security and public law enforcement had common origins and their development has only really bifurcated in more recent times — and because to understand the development of both, one needs also to understand the development of the concept of law (a very complex subject) — let's define 'law'.

According to "Black's Law Dictionary", law is "that which is laid down, ordained, or established and that which is obeyed and followed by all citizens, subject to sanctions or legal consequences." [1]

It must be kept in mind that 'law' is a general term and can be used in many concepts. For example, we have the law of gravity, 'Murphy's Law', natural laws, criminal laws, civil laws, laws of nature, the law of the jungle, etc. Our use of the term 'law' relates solely to those laws (codes of conduct) considered necessary for an orderly society.

We must not, however, confuse 'law' in this sense (i.e., a code of conduct which carries sanctions) with morality, even though in many cases laws develop from moral codes, or refine or reinforce moral concepts. For example: The moral concept 'thou shalt not steal' is defined and refined by the law in the various penal codes enacted by appropriate authority which prescribe such conduct, attach sanctions, and refine degrees of violations such as petty theft, grand theft, etc. In other areas, moral laws such as 'thou shalt not lie' are limited to application only under certain circumstances, such as lying under oath (perjury) and under certain other specified situations — it is only then that lying is 'illegal' or 'against the law' and that sanctions apply if such behavior is proven to have been undertaken.

It has been said that the establishment of laws and a means of enforcing them is essential to a well-ordered society and is a keystone of democratic forms of government.

The earliest law was probably a combination of tribal custom and the wishes of tribal chiefs. It was passed on by word of mouth (not written or codified as it is today) and its sanctions, the implementation of which were probably overseen by the tribal chief or the entire tribe, were primarily personal; which is to say, designed to satisfy the aggrieved party.

The earliest evidence of any written law does not appear until about 2000 B.C. At that time, Hammurabi, King of Babylon, compiled a legal code which dealt with the behavior of individuals amongst themselves, as well as their responsibilities to the society as a whole.

The Code of Hammurabi set forth in writing the long established customs regarding intra-group and interpersonal relationships, defined unacceptable behavior, and spelled out the penalties and punishment for violations. Penalties, for the most part, reflected the ancient 'eye for an eye' philosophy; in many cases the offender suffered a penalty similar to the hurt or wrong done the victim.

The Old Testament is replete with laws relating to intragroup and inter-personal relationships. Laws relating to property, inheritance, slaves, criminal offenses (theft, murder & prostitution, among others) can be found throughout the Old Testament.

The next significant development in the chronology of the development of law and the protection of life and property occurred about 600-500 B.C. when the early Greek city-states developed systems for guarding highways and other strategic parts of their cities, including the protection of their rulers — the earliest evidence of Executive Protection.

The Roman Empire (100 B.C. - 500 A.D.)
Significant events relating to the development of law, security and law enforcement took place with the development of the Roman Empire. The "Twelve Tablets" which covered the broad spectrum of the existing body of Roman law appeared.

Augustus (63 B.C.-14 A.D.), Emperor of Rome, formed a military unit known as a 'Cohort' to protect the city. Members of the Cohort were known as 'praetorians' and the now-historically famous 'praetorian guard' is considered by many historians as the first police force, even though its members were military personnel.

Later in his reign, Augustus formed the 'Vigiles of Rome'; its members were civilian freemen whose task was to control fires and assist in controlling crime and quelling riots.

Perhaps the most significant contribution by the Romans came under the Byzantine Emperor Justinian (483-565 A.D.), who summarized Roman law into the world's first lawbook known as "Corpus Juris Civilis" (Body of Civil Law).

Thus, by the end of the Roman period, we have seen tribal customs and trial by ordeal evolve into written laws, standardized punishments and the beginnings of such concepts as proof of guilt and fair trials.

Anglo-Saxon Period (500-1066 A.D.)
England, from whence came the foundation of the current U.S. law, was a country of instability and confusion from 500 A.D. until the late 800's. The failure of the Roman conquest of England produced several hundred years of turbulence, aimlessness and general lack of direction and forceful leadership in England.

Not until King Alfred (872-901), do we see the beginnings of legal developments in England which will continue and ultimately change and influence the entire body of legal concepts in the world of that time. The influence of Alfred is significant in two respects: He established the concept of the "King's Peace" (i.e., widespread unlimited private warfare among the various English kingdoms was inconsistent with preserving the peace within the whole of England and would no longer be tolerated) and he established a new code of law which set forth standardized forms of punishment including specific fines for certain offenses.

The Anglo-Saxon period also saw many customs and practices in the handling of the protection of the citizenry which are recognizable as the forerunners of today's practices. For example: Crime prevention and law enforcement was a community responsibility, therefore, whenever an offense occurred a 'hue and cry' went up and all persons were expected to assist in apprehending the offender. The term 'hue and cry' is still heard today and the concepts of citizen arrest and 'posse comitatus', which were first evidenced in this period, are very much alive and still in use today.

It was also during this time that the English kingdoms began to be sub-divided to meet both agricultural and societal purposes. One of the larger geographical subdivisions was called a shire, and governed by an appointed person with the title 'ealdorman'.

A smaller sub-division, the 'hundred', was governed by a person known as a reeve. Eventually, 'ealdorman' became an Earl (our present-day term "alderman", common in East Coast cities to designate a political leader, eminates from ealdorman).

The King soon appointed a person to assume primary control of the reeve; that person was known as a 'Shirereeve', and our present day Sheriff derives from the Shirereeve, and our office of Sheriff has similarities to the duties of the Shirereeve, who was responsible for tax collection, law enforcement and who served as an agent of the King.

Also during this period, we see the first primitive form of a court system. Landowners and royal officials met from time-to-time to conduct the business of the 'shire' or 'hundred' which included resolving law suits and criminal complaints. While sitting on these matters, the officials became known as "courts", and each had its own jurisdiction depending upon the composition and residency of its members.

For persons charged with a criminal offense, guilt or innocence were determined by either "ordeal" or "oath", neither of which placed any reliance upon facts, but rather relied upon some outward and resultive manifestation of God's indication of guilt.

The ordeal took many forms. An accused might, for example, be required to carry hot coals for a specified distance. If his hands healed from the burns within a specified time, this was a sign from God of his innocence; conversely, if his hands had not healed he was guilty.

Trial by oath consisted primarily of obtaining the required number of "Compurgators" to testify as to the accused's truthfulness or innocence. As might be expected, the higher the rank or position of the 'Compurgators', the greater the weight given their oath. Compurgators were essentially character witnesses; it was not required that they have any knowledge of the events in question.

While capital punishment was used occasionally; branding, mutilation and fines were more common forms of punishment. Fines were on a graduating scale: low for petty offenses and/or persons of lower rank and increased in amount for more serious offenses or persons of higher rank or class.

The Anglo-Saxon period can, with respect to law and justice, be characterized as a period when the law of private vengeance prevailed, and where the biblical law of Moses — which regarded a crime primarily as an offense against the individual rather than society as a whole — was totally accepted. Thus, a person who suffered an injury from another could seek his own redress; if a person was slain or disabled, it became the duty (and right) of his clan or village to exact atonement in kind from the transgressor.

The Middle Ages (1066-1500 A.D.)

The Middle Ages period began with William the Conqueror's successful (and last in history) invasion of England and his accession to the throne on Christmas Day of 1066, and ends with the beginnings of the modern era at the end of the reign of Henry VII (1485-1509) — the first of the Tudors. It is during this period that we see the development of many of the concepts of law, justice and legal principles which form the underpinnings of our own cherished western judicial system.

Norman Period (1066-1199)

One of the principal results of the Norman conquest was the establishment of feudalism in England. Feudalism was, among many things, a reciprocal and contractual relationship between the lord (landlord of the fief or land) and the vassal or tenant. Both parties had rights and responsibilities; one of which was for the vassal to report to the lord's court and assist the lord in the administration of justice.

It must also be pointed out that during this period, there were two distinct legal jurisdictions: the lord's courts and the ecclesiastical (church) courts. The church had an elaborate code of laws (canon law) governing the lives of the clergy and certain aspects of laymen. Lord's courts had jurisdiction over non-church matters, although there were frequent disputes as to who had jurisdiction.

The Norman conquest produced three very significant developments in England, all of which impacted upon the justice system. These three events were:
1.) The introduction of feudalism.
2.) The centralization of government, and
3.) The reorganization of the church.

Some of the direct results of William the Conqueror's leadership on the justice system were:
a. The formation of the 'curia regis', or King's court.
b. The institution of itinerant justices.

The King's courts had jurisdiction over more major matters and serious offenses such as homicide and robbery. The King's courts were generally in-session, followed their own precedents, developed uniform procedures, and tended to be more impartial than local courts.

As a result of the above factors, they became quite popular among the citizenry. Because the 'curia regis' travelled with the King on his constant journeys, it was difficult for prospective litigants to know the location of the currently sitting court. To solve this problem, the King often sent members of the 'curia regis' to various parts of the country to hold court. These justices became known as itinerant justices.

The end of the Norman period saw Henry II (1154-1189) on the throne. Henry II's reign saw a treatise on the law of England written, and we see the development of the differentiation of the various levels of crime and the first use of the distinction between felonies and misdemeanors. Other significant changes under Henry II included:
a. Widely extended jurisdiction of the King's court
b. Enlarging of the criminal jurisdiction of the King's court.

c. Extending the writ process to assure that any freeman having business before the King's court would be heard.

d. Expansion of itinerant justices.

e. The recording of court decisions and the use of previous decisions as precedent for future holdings, thus establishing a body of common law and the principle of 'stare decisis' (to stand by decided cases and uphold precedent).

Finally, and most significant, was the introduction of the forerunner of our jury system as a standard part of the King's court procedures. In fact, in cases involving land ownership, a freeman had an absolute right to trial by jury. Simultaneously, deciding cases by oath was abolished. For these reasons, Henry II is generally credited with laying the foundation of our modern system of trial by jury.

Post Norman Period (1200-1500)

The year 1215 was perhaps the apogee of the Middle Ages in the development of modern legal concepts. In this year:

a. The Latern Council abolished trial by ordeal.

b. King John issued the Magna Carta, which not only made significant changes in the relationship of the crown (state) to the people in the areas of taxation and the exercise of royal power, but more importantly in the area of the administration of justice. The Magna Carta contained language which is similar to and the foundation of the United States' fifth amendment to the Constitution, which provides that no person shall "be deprived of life, liberty or property, without due process of law".

c. Of equal or greater importance, the Magna Carta implied that the King was not above the law and provided means for redressing royal transgressions.

Edward I (1272-1307), a prolific legislator in the areas of law, is remembered in history as the "English Justinian". Among his accomplishments were:

a. Issuing the Statute of Winchester (also known as Westminster) which made harboring a felon illegal.

b. Writing the Second Statute of Westminster which:

[1] Established the practice of having legal issues decided by the courts while questions of fact were left to juries for resolution.

[2] Began citizen participation in crime prevention by 'requiring' that the hue and cry be raised whenever crimes were committed and witnessed by citizens.

[3] Established the principle that ignorance of the law was no excuse.

[4] Established the concept of "hot pursuit".

[5] Forbid strangers from lurking about at night — a forerunner of current vagrancy and loitering laws.

[6] Established a "watch and ward" system which required night watchmen or bailiffs selected from the citizenry to maintain order and prevent crime.

[7] Regulated prostitution in cities.

[8] Provided for clear areas next to roads to prevent and discourage criminals and highwaymen from hiding there and committing crimes against travelers.

[9] Required male citizens to arm themselves to the ability his station in life permitted.

c. Expanded and formalized the court system and local responsibility for administering justice.

d. Ordered free elections; forbid judges from permitting corrupt lawsuits from being pursued in court.

Under Edward II (1327-1377), we see the appointment of justices of the peace and the first use of coroners to inquire into unexplained deaths. Edward III also issued the Statutes of Treason, which made giving aid or comfort to enemies of the land treason; counterfeiting the land's currency was declared treasonous.

The Middle Ages ended with the reign of Richard III (1483-1485) and the ascendancy to the throne of the first of the Tudors, Henry VII (1485-1509). From the foregoing, it is quite reasonable to conclude that the Middle Ages outshone any other era in the number of revolutionary and significant advances made in the development of legal concepts which have survived to modern day.

Modern Period (1500-present)
The 1500s

The rule of Henry VII (1485-1509) was marked by social turbulence and the emergence of a new merchant or middle class in England which profited at the expense of both the lower (serf) and upper (nobleman) classes. Henry's having been dubbed the "Big Policeman" resulted from his major efforts in restoring law and order to England when it was threatened by social unrest and upheaval.

Henry found that trials had become corrupt and perjury prevailed. He established the Court of Star Chamber, which sat without a jury and was thus less subject to corruption; the court did its job under Henry (although it was later subject to royal abuse under Charles I) and the end of his reign saw England peaceful again; the Crown had consolidated power; the spirit of individualism flowered and the Renaissance was in full bloom.

The 1600s

Changes in the administration of justice and innovations to the system slowed down for the next couple of centuries. The 1600s saw the development of "private police" to protect the property of merchants. Parochial police were formed to protect parishes or districts within a city. Night patrols were popular to prevent crime and give early warnings of fire.

During the reign of Charles I (1625-1645), his constant feuding with Parliament over their refusal to provide him adequate funds led Charles to subvert the Court of Star Chamber into an instrument of royal abuse synonymous with tyranny.

The Star Chamber became famous for "third degree" methods; to be charged with an offense was tantamount to being condemned. Punishment was often corporal or considered "cruel and unusual". Charles was finally forced by Parliament in 1628 to sign the Petition of Rights, many of the provisions of which were restatements of the Magna Carta.

In 1641, Charles was forced to totally abolish the Star Chamber. His tyrannical rule resulted ultimately in a civil war which saw Charles beheaded in 1649.

Oliver Cromwell (1653-1658) assumed leadership after Charles' execution and was known as Lord Protector rather than King.

Cromwell maintained order by martial rule and was eventually replaced by Charles II (1660-1684). Under Charles II, Parliament rather than the King, was given the power to make new laws. In 1679, the Habeas Corpus Act was passed, requiring law enforcement officials to bring an accused before a judge to explain why the prisoner was being held. (For a modern-day comparison, refer to Article I, Section 9, and the 6th Amendment to the U.S. Constitution).

The continued emergence of mercantile establishments resulted for the first time in 1663 in the formation of a force of paid constables to protect business property at night. This force became known as the 'shiver and shake' watch.

The late 1600s also saw the proliferation of private police in the form of merchant police, parrish police, dock police, warehouse police, etc. We also see the first use of "rewards" to entice the public to report known criminals and participate in the control of crime.

The 1600s saw developments in America which paralleled those in England. Sheriffs and constables were appointed as representatives of the English King. Citizen participation in law enforcement took the English form — the night watch system could be found in Boston, Philadelphia and New York.

The 1700s

The 1700s saw an increase in the concern for individual rights; individuals were no longer "conscripted" into nightwatch service. Rather, tax revenues were used to pay for nightwatch personnel. The concept that a criminal offense was an offense against the crown or state (i.e., the whole of society) rather than a personal offense against an individual victim, which had been slowly developing since the 1600s was by now well established.

In 1748, lawyer and novelist Henry Fielding was appointed magistrate for the second district of London, the Westminster area. In 1750, Fielding published "An Enquiry in the Causes of the Late Increase of Robberies" — probably the first Security Survey. Fielding took over the Bow Street police station as chief magistrate, and proceeded to make significant improvements in the London police force, including the formation of the first plain clothes detective unit known as the Bow Street Runners — since its members ran to the scene of crimes hoping to apprehend the culprit.

1800 - World War II

The year 1829 is generally conceded as the year in which the real beginnings of a modern police system took place. It was in this year that Sir Robert Peel, Home Secretary of England, guided a bill through Parliament entitled "An Act for Improving the Police in and Near the Metropolis". This legislation authorized a new uniformed, full-time salaried 1600-member police force.

These features, coupled with other new ideas such as rigorous pre-employment screening, semi-military principles of discipline, and lifetime tenure (provided established standards were maintained) resulted in a growth of the force to over 3200 men within three years.

Of historical note is the fact that the headquarters of this new force was on a small London side street called Scotland Yard; and that the term "Bobbie" which is recognized worldwide as the nickname for London police officers, derives out of respect for Sir Robert.

In the United States, such famous lawmen as Wyatt Earp, Bat Masterson, Pat Garrett, "Wild Bill" Hickok, along with the Texas Rangers, all gained fame in the "Old West" for their own methods of bringing law and order to the frontier.

In the East, cities were growing and forming their more formalized police departments. True police agencies, following Peel's example, began to flourish in the 1800s. Police departments were established in New York (1844), Chicago (1850), Cincinnati (1852), Philadelphia (1855) and Detroit (1865).

On a national level, crime was also a problem, and we see the federal government forming investigative agencies; the Post Office Investigative Service was formed in 1828, the law enforcement arm of the Treasury Department in 1864 and the U.S. Justice Department in 1902 began its law enforcement arm which was the forerunner of the FBI — which as we know it today, began in 1932 under J. Edgar Hoover.

It was in the mid to late 1880s that modern-day private security had its beginnings.

Alan Pinkerton, who was born in Scotland, emigrated to the U.S. after his police officer father died when Alan was a small boy. In 1850, after four years as deputy sheriff in Cane County, Illinois, Pinkerton was made a deputy in Cook County (Chicago). Later, he became a special agent of the U.S. Post Office Department, and then Chicago's first and only police detective. He then left the police department to form a private detective agency, specializing in providing investigative and security services for railroads and industrial organizations.

Pinkerton's reputation as a "master sleuth" led to his acquiring a national reputation. During the Civil War, Pinkerton's and its agents provided the Union with the organization for intelligence and counter-espionage services and also served to provide personal protection for President Lincoln.

After the Civil War, Pinkerton returned to private clients, and because of the relatively few number of public law enforcement agencies coupled with jurisdictional restrictions, he provided the only investigative agency with truly national capabilities.

In 1889, Brinks Incorporated was formed to protect property and payrolls. In 1909, William J. Burns, Inc. formed a private detective agency and became the investigative arm of the American Banking Association. The Pinkerton, Brinks and Burns companies all continue in business today.

Simultaneous with the founding and growth of the 'original three', the various railroads, which had great political power, got state legislatures to pass Railroad Police Acts authorizing the railroads to establish their own security forces with full police powers. By 1914, over 12,000 railroad police agents were in operation.[2]

World War II
World War II was the real source and stimulus of the modern and complex private security industry. Private security in a sense was born of the war, went through adolescence during the Cold War period, and reached maturity in the 1960s — and continues to grow and prosper all the while developing more specialization and sophistication.

The military services in W.W.II trained thousands of men in law enforcement (MPs, SPs, CID, etc.) and in the various intelligence services (OSS, ONI, CIC, etc.). At the same time, the FBI and the Immigration and Naturalization Service (INS) and other federal agencies (and their counterparts in the other Allied nations) were expanding to counter-sabotage and espionage threats.

Additionally, thousands of others were trained as auxiliary police and plant guards to provide physical security at home and in defense plants. By 1945, there were literally thousands of businesses, plants, factories, etc. engaged in 'classified' government or war contracts. Each of these facilities required physical security, thus producing a large pool of personnel trained — to some degree at least — in 'security'. After the war, this large resource of military police, intelligence agents, auxiliary police and plant security guards entered the civilian work force with hopes of putting their wartime training to use in the civilian marketplace.

The Cold War produced, among its many ramifications, the continued need for classified defense contracts thus requiring these now civilian-orientated operations to maintain some degree of security. Additionally, the many employees who worked in these facilities needed security clearances, thus creating the need for a large force of investigators to do background investigations in order to grant security 'clearances'.

Congressional committees and government agencies of all sorts began investigating both aspects of the 'War' and contemporaneous domestic matters requiring more hundreds of investigators. Thus, while the war itself gave birth to the multitudes of personnel trained in security and investigations, it was the post-war period which provided a means for them to use their training in the civilian world.

The trend begun during the Cold War to use investigative and security trained personnel by both government and civilian agencies and private business in numbers never before visualized not only continued, but increased after the so-called Cold War years — albeit for somewhat different reasons.

As the Cold War thawed, and the need for private security normally would have abated, the concurrent increase in street crime and white collar business crime began escalating, more than taking up the slack in the need for private security and its many related specialties.

By the mid-70s, the best available statistics indicated that there were over 500,000 persons engaged in private security and that this number exceeded those engaged in public law enforcement. By 1985, estimates place the number of persons in private security jobs at 700,000 — exceeding those in the public sector by at least 100,000. Most observers agree that the private security growth will continue to outstrip the public sector.

One has only to peruse one of the numerous trade or professional publications devoted to private security to appreciate the growth of this industry. An examination of the organizations devoted to the private security profession (and it truly has become a profession) reveals both the wide-spread applications of the profession and its diversity.

Organizations range from those with a very broad membership base (e.g., the American Society for Industrial Security) to those with rather specialized interests (e.g., organizations devoted to credit card fraud, hospital security, banking security, multi-national corporation executive protection and anti-terrorism organizations, etc.).

Naturally, when considering the scope of private security and its economic implications, we must also consider all the supporting functions which accompany the practising security professional, such as training schools, equipment manufacturers, expositions and seminars, consultants, and yes, even these specialized books and literature devoted to the subject.

The Future
The future of private security is (on balance) bright, but only if some cautions are exercised. The rapid growth of our industry, over the past two or three decades, has also given rise to some challenges which our profession must meet and overcome if it is to enjoy both continued growth and the respect and confidence of its clients, the public, and governmental and regulatory agencies.

Some of the challenges facing us are:

Professionalism: The calibre of persons entering private security with a long-term commitment to grow in and with the industry continues to improve. We must encourage this trend by improving pay scales (particularly for entry level positions and uniformed guard personnel) and by offering opportunities for upward mobility for qualified persons.

Training is the key to this challenge. No longer can we hire someone and put them on assignment with only a new uniform and a pat on the back. The ASIS (American Society for Industrial Security) Certified Protection Professional (CPP) professional certification program and the efforts of the Protection Officer Security Academy's Certified Protection Officer (CPO) program directed primarily toward uniformed security officers are both noteworthy steps in the right direction.

Legal Status & Liability: With few exceptions, private security personnel have no police powers beyond those of thier fellow citizens. Their work, however, is quasi-law enforcement in nature and thus they interact with and confront their fellow citizens in adversarial situations very much like public police. Effort must be made to keep the distinction clear and to concentrate private security efforts on asset protection and loss prevention programs. When apprehensions and arrests must be made, it is essential that the procedures followed are both legal and ethical. The courts of many jurisdictions are just beginning to realize the full extent of the private security industry and how frequently its practitioners interact with the public.

These court reviews of arrest, privacy, malicious prosecution, assault and search & seizure issues to name a few are producing both constantly changing rules and laws under which private security must operate, as well as large money judgements against both security companies and individual security officers when their behavior violates often-changing and unclear 'rules of the game'.

Image: The public's perception of private security is rapidly outgrowing the 'rent-a-cop' or 'floor walker' image, but there is still room for improving both the relationship between and the perception of us by police agencies.

The International Association of Chiefs of Police (IACP) has recently officially recognized our industry and formally noted our contribution to crime prevention and control, and has urged its members to work for a closer degree of cooperation between the public and private sectors.[3]

Proprietary Security: Corporations now expect its security personnel, particularly those in middle and upper management positions, to be more than simple 'security experts'. Businesses today expect their security to come out of its traditional isolation and to get into and contribute to the mainstream of the business venture.

Certainly security expertise is still essential, but in addition security executives are expected to be knowledgeable of general business concepts, the goals of their organization, and to make a contribution in these areas. Top management is looking for a larger return on their investment of security dollars.

Contract Security: Those businesses which hire contract security are demanding more than simply a person with a uniform, badge and gun. Business is becoming more and more sensitive to its 'image' and how it is perceived by the public. The public rarely distinguishes whether a security guard is contract or 'in-house' — the guard represents and 'is' the company. Therefore, a guard who is slovenly in appearance, rude, unknowledgeable, or who makes a serious legal error in accomplishing his duties becomes either unacceptable or a serious liability — or both.

Thus, the contract officer must be well trained not only in the technical aspects of his job, but also in the expectations of the client employer, and must be a knowledgeable and courteous representative of the client. The contract security officer must be sensitive to the unique relationship that exists between he or she and the client.

Summary

Traditionally, society's efforts to prevent and control crime have been the province of public (government) law enforcement, although private 'security' efforts have been woven into the fabric of crime control since earliest times.

Beginning in the second half of the 20th century, private security (whether proprietary or contractual) has taken an increasingly larger role in crime control and prevention, so that as of 1985 the resources of money (over $20 billion annually) and personnel (over 700,000) exceeds that of public law enforcement. Indeed, the most recent trend is the 'privatization' of functions such as running jails and prisons which were previously the jobs of government exclusively.

Private security is big business (over one per cent of the GNP of the U.S.) in all free-world countries and ranges from the single owner/operator private detective agency or security consultant through national contract security guard companies and investigative agencies, to multi-national security firms and alarm companies. The thousands of proprietary security personnel, working only for a single employer and in his interests only, must also be included.

The industry, because of its size, has begun to attract the attention of legislatures and of the courts, and in those instances where self-restraint and legal and ethical considerations are neglected, the legislatures and courts are establishing the standards under which we are required to operate.

In other cases, the courts are also punishing, through monetary awards to injured parties, those private security practitioners who 'go too far' and offend public sensibilities.

The industry is also growing in sophistication and professionalism. It is attracting personnel and leaders who would be a credit to any profession. With both continued growth and professionalism, which seems assured, the future of private security and that of those in the profession, seems bright.

Footnotes:

[1] Henry Campbell Black, "Black's Law Dictionary", (St. Paul, Minnesota; West Publishing Company, 1951) P 1028

[2] Green and Farber, "Introduction to Security", (Los Angeles, California: Security World Publishing Co., Inc., 1975) p 27

[3] For a thorough discussion and detailed analysis of the relationship between private security and public law enforcement in America, see: William C. Cunningham & Todd H. Taylor, "The Hallcrest Report: Private Security and Police in America", 1985, Chancellor Press, 7316 Hooking Road, McLean, Virginia 22101.

SECURITY QUIZ
History of Private Security

1. _____ is that which is laid down, ordained or established, and that which is obeyed and followed by all citizens, subject to sanctions or legal consequences. (Fill in the blank)

2. Our modern-day law enforcement officer called the _____ is derived from the Anglo-Saxon political leader known as a 'Shirereeve'.
(Fill in the blank)

3. The court of _____, originally established by Henry VII to lessen court corruption, was later abolished under Charles I after it became the symbol of royal abuse and tyranny.

(Fill in the blank)

4. The term _____, by which England's policemen are known, developed out of respect for Sir Robert Peel who began the first salaried, full-time police force in London in 1829.

(Fill in the blank)

5. In 1985, private security in the U.S. employed more people than all of public law enforcement combined.
   ☐ T ☐ F

6. Edward I, a prolific legislator in the area of law, was known as the "English Justinian".
   ☐ T ☐ F

7. In the U.S., true police agencies, following Sir Robert Peel's example, began to flourish beginning in the mid-1800s.
   ☐ T ☐ F

8. The 'Praetorian Guard' is considered by many historians as:
   ☐ (a) the first police force
   ☐ (b) the first formal civilian guard
   ☐ (c) the first executive protection force
   ☐ (d) the first semblence of a jury

9. Lawyer and novelist Henry Fielding, in 1750, took over London's Bow Street police station, and:
   ☐ (a) created the first known plain clothes detective unit
   ☐ (b) started the "night watch" system
   ☐ (c) neither of the above
   ☐ (d) both (a) & (b) above

10. In the U.S., the first industry to have its own police force was the:
   ☐ (a) textile industry
   ☐ (b) the retail industry
   ☐ (c) the railroads
   ☐ (d) the printing industry

FIELD NOTES & REPORT WRITING

By Martin A. Fawcett CPO

Consider for a moment what our world would be like without newspapers, magazines, books or any other kind of written material. How would we learn about things that were happening in other parts of the world? How would we learn new skills, become educated or pass what we have learned on to others?

The only source of knowledge that we would be able to obtain would be that which was readily at hand to us through other people, providing they were willing and able to pass along this information. Without the written word for us to read and to learn, we would still believe that the world was flat, there wouldn't be the advances in technology that we have become accustomed to over the years such as television, radio, automobiles — and the list goes on and on.

In order for man to advance as he has and to continue to advance, there must be a written word that can be passed on to future generations in order that they will learn through our mistakes and our successes.

As you may now appreciate, the written word is an important and integral part of our personal and professional life. There is not one part of our culture that is not affected directly or indirectly by the written word. It is the foundation upon which we build our knowledge, our experience and our life.

In the Security Industry, like other professions, the written word is an important "Tool of the Trade". It is the means by which detailed, factual reports of events or incidents are recorded so that others may learn what has occurred and if necessary, take action.

A protection officer in the course of duties may encounter a myriad of events or incidents which will require the passing of factual information to person(s) who were not present at the event or incident. In order to effect this duty, the protection officer must be able to accurately observe the event and then take those observations and put them on paper in a clear, concise and logical manner.

This passing of information takes the form of **Notes and Reports.**

Unfortunately, experience has shown us that many people lack appreciation of the value of taking good notes and preparing proper reports. There are no prerequisites set by employers on notes and reports in most instances, and the matter of notebooks and the manner of report writing is often left up to the individual protection officer or his immediate supervisor's discretion.

Experience has also shown us that many inaccurate reports are the direct result of inaccurate or incomplete notes. This has led to losses in assets, information, statistical data and convictions in court.

As you can see, both 'Notes' and 'Reports' are very important and that it becomes incumbent on the protection officer to become as proficient and as professional in his/her use of these valuable tools.

Field Note-Taking

A protection officer's Notes may be defined simply as "a quick and accurate method of recording what you saw, did and heard".

Let's take a closer look at what the notebook is. A notebook should be:
1. Small enough to carry easily in your clothing.
2. Large enough for easy writing.
3. Cloth-bound with no looseleaf pages.
4. Pages numbered sequentially.
5. Protected by adequate cover.

Before looking at what should go into the notebook and how it should be put in, let's look first at why we need them.

There are five main areas of consideration when determining the purpose of keeping a notebook.

1. Assist in Preparing Reports
2. Detecting Contradictions in Statements
3. Refresh your Memory
4. Investigative Aid
5. Reflect Officer Ability

Assist in Preparing Reports

The protection officer, during the course of a tour of duty, may have occasion to investigate a number of events, incidents and people. In most instances, some form of report will have to be submitted. Some of the events that will be looked at will not necessarily be investigated at a place that is convenient to the protection officer.

As a result, report forms, desks, office areas, etc. will not be available. Notes will be made in the officer's notebook and a full report will be made at some point in time after the investigation is completed. It now becomes necessary for the protection officer to ensure that he has all the facts, details, names, addresses, etc., that will be required when it comes time to complete his report.

The protection officer cannot trust these facts and details to memory. The tendency to forget details and events with the passage of time is a well-known fact. Notes, properly made at the time, are seldom forgotten, will never change with the passage of time and will ensure that accuracy and detail are not lost.

Detect Contradictions in Statements

During any investigation, certain facts are made known by witnesses and suspects, and certain statements may be made by those persons involved. If the protection officer has conscientiously made good notes regarding the events, then any contradictions or changes in facts or details will be found and further questioning may result in the apprehension of the culprit or the recovery of assets or information.

If proper notes have not been made, then the officer must rely on memory, which may or may not be accurate. The proper use of notes in this instance makes for a more professional investigation and more credibility when questioning people regarding conflicting facts.

Refresh Memory at Later Date

As discussed earlier, man's memory is far from infallible. Notes made at the time of an event will not change and form a permanent record of events as they occurred or were observed by the protection officer.

They become an invaluable aid when trying to recall an incident or specific detail of an investigation at a later date. The notes will remind you of what you actually saw, did and heard.

This in turn assists you in report preparation, giving evidence in court, or in apprising a supervisor of what occurred. The courts have long recognized the value of the written word over memory.

Investigative Aid

In some instances, an investigation into an event or incident may take many days and many hours to complete. During the investigation, notes are being made of each step in the investigation and subsequent reports are being filed as they are completed.

Should you become involved in this type of investigation, then it becomes apparent that it is most cumbersome to carry around a briefcase filled with reports concerning the event.

The use of a notebook in these instances makes the investigator's job that much easier, as he has much greater freedom in packing around a notebook filled with facts than in carrying around a briefcase filled with numerous reports.

Reflect Officer Ability

Many times during his career, the protection officer may be required to show his notebook to any number of different people. He may be required to show it to his supervisor on a regular basis; he may be asked to produce it in court as part of his evidence.

In any of these circumstances, the protection officer's abilities may be judged solely on the basis of what is presented in his notes. (Note: While the protection officer may not be directly involved in the investigation, interrogation process, what he/she saw, did or heard is vital to the information-gathering process.)

Tips on the Use of Notebooks

While most of the rules governing the preparation and content of report writing apply to note taking, here are a few items worthy of mention.

1. Prepare your notes in a legible manner -
This means that you are able to go back anytime in the future and be able to understand what you have written. Many people are unable to go back even a week in their notes and be able to remember what has occurred because they are unable to make accurate observations from their own notes.

2. Keep your notes complete -
If your notes are legible and you are able to go back and read them and understand them, you must also ensure that there is enough detail in your notes to give you a complete picture of the event that you are detailing. Again, many people will jot down some basic facts regarding an incident, but if asked to relate what actually occurred, they are at a loss because their notes are incomplete.

3. Be Systematic -
Record your observations in chronological order; don't bounce around in your story as this becomes confusing when refreshing your memory at a later date. Also, keep the day-to-day details pertaining to your tours of duty in proper sequence. It does no good to have to look back through an entire notebook to find one day's events. If your notes are kept in proper order, it becomes easy to find specific information no matter when it occurred.

4. Abbreviations -
As long as you can remember what word or phrase you are abbreviating, then go ahead and use them. If you will be unable to remember what the abbreviation means, then use the full form of the word or phrase.

5. Use all pages and spaces -
Use all spaces and all pages in your notebook. By leaving spaces, you are not only wasting space, but you are leaving yourself open to questioning regarding the accuracy of your notes at some future time. The courts, especially, view the leaving of blank pages and spaces with extreme scepticism believing that you may have added or deleted vital information. Don't fall into this trap. Always fill in every line, even if you must draw a line as a filler.

6. Develop your own style -
Remember that these are your notes. Develop a style that

is comfortable for you to use. Everyone will have a slightly different style of using a notebook and no one way is better than another. Try different methods and use those that will be of benefit to you and discard the rest.

7. As soon as possible -

Get into the habit of making your notes as soon as possible after an event or incident. The longer you wait to record your observations, the less you will remember. The best method is to write down your observations as you make them, and to note details provided by witnesses as they give them. If this is not practical; then at the earliest possible moment, take the time, stop what you are doing and make your notes.

8. Ripping out pages -

Whenever possible, avoid ripping out pages from your notebook. Should the occasion arise that you must do this, take a page from the back of the notebook and use it. When this is done, you should note the time and date on the stub that is left.

9. Errors -

Should you make an error while making an entry, do not attempt to erase it. Draw a single line through the error and initial it, then continue. Any other method is unacceptable in a court of law.

10. Personal notes -

Personal notes have no place in your notebook. If you find that you need to jot something down and do not have any extra paper to write on, tear out a piece from the back of your notebook as discussed earlier. Never leave any personal notes in your notebook.

11. Opinions -

Opinions have no place in your notebook. Remember that your notebook is a "diary" of what you saw, did and heard, not your opinion.

12. Review -

Always try to take your notes with the idea that you will, at some point in the future, have to re-read them and be able to understand all that occurred. After you have completed your notes on an event, review them and see if they make sense, and if they tell the entire story and represent the event as it actually occured.

Remember — There is no better way to ensure accuracy than properly prepared, properly preserved and properly presented notes. This information will be invaluable to the protection officer in bridging the gap between the "First Occurence" and their "Later Use".

"The dullest pencil has a better memory than the sharpest mind."

Report Writing

The basic elements of report writing are taught in the elementary and high school years. All protection officers have had a certain level of education and must know how to lay out and write an account of their actions.

They should understand singular and plural persons, past, present and future tense; masculine, feminine and neuter gender. They should have a good vocabulary and know how to spell. In general, before they even become a protection officer, they should have a reasonable education.

A dictionary should be within reach at all times. The report requirements of a protection officer today are much more rigid than in past years — therefore, standards must be higher.

You must combine your prior learning with knowledge of security work, experience and common sense for better security reports. Remember, your written work is the mirror of your mind at the time of writing. Even more important, it may well be a permanent reflection of your thinking.

A well written report by an efficient protection officer displays not only their proper application to duty in the field, but their completeness as a competent individual in applying their academic side to their vocation. Today both qualities are not only desired, they are imperative.

Progressive protection officers who recognize a weakness in themselves in the field will attempt to improve. A recognized weakness in written work must be treated likewise.

Do not become one of the smug individuals who say to themselves, "I'm as good as, or better than, other officers. I just can't put it on paper." Do something to improve this self-acknowledged weakness. It will be easier for you to eliminate the problem than to live with it.

Who Security Reports are for:
1. The Security Supervisor
2. The Security Organization
3. The Client
4. Various Civic Organizations
5. Various segments of Industry
6. The Courts (Criminal & Civil)
7. Anyone who may request and is entitled to proprietary information.

Security reports are prepared by the protection officer in order to pass on information to those concerned parties who are not present at the time of the incident or event. The report must be complete and accurate and answer all possible questions the reader might have.

The security report that is incomplete or inaccurate will have to be sent back to the writer for clarification, which is not only a waste of valuable time, but shows a lack of professionalism on the part of the writer.

Many reports are copied and sent on to other organizations or individuals. Depending on the type of event, some reports end up being read by lawyers who may be defending or prosecuting a case based on the event reported.

Many of these people will have little if any experience with security work, and the only information available to them will be the security report. As a result, your company, yourself and other protection officers may be judged solely on the basis of the security report.

Remember this point each time you set out to write a report. Your report must be clear and concise, accurate and complete. The reader of the security report must be able to understand what has occurred based on the contents of the report.

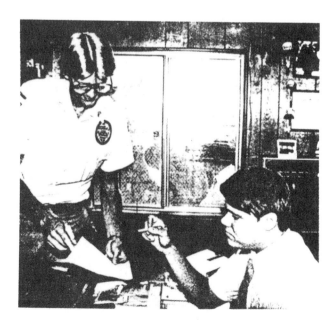

Types of Security Reports:

There are a large number of different types of security forms and reports, and each client or company will have some that are unique. Some of the more common varieties that you may encounter are:

1. Daily occurrence
2. Weekly summary
3. Motor Vehicle Accident
4. Department memorandums
5. Visitor access logs
6. Administrative policy
7. Employee evaluations
8. Event occurrence
9. Post Orders

Planning the Security Report

Before writing a security report, particularly a lengthy one, the protection officer should plan how he is going to write it before starting. All the relevant facts should have been obtained and should be readily available.

All relevant reference material, Post Orders, Directives and Dictionary, etc. should be readily available for quick and accurate reference.

You should not be rushed in compiling your information into the written format of the security report. The most common error made by protection officers is that they rush through their reports believing that they have done a satisfactory job and that their time is of more value in the field than in writing the report.

In fact, the opposite is true. The protection officer who takes the extra time to properly write a complete and accurate report is of more benefit to his/her employer than the one who races through reports and makes mistakes.

Reports should be completed as soon as possible after an event has occurred and never later than the end of the tour of duty. Leaving reports to pile up only encourages the protection officer to hurry through the reports. Remember that report writing is just as important as patrolling and should be given the same thoroughness and attention to detail.

Avoid Distractions, be thorough: Go to the area that has been set aside for writing your reports, place all your

materials down, make sure that you have everything you will need and then you will be ready to start your report.

Before beginning to write, arrange all your facts into chronological order so that the reader can progressively follow you through the sequence of events.

Refer to your notes and other reference material to verify that you have the correct information. Absolute accuracy is essential, do not trust your memory in relating facts. Check facts before committing them to paper.

Vital facts such as names, addresses, company names, vocations, times, occurrences, etc. should be emphasized in the report. This can be done in a number of different ways. Block lettering is useful in a written report, as is underlining. Choose a method that makes these facts stand out from the rest of the information in the report.

First-person conversation, when used, should be in quotation marks. A word of caution about direct conversation — if you are not absolutely accurate in reporting what was said, word for word, **don't** use quotation marks.

Start off saying that what was spoken was "words to the effect" and then write down what you believe was said. Using quotation marks at the wrong time has been the scourge of many a protection officer and could result in misleading the report reader.

Avoid abbreviations, unless they are in common use. The writer must clearly indicate which facts are attributable to their own actions or observations and which were the actions or observations of others.

If certain facts are not available at the time you write your report, then these facts must be clearly spelled out along with what action has been taken or will be taken in order to complete the report.

Never leave a report incomplete at the end of your tour of duty without authorization and without attaching a memo to indicate the date you expect to have it completed.

To ensure that your reports are submitted in the proper manner, they must be kept in a safe and secure place away from any unauthorized personnel. Confidentiality is a key component in the report writing process.

The Six Essential Ingredients

There are six main essential ingredients that must be included in most security reports. Not all security reports will contain these ingredients. Some, such as access logs, will only contain a minimum of information; however, whenever an event occurs or an incident requires reporting, then all six ingredients will be present and **must** be included in the report. These six ingredients are: **Who, What, When, Where, Why** and **How.**

1. **Who** - relates to who was involved in the event, the name of the complainant, client, witnesses, suspects, accused parties or officers.
2. **What** - relates to the type of incident or event, what actually occurred.
3. **When** - this is the time and date that the event occurred.
4. **Where** - this is the location that the event took place, or subsequent locations depending on the type of incident.
5. **Why** - this is the motive. It can frequently be determined by proper investigation. It may explain the reason for the occurrence, but can't be officer speculation or unfounded opinion.
6. **How** - how did the event come to your attention, how did it occur. This means the complete details about how the event happened from start to finish.

In a normal occurrence report outlining even the simplest event, all six ingredients will be present. Unfortunately, most protection officers fail to include all six ingredients as some of the details seem unimportant at the time.

This results in lost information that may prove valuable at

some later time and may also lead to the embarrassment of having to explain a sloppy report to an irate client or supervisor.

Always ensure that all six ingredients are properly explained in your report.

Security Reports are Important

We have been stressing the importance of submitting complete, accurate security reports, but before we go further into how to write useful reports, let's examine just what it is about reports that makes them so important.

1. Accurate and permanent record (memory bank) - Reports that are submitted become part of the "paper flow" of your organization. Every business, no matter how large or small, requires a certain amount of paper flow.

With proper record-keeping, this paper flow will allow you and every other member of your security team to instantly access information that has been stored. If proper security reports are written and filed, this storehouse of information can be priceless. This includes manual and electronic filing.

2. Detecting Problem Areas - We have already examined the reasons that the passing of information is a vital tool in our everyday lives, but in security it becomes ever more important. The submission of reports allows every other officer access to your experiences while on the job. Everything that has occurred while on duty has been properly submitted in the prescribed report format.

You are now able to access that information as far back as your file/data system allows. This can become a useful tool to the effective protection officer who sees from many reports various patterns forming regarding a problem area in the security of the facility.

It may be something as innocuous as a side door being constantly left unlocked. You may only have noticed it once and not thought much about it.

But if a number of reports pointing to the same event are filed, it suddenly becomes a serious matter, a breach in security that may indicate an employee is testing the security.

3. Statistical Data - From the security reports that are generated, it is possible to compile statistics that may eventually assist in justification of existing or future expenditures in the areas of personnel, equipment and facilities.

4. Indication of Work - This means that there is a simple and effective way to check on the amount of work and the type of work each officer has been doing.

Report Organization

The security report detailing a specific occurrence should contain an introduction, a body and a conclusion.

Introduction

The introduction should let the reader know in the briefest manner what basically occurred. It should include the date and time, the location, people involved and what happened.

Body

The body will include a detailed chronological narrative of what actually occurred, observations made, and subsequent interviews and inquiries, witnesses' names, statements and descriptions.

Conclusion

The conclusion will show what follow-up actions are still required and expected time of completion, preventative action taken, and a brief summary of any points that are not completely answered in the body of the report.

All reports, no matter how seemingly insignificant, have value. The value is the information contained. It must be remembered that information is our greatest asset in security work. We must have it to operate effectively. It is of little value if it is retained by one individual. Through reports, this information is recorded and is disseminated to the security personnel.

Every person who writes a report, fills out a form or makes a memorandum, must question in their minds what essential ingredients are required. They must ask themselves this question: "Is my work clear, concise, accurate and complete."

Every security report must be self-explanatory. It must clearly paint a word picture for the reader. If it does not, then the report has failed to serve its purpose. A well-written report must contain the following properties:

1. Clear - The language and format must be simple and to the point; facts must follow a logical sequence.

2. Legible - When handwritten or printed, the reader must be able to understand what is written; it must be easily read by others.

3. Complete - All available information will have been included in the report covering all six essential ingredients.

4. Accurate - All facts presented in the report must be accurate. To ensure accuracy, the officer must make the effort to check and double-check facts before committing them to writing.

5. Brief - Keep the report as brief as possible by eliminating excess words. The report needs to have all essential ingredients, with nothing more.

6. Re-Read - Before submitting a report, re-read it and be sure that all the questions that could possibly be asked have been answered in the report. Do not assume that the report is complete until you have proofread it. If necessary, re-write the report.

7. Prompt - Reports must be completed as soon as possible and never later than the end of the tour of duty. All reports must be handed in to the appropriate person as soon as possible in order that the information contained in the report can be acted upon quickly.

Remember, you must satisfy the questioning mind of your supervisor, who does not see you at work, and the judgement of your abilities will come from reading your reports. Your personal evaluation is often based largely on the type of report you submit, so take care in the preparation of your security reports.

A shift properly conducted, but inadequately reported, not only fails to provide the administration with the products needed for proper record-keeping, but reflects on the protection officer's total job performance. On the other hand, reports alone do not equate to an effective protection officer.

QUIZ
Field Notes & Report Writing

1. Notes and reports can be considered tools of the
_____ to the protection officer.
(Fill in the blank)

2. An officer's notes are a quick and accurate method
of recording what he _____ _____
and _____ (Fill in the three blanks)

3. Properly made notes will ensure that _____
and _____ are not lost.
(Fill in the two blanks)

4. It is important to double check and _____ .
all facts before committing them to a report.
(Fill in the blank)

5. When choosing a notebook, which of the following
should be considered:

☐ a. small enough to carry easily in clothing
☐ b. pages numbered sequentially
☐ c. durable cover
☐ d. all of the above
☐ e. none of the above

6. Notes will assist the officer in:

☐ a. preparing reports
☐ b. refreshing memory
☐ c. reflecting officer ability
☐ d. all of the above
☐ e. none of the above

7. Notes are important in ensuring that:

☐ a. facts will not be forgotten
☐ b. your supervisor knows you are doing a good job
☐ c. you will remember what shift you are working
☐ d. all the above
☐ e. none of the above

8. The protection officer must be able to observe accurately and record observations on paper in a clear, concise and logical manner.

☐ T ☐ F

9. Accurate reports can be traced back to poor notes.

☐ T ☐ F

10. Detecting contradictions in statements result from a protection officer's interrogation.

☐ T ☐ F

OBSERVATION SKILLS & MEMORY

By R. Lorne Brennan CPO

In the profession of security, as in other professions, you develop various skills which make your job easier. Observation as well as memory are skills such as these.

You will find that as your **observation and memory** skills improve, all aspects of your job become easier. This will show from the way you handle situations right through to the written report you will complete after — from the way you conduct your patrols to the way your peers and supervisors see you.

One of the differences between a professional security officer and other security officers is that the professional can and does utilize his senses, through observation and memory, in all aspects of the job.

The Professional Security Officer Will:
— Be able to see a problem situation forming and be able to take appropriate action before the situation erupts.
— Be able to give more accurate descriptions of people, places and things he encounters.
— Be able to see signs of untruths when interviewing people.
— Be able to conduct more effective patrols, both inside and outside.
— Be able to say with full confidence that he has conducted his tour of duty in the best possible manner.

Observation is the act of noticing and noting the information we gather through our senses. The degree to which we observe is what this chapter is all about. The following pages will assist you in understanding your senses as related to security and in developing your skills of observation as well as your memory.

Most people feel that our five senses and our memory are automatic and some people just have better senses and memories than others. This idea is wrong. Your five senses and your memory, although somewhat automatic in function, are skills. You can build these skills just as one would build muscles, through use and 'awareness'.

As a professional security officer, you will rely on these skills; the better you can use them, the more effective a job you can do. You need to be able to see, hear, smell, touch, and taste with accuracy and be able to remember this information for your notes, reports and discussions with fellow guards.

Your Five Senses
Your five senses are the basis for effective observation. The information these senses gather is the information you use, through your memory, in every aspect of security work.

Your ability to gather information through your senses depends fully on your awareness.

Example 1:
You are on a floor patrol and you enter the lobby of the building on your way back to the security office. There are many people and much movement. After you make your way to the office and your supervisor asks what is happening in the lobby, could you say:
— How many people were in the lobby?
— Did they all seem to belong there?

— Was all the fire safety equipment in place and in good working order?
— Did anyone need assistance or directions?

Example 2:
You are now sitting at your desk, the phone rings, the caller tells you a bomb has been placed in your building. After the caller hangs up, do you know:
— If the caller was disguising his voice?
— If the caller was calling from a phone booth?
— The approximate age of the caller?
— Did you note anything else or were you not aware and now can't remember.

You can think back to a time, probably not that long ago, when you were confronted with a similar situation. A situation we all fall into, when we look without seeing, of listening without hearing, of touching without feeling, not knowing what we smell, or not knowing what we taste.

The difference is in 'thinking' about our surroundings and being 'aware' of what is happening around us.

Sight
What can we do about sight? There are a few things we should know about seeing and perception that will improve the information our eyes are giving us.

Visibility:
The visibility of an object depends upon three things:
1) The **Distance** from the observer.
A person who has distinctive features will be recognized by friends or relatives in daylight up to 100 yards away while a person who is not known by the observer can only be

recognized in daylight up to 30 yards away. In contrast, a person can rarely be recognized beyond 10-12 yards under a full moon.

2) The Size of the object.

A large object can be recognized at a further distance because its features are more distinctive. The larger the object is, the further away the observer will be able to recognize it.

3) The Illumination of the object.

The amount of light that reflects from an object to the observer's eye determines how easily the observer will recognize the object. The observer can recognize an object easier by sunlight than by street lights.

The direction of illumination is also a factor. The observer can see much better if the light is on the object and away from the observer, than toward the observer.

The observer must also remember the color of illumination can change the color of the object to the observer's eye.

Problems related to sight in observation:

1) Night Vision — At night you use the periphery of the retina to receive light. The problem you run into is that if you look directly at an object at night, it tends to fade away because the image strikes a "dead spot" in the eye.

To solve this, look slightly above, below or to one side of the object, thus the image will not strike the "dead spot" of the eye.

2) Position of the observer — The position of the observer in relation to the object can alter the observer's perception of the object.

A seated person will often over-estimate the height of a person standing nearby. Keep this factor in mind when recording descriptions.

This problem also works in reverse. It is hard to estimate the height of a person seated close by a standing observer.

Hearing

This is an important aid in identifying persons, places of events, and things — especially at night when sight is limited. You must be aware of the different sounds which are normal at your worksite.

The following are sounds which you should learn to recognize and be able to differentiate:

1. Activity Noises — animal calling, footsteps, glass breaking, etc.
2. Voices — volume, pitch, accents, intonation, etc.
3. Motors — drills saws, foreign vehicles, domestic vehicles, etc.
4. Firearms — pistols, rifles, shotguns, automobile backfires.

Smell

The professional security officer must be able to distinguish potentially dangerous odors, as this may assist emergency personnel, as well as cut down the extent of loss through life and property.

The following are substances you should know and be able to distinguish:
— gasoline
— natural gas
— gunpowder
— gas fumes that endanger life and health, such as chlorine gas
— smoke: wood, electric or rubber

Remember that certain substances such as gas and ether may kill your sense of smell temporarily. The longer you are exposed to any smell, the less distinguishable it will be.

Touch

This sense can give you vital information which would be difficult to obtain in any other way.

The following are some of the ways touch can assist you in your job.
1. Feeling walls or glass for heat from an unseen fire. For vibrations created by sound, movement or tools in a burglary.
2. Check the pulse or heartbeat of an unconscious crime or accident victim.
3. Examine doors and windows in the dark for signs of forced entry.
4. Check tires, engines or mufflers for warmth to see if a car has been running recently.
5. To identify types of cloth or paper.

Taste

This sense should never be used on the job by anyone who has not received extensive training and then only with extreme caution.

Never taste any substance which could be narcotic or poison. You won't like the trip.

Memory

Memory is the act of recalling information.

You need this skill, and it is a skill, in order to be effective in the security field. You may have developed your senses to their peak, but if you can't recall the information they give you for your notes and later your reports for your superiors, you are not fulfilling your responsibilities.

Your memory skills, like your muscles, grow the more they are used. Therefore, you should incorporate memory tests into your everyday life.

These memory tests need not be complicated and take a lot of time, but can be extremely simple and can be done at any time of the day or night, in any atmosphere.

Here are some simple tests to assist you in improving this skill:

1. During your patrols or even when out shopping, examine a pedestrian who walks by you and mentally record their appearance. Then double back and determine how close your mental record was to the person's appearance.

As you progress, cut back on the time you take to study the person and lengthen the time you take to double back to re-examine them.

2. Use this same technique on display cases in stores or other locations which have a variety of objects.

3. Study photographs, set them aside, write lists of your observations, then compare. You can also do this with objects in a box.

4. **Discuss** with other guards what events or characteristics arouse their suspicions about situations or persons. More than increase your memory capacity, this will give you a chance to relay information you remember about specific situations and allow you to see others' views about what they remember.

How to Improve your Senses

1. Sight:

Ensure that your vision has been tested and that it is in peak medical condition. (If you require glasses or contacts, ensure that you wear them.)

Make a conscious effort to see instead of just look. Be 'aware' of what you look at. This can't be stressed enough.

Ensure you understand the various factors that affect your vision and learn how to compensate for them.

2. Hearing:

Ensure your hearing is in peak medical condition.

Know and be able to distinguish various sounds sometimes associated with crime and also those sounds which are normal for your job site.

Know your limits. Don't state that you heard a particular sound unless you are 100% sure that is the sound you heard.

When making your round, take time to stop and just listen. It's amazing the sounds you're not aware of.

3. Smell:

Know when this sense is limited, through a cold or other sinus condition. Guard against this happening to you.

Know the various danger smells and be able to distinguish them.

Be aware of what you smell; take time to give this sense justice.

4. Touch:

Don't hamper this sense by covering it with other materials.

Know when and how to use it; i.e., for feeling doors when there is a possible fire in the area.

Know the feel of different material. This may assist city police in identification of suspects you encounter.

GENERAL DESCRIPTION

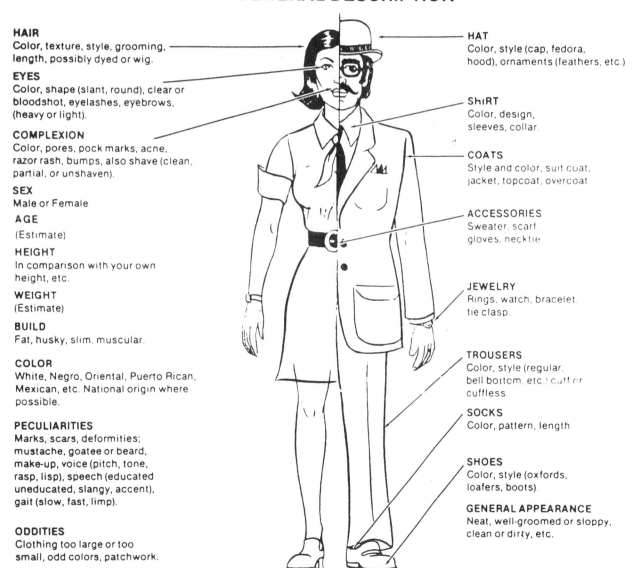

HAIR
Color, texture, style, grooming, length, possibly dyed or wig.

EYES
Color, shape (slant, round), clear or bloodshot, eyelashes, eyebrows, (heavy or light).

COMPLEXION
Color, pores, pock marks, acne, razor rash, bumps, also shave (clean, partial, or unshaven).

SEX
Male or Female

AGE
(Estimate)

HEIGHT
In comparison with your own height, etc.

WEIGHT
(Estimate)

BUILD
Fat, husky, slim. muscular.

COLOR
White, Negro, Oriental, Puerto Rican, Mexican, etc. National origin where possible.

PECULIARITIES
Marks, scars, deformities; mustache, goatee or beard, make-up, voice (pitch, tone, rasp, lisp), speech (educated uneducated, slangy, accent), gait (slow, fast, limp).

ODDITIES
Clothing too large or too small, odd colors, patchwork.

HAT
Color, style (cap, fedora, hood), ornaments (feathers, etc.)

SHIRT
Color, design, sleeves, collar.

COATS
Style and color, suit coat, jacket, topcoat, overcoat

ACCESSORIES
Sweater, scarf, gloves, necktie

JEWELRY
Rings, watch, bracelet, tie clasp.

TROUSERS
Color, style (regular, bell bottom, etc.) cuff or cuffless

SOCKS
Color, pattern, length

SHOES
Color, style (oxfords, loafers, boots).

GENERAL APPEARANCE
Neat, well-groomed or sloppy, clean or dirty, etc.

5. Taste:

Know the taste of the drinking water at your worksite. This will assist you in case of possible additives being placed in the drinking water.

Other than in this case, the sense of taste should never be used.

As you can see, the skills which have been discussed in this chapter will serve you in all aspects of your work. You, your peers, your supervisors will notice im-

provements in all aspects of your job the more you work on these skills.

The more exercises you do, the easier these skills will become. Use the diagrams in this chapter to assist in your training. The more 'aware' you become, the easier the exercises will become.

Remember to always be aware of the senses you are using at any given time, and make a point of utilizing them to their fullest capabilities. 'Think' at all times which of the senses will give you the most and the best information and then remember that information.

OBSERVE AND REMEMBER

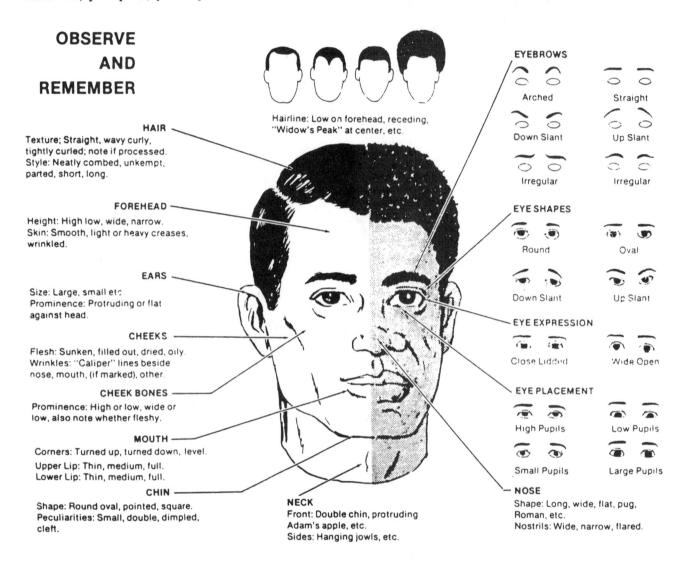

Hairline: Low on forehead, receding, "Widow's Peak" at center, etc.

HAIR
Texture; Straight, wavy curly, tightly curled; note if processed. Style: Neatly combed, unkempt, parted, short, long.

FOREHEAD
Height: High low, wide, narrow. Skin: Smooth, light or heavy creases, wrinkled.

EARS
Size: Large, small etc. Prominence: Protruding or flat against head.

CHEEKS
Flesh: Sunken, filled out, dried, oily. Wrinkles: "Caliper" lines beside nose, mouth, (if marked), other.

CHEEK BONES
Prominence: High or low, wide or low, also note whether fleshy.

MOUTH
Corners: Turned up, turned down, level. Upper Lip: Thin, medium, full. Lower Lip: Thin, medium, full.

CHIN
Shape: Round oval, pointed, square. Peculiarities: Small, double, dimpled, cleft.

NECK
Front: Double chin, protruding Adam's apple, etc. Sides: Hanging jowls, etc.

EYEBROWS
Arched   Straight
Down Slant   Up Slant
Irregular   Irregular

EYE SHAPES
Round   Oval
Down Slant   Up Slant

EYE EXPRESSION
Close Lidded   Wide Open

EYE PLACEMENT
High Pupils   Low Pupils
Small Pupils   Large Pupils

NOSE
Shape: Long, wide, flat, pug, Roman, etc. Nostrils: Wide, narrow, flared.

QUIZ
Observation Skills & Memory

1. Your ability to gather information through your senses depends fully on your _____ (Fill in the blank)

2. The visibility of an object depends largely upon _____ _____ and _____ (Fill in the three blanks)

3. _____ is the act of noticing and noting the information we gather through our senses.
(Fill in the blank)

4. The position of the subject in relation to the observer can alter the observer's perception of the subject.
☐ T ☐ F

5. To help improve your sight, you should:
☐ a) Ensure your vision is in peak medical condition
☐ b) Ensure you understand the factors which affect your vision.
☐ c) Be aware of what you look at.
☐ d) All of the above

6. When we use our senses effectively, we are:

☐ a) Aware of odor
☐ b) Aware of sound
☐ c) Aware of touch
☐ d) All of the above

7. Some aspects of your job will become easier as your observation and memory skills improve.
☐ T ☐ F

8. Which sense should almost never be used?
☐ a) Taste
☐ b) Hearing
☐ c) Sight
☐ d) Touch
☐ e) Smell

9. To be effective in security, you need to be able to:
☐ a) See a problem situation forming
☐ b) Give an accurate description
☐ c) Use Radio 10 Code if required
☐ d) All of the above

10. There is no need to know the "normal" sounds at your worksite.
☐ T ☐ F

Name 24 things wrong with this picture.

By Charles A. Sennewald, CPP

Answers

UPPER LEFT QUADRANT
- Star in front of the moon
- Corner building has 3 floors on one side, 2 on the other
- Schick misspelled
- Lady is shaving her face
- Bar Mitzvah is an event, not a location
- Theatre marquee not over a theatre
- Upper light in traffic signal is Stop, not Go

LOWER LEFT QUADRANT
- 'Walk' indicator in conflict with stop light
- Car going against one-way sign
- Bar & Grill sign hung too low
- Man crossing street with both left arm and leg forward
- Driver and steering wheel on wrong side of car

UPPER RIGHT QUADRANT
- Clock misspelled
- Clock numerals are wrong
- Storefront awnings are down at night
- Coffee shop sign says 'Open 24 Hours,' but is closed

LOWER RIGHT QUADRANT
- Hot dog stand has umbrella up at night
- Selling icecream from hot dog stand
- 24-hour coffee shop has daily hours posted
- Auto parked on wrong side of street
- No street lights

- Tractor and trailer parked in a business district
- Right lane sign not visible to approaching vehicles

Unit 2

Patrol Techniques
Safety – Security
Traffic Control
Crowd Management
Crime Scenes

PATROL TECHNIQUES

Christopher L. Vail

History of Patrol

Security work encompasses many different and various functions; however, there is one function that is common to all security agencies - the job of patrol. In order to understand the technical aspects of patrol, it is important to see how this function came about; how it developed and how it changes over time. Eugene O'Neill, a famous writer once said, "The past is the present, isn't it? It's the future, too." Therefore, to gain more insight and understanding of the patrol function today, it's necessary to see its genesis. The very word "patrol" is thought to be derived from the French work "patrouiller," which originally meant "to tramp in the mud." To many, this translation may well reflect what may be described as a function that is "arduous, tiring, difficult, and performed in conditions other than ideal."

Patrol has roots that go back to the days of the caveman. The caveman moved from the solitude of the cave to small family groups which became clans or tribes. Tribal customs developed and informal codes of conduct evolved, although laws did not follow until written records were kept. The people were the police. The chief of the tribe or clan exercised all executive, legislative and judicial powers. Eventually, the tribe or clan chief appointed members to perform such duties as that of bodyguard or enforcers of his edicts. Crimes against a member of the tribe or clan were handled by the person injured or by his family. Crimes against the clan or tribe were handled by the group itself. This led to rather harsh, barbaric, and retaliatory punishments often known as the concept of "an eye for an eye, a tooth for a tooth."

Around 2100 B.C., the first codification of customs was written by Hammurabi, King of Babylon. Under these laws of Hammurabi, it is believed that messengers were appointed to carry out the commands of the law, i.e., the first form of patrol duty. About 1400 B.C, Amenhotep, King of Egypt, developed a marine patrol on the coast of Egypt, this being the first recorded history of a patrol unit.

In early Greece, guard systems were established to protect the tower, highways, and the person of Pisistratus, ruler of Athens. Ancient Rome saw the establishment of quaestores (inquirers; also basically judicial officers) who would go to the house of the accused and blow a trumpet or horn as an indication of his arrest. In 27 B.C., under Augustus, Emperor of Rome, the Praetorian Guards were formed to protect the life and property of the Emperor, and urban cohorts were established to keep the peace of the city. The vigiles (from which the word vigilantes comes) were formed to patrol the streets and act as enforcement officers. While they were non-military, they were armed with staves and the traditional short-swords. These patrolmen were also assigned to patrol geographical precincts.

The Romans began to move north toward England, leaving Europe in a terrible state of turmoil and strife for about five centuries after the fall of the Roman Empire. Little is known of policing and law enforcement during this time. Between 450-650 A.D., the Anglo-Saxons in England developed small groups of people known as tuns (from which the word town comes). A form of individual and group responsibility for policing began to emerge through the concept of local self-government. Around 700 A.D. tithings (groups of ten families) were formed for the purpose of maintaining the peace and protecting the community. Tithingmen were elected by the group, and their responsibilities included raising the hue and cry upon learning of a crime in the group, and dispensing out punishment. Ten tithings were called a hundred and the head man was called a reeve. Several hundreds within the same geographical area were collectively called a shire (the equivalent of our county) and the chief law enforcement officer was called a shire-reeve (what we now call the sheriff).

William, the Duke of Normandy, introduced a highly repressive police system in 1066 A.D., in which collective security was deemed far more important than individual freedom in England. He divided England into 55 separate military districts and appointed an officer of his choice to be the shire-reeve in each shire, or military district. The state assumed the responsibility for keeping the peace in this system. England lived under this system until the Magna Carta (Great Charter) was written in 1215 A.D., guaranteeing civil and political rights to individuals, and restoring local control to the communities.

In 1252 in England, the watch system was established. People appointed to the duty of watchman had the responsibility for keeping the peace. They were unpaid, and were the dregs of society - the old, infirm, sick, and criminally inclined. After 1285, some watches grouped together for the purpose of safety, forming a "marching watch", which may be considered the first form of patrol organization found in our present-day system. The only paid watchmen were those paid by merchants, parishioners, and householders. In 1737, the Elizabethan Act of 1585 was enlarged to allow cities to levy taxes to pay for the night watch.

In 1748, Henry Fielding suggested that policing was a municipal function and that some form of mobile patrol was needed to protect the highways. The Bow Street Runners were formed, with a foot patrol to operate in the inner areas of London, and a horse patrol to operate in the outer areas. In 1829, the Home Secretary, Sir Robert Peel, introduced "An Act for Improving the Police In and Near the Metropolis" - the Metropolitan Police Act. This legislation forms the basis for law enforcement organizational structure in America. Setting the stage for organized patrol activity, one of the 12 fundamental principles of the Act stated that "the deployment of police strength by time and area is essential." By the end of 1830, the metropolitan area of London was organized into seventeen divisions and superintendents were appointed. Patrol sections were created, and each section was broken down into beat areas.

Basically, Peel replaced the patchwork of private law enforcement systems then in existence, with an organized and regular police structure that would serve the state and not local interests. He believed that deterrence of criminal activity should be accomplished by preventive patrol officers trained to prevent crime by their presence in the community. Hence, modern patrol was born.

America was founded along the Atlantic coast and many English systems and beliefs became the basis for our social, political, legal, and governmental systems. The New England part of America was built and developed basically under a system of commerce and industry. Communities were formed around towns and villages, which relied on constables to provide protection and keep the peace by using the watch system. The South developed differently. It was more rural and agricultural with smaller communities. The county was the primary form of government, in which the sheriff system was the prominent form of law enforcement. As the country developed further to the mid-west and west, law enforcement organizations combined the functions and roles of constable and sheriff.

Patrol activity in America can be traced to Boston in 1636, when a night watch was formed. In 1658, New York City formed a "rattle watch", so named because they used a rattle to communicate their presence, and signal each other. Philadelphia formed a night watch in 1700. Just as in England, these early watchmen were lazy and inept. Often times, people who committed minor crimes were sentenced to serve on the watch as punishment. As can well be imagined, order discipline was a major problem, leading New Haven to create a regulation that said "no watchman will have the liberty to sleep." A 1750 Boston rule said that "watchman will walk their rounds slowly and now and then stand and listen."

Following this rule - as well as making sure to look up, down, and all around, are good procedures for contemporary protection officers to follow.

Uniformed and paid police did not come about until the early-to mid-1800's. In 1833, Philadelphia began paying police officers and the New York City Police started wearing uniforms around 1855. Politics and corruption permeated police departments as America grew during the 1800's. In 1855 Allan Pinkerton founded the Pinkerton Detective Agency in Chicago, which became the forerunner of the U.S. Secret Service. As America grew, policing took on new shapes and challenges, with the addition of technological advances, new organizational and political structures, new laws requiring more police officers, societal reliance on law enforcement, and the slow growth of private police and security agencies. However, the patrol function of police and security remains the same, and is considered "the back-bone" of security and police agencies.

Security patrols may be routine and boring to some; however, the patrol activity of today is much more than "tramping in the mud," sounding the hue and cry, or shaking a rattle. The officer of today who protects a facility is responsible for the safety and security of physical - and often intellectual - assets of tremendously high value. He/she is responsible for the safety and security of a work force consisting of people who are educated, well-trained and professional - a huge investment of human worth and productivity. Today's security officer has the availability of training, equipment, and technology heretofore unheard of. We now live in an age of more random violent criminal activity, much of which is directed toward innocent victims; of drug related crime; of juvenile crime involving senseless violence; of overloaded legal systems; and, of more and more civil litigation. At the same time there is more being demanded from property and organizational managers in terms of protection from fire, disaster, and accident. Administrative agencies at the federal, state, and local level continue to enact new regulations that employers must follow. **Security officers have more responsibility now than they have ever had before.** In fact, the patrol function is more

than just the backbone of security; it is also the heart and soul of a total loss control approach.

Purpose of Patrol

The function of security is to prevent and control loss. As a means of accomplishing this, patrol officers make periodic checks around a facility. Therefore, patrol can be defined as the act of moving about an area to provide protection and to conduct observation. That is a fairly simplistic definition, since while protection and observation may be the major elements of patrol, there are numerous other functions that the officer may be called on to perform during his or her tour of duty. Based on organizational needs, there are several major purposes of patrol:

1. **Detection of criminal or unauthorized activity.** Contingent upon organizations' needs; this could include trespassing, noise violations, safety violations, lease violations by tenants, alcohol violations, parking violations, etc. In order to be effective at this, officers must be intimately familiar with organizational rules, laws, and patterns of criminal behavior, all of which are constantly changing.

2. **Prevention and deterrence of crime and unauthorized activity.** This includes projecting a security presence into the environment. Making the security program visible will at least temporarily suppress criminal/unauthorized activity.

3. **Ensure compliance with organizational policy.** At the same time this is done, public/community relations are maintained by interacting with persons in the work environment. Relations with tenants, vendors, neighboring security departments, and local law enforcement certainly come into play here! Additionally, officers may help ensure compliance with administrative agency regulations such as OSHA, EPA, or Labor Department mandates.

4. **Assess, report, and record loss causing situations or circumstances.** This could include any type of fire, safety, or health hazard, such as chemical spills, overcrowding of rooms/area, radiation leaks, coffee pots left on, leaking pipes, unsanitary conditions, congested areas, mechanical failures, etc.

5. **Investigate as directed by the central alarm station (CAS), dispatch, or supervisor in charge.** There are a host of possible lines of inquiry which can be requested of the patrol officer by management.

6. **Test and inspect the physical security system.** This includes alarms, locks, lights, CCTV, access points, and physical barriers such as fence lines. While assuming greater importance in high security installations, this is a function of patrols in all environments to some degree or other.

7. **Act as a compensatory measure during system outages.** Should there be an outage or malfunction of a physical security system component, the patrolling officer will stand by and assume a fixed post at the affected point/area until the situation is remedied. This may simply involve calling maintenance and standing by until a lock is fixed, or it may require continuous posting out in a high security facility with an alarm or power outage.

8. **Respond to emergencies.** This is where security patrol has traditionally varied from police patrol; while security emphasizes prevention, law enforcement emphasizes response to problems. Unfortunately security departments must be able to respond professionally to accidents, fights, fires, intrusions, assaults, thefts, HASMAT problems, or other reasonably foreseeable emergencies. Staffing levels, response times, training, and equipment must all support the requirement for emergency response.

9. **Performance of other services required by management.** This can include opening up areas and making

them ready for visitors. It could also include dispensing literature, conduction of formal or informal surveys of visitors, testing equipment, finding lost children, or acting as an escort.

Obviously, the needs of all organizations/facilities are unique. Shopping centers have different loss control needs than warehouses. Hospitals are different than power plants. Hotels are different than amusement parks. Military installations are different from college campuses. What activities occur and what activities are unauthorized vary considerably. Patrol may involve taking action against unauthorized personnel, suspicious persons, illegal activities, and suspicious automobiles. Pertinent state and local laws, and company policies, will dictate what security officers are to do in these situations. Depending on the officer's employer, he or she may also be required to conduct an investigation of criminal activity. The catch-all phrase of "performance of other services" may include a multitude of functions as requested by the officer's employer, the client, and/or as needed by others such as visitors, vendors, and employees. In any event, patrol is the "eyes and ears of security".

The provision of security services is not an "afterthought"; it is a business necessity. Organizations that don't take steps to protect their assets will lose them! Employers also have a legal and moral responsibility to provide a safe and secure workplace for their employees, and those who visit their organization. Insurance companies require that certain security measures be enacted. There are court decisions affecting security, particularly relating to the commission of wrongful acts or the omission of required acts. Federal, state and local laws, rules, and regulations dictate that certain security measures be placed in effect. Security, therefore, is a part of management in any company or organization. Patrol is the essence of providing those security measures.

Types of Patrol

There are two (2) basic types of patrol; foot and mobile. Within each type of patrol, different methods may be used, depending on many factors which will be discussed. Mobile patrols include the use of automobiles, bicycles, mopeds, and golf carts. Helicopters and horses are other means of mobile patrol, but are not all that common.

Foot patrols are conducted normally by one officer "walking a beat." Areas to be patrolled are both indoors and outdoors. The major advantage to this type of patrol is that officers can really learn their assigned areas well. While this is not an all-inclusive list of what a foot patrolman can learn, he or she will learn what doors and windows are normally locked or unlocked, what lights are normally left on at night, what personnel are authorized in certain areas, where emergency equipment is located, and what potential hazards exist. Such knowledge and information will assist the officer in determining if anything is amiss. It is also a good opportunity for the officers to become known to the employees and to establish a positive professional relationship with everyone they contact. One way to accomplish this is by discussing the above-mentioned items, or any other official matter, with the people involved. Another advantage of foot patrol is that an officer could place himself or herself at or near high security risk areas on a frequent and random basis, making it difficult for one with criminal intent to penetrate that area. Officers on foot patrol also have as much use of their five senses - sight, smell, taste, feel, and hearing, as their physical condition allows. If they are in excellent health, this is very advantageous, and they can actually "patrol" a larger area using one or more of these senses.

Major drawbacks to foot patrols are the small size of the area that can effectively be patrolled; the amount of time taken to conduct one round while carefully checking everything, and getting from one part of the area to another; access to emergency equipment if needed and personnel costs involved - it takes a lot of protection officers to provide adequate protection. Inclement weather conditions also sometimes restrict foot patrol activity.

Patrol officers can use a number of different methods of mobile patrol. The automobile is the most common form of patrol, however, many agencies find it economical, while providing other benefits, to patrol with golf carts, bicycles, or mopeds. The advantage of mobile patrol includes the very fact that it is mobile. The officer can patrol a much larger area. Depending on which type of vehicle is used, the officer has access to emergency equipment, and he/she can carry different amounts and types of equipment. Obviously, a car can carry a lot more than a bicycle, and this is a bona fide consideration when determining what type of mobile patrol to use. While a bicycle can't carry as much equipment as a car can, it can get to places a car can't, and can do it much more quietly. Other factors to consider in selecting what type of mobile patrol to use are:

1.   The initial cost of purchase.
2.   Ongoing maintenance costs.
3.   Size of the area to be patrolled.
4.   The need to access emergency and other equipment, such as first-aid kits, traffic control equipment, extra rain ponchos, additional radios, etc.
5.   The type of facility being protected, and the organizational image and culture of the facility.
6.   The threat model, and degree of vulnerability of the facility.

Depending on the size of the patrol area, a car, or in some cases where golf carts are used, the officer can also carry patrol dogs. Dogs enable the officer to search a large and/or complex environment very quickly, with minimal manpower. In very large areas aerial patrols may be conducted by helicopter. In rugged terrain, horses or ATVs may be used. Each of these methods has some capacity to carry equipment.

Preparation for Patrol

Preparation for going on patrol duty is not only the physical act of putting on a uniform; it also requires mental and psychological preparation. **Security officers should act and look professional not only while on duty, but also while going to work.** This not only produces a positive impression upon the people they serve, but it helps the officer to perform better. When they look and act like professional security officers, such demeanor demands more respect from others. This respect generates a positive attitude in the officer, and he or she becomes more confident and more competent in his or her work.

While people should not "judge a book by its cover," the fact remains that people do judge protection officers based on their first impression. Clothes "do make the man" so one's personal appearance is important. The officer's uniform should be properly tailored and in good condition - neat, clean, and pressed. There should be no holes, patches, or loose threads dangling from it. Shoes and leather equipment should be polished. Male officers should be clean shaven. Hair and fingernails should be clean. No items not authorized by the employing organization should be attached to the uniform.

The officer should have a positive attitude when going to work - his or her mind should be focused on the job ahead. No personal problems, hobbies, or business should be carried to work with the officer.

There should be absolutely no ingestion of alcoholic beverages or other psychoactive substances at least eight hours before going on duty. The officer should have had ample rest before going to work, as he or she will need to be both mentally and physically alert on duty. **Officers should have a positive attitude and an accompanying bearing that reflects courtesy, politeness, and a willingness to serve.** These are basic qualities of professionalism, which instill confidence in a department.

All personal and company equipment issued or used while on duty should be checked to ensure that they are in working order. For example, an officer conducting an interview or investigation while away from the office, may be embarrassed to find his or her pen has dried up. Or, the officer's radio may not receive or transmit because the battery is dead. Without having checked beforehand to see if it worked, the officer could also be dead. Officers need to know all policies, rules, and regulations that pertain to the security of the facility, and particularly, the assigned patrol post. While proper procedures for performing the job should be known, many officers have their own procedures for accomplishing a task. If used, they should be in compliance with accepted practices of the security agency, the client, and certainly, the law.

It is important when preparing to go on patrol, that the officer knows the property he or she is protecting "like the back of his/her hand."

The location and condition of emergency equipment, water shut-off valves, electrical controls, fire alarms, and telephones should be known, as the patrol officer may be the first responder to a situation requiring their use. The location of any hazardous materials, or places where hazardous materials are worked with, should be firmly implanted in the officer's mind. All doors and windows, and the condition they're normally found in, should be well known. This includes the knowledge of existing scratches or other marks which, if not known about in advance, might be a sign of forcible entry. Also, some doors and windows are frequently left open, some partially open, and some should never be open. Knowledge of the state of these exits and entrances is very valuable to the patrolman.

The alert patrol officer will know what type of conduct, organizational behavior in this case, is considered acceptable or normal at his or her facility. Conduct which is considered abnormal in one area or section, may be very commonplace in another. Examples of this conduct include such things as: what doors are normally left ajar; what vendors or service personnel use what doors regularly; what computers are left on; what certain smells or odors are normal; and, what types of people frequent the facility. The officer must first be able to determine what is customary for his or her patrol area, and then look for actions, conditions, or patterns which are unusual. Each officer must decide in his or her own mind, and to his or her own satisfaction what is suspicious. This will vary widely from one officer to another, depending on his or her experience, background, training, attitude, and type of environment in which he or she works. **A successful officer is one who is able to combine a logical suspicion with being a skillful observer, and has enough natural curiosity to investigate those conditions that he or she feels are unusual.**

If an officer works the night shift, it's advisable to visit the work site during the day. This will give the officer a fresh and clearer perspective of his/her responsibilities. For example, the officer might discover the existence of doors or windows that he or she didn't even know were there. He or she might discover that a part of the facility thought to be empty or unused, is really full of expensive equipment. Or, the officer might find that an area thought to contain valuable equipment or materials, is actually empty or full of items to be discarded. It also gives the officer the opportunity to talk with and discuss security issues about the facility with other officers, whom he or she normally doesn't meet.

Some techniques that enhance an officer's ability to detect unusual situations include:

* Getting to know people in the patrol environment. Maintain a professional - not personal - relationship with them. Have some idea what their jobs and/or functions are. Most people will gladly elaborate on what they do if asked in a tactful manner.
* Inspecting equipment. Get in the habit of checking maintenance tags on equipment. Know what the equipment does.
* Getting to know maintenance personnel and procedures. Consider taking an orientation tour with the maintenance department.
* Visiting the central alarm station, if possible. Become familiar with the alarms and CCTV in each protected point and area.

There are many different sorts of incidents that could occur to an officer on patrol that may require immediate action on his or her part or on the part of others. As the first responding authority to such incidents, the officer should be mentally and physically alert and able to respond to these incidents, making correct decisions as to what needs to be done. The officer may have to take immediate action using his or her own professional knowledge, skills and abilities, or he or she may have to direct others such as the police, EMS, fire, or maintenance personnel to the scene via the most expedient way.

In some circumstances, the officer may have to control a gathering group of onlookers and it is essential to know how to isolate them from the crisis point (problem area). Being able to block off an area quickly and efficiently is obviously important in emergencies. Since anything could happen at any time, the effective security officer knows his or her patrol area very well.

When arriving for duty, an officer should be briefed by a supervisor, or check with the previous shift for any unusual events or occurrences; suspicious activities or persons; facility problems dealing with security, fire or safety; orders, directives, and policies; and any expected VIP's, vendors, contractors, etc. Determine if there are any communication "dead areas", and where they are. In other words, to be fully prepared to go on patrol, an officer must know what has happened, what is happening and what is likely to happen.

One area of preparation often overlooked by many officers and departments is that of continuing training and education. With the many and increased demands being placed on security personnel today, it is essential for the officer to stay abreast of the latest laws, equipment, products, services, and procedures in security. This information is gained only through education or training. Companies who contract out for their security services, proprietary security departments, and security companies themselves, should provide basic and on-going training for their security officers. Companies can either establish internal training programs, send officers or require officers to attend local colleges that have security educational programs, or have their officers take home-study courses.

There are also private vendors who specialize in conducting security training programs. If a local police department has a "ride-along" program, this can provide excellent training for the security officer. Another way for an officer to gain new information and knowledge is by reading security and law enforcement related professional journals and magazines. PROTECTION NEWS, SECURITY, POLICE AND SECURITY NEWS, FBI LAW ENFORCEMENT BULLETIN, AND SECURITY MANAGEMENT are all excellent sources of up-to-date professional information.

Techniques of Patrol

As stated earlier, patrol is defined as the act of moving about an area to provide protection, and conduct observation. In the security world, the majority of patrol activity is focused on the prevention of criminal behavior. A crime cannot occur unless three elements are present: the opportunity, the desire and the tools. Patrolmen have a direct influence over the first one, and some influence over the second. An effective patrol officer, by following accepted patrol procedures, can and will hinder the first element - the opportunity to commit a criminal act. By ensuring all doors and windows are properly closed and locked, by ensuring there is adequate lighting in vulnerable areas such as where safes or valuables are kept and around the building(s) proper, and by making access difficult to possible targets for criminal activity, opportunities for the criminal are reduced or eliminated. This is the very essence of loss prevention.

While the patrol officer may not be able to directly influence the desire of a person to commit a crime, that desire is greatly hampered by the very presence of a security officer performing his or her patrol duties in a professional way. It is indeed a rare criminal who will commit a crime in the presence of a patrol officer (although it has happened), especially one who is visible,

alert, and showing confidence. The third element is not a controllable one by security personnel, however, security officers should know what tools are generally used by criminals. Guns are obviously a tool, but some people have the authority and permission to carry weapons. Screwdrivers and pry bars are common everywhere, but in the hands of a criminal, they become burglar tools. Information gathering equipment, such as photographic or recording devices, may be used to steal information. Radio transmitting or monitoring devices may also be used by terrorists and sophisticated professional criminals.

Patrol is never routine; anything is liable to happen at any time. Therefore, there are two major principles of patrol that guide the effective patrol officer. **The first principle of patrol is that it should always be done in a random fashion.** Never patrol by driving or walking in the same direction. Alter routes; change the pace occasionally; walk or drive for a while then stop to look and listen. Sometimes, turn around and backtrack your route. If someone is trying to figure out where the patrol officer will be at any given time so that they may conduct some illegal act, random patrolling will keep them off guard.

The second principle of patrol ties in with randomness - the frequency of patrol should be random. Do not go on patrol the same time each time; the officer's patrol schedule should always vary. Depending on the vulnerability of the facility being protected, the officer may want to patrol the area once every few hours, once every two hours, once an hour or more each hour. At the very least, every facility or area should be patrolled, when going on duty, and just before going off duty. Patrol should never be conducted the same way each time by timing or route; there should be nothing predictable about a patrol officer's schedule as the officer should not patrol by a set routine or pattern.

With the use of automatic monitoring systems or bar-code technology, patrols are documented. These systems generally require that officers patrol in a set sequence within an established time period. Using a random patrol route with a bar-code unit is still possible by approaching each patrol point from a different direction. Times may also be varied to some degree.

Another principle of patrol is communication. Patrol officers should always keep the command post, supervisor, back up officer or central alarm station advised of where they are and what the situation is. They must follow proper radio procedures such as:

1.   Listening before speaking into the radio.
2.   Depressing the microphone a split second before and after speaking to ensure that all syllables are transmitted.
3.   Speaking clearly and slightly slower than normal into the microphone.
4.   Not broadcasting when not necessary.
5.   Avoiding the use of profanity, horseplay, or confidential information on the radio. Scanners abound - especially with reporters.

Patrol officers must also thoroughly document their observations. There should be detailed notes taken on any unusual, suspicious or potential loss causing situation. Notes must be kept professionally and observations reported up the chain of command to the appropriate management personnel. Forms designed specifically for each environment should be on hand. Whether there is a pre-designed form or not, the important thing is to **report all situations where there is any doubt as to**

their importance.

Although it is not a patrol technique in the true sense of the word, officer survival is a **major consideration** when on patrol. One way to survive patrol is to use "sensible" patrol methods, i.e., use all five natural senses - sight, hearing, smell, touch, and sometimes, although rarely, the sense of taste on patrol. The two strongest senses the officer will use are that of sight and hearing. If riding in a motorized vehicle, an officer should keep the windows opened a little, allowing him or her to detect the sound of breaking glass or other noises of suspicious origin. He or she should not play a commercial radio loudly if the car is equipped with one as it could drown out noises that require investigation. An open window will also allow the officer to use his or her sense of smell to detect the smell of smoke or other odor that should be investigated.

Often a person is known to have a "sixth sense." This means that they seem to know "when something just isn't right", or they get a "feeling" about a person or a situation. This sense is called intuition. It develops from experience, and it permits a person to sense what is abnormal or unusual. While an officer cannot testify in court that he or she performed a certain duty by using his or her "sixth sense," it can be very accurate in determining when something needs further investigation. While it can be used as a guide to determine which action or actions are appropriate, it should never be used as the sole determining factor.

Another means of patrol survival is the use of the mental "what if? game." This game (also known as creative daydreaming or mental rehearsal) is played as an officer patrols his or her area by thinking of any possible incident, remote as it might be, that could occur at any place or time. For instance, the officer could think of what to do if someone came running out of an office or building that is supposed to be closed and locked, just as he or she gets there. The officer could think about what actions to take if he or she heard a loud explosion, or gun shots in the area. What would an officer do it he or she smelled smoke in the area, or if the officer saw a fire in progress? What would an officer do if he or she saw a chemical leak in progress? The list goes on and on. **"If this happened, what would I do?"** is the question asked by security officers playing this game. It might uncover a potential loss event that has occurred or is occurring. It will also keep an officer up-to-date on company rules, regulations, policies and procedures. It is a form of self-training, as the officer can determine his or her own needs for improvement and take the appropriate steps to correct any deficiencies in his or her professional life. Finally, it makes response to the event more efficient, should it occur. It may save the life of an officer, or the life of another.

Light and noise discipline should be practiced when on patrol. This means that patrolling officers should avoid making any more noise than is necessary. They should keep the radio turned down somewhat, keep keys and equipment from jangling, etc. They should be able to "hear others before they hear you". Note that radio net discipline is also important: over use of the radio ties up the net and depletes the battery. Extended conversations should be carried out by land line methods such as telephones or Fax phones. Note too that backup means of communication should always be considered when on patrol or fixed post duty: always have a contingency plan if the primary means of communication doesn't work.

Similarly, light discipline should be practiced. This means to avoid being silhouetted. Never sit with lights behind you or stay in a car with the dome light on. Use a clipboard light or flashlight. If there is a glare from lights, use it to your advantage if necessary! Use flashlights judiciously; don't have them turned on more than necessary (although for walking safety they should be used if other light sources are not available). "See others before they see you".

Factors that Influence Patrol Effectiveness

As patrol is an expensive loss control technique, it only makes sense to have the officer detect the greatest number of loss causing situations as possible. The WAECUP Theory of loss control can be applied here:

WASTE Patrol Officers check scraps being thrown away, look for lights, heat, and water turned on needlessly.

ACCIDENT Officers look for spills and other slippery walking conditions. Always observe all around patrol points for fire hazards, materials stacked too high, etc. "Look up, down, and all around".

ERROR Patrol officers should be thoroughly briefed prior to their shift as to what activities are occurring in their patrol environment. They should check and double-check schedules of building openings, shipments of personnel arrivals. In many cases the Security department functions as "the grease in the machine", making things run smoothly between different departments. In most organizations, Security makes sure that things don't "fall through the cracks". This is particularly true. Patrol officers can play a key role here in alleviating problems caused by simple human error.

CRIME Become familiar with criminal behaviors in the local area. Also, keep up to date on criminal trends within the industry. Speaking with local police and reading industry specific management literature are good ways to maintain one's professional education. Also patrol in a random manner and develop professional relationships with people in patrol area so that you are approachable. If people observe something that doesn't quite seem right, and they are comfortable talking with a security officer about it, they will! This can uncover numerous potential crimes.

UNETHICAL/UNPROFESSIONAL PRACTICES

Patrol officers should be wary of fraternizing with employees ("familiarity breeds contempt"). They should also be on guard for possible indications of: collusion between employees, employees who constantly work when no one else is around, gambling between employees, racist graffiti in bathrooms and elevators, employees conducting competing businesses using company resources, etc.

Since observation and perception are key to effective patrol techniques, the officer should be aware of certain internal and external factors that can influence his/her ability to perform on patrol effectively. While the officer may not be able to control all of these factors, the very realization that they exist can help the officer be more effective. Internal factors include:

Fatigue: being tired or worn out can affect the way an officer perceives things (with the use of all five senses).

Boredom: the more often a task is performed, the more it becomes routine and boring. Boredom leads to stress; stress leads to hasty, improper decisions being made. This can be a deadly distraction if not kept under control.

Personal problems: preoccupation with personal

problems distracts from keeping one's mind on the job at hand and should not be brought to work with the officer;

Known facts: officers with security or law enforcement experience will recognize things such as burglary tool marks or the smell of marijuana more quickly than an inexperienced officer.

Variety of activities: officers do many various things, many of which don't even appear to be connected and things can happen very quickly. Other employment, such as an extra job, can influence an officer's work performance (see fatigue above).

Failing senses: age or illness affect an officer's senses; the older or sicker he or she becomes, less quickly the body is able to respond to stimuli. Obviously keeping in good health aids in being more discerning on patrol. It also makes for better interactions with others; something which is critical to the success - and job survival - of the officer.

There are also external factors that can affect the ability to perform the patrol function effectively. Some of these factors are:

Environmental conditions: such as the weather, highway traffic and conditions, lighting (day patrol vs. night patrol, interior patrol and exterior patrol).

Distance: things that are closer to us are easier to perceive, and things more distant are harder to identify clearly.

Time: the more intense a person's involvement in an activity, the faster time seems to go. Also, security officers may work shift hours and often an officer needs to adjust his or her "internal clock" both at work and at home.

Duration of the input: the longer a stimulus is received, the more accurate the interpretation will be.

Fixed Posts

While not patrols in the strict sense of the word, fixed posts manned by security personnel are a part of almost every facility. In some cases these are in designated structures like those manufactured by commercial suppliers. In others they may consist of manning a desk in the lobby during evening hours. Many situations support the use of temporarily fixed posts such as at public events, at traffic control points during rush hour, or during heightened periods of security such as strikes.

Regardless of the employment, fixed posts represent a substantial amount of man hours and cost. Fixed post duties should be performed in a professional manner, bearing in mind the following:

1.   **The mission or objective of the post must be clearly understood.** The reason for the existence of the post should be specified in written post orders. These orders should be readily available to the officer manning the post.

2.   **Duties as mandated by the post orders should be read and understood.** A supervisor or auditor who inspects the post should be favorably impressed with how well the officer knows his or her duties.

3.   **Post orders should be kept neat, orderly, and secure.** Persons without a "need to know" should not be told what the orders of the post are.

4.   **Light discipline - the avoidance of being silhouetted should be maintained just as on patrol.** "See others before they see you".

5.   **All equipment, especially communications equipment, should be checked when first manning the post.** Simple tests of detection equipment (X-ray, metal detectors, explosive detectors, etc.) should be conducted as early in the shift as is practical. Manuals for the use of the equipment should be readily available. Officers must

be accountable for the presence and condition of all equipment on post.

6.   **Officers being relieved on post should brief their relief officer.** A pre-designed form can be made for this in large, complex operations, or a simple list of things to advise the relief of can be made up by the officer being relieved.

7.   **In high-threat situations such as strikes, civil disturbances, or crowds that could trample an officer, a route of retreat should always be open to the officer manning the post.** There may also be justification for concealing the post or building cover into it. Whatever the situation, safety of the officer must be the paramount value.

8.   **Comfort - reasonable comfort - should always be afforded to officers on post.** Care should be taken to ensure that guard booths are not so hot as to induce sleepiness.

9.   **Fixed posts should be visible from other posts, patrolling officers (on foot or in a vehicle) or CCTV.** This helps to ensure safety of officers, and provides overlapping visual coverage of the area being secured.

10.   **Officers should not leave the post until properly relieved.** This is of critical importance in high security installations or where a contract firm is billing a client for a fixed post officer. Officers should stay in the immediate vicinity of the post. They should check out the area near the post for unusual or unacceptable conditions, prior to assuming it.

Conclusion

The need for security is not a modern requirement. The caveman was initially concerned only for his personal well-being, then he became responsible for his immediate family's safety and security. Eventually, families became clans or tribes which evolved into communities. Security became a social responsibility. Within this responsibility, the patrol function with designated people to conduct the patrols, dates to early Egypt. Despite political, legal and other changes, the patrol function has remained the primary means of providing security services to communities, regardless of whether they are public or private entities.

Protective services in America are based on English precedents. Modern-day patrol techniques can be traced to Sir Robert Peel's reforms in 1829 in England. While there have been tremendous changes in technology, society, world political scenes, economies, and the work forces themselves, the purpose of patrol today remains as it's always been: the protection of property and lives, the prevention and detection of crime, and the performance of other services. Today's security officer has many more duties and responsibilities than his predecessors. Because of that, today's officer cannot be from the lowest level of society. He or she must be technically competent in patrol techniques; the laws, rules, and regulations pertaining to security; and numerous other areas of responsibility such as fire fighting and medical emergencies. Embracing the WAECUP theory, and putting it into practice, will go a long way towards making patrols more cost-effective and professional.

Proper training and preparation for patrol, professional work habits and attentive patrolling techniques will enhance the patrolman's skill and abilities. What was once considered a punishment for minor criminal offenses, or a job with little or no responsibility for the "down and out," is rapidly becoming a profession.

In conclusion, professional patrol performance may be considered using the following acronym:

P **Preparation**
A **Alertness**
T **Thoroughness**
R **Reports**
O **Observations**
L **Language (communication)**

References

Bopp, William J. and Schultz, Donald O. PRINCIPLES OF AMERICAN LAW ENFORCEMENT AND CRIMINAL JUSTICE, Springfield, IL: Charles C. Thomas, 1972.

Bottom, Norman R. Jr. and Kostanoski, John I. SECURITY AND LOSS CONTROL, New York, NY; Macmillan, 1983.

Brisline, Ralph F. THE EFFECTIVE SECURITY OFFICER'S TRAINING MANUAL.   Boston: Butterworth-Heinemann, 1995.

Cole, George F.   THE AMERICAN SYSTEM OF CRIMINAL JUSTICE, 7th Edition.   Belmont, CA: Wadsworth, 1995.

German, A.C., Day, Frank D. and Gallati, Robert J.   INTRODUCTION TO LAW ENFORCEMENT AND CRIMINAL JUSTICE.   Springfield, IL: Charles C. Thomas,

Purpura, Philip P. SECURITY AND LOSS PREVENTION: An Introduction, Stoneham, MA. Butterworth-Heinemann, 1991.

United States Nuclear Regulatory Commission SITE SECURITY PERSONNEL TRAINING MANUAL.   Springfield, VA National Technical Information Service, U.S. Department of Commerce, 1978.

RESOURCES

Butterworth-Heinemann has books on physical security, alarms, report writing, and security in schools, hotels, colleges, office buildings and retail stores (800-366-2665), 255 Wildwood Avenue, Woburn, MA. 01801.

Professional Training Resources has books and videos on patrol, and a multitude of other Security topics. (800-998-9400). P.O. Box 439, Shaftsbury, VT. 05262.

Performance Dimensions Publishing provides patrol books, videos and equipment. (800-877-7453), Powers Lake, WI 53159-0502.

QUIZ
Patrol Techniques

1.   List five of the purposes of patrol:
A._____
B._____
C._____
D._____
E._____

2:    An officer who works an evening shift should visit the site during the _____to see the change in activities there.

3.   Patrolling officers should check their equipment _____to going on patrol.

4.   Patrolling officers should play the "_____game" to both discover and prepare for possible emergencies.

5.   While patrolling in a vehicle, the officer should keep the _____opened so as to be able to hear and smell better outside the vehicle.

6.   Patrolling officers should look _____, _____ and all around their patrol areas.

7.   Embracing the WAECUP theory and putting it into practice will go a long way towards making patrols more cost-effective and professional.
   ☐ T   ☐ F

8.   Avoid silhouetting and "_____others before they _____you".

9.   Officers on post should always_____their relief officer.

10.   Patrols should occur at the same time every day.

   ☐ T   ☐F

SAFETY & THE PROTECTION OFFICER

By David J. DeLong CPP

The disciplines of safety and security share the same common objectives — conservation of the company's assets, human life and property alike. Each approaches the goal of providing a safe and secure physical environment utilizing the same methods, eliminating, segregating or protecting against potential hazards.

Many companies combine the disciplines of safety, security and fire protection into one single department because of their common objectives. This department is usually referred to as the loss control department or the loss prevention department usually directed by a manager or administrator.

The protection officer by nature of his duties is in a position to observe and correct unsafe conditions, unsafe acts and potential hazards. The protection officer can play a significant role in accident prevention and safety awareness.

Basic Elements of a Safety Program

The protection officer should be familiar with the basic elements of the safety program at his company because his activities may have an influence on the program.

1. **Company Safety Policy**
   A company safety policy provides a guide outlining the responsibilities of all employees whether they are hourly workers, supervisors or managers in the prevention of accidents, injuries and illnesses on and off the job site. Without a formal safety policy, the reduction or elimination of accidents is extremely difficult.

2. **Safety Committees**
   Safety committees are a vital component of a successful company safety program. Safety committees carry out the following basic functions which enhance the overall safety program:

   • Discover unsafe conditions, unsafe practices and identify hazards, and make recommendations to control or eliminate them.

   • Discuss safety policies and procedures with recommendations for management.
   • Teach safety to committee members who will in turn teach safety to all employees.
   • Review accident reports recommending appropriate changes.

3. **Safety Audits or Inspections**
   The protection officer should be familiar with safety audits or inspections because this procedure is a principal method of discovering accident causes. The safety audit or inspection uncovers unsafe conditions and work practices by means of inspection and provides the means of promptly correcting these unsafe conditions and work practices.

A safety program that initiates regular safety inspections or audits demonstrates to employees, management's interest and sincerity in accident prevention. Also, inspections enable the individual worker to make contact with loss control personnel on a one-to-one basis. The worker can point out unsafe work conditions unique to his work area that would otherwise go undetected. When a worker's suggestions are acted upon, he realizes that he has made a contribution to the safety program and his viewpoints are taken seriously.

Normally, when safety inspections are conducted, checklists are used. Each company, plant or department usually develops its own checklist. Items usually included on an inspection report are as follows: housekeeping, material handling, material piling and storage, aisles and walkways, machinery and equipment, electrical and welding equipment, tools, ladders and stairs, floors, platforms and railings, exits, lighting, ventilation, overhead valves, protective clothing and equipment, dust, fumes, gases and vapors, explosion hazards, unsafe practices, hand and power-driven trucks, fire fighting equipment, vehicles, guards and safety devices, horseplay and maintenance.

The protection officer should remember that the safety inspection is one of the best methods to prevent accidents and safeguard employees.

4. **Safety Training**
   An effective company safety program is based on proper job performance. When employees are trained to do their jobs properly, they will do them safely. Supervisors should know how to train an employee in the safe and proper method of doing a job. The immediate job of accident prevention falls upon the supervisor, thus the need for supervisor safety training. Most companies give extensive supervisor safety training programs.

5. Safety Awareness and Motivation

Safety requires constant and skillful promotion. Some methods of awareness and motivation that are common in industry the protection officer should be aware of include the following:

- On-the-job safety discussion and safety meetings.
- Safety contests with awards are effective in increasing employee safety awareness and motivation, stimulating pride among departmental employees and improving the safety record.
- Posters and displays.
- Safety campaigns serve to focus the attention of the entire plant on one specific accident problem (i.e., campaign may be undertaken to promote use of safety glasses).
- Educational materials (films, newsletters, booklets, leaflets, etc.)

6. Motor Vehicle or Fleet Safety Program

Depending on the nature and type of company, the loss control or loss prevention department may organize a complete program for motor vehicle/fleet accident prevention and operator education.

7. Accident Investigation

Accident investigation is essential in the prevention of future accidents. An effective investigation should produce information that will lead to the development of countermeasures which will prevent or reduce the number of accidents.

Obviously, serious injuries and fatalities should be investigated. The near accident or incident should also be investigated to determine cause to prevent the possibility of a future accident. Near accidents usually indicate deficiencies in the system. The investigation can bring out these problems. Thorough investigations will bring out contributory causes of supervision and management.

For purposes of accident prevention, investigations should be fact-finding and not fault-finding. The investigation should be concerned only with the facts. The investigating officer, who may be the protection officer, is best kept free from involvement with the discipline aspects of their investigation.

Key Facts in Accidents

The protection officer must be knowledgeable of the key facts in accidents. Whether or not all the key facts are present in an accident will depend upon the particular case.

Key facts taken from "Accident Prevention Manual for Industrial Operations", p.154, National Safety Council 1980.

a) nature of injury — the type of physical injury.
b) part of body — the part of the injured person's body affected by the injury.
c) source of injury — the object, substance, exposure or bodily motion which directly produced the injury.

d) accident type — the event which directly resulted in the injury.
e) hazardous condition — the physical condition or circumstance which permitted the occurrence of the accident type.
f) agency of accident — the object, substance or part of the premises in which the hazardous condition existed.
g) agency of accident part — the specific part of the agency of accident that was hazardous.
h) unsafe act — the violation of a commonly accepted safe procedure which directly permitted the occurrence of the accident event.

Other items of information closely related to the key facts the protection officer should be aware of include age, sex, type of occupation and type of work.

Remember: The protection officer must be knowledgeable of the eight basic elements of a safety program. 1) company safety policy, 2) safe rules, 3) safety committees, 4) safety audits or inspections, 5) safety training, 6) safety awareness and motivation, 7) motor vehicle or fleet safety, and 8) accident investigation.

Accidents

The protection officer should have some basic knowledge of accident types and accident causes because he may be involved in accident investigation.

Definition — An accident is an unexpected event in which physical contact is made between a worker and some object, or exposure of substance which interrupts work.

The three elements to remember about accidents are:
1. an accident is an unexpected event,
2. contact is made, and
3. work is stopped or delayed.

Accident Types

Accidents normally involve a physical contact between the worker and some object, substance or exposure. With this in mind, accidents are categorized into the following basic types:

struck by -	example: struck by a falling tool
contacted by -	example: contacted by hot steam
struck against -	example: banging your head against a low beam
contact with -	example: touching a hot pipe
trapped in -	example: trapped in a tank
caught on -	example: pant cuff caught on a board, causing a fall
caught between -	example: finger caught between car and car door
different level fall -	example: falling down stairs
same level fall -	example: slipping or tripping
exposure -	example: exposure to toxic gasses,
over exertion -	example: back strain

Accident Causes

Generally speaking, there are four major causes of accidents.

1. Unsafe Acts — Action(s) by the worker that deviate from the accepted safe work procedure that cause or contribute to an accident. (examples: horseplay or worker not wearing proper personal protective equipment)

2. Personal Factor Causes — Any personal characteristic or conditions that may cause or influence a worker to act unsafely. (examples: physical or mental conditions; extreme fatigue, intoxication, attitudes)

3. Unsafe Conditions — Any condition of structures, materials, tools, equipment, machinery or other conditions of a worker's environment that cause or contribute to an accident. (examples: inadequate lighting, poor housekeeping or lack of warning systems)

4. Source Causes — Any unsafe condition has a source cause. A source cause can contribute or cause an unsafe condition which could lead to an accident. (examples: normal wear and tear; pipes corroding from within; ropes becoming rotted creating an unsafe condition; or lack of preventive maintenance)

The Role of the Protection Officer in Safety

The protection officer is trained to observe and identify potential hazards. The majority of large companies maintain a loss prevention department with protection officers on duty 24-hours a day, seven days a week. The protection officer is in a position to report and correct unsafe acts, unsafe conditions and potential hazards while conducting routine patrols.

The protection officer who observes a safety violation by a worker should:

— Record the worker's name and advise the worker of the safety violation committed.

— Notify the worker's supervisor advising him of the safety violation committed.

— Document the safety violation and forward a report to appropriate management.

The protection officer who observes an unsafe act, unsafe condition or a safety hazard should:

— Correct the condition or report it to someone who can correct the condition.

— Mark off the condition as a hazard where immediate cortive action is not possible.

— Document the unsafe hazard or condition and the action taken forwarding the report for appropriate action.

Common Safety Hazards

There are numerous safety hazards that the protection officer should be aware of. Some of the frequently encountered safety hazards or conditions include the following:

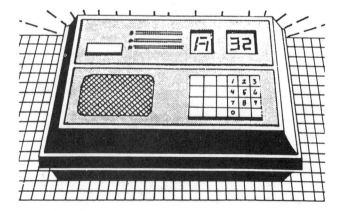

1. Fire Protection
- violation of no smoking regulations;
- unusual odors, especially smoke;
- obstructed passageways and fire door;
- inadequate exit signs;
- obstructions in front of hydrants, alarm boxes, extinguishers;
- electrical heaters, coffee pots left turned on;
- improper disposal of waste;
- flammable gasses and liquids which are uncontrolled in areas where they may pose a hazard;
- paint or painting areas poorly ventilated and not properly secured;
- gas pumping areas close to operations where an open flame may be used;
- use of flame or spark-producing equipment near flammable substances;
- missing fire protection equipment

2. Housekeeping
- missing handrails on stairways
- debris on grounds
- inadequate containers for trash
- broken glass
- obstructions on walkways; i.e., snow and ice
- oil spills or slippery substances that may cause slipping and tripping
- cables, pipe, electrical wires across aisles
- aisle obstructions
- litter accumulation on shop floors
- cracks, holes, breaks in parking lots, roadways and sidewalks

3. Doors and Emergency Exits
- burned out or missing emergency lights;
- doors that don't fit properly which would hinder emergency exit;
- improper fitting door frames;
- equipment or debris blocking emergency doors;
- improper panic hardware for doors;

4. Vehicle and Fleet Safety
   - improper audible warning devices for backing up
   - improper wheel chocking for parked vehicles
   - speeding violations
   - improper preventive maintenance procedures
   - vehicles parked in fire lane or blocking emergency exit
   - vehicles without proper signalling devices or lights
   - improper tires for road conditions
5. Personal Protective Equipment
   - improper personal protective equipment for the job
   - protective eye goggles not worn
   - safety-toed boots not worn
   - protective gloves not worn
   - hearing protection not utilized
   - respiratory protective equipment not maintained
   - proper protective clothing not worn.
6. Machinery Maintenance
   - lack of adequate guarding

   - worn belts, pulleys, gears, etc.
   - frayed electrical wiring that may result in short-circuiting
   - workers operating machinery with loose-fitting clothing
   - dangerous machinery lacking automatic shut-off devices

7. Other Hazards
   - first aid supply improperly stored and maintained
   - emergency routes not adequately marked
   - improper labelling of dangerous goods
   - broken or damaged equipment not adequately tagged.

These are the more common safety hazards encountered by the protection officer on routine patrol. The protection officer should devote one complete patrol during his shift for the observation and reporting of unsafe acts, unsafe conditions and safety hazards.

QUIZ
Safety and the Protection Officer

1. The disciplines of Safety and _____ share the same common objectives in terms of the overall protection process. (Fill in the blank)

2. The Protection Officer can play a significant role in _____ prevention. (Fill in the blank)

3. A company safety _____ provides a guide, outlining the responsibilities of all employees in terms of accident prevention. (Fill in the blank)

4. One aspect of a formal safety policy is to prevent accidents and illness on and off the job.

   ☐ T ☐ F

5. One of the main functions of a safety committee is to administer effective rescue training programs.

   ☐ T ☐ F

6. The Safety Committee has the authority to make safety recommendations to management.

   ☐ T ☐ F

7. The Protection Officer should carefully inspect the work habits of members of the workforce and report deficiencies detected.

   ☐ T ☐ F

8. A safety program that initiates regular safety inspections (audits), demonstrates to employees: (check correct answer)

   ☐ a. Management's concern for improved productivity
   ☐ b. Management's interest in accident prevention
   ☐ c. Management's concern for the off-duty worker
   ☐ d. Management's concern for an unsafe workplace

9. When a safety recommendation made by an employee is acted upon, (mark the two best answers)

   ☐ a. Management recognizes the employee's contribution to the safety program.
   ☐ b. The employee is likely to become a member of the safety committee.
   ☐ c. The employee is likely to become even more safety conscious.
   ☐ d. Management perceives this kind of action as interfering with the safety committee.

10. A Safety Checklist is useful because: (check best answers)

   ☐ a. It makes employees aware of safety hazards.
   ☐ b. It can be used by various departments to audit general safety procedures.
   ☐ c. It can be incorporated into security patrol procedures.
   ☐ d. It enhances corporate proprietary information retention.

TRAFFIC CONTROL PROCEDURES

By Arthur A. Holm CPO

An officer directing traffic at a busy site provides the most frequent contact between citizens and security personnel. The importance of bearing, appearance and attitude cannot be over-emphasized. Likewise, the skillful handling of what citizens recognize to be a difficult and hazardous job can generate and maintain public respect.

Signs and Automatic Signals

If you hold a driver's license, then your knowledge and awareness of most traffic signs can be assumed. The STOP sign is without a doubt the most important sign in use today.

Listed are three of the functions of a STOP sign which are taken for granted:

(a)   regulates traffic flow;
(b)   clarifies the question of Right-of-Way at intersections; and
(c)   reduces motor vehicle accidents at intersections.

Generally speaking, there are two main types of automatic traffic signals:

(a)   traffic lights of three colors, sometimes with an arrow for easy turning;
(b)   visual and audio warning signals commonly seen at railway crossings.

Automatic traffic signals normally provide adequate intersectional control. However, there are numerous situations which must be directed by a "point control" officer, to assure safe and efficient vehicular and pedestrian movements. Construction sites, accidents, rush hour periods, special events or any other condition which causes congestion of traffic must receive immediate attention.

Traffic duty consists of directing and supervising traffic at gates, intersections and patrolling parking areas. These duties are performed in order that traffic can be kept moving with a minimum of delay and maximum of safety.

Since traffic control duty may require an officer to remain at his post for hours, in all kinds of weather, protective clothing must be readily available. Proper protection against the elements is an important factor in maintaining efficient traffic control. It has been observed that a wet or cold officer presents a hazard to himself as well as to motorists.

Proper clothing should also include high visibility potential to increase the safety value during nighttime assignments whether the intersection is well lit or not.

Roadway Positions

The position selected to direct traffic must be suited to the particular intersection and expected traffic patterns. It must command a full view of the intersection and its approaches. In turn, the officer must be completely visible to the motorists and pedestrians. In many instances, disobedience to gestures or whistle signals is caused by the inability of the motorist to see the officer. Usually, officers assigned to traffic control will select a position in the centre of the intersection or at one of the corners.

1. The Centre of the Intersection: This position affords the greatest visibility, but is also the most hazardous. This location is usually selected when traffic signals are inoperative, traffic is not moving at a high rate of speed and where there is little pedestrian traffic.

2. The Corner Position: Intersections having heavy pedestrian or vehicular turns can be controlled by an officer standing a few feet off the curb line at one of the corners having the greatest personal safety and better pedestrian control.

Posture serves to communicate the fact that the officer is in command of the situation. He must therefore assume a military bearing, with his weight evenly distributed on both feet.

When not engaged in signaling motorists, he must stand at the 'at ease' position, facing traffic and with his hands at his sides. When directing traffic, his shoulders must be in line with the flow of traffic and his attention must be directed to the vehicular movements.

Hand Signals

Prompt compliance to hand signals is dependent upon the officer's ability to use uniform, clearly defined and understandable gestures. Intersectional control does not call for complicated choreography or wild arm movements.

Improper hand signals, although highly entertaining to bystanders, cause confusion, hesitation and lead to violations and accidents. Unusual movements undermine the purpose of traffic control and direction.

— **Stopping Traffic:** Two clearly defined motions are required to stop traffic. First, select the vehicle to be stopped. Look directly at the driver, and point in his direction with the arm fully extended. The position is held until you are observed by the driver. Then raise your hand so that the palm is extended. The position is held until you are observed by the driver. Then raise your hand so that the palm is toward the driver and the arm is slightly bent at the elbow.

Maintain this position until the oncoming traffic has stopped. With the one arm still raised, turn your head and repeat the procedure with your other hand to stop the traffic moving in the other direction. The arms are now lowered until all traffic has stopped.

— **Starting Traffic:** To start vehicular movement on the cross street, pivot a quarter turn to place your shoulders parallel with the vehicles waiting to move. When the intersection is cleared, turn your head to one side facing the waiting traffic. Attract attention by pointing to the lead car. Then, turning the palm inward, bring the hand up and over to the chin, bending the arm at the elbow.

If the driver's attention has been properly obtained, it will only be necessary to make a few motions. After traffic begins to move, the arm is dropped to the side. The opposing traffic is then started in the same manner, but with the other arm.

Slow or timid drivers may be urged to speed up by increasing the rapidity of the arm movements. However, flailing the air with wild arm gestures and shouting at the slow-moving vehicles is unnecessary and only confuses nervous drivers and may lead to greater traffic congestion or accidents.

The Whistle

The whistle, when properly used, attracts the attention of motorists and pedestrians and facilitates compliance with hand signals. Improperly used, it becomes a meaningless distraction which adds to the confusion.

To be effective, the whistle must be used in moderation. It then becomes an invaluable aid to assist in the control of the various road users. The whistle should be blown loudly and not tooted lightly. It is a means of communicating rather than a musical instrument.

One long blast is used to attract the motorist's attention to the officer's hand signals to stop. **Two short blasts** are used to give warning of unusual or dangerous conditions — turning vehicles, improper crossing and the like. The number of warning sounds should be limited as it is in this area that most improper whistle useage occurs. Normally, **three short blasts** will suffice to warn any motorist or pedestrian.

Traffic Control

For responsibility of traffic direction, you will be assigned to control for the purpose of obtaining maximum vehicular movement by preventing congestion and by safely expediting the flow of traffic. The following responsibilities must be fulfilled in order to properly carry out this assignment.

1. Regulate the flow of traffic. Give priority of movement to the most heavily travelled areas by allowing longer periods of running time. Traffic movements must be of equal and adequate time, if the intersecting streets carry an equal traffic volume. Long runs are preferable as they reduce the loss of time from frequent changes of traffic directions.

2. Control and assist turning vehicles. Supervise all vehicular turns. If traffic is exceptionally heavy or a spillback is caused by another intersection, determine the preference of traffic direction. If turning vehicles increase the amount of congestion, direct traffic to continue straight ahead during the period of the backup.

Prevent improper turns; right turns from the left lane or a left turn from the right lane must be prohibited. Not only are they illegal, but increase the potential of congestion and accidents.

Traffic backups or accidents may be caused by motorists waiting to turn left or cutting in front of oncoming automobiles. Assist vehicles wishing to turn left. Direct the waiting motorists to enter the intersection on the left turn lane. Allow approaching vehicles which present an immediate hazard to pass. Stop the other oncoming traffic and motion the vehicles turning left through the intersection.

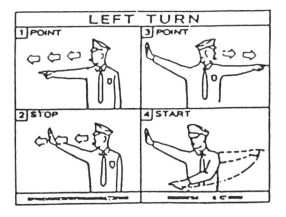

Priority of movement is determined by the amount of traffic flow in each direction. If the number of vehicles turning left is greater than the opposing traffic flow, the turning traffic is given preference. If the oncoming traffic is heavy and there are only a few vehicles waiting to turn, these vehicles are held up until a sufficient amount of traffic has been permitted to pass through. The cross traffic is not started until the intersection has been cleared.

In heavily congested situations when a large number of motorists are making right turns, hold back pedestrians to give precedence to the vehicular traffic.

3. Coordinate the flow of traffic with the adjacent intersections. Whenever applicable, allow the movement of traffic at the adjoining intersections to serve as a guide. If the vehicular movement is not coordinated, traffic spill-backs may occur by reason of traffic being stopped at the next intersection.
4. Protect pedestrians. Immediate motorist responses cannot be assured when traffic is signalled to stop. Mechanical failure, inattentiveness, or other reasons may cause failure to obey the signal. Pedestrians can then be protected only if they are held back at the curb until all moving traffic is completely stopped. Pay particular attention to children, blind or lame persons and the elderly. Escort these people across the street, if necessary.
5. Assist people seeking information. Carry a street guide or a map of the local area to assist out-of-towners or local citizens seeking directions. If an enquiry can be quickly answered, there is no need to leave the intersection. However, if a detailed explanation is necessary, direct the citizen to the curb where the answer may be given in safety. Don't leave your post, unless traffic conditions permit.
6. Assisting emergency vehicles. Stop all vehicles and pedestrian traffic when an emergency vehicle is approaching. Give the driver a "Go" signal indicating the intersection is clear. If the driver of the emergency vehicle signals for a turn, acknowledge by motioning in the proper direction, indicating that the way is clear.

There is no written, legal authorization which allows private citizens (security officers) to direct traffic on public land or thoroughfares. However, should you be requested or ordered, by a police officer, to assist him you are obligated to do so. This includes directing traffic if necessary.

On private property, the safe movement of traffic is the responsibility of the owner or someone delegated by the owner. In most cases, the delegated authority is the security officer.

7. On construction sites, assistance is required to get traffic in and out of the site quickly and safely. Highway flagmen are required for the safety of the workers and for an even flow of traffic around building or repair sites.

Gate Duty

Directing traffic from or at a gate would include such duties as — checking passes, checking trip tickets and regulating special types of traffic flow.

The position you take at a gate is determined by the design of the gate, traffic characteristics, whether daylight or night conditions, and the degree of control required. In taking up your position, keep these factors in mind:

(a)   be visible to approaching traffic;
(b)   be in a position to see approaching traffic; and
(c)   do not interfere unnecessarily with the flow of traffic.

Equipment

It is essential that you have the proper equipment when on traffic control.

1. Clothing — You must dress properly according to the weather conditions. If you are uncomfortable because you are cold or wet, you cannot perform at peak efficiency.
2. Reflective body vests and armlets. These aids help the motorist to see you and help protect your safety.
3. Flashlight — Use a flashlight with a red or orange cone on the end of it at night. This makes you more visible to the motorist and also aids in giving directions.
4. Whistle — The whistle is used to attract the attention of the motorist and is used in conjunction with hand signals.
5. Radio — The radio provides a means of communication with your supervisor or other security officers.

6. Signs — Stop and Go signs and flags are most commonly used on construction sites and highways.
7. Pass or Badge — In some situations you are required to have a pass or a badge to allow you to perform your duties at a gate, crosswalk, building or highway construction site.

General Rules for Traffic Direction

1. Select a position best suited for the intersection.
2. Use uniform signals and gestures.
3. Keep stragglers alert and rolling in their proper traffic lanes.
4. If a spill-back begins to form, look immediately for the source of the trouble and take action.
5. Be cheerful, but firm. Do not shout or argue with motorists or pedestrians.

As a general rule, protection officers are assigned to control private parking and traffic scenes. Examples are shopping centres, parking lots, sporting events, construction sites, resort areas, etc.

Each area is different and the protection officer must exhibit sound judgement in selecting his position. For example, when an extremely heavy flow of traffic is expected at a football game, a pre-game plan should be formulated.

Vehicles should be allotted space by sections ensuring one section is filled in an orderly fashion before rotating to another section. The signals to start and stop traffic are extremely important. **Practise them.**

QUIZ
Traffic Control Procedures

1. The _____ sign is without doubt the most important sign in use today.
(Fill in the blank)

2. Directing traffic from or at a gate would include such duties as checking _____
(Fill in the blank)

3. On private property, the safe movement of traffic is the responsibility of the _____ or someone delegated by the owner; e.g. a security officer.
(Fill in the blank)

4. When signalling a driver to stop, your hand should be:
   □ a) Closed
   □ b) Palm open
   □ c) Finger pointed
   □ d) Fist clenched

5. Slow or timid drivers should not be urged forward with increased rapidity of arm motion because they may over-react and cause an accident.

   □ T □ F

6. Directing traffic from the corner position is safer than a centre-of-the-intersection position.

   □ T □ F

7. Proper protection against the elements is an important factor in maintaining efficient traffic control.

   □ T □ F

8. The primary use of the traffic whistle is to attract the police.

   □ T □ F

9. General rules for traffic direction are:
   □ a. Select a position best suited for the intersection.
   □ b. Use uniform signals and gestures.
   □ c. Be cheerful, but firm.
   □ d. All of the above.

10. When on traffic control, proper equipment includes:
   □ a. Proper clothing
   □ b. Flashlight
   □ c. Radio
   □ d. All of the above

CROWD CONTROL MANAGEMENT AND PROCEDURES

By Patrick C. Bishop

Whenever people gather together in large numbers, such as at athletic events, parades, strikes, peaceful demonstrations, protest rallies, etc. there exists a potential threat for mass discord.

When disturbances do occur, it becomes the responsibility of the Police, and in some instances, that of Security Forces to restore order. Once a crowd has been allowed to get out of hand through inadequate supervision, or in spite of the best efforts by security personnel to prevent a disturbance, the task of restoring any semblance of order, protecting life and property, and the eventual disbursement of the crowd or mob is a tremendous one.

It is important therefore, that Police and Security Forces be able to quickly determine if a gathering will become uncontrollable and must be able to take immediate steps to prevent disorder. The only way this will be successfully accomplished is for the personnel of all control groups to have a good understanding of the types of crowd formations that are likely to be encountered. Also, these personnel should note the different responsibilities of Security Officer, Police and Riot Control forces.

Definitions

a) **Crowd** - A concentration of people whose present or anticipated behavior is such that it requires police action for the maintenance of order.

b) **Demonstration** - A crowd that is exhibiting sympathy for or against authority, or some political, economical or social condition.

c) **Riot** - A breach of the peace committed to violence by three or more persons in furtherance of a common purpose to execute some enterprise by concerted action against anyone who may oppose them.

d) **Disaster** - A disaster means any extreme or catastrophic condition which imperils or results in loss of life and/or property.

Formation of Crowds

a) A crowd may exist as a casual or temporary assembly having no cohesive group behavior. It may consist of curious onlookers at a construction site, spectators at the scene of a fatal accident or curious citizens who are attracted to a soap-box orator. Such a crowd has a common interest for only a short time. It has no organization, no unity of purpose beyond mere curiosity, and its members come and go. Such a group will normally respond without resentment to the urgings of a police officer to "stand back", "move on" or "keep moving". There is no emotional unity and they offer little concern.

However, even in this most ordinary and routine situation, the person in authority who is lacking in good judgement and discretion may meet with resistance. Derogatory remarks, unnecessary shoving and the like cause immediate resentment in people and become self-defeating. Impartiality, courtesy and fair play hold the key to any situation involving people.

When you instruct a crowd to "move on", it must mean everyone. If you make exceptions and allow some persons to remain, strong objections may be raised. This glaring par-

tiality may cause some of the people to defy you. Incidents such as these can rapidly change crowd attitudes, and if nothing else, impart a very poor impression of the security officer.

b) A crowd may also assemble for a deliberate purpose — spectators at a football game, a rally of some sort, or it may be a disgruntled citizen or group of citizens willing to be led into lawlessness if their demands are not met.

Members of these crowds have little dependence on each other, but they do have a unity of purpose; they are drawn together to share a common experience. If outside influences interfere with their purpose or enjoyment, it is possible for some individuals in the group to become unruly and aggressive. There are numerous instances of riots occurring during, or immediately following a sporting event or rally in which emotions run high.

Causes of Crowd Formations

1. **Basic Cause** - The basic reason for the formation of any crowd is the occurrence of an event that is of common interest to each individual. The nature of the crowd is largely governed by the nature of the event.

2. **Casual Causes** - A large and comparatively orderly 'casual crowd' may gather in a shopping area or at a sporting event. This casually-formed crowd is characterized by the fact that its members think and act as individuals. There is an absence of cohesion or organization. This type of crowd is easily controlled in its formative stages, but it may develop otherwise if the event becomes alarming, or if something occurs which causes severe emotional upset to its members.

3. **Emotional Causes** - Crowds that are formed due to events that have incited the emotions of the individual are almost invariably unruly and troublesome simply because emotion makes them blind to reason. The most frequently encountered emotional causes are:

    a) **Social** - Crowd disturbances resulting from racial or religious differences, or excitement stemming from a celebration, sports or other similar event.

    b) **Political** - A common political cause may result in attempts by large groups to gain political power or settle political disputes by other than lawful means.

    c) **Economic** - Economic causes of disturbances arise from conditions such as disagreements between labor and management, or from such extreme conditions of poverty that people resort to violence to obtain the necessities of life.

    d) **Absence of Authority** - The absence of authority or the failure of authorities to carry out their responsibilities may cause people to believe they can violate the law without fear of reprisal or hindrance.

    e) **Disaster** - Disaster conditions may result in violent emotional disturbances among people in the area due to fear, hunger, loss of shelter or injury and death of loved ones.

Psychological Factors

In addition to the factors which cause crowds to form and turn peaceful groups into disorderly mobs, it is important that people dealing with crowds understand that a small crowd often attracts a great many initially disinterested people, thereby rapidly increasing its size; this snowballing effect is caused by certain psychological factors:

1. **Security** - Certain individuals may be attracted to a crowd due to the feeling of security and safety it provides while associating with large numbers. This situation is most likely to arise during periods of civil unrest where large gangs are roaming the streets looting and threatening the safety and peaceful existence of the citizens who become fearful for their well-being and join with the gang for the security it may afford them.

2. **Suggestion** - Persons joining a crowd tend to accept the ideas of a dominant member without realization or conscious objection. If the dominant member is sufficiently forceful with their words and ideas, they are able to sway the good judgement and common-sense reasoning of those about them; there is a tendency to accept even the wildest of ideas, thus they transform the susceptible into unthinking followers.

3. **Novelty** - An individual may join a crowd as a welcome break in their normal routine and through persuasion and suggestion react enthusiastically to what they consider proper form under these new circumstances.

4. **Loss of Identity** - Similar to that of the 'security' factor. The individual tends to lose self-consciousness and identity in a crowd. Consequently, they may feel safe that they can be neither detected nor punished for any wrong-doing they may take part in.

5. **Release of Emotions** - The prejudices and unsatisfied desires of the individual that are normally held in restraint may be released in an emotional crowd. This temporary release of emotions is a strong incentive to an individual to participate in the activities of the crowd. It provides the opportunity to do things he was inwardly desirous of doing, but hitherto, has not dared.

Types of Crowds

The behavior of crowds varies widely depending on its motivation interest. Crowds are classified in accordance with their behavior patterns and it is essential that any security measures are based on recognition and in understanding of the type of crowd they must deal with. The following outline is representative of most of the crowd types that might be encountered in this country.

1. **Acquisitive** - The Members of an acquisitive crowd are motivated by the desire to get something. They are best illustrated in a crowd of shoppers seeking items in short supply or at an auction sale. They have no leaders, little in common and each member is concerned with his or her own interest.

2. **Expressive** - In this type of crowd the members gather to express their feelings such as at a convention or political rally. The expressive crowd is usually well-behaved; however, some persons in it may feel that slight disorders and unscheduled demonstrations should be condoned by the officials. When they are thwarted or restrained, resentment occurs and their otherwise cheerful enthusiasm may be replaced by hostility.

3. **Spectator** - This crowd gathers to watch out of interest, curiosity, instruction or entertainment. It is invariably well-behaved and good-humored initially, but since spectator sporting events, parades, etc. tend to stir the emotions rapidly, this type of crowd can quickly become unruly and very violent.

4. **Hostile** - Crowds of this nature are generally motivated by feelings of hate and fear to the extent they are prepared to fight for what they want. The most prominent types are strikers, political demonstrations and hoodlums or rival mobs. Hostile crowds may have leaders who direct and maintain a high degree of hostility in their followers, but not always.

5. **Escape** - An escape crowd is one that is attempting to flee from something it fears. It is leaderless and completely disorganized, but it is homogenous in that each person is motivated by the same desire, which is to escape. Once an escape crowd reaches safety, it will lose its homogenity and its members must then be handled as refugees.

Crowd Actions and Suggested Counter-Measures

The majority of crowds do not, as a rule, resort to violence; however, any crowd is potentially dangerous or at the least, aggressive. The mood of a peaceful crowd, i.e. "acquisitive", "spectator", or "expressive" may change quickly to that of a "hostile" or "escape" crowd. Since most concern is caused by a "hostile" crowd, as opposed to the other types mentioned, a more thorough study should be made of it.

A hostile crowd is usually noisy, threatening and its individual members may harrass security personnel. This kind of crowd will hesitate to participate in planned lawlessness because it generally lacks organization and leadership in its early stages. However, it may provide the seedbed for "mob" action when it is aroused by the more forceful persons who assume leadership. It may also be triggered into violence by the undesirable actions of individual protective personnel.

Aroused crowds will often vent their resentment and hostility on those assigned to maintain order. Some individuals may try to bait security officers into committing errors of judgement or displays of unnecessary force in order to discredit authorities or to further incite crowd members to commit acts of lawlessness or to oppose efforts in regaining control. Such crowd actions are usually directed toward one or two individual officers in the nature of taunts, curses and other minor annoyances. Verbal abuses must be ignored, no matter how aggravating they may become. On the other hand, immediate action must be taken to those who assault, throw rocks or attempt in any way to interfere with protective units.

In controlling a hostile crowd, sufficient manpower is basic to your success. If it appears a peaceful demonstration or other large crowd gathering is showing hostile tendencies, do not hesitate to report and call for immediate assistance. This does not, however, mean you may or should resort to the use of unnecessary force. Such action is never justified. Potentially dangerous crowds can usually be controlled by the following methods:

1. Remove or isolate individuals involved in precipitating an incident before the crowd can achieve unity of purpose. This may cause temporary resentment in a very small portion of the crowd members. It is important therefore, to immediately remove the subject from the area. Elimination of the cause of irritation will prevent an ugly incident. Remember that the injudicious use of force can well defeat your purpose and turn the entire crowd against you.

2. Fragmentizing the crowd into small isolated groups. The police often arrive at the scene of an incident or hastily conceived demonstration after a crowd has assembled and achieved a degree of unity. The close contact of the crowd members and the emotionalism of the situation causes the individuals in the crowd to become group-influenced and directed. Individual controls disappear and each person is swayed by the mood and feelings of the crowd. This collective excitement is communicated to each member of the group in what is known as the "milling process".

    The presence of an adequate force of men to disperse the crowd and break it into small isolated groups before it becomes hysterical and aggressive, is an effective method of coping with the "milling process". It is necessary for security to make a show of force which does not necessarily mean the use of force. The mere presence of an adequate number of well-disciplined and well-trained control force often suffices.

3. Removing the crowd leaders. The most excited and vocal members of a crowd establish themselves as the

informal leaders. Removing or isolating the agitators contributes greatly to eventual crowd dispersal. Isolating the more boisterous individuals should only be attempted if sufficient manpower is available. A crowd is not impressed with inadequate manpower and violence may result. Individual heroics are not only foolhardy, but dangerous as well.

4. Diverting the attention of the crowd. The use of a public address system on the fringe of a crowd, urging the people to "break up and go home" is a successful crowd dispersal tactic. Amplifying the authoritative tone of the command attracts the attention of individuals in the crowd and breaks the spell cast by the more excited crowd members.

5. A crowd that grows in hostility and defies orders to disperse can also be controlled by forcing the individuals to focus attention on themselves rather than the objectives of the group. Instead of making a direct assault on the crowd, a series of random arrests is made of individuals situated on the edge of a crowd. The crowd will soon recognize that a greater number of persons are being arrested. But the fact that arrests are threatened through haphazard selection causes them to fear for their safety and a spontaneous dispersal results.

6. Use of a recognized leader. An effective method of counteracting the developing leadership in a crowd is by using someone having greater appeal to the crowd. A trusted labor leader, a member of the clergy, a well-known sports figure or a well-known civil rights leader can often successfully plead for order and reason. Depending on the origin and cause of the crowd formation, an appropriate public figure or official may greatly assist in calming the excitement and emotions of the crowd.

7. Try to prevent panic from developing in a crowd. Panic is caused by fear and is most often found in the "escape" crowd fleeing from disaster or the threat of disaster or violence. The primary cause of panic is blockage of the escape route. Security actions should aim at providing an escape route, directing and controlling the progress of the crowd along the route, and at the same time dividing the crowd into small groups if possible. The following control techniques might be implemented:

a) Displaying a helpful, calm and confident attitude. Loudspeakers should be used to give directions and helpful information.

b) Use of rational members of the crowd to assist in calming or isolating hysterical persons.

c) By providing First Aid and medical attention to the injured and weak, particularly women and children.

d) The use of security to block off routes so as to channel movement in the desired direction. Care must be taken to ensure that the police forces do not panic a crowd by hasty action, arrogance or thoughtlessness.

8. Use of women and children. Crowds and demonstrators may resort to having women or children wheeling baby carriages at the head of their advance. If the marchers must be stopped, an attempt should be made to divert the women and children or let them pass through the ranks and then close rapidly behind them.

Security and Demonstrations

Security organizations assigned to supervise demonstrations have a two-fold responsibility. Regardless of individual convictions, they must protect the peaceful demonstrators who are exercising their right to protest.

Spectators not in sympathy with the demonstration constitute a potential threat of violence. This is often aggravated by counter-demonstration whether they be organized or spontaneous.

Control Forces must also protect the general public from demonstrators who infringe upon the rights of others. The more common problems occur when demonstrators engage in "sit-ins", etc. and violate property rights of others. Fanatical members may even lie down in the path of vehicles and refuse to move. They must be picked up and carried away at once. Use of tear gas in this situation is not generally recommended in view of the passive nature of the gathering and their relatively few numbers.

Such groups may attempt to discredit security by harassment during removal, by resorting to shouts of "brutality", raising their hands as if to ward off blows and emitting cries of pain when they are aware of the presence of news media. Such encounters will tax the patience and control of individual security officers, who must ignore all such verbal attacks.

Formation of a Mob

A crowd or demonstration will deteriorate into a mob if it has been pre-conditioned by irritating events, aroused by rumors and inflamed by professional agitators, who appeal to emotional levels rather than to reason. Hostility prevails, unity replaces confusion and disorganization.

The early frustrations engendered by agitation and rumor requires a climactic incident to unleash the mob. It may come about for any number of reasons. It may often be influenced by the apparent weakening of the strength and attitudes of security groups assigned to preserve the peace.

Responsibility and Behavior of Protective Groups

Protection must extend to all people. This means fair and equal treatment to all. Observe a position of neutrality — act with firmness — this is not beligerance or unreasonable force. After an order is given, it must be enforced for the preservation of the public peace and the carrying out of the traditional mission of protecting life and property of citizens to assure the basic rights of all people.

If you observe a hostile crowd gathering, never hesitate to request assistance. In these instances, it is definitely safer to overstate the number of men needed to restore order than to attempt to act alone or underestimate your requirements. A show of force not only has a restraining effect on the crowd, but it will also provide the necessary manpower.

Order must be established. Approaching the more vocal individuals in a crowd is an effective method of dealing with a group. When addressing these persons, be firm and carefully phrase your commands. Do not become involved in an argument. Use simple language and inform the people of the violations they are or may be committing. Request that the violations stop and that the groups disperse. Allow the crowd the opportunity to withdraw peacefully without interference. If the throng defies authority and the apparent leaders make no efforts to disperse the crowd, arrests should be made, or police assistance sought.

Whenever you are dealing with an excited or hostile crowd, remember that it is potentially dangerous and may require only a slight incident to turn it into a mob — your example and your ability to maintain order are the best deterrents to mob action.

Planning Considerations

From time-to-time, Security Personnel have the opportunity to plan for large crowd control events. An example of this may be: political rallies, sporting events, parades, and planned shopping centre events. As there is always some form of advance notice for these expected large crowd events, the following considerations should form part of the contingency procedure:

1) Is police involvement required?
2) Barriers (this includes metal fencing, ropes and stanchions, people).
3) Communications (radio and telephone, PA system).
4) First Aid staff.
5) Ambulance or first-aid rooms.
6) Doctors.
7) Location of event.
8) Fire procedures, equipment, personnel.
9) Communication Centre
10) Media observation area
11) Entry and exit location for VIP
12) Parking
13) Lavatories
14) Food concessions
15) Disabled persons areas (wheelchairs)
16) Entertainment before or after event
17) Signing
18) Timings
19) Number of security personnel and degree of expertise required
20) News releases and media pre-coverage
21) Time of year and type of environment
22) Alternate power sources
23) Size of crowd expected
24) Vehicles for movement of VIPs, etc.

As you can see, when a large crowd control event is known and sufficient time is available for pre-planning, the event should be able to take place with minimal problems for both Security staff and participants alike.

Personal Behavior

1. Stand your ground without yielding. Your job is to maintain order and protect life and property.
   a) Avoid all unnecessary conversation.
   b) Do not exchange pleasantries with the crowd or apologize for your actions.
   c) Do not give the impression you will not enforce orders to disperse or arrest individuals defying such an order.
2. Place lawbreakers under arrest.
3. Use reasonable force to enforce the law.
   a) Do not overlook violations or defiance of lawful orders.
   b) The use of unreasonable force often incites a crowd which normally would be passive or curious.
   c) Charges of brutality are often made in an attempt to discredit the security force, they will have little basis in fact if discretion is used.
4. Remain on the fringe of the crowd.
   Do not close or mix with a hostile crowd. Remain out of reach and observant of crowd and individual activities, pending the arrival of reinforcements.
5. Assist fellow officers who may be in trouble.
   If one of your members situated near you is physically attacked, go to his immediate assistance. Arrest the assailant. To permit such a person to escape will encourage others to assault or try to overpower individual security personnel.
6. Refrain from participating in crowd activities.
   a) An aggressive crowd will invariably throw a barrage of rocks, sticks, bottles, etc. at opposing forces. DO NOT throw them back at the crowd! This will only precipitate greater hostility and assures the crowd of a further supply of missiles.
   b) Withdraw to a safe distance until dispersal operations can be commenced.

Riot Control Force Deployment Procedures

Basic riot and crowd control formations used by control forces exist in the following forms:

a) **Arrowhead** - This is used to strike into and split a crowd or mob, to provide an escort for a person(s) to a given point through a friendly or disorganized crowd. The use of an additional inverted arrowhead at rear of the formation will give all-round protection.

b) **Left Flanking and Right Flanking** - Used to move a crowd or mob to the right or left, or to turn a crowd away from the front of a building, fence, etc.

c) **Line** - Used to move a crowd or mob straight back up the street.

PERSONNEL EMPLOYMENT

BASIC RIOT AND CROWD CONTROL FORMATIONS USED BY CONTROL FORCES EXIST IN THE FOLLOWING FORMS:

a) ARROWHEAD

THIS IS USED TO STRIKE INTO AND SPLIT A CROWD OR MOB, TO PROVIDE AN ESCORT FOR A PERSON(S) TO A GIVEN POINT THROUGH A FRIENDLY OR DISORGANIZED CROWD. THE USE OF AN ADDITIONAL INVERTED ARROWHEAD AT REAR OF THE FORMATION WILL GIVE ALL ROUND PROTECTION.

b) LEFT FLANKING   AND   RIGHT FLANKING

USED TO MOVE A CROWD OR MOB TO THE RIGHT OR LEFT, OR TO TURN A CROWD AWAY FROM THE FRONT OF A BUILDING, FENCE, ETC.

c) LINE

USED TO MOVE A CROWD OR MOB STRAIGHT BACK UP THE STREET.

QUIZ
Crowd Control Management

1. The majority of crowds do not as a rule resort to
_____. However, any crowd is
potentially dangerous. (Fill in the blank)

2. In controlling a hostile crowd, sufficient:

_____is basic to your success.
(Fill in the blank)

3. The protection officer should attempt to isolate or
_____ an individual trouble-maker.
(Fill in the blank)

4. If you observe a hostile crowd gathering, never

hesitate to request additional _____
(Fill in the blank)

5. A demonstration is a crowd that is exhibiting sympathy for or against authority, or some political, economical, or social condition.

   □ T □ F

6. A riot means any extreme or catastrophic condition which imperils or results in loss of life and/or property.

   □ T □ F

7. The basic reason for the formation of any crowd is the occurence of an event that is of common interest to each individual.

   □ T □ F

8. Some psychological factors in crowd formation are:

   □ a. security
   □ b. novelty
   □ c. loss of identity
   □ d. none of the above
   □ e. all the above

9. The Protection Officer when dealing with crowds, should:

   □ a. exchange pleasantries with the crowd
   □ b. give the impression you will enforce orders
   □ c. apologize for your actions
   □ d. all the above
   □ e. none of the above

10. Some riot control, force deployment procedures are:

   □ a. arrowhead, left and right flanking, line
   □ b. right flanking, bullet, left flanking
   □ c. line, bow, arrowhead
   □ d. arrowhead, bullet, left flanking

CRIME SCENE PROCEDURES

By Martin A. Fawcett CPO

At some point in time during your career as a Protection Officer you will likely discover a crime scene. Your actions, or inactions at this critical time will determine to some degree the outcome of any ensuing investigation into the crime.

In order to properly preserve and protect a crime scene, it is important that the protection officer understand what a Criminal Crime Scene is and what it is that is expected in terms of officer roles and duties.

Determining the Crime Scene

Many crimes do not have a crime scene in the sense that there is a physical location that the protection officer can see and protect. This would include crimes such as fraud or embezzlement where there is seldom any physical evidence left other than a document or various kinds of records.

On the other hand, some crime scenes can cover very large areas. On first examination, the boundaries of a crime scene may not be easily determined. It is important not to establish the limits of a crime scene until after an initial investigation. A premature definition of the crime scene may cause loss or destruction of evidence outside the established area defined as the crime scene.

Determining Boundaries

Once the boundaries of the crime scene have been established, close off the area to all persons who are not required for investigation purposes. This includes fellow officers, occupants, employees and the public. The limits established should exceed beyond what is believed to be the actual crime scene. It is better to contain too much of an area than later to discover you did not include enough, causing a possible loss of valuable evidence. The area can always be reduced, but it is difficult to expand.

Always remember that in order to commit a crime, the culprit(s) must pass from one point to another. This can be further broken down into three areas: point of entry, location of crime, and point of exit.

By following a logical sequence in the reconstruction process, it is possible to determine in most instances all three areas, thereby deciding the probable limits of the crime scene. At this point, backup, support officers or investigators (police/security) are required.

Once a crime scene is established, how can we best effect protection of the scene and at the same time preserve any evidence that may be found at the protected area (crime scene)? It can be accomplished by the observance of the following three rules:

1) Protect
2) Preserve
3) Make Notes

Protect the Scene

As the officer is usually the first person on the scene of a crime, or the first person to be called, it is imperative that he/she arrive as quickly as possible to the location of the scene. When there is a time lapse between being notified of the crime and arrival of the officer, it should be stressed to the caller not to do anything until the officer arrives. Once the officer arrives, the first priority is to prevent unauthorized access to the crime scene area.

This means that all personnel, bystanders and anyone else who happen to be in the area or stop to look, be prevented from entering the crime scene area. All unauthorized personnel must be told to leave the area and remain outside the area until told to return by security/police.

The reason for this is that people are creatures of curiosity and will often look and touch articles that appeal to them, thereby inadvertently destroying evidence.

If the location is a large one, then it is imperative that the officer summon enough assistance to ensure that unauthorized persons are kept out of the area. A word of caution: In your efforts to remove and keep out unauthorized persons, do not forget that they may have witnessed part or all of the crime and be waiting for someone to ask them for their story.

Many witnesses will silently stand around and then be sent on their way without the officer ever taking the time to question them about the crime. Remember, be polite when asking them to move away, and also ask if they know anything about the crime.

Preserve the Crime

After unauthorized personnel have been questioned or removed, the next important step is to preserve the scene exactly as it was when first discovered. Nothing must be moved, removed or altered in any way; and no evidence, real or suspect, may be added to the scene. This merely confuses the scene for the qualified experts who must, from the evidence, reconstruct the crime.

Complete crime scene protection will enhance the protection officer image and greatly improve crime solution potential.

The best way to preserve a scene is to remember: **Keep your hands to yourself.** This means that you do not touch anything. Should you have to touch, move or remove anything from the crime scene for safety reasons, such as an article on fire that has to be extinguished. It is essential to remember exactly what you did, heard or viewed respecting possible evidence. If anything was moved or altered in any way, an explanation must be provided.

If contamination has occurred in any way, it may lead investigators and technicians to false conclusions or blind leads which can prevent the successful solution of a crime.

In order to preserve a crime scene, it becomes necessary to understand what might be considered "evidence".

Making Notes

In the initial stages of protecting a crime scene, there is normally a certain amount of confusion. It is important that the officer realize that time is vital and that many details he/she has seen will quickly be forgotten unless committed to a notebook. The moment the officer arrives, he/she should commit important information to the notebook format. The date and time of arrival, the date and time of the occurence, who was present upon arrival and what happened. Also who initiated the call in the first instance, and all other pertinent information (see chapter on notebooks/reports) pertaining to the crime scene. In some instances, a small sketch in the notebook showing the scene as it was found can be of great value for future reference.

Ensure that the notes you make are accurate and complete. They may prove to be invaluable as the investigation progresses.

Reconstruct the Crime Scene

As soon as is possible after arriving at a crime scene, the protection officer should attempt to reconstruct, in his mind,

the crime scene to be protected. Reconstruction may lead to further evidence that was not readily apparent upon arrival or after an initial search of the area.

Public Relations

It is important during the crime scene investigation to not overlook the victim. During the rush of activity that follows the discovery of a crime scene, the victim is often pushed from the scene and left unattended. He/she may resent the fact that this is occurring and could become hostile.

It is important that the protection officer explain to the best of his ability just what is happening and the reasons for actions taken. This keeps the victim informed which could enhance communications and aid in the ensuing investigation. It will also show that the protection officer knows his/her job, and cares about the people he/she is responsible to protect. This step takes very little time and greatly improves public relations and the protection officer's image.

Physical Evidence

At a crime scene you can expect to discover any number of different forms of physical evidence. Physical evidence simply stated is anything that the culprit(s) could be connected to or associated with. The importance of physical evidence is that it can be used to link an accused person to the scene of a crime. Some of the more common forms of physical evidence that could be encountered are:

1. Fingerprints
2. Palm prints
3. Tool impressions
4. Footwear impressions
5. Tire impressions
6. Torn metal
7. Headlight glass
8. Torn paper
9. Penny Match cases
10. Hair & fibres
11. Blood
12. Bullets & casings
13. Paint chips
14. Cut wires
15. Dirt & soil
16. Anything that appears out of place.

The above list is by no means complete. Physical evidence

can be visible or invisible. Some forms of evidence require complex scientific procedures to collect and identify. As a protection officer required to attend a crime scene, it is important to realize that physical evidence is usually present.

It is therefore imperative that you follow the guideline set forth by your supervisors, and **Protect, Preserve and Make Notes.**

Evidence Collecting

Evidence left at the scene of a crime should be left for the trained investigator or identification technician. These professionals understand the scientific procedures for the collecting and identification of physical evidence. These experts are responsible for gathering evidence. Again, "hands off" approach.

Another factor to consider when dealing with physical evidence is that the purpose of collecting it is to link the culprit to the scene and eventually enter the evidence as an exhibit(s) in court, with a view to gaining a conviction.

In order to enter physical evidence in court, a number of procedures are required or the evidence gathered will be ruled inadmissible. In order to reduce this threat, it is best to let the professional gather and identify the evidence because they are more familiar with all the rules of the court relating to the admissability of physical evidence.

Should the occasion arise that it is impractical to await the arrival of the police or a senior member of the security force is not available, then the protection officer will have to take the initiative and gather the evidence that is found at the scene. If this becomes necessary, then there are a number of points to be remembered.

1. Assign **one** officer to collect **all** evidence.
2. Record all information in detail in notebook.
3. The 'Exhibit' officer must maintain possession of all exhibits.
4. For each exhibit, record:
   a) time
   b) date
   c) location
   d) officer's initials
5. In notebook, record:
   a) time
   b) date
   c) location
   d) who seized exhibit
   e) description of exhibit
   f) dispositon of exhibit

The admissibility of any physical evidence in court will depend in part upon the manner in which it was collected and the safeguards followed to ensure its integrity. The protection officer must be able to demonstrate to the courts that:

1. The evidence introduced can be positively identified from other items of a similar description.
2. The evidence has not been altered in any way.
3. That 'continuity of possession' (or 'evidential chain of custody') has been maintained.

'Continuity of Possession' simply means that there is an unbroken chain of possession from the first instance to presentation in court. Anyone coming into physical contact with any form of evidence joins the chain and will be required to testify in court as to his/her handling and dispositon of the exhibit.

As you can well imagine, it is not only more expedient, but much safer to limit the number of persons involved with each exhibit. If for any reason, the chain cannot be proven, then the evidence may not be accepted by the courts, and if accepted its value in the proceedings is greatly reduced.

Conclusion

When a crime scene is discovered, it is essential that the protection officer seek back-up or support personnel. The person(s) responsible for the commission of the crime may well be on or near the scene. Criminals are dangerous. Your job is to protect innocent people and yourself. Capturing suspects is a job for the police. Your job is to report and observe. Protect life and prevent loss or damage to evidence. Your report will reflect your crime scene actions. Do first things first; that means prevention, not crime detection and apprehension.

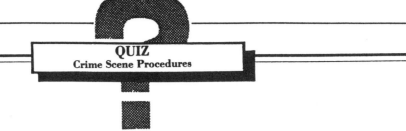

QUIZ
Crime Scene Procedures

1. Sometime during your career as a protection officer, you will be called upon to investigate a crime scene and your _____ or _____ will have a great bearing on the outcome of any ensuing investigation. (Fill in the blanks)

2. A premature definition of a crime scene may cause evidence that is later discovered outside the crime scene boundaries to be _____

or _____
(Fill in the blanks)

3. The competent protection officer will always make sure that his notes are_____

and_____
(Fill in the blanks)

4. The importance of _____
is that it may be used to link an accused person to the scene of the crime.
(Fill in the blank)

5. Elements to be considered when determining the boundaries of a crime scene are:

☐ a. point of entry
☐ b. location
☐ c. point of exit
☐ d. all the above
☐ e. none of the above

6. The protection officer's prime responsibility with regards to crime scenes can best be described as:

☐ a) Protect, preserve, arrest
☐ b) Investigate crimes
☐ c) Seize evidence
☐ d) All of the above
☐ e) None of the above

7. Once the protection officer arrives on the scene, his first priority is:

☐ a) To get the names of all those present
☐ b) To lock all the doors and wait for the police
☐ c) To preserve evidence found at the scene
☐ d) Call for assistance
☐ e) None of the above

8. Many crime scenes do not have a physical location on a site or facility.

☐ T ☐ F

9. The boundaries of a crime scene will be immediately evident once the protection officer arrives on the scene.

☐ T ☐ F

10. It is necessary to establish the boundaries of a crime scene before an investigation can begin.

☐ T ☐ F

Unit 3

Physical Security
Computer Security

PHYSICAL SECURITY PLANNING

By Denis A. O'Sullivan CPP, CPO

What is "physical security planning"? It is a recognized security process that if followed will result in the selection of physical countermeasures based on appropriateness. The countermeasures selected should also be justifiable from a cost point of view.

The process consists of the following five steps:

1. Assets are identified.
2. Loss events are exposed.
3. Occurrence probability factors are assigned.
4. Impact of occurrence is assessed, and
5. Countermeasures are selected.

Let's look at each of these steps.

1. Assets are identified: At first glance this step would appear easy; however, this is not necessarily the case. Have you ever attempted to take inventory of your personal property? The major problem seems to be "how to" — Do we include every nut and bolt. For the purpose of following the security process this is not necessary. It should suffice to group assets according to category except where an item is especially attractive (from the point of view of a thief) and valuable. The following categories should include most assets for most companies:

- land	- buildings
- heavy machinery	- production equipment
- office equipment	- office furniture
- vehicles	- cash or other negotiables
- goodwill	- public image
- raw material	- finished product

Depending on the nature of the company's activities there may be other categories. In any event there is one asset I have not mentioned, primarily because it is controversial: employees being a company's most valuable asset; however, some people do not like to group employees with all the other assets.

2. Loss events are exposed: This step consists of exposing all possible threats to the assets that we have identified. Similarly to the way we grouped assets, we will group threats according to their nature. All threats can be grouped under the following headings: industrial disaster, natural disaster, civil disturbance, crime and other risks.

Industrial Disaster — These should be easy to identify, associated threats related to on-site or adjacent activity. The following are typical industrial disasters that might affect most companies; explosions, fire, major accident and structural collapse. To correctly assess the threat, you must know intimately the nature of company activity, the nature of activity on adjacent properties, dangerous routes, flight paths, and the existence of nearby major oil or gas pipelines.

Natural Disaster — The potential to become the victim of a natural disaster largely rests with the geographic location of the company property. If property is located in the southeast of the United States, it is reasonable to identify hurricanes as possible loss events. Similarly, if the property is in California, it would be reasonable to plan for earthquakes. Other areas may suggest the need to identify flood or tornados as threats.

Civil Disturbance — Most companies either directly or indirectly can be threatened by actions that can be categorized as civil disturbances. If your company is engaged in weapons technology, or indeed any activity that might be viewed as threatening the environment, it is reasonable to expect that the company might become the target of demonstrators. All labour disputes can be categorized under this heading.

Crime — It is relatively easy to identify the crimes that might effect company operations. Any or all of the following will affect most companies: arson, assault, bomb threats, break and enter, theft and vandalism. If a company is engaged in high-tech, it would be reasonable to also identify espionage, extortion and sabotage as likely threats.

Other Risks — This is meant to be a catch-all for those threats that do not neatly fit the above categories; disturbed persons and loss of utilities to name two.

3. Occurrence probability factors are assigned: Having identified assets and exposed the threats to those assets, the next step is to quantify the possibility that the threat will occur. This is probably the most difficult step in the process. Information must be collected and carefully analyzed to determine its affect on the probability for occurrence. The following all affect probability:

- The physical composition of structures; for example, wood frame, or concrete block.
- The climatic history of the area, e.g., number and frequency of tornados, hurricanes, earthquakes, etc.
- The nature of activity at the property to be protected. For example, if the product being produced is televisions and related products, then the probability for theft will likely be high.
- The criminal history for the immediate and adjacent areas.
- Is there community conflict in the area.

An analysis of the foregoing, coupled with a review of the activity and organization of the company to be protected, will enable a determination with reasonable accuracy, to be made regarding the probability for a loss relative to specific assets or groups of assets.

The probability for occurrence will not be the same for all loss events. For this reason and to facilitate later correlation with impact factors, we must assign probability ratings. While the actual wording is not important, the following are suggested:

- Certain
- Highly Probable
- Moderately Probable, and
- Improbable

To make these words more meaningful, we can assign percentage weights to each: certain 75% - 100%, highly probable 50% - 75%, moderately probable 25% - 50%, and improbable 0% - 25%.

4. Impact of occurrence is assessed: This step is not as difficult or as uncertain as determining probability. Impact for almost all organizations has a bottom line of dollars and cents. The most important thing to remember is that dollar losses may be either direct or indirect and that they may be so high as to be crippling.

Direct costs are those that can be directly assigned as the value of the asset that has been lost or damaged. Indirect losses are those costs associated with the loss that would not have been incurred if the loss event had not occurred, for example down-time.

The final task in relation to impact is to assign levels or classifications that will allow for correlation with the four degrees of probability. Again the actual words are not important; however, the following are suggested:

- Very Serious
- Serious
- Moderately Serious, and
- Unimportant

Shortly we will see the importance of these ratings. Before we go on to the final step, let's recap. We have taken inventory of our assets, identified the threats to those assets, assessed the probability that any one of these threats will actually occur and if one of these threats was to occur, we have assessed the potential impact on company operations.

THREAT LEVEL
MATRIX

	IMPROB.	MOD. PROB.	HIGHLY	CERTAIN
UNIMPORTANT	1	1	1	1
MODERATELY SERIOUS	1	11	11	11
SERIOUS	11	111	111	1V
VERY SERIOUS	111	1V	1V	1V

LEVELS OF SECURITY

1 LOW
11 MEDIUM
111 HIGH
1V VERY HIGH

Figure 1

5. Countermeasures are selected: This is the final step in the planning process. We now have to use all the data that we have collected to use to protect our property. The initial step is to decide on the level of protection needed, the level can range from low to very high.

The simplest method to use to ascertain the desired levels of protection is a matrix as illustrated in Figure 1. For example, let's look at the threat of fire: the probability of a fire can be rated as "moderately probable" for most types of businesses; from a criticality point of view we must consider fire as potentially "very serious". Referring to our matrix, we can quickly see that the recommended level of protection is "level IV", or to put it another way, the highest level possible. This would suggest using an effective detection system coupled with an efficient suppression system.

The large number and variety of assets and associated threats mean that we will end up with a complex pattern of different levels of protection. This is not as confusing as we might expect, particularly if we think in terms of security-indepth.

Security-in-depth is a military concept that means placing a series of progressively more difficult obstacles in the path of an aggressor. These obstacles are often referred to as 'lines of defence'.

The **first line of defence** is at the property line. Methods of defence at this point may be either natural such as a river or man made such as a fence. Additionally the barrier may be psychological or physical. At a very minimum, the property boundary must be defined in some way that separates it from its neighbours. Psychological barriers such as property definition do not impede would-be trespassers; however, they do play an important role in the rights of the property owner.

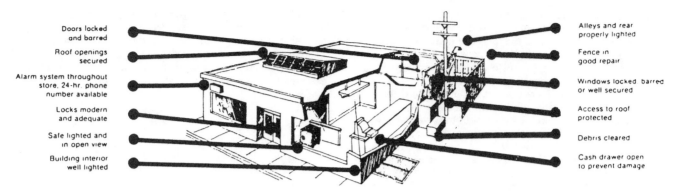

Doors locked
and barred

Roof openings
secured

Alarm system throughout
store, 24-hr. phone
number available

Locks modern
and adequate

Safe lighted and
in open view

Building interior
well lighted

Alleys and rear
properly lighted

Fence in
good repair

Windows locked, barred
or well secured

Access to roof
protected

Debris cleared

Cash drawer open
to prevent damage

The **second line of defence** is the exterior of buildings. Controls at this point should be difficult to overcome. It is important to remember that all six sides of structures (roof, floor and walls) often present weaknesses that must be strengthened. Special attention must be given to the usual points of break and enters; doors, windows and skylights. In fact, any opening greater than 96 square inches in area and less than 18 feet from grade, must be protected. It is usually at this line of defence that most use is made of electronic intrusion detection devices and electronic access controls.

The **third line of defence** is interior controls or object protection. Controls at this line of defence include electronic motion and intruder detection devices, access controls, safes, vaults, document storage cabinets, quality locking devices and fire protection.

The application of the concept '**security-in-depth**' means more than simply establishing three lines of defence that will meet all your needs. Ideally, we would apply the principle first to the property in general terms as described above, and then to each and every asset separately. For example, an industrial complex and an asset such as information.

The complex itself will be protected probably by a perimeter fence, each building within will be properly secure and there will be an electronic intrusion detection system within the buildings. In addition to this general protection, we should attempt to establish protective rings around the information. Working backwards; the information should be stored in a safe (third line of defence), the safe should be in a room that has interior motion detection (second line of defence) and access to the room should be via a door equipped with proper locking hardware and possibly with a card access system (the first line of defence).

Selecting appropriate countermeasures is a difficult task requiring considerable practical experience and extensive knowledge of the various controls, their strengths and weaknesses. Effective planning will result in a cost justifiable, integrated protection program.

An integrated protection program results from a systems approach to selecting controls. Two important points in relation to using a systems approach is:

1) The whole rather than its individual parts must be considered, and

2) Design should allow for an acceptable level of redundancy, without any unnecessary duplicaton of effort.

A systems approach is often referred to as systems engineering.

The remainder of this chapter will concentrate on the physical components of a protection program. While space will not permit great detail, we will attempt to explain the major points relative to security lighting, security glazing, alarm systems, card access systems, locks and keying, closed circuit television, safes and vaults, and fencing.

Security Lighting

Security lighting has three primary objectives:

1. It must act as a deterrent to intruders;
2. If an intrusion is attempted, it must make detection likely, and
3. Not to unnecessarily expose patrolling personnel.

Lighting systems are often referred to as either: 'Continuous', 'Standby', and 'Movable' or 'Emergency'.

Continuous lighting is the type most commonly used. Lamps are mounted on fixed luminaries and are normally lit during the hours of darkness.

Standby lighting is different from continuous lighting in that the lamps are only lit as required.

Movable or emergency lighting is portable lighting that may be used to supplement either continuous or standby lighting.

Light sources may be either: 'Incandescent', 'Gaseous Discharge', or 'Quartz Lamps'.

The common light bulb emits **incandescent** light.

Gaseous discharge lamps are street-type lighting and may be either mercury vapor or sodium vapor lamps. Mercury vapor lamps emit a strong light with a bluish cast. Sodium vapor lamps emit a soft yellow light. Both types of gaseous discharge lamps take two to five minutes to reach maximum intensity. They are very effective in areas where fog is prevalent. A word of caution in relation to gaseous discharge lamps is that they make colour identification unreliable.

Quartz lamps emit a very bright white light.

Lighting may be classified as either: 'Floodlights', 'Search Lights', 'Fresnels', and 'Street Lighting'.

The difference between floodlights and searchlights is that **searchlights** project a highly focused beam of light, whereas **floodlights** project a concentrated beam.

Fresnels produce a rectangular beam of light and are particularly suitable for illuminating the exterior of buildings.

Streetlights produce a diffused light and are suitable for use in parking areas and driveways.

Certain lighting intensities are recommended for specific situations:

- perimeter or property boundary . . . . 0.15 to 0.4 fc
- vehicle entrances . . . . 1.0 fc
- pedestrian entrances . . . . 2.0 fc
- exterior of buildings . . . . 1.0 fc
- open yards . . . . 0.2 fc

The foregoing are suggested lighting intensities only; specific circumstances may dictate different lighting intensities. To place some perspective on the intensities suggested it is necessary to explain 'fc': 'fc' means foot candle and simply refers to the amount of light emitted within one square foot from a lit standard candle.

Application Considerations

1. When designing a protective lighting system, consider approaching the task from the point of view of "three lines of defence"; the perimeter, open yards and building exteriors.
2. All accessible exterior lamp enclosures should be in tamper- or vandal-resistive housings. This means that the receptacle and lens should be constructed of a material that will resist damage if attacked, and that the mounting screws or bolts be tamper-resistant.
3. If protective lighting is to be located in an area that may be subject to explosions, then the housings should be explosive-resistant.
4. Before finalizing any decision on the installation of lighting, consider the impact that additional lighting will have on your neighbours. Failure to consult with a neighbour prior to an installation may result in costly re-design.

The foregoing is a presentation of the basics of security lighting. Prior to utilizing any of the suggested standards, please check local codes or ordinances.

Glazing

The various uses, methods of fabrication and the over-abundance of trade names, makes the selection of an appropriate glazing material appear very confusing. In an effort to simplify the process, we will address the subject under the following headings:

- Safety/Fire
- Burglar/Vandal-Resistive
- Bullet Resistive, and
- Special Purpose

Safety/Fire: Under this heading, we are basically looking at two types of glass; tempered and wired.

Tempered glass can be considered safety glass as it is several times stronger than ordinary glass. It is especially resistive to accidental breakage. If it does break, it will disintegrate into small pieces with dull edges, thereby minimizing risk of injury. Tempered glass is available in different thicknesses to suit different purposes.

Wired glass is glass with a wire mesh built into it. The wire is embedded in the glass when it is still in its molten state.

Wire glass resists impact because of its strength. It is also listed by Underwriter's Laboratories as a fire retardant material.

Some suggested uses for safety/fire retardant glass are:
- along passageways,
- entrance doors and adjacent panels,
- sliding glass doors, and
- bathtub enclosures and shower doors.

Burglar/Vandal-Resistive: Several types of burglar/vandal-resistive glazing materials are available including laminated glass, wired glass and acrylic and polycarbonate plastics.

Laminated glass will resist degrees of impact proportionate to its thickness. This type of glass is particularly valuable where the quality of transparency is important and where other types of impact-resistant material may be subject to vandalism.

Wired glass provides resistance of a limited nature; it will not resist prolonged attack.

Acrylic plastic is particularly resistive to forced attack; however, it is not as resistive as polycarbonate. It is, however, much more transparent than polycarbonate.

Polycarbonate plastic is 20 to 30 times stronger than acrylic of comparable thickness.

Bullet Resistive: Bullet resistive material is available in the form of laminated glass or acrylic and polycarbonate plastics.

Bullet resistant laminated glass consists of multiple plies of glass and plastic material laminated together.

Highly transparent bullet resistant acrylic material is suitable for many cash handling situations such as in banks.

Polycarbonate consisting of several sheets of plastic laminated together is highly resistive to ballistics; however, visibility is somewhat impaired.

Special Purpose: Under this heading, we will look at transparent mirror glass, coated glass, heated glass and rough or patterned glass.

Transparent mirror glass may be installed in a door or in a wall. From one side it is functionally a mirror, from the other it permits an unobstructed view through the mirror. The primary purpose of transparent glass is for surreptitious surveillance.

Flow-on or cement-on plastic coating is available for application to existing installed glass. This material may serve well as an interim measure until a more appropriate vandal-resistive material can be installed.

Rough or patterned glass is available with many different designs that make it range from practically opaque to practically transparent. This type of glazing is most appropriate where there is a conflict between the need for privacy and natural light.

INTRUSION DETECTION

Every intrusion detection system has one or more of the following objectives — the detection of:

1. Unauthorized entry
2. Unauthorized movement within, and/or
3. Unauthorized access to controlled areas or objects.

There are three components to an intrusion detection system:

1. detectors/sensors
2. system controls
3. signal transmission

Detectors/Sensors

Selection of the appropriate detector, from the numerous and varied options available, is a difficult task. An end user is well advised to become familiar with the different types of dectectors/sensors available. If reliance for proper selection is placed on advice from a vendor, then it is essential that the end user be able to describe accurately his objective and to make the vendor contractually responsible for meeting the stated objective.

In the following paragraphs we will look at different types of detectors: magnetic switches, metallic foil, audio, vibration, ultrasonic, photoelectric, passive infrared, and microwave.

Magnetic Switches: These are often referred to as door contacts. They may be either surface-mounted or recessed. The choice is largely an aesthetic one; however, the recessed ones do afford more protection from tampering. Switches are commonly 'unbalanced', which means that they may be defeated by substitution of a secondary magnetic field to keep the contacts in the open position while the detector magnet is moved away from the housing containing the contacts.

For high security application, a 'balanced' switch is available. This switch is designed to withstand defeat by creation of a secondary magnetic field. Magnetic switches have many potential uses in addition to their traditional use on doors and windows. They may be used on desk or file cabinet drawers or to secure equipment to a fixed position.

Metallic Foil: A narrow strip of very thin metal foil designed to break if the surface to which it is attached is attacked. It is mostly used as a glass breakage detector and is commonly seen on storefront windows and glass doors. It may also be used as a barrier penetration detector such as in a wall under gyprock. If properly installed, it should do its job well. A major detractor is that it is not considered aesthetically pleasing; this can also be overcome to some extent by the experienced installer.

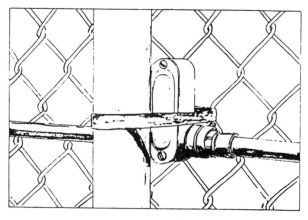

Vibration: Vibration detectors are shock sensors. They may be used to detect persons climbing chain-link fencing, breaking through walls or attacking safes or other containers. As glass breakage detectors they are very effective and not too expensive.

Ultrasonic: These are motion detectors. A protected area is flooded with an oval pattern of sound waves. As the sound waves bounce off objects, they reflect a signal back to a receiver. Any movement in the protected area will cause a change in the reflected pattern which will result in an alarm. Ultrasonic sound waves are in a frequency range that is above the capacity of the human ear. These detectors are particularly susceptible to false alarm due to air turbulence.

Photoelectric: A beam of light is transmitted to a receiver. The transmitter and receiver may be in one housing with the beam being reflected. Any interruption of the beam causes an alarm These devices are commonly used as automatic door openers or in stores to warn off a customer from enter-

ing. When used for security purposes, different methods are used to make the beam invisible to the naked eye. Either an infrared light-emitting diode is used or an infrared filter is simply placed over the light source. Either method effectively makes the beam invisible.

Infrared: These are probably the most versatile detectors currently available. Patterns of coverage are available that will protect practically any configuration of space. They can be used effectively to protect long narrow corridors, portions of rooms or entire large rooms. Infrared detectors are often referred to as passive detectors because they are the only detector that does not monitor an environment that has been created by the detector. Infrared detectors measure radiated energy. When activated, they simply establish the ambient temperature. From that point on any significant deviation will result in an alarm.

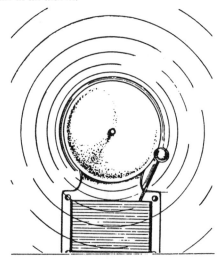

Microwave: Microwave detectors use high frequency radio waves to establish a protected area. They are particularly suitable for use in areas where air turbulence or changing air temperatures may prohibit the use of ultrasonic or infrared detectors. A major weakness with microwave is that it can penetrate beyond a protected area. Microwaves will penetrate practically all surfaces except concrete and metal.

System Controls

System controls consist of components that transform individual sensors/detectors into a network of intelligence-gathering devices. System controls include data processing equipment, signal transmission equipment, on/off and reset controls, back-up power supply, LED system status indicators and any other equipment specific to a particular system.

The data processing equipment basically acts as a receiver and interpreter of signals from the sensors/detectors and reacts to these signals in accordance with pre-programmed instructions.

The signal transmission equipment is the means by which an alarm is raised. This equipment may simply activate a local siren or it may send a signal over telephone wires to a remote monitoring location. The telephone wires may be either dedicated (the most secure system) or via the normal telephone network by use of a digital dialer transmitting to a special type of receiver/decoder.

The on/off and reset controls are either keys, toggle switches or digital key pads. The digital key pad is recommended.

The back-up power supply is essential in case the electrical power supply fails or is sabotaged.

The LED (light-emitting diode) system status indicators indicate by different colors whether the system is on or off, or if there is trouble in the system. The usual colors are red for system okay, but in the off mode; the yellow signifies trouble somewhere in the system; and green usually signifies that the system is armed and functioning correctly.

System Monitoring

There are basically three options:

1. local,
2. proprietary, or
3. commercial.

The local system is just that, a siren or bell on the outside of the protected premises. This system is not recommended due to its reliance on a passerby to actually call the police.

The proprietary system is similar to a local system in that the system is monitored on-site or remotely by employees of the owner of the protected premises. If this system is used, it is advisable to have a link from the proprietary station to a commercial station in the event of a holdup of the monitoring personnel.

The commercial monitoring falls into two categories: monitoring stations or answering services. The answering services are useful for the economical monitoring of signals transmitted by telephone dialers; however, this is not for high security systems. Commercial monitoring stations are either Underwriters Laboratories of Canada (ULC) approved or they are not. The ULC approved is the best guarantee of quality service.

Note: An initial step in planning an intrusion detection system is through a thorough understanding of building operations to identify zones of protection that will create a series of independent sub-systems. Each sub-system should:

- Be compatible with normal operations, and
- Allow for prompt response to a specific problem area.

When the functional requirements of a system have been identified, the system engineering should be left to experts.

Card Access

The decision to use, or not to use, a card access system should be based on the perceived need for accountability and the accompanying financial considerations.

An objective statement for a card access system might read:

"To economically eliminate the inherent security weaknesses in key access systems by electronically supervising and documenting the activities of persons authorized to access the property."

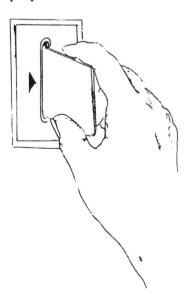

To be useful, a card access system should have the following minimum capabilities to:

- Restrict access by authorized persons to certain times and/or days of the week.
- Allow controlled after-hours access to selected areas within.
- Control after-hours access to a parkade.
- Selectively control after-hours use of elevators.
- Maintain a record of all valid and invalid use of cards.
- Provide an audit trail permitting a printout of persons on the property at any one time.

There are numerous types of cards. The most commonly used are:

- magnetic coded
- magnetic strip coded
- proximity coded
- weigand coded
- hollerity, and
- optical coded

The **magnetic coded** contains a sheet of flexible magnetic material on which an array of spots have been permanently magnetized. The code is determined by the polarity of the magnetized spots.

The **Magnetic Strip** encoding is widely used in commercial credit cards.

The **Proximity Card** is a badge into which electronically tuned circuits are laminated. The badge gets its name from the fact that it only has to be held near the reader for authorized access to be granted. The reader for this card is concealed in the wall behind drywall or panelling.

The **Weigand Coded** badge contains a series of parallel wires embedded in the bottom half of the badge. Each wire can be assigned a logic "0" or "1", the combination reveals the I.D. number.

The **Hollerith Badge** is easy to recognize because the card has small rectangular holes punched in it. It cannot be considered a high security badge.

The **Optical Coded** badge is easy to recognize if it utilizes the "bar" code as its encoding device. The "bar" code is commonly used on retail goods to assist the cashier with pricing.

All of the commonly used coded cards are reliable and, with the exception of the hollerith badge, are reasonably resistive to compromise.

Although it is not recommended, many organizations like to use their access cards as both an access card and an identification badge. The information contained in the normal employee I.D. card can easily be incorporated into any access card:

- company name and logo
- details of card holder
- name
- department
- date of birth
- signature, and
- photograph
- condition of use (restrictions)

This is not recommended; however, because if the card is lost it will be obvious to a finder that it is owned by a particular organization, which may lead to unauthorized use of the card. There are many different card readers. However, the significant difference is the addition of a secondary method of verification or confirmation such as the requirement for insertion of a personal identification number (PIN) via a numerical key pad.

The use of a numerical key pad usually offers the very valuable option of an ability to allow a user to signal that he is operating under duress.

The following flow chart, illustration 2, shows the functional operation of a card access system.

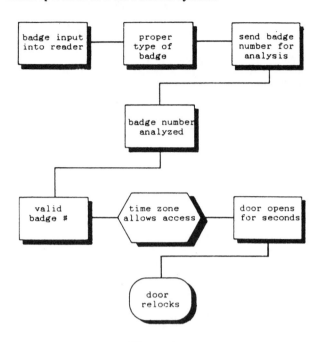

Illustration 2

Locking Hardware

Locking hardware can be categorized as either mechanical, electrical or electro-magnetic; and as either security or non-security.

Quality mechanical security locks should be used for all:

- perimeter openings
- doors that control/restrict internal movement, and
- doors to sensitive/restricted areas

Only deadbolt locks should be considered. The bolt should offer a minimum of 1'' throw; if the door is a glass metal-framed door, the bolt should be of the pivotal type to ensure maximum throw.

Electric locks are particularly suitable for:

- remote control of the after-hours pedestrian entrance door
- grade level emergency exit doors
- exit doors from stairwells to grade level, and
- all stairwell doors

Electric locks are available where the strike is normally in the locked or the unlocked position.

Electro-Magnetic locks are particularly suitable for use on emergency exit doors as there is no moving parts that can accidentally become jammed. Several conditions must be met before this type of lock can be used on an emergency exit door:

- A 24-hour proprietary control centre must exist in the protected property.
- An activation/deactivation capability must exist from the control centre.
- Activation of the fire alarm system automatically deactivates the locking device.
- Each location must have a fire pull station in its vicinity and the fact that its activation will automatically deactivate the lock.

Note: It is essential that the Fire Department be consulted prior to any final decision on the use of locks on any door that may be considered an emergency exit. Get their decision in writing and carefully consider before compliance.

Emergency exit devices that are normally used on emergency exit doors cause justifiable security concern.

If permitted, only quality electric or electro-magnetic locks should be used.

If electric or magnetic locks cannot be used, great care should be taken to ensure the emergency devices use such features as:

- deadbolts
- deadlocking latches
- vertical locking bars for pairs of doors

Remember that emergency exit devices can be connected to a proprietary or commercially-monitored alarm system. Loud local alarms are also an effective way to protect emergency exits.

Closed Circuit Television

If used selectively, CCTV can be very effective and has the potential to significantly reduce security manpower costs.

An objective statement for a CCTV system might read:

"To avoid costly manpower requirements by using CCTV to monitor several sensitive/critical areas simultaneously, thereby ensuring the safety/security of property and occupants."

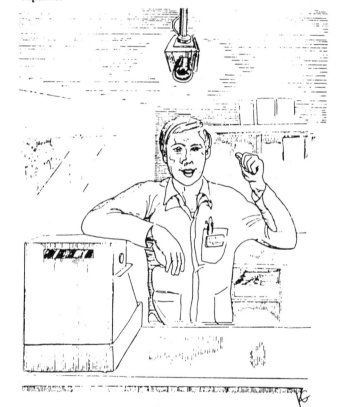

Great care must be exercised in designing a CCTV system to ensure that the objective statement is achieved. Caution is also necessary to ensure that costs do not get out of hand. This is a common problem when the system is not designed by a security expert.

Suggested practical applications for CCTV are:

- parkade areas,
  entrances/exits
  shuttle elevator lobbies
  stairwells, and
  elevators
- shipping/receiving areas
- main floor elevator lobbies
- cross-over floors
- cash handling areas

All CCTV systems are made up of several components that an end user should be, at the very least, familiar with. The following is a brief description of each component:

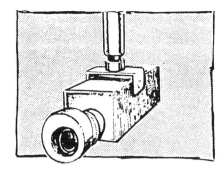

CAMERAS
The primary consideration in relation to camera selection is the available light coupled with required image quality. The two most common cameras are the 'vidicon' and 'newvicon'. The big difference is that one performs better than the other in adverse conditions. The vidicon is only suitable if the area is well-lighted and if the quality of lighting, during the time it is expected that the camera will be required to operate, is stable. Naturally, it follows that the newvicon is significantly more costly.

HOUSINGS
Several types of housings are available. They fall into two categories; aesthetic and environmental. Housings can also effectively disguise the existence of a camera.

MONITORS
Monitors are available in different sizes and in color or monochrome. When a quality image is required, it is necessary to use a high-resolution screen.

SEQUENTIAL SWITCHES
It is not necessary, or usually desirable, to have a monitor for every camera. By using a sequential switcher, the image from two or more cameras can be routinely rotated for viewing on one monitor. When required, an operator can lock on the image from one particular camera for select viewing.

MOTION DETECTORS
Cameras are available with a built-in motion detection capability. If movement occurs within the field of view of the camera lens, an alarm will sound at the control centre or a video recorder will be activated to record the activity that caused the alarm. This feature is very valuable when a large number of monitors are used.

PAN/TILT/ ZOOM
The need to use several cameras to cover an area or activity can be avoided by careful positioning of one camera and providing pan/tilt/zoom features.

CONTROLS
In addition to the normal television controls, controls will be required for whatever special features that are built into the system.

CONSOLES
The design of a control centre console that houses a CCTV system is definitely an engineering task. Care must be exercised to ensure operator comfort, particularly in relation to viewing angles and ease of accessibility of controls.

VIDEO RECORDERS
A CCTV system should be considered incomplete if it does not have the ability to selectively record events.

DAY/TIME GENERATORS
This feature has potential benefits in specific circumstances; e.g., where no immediate incident response capability is available, or if the recording may be required as evidence in court.

For an example of a typical system diagram, see Illustration 3.

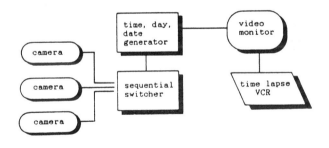

illustration 3

Illustration 3

SAFES and VAULTS

Safes and vaults are designed to offer varying levels of protection from specific risks; namely burglary, robbery and fire.

Burglary Resistive Safes

Burglary resistive safes in addition to their actual construction have a number of protective features that we should be familiar with:

- locks
- interior design
- depository

- time locks
- time delay locks
- relocking device
- extra weight
- floor anchoring, and
- counter spy dials

LOCKS:

Safes are available with three types of locking systems:

- a single combination
- a single key lock combination, and
- dual combination locks

With the single combination option, an unaccompanied person with the combination can access the contents at any time.

The second option; a key lock combination requires two persons to be in attendance to open the safe. One person has the key to unlock the combination-turning mechanism; the other has the combination to unlock the safe.

The third option is similar to option two in that two persons must be in attendance to open the safe. Each person only has one of the combinations.

INTERIORS:

Sufficient options are available in interior configurations so that the need for customizing may be avoided. Features available include fixed or adjustable shelving and enclosed compartments that may be either key or combination-locked. Available options increase proportionately to the size and cost of the safe.

DEPOSITORY:

This feature permits the inserting of property, most often cash, without allowing access to the safe contents. The depository is usually fitted with an anti-fish device to inhibit retrieval of deposited property.

TIME LOCKS:

Time locks prevent access to the safe contents for predetermined time frames by persons normally authorized for access. For example, when a bank safe is locked at the close of the business day, it cannot be opened again until the following morning. Should the bank manager be forcibly taken from his home, he cannot be forced to open the safe.

TIME-DELAY LOCKS:

This feature is designed to protect against a holdup. To open a safe equipped with this feature requires keying the lock, followed by predetermined waiting period before the locking mechanism will unlock. A safe with this feature is often used at late night convenience stores or 24-hour gas stations.

RELOCKING DEVICES:

These devices are designed to act as a secondary locking feature if the normal one is attacked. For example, if someone attacks the combination dial with a sledge hammer, the relocking device will activate; after this happens only a qualified safe expert can open the safe.

EXTRA WEIGHT:

To prevent thieves simply walking away with a safe, it is recommended that a safe weigh a minimum of 340 kg or 750 lbs. Most large safes do weigh 340 kgs, and smaller ones can be ordered with extra weight added.

FLOOR ANCHORING:

An acceptable alternative to extra weight, where extra weight may present problems for structural reasons, is floor anchoring — provided a concrete slab is available.

COUNTER SPY DIALS:

It is not uncommon for thieves to note the combination of a safe while surreptitiously viewing it being unlocked. This is often done from a building across the street. A counter spy dial prohibits anyone other than the person immediately in front of the dial to see the numbers and only one number is visible at a time.

Apart from the foregoing, obvious security features, we can tell little about a safe by looking at it; nowhere can appearances be more deceptive. For this reason, a purchaser has to rely on a particular vendor or on independent appraisal. Independent appraisal is available from Underwriters Laboratories Inc. (UL).

If a manufacturer submits a product sample to UL, they will conduct various tests and issue authority to the manufacturer to affix a specific label to the product line. The following UL labels are available:

UL Labels	Resistant to Attack From:
T.L. - 15	Ordinary household tools for 15 minutes
T.L. - 30	Ordinary household tools for 30 minutes
T.R.T.L. - 30	Oxyactylene torch or ordinary household tools for 30 minutes
T.R.T.L. - 30x6	Torch and tools for 30 minutes, six sides
X - 60	Explosives for 60 minutes
T.R.T.L. - 60	Oxyactylene torch for 60 minutes
T.X. - 60	Torch and explosives for 60 minutes
T.X.T.L. - 60	Torch, explosives and tools for 60 minutes

Safe manufacturers sometimes assign their own rating to a safe. An assigned rating will usually mean that the safe offers a level of protection that compares to what UL would say if they had the opportunity to test. A concern exists, however, that without an independently assigned rating or classification, a purchaser has no way of verifying the expected level of protection.

Burglary Resistive Vaults

Any storage container specifically designed to resist forcible entry and large enough to permit a person to enter and move around within while remaining upright can be considered a vault.

Vault construction consists of reinforced concrete walls, floor and ceiling, and a specially-constructed vault door.

Any consideration to build/purchase (a prefabricated vault is available from most large safe manufacturers) must

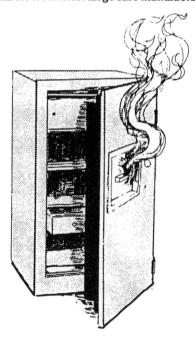

be carefully assessed to ensure cost effectiveness. The evaluation to determine need must recognize that the value of the asset to be stored in the vault will likely attract the professionally competent thief. The impact of this is that regardless of construction, the vault will only delay penetration.

In addition to applicable features as mentioned for "burglary resistive safes", the possibility that an employee(s) may be locked into the vault accidentally or deliberately in a robbery situation, must be considered. To ensure safety of employees, all vaults should be equipped with approved vault ventilators and a method of communicating to outside the vault.

Fire Resistive Containers

Insulated safes, filing cabinets and record containers are available that offer varying degrees of protection to contents from exposure to heat.

The appearance of fire resistive containers can be particularly deceptive — it must be remembered that, of necessity, the construction material is totally different from burglary safes. The insulation material used in fire resistive containers offers little protection from physical assault.

Two very important points in relation to fire resistive containers are:

- Paper records will destruct at temperatures in excess of 350°F (159°C), and
- Computer tapes/disks will destruct at temperatures in excess of 150°F (66°C).

Underwriters Laboratories tests fire resistive containers for their ability to protect contents when exposed to heat. Tests are also conducted to determine the container's ability to survive a drop as might happen when a floor collapses in a fire situation.

NOTE: It is of the utmost importance to remember that safes and vaults are only designed to delay entry when attacked; they are not impenetrable. For this reason, safes and vaults should always be protected by a burglary alarm system. Similarly, alarm systems should be used to protect the contents of record safes from theft.

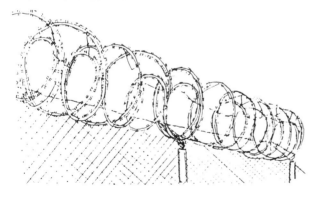

FENCING

The subject of 'fencing' is a much more interesting and important topic than most people at first realize. Fencing has been used throughout history as a defence against enemies — the walled city of Pompeii dates back to 800 B.C.; and it was not uncommon for the complete frontiers of kingdoms in China to be walled (origin of the Great Wall of China). Closer to home, the old city of Quebec remains the only enclosed city in Canada and the U.S.A.

Modern acts of terrorism and civil disturbance have resulted in innovations in the types and usage of fencing. Barbed tape (razor ribbon), a modern version of barbed wire, is a very effective (if not vicious) defensive, or should we say, offensive material. Its use is rarely justified except where the highest standards of security are necessary — for example, in a federal penitentiary.

The use of barbed tape in industrial facilities is not common in North America. Barbed tape can be used in coils along the top of fences instead of the conventional barbed wire overhang. In very high risk situations, coils of barbed tape stacked in a pyramid configuration between a double conventional fence will provide a very effective defence.

Another product of modern terrorism is the freely-rotating barbed wire fence topping recently developed in Ireland. When a would-be intruder grabs the overhang in an attempt to gain leverage, a second overhang simply rotates into place. This is more effective than the conventional overhang and much more acceptable for routine application than coils of barbed tape.

Fencing as used in most applications is the common chain-link type with a barbed wire, outward facing overhang. A major weakness with the chain-link fence is the ease with which it can be climbed. To overcome this problem, the British developed the 'welded mesh fence'. Compared to the 4-sq. inches of opening in chain-link fence fabric, the welded mesh fence has openings of 1½-sq. inches. The openings are 3" x ½" and run vertically. The narrowness of the openings makes it almost impossible for a climber to gain purchase. The width of the openings also inhibits the use of wire or bolt cutters.

Prior to making any decision on the location and type of fencing, it is necessary to conduct a risk assessment. It is also necessary to gain a thorough understanding of the enterprise's operation. For the purpose of this article, we will discuss the fencing requirements for a typical manufacturing plant located in an industrial area of a large city. The objective of the fencing program is two-fold — to control movement to and from the property and to minimize the need for costly manpower at control points. The latter is to be attained by keeping the number of perimeter openings to a minimum.

While it is true that industry is becoming ever-more security conscious, it is also true that the owners of industrial facilities do not want their property to look like a prison compound or armed camp. With this in mind, the first objective is to define the boundary of the property. Most often, this will require a combination of structural and psychological barriers.

From a psychological point of view, we are only concerned with defining the boundary — mostly for legal reasons, prevention of trespass and liability law suits. Property definition may be simply a change in landscaping, or indeed anything that distinguishes the property from its neighbour.

Somewhere between the property line and the area of company activity, it will be necessary to install a structural barrier that will act as a physical deterrence to the would-be intruder. Usually this barrier will be chain-link fence and it should be topped with a barbed wire overhang. The following are suggested minimum specifications:

1. 7' in height excluding top overhang.
2. Wire must be 9-gauge or heavier.
3. Mesh openings must not be larger than 4-sq. inches.
4. Fabric must be fastened securely to rigid metal or reinforced concrete posts set in concrete.
5. There should be no more than two inches between the bottom of the fence and the ground.
6. Where the ground is soft or sandy, the fence fabric should extend below the surface.
7. Top overhang should face outward and upwards at a 45-degree angle.
8. The overhang supporting arms should be firmly affixed to the top of the fence posts.

9. The overhang should increase the overall height of the fence by one foot.
10. Three strands of barbed wire, spaced 6" apart, should be installed on the supporting arms.
11. A clear zone of 20 feet or more should exist between the perimeter and exterior structures.
12. Where possible, a clear zone of 50 feet or more should exist between the perimeter barrier and structures within the protected area.

Vehicular and pedestrian gates in the perimeter fence should be kept to a minimum — ideally only one common entry point for employees and business visitors. Depending on the size and layout of the site, it may be necessary to install a secondary entry point for emergency use such as access by the fire department. However, this entry point should normally remain closed and locked.

All openings in the perimeter fence should be equipped with gates. Even if these gates are not to be electronically controlled initially, planning should provide for power to each gate location with provision for a remote control capability from the control/security centre.

Typically, security control is provided at the first defensible point; however, numerous facilities allow free access beyond this point to an inner control location. This may be beneficial for many reasons, especially in large, heavy traffic plants. Once inside the initial perimeter, signs would direct employees to the employee car park, visitors to an information centre and truck traffic to shipping/receiving areas. Beyond these points, a secondary secure perimeter would be established.

The employee car park should be completely enclosed; access to the area would ideally be controlled by a card access system. Access from the car park to the plant would be through a control point (manned during shift changes).

In addition to the possible need for a secondary line of defence, there may also be a need for fenced areas to provide secure overnight storage for company vehicles, secure storage for bulk raw materials or for the storage of large finished products. Waste awaiting disposal should also be stored within a fenced area. Fencing may also be required to segregate operational areas; e.g., stores, tool crib, etc.

It is important to remember that fencing is first and foremost a barrier and that as a barrier it does not have to be chain-link fencing. If we also remember that fencing will only delay the determined would-be intruder, it should be easy to be flexible regarding the material used. Hedging, poured concrete, solid concrete blocks and decorative concrete blocks are all suitable fencing material.

If fencing is required to provide a very high level of protection, its use should be supplemented by the use of fence disturbance detectors, motion detectors and patrolling guards or surveillance by closed circuit television.

QUIZ
Physical Security Planning

1. What is "physical security planning"? It is a recognized security process that if followed will result

in the selection of _____ _____
based on appropriateness (Fill in the two blanks)

2. Effective security lighting acts as a _____ to intruders. (Fill in the blank)

3. Polycarbonate plastic is _____

and _____ resistive.

(Fill in the two blanks)

4. There are three components to an intrusion detection system: detectors/sensors; systems controls; and

_____ _____ devices.
(Fill in the blanks)

5. Microwave detectors use high frequency sound waves to establish a protected area.
   ☐ T ☐ F

6. Deadbolt locks should have a minimum of a ½" throw.
   ☐ T ☐ F

7. Card access systems permit accountability.
   ☐ T ☐ F

8. The most commonly used security fencing material is:
   ☐ a. barbed wire
   ☐ b. barbed tape
   ☐ c. chain-link
   ☐ d. welded wire mesh

9. The minimum height of a security fence should be:
   ☐ a. 7 feet
   ☐ b. 6 feet
   ☐ c. 8 feet
   ☐ d. 9 feet

10. Which of the following types of lighting are only lit on an as-required basis:
   ☐ a. Continuous
   ☐ b. Standby
   ☐ c. Movable
   ☐ d. Emergency

COMPUTER SECURITY

By Professor George E. Strouse

This chapter on computer security is not included in the Certified Protection Officer (CPO) program examination process, rather is provided as an information reference source. The contained information is at times, somewhat technical and those Protection Officers without prior experience in Electronic Data Processing may experience difficulty with some of the terminology and information contained in this chapter.

All CPO candidates should, however, read this chapter carefully and retain as much of this useful information as possible. Professor Strouse has done an admirable job in making the chapter contents interesting, easily understood and relevant to the job of protecting the physical aspects of the Computer Centre and computer generated data. Once a Protection Officer has the opportunity to become involved with some facet of Electronic Data Security, this material will be more meaningful and helpful in providing better protection to proprietary information.

As the dedicated Protection Officer advances in his or her career, it will become necessary to get involved with some form of Computer Security. Use this chapter as the beginning of a new phase of learning in the challenging profession of protective security.

Introduction

— In 1984, the American Bar Association discovered that 27 percent of the 283 businesses and public agencies polled had computer crime losses for that year totalling approximately $730 million.

— According to DataPro Research Incorporated, by 1985, U.S. businesses were spending $600 million a year on computer security equipment and software. Security expenditures could exceed two billion dollars annually by 1993.

— As of 1986, the U.S. Secret Service placed the annual losses resulting from computer crime in both public and private sectors at $500 million. This figure is not unreasonable, considering that national and international electronic funds transfer systems move more than $400 billion daily.

As the economic impact of computer crime and invasion of privacy is forced upon businesses, banks and government agencies, computer security becomes an increasingly important aspect of their operations. No longer are employers satisfied with the security officer who perceives himself as just a "guard" or "night-watchman". Today's protection officer must be familiar with the aspects of computer security and be able to participate in computer security planning, implementation and review.

Computer security is any measure taken to protect computers, computerized systems and information resources against theft, invasion of privacy, misuse or physical damage. An overview of computer security includes:

— Identifying types of computer crime

— Perceiving invasion of privacy
— Recognizing signs that warn of computer crime or possible infiltration of your computer system
— Planning physical and logical security
— Conducting risk assessment
— Establishing contingency plans
— Conducting computer security reviews

Types of Computer Crime

Computer crime can be divided into four general categories: personal gain, theft of computer time, sabotage and espionage. In many instances, however, computer crimes overlap categories. For example, a disgruntled employee that furnishes a competitor contract bid information may be committing both espionage and sabotage at the same time.

PERSONAL GAIN:

1. **Theft of Data.** Usually financial data, customer lists, any data that can be used to obtain goods and services, or data that can be sold for profit is subject to theft. Computers are often used to gain access to or copies of financial accounts or programs. The stolen data is then used to access credit card accounts, manipulate or transfer funds, and gain access to goods and services. These types of theft usually go unnoticed until the end of the accounting cycle. By then, the thief has covered his tracks. Corporate data such as customer lists, commercial designs, formulas and patent information are sometimes sold to competitors for profit or revenge.

2. **Manipulating Data.** Criminal data manipulation occurs when data is purposely entered incorrectly, or existing data is altered. For example, one employee of a

large stone quarry did not record all sales, keeping a small percentage of the cash payments for himself. This went on for over 10 years until a new computer system was installed that accurately tracked sales tickets. The amount of money stolen was estimated to be in the tens of thousands of dollars. In another case, some teenagers gained access to an on-line hospital accounting system and decided to play Robin Hood. They managed to reduce several hundred patient account balances.

3. Stealing Computer Programs (Piracy). This crime usually occurs when an individual makes an illegal copy of a software program for his/her own use. Many people, and occasionally a few businesses, have then copied it for use elsewhere or even on their own premises. Sometimes the copies are taken home, distributed for use throughout the company, or simply given to friends. Occasionally the illegal software is sold to unsuspecting buyers who think they are getting legitimate copies. Recently Lotus Development Corporation filed lawsuits against two large corporations and one large university for copyright violation. Illegal copies had been made and distributed throughout organizations. The suits were settled out of court. However, if found guilty the pirates could have paid up to $50,000 each for illegal copies.

4. Altering Programs. Occasionally knowledgeable people will alter a program for personal or corporate gain. An example of this type of computer crime was committed by Equity Funding Corporation. Top-level managers from Equity Funding created fake insurance policies, then sold them along with valid policies to other insurance companies. The computer program had been altered to record only the valid policies. More than 20 people were convicted and losses were estimated to be as high as $2 billion. In some instances employees have modified payroll, expense account and other computer programs for personal gain.

5. Theft of Computer Time. Because computer systems are expensive and costly to maintain, stealing computer processing time is the same as stealing any other valuable resource. At one large university very little processing was done at night. Some personnel at the facility decided, without attaining proper authority, to rent the system out to process applications for local businesses. Thousands of dollars of illegal profits were pocketed by these individuals before the university discovered their system was being used in this manner. Programmers may 'steal' computer time to work on software that they are developing for themselves or for some other business. Authorized users from one department may use a user's password form another department to avoid or reduce the costs charged to their department or account.

SABOTAGE:

Computer sabotage involves the damage or destruction of data, programs or physical equipment. In many cases the damage is not traceable and may remain undiscovered for an extended period of time only to surface as a catastrophic event at some later date. Sabotage is one of the deadliest threats to corporate data processing security and may arise both from inside and outside the corporation.

1. Outsider sabotage usually manifests itself in two forms. The first form is physical in nature. The willful disruption of power, damaging computer equipment or disrupting support equipment can cause loss of processing capability. Destroying an air conditioning or cooling system, while only inconveniencing personnel, may bring the computer to a total standstill. The second way someone may get to your system is through access to terminals or communication lines. Extensive damage in the form of erased or altered data may occur if a saboteur gains access. Further, phone lines may be tapped or transmissions monitored, jammed or disrupted.

2. Insider sabotage often results from disgruntled employees and will usually result in more harm than outsider sabotage because they know more about the system. The following are some forms of insider sabotage:
- **Data diddling** changes, forges or destroys data.
- **Trojan horse** embeds illicit commands or instructions inside a valid program causing the computer to execute unauthorized actions when the valid program is executed.
- The **salami technique** modifies a program by a minor, relatively indiscernible logic alteration. This technique is usually applied to rounding down dollar amounts and interest computations. The rounded amount is then assigned to another account. This method is most often utilized when large numbers of transactions are performed.
- **Zapping** prevents alterations to programs. The program checks itself to see if alterations have been made, perhaps by merely asking the system to check the size of the program. If an alteration has been made, the program may erase itself, a needed file or other essential data making the program impossible to run until the original programmer is contacted to correct the situation.
- **Back doors,** sometimes called **trap doors**, are usually installed by systems personnel to bypass normal security measures. They allow system personnel to gain rapid unobstructed access to the system. Since system personnel usually have very high levels of access and authority, back doors can cause extensive system damage if used for unauthorized purposes or discovered by intruders.
- **A logic bomb** is a method of sabotage closely related to zapping. Your own system or application programmers create hidden or embedded code that will cause destruction or other operational problems at some later date or upon a specific condition. One such bomb looked for the programmer's social security number when payroll was being run. When his number was not present, it meant he was no longer working for the company. His logic bomb, embedded in the program, went out and erased not only the payroll program and its data but other essential data as well.
- **Computer virus,** an advanced form of insider sabotage, is a combination Trojan horse and logic bomb. The usually destructive commands are initially hidden within a valid program. When the program is executed, the unauthorized code is executed also. In addition to doing its obvious damage, such as erasing files, the program copies itself to another area of storage where it lies dormant until encountered again. The combination of the virus's ability to self-perpetuate while changing its position or host program, makes it not only the most damaging form of sabotage but the hardest to eradicate.

ESPIONAGE:

Another, not so obvious but prevalent, form of computer crime is espionage. A major discomforting aspect of computer espionage is that it usually goes undetected. The computer "spy" illicitly accesses data to extract copies of government or corporate strategies, customer lists, personnel information, medical data, mailing lists, contract information, formulas, research and development patent information, and any other classified or competition sensitive data without the victim's knowledge. Since the data is not modified, no trace of access remains. Consequently, the unsuspecting victim is open to repeated attacks. There are three basic forms of attack used in computer espionage. These basic forms are often combined to achieve success.

— **Scavenging** obtains either the desired data and information or pieces of data and information, such as passwords or access codes, that may be used in conjunction with other forms of espionage to attain the desired goal. Scavenging takes such forms as looking through trash or discarded papers and printouts for usable information, going through the desk of a person who has legitimate access in hope of finding passwords or other usable information, examining residual data such as typewriter ribbons or carbon paper, or just looking over a user's shoulder at the time of system sign on.

— **Piggybacking** occurs when someone gains access to the computer area or system by impersonating an authorized user. This can occur by using a lost or stolen badge or access pass, using an authorized password gained from scavenging, or simply using a terminal at which an authorized user forgot to log off. In one case access to the computer center was gained after an authorized user had inserted his badge in the entry door lock and entered his personal identification number (PIN). The unauthorized person caught the door before it closed and gained entry. Electronic piggybacking occurs when legitimate communications are intercepted, and modified communications are inserted in their place. Such substitution may occur when a user terminal is inactive for a long period of time between log-on and log-off. Messages are sent and received during the inactive period. This would most likely occur in conjunction with the next form of espionage, tapping a communication link.

— **Tapping a communication link** usually takes one of two forms, either passive or active. Passive taps are listen-only devices. With active taps, the intruder originates as well as receives data. Active tapes require extensive system and electronics knowledge, while passive tapes can be as simple as placing two or three clips on a phone line. Passive taps sometimes use inexpensive tape recorders to capture data that is later reconstructed into its physical form. Passive and active microwave taps require sophisticated equipment but can be achieved without a physical connection. Fiber optic

lines can be actively tapped but only through the use of highly technical equipment.

Perceiving Invasion of Privacy

One of the major benefits of computers is their ability to make the storage and retrieval of large quantities of information easy. This concept of easy access also provides the greatest opportunity for privacy invasion. Computer technology impinges upon two areas of privacy: organizational and individual. Organizational privacy pertains to governments and businesses, while individual privacy applies to specific information or data maintained on private individuals, such as employees, members, subscribers, depositors, borrowers, contributors, tax payers, drivers, etc.

Organizational invasion or privacy usually relates to the illegal access, manipulation, destruction, and possible disclosure of information or data that may be detrimental to an organization. This type of privacy invasion ranges from teenagers trying to access corporate and government data banks for fun to espionage. In Virginia, four men were charged with breaking into the electronic mail accounts of the National Aeronautics and Space Administration (NASA), the United Auto Workers' Union and the Raytheon Corporation. Some teenagers in New Jersey used their computers to access stolen credit card numbers and purchase computer hardware. A ring of hackers in Milwaukee gained access to such sensitive computer systems as the Los Alamos National Laboratory and the Sloan-Kettering Memorial Cancer Center. These few acts gained national attention. However, the vast majority of such crimes go undetected and unreported. In many instances, the sensitive information is accessed internally by employees or other members of the organization. The sensitive information, such as impending stock splits, mergers, government contracts, environmental studies, strategic plans, government actions, etc. may be used for financial gain, leaked to the press by "whistle blowers", or revealed to competitors by disgruntled employees.

Individual invasion of privacy is the application of computers in the unauthorized gathering, storage, disclosure or use of private details pertaining to an individual's personal history. The magnitude of data gathered and maintained on individuals is revealed by the fact that any individual's name may appear in some computer at least 40 times daily. Federal, state and local governments alone maintain more than 35 files on each and every one of us. National Security Agency (NSA) computers eavesdrop on every overseas communication made. This vast quantity of readily available information in the form of salary, marital status, net worth, address, phone number, medical history, etc. is gathered, accessed, exchanged, and stored on a daily basis. The major problem with individual privacy invasion is one of liability. In one instance, an individual's medical history became generally known. An employee accessed medical records and found out that another individual was liable for not protecting the records from intrusion. Did you ever wonder how your name appeared on some firm's mailing list? Recently a mother-to-be wrote to Ann Landers complaining about her obstetrician. It seems he sold her name, address, phone number and the information that she was pregnant to diaper services, professional photographers, baby furniture stores, etc. This resulted in a deluge of solicitation in the form of mail and phone calls. Sales of this type of information, although sometimes illegal, are an every day practice for some retailers, business registers, and mail order operations. The real problem with all this data gathering is that once collected it is seldom updated; its distribution is impossible to control; it is seldom verified for accuracy; and it is almost impossible to modify or eradicate. Even governments practice privacy invasion. The French government enlisted the aid of teenage computer buffs to gain access to Swiss banking computers. The object was to obtain information on French citizens who were trying to avoid taxes. The cash deposits by French citizens had been made into what they believed were secure, numbered Swiss accounts. The major problem to the protection officer is control of access to information resources.

Recognize Warning Signs

No computer crime has ever been committed that was beyond the capability of existing technology to prevent. Why then does computer crime exist?

First and most significant is that, security thinking has remained far behind the technology being implemented. A conservative estimate would indicate that the planning and implementation of security technology in most organizations is at least five to ten years behind current operating technologies.

Second, computer security requires a trade-off between protection and cost. The amount of resources (time, manpower and money) management is willing to expend is a direct function of the perceived value of the information or system being protected.

The third factor involves ethics. There appears to be a wide-scale departure from acceptable values and business practices. While most people and businesses would not think of stealing, breaking into someone's home or reading personal documents, some see no harm in tapping into someone else's data base, obtaining a free copy of protected software or examining detailed personal data.

The following are some of the warning signs a protection officer should be aware of:

— rapid acquiring and implementing new computer technology without the appropriate update of security

— management's unawareness or reluctance to recognize the need for protection

— employees that lack a security conscious attitude or that display a conspicuous lack of ethics

— disgruntled or recently terminated employees who have or have had access to sensitive information or computer equipment

— a programmer or other employee with access to the system who habitually arrives for work early and/or leaves late and who has shown little or no visible results for the extra hours worked

— lax physical security procedures, such as passwords written on desk tops or placed under terminals, security access doors unlocked or left open, unauthorized personnel allowed in sensitive areas, discovery of a failure to report a security breach or violation

— programmers or employees with access to sensitive data who carry printouts, magnetic media (disks, tapes, etc.), or personal portable microcomputers (lap tops) to and from work under the guise of doing work at home

— incomplete system documentation and/or procedures for system use, including guidelines for data processing personnel

— managers, functional area supervisors or other unauthorized personnel making program changes

— non-organizational maintenance personnel, e.g. phone technicians, computer repairmen, etc. allowed to work in sensitive areas without surveillance

Planning Physical and Logical Security

The protection of computer resources entails more than just restricted access and disaster planning. In many instances, the protection officer must be aware of special requirements that accompany the task of providing security for computerized information systems. These requirements can be divided into two categories -- physical security and logical security.

Physical Security:

Physical computer security involves the protection of the computer system's hardware and software, its online and stored data, as well as documentation and procedures that relate to the control and operation of the system. These must be protected from natural disasters such as fires, floods, loss of electrical power or air conditioning, etc. as well as crime, terrorism and unauthorized use. The first line of defense, and usually the first person notified, should be the protection officer.

Natural disasters, although unpredictable, require preparation and contingency planning in the event they actually occur. The ideal location for a computer system would be in its own environmentally enhanced fire-proof building. Economically, such facilities may not be feasible. In the event the system is located within another building, the building should be constructed of fire-resistant materials and should have a sprinkler system.

The computer area itself should be protected by both hand-operated and automatic fire extinguishers. The best types of extinguishers use either carbon dioxide (CO_2) or halon as their active agent to preclude water damage to both hardware and software. The protection officer's awareness of the benefits as well as the problems associated with these types of extinguishers is essential. Both carbon dioxide and halon are odorless and colorless and potentially lethal. Either gas may effectively extinguish fires without undue damage to sensitive computer equipment. When automatic carbon dioxide systems are used, a warning bell must be sounded prior to the release of the chemical to allow enough time for personnel to exit the area before the agent is released. Carbon dioxide systems work by removing the oxygen from the air and therefore are extremely dangerous. Hence, carbon dioxide is especially useful for unmanned sites. Halon, on the other hand, breaks down into dangerous chemicals only after it begins extinguishing the fire. Personnel usually recover from low concentrations of inhaled halon. Consequently, less time is needed between the sounding of the alarm and the release of the chemical.

Water damage due to natural disasters or broken sprinkler systems can be readily detected through the use of water detection cable. This cable, with its built in sensors, is strategically placed around the perimeter of the computer area. When water makes contact with the cable, it completes a circuit, and the sensing monitor sounds an alarm indicating the area being flooded.

Loss of electrical power or fluctuations in the voltage of the lines providing current to computing facilities can be damaging to sensitive computer equipment. Occurrences of this nature should be observed and recorded by the protection officer. In the event of a power failure or notification of the failure of voltage conditioning/control equipment, immediate action is essential. Severe damage can result if computer systems are allowed to continue unattended under these conditions. Procedures must be established and training conducted on a regular basis to insure effective handling of this contingency.

Heat and humidity are also factors that can plague computer systems. Most systems have functional heat and humidity ranges. If air conditioning or humidity control systems fail, it is essential that action be taken immediately.

Figure 1.
Layered In-depth Approach to Physical Computer Security.

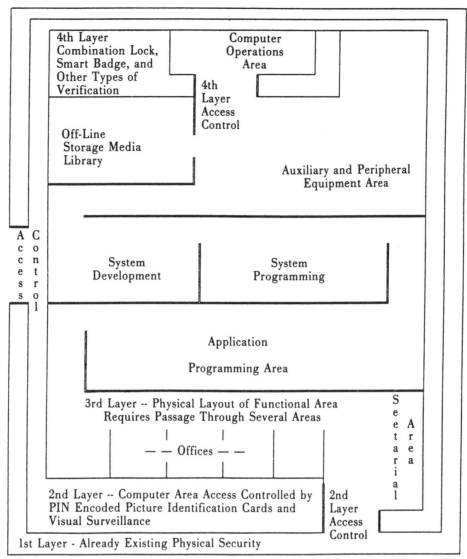

4th Layer
Combination Lock,
Smart Badge, and
Other Types of
Verification

Computer
Operations
Area

4th
Layer
Access
Control

Off-Line
Storage Media
Library

Auxiliary and Peripheral
Equipment Area

System
Development

System
Programming

Application

Programming Area

3rd Layer -- Physical Layout of Functional Area
Requires Passage Through Several Areas

— — Offices — —

2nd Layer -- Computer Area Access Controlled by
PIN Encoded Picture Identification Cards and
Visual Surveillance

2nd
Layer
Access
Control

Seetarial Area

1st Layer - Already Existing Physical Security

Access Control

Figure 2.
Security
Kernel
Concept

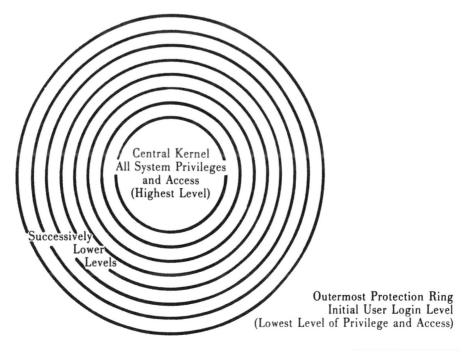

Central Kernel
All System Privileges
and Access
(Highest Level)

Successively
Lower
Levels

Outermost Protection Ring
Initial User Login Level
(Lowest Level of Privilege and Access)

Temperature in a computer facility can rise as much as five to ten degrees a minute when cooling systems fail. At this rate, a few minutes of operation could damage the system. The protection officers of a university campus in Baltimore were notified of an air conditioning failure but did not think it was important. They felt that operations could continue until the system was repaired. However, the same system that cooled the students' classrooms cooled the computer room. The result was system down-time and expensive repairs.

Humidity control prevents electrostatic build up. Control of static within a computer environment is essential. The microminiaturization of components makes them extremely susceptible to damage from static discharge. These components are designed to operate at very low voltages. The average person can build up and discharge up to 4,000 volts of static electricity without even feeling the shock of the discharge. Discharge of voltages greater than 10,000 volts are not uncommon. Many computer microchips cannot tolerate even as much as 150 volts. Simply walking down a carpeted corridor, entering a room, and touching a piece of computer equipment could result in the damage or destruction of a component.

Crime, terrorism and unauthorized use are the primary reasons for physical access control of computer facilities. Door locks, visual surveillance, identification cards and alarms have long been tools available to the traditional protection officer. It is important to protect all aspects of the information system, since a security system is only as strong as its weakest link. A high-tech assault on the system usually begins by efforts to determine the types of equipment being used and their configurations. Scavenging is the most customary approach. Internal unauthorized use may be the result of lax access controls. Assault of this type can be successfully combatted by a layered in-depth approach to physical computer security (See Figure 1.). Most organizations already have some form of access control in place as the first layer of overall system protection. The second layer involves access to operational computer areas.

The computer center itself is usually the main area of concern when thinking of physical security. However, documentation, storage-media libraries and outlying computer terminals must also be protected. If an attacker managed to gain access to any of these, or to system design documentation, any or all aspects of the system could be compromised. These areas must have additional forms of protection to guard against would-be attackers, as well as curious employees who "just want to look around". Access to operational areas is normally based on the strategic importance of the data/information being protected. Access control may be as simple as a locked door or as complex as a retinal scanner. However, the majority of second layer protection takes the form of combination locks, picture identification cards with magnetic tape encoded personal identification numbers, and visual surveillance.

The third layer protects the operations center. By design, the layout becomes a protection requiring personnel to traverse several functional areas, e.g., secretarial, application programming, system programming, system development, etc. prior to entering the operational areas of off-line storage, auxiliary equipment, peripheral equipment and finally the computer area. Personnel of each area should be familiar with all persons authorized in their area and have the ability to recognize those allowed into the next area.

Again, depending upon the value of the information being protected, the computer operations area may be protected by a fourth layer of access control consisting of combination locks, "smart" badges, voice recognition, palm scanners, retinal verification, etc.

Logical Security:

Security considerations, such as fenced-in areas and employee badges, may prove insufficient protection against unauthorized access. One of the major reasons is the wide dispersement of computer terminals normally found throughout an organization. Each time access moves a step away from the operations center, the system becomes more vulnerable to attack. Logical security uses passwords, security codes, data storage and communication encryption, limited access areas/terminals, and other techniques to prevent unauthorized use by a person who has gained physical access to the system. Logical security may also be used to preclude authorized users from accessing data or programs beyond their area of operation for example, a programmer assigned to work on accounting programs should not be able to access systems, program and data from the personnel department or any other area. This concept is usually accomplished through a security kernel.

The security kernel functions under the concept that only a very small central kernel (number of users or applications) needs *all* the system's capabilities. Perhaps only the system supervisor and his staff should have such access. The remaining users need access to only a portion of the overall system and its power. This holds true for all system privileges, programs and data. The central kernel is surrounded by concentric rings of protection that limit access (See Figure 2.). The farther a user's access is from the central kernel, the less overall access or privilege he is allowed. Proceeding from the outermost ring, as access progresses inward, the user has access to all data, programs and privileges or each successive ring and is limited only within his specific area. For example, an order entry clerk will have system access but only to the order entry program. The ordering officer may have access to use all the order entry programs and be able to examine the order data, but he cannot make modifications or access any other area.

Everyone that gains physical access to the system may attempt to sign on (called logging-in) to the outermost ring of protection as an authorized user. System access and subsequent use is not allowed until the proper usercode and password are provided. Failure to provide the proper code results in access denial. The only way for a user to progress from the outer protection rings to the kernel is by providing the proper access codes. Sometimes access and privilege is linked to the user's usercode. In these cases, when the user logs-in, he is automatically given all access and privileges assigned to him.

Usually a system will record the location and time of unsuccessful log-in attempts. Protection officers should monitor logs of such attempts. When a pattern is discovered, action can be taken to apprehend the individual trying to gain unauthorized access.

Passwords are used to limit access to specific programs and data. When a request is received by the system to execute a program or grant access to certain data, the system requests that the user provide the proper password. After the user enters the password, the system or program checks to verify the password. Some systems may require more than one password during the log-in or access procedure. If valid responses are furnished, access is granted.

Data storage and communication encryption scrambles data and programs prior to storage or transmission over networks and communication lines. There are basically two types of encryption/decryption. The first, **transposition**, rearranges the bits **(binary digits)**, characters or blocks of text that make up data into a different sequence. The other primary method of encryption is **substitution.** In this method, bits, characters or blocks of text replace the unencrypted text. In order to encrypt or decrypt data, a key (the actual method of encryption/decryption) must be used. Encryption keys are either symmetric, where one key is used for both encryption and decryption, or asymmetric, where one key is used for encryption but a different key is applied for decryption. Another less frequently used method of encryption, called **a public and private key** system, allows for both secrecy and authenticity by first encrypting the data with the public key, then encrypting it again with the private key. The receiver must first apply his private key, then decrypt a second time using the public key to transform the data to its original form. Another method of authentication frequently used is **digital signatures.** A digital signature, used almost exclusively when transmitting messages, concludes the data transmission. The receiver validates the message by decrypting the digital signature.

Limited access terminals/areas are often used to restrict access to specific programs and routines. For example, a warehouse terminal, when initially turned on, may automatically access and execute a stock control program. This method limits the use of that terminal to functions performed only by the stock control program. No other data or programs can be accessed from that terminal. Sometimes entire areas are placed in a limited access mode. A large insurance company may dedicate an entire room or floor to claims handling. Under the concept of limited access, only those programs and data related to the handling of claims could be accessed from that area.

Other frequently used logical security methods include:

— **Intercept and call-back** allows access via public dial-up phone lines. In this method, the user calls the computer from his personal phone using a portable terminal. The system waits for a password and allows a limited time for entry. The user enters his password, and the computer hangs up. After checking the password's validity and waiting a specified period of time, the system calls the user back at a pre-determined phone number. If the password is invalid, no return call is made. The problem is that the user must be at the predetermined phone location.

— **Line speed switching** can also control access from public phone systems. Under this method, the user is provided a special pre-programmed modem (modulator/demodulator used to convert digital computer signals to analog phone signals and back). The modem dials the number, furnishes the proper code and then changes to a new pre-set transmission speed at which the two systems will communicate. A password must be entered by the user within a specified period of time at the correct transmission speed or the user is logged off. This routine can be effective, since at no time during the log-in process does the main system display any information nor acknowledge the transmission in any way that would let an unauthorized user determine the access code or the new transmission speed. The entire procedure occurs so rapidly that even an experienced attacker would have difficulty determining what had occurred.

Conducting Risk Assessment

In any risk assessment of computer security, the following factors must be considered:

— What is the operational impact of partial or complete loss of the procedure, process or information?

— What is the damage to the organization financially and competitively if the information is acquired by a rival firm?

— What are the legal and psychological ramifications of the information being made public?

With this information in mind, the protection officer can begin preparing for the risk assessment analysis. There are several reasons why a protection officer must not conduct a risk assessment on his own. First, the protection officer cannot be expected to have in-depth knowledge of the entire computer system. Each functional area -- accounting, personnel, operations/production, marketing, etc. -- will have to make decisions on operational impact, cost of replacement and general vulnerability. All levels of management must be involved to determine the strategic importance of the security plan that will result from the analysis. In addition, the technical aspects of the security involved requires personnel with highly specialized technical knowledge. Therefore, the protection officer should recommend the establishment of a committee with representatives from each area.

The committee should examine the current situation, focusing on the following questions. Does a security program currently exist? If so, to what extent is its coverage? The committee should then determine how the computer security program, or parts under consideration, will fit within the organization's overall security philosophy. With these questions in mind, the protection officer and a technical person from data processing should conduct a survey of each functional area in the company of the committee representative from the area being surveyed. Participation of managers as well as other personnel within each area is extremely important. Each functional area survey should define the relative importance of every computer - supported function within the area under consideration as well as any controls already in effect.

Possible areas of compromise or weakness should be determined in accordance with potential exposure. Ideas pertaining to control, cost, and time to implement should be listed. Prior to departing each area, the survey team and the area manager should rank each item as to importance using the three factors of operational impact, potential damage, and legal/psychological ramifications outlined at the beginning of this topic. After all the functional areas have been surveyed, which could take six months or more, the committee should make a security requirements plan for submission to top management. Management will review the plan with emphasis on adherence to the organization's overall security policy and cost.

Contingency Planning

In the majority of organizations, it is prohibitively expensive to maintain a duplicate off-site system to be used in the event information processing capabilities are lost. A realistic approach, called **the Critical Factor Approach,** provides a method for damage recovery by insuring that the most critical operations continue to function when operational loss occurs. There are four steps involved in critical factor contingency planning:

— Determine the operational areas that are most critical in keeping the organization functional. These areas become the critical factors.

— Minimize the probability of exposure in these critical areas. This should be done with consideration to cost. It is senseless to spend large amounts of money to protect or duplicate inconsequential data.

— If an attack or damage results in the loss of a critical

area's ability to function, the protection system should minimize the impact. This can be done through backup systems.

— Insure that for each critical area defined, a systematic method, with documented and tested procedures, exists for recovery from the damage.

Determining critical factors is most easily accomplished during the risk analysis survey. If a critical factor survey has to be made, top level management as well as the highest level manager for each functional area must be involved. Only management can decide which areas or operations can function without information support. When conducting the survey, it is essential that critical factors be ranked as to the length of time the organization or functional area can continue to operate without support. Then, if an operational or information loss should occur, the estimated recovery time would indicate the particular contingency plans that would have to be implemented for the critical factors involved.

Minimizing a critical factor's probability of exposure is accomplished by implementing the security requirements plan from the risk analysis survey. Physical and logical security should be set up in such a way that if an intruder succeeds in gaining access to the system, the resulting damage must be limited. For example, if an intruder gains entry into a warehouse and manages to log-in on a warehouse terminal, his access should be limited to shipping and inventory data. He should not be able to access personnel, accounting or other data. Should a disaster occur, backup equipment and archival data (backup data) should be maintained off-site. Natural disasters, in the form of fire, flood, earthquake, etc., are usually localized. If backups are maintained off-site, it is likely they will not be affected. A large bank in Maryland maintains a complete duplicate system in Delaware in case an event of this nature occurs.

Minimizing the resulting damage is usually accomplished via backup systems and data. Unlike the bank in Maryland, it is not always possible or practical to maintain a complete duplicate system. The extent of the company's commitment to a backup system is a direct function of the organization's strategic dependence upon the information system. A phone company or a large bank could function for only a very short period of time without computer support. However, while a hospital may be hampered by the loss of its processing capabilities, it could continue to function. Smaller organizations and those which have less strategic reliance upon information processing usually find other methods of minimizing the damage. In some cases, organizations may make agreements to process another organization's data in the event of damage; in other cases, an organization may have a contingency agreement with a service bureau (a business that provides computer processing services for a fee) to perform critical computer operations if the need arises.

Systematic methods for recovery must at least insure that the organization can recover quickly enough to continue or resume operations as soon as possible. Protection

against disaster with dual systems, shareable sites, software backups and off-site archives is not enough. Highly detailed recovery plans with specific instructions for each critical operation involved must be developed and continually maintained to insure they are current. Recovery plans must also be systematically tested to insure that they function. Nothing could be worse than an organization relying on an out-of-date recovery plan for its continued operation.

Reviewing Computer Security

After the computer security plan has been implemented, it is essential that its adequacy continually be verified. The most viable method is to have personnel from outside the protection/security and data processing operational areas conduct an operational audit. This function is usually performed by experienced internal auditors. The purpose of the audit is to verify that the security checks and plans are still in place and functioning properly. It should identify risks, problem areas, bad practices, security deficiencies, deviations from established procedures, and guidelines that are out of date either functionally or technologically.

Large organizations usually have a group of internal auditors that specialize in data processing. Smaller organizations may hire a consultant or a firm that specializes in computer security. Whatever the approach, auditors should check the physical, logical and psychological security of the computer system. Auditors will make spot checks of physical security, attempt security violations and monitor contingency testing exercises in an attempt to verify physical and logical security. In testing the organization's psychological security, the auditors should look for a security conscience attitude in the employees that gives off an atmosphere or impression that the organization is secure. The protection officer must work closely with the auditor in helping to pinpoint areas of weakness. Auditors should be allowed to scrutinize protection officer log entries concerning security violations. At the end of the audit, the protection officer may be asked to make and/or implement recommendations to correct any deficiencies discovered.

QUIZ
Computer Security (Question Set #1)

1. Using another department's computer access code to avoid or reduce charges to your own department is an example of:
   - ☐ a. personal gain
   - ☐ b. espionage
   - ☐ c. vandalism
   - ☐ d. theft of computer time
2. The major drawback of intercept and call-back systems is that the user is restricted to:
   - ☐ a. the use of a public phone system
   - ☐ b. a pre-determined location
   - ☐ c. calling from his home phone
   - ☐ d. a specific time of use
3. The security concept that only a very small number of users or applications need all the system's capabilities is called a/the _____. Under this concept concentric rings of protection are established to control access.
   - ☐ a. security cell
   - ☐ b. security kernel
   - ☐ c. security rings
   - ☐ d. security circles
4. Within the concept of critical factor contingency planning, one of the major objectives of the plan is to minimize the resulting damage if any occurs. This is usually accomplished via backup systems. If your firm is too small to have its own backup system, which of the following would you recommend:
   - ☐ a. an agreement with another organization to process your data in the event of an emergency.
   - ☐ b. purchase a contingency agreement from a service bureau
   - ☐ c. process your data one day in advance and arrange for support within one day
   - ☐ d. either a. or b.

5. Computer security is any measure taken to protect computers, computerized systems and information resources against theft, invasion of privacy, misuse or physical damage.
   - ☐ True   ☐ False
6. Sometimes governments practice privacy invasion.
   - ☐ True   ☐ False
7. Because computer systems are expensive and costly to maintain, stealing computer processing time is the same as stealing any other valuable resource.
   - ☐ True   ☐ False
8. Scavenging takes such forms as wiretapping and designing logic bombs.
   - ☐ True   ☐ False
9. Which of the following is not a form of insider sabotage?
   - ☐ a. piggybacking
   - ☐ b. salami technique
   - ☐ c. back doors
   - ☐ d. data diddling
10. Computer virus is the easiest form of insider sabotage to detect and correct.
    - ☐ True   ☐ False

QUIZ
Computer Security (Question Set #2)

1. Computer crime can be divided into four general categories: fraud, theft of computer hardware, sabotage and impersonation.
   ☐ True   ☐ False

2. Tapping a communication link usually takes one of two forms, either passive or active. Passive tapes are listen-only devices.
   ☐ True   ☐ False

3. A computer programmer adds a routine to a transaction processing program that deposits one penny for every seventh transaction processed into a phoney account. At the end of each day, the funds are transferred into the programmer's expense account and the phoney account deleted. This is an example of:
   ☐ a. Trojan horse
   ☐ b. logic bomb
   ☐ c. salami technique
   ☐ d. data diddling

4. An employee enters a cash sales transaction, collects and pockets the money and then erases the computer record of the sale. This is an example of:
   ☐ a. manipulating data
   ☐ b. theft of data
   ☐ c. altering programs
   ☐ d. sabotage

5. There is no way a protection officer can conduct a risk assessment analysis on his own. This is primarily due to the complexity of the computer system and the wide diversity of the functional areas involved.
   ☐ True   ☐ False

6. Implementation of a good computer security plan is the final step in insuring adequate computer security for your organization.
   ☐ True   ☐ False

7. The Critical Factor Approach insures that the most critical operations will continue to function when loss of data processing occurs. This approach is used when it is too expensive to maintain a duplicate off-site computer system.
   ☐ True   ☐ False

8. A conservative estimate would indicate that the planning and implementation of security technology in most organizations is at least _____ to _____ years behind current operating technologies.
   ☐ a. 1 to 3
   ☐ b. 2 to 6
   ☐ c. 5 to 8
   ☐ d. 5 to 10

9. _____ terminals or areas are often used to restrict access to specific programs and routines. No other data or programs would be allowed to be accessed.
   ☐ a. Limited access
   ☐ b. Security
   ☐ c. Password encrypted
   ☐ d. Physical

10. The individual testing an organization's psychological security should look for a security conscious attitude in the employees that gives off an atmosphere or impression that the organization is secure.
    ☐ True   ☐ False

QUIZ
Computer Security *(Question Set #3)*

1. _____ _____ is any measure taken to protect computers, computerized systems and information resources against theft, invasion of privacy, misuse or physical damage.

2. _____ is used to obtain data and information about a computer system by looking through trash or discarded papers, going through the desk of a person who has legitimate access or examining residual data such as typewriter ribbons and carbon paper.

3. The computer area should be protected by both hand-operated and automatic fire extinguishers. These extinguishers should use either _____ or _____ instead of water as an active agent.

4. _____ is the unauthorized access of data for the purpose of extracting copies of government or corporate strategies, customer lists, personnel information, medical data, mailing lists, contract information, formulas, research and development data, patent information, and any other classified or competition sensitive data without the victim's knowledge. This form of computer crime usually goes undetected.

5. There are four general categories of computer crime: personal gain, theft of computer time, sabotage and vandalism.
   ☐ True   ☐ False

6. No computer crime has ever been committed that was beyond the capability of existing technology to prevent.
   ☐ True   ☐ False

7. Conducting a risk assessment is the first step in developing a comprehensive computer security plan.
   ☐ True   ☐ False

8. An employee obtains a copy of a customer list and sells it to a competitor for a profit. This is an example of:
   ☐ a. stealing computer programs
   ☐ b. stealing data
   ☐ c. manipulating data
   ☐ d. altering data

9. Computer security requires a trade-off between _____ and _____. The amount of resources (time, manpower and money) management is willing to expend is a direct function of the perceived value of the information or system being protected.
   ☐ a. time and money
   ☐ b. personnel and training
   ☐ c. protection and cost
   ☐ d. personnel and cost

10. Considering the layered approach to physical computer security, the _____ layer protects the computer by requiring personnel to traverse several functional areas prior to gaining access to the operations center.
    ☐ a. first
    ☐ b. second
    ☐ c. third
    ☐ d. fourth

READINGS
The following readings are recommended if the student wishes to gain a more in-depth knowledge of the topic:

Computer Security:

Enger, Norman L. and Paul W. Howerton. *Computer Security: A Management Audit Approach.* New York: AMACOM, 1980.

Freedman, Warren. *The Right of Privacy in the Computer Age.* New York: Quorum, 1987.

Hoffman, Lance J. *Modern Methods for Computer Security and Privacy.* Englewood Cliffs: Prentice-Hall, 1977.

Martin, James. *Security, Accuracy, and Privacy in Computer Systems.* Englewood Cliffs: Prentice-Hall, 1973.

Rullo, Thomas A., ed. *Advances in Computer Security Management, Vol. I.* Philadelphia: Heyden, 1980.

Schweitzer, James A. *Managing Information Security: A Program for the Electronic Information Age.* Boston: Butterworth, 1982.

Trainor, Timothy N. and Diane Krasnewich. *Computers!* Santa Cruz: Mitchell, 1987.

Data Security/Cryptography:

Denning, Dorothy Elizabeth Robling. *Cryptography and Data Security.* Reading: Addison-Wesley, 1982.

Katzan, Harry, Jr. *Computer Data Security.* New York: Van Norstrand Reinhold, 1973.

U.S. Department of Commerce. *Computer Science and Technology: Computer Security and the Data Encryption Standard.* NS Special Publication 500-27. National Bureau of Standards, 1978.

U.S. Department of Commerce. *Computer Science and Technology: The Network Security Center: A System Level Approach to Computer Network Security.* NS Special Publication 500-21, Vol. 2, 1978.

BIBLIOGRAPHY

"ATM Card Rip-offs: Who Pays?" *Money,* November 1985, p. 13.

Baier, Kurt and Nicholas Rescher, eds. *Values and the Future.* New York: Free Press, 1971.

Bequai, A. "The Rise of Cashless Crimes (electronic funds transfer systems)." *USA Today,* January 1986, pp 83-85.

Berney, K. "The Cutting Edge." *Nation's Business,* April 1986, p 57.

Comer, J.P. "Computer Ethics." *Parents,* September 1985, p. 158.

DeGeorge, Richard T. *Business Ethics.* New York: MacMillan, 1982.

Denning, Dorothy Elizabeth Robling. *Cryptography and Data Security.* Reading: Addison-Wesley, 1982.

Elmer-Dewitt, P. "Cracking Down." *Time,* 14 May 1984, p 83.

Elmer-Dewitt, P. "The Great Satellite Caper (arrest of New Jersey teenage hackers)." *Time,* 29 July 1985, p. 65.

Elmer-Dewitt, P. "Surveying the Data Diddlers (study released by National Center for Computer Crime Data)." *Time,* 17 February, 1986, p. 95.

Enger, Norman L. and Paul W. Howerton. *Computer Security: A Management Audit Approach.* New York: AMACOM, 1980.

Eskow, D. and L. Green. "Catching Computer Crooks." *Popular Mechanics,* June 1984, pp 63-65+

Filepski, A. and J. Hanko. "Making Unix Secure." *BYTE,* April 1986, pp 113-114+

Freedman, Warren. The Right of Privacy in the Computer Age. New York: Quorum, 1987.

Hoffman, Lance J. *Modern Methods for Computer Security and Privacy.* Englewood Cliffs: Prentice-Hall, 1977.

Johnson, D.W. "Computer Ethics." *Futurist,* August 1984, pp 68-69

Katzan, Harry, Jr. *Computer Data Security.* New York: Van Nostrand Reinhold, 1973.

Lewis, M. "Computer Crime: Theft in Bits and Bytes." *Nation's Business,* February 1985, pp 57-58.

Lewis, M. "Scuttling Software Pirates (Association of Data Processing Service Organizations)." *Nation's Business,* March 1985, p 28.

Mano, D.K. "Computer Crime." *National Review,* 27 July 1984, pp 51-52.

Martin, James. *Security, Accuracy, and Privacy in Computer Systems.* Englewood Cliffs: Prentice-Hall, 1973.

Morrison, P.R. "Computer Parasites." *Futurist,* March/April 1986, pp 36-38.

Ognibene, P.J. "Computer Saboteurs." *Science Digest,* July 1984, pp 58-61.

Peterson, I. "New Data Increase Computer Crime Concerns (report by the American Bar Association)." *Science News,* 23 June 1984, p 390.

Reilly, A. "Computer Crackdown." *Fortune,* 17 September 1984, pp 141-142.

Rokeach, Milton. *The Nature of Human Values.* New York: Free Press, 1973.

Rullo, Thomas A., ed. *Advances in Computer Security Management, Vol. I.* Philadelphia: Heyden, 1980.

Sandza, R. "The Night of the Hackers." *Newsweek,* 12 November 1984, pp 17-18.

Sandza, R. "The Revenge of the Hackers (animosity directed at Newsweek writer for anti-hacker story)." *Newsweek,* 10 December 1984, p 81.

Schiffres, M. "The Struggle to Thwart Software Pirates." *U.S. News and World Report,* 25 March 1985, p 72.

Schweitzer, James A. *Managing Information Security: A Program for the Electronic Information Age.* Boston: Butterworth, 1982.

Sterne, R.G. and P.J. Saidman. "Copying Mass-Marketed Software (Lotus lawsuits)." *BYTE,* February 1985, pp 387-390.

Steward, G. "Computer Sabotage (disgruntled employee at Calgary Herald)." *Macleans,* 23 April 1984, pp 59-60.

"Three Teenage Hackers Arrested in Computer Scam." *York Daily Record,* 26 July 1987, p 2A.

Tracey, E.J. "Selling Software on the Honor System (combating piracy by giving programs away)." *Fortune,* 15 October 1984, p 146.

Trainor, Timothy N. and Diane Krasnewich. *Computers!* Santa Cruz: Mitchell, 1987.

U.S. Department of Commerce. *Computer Science and Technology: Computer Security and the Data Encryption Standard.* NS Special Publication 500-27. National Bureau of Standards, 1978.

U.S. Department of Commerce. *Computer Science and Technology: The Network Security Center: A System Level Approach to Computer Network Security.* NS Special Publication 500-21, Vol. 2. National Bureau of Standards, 1978.

Weberman, B. "Book-entry Blues (potential for computerized securities fraud).; *Forbes,* 5 May 1986, p 104.

"When Thieves Sit Down at Computers (study by American Bar Association)." *U.S. News and World Report,* 25 June 1984, p 8.

Wyden, R. "Curbing the Keyboard Criminal." *USA Today,* January 1984, pp 68-70.

"Youths Charged in Computer Crime Ring." *York Daily Record,* 23 July 1987, p 6A.

Unit 4

Explosive Devices, Bomb Threats
Basic Alarm Systems
Fire Prevention
Hazardous Materials

EXPLOSIVE DEVICES, BOMB THREAT AND SEARCH PROCEDURES

By Paul J. Hawthorn

Explosives play an important role in everyday life. They are used by:

- construction crews
- quarrymen
- the military
- certain medical professions

Unfortunately, the general public usually hears about explosives when the media reports a terroristic bombing or a typical bomb scare. The security specialist on the other hand must deal with actual bomb threats, bomb search procedures and sometimes the hazardous device or bomb itself. This chapter will cover those special topics.

Individuals who misuse explosives or telephone bomb threats aren't necessarily insane or belong to a terrorist group. They can be average citizens who for one reason or another choose actual bombings or bomb threats to wreak revenge or terror on an unsuspecting business or organization.

Reasons for using or threatening to use explosives could relate to:

- A frustrated businessman who fails to close an agreement.
- An angry parent whose child must attend a school where an AIDS victim is enrolled.
- Bribes to obtain large sums of money.
- Political or moral viewpoints.

The list goes on, but whatever the reason may be, a security force must take quick and effective action to solve the problem.

Explosives and related paraphernalia can be obtained easily, usually by:

Theft -   A Senate subcommittee once stated that within one 15-month period, 31,370 pounds of explosives, 94,018 blasting caps and 101,540 feet of detonation cord (explosive fuse) were stolen. Military installations and construction sites are the primary sources.

Legal
Purchase -   With the proper credentials, forged or otherwise, an individual can obtain explosives from across-the-counter sales. One such legal document is a fire marshall's permit. This is obtained in some states after filing in a mining claim.

Mail
Order -   One firm in Colorado sells military booby-trap devices, practice hand grenades never fired, illuminating trip flares and incendiary fire starters.

Homemade
Mixtures -   Common household cleaners and chemicals used in making improvised explosives can be purchased from local grocery, hardware and lawn care establishments.

Knowledge in the use and handling of explosives is readily available through bookstores and mail order firms. Many publications go into great detail on the production of improvised explosives and hazardous devices. Therefore the security professional must realize that information relating to the use of explosives is available to almost anyone, and not restricted to any select group.

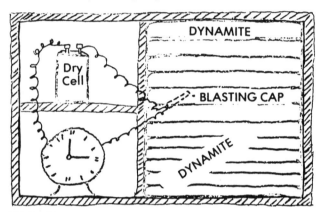

Illustration 1:
Sketch from militant book explaining how to make an "Alarm-Clock" time bomb. Such publications are readily available to the general public.

Terms

In order to report accurate findings and carry out safe, effective plans to deal with "Bomb" incidents, security officers should become familiar with the following general terms:

Bomb -   An incendiary (fire-producing) or explosive (blast-producing) device capable of causing damage to property and injury or death to individuals within a few feet or a city block from the bombing location. The extent of damage or injury would depend on the type and quantity of material used in the bomb. Distance as given here is only an example, and should not be construed as the minimum or maximum danger area.

Bomb
Threat -   A verbal or written message warning or claiming placement of a bomb or similar hazardous device.

Hazardous
Device -   Any object, which by itself or as a part of an explosive or non-explosive system, can inflict damage to property or injury to personnel.

Explosives -   Substances that, through chemical reaction, violently change and release pressure and heat equally in all directions at once. Explosives are classified as low (smokeless or black gunpowder) or high (dynamite, TNT, plastic explosive) explosives. When detonated, low explosives create a pushing or shoving effect. High explosives detonate with a higher velocity, causing a shattering or cracking effect.

Bomb - Incident Plan   A standard operating procedure which directs security or other responsible persons how to handle a bomb threat, search or actual bombing.

Blasting-Caps   An explosive initiator or detonator consisting of a small metal tube filled with a high explosive composition. Classified as electric (activated by electric current) or non-electric (activated by fuse or spark flash), blasting caps are used to detonate explosives. These devices are sensitive to heat, shock and rough handling.

Pyro-technics -   Items which through chemical reactions cause light, smoke, heat or noise. Examples are fireworks, trip flares and special training devices used by the military to simulate battlefield effects.

Explosive - Ordnance Disposal   (E.O.D.)/Bomb Squad: These organizations and certain others should be the only ones to handle or dispose of the actual bomb or hazardous device if one is found. Handling, disposing or disarming bombs and related items should **not** be the duty of untrained security personnel.

Bomber -   Any individual who uses or threatens to use an explosive device for illegal purposes.

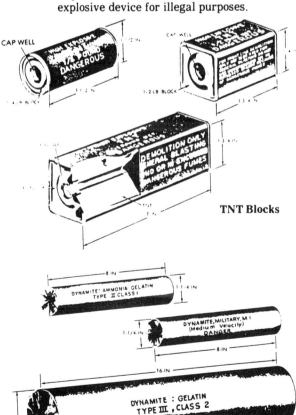

TNT Blocks

Dynamite: military, M1: dynamite, ammonia gelatin, Type H, classI and dynamite: gelatin, type III, class 2

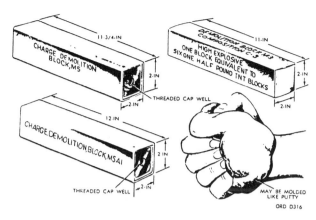

Plastic demolition charges

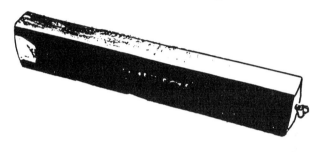

Composition C4 block charge

Explosive Firing Systems

Explosions result from a chain reaction of specific elements in an explosive firing system. There are two types: electric and non-electric. Both systems are comprised of:

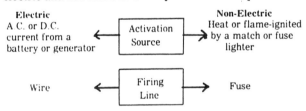

Note: A firing line is often not necessary.

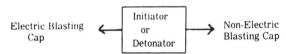

Note: Detonating/Priming cord can be used as a substitute for blasting caps and firing line in many cases. It has an asphalt or plastic sheathing and a high explosive filler. With a burning rate of 19,400 feet per second, this cord also makes an excellent cutting charge when wrapped around poles, trees or light gauge steel (such as a 55-gallon drum).

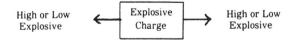

When an activation source charges the firing line, the initiator explodes setting off the explosive charge(s). Pieces of fuse, wire or actual explosive components may be found after a bomb explodes. Being able to identify such items will allow the observer to submit a more accurate investigation report. Basic components of the firing systems are illustrated throughout this chapter. However, security personnel should expand their knowledge of these items in organized classes since there are several different types of activating sources, firing lines, detonators and explosives.

"Bomb", the End Product

A bomb is basically an explosive firing system in a box or other container. This is a simple description, but there is no such thing as a simple bomb.

With the availability of electric blasting caps and miniature circuitry, the possibilities for constructing a bomb are endless. Shoe/wooden boxes, pipes, briefcases, backpacks or any other available container can be used. These items are easily recognized as possible bombs. However, appliances, lunch boxes, thermos bottles, books or even ink pens can be converted into a hazardous device. These are not easily recognized and are sometimes referred to as booby-traps. They will be discussed later.

Bombs are activated in any number of ways. Some examples are by —

Chemical
Reaction: A chemical delay device activates the detonator.
Motional: A metal ball rolls when the bomb is tilted and makes contact, closing a circuit.

Mechan-
ical: An alarm clock is wired to close a circuit at a certain time, or the winding key with a string attached pulls two flexible metal contacts together, making contact.
Frictional: Two abrasives which spark when they rub together, or a match pulled over a striking surface.
Electrical-
ly: A switch is closed either by lifting (pressure release), pushing (pressure) or simply by turning on a light switch.

Considering the possibilities of activating a bomb, certain 'Dos' and 'Don'ts' apply if a suspicious package/container is found during an initial bomb search:

Don't:
- cut wires
- submerse in water
- handle
- shake or tilt
- freeze or heat (in case thermostatic device involved)
- cut into package

Do:
- report location and accurately describe suspicious package (use telephone, not radio)
- evacuate and isolate area for a minimum of 300 feet
- notify and lead E.O.D. personnel or bomb squad to possible bomb

If time permits:
- search for a second device
- open doors and windows
- disconnect utilities
- remove flammables from immediate area
- place sandbags (double thick if possible) around bomb, or mattresses
- photograph or sketch area

Without further training, the security officer's responsibility ends upon complying with the dos and don'ts as given.

Nasty Gadgets

Explosive charges or other hazardous devices, cunningly designed to be triggered by an unsuspecting person who disturbs an apparently harmless object or performs a presumably safe act, are referred to as booby-traps (also dirty trick devices).

Booby-traps supplement bombs (or are the bomb), and may be used to impede bomb search procedures. As touched on earlier, such devices can be concealed in practically anything, but this is only part of the problem.

They are designed to maim or kill with extreme prejudice. Doors and windows can be wired with explosives to detonate when opened; hallways, rooms, roads or stairways become death traps simply by running a tripwire to an explosive device. Stepping on a loose floorboard, starting a car engine or turning on a light switch may be the last act in a person's life if they encounter such devices.

There are several precautions that can be taken in dealing with booby-traps during bomb searches:

1. Watch where you are going, observe all areas carefully.
2. If possible, examine entrances to rooms through outside windows.
3. When opening drawers or cabinet doors, do it slowly and look for tripwires or other activating devices. Treat entrance and exit doors the same way.
4. Be cautious of dark rooms; a photoelectric cell may be involved (could close switch when exposed to light).
5. Be aware of objects that look out of place or don't fit in. One example might be a Bible in a room filled with pornographic posters.
6. If a booby-trap is found, call in the experts.

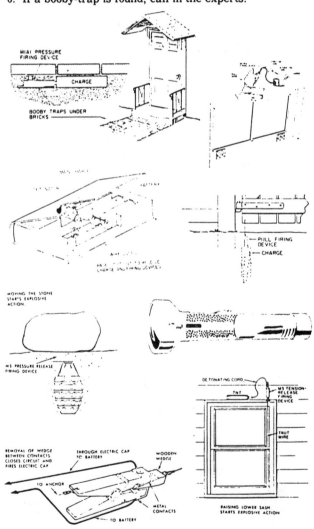

Booby-traps, the possibilities are endless.

Other Hazardous Devices

As terrorism increases throughout the world, it is not unrealistic to assume security personnel may come into contact with a terrorist situation.

Terrorists are known to use a variety of military ordnance (weapons and ammunition used in warfare). Although it would be impossible to cover all the ordnance available to terrorists in this chapter, some common items are listed below:

Grenades: Small bombs of a size and shape convenient for throwing by hand or launching from a rifle. When detonated, they can cause fires, dispense a chemical agent, smoke screen, or explode violently causing concussion and fragmentation. Grenades are also used in booby-traps.

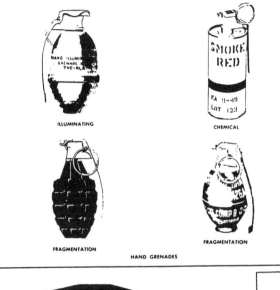

ILLUMINATING   CHEMICAL

FRAGMENTATION   FRAGMENTATION

HAND GRENADES

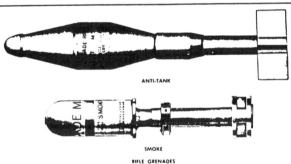

ANTI-TANK

SMOKE

RIFLE GRENADES

Representative Grenades

Claymore Mine: This device, when detonated, delivers spherical steel fragments over a 60-degree fan-shaped pattern that is two meters high and 50 meters wide. The fragments can inflict injury up to 250 meters out to the front of the mine. There is also a back blast danger area of 16 meters to the rear and sides. In what's termed a controlled situation, the weapon is aimed and manually fired. In an uncontrolled situation, it is used as a booby-trap.

66-mm L.A.W. (Light Anti-Tank Weapon): This item can be used against buildings or motorcades. It fires a rocket designed to explode on impact, killing or injuring personnel within the immediate blast area. The maximum effective range is 200 meters.

Explosive Domestics

Explosive domestics for purposes of this chapter are those situations which require security attention concerning legitimate explosive-related problems within a specific geographic area. These problems, although not in the same category as bomb threats, may present a danger if handled carelessly. Some situations could be:

Security at a National Park - If the park contains a historical battlefield, war relics may be found. Some are nice souvenirs such as a representative belt buckle. Others are not, such as an unexploded cannonball or other artillery projectile. Even though they may be over 100 years old, cannonballs have exploded when handled by an unsuspecting souvenir hunter, killing them just as dead as any modern hazardous device. If such items are reported or found, call the bomb squad.

Security in an agricultural area - Some contract security agencies and select others patrol rural areas. These locations often contain farmers who locate a box of dynamite from a past job, and want to get rid of it. The explosives involved could be years old, causing them to have a crystallized or oily surface. This is a sign that handling the explosives could be dangerous. Play it safe, even if the explosives look okay, call E.O.D. or another authorized agency.

Security around personal residences or apartments - Veterans have been known to bring home various ordnance items from foreign wars. When these show up around the house a few years later, someone may report them. Find out all the information about the device as possible. If the security officer and caller are sure the item is not dangerous to handle, it could be picked up and turned into an E.O.D. unit. If there is any doubt, or even just to play it safe, call the experts.

Security in neighborhoods - Pyrotechnics (see terms) are often reported or seen during various holidays and other occasions. If these items are found or confiscated, place all unfired items in a sealed metal container and turn them into E.O.D. Be careful not to include duds in the container. Duds are best left alone to be handled by qualified personnel.

Although technically, in many cases, persons turning over explosives and other hazardous devices could be charged with illegal possession, the security professional should consider **not** bringing such charges. This will encourage other people to cooperate with authorities, and possibly help rid the area of other hazardous devices.

BOMB THREAT REPORT FORM

INSTRUCTIONS: BE CALM. BE COURTEOUS. LISTEN, DO NOT INTERRUPT THE CALLER. NOTIFY SUPERVISOR/SECURITY OFFICER BY PRE-ARRANGED SIGNAL WHILE CALLER IS ON LINE.

Date _____ Time _____

Exact Words of Person Placing Call: _____

_____

_____

QUESTIONS TO ASK:

1. When is the bomb going to explode? _____
2. Where is the bomb right now? _____
3. What kind of bomb is it? _____
4. What does it look like? _____
5. Why did you place the bomb? _____

TRY TO DETERMINE THE FOLLOWING (CIRCLE AS APPROPRIATE)

Caller's Identity: Male Female Adult Juvenile Age ___years

Voice: Loud Soft High Pitch Deep Raspy Pleasant Intoxicated Other

Accent: Local Not Local Foreign Region

Speech: Fast Slow Distinct Distorted Stutter Nasal Slurred Lisp

Language: Excellent Good Fair Poor Foul Other

Manner: Calm Angry Rational Irrational Coherent Incoherent Deliberate
Emotional Righteous Laughing Intoxicated

Background Noises: Office Machines Factory Machines Bedlam Trains Animals Music Quiet Voices Mixed Airplanes Street Traffic
Party Atmosphere

ADDITIONAL INFORMATION: _____

_____

_____

ACTION TO TAKE IMMEDIATELY AFTER CALL: Notify your supervisor/security officer as instructed. Talk to no one other than instructed by your supervisor/security officer.

RECEIVING TELEPHONE NUMBER _____

PERSON RECEIVING CALL _____

Preventive Measures

By now, the reader has learned that it's almost impossible to prevent a determined bomber from obtaining materials or knowledge relating to explosive devices. However, one preventive measure remains that will reduce the chances of an actual bomb being placed within a security officer's area of responsibility.

That preventive measure is physical security. Physical security measures are covered throughout this manual, and should be strictly adhered to with an emphasis on package and material control, along with a personal identification system.

Bomb Threats

Threats concerning bombs come two ways — written or by telephone. If a written threat is received:

- Save all material along with envelopes or containers.
- Do everything possible to preserve fingerprints, paper used and postal marks.

- Report the threat to applicable authorities such as fire department, police and bomb squad.
- Don't take it lightly; any bomb threat is serious.

If a telephone threat is received:

- Record the call if possible.
- Keep the caller talking in order to receive as much information as possible.
- Try and learn the time of detonation, type of device, explosive used and location.
- Inform caller there are people in the building. If the caller argues, he knows the building is empty. Say there is a special meeting or something similar going on. If the bomber only wants to destroy property, this statement may prompt him to give more information.
- Note background noise (machines, music, etc.) and voice qualities such as male or female, calm, excited, or speech impediments.
- Try and write notes while taking the call.

Not only will getting all information possible help the security officer learn about the bomb, but it will also help determine whether or not the call is a hoax. Generally speaking, the more information received, the more likely a real bomb exists.

Search Procedures

After a bomb threat is received, an organized search procedure should be put into effect.

Persons most familiar with the endangered area should be the ones searching it. These individuals will most likely be selected employees, maintenance personnel or security. Police, fire department or bomb disposal teams usually will not participate in the search.

There are two basic types of searches — exterior and interior. Start outside first and then work inside, as exterior areas would probably be more accessible to the bomber.

Practically any crime scene search technique could be used for bombs, but there are specific recommendations when looking for an explosive device.

A search team of two individuals is preferred, and basic search procedures would be carried out as follows:

Exterior Search - Check:

1. The distance of 25-50 feet from the building outward.
2. Don't forget to check window ledges, air-conditioning units, signs, building ornamentation, fire escapes and the roof.
3. Street drainage systems.
4. Manholes in the street and sidewalks.
5. Trash receptacles, garbage cans, dumpsters, incinerators, etc.
6. Parked cars and trucks.
7. Mailboxes, shrubbery and stairwells.

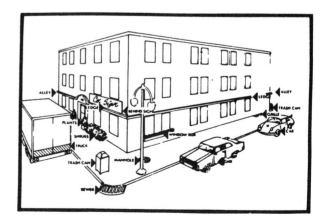

Interior Search:

1. Divide the room and select a search height.
   A. 1st search floor to hip area,
   B. 2nd search hip to chin,
   C. 3rd search chin to ceiling,
   D. 4th search suspended ceilings or hollow areas overhead.

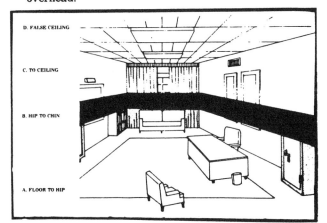

2. Search from the bottom up, starting in the centre of the room back-to-back with partner, and then work around the walls, returning to center after each pass and starting over. Do this procedure for all four height levels and room sections.

3. Utilize sight and other senses.
   A. Look for items that don't fit in, including hasty/new physical changes to room such as a dislodged ceiling panel.
   B. Listen for ticking or other strange sounds.
   C. Use sense of smell for acids or flammable liquids such as gasoline.
4. Check under rugs, air-conditioning/heating ducts, hanging light fixtures, baseboard heaters and built-in wall cupboards.
5. Open all entrance/cabinet doors slowly. A booby-trap may be involved.
6. When room search is complete, mark the door to the room with colored tape, or some other markings, so other searchers know the room has been checked.
7. If special equipment such as an explosive detector or a bomb dog are available, use them. Other items such as a flashlight or mirror may also be helpful.
8. Make sure only authorized persons have access to the threatened area, and keep security tight until after the search is completed. (This may be tough in buildings such as hospitals, but do the best job possible.)

9. Watch the time. A search team should not be in or around a building if a detonation time is imminent.

If an explosive device is found, don't touch it. Follow the suggestions given earlier in this chapter.

If an explosion occurs:

1. Call fire department, rescue squad and police (if not already notified).
2. Administer first-aid and move any injured to safe area.
3. Isolate explosion area, control fire and continue to secure area.
4. Notify special investigation personnel such as arson investigators as soon as possible.

Bomb Incident Plan

A "Bomb Incident Plan" (B.I.P.) should be available to security personnel at all times. The B.I.P. should give all the necessary information to carry out a successful response to a bomb threat. Topics and procedures covered in this plan would vary according to the type of establishment, physical layout and business/public concerns.

B.I.P.'s should not only cover threats, search procedures and what to do if a suspicious package/bomb is found, but should also include:

- How to set up a "Bomb Threat" Command or Control Centre.
- Specific Support Organizations, or those who know they are on a list to be notified in the event a bomb situation would occur at your organization.
- Communication Procedures, which would cover topics in regards to who to notify besides emergency personnel (owner/administrator, etc.) and how (paging code, telephone, etc.).
- Reporting System, for the security force handling the emergency. Included would be reminders **not** to use two-way radios in the event of a bomb threat (transmitting could set off an electric detonator), and other signalling devices such as whistles, sirens, etc. which would identify a bomb incident or other emergency.
- Any other topic or action the security professional may find beneficial to include.

Conclusion

Legitimate use of explosives can be very helpful in today's society. However, there are those who would misuse bombs and other hazardous devices to cause terror, death and unlimited destruction of property.

The 'Professional Security Officer' must learn to cope with bomb incidents, and continue to protect lives and property from falling victim to an explosive's lethal capabilities.

Most 'Bomb Threats' are a hoax, but 5 - 10% of bomb-related incidents are the real thing.

If you find an explosive or hazardous device, don't touch it, call the experts. Don't be known as a hero because you died disarming or handling a bomb. Be known as a hero because you saved other lives, including your own.

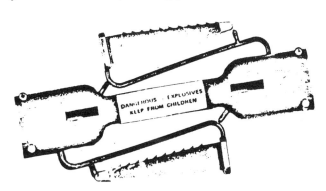

References

MOVIES:
"Bombs" 1,2,3, by Motorola Teleprograms Inc.

TRAINING CIRCULARS (TC):
Bomb Threat & Search Procedure, a Handbook by Desert Publications, Information taken from U.S. Army TC 19-5.

BOOKS:
"The Poor Man's James Bond" by Kurt Saxon, Atlan Formularies, Eureka, Ca.

"The Anarchist Cookbook" by William Powell/Introduction by Peter Bergman, Lyle Stuart, Inc., 1971

"Bomb Threats and Search Techniques" by U.S. Department of the Treasury, Bureau of Alcohol, Tobacco and Firearms.

TECHNICAL MANUALS by U.S. Department of the Army:
TM 9-1300-200, "Ammunition, General", Oct. 1969 w/changes.

SUBCOURSE MANUAL:
MMS 100, "Ammunition" by U.S. Army Missile and Munitions School, Redstone Arsenal, Ala., Sept., 1970.

U.S. ARMY FIELD MANUALS by U.S. Department of the Army:
Field Manual (FM)
5-25, "Demolitions and Explosives", May, 1967
5-31, "Booby-traps", Sept., 1965
19-30, "Physical Security", Nov., 1971
23-30, "Grenades and Pyrotechnic Signals", Dec., 1969

CATALOGUE:
Fireworks Unlimited (Lone Ranger Exhibit), 1986, 8550 rt. 224 Deerfield, Ohio 44411, (1-800-321-2400)

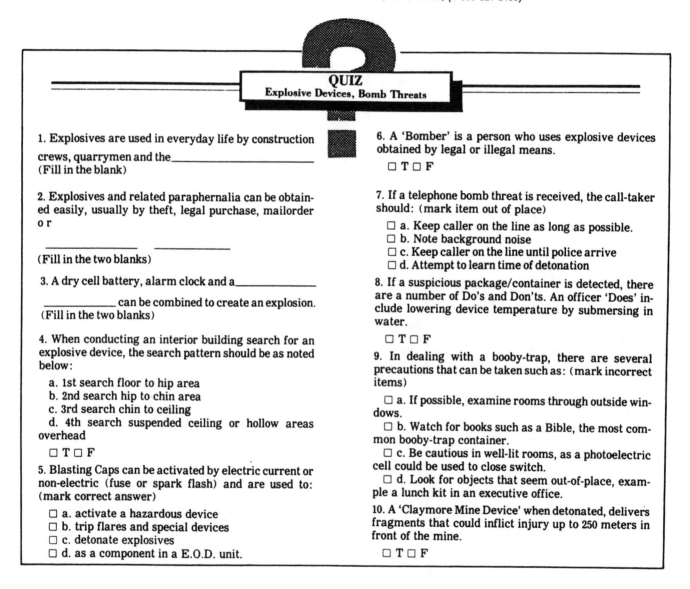

QUIZ
Explosive Devices, Bomb Threats

1. Explosives are used in everyday life by construction crews, quarrymen and the_____
(Fill in the blank)

2. Explosives and related paraphernalia can be obtained easily, usually by theft, legal purchase, mailorder or

_____ _____

(Fill in the two blanks)

3. A dry cell battery, alarm clock and a_____

_____ can be combined to create an explosion.
(Fill in the two blanks)

4. When conducting an interior building search for an explosive device, the search pattern should be as noted below:

a. 1st search floor to hip area
b. 2nd search hip to chin area
c. 3rd search chin to ceiling
d. 4th search suspended ceiling or hollow areas overhead

☐ T ☐ F

5. Blasting Caps can be activated by electric current or non-electric (fuse or spark flash) and are used to: (mark correct answer)

☐ a. activate a hazardous device
☐ b. trip flares and special devices
☐ c. detonate explosives
☐ d. as a component in a E.O.D. unit.

6. A 'Bomber' is a person who uses explosive devices obtained by legal or illegal means.

☐ T ☐ F

7. If a telephone bomb threat is received, the call-taker should: (mark item out of place)

☐ a. Keep caller on the line as long as possible.
☐ b. Note background noise
☐ c. Keep caller on the line until police arrive
☐ d. Attempt to learn time of detonation

8. If a suspicious package/container is detected, there are a number of Do's and Don'ts. An officer 'Does' include lowering device temperature by submersing in water.

☐ T ☐ F

9. In dealing with a booby-trap, there are several precautions that can be taken such as: (mark incorrect items)

☐ a. If possible, examine rooms through outside windows.
☐ b. Watch for books such as a Bible, the most common booby-trap container.
☐ c. Be cautious in well-lit rooms, as a photoelectric cell could be used to close switch.
☐ d. Look for objects that seem out-of-place, example a lunch kit in an executive office.

10. A 'Claymore Mine Device' when detonated, delivers fragments that could inflict injury up to 250 meters in front of the mine.

☐ T ☐ F

BASIC ALARM SYSTEMS

By Wilfred S. Thompson

ELECTRONICS AND THE PROTECTION OFFICER

Alarms, electronics and C.C.T.V. are valuable tools of the Protection Officer and the Corporate Security Director. It is important to understand the strengths and functions of these systems and learn how you will use them.

Develop your skills in the use of these security tools and you increase your value to the corporation you serve.

Today more than any other time in history, individuals, large and small businesses, corporations and governments are turning to alarm systems as an essential ingredient in their security programs. Many of these alarm systems may appear to be extremely complicated to the new Protection Officer.

All alarm systems are simple applications of physics and electronic programming, and are not as complex as they appear. With alarm systems being installed and operated in most facilities that the protection officer will work in, it becomes important for the officer to have a basic knowledge of the different types of systems that are commonly in use today.

It is not the intention here to instruct you in the installation or service of alarm systems, but rather to recognize, understand and use alarm systems to increase your security coverage of a given area.

As a protection officer, you should know how to arm and disarm systems, test operations (if built-in test lights are utilized) and recognize certain conditions that may result in what is usually termed 'false alarms'.

Alarm Conditions

Alarm systems are normally 'on' all the time and when an intruder enters a protected area they cause a change in the system which will activate the 'alarm'. There are a number of causes for alarms.

1. An intruder has entered the protected area.
2. A malfunction has occured.
3. Human error.
4. Undetermined.

Statistics on Alarm Conditions

(1 thru 4 above) - Based on 1,796 reported alarms.

Reason	Number of Alarms	Percentage
1.	21	0.01%
2.	354	19.69%
3.	786	45.80%
4.	635	34.50%

Malfunction: A malfunction is considered any correctable problem discovered within the alarm system that caused it to operate incorrectly, either by sounding an alarm when the conditions do not warrant it, or by failing to indicate a real alarm condition.

Human Error: A person caused the alarm condition. This usually occurs when the operator of the alarm system failed to follow proper procedures for turning on or off the system and triggered the alarm condition. Another reason may have been the faulty installation of the system in the first instance.

Undetermined: This is where no alarm system fault could be determined and no human error could be proven.

All too often, false alarms are really a detection of some condition, movements or improper application of a detector and as such are really human error and not the fault of the electronic system. We will look at some of the more common false alarm conditions that are found within each system as they are covered.

Sensing Hardware

This is the equipment that is connected by wire to a control panel and is actually what signals the presence of an intruder. Many of the systems discussed can be used in conjunction with other systems quite successfully.

Perimeter Protection

A combination of both door and window sensors comprise the basics of perimeter protection.

Magnetic contacts: On doors, windows or anything that opens, a spring-loaded switch is held closed by a magnet. As the magnet swings away with the door, the spring opens the contact and signals the control panel.

Window Bugs: Glass was originally protected by a continuous strip of metal foil, glued to the outer perimeter of a window that broke when the window was shattered, interrupting the central box circuit and creating an alarm. Today's technology has produced a 'window bug' that is a shock sensor device that when glued to a window will detect the shock of breaking glass.

Interior Protection

Motion Sensors: Motion sensors are the 'second' line of defence and are located in 'trap zones' or high traffic areas where an intruder is likely to travel through during a break-in. It is important to understand the basic principle of motion sensors, since improper selection of some types of these sensors will produce an alarm by detecting motion other than an intruder. These are often termed 'false alarms' and yet the sensor really did detect motion. It was not the fault of the sensor if improper placement placed it in a position to detect some mechanical movement. We will consider this problem as we look at each type of sensor.

A) Photo Cell:

A photo cell is comprised of a light source and a receiver that creates a beam across a room. Black light created an invisible beam that the intruder 'broke' as he walked through it. Later and present models utilize pulsed beams to defeat attempts to introduce mirrors or other light sources.

Today we can see laser models with great fog or haze penetration capabilities. These are a very stable alarm sensor. Your only problem likely as a security officer would be a system that would not 'arm'. A check will likely reveal a box or some item blocking the light path between the beam sender and receiver and creating an alarm condition.

B) Ultrasonics:

Ultrasonics sense movement in a room by a principle called the "Doppler Effect". Sound generated by a unit, above the range of the human ear, is transmitted outward into the room. The sound bounces off all objects within its range and returns to the unit. Any object moving away from, or towards the detector, will increase or decrease the rebound time, indicating motion, and trigger the alarm. Any motion then is registered as an alarm.

This system may register 'false' alarms due to the movement of hanging objects affected at various times by air conditioning vents, fans, etc., and may even detect heavy air turbulence or sounds that fall within the range of your ultrasonic detector. If your system develops false alarms, look to these as likely culprits.

C) Microwave: Microwave also works on the Doppler Effect. The difference between ultrasonics and microwaves lies in the frequency produced by the units and the fact that ultrasonic is an audio signal and the microwave a radio frequency signal. This signal, like all radio frequency signals, will penetrate solid walls and ceilings to detect motion in another room. This can be a boon for concealed detectors in large areas or for penetration into adjoining rooms and areas.

The problem faced with these systems is similar to the ultrasonics — they will detect motion from air conditioners, fans, etc., that may cause movement from displays or hanging objects, and register an alarm. Keep in mind that a microwave can "see" inside a heater to see the fan, inside pipe to see running water and through walls to see people moving outside. There are controls like "blinders" and there are range controls to limit how far it can see, but an installer must be right or you will have false alarms.

D) Infra-Red: Infra-red is the most recent state-of-the-art sensor and will present few false alarm problems. The sensors are activated by a sudden increase in infra-red energy present in the monitored area. Man and animals are an excellent source of infra-red energy. Other possible sources are fire, direct sunlight and heated elements.

The installer must consider exposure to a sunrise, electric heater elements and such when installing. A system installed in December may never see sunlight, yet in June a sunrise shines straight into a I/R receiver at 6:00 a.m., two hours before the system is normally disarmed. Result, an alarm and not the fault of the system!

E) Audio Sensors: Audio sensors are activated by loud, sharp noises within the protected area. These sensors are prone to false alarms and are not in widespread use. Some of these "audio" systems are very effectively used by central station alarm companies who use a principle of inverting the public address speakers in a school or other large building to act as microphones so they can "listen in" to sounds in the building. This is very effective in a building such as a school where every room has a speaker.

Types of Alarm Systems

Alarm systems are generally broken down into the following basic types:

Local Alarms: This system may have any number of combinations of sensors, but its alarm signal is usually a bell or siren and possibly a strobe light that is mounted outside the protected premises. It is the least expensive type of system, but its weakness lies in the fact that even if someone does hear the alarm, the authorities are seldom called.

Monitored System: Here we have taken our original "local" system and added a dialer or communicator that is capable of utilizing the existing telephone circuits to pass the alarm signal along to a monitoring station or any other location programmed into the system that can be reached by telephone.

These systems were originally a dialer that called a single telephone number by electronic pulses and then delivered a tape-recorded message. If there was no answer at the number called, the alarm would disconnect and make two more attempts. If no answer was received after the third try, the alarm would discontinue trying and the alarm would never be delivered.

Today we have replaced most dialers with digital communicators that look for a dial tone, can seize a busy line, communicate in seconds and deliver a two-way digital message with the receiving monitor and then move on to other telephone numbers to relay secondary information to numerous other sources that have been programmed into the communicator. The only weakness in this type of system is if there is a loss of telephone lines between the protected premise and the monitoring station.

An idea of the extent and use of this principle of protection lies in the fact that there are national alarm companies offering dialer monitoring across the entire United States. Computer response and communication to emergency services in every city is faster than a human operator could respond.

Central Monitoring Station: This is the best form of protection where the protected premises are connected directly by telephone line to a central station. A central station is manned by trained employees on a 24-hour, 365-day-per-year basis.

When an alarm is received at a station, the employee on duty will contact the appropriate reports of times, dates and action taken. A central station may or may not be a ULC-listed station. The U.L. designation (Underwriters Laboratory) means that the monitoring equipment, the operators, their records and the premises where they are located meet certain critical standards set down by U.L.

A system installed to ULC standards and monitored by a ULC central station is the highest degree of protection and is required by certain industries such as banks and jewelry stores. This type of system will detect a cut phone line and respond as an alarm.

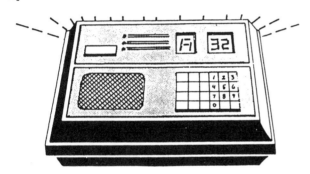

Proprietary System: This system you may well encounter in a large facility or site. An outlying building may be tied into a central communication centre by direct wire, video or combination of systems and when an alarm is indicated, will only signal the communications centre or guard post. As a security officer, you may well utilize such a system to monitor heat, air conditioning, entrance and exit, fire and emergency, flooding, and intrusion.

System Controls: All the sensors that we have been talking about depend on and operate from a control panel or box. The 110V house current is stepped down to low DC voltage used by all alarm systems. Because of this, all hook-ups are possible by low voltage wiring. The control panel sends current out through all the protection circuits in what is termed a 'series' circuit.

Any sensor detecting an intruder opens its contacts and interrupts the circuit, thereby creating the 'alarm' condition. The control unit then closes a relay to activate a siren, communicator or a central station circuit. Once triggered, the control latches until it is reset by the operator unless it is on a timed alarm setting. Some systems allow the operator either on-site or remote, to arm a system by utilizing a delay feature with a key or touch pad on the control, or even by wireless radio transmission.

Control panels today are marvels of electronic circuitry and can operate separate zones or areas, handle dozens of different inputs and react in different ways and even assist a service man in detecting what a problem is or where it lies within the system.

Wireless Alarms: We treat wireless alarm systems as a separate topic even though the sensors are the exact same as used in conventional systems. The difference lies in the fact that there are no connecting wires between the sensors and the control panel. Instead, signals are sent by low power radio transmitters and receivers. Originally, this would mean that if a sensor went dead, the owner or operator never knew it unless he tested the sensor.

Today's wireless systems can use the control to poll or speak to each sensor every few minutes to see if it is operating. It can then alarm if a battery or sensor is failing.

In some countries, where phone lines are scarce or

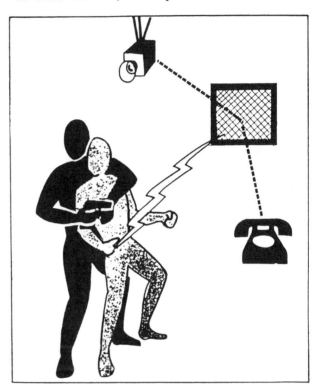

unavailable, long-range wireless alarm systems cover many miles. Such systems are appearing in the U.S. and the Arctic now, where phone systems are unavailable or too expensive. A last form of 'wireless' alarm is really not wireless! When each component is plugged into a 110V circuit, it not only draws power to operate, but sends its radio frequency signal over the power lines to talk to the control. These will even operate between buildings in certain instances, creating a 'buddy' system for holdup or emergency alarms from one store to another.

Wireless alarms today are extensively used by paraplegics or invalids to signal a communicator to dial for medical assistance.

Conclusion

As we have seen, while alarm systems appear quite complicated, they are actually fairly simple in structure and operation. Alarm systems are an excellent tool and resource in freeing up manpower and providing effective security coverage to large or remote areas and in highly sensitive areas.

The Protection Officer who takes the time and effort to learn the basics of alarm systems and in particular the one in place at his/her work site will be better prepared to take proper action on receipt of an alarm, be it bonafide or false.

QUIZ
Basic Alarm Systems

1. _____, _____ and _____
are valuable tools of the protection officer.
(Fill in the blanks)

2. As a protection officer, you should know how to

_____ and _____ alarm systems.
(Fill in the blanks)

3. A combination of both _____ and _____
sensors comprise the basics of perimeter protection.
(Fill in the blanks)

4. Motion sensors are the second line of defence and are

located in _____ _____ or high
traffic areas. (Fill in the two blanks)

5. When an alarm system has built-in test lights, it no
longer becomes necessary for the protection officer to
recognize certain conditions that may result in false
alarms.

☐ T ☐ F

6. A malfunction is considered any correctible problem
discovered within the alarm system that caused it to
operate incorrectly.

☐ T ☐ F

7. The inverting of a P.A. system in a school or large
building to act as microphones is known as the "Doppler Effect".

☐ T ☐ F

8. Audio sensors may be activated by:

☐ a. A sudden increase in infra-red energy.
☐ b. Loud, sharp noises within a premise.
☐ c. Voices and/or movements of culprits.
☐ d. none of the above.

9. Which of the following would be the best form of protection?

☐ a. A central monitoring station.
☐ b. A local alarm
☐ c. A monitored system.
☐ d. all of the above

10. Which of the following alarm sensors would be used
in a 'trap zone'?

☐ a. window bugs
☐ b. magnetic contacts
☐ c. photo cells
☐ d. all the above

FIRE PREVENTION AND DETECTION

By Charles F. Nash
Reviewed by Robert Wilson

Security plays a major role in protecting against fire. Fire has to be considered a serious and ongoing threat to the survival of any organization. History tells us just how often a fire has destroyed life and property. All security groups and individuals must make fire prevention a priority concern in terms of the overall protection process. Practice fire prevention for it most certainly will pay off, personally and professionally.

Most fires start out small and are usually easily extinguished, if prompt and efficient action is taken. Proper use of the correct fire extinguisher can make the difference between the quick extinguishment of fire, or the growth of a massive blaze that kills everyone and devours everything in its path.

We must know:
- Emergency procedures in the event of fire
- Causes of fire
- Types of fire
- Types of Fire Extinguisher
- Proper use of Fire Extinguishers

What is a Fire?

A fire is a chemical reaction called combustion, in which fuel and oxygen combine to give off large quantities of heat. In order for a fire to occur, four elements must be present:
- Fuel
- Heat
- Oxygen
- Chemical chain reaction phase

These form a four sided Geometric Figure known as a Fire Tetrahedron, which resembles a pyramid.

One of the four sides serves as the base, and represents the chemical chain reaction. The three standing sides represent heat, fuel, and oxygen.

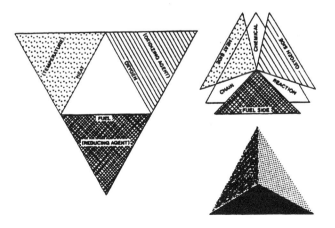

Principles of Fire Elimination

Under the theory of the Fire Tetrahedron, there are four methods of fire suppression.

Removal of FUEL
Exclusion of OXYGEN
Reduction of TEMPERATURE
Inhibition of CHAIN REACTION

Remove one or more of these essential components, and there is no fire. Always endeavor to relate to the FIRE TETRAHEDRON principle when dealing with the extinguishment of any type of fire.

Prevention Equals Good Security

By developing the ability to recognize a fire hazard and significantly reducing or eliminating that hazard, we take major strides in the art of prevention. While we must know the basics in eliminating a fire, we need to know what is likely to cause a fire. Before a fire can start, the following ingredients must be in place:

* There must be material that is flammable. This includes almost anything (e.g. flammable fluids or even fire resistant substances).

* There must be heat. How much heat depends on the material, ignition point, and temperature required to sustain the fire (i.e. smolder or blaze).

* There must be oxygen, which affects the intensity of a fire (e.g. a grass fire fanned by winds, or a smoldering rubble fire).

If we are not able to eliminate or significantly reduce the presence of any of the aforementioned elements, then we must be even more vigilant to ensure that a fire does not have the opportunity to start.

Recognizing Fire Hazards

In terms of fire prevention and detection, we can rely on our sense of sight and our sense of smell. Often it is not possible to see a fire that is in the infant stages. So we may be able to detect trouble by smelling a fire in the works. This is not to say that you should be less concerned about sighting a potential fire, rather remember that along with most fires, there are odors that can lead to death and destruction.

SOME DANGER SIGNALS:

* Look for cigarette butts that have been carelessly discarded, particularly in no smoking areas. Careless smoking has proven to be one of the most frequent causes of fire.

* Look for oily rags ... a real threat and a major contributor to accidental fire. Discarded rags, paper towels and like substances are frequently left near various kinds of equipment.

Spot them .... Remove them .... Report them.

*   **Look** for equipment overheat, a threat that is seldom appreciated in terms of real danger. Any electrical, or fuel-operated equipment can quickly overheat and result in a fire.

*   **Look** for appliances such as hot plates, coffee makers, stoves, and other such apparatus usually found in coffee or lunch rooms. Turn off ... and report.

*   **Look** for heating equipment, everything from space heaters to furnaces. Even be concerned about air conditioning equipment, designed to reduce heat, that suddenly produces heat. Take nothing for granted.

*   **Look** for the obvious, photocopiers, electric typewriters, videos, calculators, and other types of office helpers that have been carelessly left on.

*   **Look** for boxes, papers, rubbish, anything that can be termed fast burners. A cardboard box stacked against a motor, ignition ... fire, that's all it takes.

*   **Look** for improperly stored gasoline, paint, and other flammable liquid containers. Combine these liquids with excessive heat and fire has a place to start.

These are just a few of the countless kinds of fire hazards that are encountered in the administration of preventitive security. While newly designed and constructed buildings are far more fire resistant, no structure can be totally free from the threat of fire. Take nothing for granted in the fight against fires.

Fires get their beginning in many ways, and with the exception of lightning, earthquakes, and other acts of God, caused by man. At the top of the list is carelessness: Careless smoking; careless housekeeping; and carelessness in terms of paying attention to the principles of fire prevention.

CLASSIFICATION OF FIRE

It is vital that we recognize the various classifications of fire as this will provide invaluable assistance in terms of recognizing fire hazards. Attempt to relate Class A, B, C and D type fires to the facility where you provide protection.

What materials are necessary to create a certain classification of fire? Are these materials present in a hazardous form? If yes, report. Remember you are not a carpenter, a painter, an electrician, a welder, or a computer programmer. You are the eyes and ears of the organization. Report anything that seems to pose a fire threat that will endanger people and property.

FIRE EXTINGUISHERS - Classifications and Rating

There are many kinds of Fire Extinguishers on the market today. Extinguishers are the "first line of defence". It is imperative that you have a complete understanding of the types and classifications of these fire-fighting tools.

Classification of Fire

Fires are classified according to the type of fuel that is burning. There are four (4) universally used classifications designed to aid in identifying how each class of fire is to be handled.

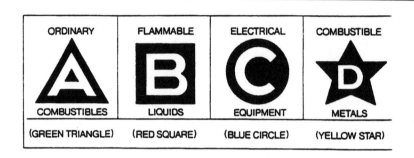

ORDINARY	FLAMMABLE	ELECTRICAL	COMBUSTIBLE
A	**B**	**C**	**D**
COMBUSTIBLES	LIQUIDS	EQUIPMENT	METALS
(GREEN TRIANGLE)	(RED SQUARE)	(BLUE CIRCLE)	(YELLOW STAR)

*Class A   -ordinary combustibles (wood, paper. cloth)
-generally deep seated
-hard to extinguish due to the re-ignition of interior of smouldering material
-cooling or quenching effect of water.
-coating effects of dry chemicals retard combustion.

*Class B   -flammable liquids and gases (gasoline, motor oil, propane)
-vapours burns above surface of liquid
-air exclusion is essential
-hotter fire - more evaporation - bigger fire.

*Class C   -live or energized electrical equipment (switch gear, computers, motors)
-non-conducting extinguishing agent of first importance
-if not de-energized, there is a source of re-ignition
-can be deep seated
-water used with great caution

*Class D   -combustible metals (magnesium, titanium, sodium)
-intense fire
-specialized techniques, extinguishing agents, and extinguishing equipment for this type of fire
-a non-reactive, heat absorbing agent required for each type of fire.

Types of Fire Extinguishers

*   **Dry Chemical**

This is probably the most common type of portable Fire Extinguishers. It can be used for all classes of fires depending upon the chemicals in each. They are clearly labelled to show which kinds of fires they will put out.

They form a cloud of chemicals which keeps oxygen away from the fire. They are very useful for electrical fires and for Class "B" fires.

*   Carbon Dioxide

Carbon Dioxide has four characteristics which make it very useful for fighting fires. It is heavier than air, it will not burn, it is very cold, and it will not conduct electricity. It puts out fires by cooling the burning material and by smothering the material with a layer of carbon dioxide gas. It is very good for Class "B" fires and it is good for Class "C" fires since it will not conduct electricity.

*   Water

You may have water in a water pump extinguisher or only a bucket you can fill. Water is the oldest kind of fire extinguisher. If nothing else is available, use it. It is very good for Class "A" fires. Do not use it for Class "C" fires because water conducts electricity.

*   Soda Acid   This extinguisher contains water and Bicarbonate of Soda. It also has a small bottle of acid. To use the extinguisher, you simply turn it upside down. When you do this, the acid mixes with the water and bicarbonate of soda and produces a lot of carbon dioxide gas. This gas forces the water out of the extinguisher. This kind of extinguisher is good for Class "A" fires. It should never be used on electrical fires unless the electricity has been turned off. This kind of extinguisher will freeze in cold buildings.

*   Anti-Freeze

This extinguisher works in just the same way as a soda acid extinguisher. The only difference is that this extinguisher will not freeze. It is most useful for Class "A" fires. Like the soda and acid extinguisher, this one should not be used on electrical fires.

*   Foam

These extinguishers put out fires by blanketing the fire with a layer of foam. This foam keeps the oxygen away, and therefore the fire goes out. These extinguishers are best for Class "B" fires - flammable liquids. They can also be used for Class "A" fires. They should not be used on Class "C" or "D" fires.

*   Halogenated Agents (Halon)

Halogenated agents extinguish fires by inhibiting the chemical reaction between fuel and oxygen. Halogenated agents simply act as "chain breaking" agents which break down the chain reaction of the combustion process. Presently there are two basic halogenated agents used commercially: Halon 1211, a portable extinguisher; and Halon 1301, a Halon Suppression System. They are most often utilized in hi-tech environments where the protection of the electrical components or valuable materials is a must. Generally very little after-fire damage is incurred through the use of these systems, however they are also very expensive to install and recharge.

More About Fire Extinguishers

Not only is it imperative to know the location of each and every fire extinguisher, but to be dead sure they are in proper operating condition. This does not happen by accident. Again, history will tell us how many times there has been an attempt to kill a fire with a defunct piece of fire fighting equipment, usually an extinguisher needing a "recharge".

Don't take any chances with fires:

*Ensure that each Fire Extinguisher is easily accessible

*Ensure that each Fire Extinguisher is operative

*Ensure that each Fire Extinguisher is clearly labelled

View all Fire Extinguishers as tools of your trade. And remember the purpose of an extinguisher. It is meant to be the first line of defence, and should be used as such. Never attempt to tackle a big fire alone; follow these steps, very carefully:

Should a Fire Occur:

*Appraise the situation. Unless the fire is in its infant stages and can be quickly extinguished, summon help: dispatcher, supervisor, or whatever method will result in the attendance of Professional Fire Fighters.

*If your judgement call results in first officer action, go for it, but do first things first:

(a)Select correct Fire Extinguisher - Read the label
(b)Activate Fire Extinguisher
(c)Direct Fire Extinguisher contents on fire as per instruction
(d)Do not deactivate Fire Extinguisher until fire is completely out
(e)Keep an exit to your back, take no chance on being trapped

When you undertake a fire by yourself there are inherent dangers. Make every attempt to get assistance and only act alone as a last resort and when you feel sure that the fire can be quickly extinguished. Your life and the life of others are the first concern, in making this judgement call. It may be advisable to summon help and then tackle the fire, only if you are sure it can easily be extinguished. Your first consideration should be to sound a fire alarm. If this course of action is not possible and help cannot be summoned immediately, you may have grounds to attempt to put it out.

*   Sprinkler Systems

These systems are designed to spray water on a fire. The system uses sprinkler heads which are activated by detection devices. These devices include the following:

Fixed Temperature Detection
A fusible link sprinkler head with a fixed temperature solder type link that will melt, allowing the sprinkler head to activate.

Rate of Rise Detection
A heat activated device operating on air pressure increases.

Smoke Detection
Detects smoke by means of a photo-electric cell (electric-eye).

Flame of Flash Detection
Uses a photo-electric cell to detect flash fires in extremely hazardous occupancies, where fire extinguishment must start instantaneously.

Vapor Detection
Indicates the concentration of combustible gases in the air. When concentrations reach about 75% of the lower explosive limit of the hazards being stored, the fire protection system operates.

Sprinkler systems have proven very effective in reducing the loss of life and property damage due to fires.

*   Fire Doors

Fire doors are frequently abused, either by accident or on purpose. These doors are specially constructed and are fire-resistant. They are invaluable in reducing the spread of fires. Fire doors usually are located so as to separate different sections of a building, to ensure that fire will not move from one section to another. When these doors are closed, they form a fireproof barrier.

But fire doors will not work when they are open. If fire doors are used for entrance and exit, they must be closed when not in use. Some fire doors are designed so that they can automatically close in the event of fire. Fire doors form an intricate part of every security program. It is essential to know the location of these fire prevention tools.

*   Stand Pipes

Stand pipes are similar in design to a sprinkler system. They are equipped with a riser, which supplies water to the system. Each section of the building, i.e. all floor levels are equipped with a hose rather than a sprinkler head. Not unlike Fire Extinguishers, these systems must be checked to ensure that they are operational.

MODERN BUILDING - In Case of Fire

Modern building codes have resulted in structures that are far more fire-resistant than older structures. Fire Doors, or smoke doors, protect enclosed stairways which are designed to prevent the spread of fire. Additional features are Fire Stops, Fire Dampers, Activated Smoke and Heat Sensors, Sprinkler Systems, and Fire Alarm Systems with heat and smoke sensing devices. Fire in these buildings is usually successfully confined to a particular room or floor level.

It is important to understand that a fire in an office building is not cause for panic. The Fire Department responds to all fire alarms. They are well trained and

knowledgeable professionals. Upon their arrival, they will effect any necessary rescues; confine and control the fire, and ventilate smoke fumes from building.

It must be realized that if a fire occurs within a particular office, or on a nearby floor level, it may be necessary to seek refuge as soon as possible. This is where it is important to follow a well-designed evacuation plan.

The following key personnel should play an essential part in any fire evacuation plan:

- **Evacuation Control Officer**
- **Floor Wardens**
- **Assistant Floor Wardens**

Here are a few key components to an effective evacuation plan:

*Most office buildings have fire alarms that signal evacuation. Know alarms' locations and evacuation routes.

*Evacuation plans and reporting procedures vary from building to building. Usually an alarm signals all occupants to leave the building immediately, or go temporarily to an "area of refuge". Pre-planning is essential.

*If an alarm sounds, all occupants must leave the building at once. Ensure that all doors are closed upon exiting.

*At this point, emergency fire fighting equipment may be a consideration. Adhere to all possible safety precautions.

*If you become trapped in a particular area, Don't Panic. To protect from heat and smoke, close door and seal off cracks, then open window for air and signal for assistance.

All employees and personnel occupying any facility must be conversant with evacuation procedures. Plans must include action to contain or delay fire, pending arrival of the Fire Department. Valuable minutes can be saved by connecting the building fire alarm system to an approved Central Fire Alarm System. Local Fire Prevention Officers, from Municipal and other Fire Departments, are usually helpful in developing fire prevention and evacuation procedures.

Conclusion

Fire Prevention, Detection, Containment, Elimination and Evacuation, are all grave considerations for the Security Professional. The role of Security in developing and maintaining an environment free from the danger of fire is an important task - one that will never be totally achieved. Striving to prevent and protect from Fire is a prime consideration for the Protection Officer.

QUIZ
Fire Prevention and Detection

1. Fire prevention equates to good_____.
(Fill in the blank)

2. Reducing the opportunity for fire to start relates to fire_____.
(Fill in the blank)

3. Having a keen sense of _____ and good _____ can prove very beneficial in fire prevention.
(Fill in the blanks)

4. Metal falls under the category of a Class _____fire.
(Fill in the blank)

5. There are four essential elements to any fire.
(Mark correct items)
- ☐ a.)Flammables
- ☐ b.)Heat
- ☐ c.)Gasoline
- ☐ d.)Fuel
- ☐ e.)Oxygen
- ☐ f.)Ignition Source
- ☐ g.)Chemical Chain Reaction

6. Halon Extinguishers are effective because they break the "chain reaction" of the combustion process.
☐ T   ☐ F

7. One of the greatest fire threats is:
- ☐ a.)Smoking
- ☐ b.)Housekeeping
- ☐ c.)Defective sprinkler systems
- ☐ d.)Oily rags

8. Class "A" fires consist of flammable liquids.
☐ T   ☐ F

9. Class "C" fires consist of:
- ☐ a.)ordinary combustible material
- ☐ b.)metal
- ☐ c.)flammable liquids
- ☐ d.)electrical apparatus

10. Carbon Dioxide Extinquishers are useful because they have a cooling effect, are heavier than air, and have a smothering effect resulting from vaporization.
☐ T   ☐ F

HAZARDOUS MATERIALS

By Thomas E. Koll, CPP

Chemical substances have been used by mankind for thousands of years. From the paints used by ancient cave dwellers to the secret potions of the Alchemists, we have always found ways to use chemicals to make our life better. With the birth of our present technological age came an explosion in the number and type of chemicals in common use. There are now more than 500,000 different chemical compounds in use with hundreds of new compounds being created every month. Chemicals are here to stay and to a large extent they have made our modern civilization possible.

Chemicals can be viewed as being similar to fire in that when their use is safely controlled, they are a benefit to civilization; however, if allowed to get out of control they can cause damage and destruction.

It should be said here that the majority of chemicals and other substances considered "hazardous materials" are not inherently dangerous in and of themselves. So what are hazardous chemicals or hazardous materials? Hazardous material definitions range from a few sentences to several hundred words in length. For the purpose of our discussion a hazardous material is any substance that has the potential to cause people, or the environment (plants, animals, and waterways) harm if allowed to be released in an uncontrolled manner.

Some common examples of hazardous materials include acids, cyanide, cleaning solvents, propane gas, and even gasoline. These and many other hazardous materials are commonly used on a daily basis throughout industry and commerce. When their use is strictly controlled, through piping systems, storage tanks, and safety devices, they present no danger; however, if an uncontrolled release of the substance is allowed to occur, the results can range from stoppage of work to fires and explosions which can destroy a facility. Ultimately, all uncontrolled releases can be traced to one or a series of human failures that lead up to the release. Whether it's a machine operator who wasn't paying attention to safety procedures or a faulty maintenance program that didn't provide for proper equipment inspections, or willful negligence as in the case of so called illegal toxic dumps, the results are always the same. Human error caused the release of the toxic material.

Methods of Response

There are several methods of possible response to an uncontrolled release of a hazardous material. For decades hazardous materials have been used with little or no training provided to the end users or those individuals charged with responding to a hazardous material release.

The common point of view was that dilution was the solution to pollution. This theory held that no matter how hazardous a substance was, if you were able to dilute it enough (usually with water), it would be rendered harmless. In the event of a hazard release, the common response was to call the local fire department or plant fire brigade, who would then wash the contaminated area down in an effort to decontaminate the area. In the process, the contaminated water was usually washed into the sewer systems and surrounding ground and ultimately into the environment.

To a limited degree this method worked, for a while. The problem is that after diluting so many hazardous materials into the environment for so many years, the environment has become saturated and, as a result, traces of those same substances are appearing in our food and water supplies today. To say nothing of the risk that untrained firefighters were placed in.

Today government and industry agree that, just as fire fighting requires specialized training, also, response to hazardous materials requires specialized knowledge and training to be handled in the safest manner possible.

Today specialized hazardous materials (HazMat) response teams are used to respond to the uncontrolled release of a hazardous substance. Usually, though not always, these teams are part of the local fire department or industrial fire brigade.

The Initial Response

Whether or not a facility has a HazMat Response Team in place, there are some basic steps that must be followed. These steps are:

1. Activate the Contingency Plan.
2. Identify the substance released.
3. Determine the quantity of the released substance.
4. Determine the extent of the damage.
5. Perform "Site Security"

Activate the Contingency Plan

In many countries facilities are required by law to have a HazMat Contingency Plan in place that would be activated in the event of an uncontrolled release of a hazardous material. In the United States this is covered by the Occupational Safety and Health Administration (OSHA) Hazardous Waste Operations and Emergency Response (Hazwoper) Standard[1].

If there is no legal requirement for a Contingency Plan or for another reason your facility does not have one, notify the public agency involved in handling HazMat incidents for your area. This will usually be the local fire department. When they arrive on the scene they take command and control of the situation. You would then be directed by their Incident Commander.

Identify the Substance and Quantity Released

The first thing that you must do is to determine what the released substance is and how much of it has been released. To illustrate, the uncontrolled release of 8 oz. (1 cup full) of acetone, while requiring caution in cleanup, does not necessitate response from a HazMat Team. The same quantity of cyanide or a high explosive would. By determining what substance or substances has been released as soon as possible, more time is bought for the HazMat Team to decide what course of action they must take.

There are several ways you can safely determine what has been released. The easiest way is to ask the person who was using it in the case of an employee related spill. This may not always be possible as the employee in question may have been injured. So how can you identify the substance? There are several safe ways to determine what a released substance is.

If the release is a liquid or solid, and has occurred in a more or less open area it may be possible for you to see where the substance is leaking from. Under no circumstances are you to go near the area unless you have been properly trained and have the proper Personal Protection Equipment or PPE otherwise you may become another victim of the incident.

Hazardous materials, when transported, are identified on their containers by the International Classification System. Under this multinational system chemical containers have a diamond shaped placard label placed on them which can be used to identify the basic type and class of chemical. It may be possible to read the

placard from a safe distance with or without the use of binoculars. The placards may either name the class, such as "Poison Gas" or may have the Class or Division number, or they may have both. These classes, while not all inclusive, will give the Hazardous Material Response Team a valuable guide as to what they are dealing with.

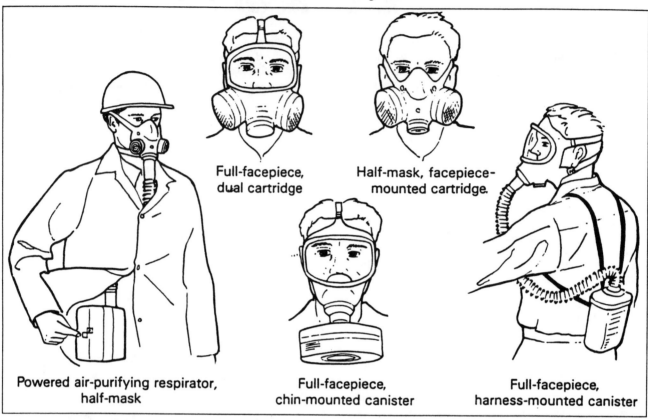

Powered air-purifying respirator, half-mask

Full-facepiece, dual cartridge

Half-mask, facepiece-mounted cartridge.

Full-facepiece, chin-mounted canister

Full-facepiece, harness-mounted canister

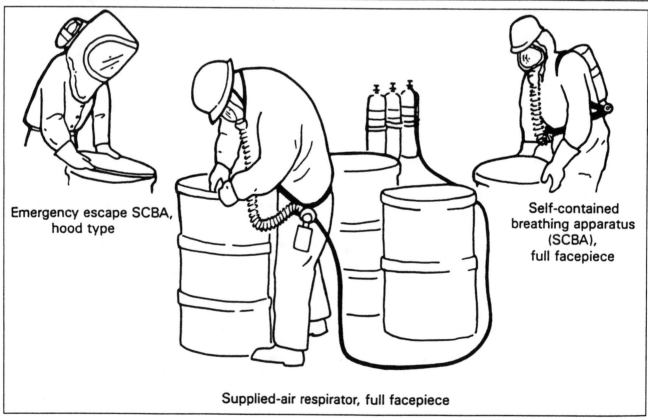

Emergency escape SCBA, hood type

Self-contained breathing apparatus (SCBA), full facepiece

Supplied-air respirator, full facepiece

Determine the Damage

Now that you have determined what has been released and how much has been released, you need to make a basic evaluation as to the extent of any damage that may have been caused. You need to know if there are any fires or fumes being spread by the release.

It is extremely important to keep clear of the area and to keep others clear until this determination has been made. The smoke produced by a fire can carry the contaminating substance for hundreds of feet and sometimes even for miles. Try to determine what path any fumes or smoke are taking from a safe distance. Haz-Mat Response Teams, even if composed of employees, are often not familiar with areas of the facility outside of their normal work area. As a Protection Officer, you are in the unique position of routinely patrolling all areas of your facility. Your knowledge can be invaluable to the HazMat Team in helping to direct their response properly.

Any injured persons should be treated by qualified First Aid or medical personnel as soon as they are safely removed from the contaminated area. A word of caution is needed here though. The injured person, if contaminated, will need to be decontaminated before treatment can be rendered.

Fully-encapsulating suit

Apron, gloves, hardhat, faceshield, boot covers

Perform "Site Security"

What we mean by site security in this context is simply keeping onlookers and bystanders out of the contaminated area. This can be a bigger challenge than it sounds.

No matter how well you communicate to your co-workers or to the general public that there is a hazardous area, and that they must keep away for their own good and the good of others, people seem to have a deep seeded belief that no matter what they do, no harm will come to them.

The logic is simple yet flawed: "accidents don't happen to me; that's something that happens to someone else." Invariably the people with this logic eventually end up getting hurt. Often they are the ones who get seriously hurt and force rescue workers to jeopardize their own safety to save these poor fools.

The most notorious abusers of this type of behavior are the news media. Reporters and camera crews will take risks that most normal people would never dream of just to "get that scoop" on their competition. Reporters have been known to cross barricades and sneak past security to get a close shot of the incident area.

This poses several problems that you must be aware of. First of all, they interfere with the HazMat Team's operation by attempting to talk to them and generally get in their way.

Secondly, they will tend not to follow any type of safety precautions and risk becoming exposed themselves. When this happens, the news crew becomes part of the list of victims and must be treated themselves. This has the effect of putting an even heavier workload on response personnel who may already be strained to adequately handle the situation. Another problem is that their entering restricted areas encourages curiosity seekers to also go beyond safety barricades.

For some unknown reason, people like to watch others dealing with problems. Whether it is a sales clerk dealing with a boisterous, irate customer, a fireman at a fire, or even someone changing a flat tire on the side of the road, we love to watch others deal with their problems. Perhaps it helps us forget about our own or perhaps deep down it makes us feel better to know that other people have troubles of their own. It has always amazed me how on a crowded highway, drivers will also slow down to take a closer look at a car along the side of the road with its hood open, as though they had never seen such a sight before! This same compulsion draws onlookers to the scene of a hazardous materials incident.

Figure 2 shows a typical layout for site security around a hazardous material contaminated site. At the top left of the diagram is the area of highest contamination, also called the *Hot Zone* which ends at the *Hot Line*. From the hot line there is an area called the *Contamination Reduction Zone (CRZ)* or *Warm Zone*. The contamination reduction zone ends at a line known as the *Contamination Control Line*.

Beyond the contamination control line is the area known as the *Cold Zone*. The Cold Zone is where all of the incident activities are directed from. Every effort should be made to keep all nonessential personnel clear of the contamination control zone and the Command Post where the Incident Commander directs all of the operations.

The specific distances from one zone boundary to another are determined by the Incident Commander and vary from incident to incident due to specific conditions such as wind speed and direction. Whether the incident is contained indoors or not, there is potential for fire or explosion.

Once the release has been safely controlled, contained and cleaned up (decontaminated or DECONed for short), the Incident Commander will make the determination that the incident has been resolved and the area may be re-entered without the use of personal protective equipment (PPE). This entire process may take anywhere from a few hours to several days. By the time the incident is completed, the HazMat Team will have followed most or all of the steps diagrammed in figure 3. The important thing to remember is that if all activities are conducted with safety in mind, almost any incident can be resolved with little or no injury.

Footnotes:
1. *29 CFR 1910.120*
2. *Source: United States DOT 1990 Emergency Response Guidebook*

Figure 2

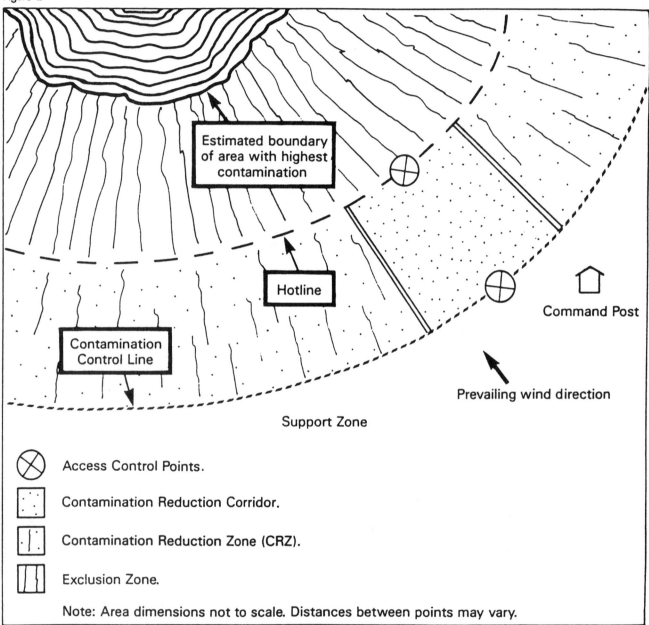

Estimated boundary of area with highest contamination

Hotline

Contamination Control Line

Command Post

Prevailing wind direction

Support Zone

⊗ Access Control Points.

Contamination Reduction Corridor.

Contamination Reduction Zone (CRZ).

Exclusion Zone.

Note: Area dimensions not to scale. Distances between points may vary.

Figure 3

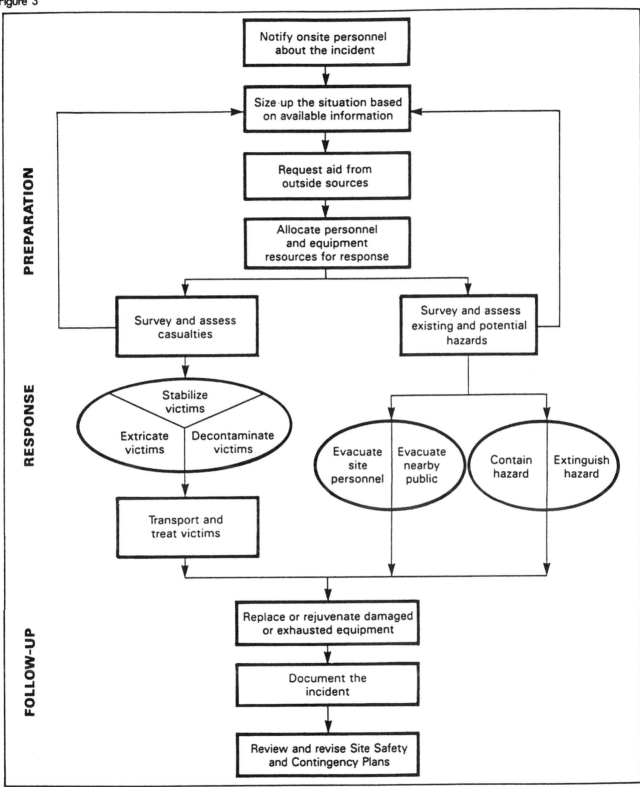

HAZARD IDENTIFICATION SYMBOLS

CLASS	WHMIS SYMBOL	T.D.G. LABEL	CONSUMER PRODUCTS SYMBOL
COMPRESSED GASES	CLASS A		DANGER WARNING CAUTION
FLAMMABLES AND COMBUSTIBLES	CLASS B		DANGER WARNING CAUTION
OXIDIZERS AND PEROXIDES	CLASS C		NO SIMILAR CLASSIFICATION
ACUTE TOXINS	CLASS D(1)		DANGER WARNING CAUTION
CHRONIC TOXINS	CLASS D(2)	NO SIMILAR CLASSIFICATION	DANGER WARNING CAUTION
INFECTIOUS AGENTS	CLASS D(3)		NO SIMILAR CLASSIFICATION
CORROSIVE MATERIAL	CLASS E		DANGER WARNING CAUTION
DANGEROUSLY REACTIVE	CLASS F	NO SIMILAR CLASSIFICATION	NO SIMILAR CLASSIFICATION

THERE ARE NO COMPARABLE CLASSIFICATIONS IN WHMIS OR THE CONSUMER'S PRODUCTS FOR THE FOLLOWING TDG CLASSIFICATIONS:

 EXPLOSIVE RADIOACTIVE MISCELLANEOUS

 *Workplace Hazardous Materials Information System*

WHMIS IS A CANADIAN STANDARD.
IN THE U.S.A. CONTACT OSHA FOR MORE INFORMATION.
ADDITIONAL WHMIS INFORMATION CAN BE OBTAINED FROM:
AASP/CCSP PROVINCIAL BODY
P.O. BOX 262 MPO
EDMONTON, ALBERTA T5I 2J1

QUIZ
Hazardous Materials

1. A common view used to be that _____ was the solution to pollution.

2. Hazardous Material or _____ response team are used to deal with an uncontrolled release of hazardous materials.

3. Determine the _____ of released substance.

4. Identify the _____ released.

5. For years the police were called to handle HazMat spills.
☐ T   ☐ F

6. The ultimate cause of uncontrolled release of hazardous materials is caused by the human factor.
☐ T   ☐ F

7. In a crisis involving the release of a hazardous material, the first thing that has to be done is to identify what has been released and in what quantity.
☐ T   ☐ F

8. A hazardous material is:
☐ a) something that members of the private sector may find objectionable.
☐ b) any substance that has the potential to cause people or the environment harm.
☐ c) materials that have been stored too long and should be deposited with the fire department.
☐ d) various kinds of solutions that unless diluted could cause danger to private and public facilities.

9. One stage of the initial response by the HazMat Response Team is to:
☐ a) call all available off duty workers.
☐ b) alert local civil defence personnel.
☐ c) determine the extent of the damage.
☐ d) develop the contingency plan.

10. There are several ways that you can determine what hazardous substance has been released in an employee related spill, the best way is to:
☐ a) ask bystanders and onlookers.
☐ b) contact the local fire department as quickly and practically as possible.
☐ c) assemble senior members of the HazMat response Team.
☐ d) ask the person who was using it.

Unit 5

Labor Relations
Emergency Planning
V.I.P. Protection

STRIKES, LOCKOUTS LABOUR RELATIONS

By David J. DeLong CPP

The protection officer should have a thorough knowledge of the security practises and procedures in existence at his place of employment and their role in the labor relations process. Labor relations are a subsection of industrial relations in existence at any company, particularly those with unionized employees. Labor relations include the employer/employee relations dealing with matters connected with collective bargaining and associated activities.

The role of the protection officer and his activities can have a major influence on labor relations at any given company. Security's role in the following activities can have a major influence on labor relations: strikes, searches, employee discipline, employee misconduct and dishonesty, arbitrations and interviews.

Strikes

Strikes are a part of carrying on business. It is an almost inevitable occurrence for many unionized companies. Indeed, it may be argued that for such companies, strike costs are an integral part of the labor costs to maintain the operation.

Work stoppages as a result of labor relation activities and difficulties will arise primarily in three instances:

1. The wild-cat strike — illegal walk-out — this type of strike is an unauthorized work stoppage which is in violation of the law and/or a collective agreement in existence.

   The most common reason for a wild-cat strike is the result of a union member being discharged for what the union considers unjust cause or reason.

2. Lawful strike — this type of strike takes place in accordance with applicable laws and the collective agreement in existence.

   The lawful strike is usually as a result of terms and conditions of employment. For example, at the expiry of an existing collective agreement, a strike may result after a strike vote has been taken. Wages or certain aspects of the collective agreement such as health and safety may not be satisfactory to members of the union with a resulting strike.

3. Lock out. This type of work stoppage takes place in accordance with applicable laws and the collective agreement in existence.

   The lock out refers to the refusal by management to allow members of the bargaining unit on the company property. The purpose of a lock out by management is to put economic pressure on members of the union to cause a behavior change that members of the union were not willing to accept.

The protection officer should be familiar with the company strike plan and manual that is in existence. The strike plan will highlight and provide guidelines for the protection officer to follow. Normally, the strike plan is designed and updated to eliminate problems that occur during a strike and provide guidelines for security and management.

The protection officer should be aware of the following security procedures during or prior to a strike, whether they are covered in a strike manual or not.

(a) **Access Control**

Will locks be changed on all gates surrounding the property? How will premise access be handled? Normally, the majority of company vehicles are left within the plant main gate. The fewer the number of company vehicles crossing the picket line the better. Non-union employees who travel to work should travel in a fleet and cross the picket line at the same time.

Besides those non-union people working, who else may desire access to the property?

(b) **Escorts**

Any union member desiring access onto the property should be escorted by a protection officer at all times. An employee may want access to the property for a variety of reasons (i.e., employee has quit and wants to remove tools, etc.)

Any visitors who have authorization to access the property should be escorted by a protection officer from the property line to their contact on the property, and escorted off the property once business has been conducted.

(c)Chain of command

The protection officer should be fully conversant with the chain of command in existence during a strike. Normally, the site security supervisor or the security chief will be responsible for all security and fire watch responsibilities.

(d)Police Assistance

The security department should notify the police ahead of time of the labor situation should a strike appear inevitable. Arrangements should be made for the police to be present at the picket during shift changes to avoid problems.

(e)Communications

The main security gatehouse is normally designated as the command post because of its rapid response capabilities. This command post is occupied 24 hours a day by a protection officer.

(f)Pre-Strike Vandalism

Employees may attempt to sabotage operations just prior to the strike commencing, especially if they know the company intends to continue production. The protection offficer must be especially alert on patrol rounds for any indications of sabotage.

(g)Fire Safety

The protection officer may have fire responsibilities in the absence of a fire crew or maintenance crew during a strike. These responsibilities may include inspecting extinguishers, testing sprinkler systems, inspecting fire alarms, hoses and fire equipment.

(h)Building Security

The security department recovers keys from all but essential persons prior to the strike commencing. If there is any reason to believe that strikers have keys for exterior doors, then the locks should be changed. It is common for strikers to make locks non-functional by driving spikes into key ways or filling the lock with glue. Plenty of spare locks should be available.

(i)Security Lighting

All security lighting should be checked prior to a strike. All perimeter and yard lighting should be operative. Backup light plants should be available.

(j)Purchasing

The purchasing department ensures that there is an adequate supply of raw materials available for any work that is to be continued during a strike. Constant communications exist between purchasing and security in the event that special shipments may need access to the property.

(k)   Threatening Phone Calls

Frequently strikers or their sympathizers will telephone threats to the Company or to officials' homes. The protection officer should record such phone calls and be prepared to be part of a security investigation.

(l)   Crossing the Picket Line

The protection officer may be required to cross the picket line for a variety of reasons. The protection officer should keep in mind the following points when crossing a picket line:

1.   Cross the line only if necessary.
2.   Do not cross on foot.
3.   Try not to cross the line alone. Two witnesses to an incident are better than one.
4.   Move slowly and steadily in your vehicle trying not to stop.
5.   Only stop when directly confronted by picketers who are in front of your vehicle.
6.   Don't leave the vehicle if stopped.
7.   Keep vehicle windows up and doors locked.
8.   Be cautious about verbal exchange with picketers. Be aware of the mood of the picketers.
9.   Observe and report any picket line infractions.

(m)   Picket Line Surveillance and Documentary Coverage

Surveillance of picket line activity is crucial during a strike to monitor and gather appropriate evidence that may be used in supporting company discipline imposed on an employee, supporting criminal charges, supporting or defending complaints about unfair labor practises and supporting obtaining an injunction. An injunction is a court order requiring a party to do or refrain from doing a particular act. For example, a company may obtain an injunction to try and limit the number of pickets on a picket line.

One of the primary functions of the protection officer during a strike is picket line surveillance. The security department will normally maintain surveillance on the picket line 24 hours a day for all or part of the strike. The protection officer should be trained in the use of still and movie cameras with telescopic lens. Pictures cannot be accused of lying and they are difficult to contradict. The protection officer should also have a tape recorder to keep a running verbal account of picket line activity. If a tape recorder is not available, then a detailed written diary of events should be kept on at least an hour-by-hour basis.

The following should be documented:

1. Location of pickets (attach plan showing pickets by company property lines and gates), and whether pickets are on company property.
2. Number of pickets, location (i.e. whether spread out or in a group) and description of their conduct.
3. Time and place that picketing commenced and ended.
4. Identity of pickets and union affiliation. License numbers of any vehicles at or near the picket line.
5. Number, size, wording of placards and general description.
6. **Conversations with pickets:** Caution should be used. It is quite proper to ask the pickets their names, who sent them, how long the picket line will last and its purpose. Relate conversations overheard between pickets or between pickets and other persons. Make notes of all conversations.
7. **Behavior of picket lines:** Provide details of whether pickets are stationary or walking, whether talking to employees or other persons. Note any threats, threatening behavior, damage to property, acts of violence, etc., and make notes. Provide details of any vehicles which have been unable to enter or leave company property.
8. **Photographs:** It is recommended that color photographs be taken with a polaroid camera. Each should be marked on the reverse side with the name of the photographer and the date and time with a brief explanation.
9. **Witnesses:** Full names, addresses and occupations of other persons who have witnessed any illegal activity on the picket line should be recorded.

The role of the protection officer is essential prior to and during a strike. His role can be vital to the protection of company assets, **especially during a strike.**

Searches

There is not much literature available on searches and labor relations for the protection officer. The protection officer should only conduct searches under the following conditions:

1. If an employee consents, a search can be conducted of his effects.
2. The employer or his representative, who is usually the protection officer, can conduct a search of an employee or his effects if there is an expressed term in the collective agreement. Also a search can be conducted of an employee or his effects if there is an implied agreement or implied term. An implied term can be derived by the company developing a formal search policy which is practised regularly, consistently and in a non-discriminatory manner.
3. If no expressed or implied term exists on employee searches in a collective agreement, the protection officer should have reasonable and probable grounds before conducting a search.

The protection officer may ask himself why he must conduct searches at every shift change at his plant or facility. **Remember, every company has a right to protect its assets.** A protection officer conducting searches of employees and their effects on a regular basis can help a company protect its assets in the following manner:

1. May reduce accident rates (alcohol and drug-related).
2. May reduce company material loss through theft and through employees hoarding materials in their lockers.
3. May reduce the use or possession of contraband on company property.
4. May increase employee morale because employees will feel that the company is concerned about maintaining a safe and secure physical environment.
5. May develop an employee awareness about theft. Regular searches conducted by protection officers deter employees from taking material off a property. **Remember,** the key to a good security is **prevention,** not apprehension.

Employee Misconduct and Dishonesty

There are a number of types of dishonesty and employee misconduct that occur at the workplace which the protection officer may be involved in. The protection officer should be aware of these types of dishonesty and employee misconduct.

1. Employee theft
2. Employee fraud - falsification of employment records, falsification of time cards and employee rebates, or falsification of workmen's compensation claims.
3. Sabotage
4. Conflict of interest - kickbacks; selling information
5. Fighting, assault
6. Alcohol and drug use
7. Insubordination
8. Sleeping on the job
9. Safety violations
10. Leaving work early
11. Horseplay

All of the above types of dishonesty and employee misconduct may merit some form of discipline. The protection officer should be aware of the variety of discipline available to his employer.

Employee Discipline

The protection officer should be aware of the types of discipline available to his employer because:
- The type and severity of discipline imposed may depend on how thorough the protection officer's investigation was.
- The protection officer may be in a position to recommend the type of discipline to be imposed.
- Discipline is an effective deterrent in the assets protection program.

Types of Discipline:
1. **Verbal Warning** - This type of discipline is given by an immediate supervisor where normally there is no documentation of the conversation.
2. **Written Warning** - A formal warning is given by the immediate supervisor and placed on the employee's file as a record of discipline.
3. **Suspension** - This type of discipline is normally the first steps towards discharge. The time off provides the employee an opportunity to think about the infraction(s) committed and whether the employee wishes to pursue employment with the company.
4. **Demotion** - This type of discipline is used infrequently. An employee may be removed from the job for discipline reasons or because of physical or emotional difficulties in performing the job.
5. **Termination or Discharge** - This type of discipline is the most severe available. Before terminating an employee, a company must consider the following factors:

   a) The age of the employee
   b) Company seniority
   c) The marital status of the employee
   d) The previous work record of the employee with the company
   e) The severity of the offense (i.e., extent of damage to equipment in case of negligence)
   f) The willingness of the employee to cooperate with the company investigators
   g) Whether the employee shows remorse or not
   h) Whether or not the offense was premeditated or a spur of the moment act
   i) Whether the discipline is in accordance with past practise. (i.e., Do all employees receive the same discipline for the same act?)

Arbitration

The protection officer may find himself involved in an arbitration case as a witness of a breach of a company rule or policy where discipline has been given. The union respresenting the penalized employee may feel that the discipline is too severe or unjust, thus taking the case to arbitration.

An arbitrator acts as an impartial third party to determine whether the discipline was just. Both the company and the union reach agreement in choosing an arbitrator.

The arbitrator is not bound by formal rules of evidence so the arbitration is less formal than courtroom proceedings. In an arbitration hearing, it is a principle of common law that the onus is on the company to establish the existence of just cause. In other words, the company has to show good reason why an employee may have received the type and nature of discipline.

Remember: The protection officer could find himself going to court and going to an arbitration over the same employee offense.

Interviews

The protection officer should keep in mind that a union representative should be provided if a witness or a suspect makes such a request. The protection officer may face accusations of harrassment or unfair labor practices should a union representative not be provided.

Summary

The protection officer must be aware of the union in existence at his plant or facility and the influence it may have on the following security functions — strikes, searches, employee misconduct and dishonesty, employee discipline, arbitration and interviews.

QUIZ
Strikes, Lockouts, Labor Relations

1. Labor relations include the employee/employer relations dealing with matters pertaining to

_____ bargaining & associated activities.

(Fill in the blank)

2. The role of the protection officer has an influence

on the labor _____ climate at any given company. (Fill in the blank)

3. A _____ by management is a form of legal work stoppage. (Fill in the blank)

4. A wildcat strike is a legal strike

☐ T ☐ F

5. Work stoppages as a result of labor relations difficulties will arise when union officials order production limitations

☐ T ☐ F

6. The protection officer should be aware of the types of discipline available to his employer because:

☐ a) The protection officer may hand out discipline.
☐ b) The protection officer will be disciplined if he doesn't know the types of discipline.
☐ c) Discipline is an effective deterrent.
☐ d) The protection officer should know what is going on.
☐ e) None of the above.

7. Which of the following is not illegal during a legal strike:

☐ a) picketing of residences
☐ b) obstructing highways
☐ c) carrying placards
☐ d) picketing within the premises

8. An incident of theft whereby an employee is discharged can become an issue in:

☐ a) civil court
☐ b) criminal court
☐ c) arbitration hearing
☐ d) all of the above
☐ e) 'b' and 'c' only

9. The strike plan is designed and updated to eliminate problems that occur during a strike and provide guidelines for security and management.

☐ T ☐ F

10. When stopped at a picket line in your vehicle, you should:

☐ a) cross the picket line on foot
☐ b) roll down the window and demand that you be let through
☐ c) remain in the vehicle and proceed with caution
☐ d) unlock the windows and doors
☐ e) none of the above

EMERGENCY PLANNING AND DISASTER CONTROL

By Michael Krikorian CPP

Summary: Advanced planning is the key to controlling emergencies and disasters in any workplace. For this reason such a plan should be a basic part of every loss prevention program. The author first presents the general guidelines to follow in setting up a disaster-control plan and then presents a step-by-step outline of specific actions to be taken — including an organization chart showing how to assign individual responsibility for each step in the plan. Highly valuable as a checklist.

Introduction

A basic necessity for every loss prevention program is the provision made for emergency and disaster planning. No plant or workplace should be without such a plan — there will be no time for plans or details when the emergency occurs.

The lessons taught by the adverse experiences over the years — and repeated much frequently as of late, emphasizes the importance of a well-planned program which encompasses all of the aspects of an adequate emergency plan. **Advance planning is the key.**

And by 'emergency plan' is meant considerably more than providing a first-aid kit, a fire extinguisher, a stretcher, emergency shower and eye-wash fountain, or fire blanket.

Instead, there should be a written plan of action for every facility detailing (to the extent possible) those actions that will be taken when an emergency occurs, so that an effective response will be insured when it becomes necessary to face an extraordinary circumstance.

The effectiveness of any of these plans will usually be proportionate to the thoroughness and soundness of the planning effort. One of the management's major responsibilities today is to plan ahead of time for as many as possible of the actions to be taken for the different kinds of emergencies.

The time devoted by security professionals and others to the preparation of an adequate plan will enhance speedy decisions and actions at the time of an emergency, and can result in lives saved and limits to the extent of damage. It will also provide the means for those responsible for the direction of these plans to concentrate on the solution of major problems and not be required to spend an undue amount of time attempting to bring some organization out of chaos.

Justification for emergency planning and disaster control becomes readily apparent with a study of the statistical evidence of fires, explosions, floods, and social disorders which produce riots, civil disturbances and other hostile and destructive acts.

The dollar losses from these occurrences are counted in the billions of dollars, while in terms of lives lost and individuals injured, the numbers are substantial.

The information here is an outline of those items considered important to the establishment of emergency plans. It will prove of value to anyone who is involved with emergency disaster conditions.

The security practitioner should assume leadership and actively participate in the development of these programs.

General Guidelines

(1) It is recommended that every facility have an emergency plan in writing.
   a. These plans should be developed locally.
   b. They should be comprehensive enough to cope with all eventualities, and
   c. It must be an effective plan.
(2) The Emergency Plan must provide for:
   a. The protection and safeguarding of company employees on company properties;
   b. The protection and safeguarding of company customers, members of the public and others on company premises at the time of an emergency;
   c. The protection and safeguarding of company property, while keeping damage and loss to absolute minimum;
   d. Periodic review and updating as necessary;
   e. Resumption of partial or complete business activity;
   f. Rehearsal of plan as necessary; and
   g. A basis for orderly actions and decisions to control damage and loss.

Keep in mind that management has the responsibility to take all possible and practical steps to protect the interests of employees, customers, members of the public and the property under its control.

Types of Emergency Situations

Figure 1

● NATURAL OR ENVIRONMENTAL
● ACCIDENTS
● MAN CAUSED
● ENEMY ATTACK

(3) The emergency plan and disaster control program must be flexible enough to meet a variety of complex emergency situations, either those that are man-made or acts of God such as:

a. fire
b. explosion
c. civil disturbance (riot or labor strife)
d. hazardous chemical and gas leaks or spills
e. earthquake
f. building collapse
g. hurricane
h. tornado
i. flood
j. nuclear holocaust, radiation accident, etc.
k. terrorist act
l. bomb threats

Emergency action plans are generally basically similar for all exposures. Details depend not only on the anticipated disaster, but to a certain extent on the size of the facility, its geographic location, and the nature of its operation. An important consideration when developing an emergency action plan is that it has to work under disaster conditions. Many commonplace conveniences — such as water, telephones, light, power or normal transportation methods — may be nonexistent.

Outline of Action

In approaching the problems of disaster control and plant security, the following outline of recommended action should be considered.

It is essential that security personnel have an integral role in the development and maintenance of the emergency and disaster plan. Security officers will be the key players in any emergency situation; therefore it is essential that each officer fully understand the overall emergency response process and their individual contributions to plan implementations.

A. Contacting the Authorities.

Liaison should be established and maintained by security officers. Get in touch with the local law enforcement agency, fire department, Red Cross and civil defense director.

(1) Determine extent and direction of emergency planning.

(2) Determine ability of those groups to cope with a serious disturbance and the degree of co-operation and the extent of protection which can be expected.

(3) Maintain liaison with these groups.

(4) Utilize their intelligence for a better evaluation of potential problems and to ensure proper co-ordination.

(5) Wherever possible, utilize these groups for advice and guidance on your individual emergency plan.

(6) Routinely communicate essential plans to the employees.

Base your plan on as much self-help as possible, keeping in mind that governmental units may not be available during certain types of emergencies.

Exhibit 1 — Organization Chart. Assign individuals to specific responsibilities — Select alternates for every position.

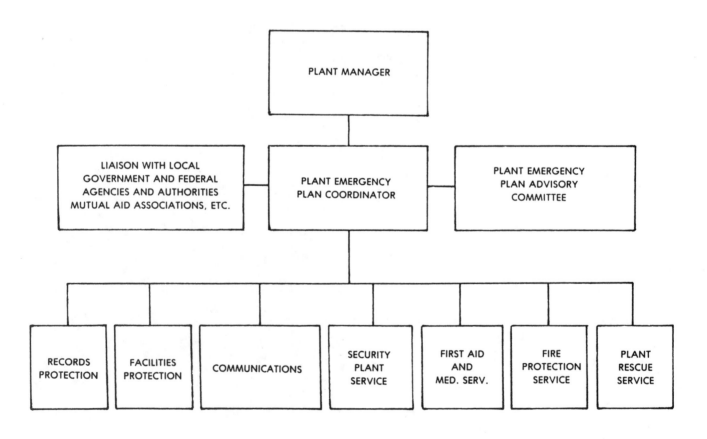

B. Delegation of Responsibilities.

Establish responsibility and authority for implementing the plan so that action can be immediately taken by local management, as follows:

(1) Prepare a policy statement assigning final authority for physical security of the location and for arranging appropriate delegations to insure that a 'single individual' in authority will be available under any circumstance to place the plan in action. Select also a competent individual to serve as plan coordinator or director (see Exhibit 1 — Organization Chart). Always provide alternates for backup to assure continuity of operations.

(2) Appoint a disaster advisory committee representing various departments of the plant to assist the emergency plan coordinator in the development of the various phases of the program.

(3) Wherever possible, utilize to the maximum present departments and key management employees — such as plant protection, fire and emergency brigades, maintenance, engineering, safety, medical, personnel, etc. as an organization framework.

(4) Inventory skills of employees and of available emergency supplies.

(5) Provide for a plan of action designating under what conditions the plan is to be put into effect. Furnish procedures for advising employees of the decision to activate the plan.

(6) Provide for the orderly termination of the emergency measures after cessation of the disturbance or emergency.

C. Limiting Facility Operations.

Provide specific criteria for determining at the time of the emergency whether the location will be: (to be determined by type of emergency)

(1) Operated on a normal basis (possible with some modification to guard and protect tours).

(2) Operated on a limited basis (designate those functions that will operate).

(3) Closed down and manned by supervisory and plant protection personnel.

(4) Closed down and unmanned for the duration of the emergency (with or without plant protection personnel). Among the factors to consider in making these determinations are:

a. Extent of damage to facility, utilities, declaration by government officials of state of emergency, etc.

b. Location's proximity to or distance from the center of a serious disturbance.

c. Anticipated emergency service demands on the location.

d. Availability of the workforce.

e. Extent of protection to be supplied by enforcement authorities.

f. Availability of security or plant protection personnel and type of guard protection.

g. Labor, political, and moral climate in the area.

h. Possible involvement of identified employees.

D. Plant Warning and Communications System.

(1) Arrangements with suitable alternatives should be made to quickly communicate a warning or alarm to employees, police and fire department officials and others as necessary.

(2) Every facility should insure that the internal alarm or warning systems is adequate to meet all needs. They should also be sure that they have a means to receive an alarm from outside the facility.

(3) Communicate the warning plan in writing to all employees; be sure they understand it, what it means and what action is to be taken if the warning signal is given. If an emergency occurs during, before or after normal working hours, employees not assigned to emergency service should receive prior instruction on actions they are to take.

(4) Maintain a roster with current telephone numers of key company personnel, union officials, law enforcement, hospitals, civil defense and fire department contacts to minimize any delay in making emergency contacts. Keep in mind that during emergencies, telephone switchboards are likely to be overloaded. Make plans for unlisted numbers and for alternate means of communications.

(5) Other points to consider:

a. Use of plant public address system.

b. Use of internal emergency telephone numbers and use of switchboard.

c. Warnings to remote or field operations.

d. Use of local radio or TV station (spot announcements at designated times).

e. Telephone committees.

f. Key employee list: maintenance, plant protection, engineering, services, etc.

E. Establish Facility and Perimeter Security and Guard Force Preparation.

(1) Select and designate entrance and parking facilities to be used by personnel expected.

(2) Arrange for police protection at designated entrances and/or roadways where possible. It may be desirable to solicit the advice of the police department before selection of an entrance is made.

(3) Secure all entrances that will not be used; if property is fenced, each gate opening not being used should be closed and securely locked, as should doors, windows and

other openings. Master key should be located centrally for emergency use by authorized personnel.

(4) Determine the availability and the total number of security officers that may be needed. This could involve round-the-clock tours which may require the services of additional personnel.

(5) All security officers should be thoroughly briefed regarding their emergency assignments, tours, behavior and responsibilities. Discuss especially their scope of responsibility during riots or civil disturbances. If security officers normally carry firearms, the practice is to be continued; if on the other hand they do not, then we recommend that they do not be given firearms. Security officers must be instructed to stay on company property and not go onto public property.

(6) Location of security officers should be considered for maximum enforcement; the presence of a guard at a strategic point may prevent trouble.

(7) Where the location is not fenced, security officer's activities should be confined to the inside of the buildings.

(8) Arrangements may have to be made for living-in by security officers and other personnel, should local conditions warrant.

F. Some Other Points to Consider in Local Plans:

(1) Photographic equipment to compile photographic evidence of conditions during the emergency. Thorough documentation in both video and still photography is recommended. Since the appearance of a camera could incite additional trouble, it is recommended that, where possible, photographers operate from protected positions.

(2) Provide for an alternate operating location away from the disturbance area — for use by key management personnel.

Figure 4

(3) Transportation service: provide for the protection of incoming and outgoing truck and rail shipments. Provide for the diversion of incoming shipments to locations outside the disturbance area should this be warranted by local conditions.

(4) Medical service: provide for in-plant emergency medical services or suitable alternates which would be capable of treating personnel casualties in the event of any emergency.

(5) Employee training: provide for first-aid, medical self-help, firefighting, rescue, etc. of employees.

(6) Review and update employee identification program as may be necessary.

(7) As necessary, conduct disaster-control drills: practice evacuation of facility, extinguishing fires, emergency rescue techniques, etc. Make necessary revisions in plans as indicated by tests and to meet changing local or national conditions.

(8) Maintain a record of all conversations with government officials, requests for assistance and others, including a complete record of all emergency actions taken.

(9) Provide for emergency lighting of aisles, exits, special processes, etc., in the event of power loss or failure during regular working hours.

(10) Investigate mutual-aid programs with other industries in your area.

(11) Have available at the facility and in a remote location up-to-date maps, layouts, specifications and similar essential data on utilities, hazardous processes and underground installations.

G. Protecting Propriety and Classified Company and Government Documents.

(1) Establish a records-protection program: duplicate vital records and store in a remote location. Essential records such as accounts payable and receivables, process data, models, blueprints, payroll accounts, propriety data on machine designs and processes should be microfilmed and placed in storage in safe location. Secondary or off-site data storage is essential.

(2) Plants with government contracts should follow the recommendations of the cognizant government contracting agency for necessary security procedures.

H. Legal Aspects and Requirements.

(1) It is primarily the responsibility and function of the local law-enforcement agency to maintain law and order, to protect life and property, and to protect civil rights in the public interest.

(2) Local management should ascertain if local statutes have been passed concerning plant-protection requirements.

(3) Conduct a review of property and liability insurance against potential loss of obligations resulting from riots and other acts of civil disobedience.

REFERENCES

1. National Association of Manufacturers; "A Checklist for Plant Security", Washington D.C. 1968.
2. Machinery and Allied Products Institute; "Company Planning with Respect to Riots or Other Civil Disorders", Washington D.C. 1968.
3. American Association of Industrial Management/NMTA; "How to Cope with a Crisis", Melrose Park, PA. 1968.
4. U.S. Department of Commerce in cooperation with the Department of Defense/Office of Civil Defense; "Preparedness in the Chemical and Allied Industries", Washington D.C. 1968.
5. Healy, Richard J.; "Emergency and Disaster Planning"; John Wiley and Sons, Inc., New York, NY. 1968.

1. A basic necessity for everyday safety and accident prevention program is the provision made for

emergency and _____
(Fill in the blank)

2. Lessons taught by adverse experiences over the years emphasize the importance of advanced

_____ in the development of an emergency plan. (Fill in the blank)

3. A management responsibility is to plan ahead of time for as many as possible of the actions to be taken

for different kinds of _____
(Fill in the blank)

4. The dollar loss from such disasters as fires, floods, explosions, riots, civil disturbances and other hostile acts runs in:

☐ a. Thousands
☐ b. Millions
☐ c. Billions
☐ d. Trillions

5. It is recommended that every facility have an emergency plan in writing and: (choose incorrect answer)

☐ a. These plans should be developed locally.
☐ b. These plans must be confidential.
☐ c. These plans should be comprehensive enough to cope with all eventualities.
☐ d. These plans must be effective.

6. The emergency plan must provide for: (choose incorrect answer)

☐ a. Continual corporate executive rehearsal.
☐ b. The protection of company employees and property.
☐ c. Periodical updating and review.
☐ d. Resumption of partial or complete business activity.

7. Management has a responsibility to include the protection of certain groups and individuals when developing the plan. (List priority group)

☐ a. executive families
☐ b. non-affected individuals
☐ c. employees
☐ d. visitors to facility

8. Emergencies can be man-created or be acts of God.

☐ T ☐ F

9. Explosions are invariably described as "acts of God" kinds of emergency situations.

☐ T ☐ F

10. If disaster strikes a facility, it may not be uncommon to expect to be required to function without water, telephones, power and transportation.

☐ T ☐ F

COUNTER TERRORISM AND VIP PROTECTION

By Christopher A. Hertig, CPP, CPO

Concerns with terrorism and workplace violence have been growing over the past several decades. We have seen spectacular terrorist acts, such as the bombing of the World Trade Center. We have also seen disgruntled current or former employees opening fire in their workplaces. We have seen assaults on staff at abortion centers, and we have seen acts of violence perpetrated in our courthouses.

Protection officers play an important role here, as they are often the ones controlling access to facilities, guarding payrolls and armored trucks, driving executives to the airport, escorting VIPs through crowds at public affairs, and maintaining the physical security at airports, courthouses, power plants, corporate headquarters, and military bases. In order to play this role safely and professionally, they must have a basic understanding of the threat(s) confronting their work environments. They also need to be competent in crucial tasks such as operating detection equipment, searching personnel and vehicles, driving vehicles, etc.

Terrorism

Terrorism is a strategy employing the use or threat of force to achieve political or social objectives. It is a form of coercion designed to manipulate an opponent (government or private organization), so that the opponent plays into the hands of the terrorists. Terrorism is systematic; actions are sufficiently cohesive so that long-term objectives can be met. Terrorism is theatrical, creating specific reactions by the 'audience' (population), through the use of intimidation and propaganda. Some of the reactions which terrorists attempt to cultivate in the 'audience' include:

1.   Lack of confidence in the opposing organization's ability to stop the terrorists from doing what they want.
2.   Feelings of oppression caused by government or corporate over-reaction to the terrorists.
3.   Sympathy with the terrorist's cause.
4.   Sympathy with terrorists themselves. ("One man's terrorist is another man's freedom-fighter".)
5.   Support of, or submission to, the terrorists. In some cases local populations are intimidated by terrorists; in others they have no strong ideological differences with the terrorists. In this sense it is important to understand group behavior as it relates to terrorism. All groups have what might be termed core members. These are the individuals who have the strongest convictions, lead the group, and are most active. The second type of group member is an active member. This person belongs to the group, supports it, and does what is asked of him. Active members are more numerous than core members. The third type of group participant is the supporter. These people don't belong to the group, but supply the moral, economic, intelligence, and political power for the group to operate. Supporters in the community at large are what allow any group to flourish. Whether we are discussing political parties, community crime watches, or revolutionary movements, community support is essential.

The problem is that terrorism can also include kidnappings and robberies that are designed as "fund-raisers" for the group. These specific acts have little or no ideological basis. Moreover, the use of terror tactics is not limited to those wishing to advance some type of political or social agenda. Terror is created by a host of threat groups; some of which have little or no political or social consciousness. Some of these threat entities are:

*   **Disgruntled current or former employees.** There are various types of individuals who create workplace violence, ranging from young males who assault their managers, to "workplace avengers", 35-45 year old males who enter with guns and shoot their supervisors and employees. Other disgruntled employees commit acts of sabotage, vandalism, phone in bomb threats, or pilfer to 'get back at the boss'. In many cases hateful graffiti, notes, and messages are signs of intense dislike. The protection professional must keep "a close eye" on such messages! They must be photographed and documented. Harassment - be it racial, religious, or sexual - is often a precursor of more extreme violence within the workplace.

*   **Robbers.** Convenience store robbers who may be after quick cash with which to buy drugs, can be violent. So too can the older, more experienced bank, payroll, and armored car robbers. **Robbers account for the bulk of workplace violence.** Many of them simply do it for the money, although some are disgruntled employees who want to exact revenge. Others are motivated by the desire to raise money for a terrorist cause. Most robbers want an easy target, where unimpeded access and egress are afforded to them. They must be deterred via physical security and environmental design, but never resisted. Robbers who feel pressured, threatened, or as though they have been tricked, may carry out their threats of violence. Employee training in how to calmly and safely respond to robberies is essential.

*   **Environmental activists.** These individuals target corporations that they perceive are harming the environment. Most are non-violent, but there have been instances of tree spiking - placing spikes inside trees so that loggers' chain saws break - and other activities which imperil people. Antienvironmentalists are another source of concern. Attacks on the logging industry by environmentalists have been met by right-wing "patriot" type groups counterattacking the environmental groups. As environmental issues are not going to go away; terror tactics by fanatical extremists within the environmental movement are likely to increase.

*   **Animal rights activists.** These people may stage raids on laboratories where animals are used in product testing, or throw blood on those wearing fur coats. They may conduct covert intelligence gathering operations, and various acts of property destruction. In most cases, extensive violence against persons is not used. Animal rights activists are difficult to deal with, as they run the gamut of the demographic spectrum: some are old, some are young, some are prosperous, some are not. There seems to be no dominant organizational subculture present within the ranks of animal rights activists. They are not at all easy to spot.

* **Right-wing religious hate groups.** While the Ku Klux Klan has been on the wane, other racist hate groups have sprung up in its place. Sometimes these people are allied with the militia movement in the United States, sometimes they may not be. Right wing groups have assassinated police officers, robbed banks, and were responsible for the Oklahoma City bombing in 1995. These groups have taken to using the Internet for advertising and recruitment.

* **Youth hate groups.** There are many of these groups; the best known is the Skinheads. These are generally working-class youths who believe that immigrants and minorities are displacing them economically; that jobs are going to minority group members instead of to them. Not all young white males who participate in this culture are criminal, however, some simply follow the music, dress, etc. Some tendencies of this group are avowedly racist and have a distinct subculture, with Doc Marten boots, suspenders, close cropped hair and a certain taste in music. It must also be remembered that some of these groups are the 'junior varsity' for the adult hate groups.

* **Youth gangs.** Protection officers in schools, parks and shopping centers may be confronted with violent youth gangs. These gangs are often surrogate parents for kids from broken - generally fatherless - homes. The gang replaces the family. The gang may become involved in drug trafficking, extortion, vehicle thefts, etc. Gangs are primarily social groups which have their own unique subcultures. Protection officers should become educated in the symbols (hand gestures or graffiti), language, dress, and activities of gangs in their areas. Forming a liaison with local police regarding the teenage gang problem is an obvious first step to take in understanding gangs. Protection professionals may also want to read some newspaper reports and sociological/criminological literature on gangs.

These are just some of the threat groups/individuals. The nature of the threat is ever changing. Variables such as the public image of the organization, legal changes, economic factors and demographics, affect the types of threats facing an organization. It is a fluid, rather than a static situation, with which the protection professional must keep current.

Left-wing vs Right-wing Terrorists

There are certain general characteristics which left-wing and right-wing terrorists seem to have. The diagram below provides a very general comparison between these two types of terrorist organizations. Again, terrorist and other threat groups and individuals change over time. To truly understand the phenomenon of terrorism, one must have a foundation of knowledge in religion, history and political science.

	Left-wing groups	**Right-wing groups**
Ideology	Communist/socialist orientation. Seek to overthrow governments.	Nazi/fascist. May seek isolation from government, rather than overthrow.
Gender	Male or female members.	Predominantly male.
Age	Young; generally under 45. Leaders may be older.	Older, including retirees, although teens may be involved in youth hate groups.
Education	Usually college educated to some degree. Literacy skills.	High school education or less. May have technical skills, computer skills. Some are former military.
Religion	Religion often not a large factor. Agnostic or Atheistic belief systems are common in North America.	Christian fundamentalist. Protestant. Often anti-Semitic.
Social and Economic Class	Upper class or upper middle class.	Working class; blue-collar. Often economically disenfranchised.

Terrorist Actions and Activities

Terrorist activities are contingent upon the capabilities of the terrorist organization, the philosophy of that organization and the area in which the action takes place. While Middle-Eastern terrorists drive car bombs into targets areas, European groups may attack police stations, airports, etc., and North American terrorists may plant bombs, murder members of certain ethnic or professional (police, doctors at abortion clinics) groups, and rob banks or armored cars.

One cannot assume what terrorists will or will not do, but counterterrorist security personnel should be familiar with the groups in their particular area. This will provide them with sufficient information, from which an accurate assessment can be made.

Task B, Element D in "Nuclear Security Personnel for Power Plants: Content and Review Procedures for a Security Training and Qualification Program" (NUREG 0219) lists the following characteristics involved in the planning and execution phases of a terrorist attack:

1.   Terrorists will learn as much as possible beforehand about the engineering details of a facility.
2.   They will assess power plant security ahead of time by observing the plant, talking to plant personnel, talking to an insider, and intercepting radio transmissions.
3.   They will attempt to recruit an accomplice on the security force.
4.   Terrorists will also try to recruit non-security employees as accomplices.
5.   They will consider kidnapping an employee or an employee's family member prior to an attack.
6.   They may take hostages during the attack to force cooperation.
7.   Terrorists will isolate the target site by cutting off communication and power supplies.
8.   The group will assemble the necessary weapons and equipment to use in the attack (this can include firearms, military issue shoulder weapons, SMGs, antitank rockets, high explosives, radio jamming or monitoring devices, power tools, construction equipment, incapacitating agents).
9.   The terrorists may use diversionary tactics such as sniping or detonating explosives.
10.   They will try to intercept, delay, or destroy responding police forces so that security personnel should not rely on local law enforcement assistance.
11.   They may use unknowing personnel as part of an attack plan, such as duping truck drivers into carrying explosives.
12.   Terrorists will take advantage of periods when security performance is lowered such as adverse weather (rain, snow, fog) or when there are workers onsite.
13.   The terrorists will plan and rehearse the attack.
14.   The attack will be planned to take the final objective in less than three (3) minutes.
15.   Terrorists will not attack unless they are 100% confident that they will be successful.

While the foregoing was written with nuclear power plants in mind, the concepts are applicable to virtually any fixed site facility, such as a bank, airport, or residence. Attacks against vehicles for the purpose of securing hostages also utilize the elements of surprise, speed, diversions, and ultimately violence. What can be gleaned from this is:

1.   Communication and computer security are paramount. Communication security protects against the compromise of information to terrorist/adversary groups. It also plays a key role in maintaining an effective physical security posture. Disgruntled employees/customers/terrorists will undoubtedly target computer systems more in the upcoming decade than they have previously.

2.   Confidentiality of information is essential! The less a terrorist or other adversary can learn about an organization and its defenses, the less likely that an attack will be planned.

3.   Personnel security - the protection of the workforce from infiltration by terrorists, foreign agents, criminals, and competitors who wish to steal proprietary business information is important. Most of the workplace violence issue revolves around the screening and management of employees.

4.   Access control - over both personnel and vehicles - must be designed into the physical security system, and maintained through the efforts of protection officers. Terrorists can be deterred from selecting a facility as a potential target if they perceive that target as being too well protected.

Counterterrorist Strategy

In essence, defending against terrorism is no different than defense against other types of threats. Even though terrorism is complex insofar as assessing the threat is concerned, the physical security planning process is the same as would be used with any other threat or situation. Physical security must always be planned in several stages. These are:
1.   Assets are identified. What has value to the organization? What has value, either strategic, monetary, or symbolic to threat groups/individuals?
2.   Loss events are exposed. These include bombing/arson, as these are easily employed tactics which can be performed by a single individual, and which have a substantial impact on the organization. Assassination, kidnapping for "fund-raising" or publicity; sabotage of machinery, implantation of computer viruses, or product tampering.
3.   Occurrence probability factors are assigned such as: certain, highly probable, moderately probable, and improbable.
4.   Impact of occurrence is assessed. Direct (replacement), indirect (loss of business), and extra-expense (added advertising fees, room rentals) costs are identified.
5.   Countermeasures are selected. These can include following a Risk Management approach.

Risk avoidance includes not operating in a hostile country or having a business operation which is prone to attack.
Risk reduction includes target hardening by patrols, locks, lights, barriers, etc. It is usually the most expensive means of risk management. It is also inconvenient to employees, customers, etc. As such it should not be employed without first considering alternative approaches to addressing the risk!
Risk spreading would be having several facilities in different areas so that if one facility - or key executive - is destroyed, the entire organization is not crippled.
Risk transfer means transferring the financial risk of the loss event to another entity. Generally this is via insurance coverage. Kidnap insurance policies have been used for well over a decade by major corporations. All organizations must assess the potential costs of extended business interruption, civil litigation in the event of death and negative publicity. Once this is done, various modifications to existing insurance coverage can be made.

Counterterrorists Techniques by Organizations/Facilities

Using the physical security concepts of deter, delay, deny and detect, in regard to terrorist attack include:
1.   Techniques used to deter terrorist activity include hardening the target so that the terrorists do not have a 100% chance of success. Checking IDs, packages, and vehicles before they enter a secured area, making patrols or routes of travel unpredictable, and maintaining confidentiality, are all target hardening approaches.
2.   Terrorists can be delayed by the use of barriers, locks, and response forces. Vehicular access to potential targets should also be controlled as much as is practical under the circumstances. This can be accomplished via barriers, as well as access/parking arrangements that don't allow quick and easy access to the target.
3.   Denial of terrorist objectives can be accom-

plished through the use of contingency plans for dealing with the media, and negotiating for hostages. These deny the terrorists the use of widespread panic and media leverage, which they attempt to exploit.

4.   Detection of terrorist activity can be accomplished through the analysis of threat intelligence. It can also occur by conducting entry searches, using detection equipment (x-ray, metal, explosive), CCTV, alarm systems, lights, patrols, and access control systems.

Specific Techniques for Counterterrorist Security

Some specific techniques that counterterrorist security personnel (Personal Protection Specialists, airport, power plant, military security officers) may utilize include:

1.   Become thoroughly familiar with any and all security equipment. While this sounds overly simple, routine audits at airports and nuclear facilities commonly reveal that equipment is not being properly used for any one of a number of reasons.
2.   Check and test equipment frequently. Develop overlapping auditing systems for the equipment, such as having technicians, officers, and supervisors all performing their own tests.
3.   Rotate personnel assignments as often as is practical, take notes and perform communication checks to maintain and ensure personnel alertness.
4.   Check all areas that the person or materials being protected are about to enter before they enter.
5.   Maintain weapons and other emergency equipment positions, so that they can be employed instantaneously. If they can't be, something is seriously deficient.
6.   Ascertain the legal implications of carrying or using weapons before they are carried. Never assume something is legal; check it out first.
7.   Be familiar with what belongs in an area, and what doesn't, so that explosives, weapons, and surveillance devices can be detected.
8.   Use cover and concealment to their utmost. Stand behind objects which can shield you from bullets, and have the protectee do the same whenever possible. Hide movements via darkness, tinted glass, or drawn blinds. Maintain light and noise discipline at appropriate times, such as on patrol.
9.   Select positions that provide the greatest visual vantage points.
10.   Stay close enough to persons who are being protected, so that effective defensive actions can always be taken, yet not so close as to intrude on the principal's personal space.
11.   Plan for communications failures, and develop alternate means of communication.
12.   Practice duress codes (verbal and non-verbal) so that secret, emergency messages can be transmitted at all times.
13.   Take appropriate action in a tactful manner to ensure that counterterrorist security personnel (airport or nuclear plant guards; personal protection specialists) do not become occupied and burdened with non-security duties.
14.   Vehicles should be driven so that there is always room to maneuver in case escape is necessary. Drive on the left side of the road to prevent the vehicle from being forced off the shoulder. Protective services personnel who drive should have specialized training!
15.   Always keep parked vehicles locked and secured as much as possible with alarms, guards, or other techniques.

16.   Check out the vehicle prior to departure for basic mechanical soundness (gas in the tank, fan belts and tires in good condition). Have a detailed check done regularly by a mechanic.

17.   Check vehicles for the presence of unauthorized personnel in or around them, attempts at tampering with the engine, gas tank, doors, tires, or undercarriage before departure.

18.   Assess the security of the route and location being travelled prior to departure.

19.   Establish and maintain positive working relationships with agencies or departments that can provide support services. Be friendly, polite, and tactfully inquisitive enough to find out how much, and what type of, assistance they can and will provide.

20.   As searching is almost always part of the security function, keep in mind and practice the principles of searching, which can be applied to any type of search:

a: Identify the search object; know what is being looked for. The more that is known, the better!

b: Establish parameters for the search; know boundaries for the search.

c: Assess the environment to be searched for obvious items, as well as the development of a search system.

d: Devise a systematic method for conducting the search, such as top to bottom, front to rear (with bomb searches, go bottom to top) after analyzing the search environment.

e: Search thoroughly using visual assessment, touch, hearing, and aids such as detection equipment, dogs, flashlights, and mirrors.

f: Continue searching until the entire area has been searched - don't stop after finding one item (or person if it is a building search).

g: Disturb the environment as little as possible during the search, try to observe before you touch something.

h: Be as polite, considerate, and courteous as possible. Professional conversation with searchees make the search more efficient (interview the searchee), and creates a lasting impression.

Professional Development for Personal Protection Specialists

Counterterrorist security personnel must have highly developed professional knowledge and skills in order to be effective. They must think in terms of the various areas of competency required. By focusing on these competencies, the protection officer can better chart a course for continuous professional development. In general, the following areas of proficiency must be present in counterterrorist security personnel operating in any environment (i.e., personal protection specialists, nuclear security officers, airport security officers, etc.):

1.   Knowledge of physical security concepts and techniques. A Personal Protection Specialist or other counterterrorist security person should be a physical security specialist first and foremost. An understanding of the theory of physical security and risk management, including various responses to risk and the physical security planning process, are crucial to the success of his/her mission.

2.   Knowledge of terrorism, especially of terrorists operating in the immediate work area. Reading various newspapers is essential! So too is keeping in contact with professional groups such as the local chapter of the American Society for Industrial Security, or state crime prevention officers associations.

3.   Public relations skills, so that security can be maintained unobtrusively. Manners, etiquette, and public speaking are all essential.

4.   Sufficient (college) education to communicate, understand, and record information that is learned during training, or encountered on the job.

5.   Physically fit so as to be able to perform strenuous tasks during emergencies, and so that martial skills can be learned (one must be fit to fight).

6.   Martial skills, such as the practical use of weapons and defensive tactics. Training for the "five second fight", where the adversary is neutralized as quickly as possible, or as a means of low-key, almost invisible, control over a disruptive person who is approaching a principal, is important.

7.   Familiarity with explosives and the weapons of terrorists, so as to be able to identify dangerous items. This means knowing standard military and commercial explosives for a start. It also means keeping abreast of the latest means of employing explosives.

8.   Knowledge of security equipment. The application of technology can be a great asset - but only when it is done correctly. Attending professional meetings and trade shows can help a great deal. This is a key area of competency in counterterrorist security. Unfortunately, it is often ignored. Counterterrorist security personnel should read a lot of equipment manuals!

9.   Searching skills used for bomb, personnel, building, package, and vehicle searches.

10.   Professional dedication to enable one to put up with boredom, long hours, and uncooperative persons.

Personal Protection Specialists (PPS)

Many people still think of the "bodyguard" as being a physically tough individual who has an imposing appearance and/or highly developed martial skills (martial arts, firearms, other weapons). While there may be a need for such an individual, and martial skills have practical application, there is a whole lot more to the makeup of a Personal Protection Specialist. Like other counterterrorist security personnel, the Personal Protection Specialist must be a security practitioner first, and a "trained killer" second. Of even greater importance to the PPS is to have highly developed communication, and human relation abilites. He or she must be highly polished. Etiquette and the ability to blend in with the protectee is more important than being able to destroy all opposition.

Knowledge of the protectee's business and personal habits is very important. Personal Protection Specialists must be able to plan out security measures in accordance with the principal's business and personal lifestyle. He or she must be able to devise protective strategies that are reasonable and unobtrusive.

Driving skills and knowledge of vehicles are especially important to the Personal Protection Specialist. Much of the time is spent guarding executives and other VIPs while those persons are travelling. Specialized driving classes should be attended. Knowledge of airline customs and regulations should be acquired, and kept up to date. In effect, Personal Protection Specialists should be "travel consultants"!

Personal security from crime must be studied and mastered. In many areas, attacks from local criminals are the most probable threat. PPS should be adept at performing home security surveys. They should be able to set up security systems at residences, hotel rooms, and apartments.

Emergency medical skills must be developed. Every PPS should be certified in first-aid and CPR. They should be aware of, and plan for, any medical problems that the protectee might have. Advanced emergency medical training is a real plus for Personal Protection Specialists, as medical emergencies can arise at any time.

Martial skills are important. These skills must be practiced and refined. In order to learn them adequately and safely, security personnel must be in good physical condition. In order to use these skills in an emergency, Personal Protection Specialists must be in excellent physical condition. Some tips on physical training are:

*   Develop endurance and stamina through running, swimming or sport activity.

*   Develop explosive power by sprinting, lifting light weights rapidly, lifting heavy weights, and maintaining flexibility. Plyometrics are often used by athletes and can certainly be adapted to emergency skill development.

*   Static strength, or the ability to apply force for an extended period of time, can be developed by practicing holding weights up, or remaining in push-up or pull-up positions.

*   Hand strength, which is important for grabbing and using any type of weapon, can be developed in any one of a number of ways. Squeezing a rubber ball is the most effective. Crumbling up newspaper pages with one hand, doing fingertip pushups/pull-ups, and virtually any type of weight-lifting involving a pulling type of motion, are other approaches.

*   Flexibility is important not only because speed is increased; but because injuries are prevented, and body tension caused by stress may be reduced. Stretch first thing in the morning! This "sets" your body's range of motion for the rest of the day. Stretching should be done after a warm-up that gets blood flowing to the muscles. During all workouts stretch and contract muscles. Once the muscles have been contracted, stretch them. Ten repetitions of a stretch, taking care to stretch a little further each time, develops flexibility. At night to relax, static-passive stretching can be employed. Try holding a stretch position for at least 30 seconds. This will make the muscles grow longer, and relax the PPS.

Manners, deportment, and decorum will "make or break" a PPS more quickly than anything else. Proper dining etiquette, and the ability to understand such aspects of corporate protocol as the conduct of meetings, are the everyday issues that Personal Protection Specialists are confronted with. In many cases, persons with a Criminal Justice background have great difficulty adjusting to upper class society. Some who previously had to adjust to lower class society must now switch gears and join the upper crust of society. This "double whammy" is quite stressful. Anyone wishing to become involved in Executive Protection must become adept at manners and dress. A trip to the library or world wide web for some information on this might be the most important career investment that an aspiring PPS can make.

Protecting the Principal

The operational aspects of guarding executives encompasses a wide range of tasks and duties. Personal protection is a speciality which requires immense dedication. A few things to bear in mind when acting as security escort include:

1.   Never leave the protectee unguarded.
2.   Always be alert and ready to respond to emergencies.
3.   Position yourself between the protectee and possible threats.
4.   Enter rooms first to make sure they are safe. Completely scan the room. Consider closing the blinds to avoid being visible from outside adversaries.
5.   When trouble starts, move the protectee to safety immediately. He or she is your first and only responsibility.
6.   Carry items such as briefcases, etc. in the non-gun hand.

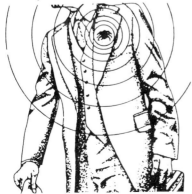

7.   Always watch the hands of potential assailants.
8.   Review the itinerary, and prepare for the day's activities well beforehand. Know it! At the same time, be able to make necessary changes and adjustments.
9.   Become acquainted with a wide range of sports and hobbies that the protectee may engage in so that you may accompany him/her.
10.   Conceal your position as a Personal Protection Specialist from everyone except those who need to know. Blend in and be part of the principal's team, not an unwanted appendage! Bear in mind that one of the biggest threats to executives is embarrassment.

Hostage Situations

The taking of hostages has become a serious problem. The criticality of these incidents, (a life or lives are threatened) coupled with the myriad of emotional, legal, and public relations problems that accompany them, make hostage incidents a concern for all security practitioners. In short, the direct and indirect costs of these incidents make them a serious problem! Security personnel must be prepared to deal with these situations; they are simply too dangerous not to worry about.

While there are many types of hostage takers, and an infinite variety of hostage situations present, there are some basic steps that can be taken. One does not need to be a qualified hostage negotiator to utilize a few basic 'first-aid' techniques in the event of an incident:

1.   Isolate the area of the incident (crisis point). Keep the perpetrators contained, and don't allow anyone except negotiators or tactical personnel near the area.
2.   Obtain as much information as possible. Use a pre-designed threat form when receiving a hostage/extortion call. Question available witnesses. Find out as much as possible about the hostages. hostage takers, and the immediate physical environment. This includes their prior life history, medical condition, and emotional condition Building layout with access/egress points, structural strength, and utilities must also be collected. Intelligence data is crucial to the successful handling of a hostage incident. Security forces play a key role, in having this information available to hostage negotiators and special response teams!
3.   Notify the central alarm station or dispatcher of the incident, and keep the information flowing.
4.   Maintain perimeters, supply information, keep a low uniformed officer profile, and await further instruction.

Don't try to make a play or be a hero, simply contain the problem and report.

Hostage Threat Receipt

According to the U.S. Nuclear Regulatory Commission (NUREG 0219 Task 57), the following procedures should be followed whenever a hostage threat call is received:

1.   Stay calm.
2.   Attempt to verify that the caller actually has a hostage, by asking for information about the hostage, and asking to speak to the hostage.
3.   Record precise details of the call.
4.   Notify the central alarm station or the security shift supervisor.

Obviously there should be a hostage threat contingency plan which is operational and updated periodically. A hostage threat report form should be readily available to security officers and telephone operators.

If Taken Hostage...

If a security officer is taken hostage, or is in close proximity to the hostage taker, there are several key points to bear in mind:

1.   Do not do anything to excite or aggravate the hostage taker. Accept your fate, speak little, lower your voice, and assume a passive/supportive body posture. Display palms, keeping hands at your sides or folded in your lap. Shoulders should be rolled slightly forward and your head a bit forward and down.

2.   Identify yourself by your first name, and use the hostage taker's first name. This will aid in having him or her view you as a person rather than an object with which to bargain.

3.   Don't speak unless spoken to, and weigh your words carefully. As with any emotionally charged individual, avoid the words "you", "should", and "why". These are too direct/pointed, and tend to place the person's reasoning process on trial.

4.   Be patient, remain calm and try to rest. Conserve your energy! This helps to prevent becoming stressed out, preserves your ability to think objectively, and prepares you for what will probably be a long ordeal.

5.   Analyze the hostage taker(s) as much as possible. Try to see things through his/her eyes. Empathic listening is key.

6.   Analyze the physical environment as much as possible.

Managing the Hostage Incident

Management of a hostage situation - or other crisis event - consists of several key elements. These are **control, coordination, communication, and information.** By employing each of these concepts, the incident can be successfully negotiated without anyone getting hurt:

1.   Control access to the area. Set up an inner perimeter around the crisis point where only negotiation and tactical personnel are authorized to go. An outside perimeter excludes members of the public, and any other unauthorized personnel. Within the outside perimeter is the command post. All communications and agency liaison emanate from the command post. Media personnel should be restricted to a secured location within the outer perimeter, that is not too close to the command post. The media's needs should be facilitated as much as possible in terms of access to power supplies, office/work rooms, and telephones. Their comfort and work needs should be met, as much as possible, by a Public Information Officer. They need to do their job, yet they cannot be allowed to roam around unescorted.

2.   Coordination is also handled through the command post. Persons who have a 'need to know' information should be supplied with that information.

3.   Communication is centered in the command post. Communication with the hostage taker should be set up immediately, preferably by telephone. The communication monitoring capabilites of the hostage-taker, and the media, must be carefully assessed and restricted.

4.   Information is the key to successful resolution be it through negotiation, or assault. Everything possible concerning the psychological, physical, and background characteristics of all those involved in the incident, should be collected at the command post. Details regarding the physical layout of the crisis point, such as the location of utility lines, room layout, and building structure, should be obtained.

Negotiation

While hostage negotiation is a complex professional skill demanding education in psychology, and years of interviewing experience capped off by specialized training, it is important for security personnel to understand something about it. Security personnel must be able to render "first-aid" - they must be able to provide immediate, necessary actions to reduce the level of violence. Hostage negotiators may not be immediately available.

Hostage takers may initiate the negotiation process with someone close at hand, and simply not want to talk with negotiators when they arrive. The basic concepts of negotiations are:

1.   Stall for time as much as possible. Say that you have to check with your boss.

2.   Don't give the hostage taker something without getting something in return.

3.   Make the hostage taker think. Wear him out mentally, by forcing him to constantly decide things.

4.   Never give hostage takers weapons or intoxicants.

5.   Don't make promises or threats which you cannot keep.

Conclusion

COUNTERTERRORISM and VIP Protection will continue to evolve with the threats that confront Protection Officers. In order to meet the challenges of the future - and be a part of that future - there must be a greater emphasis on:

1.   The study of various types of threat groups and individuals, by individual Protection Officers. There must also be research on this subject, published in the professional literature!

2.   The development of theoretical and practical aspects of conducting searches, so that training programs can produce graduates who are truly proficient and professional at the searching function. This must be studied!

3.   An emphasis on manners and deportment by Protection Officers, so that they can join management teams, and have a "voice in the organization".

4.   More academic programs in Security and Loss Control at colleges and universities, so that both theory and technology can be studied. This will also aid in making Security a more visible career option to students, who are the future of the industry.

5.   Embracing of the principles of Risk Management by Protection Officers. This assists in more creative solutions to threat problems. It also helps to marry Security to Insurance, and accepted business practices.

References

Abanes, Richard. 1996. AMERICAN MILITIAS: REBELLION, RACISM, and RELIGION, InterVarsity Press, Downers Grove, Il.

Anti-Defamation League. 1996. THE WEB OF HATE: EXTREMISTS EXPLOIT THE INTERNET. ADL, USA.

Braunig, Martha. 1992. THE EXECUTIVE PROTECTION BIBLE. Executive Security International, Inc. Basalt, CO.

Kobetz, Richard W. 1991. PROVIDING EXECUTIVE PROTECTION. Executive Protection Institute. Berryville, VA.

Kobetz, Richard W. 1994. PROVIDING EXECUTIVE PROTECTION VOLUME II. Executive Protection Institute.   Berryville, VA.

Pierce, William L. 1980. THE TURNER DIARIES. New York, NY Barricade Books.

Strentz, Thomas. 1990. "Radical Right vs. Radical Left: Terrorist Theory and Threat". THE POLICE CHIEF, August 1990.

U.S. Department of Justice 1993. TERRORISM IN THE UNITED STATES: 1982 - 1992. Federal Bureau of Investigation. Washington, D.C.

United States Nuclear Regulatory Commission. 1978. NUCLEAR SECURITY PERSONNEL FOR POWER PLANTS; CONTENT AND REVIEW PROCEDURES FOR A SECURITY TRAINING AND QUALIFICATION PROGRAM. U.S. Nuclear Regulatory Commission, Washington, D.C.

Resources

BSR (304/725-9281) provides training in Evasive Driving and Executive Security Training.

Butterworth-Heinemann (800/366-2665) has books such as AIRPORT, AIRCRAFT AND AIRLINE SECURITY, CCTV SURVEILLANCE, ELECTRONIC PROTECTION AND SECURITY SYSTEMS, EFFECTIVE PHYSICAL SECURITY and a video WHEN IT TURNS SERIOUS; COUNTER-STALKING AND THREAT MANAGEMENT IN HIGH RISK SITUATIONS.

Executive Protection Institute (540/955-1128) offers numerous programs relating to Executive Protection, Corporate Aircraft Security, etc.   They also publish PROVIDING EXECUTIVE PROTECTION and PROVIDING EXECUTIVE PROTECTION VOLUME II. In addition, the Institute administers Nine Lives Associates, a professional organization of Personal Protection Specialists.

Executive Security International (800/874-0888 or 303/927-3383) provides training courses in Executive Protection and Counterintelligence.   They also offer THE EXECUTIVE PROTECTION BIBLE and distance education courses.

Scotti School of Defensive Driving (800/343-0046 or 617/395-9156) offers courses in driving and other aspects of Executive Protection.

QUIZ
Counterterrorism and VIP Protection

1.   Personal Protection Specialists should attempt to _____in with the principal's entourage.

2.   Members of environmental activist groups are often the "junior varsity" of right-wing hate groups.
☐ T   ☐ F

3.   In many cases, embarrassment is the greatest threat to executives.
☐ T   ☐ F

4.   To truly understand terrorism, Protection Officers must have a foundation of knowlege in _____, history and _____science.

5.   The first principle of searching is to identify the search object.
☐ T   ☐ F

6.   Every PPS should be certified in _____and _____as _____emergencies can develop at any time.

7.   Right-wing hate groups are often led by women.
☐ T   ☐ F

8.   Terrorism is both systematic and _____.

9.   To better understand the activities of youth gangs, the Protection Officer should develop a relationship with local _____who are knowledgeable on this problem.

10.   When searching, the search effort may be abandoned after a single suspicious item has been found.
☐ T   ☐ F

Unit 6

Human Relations
Interviewing Techniques
Stress Management
Crisis Intervention

HUMAN RELATIONS

By Dr. Kenneth C. Hollington

The security officer is a first-line of protection. In various analyses of his role undertaken in connection with professional training and development activities, it is clear that this role is a complex and varied one.

In fact, the bands of expertise required by both the security officer and the police patrol officer are much wider than jobs higher up in the organization. As one progresses in the organization, his role tends to diminish in terms of the security technical requirements and expand in terms of the supervisory and management content.

Thus, as has often been pointed out, the boss becomes somewhat technically incompetent as he turns his focus more to problem-solving and prevention. But, the effective supervisor, chosen for his knowledge of people and human relations, should know the broad details of the various jobs in the security organization and have a clear grasp of end results.

The purpose of this chapter is to focus on the human relations aspect of the security officer's role and to, hopefully, help the officer to become more effective in his dealings with the client and others.

Analysis of Security - Human Relations Skills

An analysis of the human relations skills required of the security officer reveals the following categories which are generic to most situations:

- Utilize common sense and discretion.
- Display a positive attitude in terms of values and motivation.
- Know the purpose and goals of the organization.
- Know own role and purpose - the whole job.
- Manage stress and conflict.
- Employ effective public and human relations.
- Be observant/have a good memory.
- Deal with unusual and abnormal behavior/alcohol; drugs.
- Manage time and schedules.
- Understand cultural/language and individual differences.
- Maintain proper dress, decor, punctuality.
- Work as a team member/be sensitive to others.
- Transfer knowledge to co-workers.
- Display leadership ability.
- Communicate effectively - written, oral, non-verbally.
- Interview effectively.
- Maintain physical fitness (defensive tactics).
- Be involved in professionalism and the learning process.
- Assist and aid persons in distress.

Obviously, these skills are different than the operational, legal and other job content skills required to perform the security function. The remainder of the manual focuses on those particular competencies.

Leadership Skills:

The behavioral sciences have focussed in recent years on the fact that there is no one 'ideal' leadership approach. One must understand variables in himself, the client and the situation to respond to a situation intelligently. A good place to start is with an understanding of basic human needs.

Maslow (1954) Figure 1 developed a hierarchy of human needs which suggests that basic needs must be fulfilled to a reasonable level before such needs as esteem and self-actualization come into play.

The implication of this is that our needs hierarchy causes each of us to view the world somewhat differently. For example, someone who is broke, hungry, angry or under great emotional stress will react quite differently to a security officer who is relatively satisfied and motivated.

Figure 1 illustrates three different needs levels: Figure 2 shows the complete hierarchy; lower order needs are strongest.

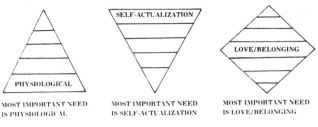

Figure 1

MASLOW'S HIERARCHY OF NEEDS

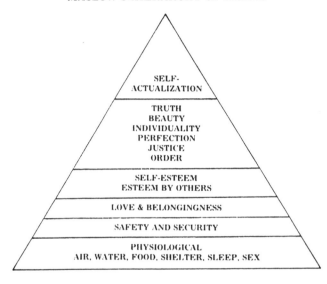

Figure 2

Hershey and Blanchard have identified four distinct types of leadership approaches. Incidentally, leadership may be described as an influence process in which you try to get someone else to do something that you want done because he/she wants to do it. Do you remember how Tom Sawyer used his knowledge of psychology and leadership to get others to whitewash Aunt Polly's fence because they wanted to do it! Imagine, they even paid Tom for the privilege!

Leadership Styles Explained

Tell 'em: The security officer spells out clearly what he wants the subject to do. There may be an urgent time factor: ''Get the hell out of here - the place is on fire!'' There is no time or need for human relations — the task is all-important. This method works well in time of urgency, stress and danger, and where a quick response is required. The officer uses his authority and, hopefully, his audience trusts him and heeds his direction. This is a Parent to Child approach and works when the client is unwilling or unable to undertake a task. Of course, if the subject does not res-

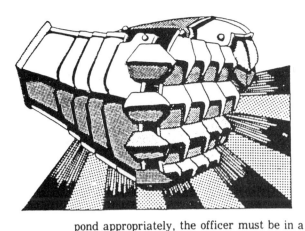

pond appropriately, the officer must be in a position to use such sanctions or power authorized and indicated by the situation.

Sell 'Em: In this mode, the officer wants the client to comply, but is determined to use good human relations psychology, stroking and support to achieve the goal. He still structures the task. However, he realizes that honey is more effective than vinegar, and uses his knowledge of human behavior to achieve compliance. The approach here is all-important. It is still a Parent to Child approach because the client does not know or is unable to perform the required task and needs structuring and guidance. You are involved in a teaching, guidance role as you both direct and support movement towards the goal. In modern policing and security, we tend to spend much more time selling, convincing and supporting than we do telling. As the client or subject learns the requirements, we can move to the next step.

Participating: Police and security have used this method in crime prevention activities. There is a realization that the public can be of great assistance in protecting assets. This is an adult approach in which the security officer forms a partnership with the public based on support and mutual concern for creating a safe and productive environment. Police block watch programs and security/employee/management committees are examples. The aim is to identify potential problems prior to their becoming actual problems and focussing on preventative strategies. On an individual basis, the security officer may enlist the help and support of the client through the principle of involvement.

Delegation: This system works well in an established security function. One example would be where certain security functions can be managed by individual managers with the security officer acting as a guide or consultant. This suggests that the managers are very clear on their security roles and have the adult maturity to see end results and act independently. It is not abdication, but means that the security officer can 'manage by exception'. That is, he can focus on activities which are more important and delegate the more routine matters. Figure 3 proves a summary of leadership style.

LEADERSHIP STYLE:

APPROACH	SITUATION	METHODS

Authoritative/
(Tell'Em
Sell'em
Parent Child)
	A. Urgent time factor
	B. Stress & danger
	C. Large number of men
	D. Condition to
	  quick response
	E. Dealing with less
	  mature persons
		A. Authority
		B. Discipline
		C. Communication
		  down chain
		  of command
		D. Delegation
		E. Sanctions
		F. Trust
		G. Persuasion/
		  Selling/
		  Support

Participative
Democratic
 	
Adult/Adult
	A. Teaching Complex
	  skills
	B. Under hardship
	  & personal difficulty
	C. Interviewing &
	  Counselling
	D. Non-Stress everyday
	E. Mature persons
		A. Learning
		  process
		B. Principles
		  of instruction
		C. Psychological
		  support
		D. Encouragement
		E. Inspiration
		F. Motivation

Free Rein/
Delegation
 	
Adult/Adult
	A. If subordinates are
	  skilled, well-motivated
	  highly mature, meet
	  standards, or accept
	  & attain objectives
		A. Influence
		  available
		  but watch-
		  fully with-
		  held pending
		  need to tighten
		  the reins

Figure 3

Transactional Analysis

The writer in numerous classes with police, correctional and security officers has found Transactional Analysis (TA) to be of significant value in explaining the communication process. It is particularly valuable in allowing the officer to see "where people are coming from". The following explains the basic theory and steps involved. Some practical examples will further amplify the process of TA.

Principles:

TA is a positive, humanistic philosophy which may be used for a wide variety of applications, such as interventions in the justice field. It operates on the basic assumption that almost every human wants to grow and self-actualize. Another premise of TA is that each person decides upon his own life plan, and each alone is responsible for maintaining or changing it. Therefore, the ultimate responsibility for a person's behavior and functioning lies on his shoulders.

TA is primarily interested in studying ego states in what is called structural analysis. An ego state is an inseparable system of thoughts and feelings. (Berne, 1972; 12) Each human has three ego states.

i. Every individual has an ego state that is a replica of the ego states of his parents - called "Parent"
ii. Every individual is able to process information objectively, in the Adult ego state - called "Adult"
iii. Every individual was once younger than the present time, and he carries these earlier ideas with him in the Child Ego state - called "Child"
(Berne, 1964; 24)

Each of these three states has an equal and legitimate place in a full life. The Parent state has two functions. First of all, it promotes survival by enabling the individual to care for actual children.

Secondly, the Parent saves time and energy by making some responses automatic by doing things in a certain acceptable manner. The Parent provides a routine of performing trivial tasks in everyday life. The Parent may be seen in two forms, direct or active, and indirect or influencing.

In a directly active adult, the individual's response would be that of his own parent. In the form of indirect influence, the individual would respond as he knows that his parent would want him to. (Berne, 1964; 26-27)

The Adult ego state is essential for survival. The individual here has the ability to reason and incorporate information on an ongoing basis to deal effectively with the outside world. Also, the Adult acts as an objective mediator between the Parent and Child, and regulates their activities.

The Child state is one which provides intuition, spontaneity, and enjoyment to life. The Child can be seen in the forms of either adapted or natural. When a Child modifies his own behavior because of parental influence, he is the adapted Child. The natural Child expresses himself spontaneously. (Berne, 1964; 26-27)

Seen below are structural diagrams of the ego states:

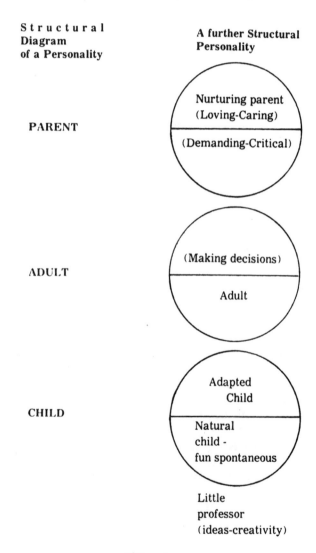

Structural Diagram of a Personality	A further Structural Personality
PARENT	Nurturing parent (Loving-Caring) (Demanding-Critical)
ADULT	(Making decisions) Adult
CHILD	Adapted Child Natural child - fun spontaneous

Little professor (ideas-creativity)

Figure 4

(Berne, 1972; 12-13)

When the ego states of one person interacts with the ego states of another, we have a transaction. A transaction is initiated when two or more people are gathered and one of them acknowledges the other in some way. This is called the transactional stimulus. The transactional response occurs when another person reacts in some way to the stimulus.

The concern of TA is with analyzing which ego state stimulated and which responded in the transaction. Incidentally, these responses may be at the verbal or non-verbal level.

There are three possible types of transactions. Complementary transactions constitute one of the basic transactions. In complementary transactions, the response is appropriate and follows the natural order of a healthy relationship. The simplest transactions occur when both the stimulus and response are implemented from an Adult level. There are nine possible complementary transactions, which are graphed below:

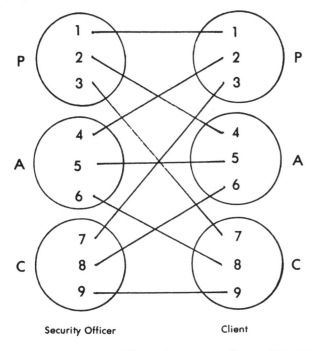

Security Officer   Client

Figure 5   (Berne, 1964; 32)

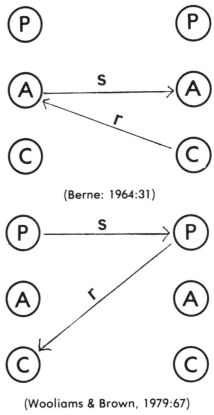

(Berne: 1964:31)

(Wooliams & Brown, 1979:67)

Figure 6

Communication will proceed smoothly as long as transactions are complementary, and may in principle go on indefinitely. Communication breaks down when crossed transactions occur. In a crossed transaction, many problems occur and this the primary concern of the transactional analyst. (Berne, 1964; 30-31)

During a crossed transaction, the response is inappropriate and unexpected to the stimulus. The individual does not respond in the same ego state in which he was addressed. In crossed transactions, the communication lines are not parallel as was seen in complementary transactions.

The effect of crossed transactions is not always detrimental. A deliberate crossed transaction may motivate the client to change ego states. An illustration of two of the 72 possible combinations of crossed transactions is found below: (figure 6)

The third type of transactions are ulterior transactions. In an ulterior transaction, there is a social and psychological or hidden message. (See Ego State)

Strokes:

A stroke is something which provides attention and stimulation to the receiver. The three different types of strokes are positive, negative and filtered. Positive strokes give the receiver a "You're Okay" message. These will usually promote self-growth and self-esteem. Negative strokes are saying "You're not Okay" and are painful.

Positive strokes which have no meaning for the participants are called "plastic" strokes and will not usually last for any significant time. Filtered strokes are those that are composed of irrelevent or distorted information.

(Wooliams and Brown, 1979; 46-48)

Strokes may be given for a variety of reasons. The unconditional strokes are given for just being, and cannot be earned. The ultimate positive unconditional stroke is "I love you". These types of strokes are very much desired by every individual. Negative unconditional strokes are destructive.

It is discouraging that while an individual usually wants positive strokes, negative strokes are those that have the most stimulation power. This disparity is a result of the fact that negative strokes are usually expressed more loudly and powerfully than positive strokes. Stroke power depends on the verbal and non-verbal content of the message given.

Strokes are necessary for communication in any life script. They may communicate one of the four possible life positions:

1. I'm not O.K. - You're O.K. - child like; insecure
2. I'm not O.K. - You're not O.K. - defeated, suicidal
3. I'm O.K. - You're not O.K. - I'll take what I want!
4. I'm O.K. - You're O.K. - healthy

(Harris, 1967; 43)

By the age of 2 or 3 years, a child decides that he belongs in one of the first three positions. During the first year of life, all infants believe in the first position that he is not okay. The person who gives him strokes and who is superior in size and power to him is okay. An individual may live out his life by confirming through himself and others that he is not okay.

(Harris, 1967; 43-46)

Value of TA to the Security Officer

We learn from TA that all transactions whether verbal or non-verbal may result in complimentary patterns which mean that we can continue communication. But, if the person we communicate with does not accept our message, we have a **crossed** transaction. This results in hurt feelings and blocked communication. Double messages or saying one thing and meaning another are **ulterior** transactions and are often "put-downs". Thus, when you communicate in a "tell 'em" approach, they may be resentful or rebellious, because it is parent to child. So, plan your communication to get the intent you want.

Secondly, most people respond well to positive strokes. A pleasant attitude, smile, remembering a name, are all types of positive strokes. Some persons will take negative strokes because that is the only kind they can accept. This causes a special problem for the security officer and a test of his human relations skills.

Berne discussed the games that people play. A game needs several players — one to be a winner and one to be a loser. In one type of game, we set someone up and then pounce on him. This is called NIGYSOB. So watch for games that set you up. Games tend to be parent to child and often can be avoided. Don't play them and activate your Adult common sense self to see the possible outcomes in situations.

Because TA is such a valuable approach, you are encouraged to follow up. See in particular "Staying OK", Harris and Harris, Harper & Row (1985).

Ego State Reaction Examples

The following comments or stimulus originates from an individual occupying one of the three ego states, i.e.: PARENT, CHILD or ADULT. Try to understand the reason for the appropriate choice in each instance.

A Security Officer loses an important letter:

A. "Why can't you keep track of anything you're responsible for?"   **"P"**
B. "Check each person who may have used it in the past two days and try to trace it."   **"A"**
C. "I can't solve your damn problems, I didn't take the bloody thing."   **"C"**

A patrol vehicle breaks down:

A. "See if you can contact the Division Mechanic as soon as possible."   **"A"**
B. "This old rattle-trap is always breaking down, it should be junked."   **"C"**
C. "The patrol operators should be more careful. They need a driver-trainer course."   **"P"**

Coffee break rumors report a fellow security officer is about to be transferred:

A. "Tell me more, I'd like to get the chance to report a couple of things to the Chief before he goes."   **"C"**
B. "Let's not spread a story that might not be true. If we have a question, let's ask Personnel."   **"A"**
C. "We really shouldn't talk behind his back. After all, he has so many troubles - financial and marital."   **"P"**

In selecting the correct ego state, try to determine Vocabulary, Gestures, Attitude and Voice as depicted in the following chart.

TRANSACTIONAL ANALYSIS CLUES IN IDENTIFYING EGO STATES

Vocabulary	Gestures	Attitude	Voice
Nurturing Parent			
Words that are:	Hugs	Caring	Soft
Consoling	Open arms	Giving	Comforting
Comforting	Hands extended		
		Loving	Concerned
Reassuring	Holds, kisses		
Critical Parent			
Don't you	Frowns	Judgemental	Critical
You should	Finger-pointing		
		Moralistic	Condescending
You might	Slaps	Authoritarian	Loud
You never	Hands on hips	Rigid	Disgusted
You'd better		Martyrdom	Scheming
You always		Demands respect	Whining
		Demands love	
Adult			
Constructive	Natural	Flexible	Appropriate
Direct	Relaxed	Confident	Modulated
Relevant	Giving	Supportive	Corresponds
Questions: how, what, when,		Reality testing	to feelings
who, why		Alert	
Suitable		Open	
Owns statements ("it seems to me")			
Adapted Child			
Compliant words	Pouting	Compliant	Repetitive
Defiant words	Show off	Demanding	Annoying
Rebellious words	Withdrawing	Jealous	Sweet
	Conforming	Ashamed	Placating
	Placating	Seeking attention	
			Angry
	Procrastinating		
		Seeking power	Defiant
		Seeking revenge	
			Rebellious
Little Professor			
Calculated	Manipulative		Wheedling
Scheming	Creative	Innovative	Innocent
Original	Innovative	Spunky	Naive
Natural Child			
Wow Gee, I can't	Spontaneous	Impulsive	Laugh
I won't, I want	Free	Uninhibited	Cry
I hope, I wish		Any feeling: happy, sad, mad, scared	Rage

Communicating with People

You should be aware of the fact that communication is a complex process which is complicated by various factors. For example, as the following diagram suggests, communication occurs in a context of a number of variables:

| Security Officer sends a message he must encode | Noise Bias Discrimination | Offender, violator or citizen receives a message and provides feedback. He must decode. |

Figure 7

What are the skills of the security officer to frame the request in language which is acceptable to the subject? How successful is he in sending the message and what are the barriers to its reception?

Now, what are the skills of the subject to receive the message and translate it into the desired action? Is it a message which, if understood, will lead to the desired action?

Let us look more closely at the great barriers to effective communication:

1) The security officer is not skilled in framing the message because of language, speech difficulties or an inability to convert the message into meaningful dialogue.

2) Considerable distraction occurs because of the nature of the situation; panic, fire, danger, threat, emotionalism, drug and alcohol abuse, rage, noise, prejudice and bias, failed communication equipment and a host of other reasons.

3) The receiver is unable or unwilling to receive the message for language, personal, status or other reason. For example, the subject may despise security officers, authority figures, people in uniform and people he perceives as "inferior" to him. Also, in many foreign countries, persons in uniform are associated with nocturnal visits, torture and disappearances. Thus, recently arrived immigrants may have a well-founded foreboding when dealing with uniformed figures.

Given these factors, which have been well-identified by psychologists, the security officer must try to plan his approach and assess the impact of his intervention. For example, an off-hand comment may spark an incident far out of proportion to the intent.

Our clients, unfortunately, might often be compared to "walking time bombs" just waiting for someone to ignite the fuse.

In our approaches, we have no idea of pressures being exerted on an individual. These may be marital, financial, job-related, health concerns and a myriad of others. Any one of these can knock the individual out of his adult functioning and render him 'TNT-like'.

One of the commonly used cliches of human relations is that we ought to use "empathy" when dealing with others and put ourselves in the other person's shoes. The idea has merit, but needs to be examined closely. Our aim is to seek and insure compliance to maintain order and protect assets. The Webster Dictionary defines "empathy" as:

Empathy ..."The action of understanding, being aware of, being sensitive to, and vicariously experiencing the feelings, thoughts, and experiences of another of either the past or present without having the feelings, thoughts and experiences fully communicated in an objectively explicit manner. (p.407, Merriam Webster, 9th edition)

Now, we do not have time for this degree of introspection. What we must do is try to use our observational processes to determine "where is this guy coming from" and "what is he liable to do?" For example, you bang on a door. On a scale of one to ten, what is the danger in the situation? Is the occupant friendly, hostile or armed? We must think through the various possible responses.

Thus, while we utilize an appropriate approach depending on the situation, we are leaping ahead to examine a vital proposition. If I do this, how will the person react? We may measure possible reactions in terms of an intervention scale. (figure 8)

SECURITY INTERVENTION SCALE

POSITIVE IMAGE

| MEET | GOOD P.R. | RIGHT AMOUNT OF POWER | ARREST |

0 ———————————————————————— 100

| WITHDRAW | BAD P.R. | TOO MUCH POWER | ASSAULT |

NEGATIVE IMAGE   (FORCE APPLIED THIS WAY)→

Figure 8

You must then visualize what you want to achieve. If you use too much power and authority, it is hard to "back-off" without losing face.

Levels of Communication

Carkhuff (1965) has developed a very useful scale of measuring empathic understanding in the interpersonal processes.

Level I - When the security officer communicates with the subject, he shows virtually no understanding of the feelings of the second person. The officer, in this situation, seems uninterested and his actions detract from the problems or concerns being expressed by the client.

Example: A Security officer is at his post when an obviously distraught executive asks something of him; the officer fails to recognize the 'state' of the executive and shows boredom, disinterest and total lack of sensitivity to the other person. The result may be a black mark against the officer and his company and a re-examination of that organization's suitability.

Level II - In this instance, the security officer may communicate some awareness of the surface feelings of the client, but any meaningful dialogue is prevented because the two people are on a different 'wave-length'. Thus, the feelings of the second person are subtracted noticeably by the officer (i.e., Parent/Child ego state).

In the case of the executive, there is a response to his request, but the security officer misses the opportunity to understand more precisely the needs of the client. If one is to get information from people, there is a requirement to establish rapport.

By using effective interviewing techniques such as paraphrasing and reflecting and probing, the officer can more accurately service the client and through his empathic responses, gain a supporter for himself and fellow officers.

Level III - In this situation, the security officer is attuned to the needs of the client and responds with accurate understanding. The communication is essentially interchangeable, although there is no attempt to respond to the feelings of the client. This represents the level at which the officer can actively help the client at the interpersonal level. Usually, the officer in the work situation will not get beyond this level because he may be at a busy work station. Sometimes, a client in trouble will require some one-on-one attention because of difficulties he is having. If the officer is able to assist, this may be considered, or perhaps, referral to a skilled professional is indicated.

Level IV & V - At these levels, one is adding noticeably or adding significantly to the feelings of the other. These approaches are used in counselling situations and such interventions as case work management and domestic crisis; dealing with children, and victims.

Decision-Making

As discussed in connection with the skills of the security officer, making effective decisions is of key importance. A successful officer impacts on people and situations in the way he intends. If he finds that he is constantly being misunderstood or misinterpreted, he must examine his own behavior. Two aspects of completing a job or task are enhancing public relations and/or insuring compliance to regulations or laws.

The latter may be concerned with matters of public safety, misdemeanors, or more serious breaches of the law. As matters of law are discussed elsewhere, let us for a moment concentrate on some aspects of effective decision-making and management of the human element.

Behavioral sciences have been instrumental in identifying aspects of models of human behavior in the past 25 years, which have fundamentally changed our modes. Police and security training have profited from these findings and this chapter will try to highlight some of the principles valuable to effective human interaction. In our decision-making, we should try to understand what is motivating and frustrating people. (See Chapter on Stress for more detail.)

All persons in positions of responsibility and, particularly, those who wear uniforms tend to be perceived as authority figures. As an authority figure, it is interpreted by the individual that you are placed on earth to: a) help and assist, or b) block and frustrate him. The decision as to which category you fall into is processed rapidly as follows:

OBSERVATION ⟶ INTERPRETATION ⟶ CONCLUSION

Figure 9

Both the security officer and the client/offender engage in the process simultaneously with potentially dangerous results. For example, we may see the individual as an intruder, desperado or potential terrorist intent on blowing the place up. In this day of ultra-sensitivity to world-wide events, we may tend to end up on the side of suspicion and defensiveness.

We are conditioned by the media and the immediacy of events around us. These pre-conditioning events may cause us to take action which is correct, or perhaps, overly reactive. Similarly, the person we confront may be trustworthy, respectable, under the influence of substances, a walking 'time-bomb', or indeed, a disgruntled employee intent on vengeance. Worse yet, he may be a dangerous threat to the physical and human resources you are obligated to protect.

How we make decisions is important. We must recognize the fact that we are susceptible to past biases, prejudices and emotions when observing situations.

Defense Mechanisms

All individuals have specific ways of managing tension and pressure. Most often, if one is skilled at recognizing body language, ample clues are provided as to where the individual is 'coming from'. The student is advised to consult some literature in this connection. "How to Read a Person Like a Book" (Julius Fast) is an excellent starting point.

Beyond the normal physical signs, an individual under stress utilizes a system of defense mechanisms to protect his person. These are a type of self-deception which the individual uses to distort reality and protect a frail ego. The following are examples that the security officer should be aware of.

Summary Chart of Ego Defence Mechanisms

REPRESSION	Unconscious preventing of dangerous or painful thoughts from entering conscious process.
DENIAL OF REALITY	Protects self from unpleasant reality by refusal to perceive or face it, often by escapist activities like getting 'sick' or being preoccupied with other things.
FANTASY	Gratification of frustrated desires in imaginary achievements.
COMPENSATION	Covering up weakness by emphasizing desirable trait or making up for frustration in one area by over-gratification in another.
IDENTIFICATION	Increased feelings of worth by identifying self with person or institution of illustrious standing.
RATIONALIZATION	Attempting to prove that one's behavior is 'rational' and justifiable and thus worthy of self and social approval.
PROJECTION	Placing blame on others or attributing one's own unethical desires to others.
REACTION FORMATION	Preventing dangerous desires from being expressed by exaggerating opposed attitudes and behavior and using them as barriers.
DISPLACEMENT	Discharging pent-up feelings (usually of hostility) on objects less dangerous than those which aroused the emotions.
EMOTIONAL INSULATION	Withdrawal into passivity to protect self from hurt.
REGRESSION	Retreating to an earlier developmental level involving less mature responses and usually a lower level of aspiration.
ISOLATION	Cutting off affective charge from hurtful situations or separating incompatible attitudes by logic-tight compartments.
SUBLIMATION	Gratification of frustrated sexual drive in substitutive non-sexual activities.

Some generalizations about Defense Mechanisms:
1. Common to everyone — abnormal only when excessive.
2. Not consciously selected and exercised by the individual — rather a function of the situation calling them forth and the individual who needs them.
3. Each individual builds up a pattern of mechanisms most useful to himself.
4. a) Have beneficial effects — e.g., may delay threat long enough to muster ego strength.
b) Have detrimental effects — if used too much, may prevent person from seeing reality and coping with it.

SUMMARY:

It is difficult to summarize human relations for the security officer, but one should be aware of the following.

— The security officer must practice good human relations at all times.
— He must be prepared for emergency situations through training and knowledge.
— He must make effective decisions and think through situations to see the end results.
— He must impact on people in the way he intends.
— He must be a good role model for others.
— He must improve his professional standing and ability.
— He must be an effective leader of others and inspire confidence.
— He must be physically fit.
— He must be emotionally fit and understand himself and others.
— He must use power and force judiciously and in a planned way.
— He must understand human psychology and the management of his and others' stress.

CONCLUSION

This matter of the Security Officer's understanding and often the control of human behavior in the workplace is indeed a demanding task and of course a complex undertaking. Readers have experienced difficulty in fully comprehending this chapter should refer to the chapter on Study Habits and Learning Skills. Apply those principals of learning to this chapter as you review it as many times as necessary to grasp this important information.

Taking into consideration all of the variables that influence human behavior, it often becomes difficult to understand where an individual is coming from; i.e., is he/she in the Parent, Adult or Child Ego state.

An enriched understanding of people and how they behave makes for a better quality of work and personal life.

This chapter should arouse your curiosity and prompt you to strive to gain more knowledge about this fascinating subject. Read one or more of the suggested books, attend a course at a college or university; become a true Professional Protection Officer.

References

Berne, E. (1961). "Transactional Analysis in Psychotherapy" New York: Grove Press.

Berne, E. (1964). "Games People Play" New York: Grove Press.

Berne, E. (1972). "What Do You Say After You Say Hello?" New York: Grove Press.

Corey, G. (1977). "Theory and Practice of Counselling and Psychotherapy" California: Brook/Cole Publishing Co.

Hersey, P. & Blanchard (1977). "Management of Organizaitonal Behavior" N.J. Prentice Hall.

Harris, T. (1967). "I'm OK, You're OK" New York: Harper and Row.

Steiner, C. (1964). "Scripts People Live" New York: Grove Press.

Wooliams, S. & Brown, M. (1979). "The Total Handbook of Transactional Analysis" New Jersey: Spectrum Books.

QUIZ
Human Relations

1. Self- _____ is the ultimate level of personal fulfillment in Maslow's "Hierarchy of Needs"
(Fill in the blank)

2. Leadership styles are described as: "Tell-Em",

_____   _____

and _____ (Fill in the blanks)

3. When dealing with less mature individuals, it may be necessary to "Tell-Em" and "Sell-Em", which would

be termed an _____
style of leadership.
(Fill in the blank)

4. Transactional Analysis means a direct communication initiated by the Security Officer and directed to another individual in a manner that exhibits empathy.

☐ T ☐ F

5. Individuals functioning in the Adult Ego state are easier to communicate with because:

☐ a. They are always sympathetic to your position of authority.

☐ b. They are easier to persuade than those individuals occupying a Child or Parent Ego status.

☐ c. They maintain a mature posture and are likely to be more reasonable.

☐ d. They usually assume a command role and take charge of the situation.

6. When the ego state of one person interacts with the ego state of another we have a Transaction.

☐ T ☐ F

7. When a "crossed transaction" occurs, that individual does not respond in the same ego state in which he/she was addressed, then the results are likely to be:

☐ a. A complimentary transaction.

☐ b. An inappropriate and unexpected stimulus.

☐ c. A motivation to revert to the Adult Ego state.

☐ d. An unexpected, social and psychological hidden message.

8. The ultimate positive unconditional stroke is "I hate you".

☐ T ☐ F

9. There are four possible life positions that one may communicate from. A life position such as "I'll take what I want" initiates from which one of the following:

☐ a) I'm not OK - you're OK

☐ b) I'm not OK - you're not OK

☐ c) I'm OK - you're not OK

☐ d) I'm OK - you're OK

10. In terms of Ego Defense Mechanisms, when one rationalizes an attempt is made to prove one's behavior is justifiable and thus worthy of self and social approval.

☐ T ☐ F

INTERVIEWING TECHNIQUES

By R. Lorne Brennan CPO

Much of a Protection Officer's time is spent giving directions, answering questions and dealing with the various enquiries related to the facility he/she is working at.

In the course of their duties, the Protection Officer is also required to investigate numerous complaints and offenses involving any number of people. The Protection Officer must assemble information gathered from these various sources, obtain the facts necessary to conduct the investigation, and ultimately to submit a complete report giving an accurate account of actions taken.

In order to fulfill this role, it is necessary for the Protection Officer to have a basic understanding of proper interviewing techniques. It is imperative that the Protection Officer control the conversation and keep control until the termination of the interview. Without control, time will be lost, facts may become distorted or forgotten and the Protection Officer may lose the psychological advantage of being "in charge" of the interview.

The content of this section can be used in part for interviewing witnesses to an offence, crime victims, suspects and potential employees. This is an overview of basic techniques that can be applied to most situations encountered by the Protection Officer. First, let's take a look at some of the areas that will be covered:

Conducting the Interview
1. Getting acquainted
2. Developing rapport
3. Motivating the subject
4. Keep the subject talking
5. Listen to what's said

Obstacles to Conversation
1. Avoid specific questions
2. Avoid yes/no questions
3. Do not use leading questions
4. Avoid rapid fire questions

Encouraging Conversation
1. Open-ended questions
2. Use of the long pause
3. Non-directive approach

Ending the Interview
1. Winding down

Preliminaries: It is important for the Protection Officer to go into an interview with a game plan in mind and with all the facts that are available to him readily at hand. The success or failure of an interview is dependent on many factors, some beyond the control of the Officer. The more factors that can be controlled by the Officer, the greater the chances are for a successful interview.

Your first approach to the subject is very important. Many people will be emotionally upset, angry, hostile, physically injured, etc. It will be necessary in some instances to tend to the subject's needs first before attempting to conduct a meaningful interview. Try to calm the subject, make him/her more comfortable and enlist their active cooperation. Do not be rushed into an interview by the subject. Take your time, obtain all the facts and as much background information as possible before taking any action.

At times this approach will upset the subject, who feels that you should be taking swift action on his behalf; however, it is important to remember that you are in charge and you are responsible for actions that you take.

Make sure you have **all** information before committing yourself to a course of action. If at all possible, the location of the interview should be one that is chosen by the officer and should be as free of distractions as possible.

Conducting the Interview

Getting Acquainted: The greeting should be cordial and sincere. Identify yourself, and if not in uniform, produce your identification. Your initial approach can be formal or informal, depending on the circumstances.

Attempt to set the subject at ease by entering into a general conversation with him/her before getting to the matter at hand. People like to talk about themselves and their interests and this is a useful tool in obtaining information regarding your subject and locating a common ground for communication with the subject. At this stage, allow the subject to become accustomed to your presence and to the surroundings by setting the pace.

Developing rapport: Your immediate objective is to establish a common ground on which you can communicate with the subject. By following the preliminaries, you should have a good idea of what the subject's educational background is and at what level it is best to talk with him on. If you are dealing with a laborer, you are not going to speak down to him by using terminology and words that he is not accustomed to.

By the same token, you would not speak to an executive as you would the laborer. Find your common ground and speak to the subject at his level. By finding areas of common interest, such as sports or hobbies, you can establish a rapport with the subject which will lead to easier communications.

In developing a rapport with another person, you must be able to put aside your personal feelings, respect the subject as a person and show your understanding of the subject and the circumstances which have brought you together. If you are unable to establish a rapport with the subject, an unbridgeable gap will be created that will make further communication difficult, if not impossible.

Motivating the subject: Most people you will be interviewing will be in a strange and stressed situation which makes them uncomfortable. It will be necessary for you to remove any fears they may have. Many people are afraid of "authority" as presented by the uniform, appearing as a witness, incriminating themselves or others, or may simply be unsure of what they are to do.

If you have developed a rapport with the subject, it is a simple matter to convince the subject of the need to tell the truth and enlist their active cooperation.

Keep the subject talking: Once rapport has been established and the subject is motivated, turn the conversation towards the topic you wish to discuss. Allow the subject to give a complete account of their involvement without interruptions, but be alert for inconsistencies or omissions.

At times, you may have to interrupt to guide the subject back in the direction you wish the conversation to go. You must control the conversation to the extent that the subject keeps talking until you have all the information you require.

Listen to what is said and how it is said: The Officer must not only induce the subject to freely relate information he may possess, but he must also evaluate the person and the conversation. In many instances, it is not what the subject says that is important, but the manner in which he says it or what he does not say.

The Officer must be constantly alert for signals from the subject that indicate he/she is telling the truth, lying or merely withholding information. A wealth of information is available to the Officer who wishes to advance his interviewing abilities by learning how to interpret body language.

Obstacles to Conversation

In most instances the content of an incident will be covered in more than one conversation. The subject will be asked to repeat his story again in order to properly fill in gaps and correct statements. It is important that the Officer not interrupt the subject during the initial stages and that the subject be allowed to recount his version in full.

After the initial story has been told, the Officer may then ask the subject to repeat the story, this time taking notes and stopping the subject from time-to-time in order to get the "full" story "straight". It is important to note that most people will never include all the details in the first attempt as they usually blurt out the information in rapid fire succession. After the initial telling, they will relax a bit and become more specific and provide greater detail.

Avoid specific questions: By asking specific questions, the Officer diverts and limits the interview rather than letting the subject give a narrative of the whole, or part of the story. Direct questions may also lead the subject into a false line of thinking as to what you consider to be important areas of the story and as a result, the subject may omit some details in an effort to supply the information that he/she "thinks" the Officer considers important.

Direct questions do have a place in an interview, but they should not be asked until the subject has given a complete narration. Direct questions can then be used to clear up various areas within the narrative. If the subject hits a block and stops talking, then a direct question can be used to lead him back into the conversation.

Avoid yes/no questions: In order for the Officer to obtain full and detailed facts, the subject must respond with an explanation detailing the events. If a question is asked that only requires a yes or no answer, the subject will normally respond with a yes or no, and information that may have been gained will be lost.

By avoiding yes or no questions, you also eliminate problems with the subject not understanding your question, agreeing or disagreeing based solely on what they perceive the Officer wants to hear, or what the subject wants to tell the Officer.

Do not use leading questions: Leading questions have the same effect as yes/no questions. They may cause the subject to give false or misleading information to the Officer. This may be done either mistakenly or on purpose.

Avoid rapid fire questions: These may seem appropriate to the inexperienced investigator; however they only lead to confusion, emotional tenseness and resistance to the rapport that may have been developed. It also stops the cooperative witness from completing his statement, thereby possibly losing information.

Encouraging Conversation

Open-ended questions: By asking a series of questions in the early stages of an interview, you may be conditioning the subject to believe that if you want to know any information he will be asked, no information is expected.

On the other hand, asking relatively few questions leading into a conversation will give the subject the feeling that everything he tells has significance. Any questioning of the subject's narrative is withheld until he has finished his story.

Typical of open-ended questions are general queries such as "Tell me what you saw"; "Can you tell me more about that?"; "What happened next?" These types of questions do not permit yes or no answers and allow for no misunderstanding of what the Officer wants. The subject is forced to give a narrative in order to answer the question.

The use of the long pause: Sometimes during an interview, the subject will stop talking and a silence will descend on the room. To the inexperienced Officer, this can be unnerving and cause the Officer to lose control of the interview and start talking. Pauses in conversation are normal and are never as long in duration as they seem to be.

The subject is as ill at ease as you are during these silences, and the experienced Officer will use these to advantage — be patient and wait — many times the subject will resume talking and will frequently volunteer additional information just to break the silence.

Non-directive approach: The non-directive approach is a technique which turns the subject's statements into questions calling for more information. In using this method, simply repeat the subject's last phrase, but with a rising inflection on the last word so that it becomes a question.

During such an interview, control your emotions, do not register surprise or anxiety, but merely restate the subject's statement. The effect of this technique is that further information is drawn out without giving direction or restricting the thinking as in direct questioning.

Ending the Interview

No interview should be abruptly terminated with a curt dismissal of "Thank you" or "O.K.", etc. When it is apparent that the interview is ending, close the conversation in a courteous and friendly manner. You may wish to summarize what has been said and ask the subject if there is anything else he/she wishes to add.

Let the subject know that you appreciate what he/she has done and that he/she has performed a valuable service. Thank the subject for their time and assistance. Treating the subject with concern and good manners will help in assuring that, should you or another Officer need to speak with the subject in the future, the subject will be more cooperative and ready to assist instead of resist.

Recognition to Sgt. Steve Cloonan, Michigan State Police (Ret.) for assistance in development of this Chapter.

QUIZ
Interviewing Techniques

1. It is important for the protection officer to establish

common _____ during an interview.
(Fill in the blank)

2. It is important for the protection officer to go into an

interview with a game _____ in mind.
(Fill in the blank)

3. Leading questions have the same effect as

_____ and _____ questions.
(Fill in the two blanks)

4. By asking specific questions, the protection officer

may divert or _____ the interview, rather than letting the subject give a narrative of the whole story. (Fill in the blank)

5. Direct questions do not have a place in an interview.
   □ T □ F

6. Leading questions have the same effect as direct questions.
   □ T □ F

7. Any questioning of a subject's narrative need not wait until he has finished his story.
   □ T □ F

8. While conducting an interview, the witness stops talking. You should:
   □ a. start talking yourself
   □ b. tell the subject to start talking
   □ c. be patient and wait
   □ d. none of the above

9. During an interview using the non-direct approach, you should:
   □ a. control your emotions
   □ b. do not register surprise
   □ c. re-state the subject's statement
   □ d. all the above

10. Yes and No questions should be avoided because:
   □ a. the subject may agree with you
   □ b. the subject may not understand your question
   □ c. the subject may disagree with you
   □ d. all the above

STRESS MANAGEMENT

By. Dr. Robert C. Harris

STRESS: IT CAN DEVASTATE MODERN MAN

Stress and 'burn-out' were one of the major topics of discussion in the 1960s and 1970s. Whether at work or play, people were telling each other how burned out they were. Unfortunately, many people became rather jaded with the subject and more recently have begun to ignore the topic.

Nature was not optimistic about the capacity of early man to make good judgements about how to survive in life-threatening situations. So the physiological stress reaction was established to work incredibly fast.

This is unfortunate especially for those persons in the justice system who must carry much of the stress of disciplining modern society. The security officer must often stand alone and take personal risks when confronting members of society, whether they be little old ladies in a shopping centre or thieves in an industrial plant.

Both these events may be equally stressful to an officer as it is ones' own attitudes, thoughts and feeling about an event that may cause one to react in a stressful manner. It is not so much the event as how one views the event that creates the stress.

Skiing is a case in point. One endeavors to come as close to 'wipe-out' as possible in order to have the maximum joy. To another person, the same slide down the mountain would literally frighten them to death.

Stress reaction is personal. It may be triggered by ego threat or physical threat or even ones' imagination during periods of boredom. However, once triggered, the stress reaction acts in a psychobiological pattern designed by nature.

Nature developed the stress reaction early in the life of the human species to protect the individual from life-threatening situations. Being designed for dire physical threat, the stress reaction is an extreme response. There are over 1400 physical changes that occur to prepare the body for fight or flight once the alarm is sounded.

It is somewhat akin to having a gun response to every situation with which a security officer must deal. Thus, like good security training, one needs to spend time learning about the response and anticipating the situations that may trigger it for oneself and practice dealing with those situations.

This chapter will outline much that is known about stress in reasonably simplistic terms and will give some suggestions for developing your own coping mechanisms.

To discuss stress at all requires that we acknowledge the work of Dr. Hans Selye, a noted Canadian scholar, who worked at the Universite de Montreal in the Province of Quebec. Much of the material in this article originates with Dr. Selye's work, although specifically where is hard to acknowledge after so many years of working in the field. As a young medical student, Dr. Selye noted that all disease starts with a general state of being sick. Being sick, those common symptoms of flushed skin, perspiration, heart speeding up, general loss of energy and so on.

The reader knows most of them as the flu. Dr. Selye began to research the factors that contributed to this condition and spent a lifetime gathering data on stress that each of us may use to improve our own lifestyles. Each of us may develop values and a personal philosophy of life that allows us to establish an area of comfortable stimulation where we can effectively cope with life.

Stress is a natural adaptive reaction of the body to any stimulation. The human being must have stimulation to exist. Non-stimulation is dead. Whether any serious demand made of the body is a good experience (eustress) or a bad experience (distress), is a personal choice. One needs, therefore, to learn how to control this non-specific response of the body to the demands of life. Stimulation may be thought of as being on a continuum from low stimulation to high stimulation.

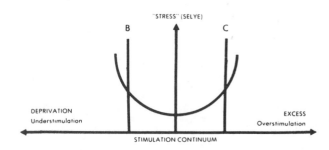

Figure 1

The graph of stress is an asymptotic curve 'A'. Somewhere in the middle of the continuum is an area unique to each of us where we have maximum comfort, enjoyment and productivity.

In Figure One, this area is shown as lying between boundary lines 'B' and 'C'. Healthy persons, mentally and physically, have very wide boundaries of stress tolerance. Less healthy persons have much more restricted areas of tolerance. As one gets "stressed", the boundaries of the productive area narrows.

Dr. Selye considered that each person is born with a limited amount of adaptive energy. As that energy gets depleted through life experiences, the individual becomes more vulnerable to distress reactions. It should be noted that in Figure One, the right-hand range is labelled 'overstimulation', not over-work.

Most North Americans are most stressed from boredom. Most of us are a long way from the classification of overwork. In fact, wartime experiences have shown that man has an incredible capacity for work that he considers to be important for survival.

Nature was not optimistic about the capacity of early man to make good judgements about how to survive in life-threatening situations. So the physiological stress reaction established was to work incredibly fast.

If you were walking along the beach and glanced out to sea where there was a huge wave coming in, you do not want to stand there admiring the wave and wondering if you could outrun it or even swim in it. Your stress reaction would set up and would prepare you for flight or fight **now**. Figure Two diagramatically indicates the organs of the body that may be mobilized to save you.

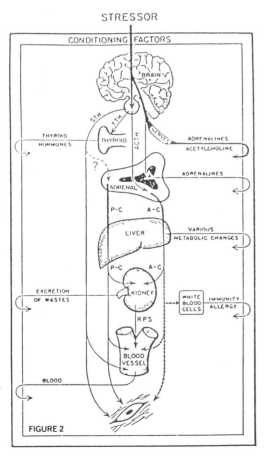

Figure 2

Simply stated, the reaction is that the stomach vacates (oops, not in a neatly-pressed uniform). Thus, the neat, modern security officer has a second stressor that heightens the reaction to the first stressor. The survival system rushes into action. After all, if that wave were to hit you, you would need all the energy you could muster.

We already established the pessimism of nature in the question of survival. So if that wave were to hit you and nature thinks it would, you would get tumbled on the rocks and cut up somewhat. So you would need to have the clotting capacity of your blood set up as well as the infection fighting capacity of the immune system.

The body starts these processes immediately while the decision to run is still being taken. Of course this incident on the beach required you to run like all get out and you make it to high ground, fell down exhausted and felt really great that you once more outwitted the elements.

The same process happens in less life-threatening situations. Seeing the little redhead walking towards him is as stimulating to Charlie Brown as the wave was to you. But sitting in the console room of his security station, he cannot run or fight. No wonder so many modern Charlie Browns have heart attacks or strokes, or at least undue absenteeism due to flu.

The stress reaction was established for the physical protection of primitive man by instantly preparing him for fight, flight or freeze. Modern man has retained the stress mechanisms, but transferred the stressor qualities to psychological and social situations. Modern man now has a fear of actual or anticipated injury, pain or death to the psychological self and social self as well as occasionally the physical self.

The problem is that the natural responses of fight and flight are not normally available to civilized man as coping mechanisms. Charlie Brown cannot "bop" the little redhead to tell her he cares, and he will never meet her if he keeps running away. He has to develop sophisticated social skills to cope with this stressor or, as he seems more prone to do, fantasize about his relationship with her.

As the body functions through electrochemical processes, the model for the stages of stress is an electrical model. The **first stage** is the alarm. The stress reaction goes into action. The claxon sounds all hands to battle stations and the whole body comes to the alert with chemical changes rushing to the ready.

The **second stage** is the resistance stage, ideally the battle itself. The **third stage** is the post-battle exhaustion during which one rests and cleans up the debris.

Biologically, the alarm means that threatening physical and psycho-social stimuli elicit, non-specifically, the same battery of neuro-endocrine responses — in particular the heightened activity of the adrenal cortex and the sympathetic nervous system.

The stressor acts upon the hypothalamus, a coordinating brain region, and the pituitary (a small endocrine gland embedded in the bones at the base of the skull). These in turn act upon the adrenals which are endocrine glands found one on each side of the body just above the kidneys. These act upon the lymphatic tissue, defensive organs found in the lymph nodes in the groin, armpits, the tonsils and the thymus in the chest.

The white blood cells come from the lymphatic organs and the bone marrow. These cells are important in defense of the body, especially against infections. This is diagramatically presented in Figure Three.

Figure 3

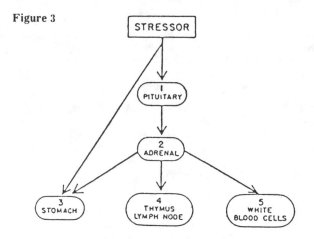

Actually, the neuro-endocrine responses elicited by the stressful experiences is the stress itself in Selye's terminology. In popular language, the word 'stress' has come to mean the experiences and the complete syndrome of reactions to those experiences.

Recent research has shown the concept of a totally non-specific stress response to be too simplistic. The extent of the responses of the different hormones may vary considerably depending on the nature of the stimulus. For example, rage is almost always associated with increased activity of the sympathetic nervous system, whereas fear is often accompanied by the inhibition of the sympathetic nervous system, resulting in fainting.

The sympathetic nervous system is activated in situations associated with arousal and aggressive attempts to maintain status. Situations of social interaction which lead to defeat and feelings of frustration and depression mainly activate the adrenal cortex. (Vander, 1981)

The sympathetic nervous system which is most associated with the fight or flight reaction is a communications system of nerve cells that spread throughout the body. They innervate the glands, the heart, the smooth muscles surrounding blood vessels, the gastro-intestinal tract, the bladder, the pupils of the eyes, and more. This is done by a chemical norepinephrine released from the nerve fibres.

The adrenal medulla, a component of the sympathetic nervous system, secretes epinephrine (adrenalin) into the blood stream. This is rapidly pumped throughout the whole body and becomes a generalized response.

"The heart's rate and force of contraction increases, resulting in the pumping of more blood; breathing is stimulated, providing more oxygen and eliminating carbon dioxide more rapidly; the blood vessels of the internal organs (like the gastro-intestinal tract and kidneys) constrict while those going to skeletal muscles dilate — thereby distributing blood preferentially to the latter; the central nervous system is aroused, becoming more alert and responsive and less cognizant of fatigue; both glycogen (the storage form of carbohydrate and fat deposits) are broken down to glucose and free fatty acids, respectively, supplying fuels for exercising skeletal muscles and preparing the body for a period of fasting (a fleeing or fighting animal obviously is not eating); the blood becomes more coagulable (mainly because of a change in blood platelets), reducing potential for wound-induced blood loss." (Vander, 1981, pp 199)

While the adrenal medulla secretes epinephrine, the other adrenal gland, the adrenal cortex, secretes the corticosteroids, the most well-known is cortisol (cortisone). This chemical has the major effect of permitting the small blood vessels to remain partially constricted for long periods of time.

Lacking cortisol with even moderate stress may cause low blood pressure and even death.

Figure 4   Pathway which controls the secretion of cortisol.

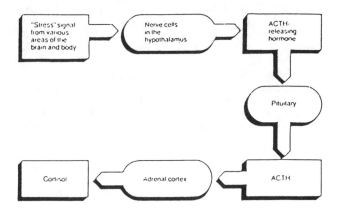

The second stage is the resistance stage in which the materials and energy released for the battle are consumed through action. However, modern man is "nice" and can no longer go into the resistance stage through battle as did the more primitive man. Thus, modern man is forced to stay in the heightened arousal stage for long periods due to the sustained and repeated alarm response with no resistance.

Continued long enough, fatty acids enter the blood, causing heart problems, the hydrochloric acid in the gastro-intestinal tract may cause ulcers or colitis, and continued use inhibits the immune system response making him vulnerable to disease.

Even urinary dysfunction and circulatory problems result, causing headaches and possibly strokes. Of concern to the marriage relationship is the fact that a sustained heightened response depletes the hormone function resulting in lowered sexual interest.

Figure 5   Hypothesized pathway from stress to disease.

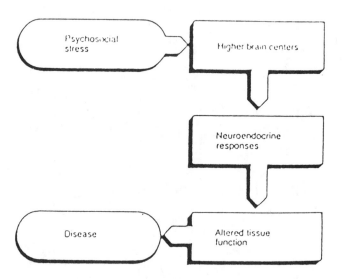

The last stage is the post-battle stage of exhaustion. The energy and materials are all used up and the body returns to its normal state of life. But what if there is no battle? All that action to prepare for battle and nothing released through action. An effort is made to return to normal, but it is very difficult to do so. Especially if another alarm goes soon.

Excessive use of the stress reaction alarm, resistance and exhaustion without being able to pass through the complete cycle uninterrupted, may lead to on-the-job burn-out. Essentially, the burn-out process may be summarized as:

1. The initial enthusiasm for the job with a great expenditure of energy.
2. The fuel shortage which may cause job dissatisfaction, inefficiency, fatigue and sleep problems.
3. The chronic symptoms of exhaustion leading to illness, acute anger and depression.
4. The crisis stage of pessimism, self-doubt and obsession with problems that may lead to:
5. Career dissolution and life-threatening health problems.

Neiderhoffer (1969) and Maslach (1976) found that continued stress reaction had very negative psychological consequences. The individuals showed suppressed anger. They were cold and impersonal. They were irritable with their families and negative to their clients. This reaction increased as the stress increased.

Lazarus (1981) found a high correlation between the number of everyday life hassles and the amount of personal depression, exhaustion, anxiety and illness. His result indicated life hassles were even more stressful than major life changes.

Figure 6

Psychosocial Situations Shown to be Associated
with Increased Plasma Concentration or Urinary Excretion
of Adrenal Cortical Steroids

Human beings

1. Normal persons
    A. Acute situations
        1. Aircraft flight
        2. Awaiting surgical operation
        3. Final exams (college students)
        4. Novel situations
        5. Competitive athletics
        6. Anticipation of exposure to cold
        7. Workdays, compared to weekends
        8. Many job experiences
    B. Chronic life situations
        1. Predictable personality behavior profile: aggressive, ambitious, time-urgency
        2. Discrepancy between levels of aspiration and achievement
    C. Experimental techniques
        1. 'Stress' or 'shame' interview
        2. Many motion pictures
II. Psychiatric patients
    A. Acute anxiety
    B. Depression, but only when patient is aware of and involved in a struggle with it

Source: A.J. Vander, J.H. Sherman and D.S. Luciano, Human Physiology: The Mechanisms of Body Function, 3rd Ed. (New York: McGraw Hill, 1980)

On one occasion, I had the opportunity to present an all-day workshop on stress in a firehall classroom. Due to shortage of hands, the classroom members volunteered to respond to call out. This was the most trying day I have spent in many years. The alarm would sound, the men would all rush to gear up and leap onto the trucks. They would get about a block from the firehall and be informed it was a false alarm. Back they would come and settle down to the dulcette tones of my class. (Be careful that you read dulcette, not dull set. Criticism is a stressor to a professor.)

Soon the whole scramble would happen again and again they would come back to class. That day we had 11 false or minimal alarms with not one situation where the men could actually swing into battle and do what they were so highly trained to do.

By 1600 hours, the men and I were exhausted and I was stressed to almost unbearable limits. The men laughed and stated that every day was like that for firemen. I had experienced very vividly the stress model in action and gained a new respect for the men who serve their community in occupations that require such wide and frequent swings of action.

Of course security officers and others in the justice professions experience similar situations on many occasions. The survival skill is to be able to control the alarm or build a resistance behavior into the situation.

In the case of the firemen, I suggested they hang ropes in the hose-drying tower and climb up and down after each run before going back to their resting state activity. The men soon found it easier to return to the normal routine after each run.

To survive happily in a world of hassles and the ensuing stress, the individual must develop coping mechanisms. One needs to start with a healthy personal lifestyle based on values and attitudes that lead to the appropriate use of time management, exercise, sleep, vacations, intimacy and family life. Relaxation techniques can release enorphin, a powerful natural tranquilizer that can turn off the alarm.

One must develop coping mechanisms and a healthy lifestyle based on appropriate self-oriented values and attitudes. What an easy sentence to write and read, but what a difficult task to carry out!

Each of us has spent years developing our lifestyle, including our self-destructive behaviors. A re-examination of our lifestyle may indicate that the very things we are best at are the things that are most destructive to us. When we are experiencing stress, we fall back on those skills that we are most comfortable with, often the very ones that are creating the problem.

The list of these behaviors is well known; excessive alcohol, drugs, work, exercise, religion, self-pity, family arguments, annoyance with the children, fear of the economy, and so on to the extent of man's creativity. Most of us have developed concepts to begin to re-work our lifestyles.

We all have experienced the pain of sore muscles when we began getting back into physical shape after a long layoff. The same process may be in store as we rebuild a healthier mental and emotional lifestyle.

Back to the basics for some of us means starting with definitions. How do you define needs and wants? A need is something vital to sustain life, whereas a want is a luxury to be striven for; to be enjoyed as ones' own right when attained.

"To want" is socially imposed behavior that may have become significant as proof of our worth as individuals. It is this last factor that creates so many problems for us.

Socially imposed behavior is always subject to change factors external to us and sets us up for threat to our psychological and social selves. Each one of us have wants that motivate us, but occasionally we need to examine them against a good needs theory in order to make sure we are not unnecessarily on "the merry-go-round".

The model of needs that I find most useful is Abraham Maslow's hierarchy of needs. (Maslow, 1970)

Figure 7	
	SELF-ACTUALIZATION
	Truth
	Goodness
	Beauty
	Individuality
	Perfection
GROWTH NEEDS	Justice
	Order
	Simplicity
	Intimacy
	Playfulness
	Self-sufficiency
	Meaningfulness
	SELF-ESTEEM
	Esteem by Others
	Love and Belongingness
	PHYSICAL SAFETY:
BASIC NEEDS	Phychological Security
	Physiological Needs:
	Air, Water, Food, Shelter, Sleep

The external environment must provide the challenge or stimulation to activate the search for needs fulfillment; i.e., stress.

Hierarchy means one starts from the bottom and works up. While this chapter is not the place for an extended discussion of Maslow's model, some brief comments are very relevant to a discussion of stress coping ideas.

As infants, we learn our basic social behavior while having our basic physiological needs for food, shelter, etc., met. In our early years, our needs for physical safety and psychological security are met through the significant others in our lives. If one thinks about it, one realizes that the basic physiological needs are constantly re-occurring appetites. The basic need of safety and security can only be met for the child by other people.

These two facts create a fascinating paradox for us. If our basic needs are adequately met when we are children, we

can continue up the needs hierarchy to an adult state where we really meet our own needs through self-growth activities.

The chart in Figure 8 uses some fascinating words to describe self-growth. These words also describe eustress conditions.

If for some reason our basic needs were not met or only very conditionally met while we were young, the appetite condition and the importance of the approval of others seem to become attached to the higher order growth needs. Hence, playfulness for example can only be satisfying if it is accompanied with the approval of others.

This is the paradox. While mature humans need to be self-approving to achieve their higher order needs, many of us are locked unnecessarily into the approval of others. The irony of this is that we do not seem to trust others when they do grant us approval.

To learn to cope with our stress, we need to develop skills that help us as adults to overcome this undue dependance on others to meet our esteem needs. These skills will free our psychological and social selves to grow in healthy eustress ways. This is not to say that we do not need other people to share our lives and to meet our esteem needs. We do, but not at the cost of excessive stress.

A courageous re-examination of ones' needs and wants may well be the first step towards good stress control and freedom from the externally imposed and never satisfied wants motivation. Having established ones' motivation based on needs and much less driven by wants, one may then examine the factors that contribute to stress, generally and specifically.

The factors that are most significant as stressors are well known, but generally ignored by ourselves and all too frequently our employers. However, it is we who suffer stress and, thus, it is we who should do what we can to minimize it.

A significant factor is boredom. Overwork is rarely a major cause of stress if one feels what he is doing is important.

We have the incredible work effort of the Second World War as evidence of mans' ability to work. It is when one feels his work is not important or appreciated that boredom and stress comes in. Boredom can be confronted head-on by identifying the purpose for what we do.

Victor Frankl (1959) states that a person can handle incredible difficulties and boredom if he knows why he is doing it. Frankl suggests there are three possible solutions to finding a meaningful and happy life. They are to find a purpose in what you are doing, fall in love, or discover your relationship with God. Simple, but effective ways to add meaning to your life without having to rely on someone else to make your life less stressful.

Many of us find ourselves in situations of role ambiguity and role conflict that have the potential for stress production. My experience has been that my employers appreciated any efforts I made to clarify my role.

In many occupations there are unclear goals and roles, but a little effort to clarify just what it is you are expected to do will pay real dividends in stress reduction.

The security officer is expected to maintain the security of his employer's property and be a reasonable public relations person at the same time. With some people, this becomes a very ambiguous and difficult task. However, time spent clarifying priorities allows the officer to do both roles with a minimum of stress.

Role conflict situations are frequently a function of unclear values rather than true conflict. As a supervisor, you may be required to criticize the work of someone who is a personal friend. At first glance, this may be role conflict and a source of stress. Clear values would help you to see that you are accepting pay for doing the job and a friend would surely realize this. Besides, a true friend supervisor would surely not allow anything but the best from his worker friend out of mutual loyalty to the employer.

These are simple examples of situations in which the employees can lower their stress levels on the job through clarifying discussions without any involvement of the employer. Clarify your values and goals for working, communicate this to others, and your own behavior are good first steps to stress reduction.

The factors are interpersonal and can be altered by you in your own life situation; i.e., the lack of social rewards. By this is meant the 'atta boy' comments, not money. We all need to be complimented regularly to maintain our self-esteem. So if each one of us resolved to compliment those around us appropriately, we would all have our social reward need met.

The problem is that if we just hand out compliments, we soon begin not to trust each other and wonder what is wrong. Unless we receive accurate feedback on what we do inadequately, we do not trust the positive feedback. Stress comes from real or imaginary threat to oneself.

We each know our shortcomings and if they are not acknowledged, we seem to begin to doubt ourselves and to magnify our weaknesses. We need friends and supervisors who will accurately and gently tell us our weaknesses as well as our strengths. To be able to do this is a major skill worth working on.

If each of us is important and want to be recognized for our importance, then interpersonal conflict is inevitable. We need to work on skills of dispute to develop fair and honest ways to disagree to minimize stress for each of us. Responsibility to start developing these skills lies with each one of us. If I can treat you honestly and fairly, you will undoubtedly do the same for me.

The identification of personal stress and stressors is essential to successful stress management. A technique to use is to list the external and internal stressors you face. Do this a couple of times a year.

Having made a list, go over each item of distress. Study the distress list and identify those items you can honestly let go and rank-order the rest of the items from least stressful to most stressful. Starting with the least stressful items, work out ways to solve the stress.

You will find that you finally have a rather short list of items that you have to learn to live with, and some of them may frequently be avoided.

Internal stressors are more philosophical and, perhaps, more difficult to examine. You may need help from your family or friends. List the ways that you expect too much of yourself. List the values and beliefs that you hold that are different from those around you. List what you are really afraid of.

Just listing them will identify things you can alter. Next, go back to the external stress lists and examine the items in the context of your internal stressors. It will be obvious that some of the major stressors in your life are unnecessary baggage from your past.

Of course, that mind exercise will only identify stressors. The real task is doing something about them. Resolve to make time your ally and to take charge of your life. Manage your life as you would a business. Diversify and seek rewarding experiences in all dimensions of living.

To do this, you will need more energy, so examine your physical condition and lifestyle. If you smoke, stop. If you use liquor, make sure it is only occasionally and that you not the liquor is in charge. Eliminate the use of recreational drugs; they are killing North American industry (Time, March 17, 1986). Minimize the use of tranquilizers, sleeping pills and headache pills — they are depressants and block problem-solving.

Replace all these artificial problem-solvers with physical exercise and good diet. Start out mildly and work up to a good appropriate physical schedule for you at your age. The bookstores are full of good exercise and healthy diet books.

Psychologically, it is essential that you guard your freedoms; the freedom to choose your friends, the freedom to live with and/or love whom you choose, the freedom to think and believe as you choose, the freedom to structure your time as you see fit and the freedom to set your own life goals.

As with all freedoms, they carry responsibilities with them; in this case, the responsibility to know yourself. This task may be aided by learning meditation or relaxation techniques. It is essential to build a good interpersonal support system.

The triangle is the most stable figure, so use a human triangle to support yourself. Intentionally seek out friends from varied walks of life to form relationships of high quality with, people you can trust and be yourself with. Give some time each week to maintaining and strengthening these relationships.

Philosophically and spiritually, find some time every day — even 10 minutes — for complete privacy; a chance to be alone with your thoughts; a chance to tell yourself that you at least approve of and care for you. Self-relaxation is an excellent skill to learn. One of the best books on the subject is "Self-Hypnosis" by Dr. Brian Alman. This book may be ordered from International Health Publications, P.O. Box 17535, San Diego, Calif. 92117.

The essence of auto-relaxation is the following seven steps.
1. Take three slow deep breaths; do not force them.
2. Shut your eyes and as you breathe out, think "I am relaxing now".
3. On each breath, think "relax now" and go deeper into yourself.
4. Count to ten as you breathe and imagine your favorite private spot — if you don't have one, now is the time to invent one; a spot where you are completely private.
5. In this private spot, think to yourself, "I relax quickly and deeply and enjoy each day with confidence".
6. Use this private place to completely relax and to deal with yourself in a positive way. Think, "It is okay to care for myself; it is okay to know I am the best I can be; it is okay to be healthy."
7. After a few minutes (five or ten), breathe yourself up to the count of three. Think as you do, "I feel good in every way". Then stretch and flex.

There is no magic in self-relaxation. It is a conditioned response that allows one to truly relax quickly and effectively. Most people do not do this, and in fact do not believe it is such an easy thing to do. This is because we do not learn to take a few minutes for ourselves. We have learned to sit in front of the T.V. or to vegetate in an easy chair.

Why can we not learn to take a few minutes to do something for ourselves? Try it, you will like it, and take my word it is good for you and does not need a prescription filled to accomplish it. For those who are religious, a deep relaxed state is a great way to say your prayers and mobilize your oneness with the Supreme.

Knowing the physiological characteristics of stress, it is soon obvious how auto-relaxation works for you. The characteristics of deep relaxation are:
1. Your breathing becomes slower and deeper.
2. Your heart beats more slowly.
3. Blood flow increases to your hands and feet.
4. Your muscles relax.
5. Your metabolism slows and normalizes.
6. Your hormonal activity becomes balanced.

All these conditions are the opposite of the stress reaction. It is not possible to feel two opposing physical states at the same time. It is possible to be emotionally confused, but the body does not normally accept confusing physical states.

If you can create one portion of the relaxation response, the chain of the other responses will follow automatically. Deep, slow breathing may be one of the easiest of the control effects for you to learn.

Again I must point out this is not magic. It is merely a good effective conditioned response controlled by yourself. Take several deep, satisfying breaths. This deep breathing initiates the relaxation response. Focus your attention on your counting or your hand or on a color.

Whatever works for you encourages your body to relax even more. In your private imaginary space, visualize the stress and tension that has built up in your muscles as constricting layers that can be peeled away. Layer by layer, you can peel away the tightness of stress.

With practice, further levels of relaxation may be achieved causing many other changes to occur. These changes are positive feelings of good health and they will improve the quality of your life.

Organizationally, we may learn to handle stress by learning problem-solving techniques, time management and arranging to do more of what we enjoy.

Rather than end with a focus on the manifestations of ill health, let's identify the characteristics of the healthy personality. They are:
1. A high level of self-esteem.
2. Action-oriented behavior that identifies what needs to be done and does it.
3. A high level of internal control; taking responsibility for what happens to oneself in life.
4. Capable of establishing priorities and working on what is important.

An effective way to put life in perspective and lower ones' stress may be to follow what I tell my children are 'Bob's rules':
1. Each day identify one way I can make life easier for me and someone else.
2. Each day, observe some living humor.
3. Each day, see a kind act.
4. Each day, observe some beauty in your life.

Stress is all too often a state of mind. If you do not like the state you are in, do what so many of our parents did: immigrate to a new state and build a new life.

References
Alman, Brian M.; Lambrou, P.T. (1983) "Self-Hypnosis: A Complete Manual for Health and Self-Change". San Diego - International Health Publications.

"Battling the Enemy Within". (1986, March 17) Time, p.40.

Frankl, V. (1959) "Man's Search for Meaning". New York: Washington Square Press.

Lazarus, R.S. (1981, July) "Everyday Hassles can be Hazardous to Your Health". Psychology Today.

Maslach, C. (1976, September) "Burn-Out". Human Behavior.

Maslow, A.H. (1970) "Motivation and Personality" (2nd Ed.) New York: Harper.

Neiderhoffer, A. (1969) "Behind the Shield: The Police in Urban Society". New York: Anchor Books.

Selye, H. (1956) "The Stress of Life". Toronto: McGraw Hill.

Selye, H. (1976) "The Stress of Life"-(Rev.Ed.) Toronto: McGraw Hill.

Vander, A.J. (1981) "Nutrition, Stress & Toxic Chemicals". Ann Arbor: University of Michigan Press.

Vander, A.J.; Sherman, J.H.; Luciano, D.S. (1980) "Human Physiology: The Mechanism of Body Function" (3rd Ed.) New York: McGraw Hill.

QUIZ
Stress Management

1. One's stress reaction is _____
(Fill in the blank)

2. The stress reaction was developed to _____ the individual. (Fill in the blank)

3. Good stress is called _____ and

bad stress is _____
(Fill in the blanks)

4. Very few persons are distressed from _____

The most common stressor is _____
(Fill in the blanks)

5. The stress reaction is a learned response that takes time to set up.
   ☐ T ☐ F

6. Stress was established in man to prepare for fight or flight.
   ☐ T ☐ F

7. For some security officers, a beautiful girl may be as much a stressor as a man with a gun.
   ☐ T ☐ F

8. Modern man has:
   ☐ a) retained the stress reaction
   ☐ b) changed the stress reaction
   ☐ c) changed the stressors
   ☐ d) eliminated stress
   ☐ e) given up

9. The human body functions as:
   ☐ a) toy
   ☐ b) machine
   ☐ c) an electrochemical processor
   ☐ d) a model ship
   ☐ e) battery operated clock

10. The stress reaction operates on:
   ☐ a) one organ
   ☐ b) all organs and hormones
   ☐ c) a select few organs
   ☐ d) only the hormones
   ☐ e) only the brain

CRISIS INTERVENTION

By Michael A. Hannigan, CPO

Introduction

Over one hundred years ago, Walter Bagehot, a British journalist wrote, "violence heads the list of inherent fears that are experienced by mankind." It is safe to say that the risk that violence may be perpetrated against individuals in our moderate workplaces has to be a major security/loss control concern.

The Protection Officer, by the nature of his/her job function, must deal with individuals that present the threat of violent behavior for reasons such as involvement with alcohol or drugs, being a victim of a crime, suffering from an accident, illness, an argument with their spouse or even the loss of a loved one. These individuals not only pose a serious threat to themselves, but most certainly to employees, the public and of course protection personnel.

There is a technique which can be used to allow more control of the outcome of a situation that involves a person that is behaving in a violent manner. A positive outcome can be achieved by suggesting certain proactive behavior to these individuals by actions or what you say and how the message is verbally or non verbally communicated. This technique is Behavioral Management or perhaps better known as Crisis Intervention. Crisis Intervention is a relatively safe technique designed to aid in maintaining the best possible care and welfare of agitated or out of control individuals while lending maximum safety to protection personnel.

Causes of Disruptive Behavior

The reasons people become violent or disruptive vary greatly but most frequently fall into at lease one of the following categories:

1. Illness or Injury:

Persons who are suffering from insulin shock, have severe breathing problems or are in need of a particular medication and can become physically violent until they receive medical attention. Sustaining a head injury, for example, could cause a person to become aggravated. In all of these situations the affected individual may not have control over their actions or even remember what they have done.

2. Emotional Problems or Mental Illness:

Persons with these types of problems may become physically violent or verbally affronting. They could be suffering from severe depression, psychosis, or schizophrenia. These individuals require prompt professional attention. The psychiatric or medical professional may order medication or a change in medication.

3. Substance/Alcohol Abuse or Medication Reaction:

Those who abuse alcohol or other substances such as P.C.P. (animal tranquilizers), cocaine, L.S.D., heroin, the list goes on, are prime candidates for violence. It is not possible to predict behavior patterns without having some indication of the kind of substance involved.

4. Stress:

Stress is often referred to as the "silent killer". Everyone suffers from various levels of stress from time to time. Stress more frequently leads to depression that remains a personal matter. However, individuals that are not able to manager personal stress may be susceptible to severe aggravation which can precede violence directed against others.

5. Anger/Frustration:

These conditions are often exhibited by individuals who lack the common decency to behave in a manner that is socially acceptable. Often the level of individual maturity will dictate the extent of objectionable conduct. But in some cases, the anger and lack of emotional control can lead to any number of violent reactions on the part of the subject.

Stages of Management of Disruptive Behavior

The management of disruptive or violent behavior consists of five states which are conditions a Protection Officer must learn to recognize. They are:

1. Evaluation:

What is going on? Why? Who is involved? Is the Protection Officer, disruptive person or others in immediate danger? Is support needed from fellow officers or resource personnel such as supervisory staff, social worker, medical personnel or police?

2. Planning:

Now that I know what is going on, what do I need to do? How do I do it? Do I have the resources available such as people or equipment? Remember that situations usually start out one-on-one, but should never be permitted to stay that way for long, no longer than it takes to get back-up personnel. Once you have determined your plan of action, whether it be to continue talking, containment, restraint, removal of the person(s), referral or arrest, communicate your decision to team members. When planning seek input from others when possible.

3. Implement:

Put your plan into action. At this state, things may not go the way you anticipated, but regardless, remain calm. A contingency plan can be activated that may be more fitting for the circumstances. In all crisis situations your personal safety is of prime importance. Your actions should be dictated accordingly. Do not attempt to resolve a volatile situation alone. Observe exactly what is happening and position yourself with personal safety in mind and await support staff.

4. Document:

Effective documentation of a crisis incident is vital for future reference and guidance. A well documented report will also serve to provide litigation protection should legal actions result from actions or inactions on the part of crisis respondents. The final report should include the standard WHO, WHAT, WHERE, WHEN, HOW & WHY. Address each of these questions carefully so that the report can be read and understood by all individuals and organizations involved.

5. Review:

This is the final stage of the crisis management phase, but by no means any less important. This is when you critique the entire crisis event. Carefully examine all documentation. It is imperative to openly discuss exactly what happened. It gives all protection personnel involved, the opportunity to vent feelings and frustrations and gain the needed confidence to deal with future similar situations. Talk openly about what happened, why it happened and if it could have been prevented. Could it have been handled more effectively, if so how? This is the reconstruction state that must be managed in a positive manner. It is not a "fault finding mission", rather a time to reflect positively on the actions taken and develop safeguards for future occurrences.

Crisis Development Behavior Levels

During a Crisis Development situation, there are four distinct and identifiable behavior levels:

1. Anxiety
2. Defensive
3. Anger/frustration
4. Tension reduction

For each level there is a demand for a specific response to provide the maximum chance of defusing the crisis:

1. Supportive
2. Directive
3. Non-violent physical crisis intervention
4. Therapeutic rapport

It is important to relate each behavior level to a specific response:

Behavior Level	Response
1. Anxiety: A notable state of dismay/torment.	1. Supportive: Active, friendly, emphatic attempts to alleviate observed behavior.
2. Defensive: Beginning stage of loss of rationality. Unreasonable and challenging.	2. Directive: Set limits, suggest expected outcomes.
3. Anger/frustration: Loss of control, physically acting out.	3. Non-violent Crisis Intervention: Safe, prudent control and restraint techniques.
4. Tension Reduction: Regaining of rationality after physically acting out.	4. Therapeutic Rapport: Communication with individual during reduction.

Protection Officer Guidelines

Written policy and procedures will vary from one organization to another, but there are three basic guidelines that are applicable for any situation. They are:

1. **Remain calm**
2. **Act appropriately**
3. **Be objective**

Do not allow the subject to make you angry or to act inappropriately. To lose your composure will most certainly intensify the situation. Don't become complacent and take anything for granted. Always be alert. In terms of personal protection, never stand directly in front of the individual, this could make them feel threatened. Stand just off to the side, at an angle; this is considered a non-threatening position. Use the person's name, treating them with respect. Keep a minimum of three feet distance between yourself and the subject. This serves two purposes. First it will preserve the individual's personal space and second, it will give you time to react if the individual begins to physically act out. Remember the amount of personal space may vary according to the individual and the situation. For example, if the person is highly agitated, he/she may need more room and coming closer may intensify the crisis. On the other hand, a troubled person may want to have you closer; your presence may be reassuring. Identify the amount of space needed to develop a calming effect.

How to react and how quickly to react will depend on the nature of the disturbance and if there is an immediate threat constituting a safety hazard. If you do not perceive such a threat, use the time to attempt to calm the subject and to continue your evaluation of the situation. If you have an audience, move them or move the situation. Only people that could provide probably support should be allowed to remain in the area. Not spectators.

It is important to know how and why the situation started and always make sure help is available.

Verbal and Physical Disruptive Behavior

When a person is verbally acting out, they may or may not be fully aware of what they are saying or doing. They may express anxiety or defensiveness, make demands or threats or use abusive language. This is especially true when the subject is in insulin shock, having severe breathing difficulties (lack of oxygen to the brain) or has suffered a head injury. These individuals are not usually able to control their actions and may suffer memory loss.

Subjects that are physically violent and require preventative measures can be easily detected by the protection officer. Typically they throw objects or use them as weapons, kick, or attempt to grab or strike other individuals. These physically out of control persons may even try to barricade themselves in a room or a particular area.

Protection Officers need to be aware of the indistict signs of physical acting-out (violence). Certain signs are likely to precede more combative behavior. Watch for indicators such as gritting teeth, closing and opening hands and tensing. These are strong indicators of a possible outbreak of physical aggression.

Emphatic Listening

Emphatic listening is an active process to see through what the person is saying. There are five measures that will enhance the listening and understanding process.

1. Don't be judgemental - Never come on with the attitude, "you caused your own problem". Don't adapt the position that the subject's actions have been carefully thought out with a view to inflict pain or injury to others.

2. Don't fake attention or ignore - If you do ignore the individual, you will not only make them upset, but you will experience difficulty in learning what is really happening. Encourage free flowing communications.

3. Carefully listen to what the subject is really saying - This gives you the opportunity to gain accurate insight into what is actually happening and what may have caused the crisis to develop. Listen for verbal clues that may be used to help defuse the situation.

4. Use silence and listen carefully to clarify message - This technique serves two useful purposes. First it provides you with the opportunity to better understand what the subject is actually trying to say and secondly it indicates that you are genuinely concerned.

5. Reflection can be used to reinforce - When the individual completes their statement, simply communicate words that leave no doubt in the subject's mind that you understand their message. Simply convey to the person that you understand what they have said.

Nonverbal Communications

Nonverbal communication deals with body language. A message that is conveyed to someone without words. Subtle or obvious body movements or gestures that can provide clear indications as to what another person might be thinking. Only 15% of what is said is conveyed by the use of words, while at least 85% of interpersonal communications are nonverbal. Individuals that are functioning under a stressful or emotional state of mind will often communicate even more useful information in a nonverbal manner. Practice identifying what people are saying without words. Some useful points to consider are:

Proxemics or personal space - Respect the subject's personal space which is considered to be 1½ to 3 feet in distance.

Kinesics - Body posture and movement is critical in a crisis situation. Avoid toe to toe or eye to eye gestures that can be presumed as challenging.

Supportive stance - Approximately one leg length away, on an angle and slightly to the side of the individual. This avoids any feelings of encroachment, invasion of personal space and enhances officer safety.

Controlling Disruptive or Violent Behavior

There are a number of useful methods that can be applied to control violent or aggressive behavior such as verbal communications, use of chemicals, physical force or a combination of all three.

Verbally - Assume a neutral body stance, let the individual talk and listen to what they are saying. Do not argue or threaten. Acknowledge feelings and thoughts. This can be achieved without agreeing or disagreeing. Consider voice tone, volume and rate when communicating verbally. Use the person's name and maintain eye contact. It may be necessary to make the subject aware that his/her actions are inappropriate and they will be held accountable for their actions and responsible for the outcome of the situation.

Chemically - In most crisis situations that occur, the Protection Officer seldom has the use of chemicals as a viable option. The decision to chemically control an individual can only be made by qualified medical or psychiatric personnel. Medications that could be used in these instances are generally depressants such as valium, thorazine or haldol. There are other medications to choose from and the qualified medical professional will use what is felt to be most effective after evaluating the behavior of the individual.

Physically - Physical control techniques are used to prevent harm or injury to the individual or others in the immediate vicinity of the incident. Application of physical force should be considered only if no other feasible options are possible. If an individual has to be restrained, non-violent techniques are the logical choice. These techniques are intended for personal safety and self defence and must be taught by a qualified instructor. The primary focus is to protect employees and clients from injury.

Other - Whether or not to use such devices as chemical mace, stun devices or lasers is a question to be addressed by local laws, ordinances and organiztional policy. Intensive training is a must before any consideration can be given to the use of these kinds of protective equipment.

Team Intervention

Team intervention is considered to be the best approach to be used during crisis development. Personnel should use the least restrictive method to control aggressive/disruptive individual(s). The objective, as in almost all volatile conditions that require security intervention, is to defuse the situation in a manner that reduces the risk of guilt, pain or injury.

Positive Factors Resulting from Team Approach

The team should consist of no more than five people which are capable of dealing with a crisis situation. More than five members tends to lead to confusion and a lack of unit cohesiveness. When team action seems inevitable, reserve/resource members should remain out of sight, nearby and ready. Advantages of the team approach are:

1. Team members enjoy more personal safety and a feeling of security resulting from the presence of fellow officers or other support staff.

2. Team members are able to maintain a professional profile becuase of the support and reliance that results from team member interactions.

3. Team members do not feel that the violence or unruly behavior is directed against them personally, rather the team as a whole.

4. Team members can provide verification of actions and inactions which tends to support a legal position in the event of later litigation proceeding being initiated by affected individual(s).

The manner in which you get the team to the scene is vitally important. A mass convergence of staff will be perceived as a show of force and have an unsettling effect on the disruptive individual(s). Try to avoid the attraction of a crowd. Protection Officers should carry two way radios which facilitate effective communication with other team members.

Resource staff that are involved in deployment to the scene must receive pre-incident training and instruction in all facets of the intervention process, particularly methods of communications.

Leadership in the Team Approach

As in any kind of team work approach there has to be a leader/captain. The team leader can be anyone that has special skills, training or expertise that will lend strength and unity to the team. When the leader arrives at the scene, he/she must be prepared to "take over". Additional points to consider when selecting a team leader are:

1. The leader will likely be the first person on the scene. Accessibility to the scene is an important consideration.

2. The leader must be confident.

3. The leader must be familiar with personnel that occupy the facility or facilities that may be a target for a crisis.

4. The leader must be familiar with the physical layout of the facility.

When the event occurs and team action is called for, the team leader must take charge and ensure that the following measures/steps are taken as quickly and prudently as possible.

1. Assess the situation, then determine what action will be taken.

2. Formulate the action plan and put it into play as quickly and effectively as conditions allow.

3. Appraise the team of what is happening. Each team member must know his/her responsibilities. In the event practice/drills have not been conducted the leader must improvise.

4. Begin the communication process. Assess the situation. Take whatever remedial actions are warranted. Activate contingency plan(s) as required. Keep team members appraised.

Safety Considerations in Crisis Intervention

The goal in any crisis situation is to neutralize the threat/risk while maintaining the safety and welfare of everyone involved. Mentally deranged or violent individuals will often resort to throwing objects or try to grab or strike the person they invision as a threat, usually the person in charge, most often the Protection Officer. In these instances, be resourceful, protect yourself with a pillow, chair back, cushions or any object that is readily available. A blanket or coat can be used to help restrain an individual while distracting their attention.

Note the location of windows, doors and furniture in the area. Normally you would not want to block a door with your body, nor would you want the disruptive person between you and the door that may be your only escape route. Stay away from windows. Try to keep the subject away from things that can be used as weapons; chairs, water pitcher, phone, glass, desk accessories and any kind of blunt or sharp objects.

Conclusion

Disruptive individuals can have a serious adverse effect on organizational operations. If such incidents are perceived as a threat by employees it will reduce productivity, lower morale and instill a sense of fear. The presence of a capable, confident Protection Officer, willing and able to effectively communicate with employees will have a stabilizing effect in the workplace.

In a post crisis intervention situation, you, the Protection Officer, may experience anger, fear or frustration; this is a natural reaction that must be controlled. It is not uncommon for the officer to feel that he/she has been the victim. This can result from a real or perceived lack of management support during and after the crisis or being exposed to the crisis for a prolonged period of time. Do everything possible to resolve the crisis in an expeditious manner which will reduce team frustration and apprehension.

Waste no time in committing your thoughts to paper. By prompt-ly composing a well written report you can vividly recall what exactly has happened. Documenting the report will provide a vehicle to vent frustration. Discuss the matter with other team members and most of all do not get discouraged and maintain a positive attitude.

Remember, when crisis intervention is required, stay calm, be objective and act appropriately. Let common sense prevail. Remember the plan for success: EVALUATE, IMPLEMENT, DOCUMENT and REVIEW.

QUIZ
Crisis Intervention

1. Crisis Intervention is a technique of behavioral management which is done by suggesting certain _____ _____ whether by action or what you say.

2. Persons suffering from insulin shock may physically act out and may not have _____ of their actions.

3. Illness or _____ may cause an individual to behave in a disruptive manner.

4. Being complacent during a crisis situation is good; it allows the individual not to know what you are thinking.
☐T ☐F

5. The best stance during a crisis situation is just off to the side at an angle
☐T ☐F

6. Indistinct signs of possible physical acting out, such as gritting teeth, closing and opening of hands and tensing, may preceed more combatitive behavior.
☐T ☐F

7. Experts say that 50% to 65% of the messages we convey are nonverbal.
☐T ☐F

8. Paraverbal communications - how we deliver our words or verbal intervention includes which of the following.
☐ a) Tone
☐ b) Volume
☐ c) Rate
☐ d) All of the above

9. Persons who are behaving in a physically violent manner may be controlled in all of the following ways except:
☐ a) Verbally
☐ b) Challenged
☐ c) Physically
☐ d) Chemically

10. When involved in a one-on-one situation, your first action taken should be:
☐ a) Make a plan of action
☐ b) Do not block the doorway
☐ c) Communicate with the individual
☐ d) Be sure assistance is enroute.

Unit 7

Security Awareness
Security Investigations
Managing Employee Honesty
Substance Abuse

SECURITY AWARENESS

By Charles A. Sennewald CPP

Perhaps the most understated or least appreciated phrase in our industry today is "Security Awareness". Understated because the very thrust, the very objective of any given security program evolves around the issue of awareness of the security efforts' existence.

Consider this. Why do security officers wear a distinctive uniform? Or why do the vehicles they drive bear distinctive markings? Obviously the answer is for visibility, and through that visibility, create awareness in the mind of the observer as to the presence of security.

Webster's Dictionary defines 'awareness' as: 1) Watchful, wary; and 2) Having or showing realization, perception or knowledge.

Interestingly, both definitions apply to security awareness. The potential law-breaker, **if security awareness** has been established, is going to be watchful, is going to be wary of committing a crime where security is present — isn't he? He'll certainly think twice before engaging in an unlawful act.

With respect to the second definition, if a potential culprit realizes security is present, or perceives or believes that security is present or **knows** security measures are in place, the likelihood of crime is certainly reduced, particularly an overt or otherwise conspicuous act.

Security Awareness is a state of mind, based on a reality, a viable reality. That is to say, "I'm going to be wary, as a robber, of the closed circuit television camera in the 24-hour-a-day convenience store. If however, I discover the camera is a dummy, then I need not be watchful or wary of security." Isn't that true?

So the level of quality or impact of Security Awareness, as a state of mind in the eyes of the beholder is directly related to the reality of the security program. Let's examine this issue of reality.

The Reality of Security

Security as a protective program or strategy must be real. Let's use the government mint as an example. Everyone will agree that the mint (the location where our currency is printed) is protected by a security program. There's no question in anyone's mind about that. Everyone is aware of security; hence security awareness!

On the other hand, how many facilities exist where there's no or very little security presence? So 'presence' is a key factor in reality. That is to say, there is physical evidence of the existence of a security program. Back to the uniforms and marked patrol vehicles. There's proof positive. It's for the world to see and recognize that the premises are under the protection of a structured program.

Imagine, if you will, the following facility — an eight-story building surrounded by a parking lot. Entrance to the surrounding lots is through a gate, controlled by a uniformed security officer. On the four corners of the building are exterior-mounted CCTVs monitoring the lots. When you enter the building you're stopped by another uniformed officer. You sign in and are issued a badge. The party you wish to visit is contacted by phone by the officer, and that person comes down the elevator and escorts you to his office. When you leave you are required to sign out and your attache case is inspected.

Compare that to the same facility: an eight-story building surrounded by a parking lot. In this case, however, there's no fence enclosure around the lot. You may enter the property from any number of driveways and park where you please.

There's no obvious or conspicuous CCTV cameras monitoring the lot. When you enter the building, there's no security desk or officer — just a building directory. The visitor locates the office of interest and takes the elevator to the desired floor, and leaves without check or control.

In the first example, there's a security presence. In the second, no presence. In the first example, not only is there a presence, but a **real** presence.

Now it might be determined, over a period of time, that it's not as real as it appears. That is to say, all the security checks and controls are meaningless because you could carry out an IBM electronic typewriter and the guard wouldn't stop you and verify you were entitled to carry it out. And that happens. But by and large, the first example has every appearance of being viable and real.

Now in comparing the two examples — in which facility would it be less likely that a woman would be sexually assaulted in a stairwell or a man robbed at gun-point in the parking lot? Or where a desk-top computer would turn up missing on Monday morning?

Making the Reality of Security Credible

Many organizations fail to buttress or otherwise make the security efforts credible. Put another way, they don't blow the security department's own horn. And they should!

When a robber in the parking lot is thwarted and caught by security; when the guy posing as a computer repairman was intercepted by security as he was leaving the lobby, computer terminal in hand (or on a dolly); when the just-fired employee of the third floor was caught with corporate documents and calculator in his attache case as he was leaving the building, and these instances or success on the part of the security are made known throughout the facility, the security program becomes credible — it works, it's real!

Security awareness is what makes the difference in the mission of the security program; i.e., 'crime or loss prevention'.

Prevention is the bottom line of the security effort. Security departments and their various programs only exist for the purpose of preventing unwanted, undesirable incidents or crimes.

How is this accomplished? Simply stated, 'Prevention through Deterrence'. Deterrence based on security awareness; such awareness created in large measure by presence, real presence.

A few more words about 'real' presence. Real in the sense of this message is essentially qualitative in nature. Certainly, to see a security officer walking through the parking lot, such existence of that officer is real, but if the officer is not alert, not paying attention to his surroundings, not observing the area as he passes through, then his presence loses some value.

The perceptive would-be criminal can tune in to that. So, it is with the officer assigned to a fixed post on the first shift. If he's in the guard shack reading or watching television, he is **present**, but not really in terms of his mission. The same is true with CCTV cameras. Even if they're live and functional; if they're not being monitored, then the security presence is more of a facade and less viable.

So it should be clear that to have a climate or establish a climate of good 'Security Awareness', it must be based on a real presence of security. That means the security officer and his department are the very foundation upon which security awareness is built.

Quality security officers supported by quality equipment. Quality is best measured by three factors (as it pertains to personnel): The care and effort in the selection process (selection of officers); the care and effort in preparing the officers for their work (training of officers), and the daily performance of officers.

If a department hires quality people, adequately trains them, and they conscientiously perform their duties as prescribed by security management, and they have good equipment, then you have a program upon which you can build 'Security Awareness'.

Creating Security Awareness Among Employees

Security awareness, that state of mind on which this chapter has been focusing, is not limited to employees or non-employees, but rather spans the whole spectrum of persons who have occasion to come onto company property.

Typically, the obvious presence of security, and the apparent efficiency of the security officers is sufficient for the infrequent visitor in terms of creating a security awareness.

Employees, on the other hand, pose a different challenge. That's because they frequent the premises on a routine basis and among other reasons, tend not to see the obvious or understand what security is really all about.

Thus management, through a well prepared and structured manner must embark on an education program among employees to ensure a 'Security Awareness' is created and maintained in the work environment.

Anything less than that is not only non-productive, but is counter-productive to the interests of the enterprise. There must be a security awareness program aimed at the employee population.

Various Strategies to Create & Sustain Security Awareness

1) Background Checks

Applicants seeking employment should understand that the security department conducts background investigations to verify former employment and other information given in the application.

That very initial exposure to the existence of security lays a foundation upon which the full impact of 'Security Awareness' can subsequently be built. There are several ways in which this can be communicated — in the employment office, a counter-top sign (or any other kind of sign) could read "Applicants are subject to Bonding"; or "Applicants must submit to a background check by our Security Department".

Another way is on the application itself. Every application I've ever seen requires the applicant's signature. The little paragraph that preceeds the signature frequently is a statement to the effect, all information above is true and accurate and the applicant agrees to having that information verified by the prospective employer.

That statement could be printed in red. Or encircled with a red pen or pencil. And it could be worded to include the word 'security'.

A third way in which this message can be transmitted to the applicant is by the interviewer, who after reviewing the application, could verbally inform the person that his or her background is subject to verification by security.

2) New Employee Orientation

New hire indoctrination programs should include material about the security department. Typically, every new employee — be he the only new hire or be there a group all starting on the same day — go through some form of structured orientation including the typical paperwork of tax withholding, who to contact in emergency, etc.

This is the ideal time to talk in positive terms about the security at the facility, from parking, to badges and all other rules as they pertain to security. This can be particularly effective if done by a uniformed security officer. The subtle impact here is: If it's important enough to talk about, it must be important.

Every new job means new rules to follow. Some employees may resent some of the new rules, such as wearing a badge. If the reasons are explained and if, as an example, no badge -no entry - rules apply, the new employee will not resent the security officer who denies entry, but rather will be angry (if at all) with himself for not following the rules.

More importantly, it makes the security function stand out as an important part of the company (anything that affects the employee personally ...like not getting in to work because of not wearing a badge, is important), and that enhances Security Awareness.

3) Security Signing and Posters

The conspicuous placement of security messages, such as cartoon posters, very subtly re-enforces the level of security awareness in the employee population. Some posters and messages are generic or off-the-shelf, available for purchase by any company, e.g., "Secure our Future by Securing your Files from Prying Eyes".

Or the messages/posters can be unique to the company, e.g., "Security at North Star is Everyone's Business; not Just Security's".

The point is: The 'presence' of the posters and signs underscores the efforts of maintaining awareness of security.

4) Paycheck Messages

Today in our computerized world, how easy it is to program the printing of paychecks to include security messages which will help perpetrate security awareness. Most checks have a tear-off part or stub, typically showing deductions from the gross salary/pay. Computer-typed across the stub could be such messages as: "Shortages erode Profits"; "From Profits come Expansion"; "Expansion means more Jobs & Opportunities for Advancement"; or "Everyone's Goal should be to Help Reduce Losses".

5) Communicating Security Events Through Policy

This fifth way of contributing to Security Awareness is through the adoption of company policy that requires communicating, in some detail, security-related events down to the line employee. Too often in the past security incidents in the company were viewed as confidential. Yet, some of the information would leak out into the grapevine and more often than not, get distorted.

Such distortion usually went against management's best interests. Example: Harry Doe, a janitor, was caught stealing by hiding parts in the trash which he pushed from the facility early every morning. The janitorial supervisor and other janitors didn't know what Harry did. All they know is he was fired. Speculation among the janitors was the company just wanted to reduce the staff and they looked for a reason to fire someone. Harry was caught taking the trash out of the wrong door so Security had him fired.

The policy of having the janitorial supervisor called to the office and advised by management that one of his janitors had just been caught stealing by the security department, and was at that moment on his way to jail has many benefits.

Note the fact I said "one of his janitors". Never identify an employee (or ex-employee) involved in a crime, by name. Now this supervisor knows the capabilities of the security department; i.e., they are not just a scarecrow, they have detection skills.

The policy then should require the supervisor to call his employees together that day or the next most opportune time and advise them that one of their ranks was caught by the security department stealing. Incidentally, everyone will know the identity of the culprit; it's just that management doesn't say it. Now the entire staff knows what actually happened. No room for unfair rumors which mitigate against management or security. And they all know what the supervisor knows — security has talent. That's positive presence. That's good Security Awareness.

6) Communication Through the Written Word

Many companies publish a newsletter or monthly magazine. This is an ideal instrument through which word about the security department, its concerns, problems, objectives, successes and its needs can be transmitted.

No company publication should be without at least one article about the security department or one of its interesting cases.

I'm a great supporter and advocate for a regular column, usually written by the Security Chief or Director of Security. The column could include the chief's photo so people recognize this executive. Such visibility, such recognition of the security department's 'presence' in the company, creates and perpetuates Security Awareness.

If, by chance, the company doesn't have its own monthly publication, the security department could prepare its own newsletter, depending of course on the size of the company and the number of employees.

I ran a security department with approximately 200 employees working in a firm with over 20,000 employees scattered over 50 sites in several states. The company itself did not have a publication, so I wrote a newsletter (ostensibly for security people only) about what was happening throughout the company as it related to security. That publication gained such popularity it was sought after by management generally, and subsequently the contents were shared by company management with their employees (non-security personnel).

Later, the company came out with its own non-security publication, but it carried messages regarding security and the importance of loss prevention. The power of the written word is something to reckon with.

7) Security Awareness Through the Spoken Word

One of the most interesting and dynamic ways of communicating to the employee population is through the spoken word, the personal presentation of a security department representative. Such representative need not necessarily be the chief or director, it could be any security employee who is comfortable and competent to speak before groups.

Every organization of any size has a continuum of inter-company meetings regarding all sorts of topics. Whoever is responsible for conducting such meetings has the difficult task of laying out an agenda to cover the topics required and at the same time to make the meeting interesting. If the meeting is interesting, everyone is happy and complimentary of the meeting's organizer. If the meeting is dull, the organizer takes criticism and flak.

What could be more interesting than to have an articulate and personable security employee speak at the meeting of supervisors about the two teenagers who were caught pulling products out through the skylight by rope last Sunday? Caught by Security!

Imagine the comments later. "Who would ever think of getting stuff out of this plant that way?" "I wonder if that's what happened to some of the missing materials in my area." "You gotta give the security department a hand for that one!"

No question, this interesting bit of information will be passed on to the vast majority of employees. And the question of presence and the issue of security's capabilities, the whole protection program is again in focus for the employee population. And the bottom line, again, is 'Security Awareness'.

Now it's important to note, before I leave this subject that the purpose of the presentations isn't simply to glorify security or to tell interesting war stories. There's a message for every presentation.

As an example, if the meeting was for supervisors of the company, the ultimate message by the security representative could well be that of "Every supervisor shares in the responsibility of protecting the assets of this company". It's part of being a supervisor. Supervisors need not view themselves as company policemen, but on the other hand as management's representatives. They have a duty to prevent loss through good supervisory skills, by being alert, and letting subordinates know they are alert, by reporting suspicious circumstances on up to their bosses or directly to security, by setting a good example, by correcting or not allowing griping about security rules and regulations, etc.

No matter what section or department of the company meets to discuss their particular areas of interest and concern, it will somehow tie-in with a security message. If it's the engineering department, levels of illumination for better security could be the message. If it's personnel/human resources people, perhaps the message could be about the selection of applicants. There's virtually no area of any company where security doesn't impact, directly or indirectly.

8) Employee Involvement and Participation

Surely an outstanding example of perpetuating Security Awareness among employees is to get them involved, get them to share in the security effort.

One way to do that is to form a Security or Loss Prevention Committee, comprised of representatives from all areas of the company, e.g., shipping, manufacturing, receiving, quality control, personnel, office administration, finance, etc. The purpose of the committee is to review security procedures and practices as they exist and how they might be modified, altered and/or improved.

That's called giving employees "ownership". If you own something, then you become possessive or protective — right? So if the security activities, policies, programs and problems belong to the employees, they are far more supportive of such effort than if the security department was perceived as an arm of management.

Such security committees are particularly useful in bringing about desired change. Example: It appears as though the best control of theft of hand tools and small parts would be through a lunch-pail inspection program (hand-carried containers). The initial discussions about such change could be held by the security committee. Once the committee adopts the plan, they can be charged with the task of going out into the plant and 'selling' the idea to all employees. The 'sell' is usually along the lines of "If you open your lunchbox for inspection, you'll never be suspected of theft".

On the other hand, if management simply makes the decision to inspect containers, the adverse reaction by the employee population could be a problem.

As an alternative to forming a security committee, consider converting the existing safety committee into a combined Safety & Security Committee. It can deal with both safety concerns (as they pertain to injuries and accidents), as well as security (crimes).

In this case, both the committee's existence and employee membership and involvement represent Security Awareness.

9) Employee Recognition Programs

There are a number of programs that sustain security awareness through recognizing employee involvement or assistance.

One example would be a security-oriented contest, such as seeking entries to a company-wide security poster contest. The winner would receive some pre-determined prize such as $100 and his or her security poster would be duplicated and displayed throughout the company.

Another possibility is an employee reward/award program whereby employees who assist security, provide confidential information leading to the arrest and/or recovery of company property or in some other fashion materially benefits the company's efforts to reduce loss, prevent crime or solve security-related problems, receive monetary recognition.

In some such programs the recognition can be public; i.e., in front of all employees. In others, particularly the program where confidential information is provided, the individual recognition cannot be made, but it can be publicized in the company or security newsletter that a $1,500 award was just made to an employee who shall remain anonymous. Very effective, in terms of sustaining Security Awareness in the company.

Conclusion

Security Awareness is essentially a state of mind, a recognition of the presence of a security program aimed at reducing loss and preventing crime on company property. The security program must be perceived as real and credible.

Security awareness is important in discouraging 'outsiders' as well as employees, but particular effort is required to sustain such awareness among employees.

Suggested ways to accomplish that include:

1) Background checks;
2) New employee orientation;
3) Security signing & posters;
4) Paycheck messages;
5) Communication through policy;
6) Communication through the written word;
7) Through the spoken word;
8) Employee involvement and participation; and
9) Employee recognition program.

QUIZ
Security Awareness

1. Security awareness is a _____ of mind. (Fill in the blank)

2. For security awareness to exist, security must have

a _____ (Fill in the blank)

3. Employees who participate on a security committee

feel they have some _____ in the security program. (Fill in the blank)

4. If there's a real presence of security, it is less likely a crime will occur.

☐ T ☐ F

5. Uniforms help create security awareness.

☐ T ☐ F

6. It's probably best to conceal CCTV cameras so no one knows they're present.

☐ T ☐ F

7. Employees automatically have Security Awareness.

☐ T ☐ F

8. Security awareness helps:

☐ a) increase productivity
☐ b) decrease morale
☐ c) reduces crime
☐ d) none of the above

9. Employees feel "ownership" when:

☐ a) they're advised what's happening
☐ b) they're involved in the decisions
☐ c) they're recognized for what they do
☐ d) none of the above.

10. Security committees should:

☐ a) be involved in security plans
☐ b) not be involved in security plans
☐ c) not be connected with safety
☐ d) should only be made up of security people

SECURITY/LOSS CONTROL
INVESTIGATIONS

Christopher A. Hertig, CPP, CPO

Many people greatly underestimate the importance of investigation within the security field. There seems to be a feeling that investigation is a highly specialized process which is performed only by police or supervisors who wear trench coats with their collars turned up and have cigarettes dangling from their lips. Perhaps this perception results from being inundated over the years by movies and television. Perhaps it is rooted in a condescending attitude towards security officers. Whatever the cause(s); there needs to be a readjustment of attitudes if security practitioners are to accomplish any meaningful loss control objectives.

Investigation is an integral aspect of a protection officer's job function

Investigation and loss control go hand-in-hand.

Protection officers serve as management representatives, enforcement/compliance agents, and intelligence agents. As intelligence agents, protection officers collect information for management. This can relate to crime, unauthorized activity, or any other potential loss causing situation (Waste, Accident, Error, Crime and Unethical/ Unprofessional Practices).

Investigation has nothing to do with attractive members of the opposite sex, great clothes, gunfights, or flashy cars. It is not glamorous. It is tedious and exacting. It has to do with fact-finding and research. **Investigation is simply an objective process used to discover facts about a situation, person, or behavior.** Once those facts are discovered, they are recorded in an appropriate manner. Investigation has a great deal to do with writing reports.

Investigation is important because without facts, management cannot make the correct decisions. As the security officer is an *adjunct member of the management team*, it is his/her duty to provide management with information. He/she reports this information after conducting some type of investigative activity (searching for something, questioning people, observing something, etc.).

Preliminary Investigations
This is the most important aspect of the investigative process. It is also the investigative stage that security personnel (or uniformed police officers) generally get involved with. The preliminary investigation is the initial fact-finding component of the investigative process. It is performed when the crime or incident is first discovered, and is crucial to the success of the follow-up investigative effort. Preliminary investigation consists of several key steps.

1.   Attending to injured persons. This must be the first priority!
2.   Detaining those who have committed the crime, being investigated.
3.   Finding and questioning witnesses.   A neighborhood canvass of the area to seek out witnesses should be performed as soon as possible.
4.   Preserving the crime/incident scene for evidentiary purposes. **Protect, preserve, make notes.** Control access to the scene, take photographs, and note your observations.
5.   Forwarding information about the incident to the dispatcher, central alarm station, (CAS) or the shift supervisor.
6.   Completing a preliminary report, so that the follow-up investigators have adequate information with which to proceed.

Follow-Up Investigation
This step in the process begins where the preliminary investigation ends. It is a process of examining the information provided by the preliminary report and proceeding to uncover additional data until the case is solved - a complete understanding of the event is attained. Obviously, the success of the follow-up investigation is heavily dependent upon the preliminary investigative effort. Without adequate records, evidence or witnesses, little or nothing can be determined; even if the follow-up investigator is extraordinarily proficient.

Follow-up investigations may be completed by the officer who performed the preliminary investigation, but in most cases they are handled by investigative specialists, police detectives or supervisory personnel. For this reason, close liaison must exist between those conducting the preliminary investigation and those with follow-up investigative duties.

Notes and Reports
Notes are the foundation of a report. It is sometimes said that testifying - *the last* step in the investigative process - begins with note taking. Without adequate notes on the crucial details, there can be no effective report, follow-up investigation, or testimony. Reports are what make or break investigators. They are the summation of the investigators (or protection officer's) work. The saying **"You are what you write."** is very true. Key points on note-taking and report writing are:

*   Think of notes as aids in remembering key details. Don't think of them as another chore to do.

*   Periodically check notes. Summarize what is written to witnesses giving statements so that you are sure to get the information correctly recorded. This should always be done at the conclusion of an interview; it can also be done at various junctures throughout the interview process.

*   Use abbreviations judiciously. If they are commonly known abbreviations, use them, Make certain that the abbreviation used is correct and that

anyone reading the notes would understand it. *"If there is any doubt, spell it out"*.

* Use rough sketches in notes to pictorially represent incident scenes.

* **Treat notes as the part of the official record that they are.** Start each set of notes on a new page. Number each page. Write in ink and cross out and initial each correction that must be made.

Auditing

Auditing is something in which loss control personnel should be involved. An audit is simply a check (or investigation) as to whether or not operations are proceeding as expected. There are operations audits which determine if procedures are being followed as well as financial audits to see if there are any fiscal irregularities. Audits can take many forms, depending upon the organization's present need:

* Security officers audit locks and alarms to maintain the integrity of the physical security system. They may also do audits of the fire protection system or of safety procedures on a weekly/monthly/quarterly basis.

* Security supervisors audit reports, procedures, personnel performance, and training/certification records of protection officers to ensure that things are being done the way they are supposed to be.

* Security managers audit policies, procedures and training records to see that services are being properly given to client firms.

* Increasingly, we will see managers and supervisors auditing for compliance with standard setting organizations such as government agencies, insurance carriers and the Joint Commission on the Accreditation of Health Care Organization, International Association of Campus Law Enforcement Administrators, etc.

* Accountants and/or fraud examiners perform financial audits of records such as payroll, accounts receivable, purchasing, or petty cash.

* Forensic accountants may review individual points of sale in retail facilities, parking garages, or bars/restaurants.

Audits enable the auditor to spot irregularities. This can mean a lack of commitment to proper work procedures caused by inadequate training, poor supervision, or demoralized job holders. It may mean that the level of service being given by the organization is not up to standard and changes are necessary! It can also signal attempts at thefts, completed thefts, or simply the opportunity to commit thefts. Audits are often the starting point of an investigation; the basic leads being uncovered during routine audits. In other cases, they are part of the follow-up investigation. In these instances, the investigator needs to either expand or narrow the focus of the inquiry. Conducting an audit can help to make this determination.

When conducting an audit, there are several important points to remember:

1. Compare the job behavior, procedures or conditions with clearly defined, measurable standards, such as written instructions, procedures, post orders, etc. The analysis of the job behavior (e.g. not signing in visitors) or conditions, (e.g. faulty alarms) must be the objective.

2. Communicate the purpose of audits to all employees. Obtain the positive cooperation of those who have input into the audit process.

3. Conduct audits in a fair and uniform manner with a set standard that relates to everyone and is used to evaluate everyone.

4. Utilize a variety of techniques. Each technique gives the investigator a specific type of information. Each provides the auditor with a particular perspective. Use a combination of techniques to see the whole picture.

5. Document the results of audits. Professional reports are essential.

6. Evaluate and review audits with relevant personnel. An exit briefing is one means of doing this. In an exit briefing, the auditor briefly discusses his or her findings with management prior to the submission of a complete report. This gives management rapid feedback upon which to make necessary modifications.

7. Follow the chain of command, be tactful, and make sure that the information gets to the right people - and only those people.

As with any type of investigation, there are a variety of approaches to auditing. Each approach has its strengths and weaknesses; each has its time and place. Some that may be of use include:

1. Document review by either systematic (every document in a set) or random selection (a sample of documents in a set).

2. Deliberate error technique where an error is deliberately made to see if it is detected. An example would be a mis-priced item at a point of sale (POS) terminal.

3. Drills are good ways to evaluate the performance of both systems and personnel. These must be done safely, and in such a manner that they are not overly disruptive! In most cases, drills can be 'compartmentalized' so that someone only needs to describe (orally or in writing) the procedures to be followed. Another method is to have the scenario limited to a single department or unit. Full-scale scenarios are often not feasible, even though exercises involving the entire protection operation and outside agencies are the best "final examination" possible for a security system.

4. Observation of job behavior or systems is a simple technique which can still provide useful information. This can be with the unaided eye, or by reviewing videotape (openly taken) of someone performing job tasks.

5.   Interviewing personnel is a method which may be used to investigate job practices. In addition to one-on-one interviews, survey forms can be used.

6.   A conference held with supervisors is a technique often used by managers to investigate workplace problems, practices, and procedures. This can be scheduled within regular supervisor meetings or as a separate meeting prior to an external audit by a government agency or accrediting body.

Interviews

The conducting of interviews is something that security officers do all the time. In many cases, these interviews are conducted informally. Whether formal or informal, an interview is a conversation with the objective of obtaining information. Loss control practitioners who are adept at their jobs can collect information from *every conversation*. Some basic rules of interviewing are:

1.   Be pleasant, friendly and helpful to the interviewee. They are taking their time out to help you!

2.   Thank people for their help, and always end an interview on a positive note. Providing them with a business card to contact you with if they can think of anything else is a positive way to continue the relationship.

3.   Ask open ended questions which require an explanation rather than a simple yes or no answer.

4.   Use silence - "the long pause" - after a person has answered a question. Most people will feel obligated to continue the conversation and add more detail.

5.   Interview in a private, quiet setting.

6.   Take notes in a manner that records the key data but does not impede the interview by making the interviewee uncomfortable.

7.   Put the person at ease with a smile, joke or off-the-subject questions (sports, family, current events). Also make the person comfortable; offer them a seat and sit next to them (picture the seating arrangements that TV talk show hosts use). This helps to establish rapport.

Interrogation

Interrogations are different from interviews in that an interrogation is an interview which focuses upon a person as a suspect. It is conducted after a substantial amount of information from other sources indicates guilt of an individual. Interrogations are conversations with the purpose of acquiring information, but with the obtaining of admissions of guilt, or a full confession from the subject, as the final objective. They are focused interviews. They should not be conducted by inexperienced and untrained individuals! Unfortunately, there are instances where a protection officer may come upon someone committing a crime or policy violation. In these cases a brief focused interview is appropriate.

Some techniques for interrogation are:

1.   Be non-accusatory. Do not blame or accuse the subject. If the facts are wrong and they are not guilty there is an obvious problem. Additionally, setting up a hostile relationship does no good. The investigator must 'sell' the subject on telling the truth.

2.   Discuss the seriousness of the incident with the person being interrogated. This is helpful in those cases where the individual falsely believes that they can act with impunity, that it is "no big deal".

3.   Request that the subject tell the story several times. Inconsistencies can be better noted in this way.

4.   Appeal to the emotions of the subject. Let him/her know that everybody makes mistakes. Allow the subject to rationalize what they have done. Allow them to minimize the harm that has occurred. Allow them to project blame onto someone or something else.

5.   Point out inconsistencies in the story to the subject.

6.   Confront the subject with part of the evidence. Be careful! Never show your whole hand.

There are various legal restrictions active during interrogation. Basically these standards do not allow any use of force, threats or intimidation. The Miranda decision required all law enforcement personnel in the United States to advise suspects of their rights before asking them any questions which focus upon them as the suspect, and which are asked in a "custodial" setting. Failure to follow these procedures will result in all evidence obtained via the illegal questioning being excluded from criminal proceedings (Exclusionary Rule).

While in most states, private security personnel are not bound to the Miranda decision, a few courts have placed this obligation upon them. All U.S. courts place Miranda standards upon private persons who are acting at the direction, request, or in close cooperation with public law enforcement personnel. Obviously, Miranda relates, if the security officer has any type of police powers.

Another standard which the United States Supreme Court imposed upon employers is the Weingarten Rule. Under Weingarten, any time that an interview is held with an employee that could reasonably be expected to result in disciplinary action, the employee is entitled to representation by a union steward or other individual. This rule is limited to those employees who are represented by a collective bargaining unit. Failure to comply will result in an unfair labor practice charge being filed through the National Labor Relations Board. Discipline imposed as a result of the illegal interview will be set aside in an arbitration hearing.

While unlike Miranda, in that management is not obligated to advise the employee of this right; once the employee asks for a representative (union steward or co-worker), the interview must cease until the representative arrives - provided the representative is reasonably available. Employees cannot ask for a rep. on vacation simply to avoid being interviewed! In these cases, the, interview may proceed without the representative present.

There are legal obligations to caution persons being interrogated. There are also other considerations to be addressed within the legal arena. As a general rule, the following procedures can save security practitioners a considerable amount of trouble in court:

1. Review the case thoroughly before starting the interrogation. The more that is known about the incident or scheme, the better. This is where good preliminary investigation comes into play.

2. Interrogate in private, but remove all possible suggestions of duress such as weapons, locked doors and intimidating individuals.

3. Avoid making threats or promises.

4. Never physically touch a subject!

5. If the subject is of the opposite sex, do not question alone. Have a member of the same sex present.

6. Advise the suspect of his/her rights, if there is any chance of an obligation to do so.

7. Have the suspect sign each page of the statement and initial all corrections. (There should be some corrections so that the integrity of the document can be clearly demonstrated in court).

8. Have someone witness the statement.

9. Use the statement as supporting evidence; not the entire case!

10. Make sure the statement is in the subject's own words; that it is dated and signed.

Informants
Informants are a key tool in many types of investigation. Often informants provide basic leads which alert loss control personnel to the presence of a problem. They are of particular importance when investigating the activities of a social network such as substance abuse, sabotage, gambling, and internal theft investigations. There are several kinds of informants operating under different types of motivation:

1. A desire to assist the investigator, either through public spiritedness, or a feeling of indebtedness to the investigator.
2. A need to 'play cop'.
3. Revenge against a criminal competitor.
4. Manipulation of the investigator.
5. Financial gain.
6. The investigator 'having them over a barrel' and the informant wants leniency.

Investigators using informants should try and understand their motivation. They should investigate their background and fully comprehend any and all relationships that they have had with the subjects.

Other tips for dealing with informants include:

1. Treat all informants with dignity and respect. While most informants are good people, the occasional criminal informant will also be used for leads/information. Avoid using demeaning terms to describe informants; they perform a valuable service! Also, the use of such terms is hardly professional.

2. Keep informants 'at arm's length'. Avoid close personal involvement with them. Many informants are master manipulators who attempt to obtain confidential information from the investigator.

3. Closely evaluate the value of the information that has been given by them.

4. Attempt to verify through independent sources the accuracy of the information. Don't rely solely on the information that an informant provides to build a case for prosecution! Corroborate with other evidence.

5. Keep a 'tight rein' on the informant; don't let them represent themselves as members of the security or police organization. Don't allow them to do anything that is unauthorized or illegal - some informants perceive that they have a license to commit crimes!

6. Take care of the legitimate needs of the informant. Assist them when possible in finding work, transportation, child care, etc.

7. "Telephone tipsters" should be kept on the line as long as possible! They should be interviewed. They should NOT be given any confidential information. They should be thanked and asked to call back in the future if they have any additional information.

Undercover Investigations
Occasionally there arises the need for an undercover investigator. Generally, there is no need for them, except when other techniques (surveillance, informants) have failed to yield information, or when the special perspective available to an undercover operative is needed. Undercover investigation is a very expensive and risky method to use! For this reason, it should not be used unless it is absolutely necessary. It should only be performed by competent professionals who specialize in this type of work. In order to use the technique to the greatest advantage, the following considerations must be weighed:

1. The objectives of the investigation must be clearly defined.

2. The entire situation must be carefully weighed from all angles (legal, labor relations, economic, operations). UC investigations can easily cause more serious problems than they rectify!

3. Strict confidentiality on a 'need to know' basis must be maintained. Many operations are compromised due to the persons being investigated finding out about it.

4. The proper agent must be selected. They must have the necessary job skills to fit in with the work environment. They must be sociable and dedicated enough to see things through when difficult decisions (turning in friends, accompanying suspects during illegal activities, staying on the job when illegal activities are not occurring) must be made.

5. Liaison with law enforcement agencies for the purpose of gathering information or prosecuting suspects. This can compromise the agent. It can also create numerous other problems if not done properly.

6.   Corroborate the agent's testimony with other evidence. Agents may not be creditable with arbitrators, judges or juries!

Surveillance

Surveillance is an essential investigative activity to loss control practitioners. It can be stationary ("plant" or "stakeout"), mobile or contact (electronic tracking devices or invisible dyes). There are various objectives that surveillance can accomplish:

1.   Identify suspects in a crime.
2   Record the movements and associations of suspects.
3.   Identify patterns of criminal or unauthorized activity.
4.   Collect information for prosecution.
5.   Locate and apprehend suspects.
6.   Prevent crimes from being committed. This can be done via overt or covert surveillance.

Once objectives have been identified, the planning process can begin. The entire planning process consists of the following steps:

1.   Establish the objective of the surveillance. Write a clear, concise sentence or two as to why you are doing this.

2.   Reconnoiter the area that the surveillance will be conducted in. Examine it for avenues of entry and exit as well as vantage points from which to observe. There should be several of these!

3.   Collect as much information as possible on the background(s) of the subject(s).

4.   Calculate the personnel requirements. A minimum of two (2) people will be needed if the surveillance lasts for any appreciable period of time or if there is danger present.

5.   Establish communication. Cell phones, radios and phone booths as a back up method can all be used.

6.   Calculate equipment needs. Equipment may consist of binoculars, videotape units, log or report forms, possible weapons and disguises.

If surveillance operations are planned properly, the chances for success are much higher. As the costs of initiating surveillance activities are high, it certainly behooves the loss control investigator to carefully scrutinize all aspects of the operation before precious time and money are wasted. Special attention must be devoted to communications, and the response to incidents. Investigators must decide what may occur, and how they will react to it. When this is considered, personnel, and equipment needs can be addressed in a logical manner.

Recording of activity observed during a surveillance must be done with care. A sample log for a stationary surveillance is as follows:

Location/Objective (an introductory paragraph):

Date:

Time (all activity occurring at a specific point in time is detailed):

Attachments (photographs, sketches, etc.):

Summary (brief concluding comments on observations):

Behavior Analysis

Another tool which investigators can use is behavior analysis. Whenever there is a crime or accident, the behavior of the perpetrator and/or victim can be examined and analyzed. The behavior can be divided into three (3) segments.

1.   **The behavior which occurred before the incident.** This can provide valuable insight into the criminal method of operation, and can also be used for analyzing vulnerability. A better understanding of what took place can be developed, and future prevention efforts can be more effectively developed. Examples of this might be the approach/entry used by a robber at the target. What protection was given to the target? Who would know what the target was? Who would be attracted to that type of target ("score")? What kind of insurance coverage was held by the victim? When applied to crimes or accidents, contributing factors to the event can be identified. What was the physical, mental and emotional condition of the victim? What was the lighting and noise level? Would anyone gain by making a false report? What was the victim doing at the crime/accident scene?

2.   **The actual incident itself.** What actually took place during the robbery? What did the robber say and do? What happened during the accident? What did the burglar do when inside the premises?

3.   **The behavior immediately after the incident should be identified and examined.** How did the robber make his escape? Where did the burglar exit from? How was the accident handled? What did the victim or perpetrator say? Who reported it? To whom was it reported? When was it reported?

Once all the behaviors in an incident are identified, it becomes much easier to analyze and understand the incident. Developing a list of questions for each phase of the event also helps to unfold lines of inquiry and perform a more complete investigation. While this technique is commonly used to investigate robbery, burglary, and homicide, there is no reason to limit its application to all types of cases. Embezzlement, passing bad checks, credit card fraud, accidents, bombings, fires, and chemical spills can all be dissected in this manner.

Testifying in Legal and Quasi-Legal Proceedings

Once a case has been investigated, it may become necessary to present it in a court, disciplinary hearing or labor arbitration. Officers are also called upon to give depositions in civil suits. In many cases, the officer will testify in several different legal arenas: one never knows precisely where an incident will be decided! Each of these procedures has a different format, and takes place in a different environment; but all require the providing of factual information in a professional manner. Each of these proceedings places the officer on the opposing side of the defendant, plaintiff, etc. It is usually "your word against his". During these proceedings, the successful investigator does everything possible to win the battle of credibility.

Some things to bear in mind when testifying in court are:

1.   Always be positive. Project a positive, affirmative image. Sell yourself to the judge, magistrate, jury, etc.

2.   Be neat, clean and conservatively dressed: "dress as if going on a job interview". Project a businesslike, professional image. Avoid dressing or talking like a cop or soldier.

3.   Sit and stand erect with shoulders squared. Face and look at the jury and judge. Be serious! You are accountable for what you say.

4.   Project your voice to the jury or judge. Maintain eye contact with them. Address them when you're talking to them.

5.   Answer 'yes' or 'no' to questions posed by counsel or the judge. Don't clarify or elaborate on your answers unless it is necessary to do so. If you must clarify a point, choose your words carefully, and know what you're going to say before you open your mouth. Consider before the proceeding what questions you may be asked!

6.   Have the case prepared before trial. Any reports or evidence presented must be carefully prepared. Consult counsel about the case beforehand to ensure that preparation is adequate. Go over the case, review evidence and plan a strategy with the guidance of counsel. Review your notes before the proceeding starts.

7.   Any notes or reports taken to the stand may be examined by the opposing attorney. Be critical of, and careful with, notes for this reason. Don't simply read from notes; consult them only if necessary. Don't take something that could cause embarrassment and a loss of credibility. Be critical of notes and reports!

8.   Avoid any show of sarcasm, conceit, or disgust with the defendant. Be objective and unemotional. Don't be afraid to say something positive about the defendant.

9.   Never try to argue with the judge or attorney. Be polite and professional, addressing them appropriately as "Sir", "Ma'am", or "Your Honor", etc. Find out how to properly address them beforehand.

10.   If unsure as to what occurred, say so. Don't be afraid to admit you don't know something or aren't sure. If you are sure, state so in a positive, affirmative manner. Try to avoid saying "I think" or any other expression which displays uncertainty.

11.   If you don't understand a question, ask that it be repeated, or that you simply don't understand it.

12.   Don't be afraid to admit that you're wrong, and be honest in all matters.

Managing Investigations.

Just as investigation is an integral part of management, so too is management an essential element within the investigative process. If the investigative effort is not carefully controlled, man-hours will be wasted, confidentiality may be compromised, and objectives will not be met. To begin with, the individual investigator must have personal management skills. He or she must set objectives, make daily priorities, and manage time effectively. Proper filing and administration of records is important. Critically evaluating one's own work is crucial.

In an organizational sense, investigations must be managed by a series of procedures and controls. Some of the techniques that should be considered when supervising an investigation include:

1.   Selecting and assigning investigators properly. Only the most qualified and efficient personnel should be entrusted with investigative duties. Individual cases should be assigned in accordance with the individual expertise of the investigator.

2.   Investigators must be properly trained in the basics of investigation (interviewing, report writing, surveillance, interrogations, etc.) before assuming investigative responsibilities. They must also be trained in specialized areas (narcotics, fraud, espionage, undercover, etc.) should they be assigned these investigative duties. Training needs must be analyzed carefully. Periodic upgrading must be done in regards to legal and technological development.

3.   All investigations should have clearly defined objectives. These objectives should be observable and measurable. The effectiveness of the investigative effort can be gauged by assessing whether or not the objective was met, how quickly it was met, and what the total costs in man-hours expended and other expenses were.

4.   Case work sheets should be designed to meet the needs of individual organizations. These forms list dates, investigator's names, case numbers, persons contacted, time invested, expenses, and results of contacts. Their efficient design and utilization are a must for the investigative effort to be properly administered in a cost-effective manner.

5.   Forms for efficiently reviewing reports can also be used to great effect. These forms enable supervisors to objectively audit reports submitted by security officers or investigators. Their use helps to streamline the investigative process while at the same time ensures that errors are caught early enough to prevent disaster.

6.   Coordination of the investigation with persons who have a "need to know" is important. Law enforcement agencies and victims should be kept informed of the progress of the investigation for several reasons, such as maintaining supportive relationships, and receiving additional information. Special concern must be given to the victim who needs moral support and a clear explanation of judicial procedure if they are to feel comfortable with seeing through the prosecution process.

Investigations can be supervised and evaluated through a number of techniques. As with auditing, no single technique is adequate to provide a complete assessment. Using several methods in concert with each other provides the best results.

1.   Statistical analysis of numbers of apprehensions, conviction rates, recovery amounts, and numbers of complaints against the investigator, can also be used as indicators of job performance.

2.   An on-the-job visit can always be used as a technique. As it is limited in its effectiveness, and lacks objectivity, it must be used in conjunction with other evaluative methods.

3.   Review of investigative reports. This gives the supervisor a quick feel for how the investigator is performing.

Resources:

American Society for Industrial Security (703) 522-5800 or www.asisonline.org has a Standing Committee on Investigations. The Society also has an extensive library of books and videos for members to borrow or purchase.

Association of Certified Fraud Examiners (800) 245-3321 or www.cfenet.com The Association sponsors the Certified Fraud Examiner (CFE) designation, as well as produces a number of computer-based home study programs. There are also local chapter meetings and seminars in various locations.

Butterworth-Heinemann (800) 366-2665 or www.bh.com/sec. offers numerous investigative texts such as LEGAL GUIDELINES FOR COVERT SURVEILLANCE IN THE PRIVATE SECTOR, CORPORATE CRIME INVESTIGATION, THE ART OF INVESTIGATIVE INTERVIEWING, REPORT WRITING FOR SECURITY PERSONNEL, and many others.

CRC Press Inc. (800) 272-7737 offers several investigative texts. THE RETAILER'S GUIDE TO LOSS PREVENTION AND SECURITY, by Donald Horan, is an outstanding book with chapters on Investigation, Audits, and Employee Dishonesty.

International Foundation for Protection Officers (360) 733-1571 or www.ifpo.com publishes CAREERS IN SECURITY AND INVESTIGATION, as well as THE PRIVATE INVESTIGATOR'S PROFESSIONAL DESK REFERENCE. The Foundation sponsors both the Certified Protection Officer (CPO), and Certified Security Supervisor (CSS), designations and has membership opportunities available to protection officers and investigators.

Professional Training Resources (802) 447-7832 or ptrbooks@sover.net, publishes a wide variety of investigative texts. Charles Nemeth's PRIVATE SECURITY AND THE INVESTIGATIVE PROCESS contains numerous forms for investigators and discusses aspects of investigation not found in most texts.

QUIZ
Security/Loss Control Investigations

1. When testifying in court, it is important not to argue with the opposing_____.

2. When preparing a case for trial, arbitration hearing, etc., it is important to review all of the _____.

3. The two most important areas of basic training for an investigator are espionage and narcotic investigation techniques.
  ☐ T   ☐ F

4. Personal management skills that the individual investigator must have include:
  ☐ a.)financial management
  ☐ b.)accounting
  ☐ c.)computer programming
  ☐ d.)time management

5. Interrogations should be non_____in nature.

6. When testifying in court, it is important to answer questions as briefly as possible, without elaborating on unnecessary details.
  ☐ T   ☐ F

7. Analyzing pre-event behavior and conditions can identify all of the following except:
  ☐ a.)vulnerability to loss
  ☐ b.)reporting procedures
  ☐ c.)criminal method of operation
  ☐ d.)causal factors

8. When dressing for a court or hearing, the protection officer should dress as if going to a_____ _____interview.

9. Security Officers conduct _____all the time. The proficient security officer/investigator makes every conversation an _____.

10. Individual case assignments should be made on the basis of:
  ☐ a.)investigator qualifications and efficiency
  ☐ b.)an analysis of investigative experience
  ☐ c.)an analysis of what training the investigator has undergone
  ☐ d.)past performance of the investigator

EMPLOYEE DISHONESTY, CRIME IN BUSINESS

By Dr. Norman R. Bottom, CPP, CPO, CST

Some employees will steal. The more opportunity we allow for theft, the more theft. Dishonest employees tend to steal what is most available to them. Computer people steal computer time. Cashiers steal cash. Warehouse employees take merchandise passing through their hands. Office personnel steal office supplies.

Managers steal, supervisors steal, and line employees steal. Protection officers have been known to steal too. Many times, dishonest employees use external accomplices such as family members and friends to help them steal. An employee can steal on his own, or several employees may conspire to commit theft for their mutual benefit.

People steal from their employers for many reasons. Criminologists study the causes of crime. You and I do not need to know the competing theories of employee crime causation. It is our job to prevent as much theft as possible. (If you are interested, I think people steal from employers on economic ground; they are greedy!)

Opportunities for employee theft come about because of waste, accident, error, crime, and unethical or unprofessional practices. The first letters of these opportunities (threats, really) come together to form the acronym 'WAECUP'. (WAECUP is pronounced wake-up.) Below is a list of WAECUP loss threats with several examples of each.

A. Waste
1. Protection officers who waste time create opportunity for employees to steal.
2. Waste containers are favorite stash places for employees who steal.

B. Accident
1. The confusion that surrounds an accident scene may be used to screen an employee theft.
2. Arson has been used by employees to cover up theft. (What seems to be an accident can actually be a crime.)

C. Error
1. Protection officers who err in following procedures, such as in failure to make an assigned round, create opportunity for undetected theft.
2. Other (non-security) employees who fail to follow security-related instructions such as failing to lock up storage areas or exterior doors, create opportunity for theft.

D. Crime
1. If protection officers allow employee theft, other employees will get the idea that it is all right to steal and commit other crimes.
2. Failure to recognize valuable merchandise allows more crime. (You will not be watching the right stuff.)

E. Unethical/Unprofessional Practices
1. A general feeling among employees that it is okay to pilfer (steal) will result in more theft.
2. Unprofessional practices by management create resentment among other employees leading to deviant acts like theft.

What Society Thinks About the Thief

Employee theft is a crime repugnant to society as a whole and to the employer as an individual. Property rights are fundamental to our way of life. We want to keep what belongs to us. So does the businessman.

Theft is a violation of property rights and universally condemned by right-thinking persons. Stealing from an employer is simply an ungrateful, criminal act. It is not a right. It is a wrong.

The Realities of Theft Prevention

Not all internal (employee) theft is preventable. We will learn below some ways to minimize, moderate and control this criminal activity. Thus we become better protection officers.

Protection officers can have an impact. They can prevent theft. They can deter and displace theft. When security is tight, thieves look for another place to steal. We can make theft so difficult and so much trouble that the would-be thief will decide against it.

Theft prevention is a good idea at any time. Today it is even more important. Many business enterprises teeter on the verge of going out of business. Times are tough. Preventing theft can save many jobs, and that includes your own.

Objective

Protection officers **must** reduce employee theft. This chapter focuses on practical methods to reduce this theft. However, it takes more than your presence, standing around in a sharp uniform or strutting through an area. You must know what to look for, what to report and what actions to take. You must know, also, what actions not to take.

Thieves can be clever, and new opportunities for employee theft will develop. This chapter is only a beginning. You must continue to study employee-theft prevention as long as you are a protection officer. The **objective** of this chapter is to whet your appetite on the scope of employee theft prevention and widen your knowledge.

This chapter will give you some tips on observation. For example, employees who bring in empty or almost empty shopping bags, (then leave with bags bulging) should be viewed with suspicion. Those bulging bags may contain company property. As a general rule, always look for the unusual and out-of-place; then investigate discreetly.

Also this section will explain some things about reporting and discuss what to report and to whom. For example, doors propped open (that are normally locked) may be used by thieves as access points to sneak company property outside. Such things should be reported and written up.

Also this will be a discussion of actions to take and actions not to take. For example, managers and other executives often work at home during the evening. They are usually permitted to take company property home to do this. Hourly workers (shift workers) seldom have the right to take company property home. Know company rules before you act or accuse.

Definition of Employee Dishonesty

What is employee dishonesty? It is theft. It is cheating customers. It is committing industrial espionage. It is lying on employment applications and falsifying time records. It is claiming sick leave when there is no sickness. Anything that can be moved, or taken apart and the pieces moved, is a candidate for employee theft.

We are going to learn some things about **Theft Prevention** in this chapter. Other types of employee dishonesty will be covered elsewhere in this Manual or in later supplements. Theft of **visible** items is our theme. Illegal computer access or electronic data intercepts will not be discussed.

Protection officers can reduce the theft of visible items of company property. They can catch thieves, of course. But, it is better to reduce **opportunity** for theft than to catch thieves.

Each company has its own types of property. That property includes personal (movable property) and fixed (real property). Real property, such as permanent buildings and land, cannot be carried off. In this chapter we need worry only about personal property.

Personal property, in business usage, is not what you or I mean by our 'personal effects'. Business tries to protect the machinery or means of production. The materials or equipment used for production (or sale) of goods and services need protection. And, those goods, services and products, etc. offered the public must be guarded.

Business wants to protect and keep its **reward** — the income received for selling its products, of course. Those categories are what we mean by business personal property.

Some business is devoted to manufacturing. Here the threat of employee theft takes place at several stages. Those stages occur from the time that machines are installed, and raw materials purchased, through the entire production process — and until the finished goods are delivered.

Other companies specialize in storage and transportation. They warehouse and distribute manufactured products. These companies worry while goods are stored. Every time goods are handled by employees causes theft concern too. Goods in transit present additional possibilities for theft.

We all shop at the malls and other retail stores. Retail is certainly a familiar business to all. There are also wholesale outlets that specialize in selling quantities to the trade. Each retail store, and each wholesaler, worries about losing that property they hope to sell. Employee theft is one way the property can be lost to these owners.

Institutions like hospitals have special employee theft problems. These include the unauthorized use or taking of narcotics and theft of patient's property. Banking institutions worry about their cash, naturally. The point to remember is that all businesses need protection against employee theft. That protection need demands proper security and loss control effort by protection officers.

First Steps

The first step in employee theft prevention is to learn what can be stolen. A list of property categories is useful for reference. All protection officers need such a list to help them identify company property.

Sample List — Retail Establishment

Office Area:
1. Paper products
2. Typewriters, calculators, computers, telephones
3. Desks, chairs, bookcases, file cabinets
4. Rugs, paintings
5. Petty cash

Stock Room
1. Sales merchandise of various types
2. Shelving
3. Materials, handling equipment
4. Some office supplies

Sales Area
1. Merchandise to be sold
2. Shelving and cabinets
3. Cash registers/computerized sales terminals

4. Product displays
5. Sales receipts (cash, checks, etc.)

Parking Areas & Outbuildings
1. Exterior merchandise displays
2. Equipment stored outside (in the open or in outbuildings)
3. Company vehicles
4. Trash and refuse containers

A similar category list can be drawn up for any work environment. Buy a notebook and make your own list, especially if there is no master list available. Test your powers of observation by comparing your list with those of other protection officers. Update your list as new property arrives and old property is replaced.

It is good to know as much as is possible about all company property including value. More valuable items, especially if easily moved (portable), deserve special theft prevention effort.

Markings

Life becomes difficult if company property is not marked to indicate ownership. Learn what marking system, if any, is used to mark all equipment. That includes office typewriters, computer equipment and so on. Sale merchandise should be marked too with special tags.

Some marking systems use stick-on labels. Other marking systems involve stamping numbers on metal. Paint and stencil are used by some companies for identification purposes. There are chemical compounds that can be painted (or sprayed) on. These compounds leave markings visible only in certain light.

If valuable items are not marked, you should ask "Why not?" Your supervisor might give you a good explanation. He may commend you for an idea whose time has come. A good protection officer learns how to recognize company property.

A general reminder: Learn, learn, learn — continue to ask good questions. Keep written records of the answers. In that way you will not have to ask the same question twice. And, you will have a ready reference when there is no supervisor available.

Concealment

Hide and Seek is a children's game familiar to most of us. The basic instructions call for someone blindfolded to count while other children hide. Then the counter opens his eyes and tries to find the others. It may help to think of employee thieves as the other children with time to take and hide your

company's property. The protection officer should not, of course, have his eyes closed while this theft and concealment goes on.

Trash and garbage containers are time-honored hiding places for employee thieves. Plastic garbage bags are another useful item for thieves. Modern garbage bags are sturdy, unaffected by moisture, and they are opaque; that is, you cannot see through them. The protection officer should look for garbage bags in containers, both inside and outside the building. And, garbage bags will be found in corners and adjacent to doorways.

Periodically check all garbage cans, dumpsters and sealed garbage bags for stolen merchandise. Be especially alert to those employees who take garbage and trash outside. That activity is a critical junction. It is critical because stolen merchandise can be hidden in the trash. It is a junction because the merchandise is leaving the premises. Normally, only a few trusted employees are allowed to take trash outside. Know who those are.

Another trick of the employee thief is to take a particular item and hide it for later pickup. Remember that everything has its place. And everything should be in its place. Be alert to the out-of-place item concealed in a strange or unusual location. That may be an indication of employee theft in progress. Look behind shelved merchandise. Examine storage rooms and broom closets.

Examples:
1. Valuables, like watches, normally under lock and key, found on open shelves tucked behind cheap items.
2. Office equipment and/or office supplies stashed in an area where there is no desk or clerical work performed.
3. Valuable merchanise found in areas set aside for employees to leave their purses and other personal belongings. The same goes for employee locker area.
4. Sheds, lean-tos, truck courts and other locations outside main buildings but on company property. Company property found at these locations should be appropriate to the area. For example, office typewriters do not belong in a garden shed.

Briefcases, lunch boxes, purses, shopping bags and even stranger containers will be carried to work by employees. Thieves use these containers to remove company property from the site. You realize, of course, that such personal items are entitled to reasonable privacy. You had better remember this, or your search will only cause trouble to you. Always check with a supervisor before searching an employee or his property.

Many companies have rules about what type of items can be brought onto company property. Know these rules. You may prevent a theft by advising an employee that the gunnysack in his hand cannot be brought in.

Vehicle parking is another factor in concealment. The personal vehicle of an employee should not be parked next to the storeroom door, for example. In fact, employee parking should be at some distance from buildings and doorways. Company policy establishes the parking rules. But, you should point out parking hazards that make employee theft easier.

Employee thieves may use their own car or truck. They may also use a company vehicle to get the stolen merchandise away. For example, a driver may load a few extra cases on the truck, cases not listed on the manifest. These will be sold for his personal profit and the company's loss.

Some thieves are very bold. They will attempt to walk out with stolen merchandise in their hands. Employees who attempt to remove company property from the premises should have a pass or other authorizing document. Since pass forms may be stolen or counterfeited, it is important to know and recognize authorized signatures. When in doubt, check with your supervisor. And make sure that the pass covers each and every item. If the pass says "six" items, do not let the employee remove seven.

Reporting

All suspicious activity observed, and especially that involving employees, should be immediately reported.

Remember that all observations and concealment findings are a waste of time unless your results are promptly reported. Along with the need for **timely reporting**, there is a second thing to remember.Get report results to the **right person(s)**. The right person or persons will be able to take the necessary action.

So far, we have three main points to remember. First, reporting must follow observation. Observation may involve the sight of suspicious activity on the part of employees. Observation may involve threat potential such as open doors. Or, the protection officer may have discovered concealed company property. First **observe**, then **report**.

The second main point is timely reporting. If you wait too long to report suspicious activity, the theft will take place. If you wait too long to report a suspicious open door, stolen items will exit through that door. If you wait too long to report a concealed item, it will be removed by the thief.

The third main point is reporting to the right person(s). The right person will be able to react properly to the threat you observed. The right person will authorize or take corrective action in timely fashion. The right person will see that your work is not wasted. **Who is the right person(s)?**

Your supervisor, if available, is the right person. The non-security supervisor in the hazard area is another right person. Each company, each business, will have a chain of command or leadership tree. Protection officers must know the responsibilities of various managers. They must know how to reach managers in case of an emergency. Emergencies include a serious threat of employee theft.

Reports about employee theft should be both verbal and written. The need for verbal reporting often increases with

rapidly unfolding events. The need for written reports is twofold. First, **clarity**. Verbal information often becomes distorted when relayed from one person to another.

Second, **record-keeping**. Written reports serve as the basis for planning by the security and loss control staff. History tends to repeat itself, and hazards repeat unless records are kept and used.

Written reports from protection officers are sometimes hastily read by management, if read at all. This is especially true of shift reports. It is hard to say why these reports are not properly used. Sometimes it is the protection officer's fault.

Reports are not valuable if poorly written, or if the handwriting is illegible. Other problems relate to forms that are poorly designed. At other times, the boss means well, but just cannot seem to get around to reading activity reports until they are stale.

A protection officer may develop a negative attitude about reporting his observations (to include employee theft hazards). Perhaps nobody asked for an explanation of important observations. No pats on the back or 'attaboys'. Or, nothing seems to have been done to reduce the reported threat. Many protection officers, especially those working midnights, never see the protection boss or his deputies. That shift especially may wonder if their reports are ever read.

What can be done? Report suspicious activity, and other employee theft potentials, verbally. Discuss your written reports with supervisors whenever you can. Once in a while, take some initiative and call the protection office when you are off-duty and the boss is in. Show your concern for your duties and for your reports. That is **dedication** often rewarded.

The protection officer bears responsibility for his observations on employee theft or the potential for that theft. They must be understood by the top ranks. No excuses, or moaning about lack of communications will help the situation.

Preventive Actions

Observation and reporting are crucial in employee theft prevention as we have seen. Preventive action is also important. But, actions can be hazardous. The wrong action can bring unnecessary embarassment to an employee, the protection manager and to the individual protection officer.

Wrongful action can expose you and your company to civil suit. For example, an employee falsely accused of theft can bring suit for monetary damages. Some wrongful actions lead to criminal prosecution and jailing of the protection officer. Be careful in accusations. Be especially careful in conducting searches. Search actions are the most troublesome preventive actions.

Preventive actions do not always mean trouble. Many preventive actions are pleasant. They involve heading off employee theft at an early stage. Never forget, the essence of protection is prevention of employee theft. Cultivate a good liaison with as many senior employees as you can. Let these employees be additional eyes and ears.

Search Policy

You may feel it necessary to search a lunch bucket or a purse. You may decide an employee locker contains stolen merchandise. There may be an excellent reason to suspect company property is in an employee's personal vehicle. Before you take action, before you search, know your company policy. And, always follow policy.

Do not take actions in conflict with company policy. Policy may state that employee packages or vehicles can be inspected **on demand**. Or, policy may authorize **periodic** and **random** searches of employee parcels, briefcases, and purses. A company without a written and well-communicated policy is buying trouble for itself and the protection staff. When in doubt about search policy, ask your supervisor. Remember that an error on your part could result in your termination and court action.

Searching a company vehicle is less hazardous. But, company policy still rules. It may be necessary to break a door seal. A search could delay delivery of overdue merchandise. The union contract may set limitations or requirements. For example, rules may require the presence of a union steward or a supervisor during the search. **Know the rules and follow them.**

Searching other areas, such as storage sheds or checking trash containers and garbage bags is normally simple. But it is wise to ask your supervisor if such routine checks can be done without giving prior notice — to the protection office or some supervisor. Routine searches should be done at different times, of course. If you check a trash container always at 4 p.m., employee thieves will wait until 4:10 to stash the stolen goods.

Protection officers may not be allowed in some areas unless invited. Such areas often include the research laboratory and executive offices. Barging into a research laboratory could ruin experiments in progress. And remember that company executives do not want protection officers poking around when important business is under way.

Public relations is the key to almost everything the protection officer does. This is never more true than in searching an employee's bag, briefcase or vehicle. Your attitude during a search must be professional and non-threatening. Remember that you must work tomorrow with the same employees you search today. An overbearing or nasty attitude will make enemies you cannot afford.

Employee Liaison

No protection officer can be successful without help. Help will come from the protection staff of course. There is another type of help. That comes from the non-security employee. It is necessary to cultivate the respect of those employees who can assist you to estimate employee theft threats.

Morale is a good indicator of theft potential. When overall morale is high, there tends to be less employee theft.

When morale is low, more theft is likely. The protection officer needs to keep his finger on the pulse of employee morale. This can best be done through contacts in the work place.

Often, non-security employees will witness an employee theft, but fail to report it. That can go on for a long, long time. If the protection officer has the respect of key employees, hints will be forthcoming about the deviant activities of employees. These hints are golden.

Liaison with non-security employees has other benefits. A roving protection officer will never know an area, or the activities taking place as well as employees who work there.

For example, changes in the work-place environment can raise the potential for employee theft. Some examples follow:

1. The arrival of new, valuable items.
2. Plans to open a door previously sealed.
3. The hiring of temporary staff.

New, valuable items represent something additional to observe. Opening a previously sealed door means another access route to remove stolen merchandise. Temporary staff may themselves steal or be blamed as regular employees attempt theft.

Summary

This chapter presented some lessons about controlling employee dishonesty. Employees at all levels may steal from their employers. Most employees steal what is immediately available to them. Opportunities for theft come about because of waste, accident, error, crime and unethical/unprofessional practices (WAECUP).

Society is against theft on principle. Protection officers cannot prevent all employee theft, but they can have a positive impact. Theft prevention is a good idea at any time. Today it is especially important due to the economic climate.

Practical methods to prevent theft were explained. These include tips on what to look for, what to report, and what actions to take. As a general rule, always look for the unusual and out of place. But, be prudent in taking action. An employee may have permission to take company property off premises.

Theft of visible items is the focus of this chapter. Protection officers can reduce the theft of visible items, but it is better to reduce opportunity for theft than to catch thieves. Theft reduction requires knowledge of company property, how it is marked, and its value. Make a property list to aid your memory.

Concealment often comes before removal of company property by the employee thief. Trash and garbage containers and bags are favorite hiding places. The thief may conceal valuable merchandise behind less valuable items. Everything should be in its place. Look behind shelved merchandise; examine storage rooms and broom closets.

Know the rules about what employees may bring onto company property. You may be able to prevent a theft simply by advising an employee not to bring a container in. Vehicle parking is another factor. Point out parking hazards which make employee theft easier.

Suspicious activity should be reported. There should be a verbal report and a written report. Timely observation is critical to the right person or persons. Know who the right person is. Follow up your reporting in discussions with protection supervisors.

Preventive actions are important to employee theft prevention. Wrongful actions by protection officers can lead to civil and criminal problems. Care is needed in making searches and in making accusations. Some preventive actions are pleasant. Employee liaison is an excellent way to prevent employee theft. Liaison with senior employees means additional eyes and ears.

Company search policy must be understood and applied. Know whether policy allows random searches or searches on demand. A written search policy is essential. Search of company vehicles may be easier. But complications can arise with respect to seals, delays or contract provisions. Always follow the rules.

Search of trash or storage areas is usually without complication. These searches should be done at staggered times.

Some areas, such as research labs and executive offices need prior permission to enter — even by the protection officer. There are valid reasons for these restrictions.

Public relations is always an important skill. This skill is important during any search involving an employee. Remember, you must work tomorrow with the employee you search today. Cultivate the respect of senior employees who can help you recognize employee theft potential. Morale is a good indicator of theft potential. Low morale is likely to mean more employee theft problems.

Sometimes employees witness theft, but do not report it. If the protection officer develops the respect of key employees, hints of employee deviancy will be given. Liaison with non-security employees has other benefits. Changes in the workplace environment can raise the potential for employee theft. Good liaison will keep you up-to-date on such changes.

The Protection Officer can do a good job in preventing employee theft. But only if he follows the methods outlined, and company policy.

QUIZ
Employee Dishonesty

1. The more _____ we allow for theft, the more theft. (Fill in the blank)

2. WAECUP stands for:

_____ _____ _____

_____ _____

(Fill in the five blanks)

3. As a ground rule, always look

for the _____
(Fill in the blank)

4. The activity of removing trash and garbage is a

critical _____ (Fill in the blank)

5. What step must immediately follow observation of suspicious activity? (check correct answer)
   - ☐ a. Marking
   - ☐ b. Concealment
   - ☐ c. Reporting
   - ☐ d. Liaison

6. Liaison with non-security employees has many benefits to the protection officer.
   ☐ T ☐ F

7. Protection officers may visit any office or activity without notice and at the officer's convenience.
   ☐ T ☐ F

8. Employee package policies usually include:
   - ☐ a. Search on demand
   - ☐ b. Periodic or random search
   - ☐ c. Neither of the above
   - ☐ d Either a) or b)

9. Suspicious activity should be reported only in writing.
   ☐ T ☐ F

10. Reporting observations to the right person or persons is vital.
   ☐ T ☐ F

SUBSTANCE ABUSE

By Francis J. Elliott, CPP

Today, we live and work in a society where substance abuse is omnipresent. It is a major domestic problem confronting the United States and the leading cause of crime, health problems, and child abuse. Substance abuse adversely affects our schools and the education of our children, it divides and destroys families, drains the economy of entire communities, and jeopardizes the ability of business and industry to be competitive. Substance abuse is a threat to our security and public safety. It destroys the human will and denies dreams. Substance abuse does not discriminate. It favors no race, age group, intelligence level, social or economic status, or sex. It consumes anyone who dares to embrace its false promises for perpetual self-gratification and well-being.

This chapter is aimed at elevating the protection officer's awareness about substance abuse in the workplace, and about psychoactive drugs and the behaviors resulting from their use and/or abuse. This chapter also identifies the risks that these behaviors pose for employees and the employer, and the methods by which to prevent or confront these risks. As a security professional, you must be prepared to deal with substance abuse on the job, and effectively communicate your observations and information to your supervisor. Because of your daily interaction with employees, and others who visit your workplace, you must be able to recognize conditions that may point to a security risk or vulnerability.

For purposes of this chapter, the phrase substance abuse refers to the use, usually self-administered, of any psychoactive drug in a manner that deviates from the approved legal, medical, or social patterns within a given culture. A drug is defined as any substance which by its chemical nature, alters the structure or function of the living organism. A psychoactive drug is one which alters the structure or function of the brain. Psychoactive drugs alter mood, perception, or consciousness. Examples include nicotine, alcohol, marijuana, cocaine, biphetamine, LSD, and many others, which will be described later in this chapter.

Because our focus is on drugs that directly impact performance and behavior on the job, nicotine will not be a focus of this chapter. However, it is important to note that nicotine consumption produces classic drug dependence characteristics. Along with alcohol, it is considered a gateway drug for those who ultimately use other dependence producing drugs, such as marijuana and cocaine. Finally, nicotine has been clearly identified as an insidious substance responsible for hundreds of thousands of deaths annually.

IMPACT ON BUSINESS AND INDUSTRY

Recent studies reveal that 74% of illicit drug users and 90% of alcoholics are employed in the American workplace. Many of these employees are poly-drug abusers. They abuse more than one drug in the course of their drug taking behavior. Employees with alcohol and other drug problems represent 10% to 20% of any given workforce. Within this workforce the highest concentration of abusers is within the 18 - 25 year old age group. A recent study shows that 20% of workers 18 - 25 use drugs on the job, while the rate for 27 - 34 year olds is 13%. The economic cost of this extensive involvement with mind altering drugs is in excess of $1 billion annually to the American business community. The annual cost for a single employee with a substance abuse problem is $7,621.00. Aside from the substance abuser population, there exists an unspecified number of employees who are co-dependent. These employees do not abuse drugs. However, they share a common thread. They are the spouses, children, and significant others who arrive for work each day preoccupied with the physical and emotional condition of their loved ones.

Some of the tangible costs generated by the substance abuser include:

1.   **Decreased productivity** - They are 25% less productive.

2.   **Accidents** - They are three to four times more likely to have an accident on the job. Fifty percent of all accidents are attributable to substance abusers. Forty percent (40%) of industrial accidents resulting in fatality are linked to alcohol consumption and alcoholism.

3.   **Absenteeism** - They are absent four times more often. Also, they are more likely to be away from their assigned locations during regular work hours.

4.   **Theft** - They are responsible for 50% - 80% of employee thefts.

5.   **Workers' Compensation** - They are five times more likely to file a workers' compensation claim.

6.   **Health care costs** - They use medical benefits five times more often and the family members of substance abusers generally have higher than average health care claims.

Aside from the tangible costs of substance abuse, many hidden costs exist for which a dollar figure cannot be assigned. Such factors include:

*   Morale problems
*   Intimidation of managers and employees
*   Wasted supervisory time
*   Overtime costs
*   Grievance costs
*   Training and replacement costs
*   Decrease quality of products and services

To successfully address the adverse consequences of substance abuse in the workplace, we must elevate awareness and change existing attitudes and procedures which enable the problem to perpetuate itself. There is no single solution. The greatest success will come through the selection of various prevention and remedial components, which complement a company's particular philosophy and culture. These components include policy development, training and education, employee assistance programs, the security function, and drug testing measures.

SUBSTANCE ABUSE: WHAT IS THE MOTIVATION?

Time and again the question is asked: "Why do people abuse drugs?" The reasons are usually complex. Early drug use, at any age, may be a result of peer pressure, low self-esteem, insecurity, or various other social, environmental, psychological, and biological factors which induce stress and anxiety. In all likelihood some combination of these variables stimulates the initial use and abuse of psychoactive drugs. Initial use is usually re-inforced as a result of 1) their pleasant effects, 2) a perceived control over the drug, 3) peer acceptance and recognition, and 4) myth and misinformation. What we know is that drugs can quickly relieve unpleasant feelings. Mind altering drugs quickly affect the pleasure centers of the brain so that the user who is feeling good will feel better, and those feeling badly will feed good. The result is nearly immediate self-gratification, but it is only temporary. In reality, sooner or later, the user and others always pay the price.

Continued use of a psychoactive drug will most often result in problematic behavior such as drinking and driving, job jeopardy, or splitting with the family. Ultimately, repeated use can lead to physical and/or psychological dependence. As use continues there are usually three anticipated outcomes. The substance abuser will either:

1.   Return to a drug free lifestyle.

2.   Continue to abuse drugs avoiding dependence, but exhibiting problematic behavior at work, home, or the community.

3.   Continue to abuse drugs to the point of dependence and most likely die from his/her disease.

How each substance abuser will land is unpredictable, and is often guided by circumstances beyond anyone's control.

HOW PROBLEMATIC BEHAVIOR AND DEPENDENCE DEVELOP

Today, drug dependency is viewed as a disease, with identifiable causes, signs, and symptoms. It follows a predictable course and outcome, and it is treatable. The disease of drug dependence is:

*   **Primary** - it is not simply the symptom of some other problem(s), it is in itself the problem.

*   **Contagious** - it attracts others who are vulnerable.

*   **A family disease** - it effects their families, and not just the individual abuser.

*   **Chronic** - it is difficult to control, is quite often recurring, and although treatable, it is incurable.

*   **Fatal** - it takes hundreds of thousands of lives annually.

Drug dependence may be physical or psychological, and represents an individual's loss of control. Physical dependence occurs when a person cannot function normally without the repeated use of a drug. If the use of the drug is abruptly discontinued, the person experiences severe physical and psychic disturbance, known as withdrawal. Psychological dependence provides a strong psychological desire to continue the self-administration of drugs for a sense of improved well-being.

A great number of programs and treatment approaches exist for the treatment of drug dependencies. What we do know about these various programs is that no single approach or program is effective for every drug dependent person. We also know that there are not enough of these programs to meet the needs of the afflicted. In spite of the various programs and models, we know that recidivism rates are high. So, for all that is known, the experts still have much to learn and continue to do so each day. There is, however, a solid body of evidence pertaining to the stages of dependency and associated behaviors which the protection officer should know. An understanding of the process is critical to prevention and rehabilitation efforts.

Drug dependence follows a predictable course of action which, most often, begins with experimentation. This may be the result of curiosity, peer pressure or a variety of other variables or combination of variables. Everyone is susceptible to the abuse of drugs; some, more so than others, due to a host of social, environmental, psychological and biological issues, or in some cases, heredity. What is significant is that each incidence of use makes the user more susceptible to continue use, up to and including dependence. Further, the earlier drug use begins, the more likely it is to progress to abuse, and dependence.

Another facet of dependence is recovery. The individual user has a greater opportunity for a full recovery if treatment begins before dependence sets in. The longer one uses a drug(s), the more complex the physical and psychological symptoms become. As a result, recovery for the dependent person, or daily user, is a greater challenge in most instances than recovery from occasional use or experimentation. This is why early intervention is significant.

Whether an intervention occurs at home, work, school, or in the community, it is certain that the earlier the intervention takes place the greater the opportunity is for recovery.

HOW IS SUBSTANCE ABUSE PERPETUATED?

There are essentially five (5) reasons why substance abuse continues to be a problem in the workplace. These include:

1.   Denial
2.   Mixed messages
3.   The "harmless" theory
4.   Drug use is controllable by the user
5.   The problem is viewed as controllable through attrition

Denial - provides the biggest single roadblock to successfully addressing the problem of substance abuse in society or the workplace. Parents, teachers, husbands, wives, managers, and users themselves all tend to deny the problem exists, even in light of hard evidence. Some familiar phrases illustrate the point: "Not My Kid", "What Is Wrong With A Few Drinks", "Not In My Company", "Not Joe, He's Just A Good Natured Guy", "It Must Have Been Entrapment".

Mixed messages - are heard daily, and are confusing to the lay person. Some promote the use of certain drugs for "recreational" purposes as harmless. Others say that the same drugs contribute to many individual, social, and occupational ills. For instance, some marijuana advocates say that this drug is harmless and does not interfere with one's work. Others claim that the drug has a negative impact on education, motivation, and the ability to remember and perform complex or new tasks. Hence, marijuana use may contribute to industrial accidents.

The "Harmless" theory - contends that the use of drugs such as marijuana, cocaine, and alcohol is considered by many to be an innocuous activity, on or off the job. In fact, some forces are aggressively moving to legalize all psychoactive drugs. In reality, no drug can ever be considered harmless. Any drug is harmful when taken in excess; e.g. even aspirin, and of course, alcohol. Some drugs can also be harmful if taken in dangerous combinations like barbiturates and alcohol. Some drugs, like over-the-counter medications, can be harmful in therapeutic doses if alertness is diminished, or drowsiness results. Finally, certain drugs taken by hypersensitive people can be lethal; e.g. penicillin. Given the potential harmfulness of some legal, prescription, and over-the-counter drugs, one must realize the increased potential for harm, impairment, and death with illegal street drugs, whose composition is never truly known.

Controllable use - is some people's belief that drug use can be "recreational" providing one controls his/her intake of a given psychoactive drug. However, this argument is academic because even so-called "social", "recreational", or "controlled use" of psychoactive drugs on the job often leads to impairment, which in turn leads to diminished performance, accidents, and other adverse consequences. Everyone pays a price for his/her drug use. Some pay earlier than others, and all too often innocent people suffer first.

Attrition - in industry is often seen as a solution to the drug problem. Unfortunately, tomorrow's workforce is intimately involved with drugs today. Consider the following:

* After several years of declining abuse among high school aged children, the rate of abuse in the U.S. for 12-17 year olds rose 78% between 1992 and 1995 and it continues to rise.

The data clearly shows that tomorrow's workforce is intimately involved with the use and abuse of alcohol and other drugs today. Unless we heed the warning of history we will once again be confronted with a new generation of young people predisposed to tolerating the use and abuse of psychoactive drugs. For this reason, the business community must gather its resources to establish sound drug free workplace programs that will meet this challenge.

CONDITIONS ADVERSELY AFFECTING THE WORKPLACE

As substance abusers arrive for work each day, they generally fit into one or more categories that present threatening conditions for employees and their employer. Some employees will:

1.   Appear for work under the influence of drugs and will be openly and obviously impaired, or intoxicated and unfit for duty.

2.   Possess and use drugs on the job. Although they are impaired, it will not be evident.

3.   Sell or otherwise distribute, or transfer illegal drugs, or legal drugs illegally, while on the job.

4.   Display impairment due to the residual effects of drugs taken hours or even days prior to coming to work. These effects may include emotional outbursts, personality changes, irritability, combativeness, memory problems, and the inability to complete assignments.

5.   Have co-dependent loved ones working at jobs where they will be less productive.

Keeping in mind that the protection officer is not a diagnostician, recognizing impairment due to sustained low dosages and residual effects, or co-dependence, will be unlikely unless he/she is informed of this information by a third party. If third party information is received, then the protection officer should bring this intelligence to his/her supervisor immediately. These conditions are best left to supervisors and managers who can evaluate these issues as a matter of job performance and make the necessary referrals, or take disciplinary action when performance is considered to be deteriorating. However, the protection officer should be alert for the outward signs of drug possession, use, and distribution, which are often overlooked by the lay person. These signs include the:

1.   Observation of drugs and/or drug paraphernalia in the workplace;

2.   Observation of suspicious activity especially in secluded areas of the facility or parking lots. Whenever suspicious activity is observed you should immediately contact your supervisor and request back-up before approaching. However, immediate action may be necessary if a threat to personal safety exists;

3.   Scent of chemical odors not commonly present in the workplace;

4.   Observation of abnormal behavior including the signs of intoxication. Keep in mind that not all abnormal behavior is an indication of substance abuse. Some employees may have legitimate medical problems which can result in behavior similar to intoxication. Regardless of the cause, immediate action is required to protect the employee, co-workers, and the company's property and interest.

HOW MUST INDUSTRY RESPOND?

The workplace plays an integral part in the fight against substance abuse. When continued employment is conditional upon being drug free, then employment becomes a powerful incentive in support of a drug free workplace. When a company demonstrates commitment to a comprehensive program in support of a drug free workplace then the opportunity to affect attitudes, behavior, and the lifestyles of employees is significant. Through the influence of these programs employees are likely to make healthier choices. Employees who are educated and committed to a drug free lifestyle convey this attitude to their families and friends. In effect, the employee not only serves to reduce substance abuse at work, but he/she serves to improve the health of his/her family and community.

Until now, the workplace has been underutilized in the fight against substance abuse. Recently, however, government mandates and current trends are requiring aggressive action. To respond effectively, a multi-dimensional approach is necessary. A company should consider five components in the development of a comprehensive drug free workplace program. These include:

1.   Policy development
2.   Training and education
3.   Employee assistance
4.   Drug testing
5.   Security measures

A company policy is the first step upon which to build an effective drug free workplace program. It must clearly state the company's purpose, what will and will not be tolerated, how the company will respond to violations, and what training and treatment support are available. It should also describe the company's drug testing policy, if they chose to conduct these tests.

Training and education should be provided at all levels of employment, especially supervisors and manager, for they represent a company's first line of defense. Training and education should focus on a review of the company's policy, and provide a clear understanding of the nature and scope of substance abuse, and the required response to prevent and properly address the problem.

Employee Assistance Programs (EAP) are most often a resource offered by large companies. However, more and more smaller sized companies are forming consortiums, and thereby making the availability of EAP services cost effective. An EAP may be an in-house function or contracted out through an independent service. These programs assist employees and their families in addressing a wide range of personal problems, including substance abuse. In addition, they offer training programs, consult on matters pertaining to troubled employees, assess employee problems, make referrals for treatment and counselling, and in some instances, oversee drug testing programs. Current data reveals that each dollar invested in an EAP can save a company $5.00 - $16.00 dollars in the long run. Where an EAP is not available, a company may provide insurance coverage that will allow an employee to seek community resources.

Drug testing programs like the EAP have traditionally been employed by large companies. One of the restrictive factors for a small company is, of course, cost. As with EAP's, smaller companies are banding together to form consortiums in order to make drug testing more cost effective. The purpose of drug testing is to deter substance abuse, prevent the hiring of substance abusers, and provide for the early identification and referral to treatment of employees with a substance abuse problem.

Several types of testing can be performed by a company, depending on their needs and collective bargaining or legal restrictions. These include pre-employment, post accident, follow-up to treatment or counselling, reasonable suspicion, and random. Urinalysis has been the predominant method used to test for the presence of controlled substances. However, other testing materials being evaluated and/or used include blood, hair, and saliva.

Each of the components discussed above plays an integral part in a drug free workplace strategy. However, these components cannot address all situations. Sometimes a security response is required. This is true when reckless and wanton behavior places the safety of employees and the interest of the company at great risk. Protection officers should clearly understand why and when the security response is necessary.

There is a small percentage of substance abusing employees, perhaps 4% - 10%, who will not accept or benefit from an offer of assistance in the way of treatment or counselling. These individuals include drug dealers who may or may not use drugs on the job, and users who are not interested in or ready for recovery, because they are in denial. Employees who deal drugs are engaged in criminal activity that cannot be tolerated. They make available the supplies on which troubled employees depend and they establish new opportunities for other types of criminal activity such as gambling, prostitution, and theft. A survey conducted with substance abusing employees revealed that 44% had sold drugs on the job. They sell their drugs in bathrooms, parking lots, vehicles, and secluded areas.

In some cases, major drug trafficking organizations have directed dealers to secure jobs in industry and to develop a clientele. Why? Because 1) there is low police visibility, 2) security forces are well known and predictable, and 3) there is a ready made clientele. These types of employees create morale and safety problems and, in many cases, create a great deal of intimidation for employees and managers alike.

Theft is a major problem for both employers and employees. Employees who use drugs on or off the job need to support that use. In many cases the cost of drugs is very high. For instance, the average weekly expenditure for cocaine may be as high as $637.00. To support this need, the theft of valuables such as equipment, money, and trade secrets, are a few methods which have been exploited. On the other hand, a person who spends $20.00 - $40.00 a week for marijuana and/or other drugs, can effectively supplement their income by removing valuable equipment or money from the employer or other employees.

To counteract the activities of drug dealers, the company's security department or independent contractor may have to employ certain investigative techniques. For the most part, these techniques include interviews with employees, undercover operations, covert surveillance, or searches conducted by drug sniffing dogs or chemical process.

Interviews are conducted for the purpose of gathering intelligence that may dictate future action, such as policy changes or the selection of an investigative technique. Employees quite often possess critical information, but may not recognize its significance unless questioned by a trained investigator.

An undercover operation is a specialized investigative technique. It is employed for the purpose of covertly infiltrating a workforce in order to identify violations of company policies or law. These investigations are usually initiated when there is a suspicion or clear knowledge that drug dealing is taking place, but the source and the degree are unknown. Even if a source was identified, in many instances an undercover operation may be necessary to gather the required evidence to take disciplinary or legal action.

Covert surveillance or hidden cameras are used when the activity in question is confined to an individual or specific location. When these circumstances exist then a special surveillance camera can be covertly secreted inside a ceiling, wall, fixture, or a variety of other areas restricted only by one's imagination. The greatest advantage to the hidden camera is the undisputed nature of the evidence, a picture of the event and those responsible.

The act of searching a work area or entire workplace is not a common practice in most industries. When a search is performed it is usually carried out by drug sniffing dogs, or by chemical analysis. Most employers reject searches by dogs, based on the perceived negative impact it would have on employee morale. However, these searches can and do detect the presence of controlled substances in the workplace. Once detected, a host of questions are raised regarding what legal or disciplinary action may be justified or taken. The action to be taken can only be determined, on a case by case basis, after analyzing a variety of factors.

The second type of search is less intrusive and much more discrete. The chemical analysis search involves sweeping an area and analyzing the contents for the presence of a controlled substance. The chemical analysis is, however, restricted to the identification of a limited number of drugs. The same legal and disciplinary issues apply, as mentioned above.

DRUGS OF ABUSE, PARAPHERNALIA, AND DEFINITIONS

Although there are many drugs that will fall within the psychoactive classification, it is important that protection officers have an awareness of those which are most prevalent in the workplace. In order of significance they are:

1. **Alcohol**

2. **Cannabis**

3. **Stimulants**

4. **Depressants (other than alcohol)**

5. **Narcotics**

6. **Hallucinogens**

To facilitate a review of the most popular drugs of abuse within each class, a controlled substance chart is provided which identifies specific drugs, trade or other names, medical uses if any, its potential for producing dependence and tolerance, duration of effects, routes of administration, and possible effects of abuse, overdoses, and withdrawal.

Before continuing, it will be helpful to review the following definitions:

Tolerance: Refers to a state in which the body's tissue cells become accustomed to the presence of a drug at a given dosage and eventually fail to respond to this ordinarily effective dosage. Hence, increasingly larger dosages are necessary to produce the desired effect.

Physical Dependence: Often referred to as addiction, this occurs when a person cannot function normally without the repeated use of a drug. If the drug is withdrawn, the person has mild to severe physical and psychic disturbance, known as withdrawal.

Withdrawal: Is characterized by symptoms that occur after drug use is abruptly discontinued. Symptoms may be mild or severe and include seizures, restlessness, irritability, nausea, depression and more. In some cases, as with alcohol and other depressants, withdrawal can be life threatening.

Psychological Dependence: The result of repeated consumption of a drug which produces psychological but not physical dependence. Psychological dependence produces a strong desire to continue taking drugs for the sense of improved well-being. Psychological dependence is the most difficult to treat.

Potentiation: Concurrent use of two or more depressant drugs with the same action which produce a multiple effect greater than the sum of either drug when taken alone. For example, use of barbiturates/alcohol. Potentiation can result in unexpected lethal overdose.

Look Alike Drugs: Drugs (tablets, capsules, and powders) which are manufactured to closely resemble the appearance of well-known, brand name drugs, e.g. Dexedrine (dexies), and Biphetamine (black beauties). They generally contain drugs found on over-the-counter medications, but usually in larger amounts to provide greater potency.

A WORD OF CAUTION: You should never taste, smell, or directly touch an unknown substance. IT COULD BE HAZARDOUS TO YOUR HEALTH!

INDICATORS AND COMMON SIGNS OF ABUSE

There are various indicators which suggest or positively identify drug involvement in any environment. These indicators include:

1. Presence of a drug and/or drug paraphernalia
2. Physical signs (needle marks, dilated pupils)
3. Behavioral signs (slurred speech, irritability, personality changes)
4. Analytical tests (saliva, urine, blood, hair)

There are many signs of substance abuse which can be identified by the protection officer. However, keep in mind that some people have legitimate reasons for possessing a syringe and needle (diabetics), or having capsules and tablets (valid prescriptions). Having the sniffles and running eyes and nose may be due to a head cold or allergy, and not cocaine use. Unusual and odd behavior may not be connected in any way with drug use. For these reasons protection officers cannot and should not view themselves as a diagnostician. The protection officer's role is to observe and report suspicious conduct or behavior to the appropriate supervisory contact within the company, so that they can evaluate each incident and follow through in the appropriate manner.

SIGNS AND SYMPTOMS: CONTROLLED SUBSTANCES

The following are specific characteristics attributable to each drug class.

Cannabis: Marijuana, Hashish, Hashish Oil

1. Initially, the person may appear animated with rapid loud talking and bursts of laughter. In later stages, he/she may be sleepy.
2. Pupils may be dilated and the eyes bloodshot.
3. Use results in distortion of depth and time perception making driving or the operation of machinery hazardous.
4. Smokers may be impaired for as long as 24 hours following intoxication which may last 1 - 2 hours.
5. Short term memory is impaired.
6. Long term use of marijuana is associated with mental deterioration in some users, and presents a significant health risk to adolescents, the unborn, diabetics, the emotionally disturbed, and those with respiratory problems.

Marijuana is the most commonly used illicit drug in the workplace, because it is easily concealed and use can be accomplished quickly.

This drug is often a brown herbaceous substance, but may be shades of brown, red, green, or yellow depending on its origins. Marijuana is smoked as a "joint" (cigarette) or through various types of pipes. When the "joint" is reduced to a butt and can no longer be held with the fingers it is referred to as a "roach" and held with a "roach clip" for continued smoking. Another method used to smoke marijuana is to hollow out a cigar and fill it with the marijuana. This preparation is referred to as a "blunt".

Marijuana may also be taken orally when used in the preparation of food or drink. However, smoking is the preferred route of administration.

Cost is based in large degree on availability and/or its potency which is determined by the percentage content of the psychoactive chemical called THC (Delta 9 Tetrahydrocannabinol). It is often packaged in clear plastic baggies, but any type of container may be used.

Marijuana users attempt to avoid detection on the job by smoking small amounts of marijuana, called "sustained low dosages", throughout the work day. This enables the user to avoid intoxication and therefore detection, because the euphoria or impairment is not outwardly obvious. The user experiences mild effects along with a level of impairment that can adversely effect one's fitness for duty and safety on the job.

Hashish and Hashish Oil contain concentrated levels of THC which result in increased potency over marijuana. These forms of cannabis are generally not consumed at work because of the preparation required, but they are readily distributed.

Stimulants: Cocaine, Amphetamines, Look Alikes

1. The user may be excessively active, irritable, ar-

gumentative, nervous or restless.

2.   The user generally shows signs of excitation, euphoria, talkativeness and hyperactivity.

3.   May perform the same tasks repeatedly.

4.   Dilated pupils and dry mouth are common.

5.   Regular users can go long periods without sleeping or eating. This can result in fatigue, depression and weight loss.

6.   Long term heavy use can produce delusions, psychosis, paranoia, or death.

7.   Specific to cocaine - the user may exhibit runny nose, sniffles, watery eyes (symptoms similar to the common cold), and ulcerations of the nasal passage.

8.   Paraphernalia consists of razor blades and mirrors for chopping cocaine into fine particles. Straws and small spoons are then used for snorting.

COCAINE: is a drug produced by chemically processing the leaves of the coca bush which is indigenous to South America.

Cocaine is usually a white crystalline substance which looks like snow. When sold and used as "crack", it takes the form of solid matter and resembles small rocks or pebbles. Various containers are used to conceal or store the drug, such as tin foil, paper, and small glass vials.

Cocaine is taken by various routes of administration, including snorting (the most popular route), injection, and smoked as "crack". On the job use is usually confined to snorting which can be accomplished quickly and surreptitiously.

Cocaine can be snorted with the use of a coke spoon, a straw or by using the corner of a match book cover, or the end of a long fingernail. When using a straw, which might be a rolled up piece of currency, the user refers to this as snorting a line of cocaine. In addition, there is paraphernalia available today that is disguised as common sinus inhalers, but are used to dupe unsuspecting employers into believing the user is treating a cold. In some cases employees have been dismissed on sick leave to address their symptoms!

Although traces of cocaine remain in the body for up to a week, its mind altering effects, which users seek, last only 15 - 30 minutes. This is important because following this brief drugged state, the user experiences varying degrees of depression, exhaustion, and dullness, due to chemical disturbances in the brain which reinforce re-administration of the drug. This may lead to continued or compulsive use, and quite often to new routes of administration to achieve a more potent effect. The high cost is a powerful force which can lead to theft, drug dealing, and other criminal activity in the workplace.

AMPHETAMINES: are produced by both legitimate pharmaceutical companies for medical purposes and by clandestine laboratory operators (drug traffickers) in make-shift laboratories located in bathrooms or garages, or in elaborate facilities including workplace laboratories. Their effects are similar to cocaine with one important exception, they last for hours rather than minutes. When these drugs are used for non-medical reasons, they are commonly obtained through 1) pharmacy theft, 2) clandestine manufacturers, or 3) from unscrupulous doctors who write illegal prescriptions for monetary gain.

Some of the more popular amphetamines are Methamphetamine (Speed), Biphetamine (Black Beauties), Dexedrine (Dexies), and Benzedrine (Pink Hearts). Ritalin and Preludin are amphetamine-like substances which are also popular.

Amphetamines are taken orally as tablets or capsules which vary in color, shape, and size. Some, like Methamphetamine or Methcathinone (CAT), are available in powder form and are injected, snorted, or taken orally.

Aside from the drugs listed above, a whole new class of substances referred to as "Look Alike" drugs have become problematic. Initially utilized by truck drivers and students, these substances have now infiltrated the workplace and are taking their

toll. These substances can be distributed legally. They consist of capsules, tables, and powders which contain legal, over-the-counter stimulants such as caffeine and ephedrine. They are marketed as "stay awake" and "stay alert" drugs. However, their use can, and has caused, irritability and fatigue which in turn has contributed to morale problems within the workforce.

The use of stimulants, often referred to as "uppers" or "speed", on the job, poses three serious problems. First, being under the influence of these drugs gives one a false sense that they are capable of achieving any task or conquering any challenge. In this condition, employees may use poor judgement or attempt tasks which are beyond their training and knowledge, resulting in wasted time, property or personal damage, safety infractions, and accidents. Secondly, in a stimulated, talkative and hyperactive condition, users often disrupt co-workers, thereby creating employee morale problems. Finally, stimulant users tend to repeat tasks. This reduces productivity and quality control, and can affect morale in an environment dependent upon a team effort.

NOTE: Many precursor chemicals necessary to manufacture illegal drugs are legitimately used in private industry. To avoid theft of these chemicals by drug traffickers, a company should establish safeguards. Also, the workplace has been used to manufacture illegal drugs. This not only creates an image problem, but also a safety problem, because many of the necessary precursor chemicals are highly flammable and/or explosive.

Depressants: Alcohol, Barbiturates, Tranquilizers, Rohypnol

1.   Behavior like that of alcohol intoxication, but without the odor of alcohol on the breath.

2.   Staggering, stumbling, or decreased reaction time.

3.   Falling asleep while at work.

4.   Slurred speech.

5.   Constricted pupils.

6.   Difficulty concentrating and impaired thinking.

7.   Limited attention span.

These drugs, with the exception of alcohol, are produced and obtained in the same manner as amphetamines.

The most commonly abused drugs in this group, aside from alcohol, are the barbiturates, such as Seconal (Red Devils), Tuinal (Rainbows), and Nembutal (Yellow Jackets), and the benzodiazepines, such as Valium and Librium. Another popular drug in this classification is Rohypnol.

The depressants possess two important characteristics which bear mentioning. First, as stated in the definitions at the beginning of this section, they are potentiating when combined with other depressant drugs. Secondly, the withdrawal from alcohol and other depressants is life threatening, and should always be done under medically supervised conditions.

Valium and Librium are the most widely prescribed and abused tranquilizers. They are also potentiating when combined with alcohol, barbiturates, or other tranquilizers.

"Look Alike" substances containing antihistamines and analgesics like acetaminophen are also available as described for the stimulants.

Rohypnol is one of the latest fad drugs of the 90's, which is becoming increasingly popular with young people. It has Valium-like effects and is referred to as "Roofies".

Depressants are taken orally and no specific form of packaging is outstanding.

The use of depressants diminishes alertness and impairs judgement, making the operation of machinery difficult. Manipulative skills and coordination are also affected. This type of impairment can lead to accidents and poor quality control, as well as diminished work performance.

The depressants are frequently referred to as dry alcohol,

and alcoholics routinely substitute these drugs for alcohol during the work day in order to avoid detection from alcohol's odor.

NARCOTICS: Heroin, Dilaudid, Percodan
1. Scars (tracks) on the arms or on the backs of the hands, caused by repeated injections.
2. Pupils constricted and fixed.
3. Scratches oneself frequently.
4. Loss of appetite.

5. May have sniffles, red watering eyes and a cough which disappears when the user gets a "fix" (injection).
6. User often leaves paraphernalia such as syringes, bent spoons, cotton balls, needles, metal bottle caps, eye droppers, and glassine bags in lockers or desk drawers. They may also be discarded in stairwells, remote areas of a parking lot, or a secluded location within the workplace.
7. Users, when under the influence, may appear lethargic, drowsy, and may go on the "nod" (i.e. an alternating cycle of dosing and awakening).

Natural narcotics (opium, morphine, codeine) are a product of the opium poppy, which is cultivated for the purpose of extracting these powerful drugs for medical use. Major growing areas include Southeast Asia, Southwest Asia, Middle East, South America, and Mexico. In addition, semi-synthetics like Heroin and Dilaudid, and synthetics like Demerol, Percodan, and Fentanyl, are popular.

Narcotics are usually available in tablet, capsule, or powder form, and can be injected, smoked, snorted, or taken orally. In addition, capsules may be used to conceal heroin in powder form to produce a legitimate appearance. Heroin is generally packaged much like cocaine in tin foil, paper, balloons, baggies, and vials. Heroin is usually white, brown or black ("black tar"), or in color or shades of these colors. Synthetic and semi-synthetic tablets and capsules appear in various colors, shapes, and sizes.

The narcotics are not popular drugs of abuse in the workplace, because their use suggests a long history of abuse, which contributes to unemployment and criminal careers. The time required to prepare an injection is another factor discouraging heroin use on the job. However, the administration of heroin by the method of snorting, is becoming more popular. If this trend continues then heroin may become as popular as cocaine. Aside from the issue of use, the narcotics are quite often encountered for sale and distribution on the job.

Hallucinogens: LSD, PCP, DMT
1. Behavior and mood vary widely. The user may sit or recline quietly in a trance-like state or may appear fearful or even terrified.
2. Rapid eye movement, drooling, flushed and sweaty appearance, trembling hands, and dizziness.
3. There may be changes in sense of light, hearing, touch, smell, and time.

Hallucinogens are rarely utilized by employees on the job because of their long duration of effects (2 - 12 hours) and their unpredictable nature. Also, impairment is total, therefore obviating any degree of productivity. Hallucinogenic drugs are especially popular with 18 - 25 year olds, and are frequently available at the workplace for distribution in their various forms. The most popular hallucinogens include LSD and PCP.

Hallucinogens, often called psychedelics, are a group of drugs that alter perception and awareness. Their effects are generally unpredictable and in some cases bizarre. The nature and intensity of the drug experience is determined by the potency and amount taken, the user's personality, mood expectation, and the social and environmental setting.

The LSD experience is labelled a "trip" which is characterized as "good" or "bad". The nature of the trip can only be determined after ingestion, and can last as long as 10 - 12 hours.

The "good trip" is characterized by a passive trance-like state with pleasant hallucinations, perhaps a kaleidoscope of colors and altered sensations. Senses sometimes cross so that the user sees sounds and hears colors. These characteristics result in the hallucinations being touted as mind expanding drugs. The "bad trip" is characterized by unpleasant experiences including terrifying hallucinations, panic, and irrational acts, which have resulted in injury and death.

LSD is sold on the street in tablet and blotter form. As tablets, they are commonly referred to as "microdot acid", and are sold in variety of colors, shapes, and sizes. When liquid LSD is dabbed on blotter paper it is called "blotter acid". Because of LSD's negative reputation as an unpredictable and bizarre drug, it is commonly sold to unsuspecting buyers as THC or Mescaline.

Mescaline (Mesc), PCP, Psilocybin (mushrooms), and DMT (Dimethyltryptamine) are other commonly used hallucinogens.

INHALANTS: Glue, Gasoline, White Out
1. Odor of substance inhaled on breath and clothes.
2. Excessive nasal secretions and watering of the eyes.
3. Poor muscular control.
4. Drowsiness or unconsciousness.
5. Presence of plastic or paper bags or rags containing saturated quantities of the inhalant.
6. Slurred speech.

Inhalants represent a diverse group of psychoactive chemicals composed of organic solvents and volatile substances. These chemicals like glues, paint products, gasoline, and white out, can be readily found in the home and workplace. Their easy accessibility, low cost and ease of concealment make inhalants, for many, one of the first substances abused.

Inhalants are usually sniffed directly from an open container, or from a rag soaked in the substance and held to the face. This is usually referred to as "huffing". Some users have been known to place open containers or soaked rags inside a bag, where the vapors can concentrate, before being inhaled. These substances are rapidly transported to the brain, and can result in unconsciousness or death.

These substances are not widely abused in the workplace. However, incidents of abuse in the workplace have been reported. Many of the chemicals used by some businesses can and are diverted for the purpose of inhalation. In some cases, the diversion and subsequent use has resulted in death on company property.

For further information on drugs of abuse, a comprehensive description and colorful photographic collection of drugs and paraphernalia can be found in "Drugs of Abuse", published by the U.S. Department of Justice, Drug Enforcement Administration, Edition 1996.

Protecting People and Assets
The role of any protection officer is that of protecting people and assets. The protection officer accomplishes this responsibility by observing and reporting incidents or situations which present a threat to the people and assets he/she has a duty to protect. Substance abuse is one such threat, and the protection officer represents a critical component in a company's effort to combat this threat and maintain a drug free workplace. By understanding the scope and nature of this problem, along with the specific security related concerns, the protection officer will be prepared to recognize and report substance abuse situations which undermine safety and security.

Finally, every protection officer should communicate his/her knowledge about the causes and effects of substance abuse beyond the confines of the workplace. By sharing this vital information about the perils of abuse, the protection officer can influence his/her family and community in a most positive way.

Controlled Substances: Uses and Effects

National Drug Institute

Category	Drugs	Trade Or Other Names	Medical Uses	Dependence: Physical	Potential: Psychological	Tolerance	Duration of Effects (in hours)	Usual Methods of Administration	Possible Effects of Abuse	Effects of Overdose	Withdrawal Syndrome
NARCOTICS	Fentanyl	Innovar, Sublimaze	Analgesic anesthetic	High	High	Yes	10 to 72	Injected	Euphoria, drowsiness, respiratory depression, constricted pupils, nausea.	Slow and shallow breathing, clammy skin, convulsions, coma, possible death.	Watery eyes, runny nose, yawning, loss of appetite, irritability, tremors, panic, chills, and sweating, cramps, nausea
NARCOTICS	Morphine	Morphine	Analgesic	High	High	Yes	3 to 6	Oral, Smoked, Injected			
NARCOTICS	Codeine	Codeine	Analgesic, antitussive	Moderate	Moderate	Yes	3 to 6	Oral, Injected			
NARCOTICS	Heroin	Diacetylmorphine, Horse, Smack	None in U.S.	High	High	Yes	3 to 6	Injected, Snorted			
NARCOTICS	Methadone	Dolophine, Methadone, Methadose	Analgesic, Heroin substitute	High	High	Yes	12 to 24	Oral, Injected			
NARCOTICS	Other Narcotics	Dilaudid, Darvon, Demerol, Percodan	Analgesic, antidiarrheal, antitussive	High	High	Yes	3 to 6	Oral, Injected			
DEPRESSANTS	Chloral Hydrate	Noctec, Sommos	Hypnotic	Moderate	Moderate	Yes	5 to 8	Oral	Slurred speech, disorientation, drunken behavior, stumbling.	Shallow respiration, cold and clammy skin, dilated pupils, weak and rapid pulse, coma, possible death.	Anxiety, insomnia, tremors, delirium, convulsions, possible death.
DEPRESSANTS	Barbiturates	Amytal, Nembutal, Phenobarbital, Seconal, Tuinal	Anesthetic, anti-convulsant, sedation, sleep	High-Moderate	High-Moderate	Yes	1 to 16	Oral, Injected			
DEPRESSANTS	Glutethimide	Doriden	Sedation, Sleep	High	Moderate	Yes	4 to 8	Oral			
DEPRESSANTS	Alcohol	Ethyl Alcohol, Ethanol	Ingredient in some medicines	Moderate	Moderate	Yes	2 to 8	Oral			
DEPRESSANTS	Benzodiazepines	Ativan, Halcion, Equanil, Librium, Miltown, Serax, Tranxene, Valium, Verstran	Anti-anxiety, sedation, sleep	Moderate	Moderate	Yes	4 to 8	Oral, injected			
DEPRESSANTS	Other Depressants	Equanil, Dormate, Noludar, Placidyl, Valmid	Anti-anxiety, sedation, sleep	Moderate	Moderate	Yes	4 to 8	Oral			
STIMULANTS	Cocaine	Coke, Snow, Flake, Crack	Local anesthetic	Possible	High	Yes	1 to 2	Injected, Snorted, Smoked	Increased alertness, excitation, euphoria, dilated pupils, increased pulse rate and blood pressure, insomnia, loss of appetite.	Agitation, increase in body temperature, hallucinations, convulsions, possible death.	Apathy, long periods of sleep, irritability, depression, disorientation.
STIMULANTS	Amphetamines	Benzedrine, Biphetamine, Ice, Desoxyn, Dexedrine, Meth	Hyperkinesis, narcolepsy, weight control	Possible	High	Yes	2 to 4	Oral, Injected, Smoked			
STIMULANTS	Phenmetrazine	Preludin	Weight control	Possible	High	Yes	2 to 4	Oral			
STIMULANTS	Methylphenidate	Ritalin	Hyperkinesis, Narcolepsy	Possible	High	Yes	2 to 4	Oral, Injected			
STIMULANTS	Other Stimulants	Tepanil, Didrex, Ionamin, Plegine, Sanorex, Adipex	Weight control	Possible	High	Yes	2 to 4	Oral, Injected			
HALLUCINOGENS	LSD	Acid, Microdot	None	None	Degree Unknown	Yes	8 to 12	Oral	Illusions and hallucinations (with exception of MDA); poor perception of time and distance.	Longer, more intense "trip" episodes, psychosis, possible death.	Withdrawal syndrome not reported.
HALLUCINOGENS	Mescaline and Peyote	Mescal, Buttons, MESC	None	None	Degree Unknown	Yes	8 to 12	Oral			
HALLUCINOGENS	Amphetamine Variants	MDA, STP, Ecstasy, DOM, MDMA	None	Degree Unknown	Degree Unknown	Yes	Variable	Oral, Injected			
HALLUCINOGENS	Phencyclidine	PCP, Hog, Angel Dust	None	Degree Unknown	High	Yes	Days	Oral, Smoked			
HALLUCINOGENS	Other Hallucinogens	DMT, DET, Psilocybin	None	None	Degree Unknown	Possible	Variable	Oral, Injected, Smoked, Snorted			
CANNABIS	Marijuana	Pot, Grass, Sinsemilla, Thai Sticks, Marinol (Synthetic THC)	Marijuana - None THC, Antiemmtic	Degree Unknown	Moderate	Yes	2 to 4	Oral, Smoked	Euphoria, relaxed inhibitions, increased appetite, depth and time perception distorted.	Fatigue, paranoia, possible psychosis.	Insomnia, nervousness and decreased appetite
CANNABIS	Hashish & Hashish Oil	Hash, Hash Oil	Hashish - None	Degree Unknown	Moderate	Yes	2 to 4	Oral, Smoked			
ANABOLIC STEROIDS	Testosterone	Depo-Testosterone, Delatestryl	Hypogonadism	Degree Unknown	Degree Unknown	Degree Unknown	14 to 28 days	Injected	Virilization, acne, edema, aggressive behavior. Testicular atrophy Gynecomastia	Unknown.	Possible depression.
ANABOLIC STEROIDS	Nandrolone	Nortestosterone, DECA	Anemia, Breast Cancer	Degree Unknown	Degree Unknown	Degree Unknown	14 to 21 days	Injected			
ANABOLIC STEROIDS	Oxymetholone	Anadrol - 50	Anemia	Degree Unknown	Degree Unknown	Degree Unknown	24	Oral			

QUIZ
Substance Abuse

1.   Drug dependence is a primary disease.
     ☐ T   ☐ F

2.   Which of the following applies to drug dependence?
     ☐ A)it is fatal
     ☐ B)it is a family disease
     ☐ C)it is contagious
     ☐ D)all of the above

3.   The biggest single roadblock to addressing a person's substance abuse problem is _____.

4.   A company can effectively fight substance abuse by just starting a drug testing program.
     ☐ T   ☐ F

5.   A person who does not use drugs, but is preoccupied with a loved one who does, is said to be _____.

6.   The first step in developing a Drug-Free Workplace Program is to:
     ☐ A)provide education
     ☐ B)start an employee assistance program
     ☐ C)write a policy
     ☐ D)start drug testing

7.   The most widely used drug testing material in use today is:
     ☐ A)blood
     ☐ B)saliva
     ☐ C)urine
     ☐ D)hair

8.   Psychoactive drugs affect the _____.

9.   Nicotine and _____ are referred to as a gateway drugs.

10.   Your job as a Protection Officer is to observe and _____ substance abuse behavior activity.

Unit 8

Legal Aspects in Security
Protection Officer and the Law (American)
Protection Officer and the Law (Canadian)

THE LEGAL ASPECTS OF SECURITY

By David L. Ray LL.B.

Introduction

The purpose of this section of the manual is to introduce the student of security to the law. The law is a complex and constantly changing field and the security professional cannot be expected to have more than a fundamental understanding of the basics. It is important, however, to understand the rights and duties which are exercised in the everyday security roles.

This chapter will look at what the law is, the sources of our laws and the differences between some of the more important parts of the legal framework. It will look at some of the powers of the security officer including arrest and search, and it will also look at some of the duties that come with those powers.

Objective

The objective of this section is to help you to understand the authority that is provided to you with your duties. The security officer who understands the nature and extent of personal authority do the best possible job for their employer without unnecessary exposure to liability.

Court actions for false arrest and illegal search can be costly in terms of legal fees and damages if the case is lost. It is the duty of every security officer to minimize the risk of exposure to those actions by acting within the law.

What is the Law?

There have been many attempts to define what the law is, but there has never been a universally-accepted definition. The word 'law' is used to describe a wide variety of things, from individual statutes (e.g., immigration law) to a whole system of justice (e.g., the law of England). It is also used to describe things outside the justice system (e.g., the law of gravity).

For our purposes, here we will describe laws as follows:

LAWS ARE RULES GOVERNING SOCIETY

Laws are everyday guidelines established by us, by our forefathers and by the governments elected to rule us. Laws govern all of our everyday behavior — from the way we do business to the way we spend our leisure time. The purpose of our legal system is to:

1. Set down our obligations to each other
2. Set penalties for breaching those obligations
3. Establish procedures to enforce those obligations

The Source of our Laws

We tend to think of laws as being words written in books and passed by a government authority, but actually that is only one source of our laws. There are actually three —

1. The Common Law
2. Case law
3. Statutes

1. The Common Law:

Before the introduction of a justice system in England, people went to the feudal lord to resolve disputes. The lord was expected to be consistent in his decisions from one trial to the next and he would rely on local custom. It was therefore believed that laws were **common** throughout the land, even though they were not written down. In fact, this was far from true and many disputes were settled by combat or by ordeal so that the lord would not be required to make a decision.

Even after the establishment of the royal courts, throughout England the judges met at the Inns of Court to discuss their decisions and ensure some degree of consistency in the whole jurisdiction. The common law eventually found its way to North America and even today plays a strong role in our judicial system.

The common law still provides authority which is not set down in statute, it provides defences at criminal trials and it provides interpretation for statutes. The common law is still changing to adapt to changes within our society.

2. Case Law

Discussions by judges at the Inns of Court in London during feudal times was the first example of the attempt to ensure that they follow each other's decisions. Once cases were reported in books, it became much easier to refer to those decisions and follow universal principles. This 'case law' is also referred to as 'precedent' or 'the doctrine of stare decises'.

The principle of case law is fairly simply stated:

A Court Must Stand By Previous Decisions

In application, however, the doctrine becomes extremely complex. The weight that will be given to any previous decision will depend on a number of factors:

- Whether the court was the same legal jurisdiction;
- The level of the court where the decision was made;
- The similarity of the facts

3. Statutes

Statutes are the law in black-and-white. In feudal times, statutes would have been of little use because the common man could not read or write. As education became more commonplace, the government authorities began to pass statutes which would guide everyday life.

Statutes may be passed by any one of several levels of

government from municipal right up to federal. Like the common law, statutes are constantly being amended, new statutes are passed and old ones are repealed. Our society is constantly changing and so it is necessary that statutes change to meet new requirements. They are created to fill a need in our society. Sometimes the need is economic (for example, an amendment to income tax laws, to 'plug a loophole') and sometimes the need arises as a result of changes in society (for example, new computer crime legislation).

4. Conclusion

The security officer exercising the authority to arrest someone will not have to understand whether that authority comes from statutes or common law, or whether case law will uphold the matter in court. It must simply be understood that authority comes from one of several sources.

Types of Law - Criminal and Civil

The security officer should also understand the fundamental difference between criminal and civil law.

1. Criminal Law:

Many criminal laws may appear to be set up to protect people. For example, it is an offence to assault someone. But, the criminal law is set up to protect the state, not the individual. A crime is an act against society and it is the state which will take action to obtain punishment (although in some cases, there are provisions for private prosecutions).

In general, the prosecutor will act on behalf of the state, not on behalf of the victim. Any fine that the accused pays will go to the state, not to the victim and he may be sentenced to serve a sentence in a government institution.

2. Civil Law

The purpose of civil law is to protect private rights and not public rights. It is the individual who has been wronged, who must undertake the civil action. The prosecutor will not make that decision for him. He must pay for his own lawyer and hire an investigator if one is required. Any amount of money that the court orders the defendant to pay will go to the victim and not to the state, as in the case of a fine.

Often a particular action will be both civil and criminal. If a security officer were assaulted, the police may be called in to investigate a criminal assault and the person responsible may be charged with that criminal offense.

At the same time, however, the security officer may decide to sue civilly for damages for the assault and battery. Both cases may proceed at the same time although through a different court system. The person responsible may be sentenced to jail in the criminal court and ordered to pay the officer damages in the civil court.

There are several major areas of the civil law. Some of them are:

Area:	Example:
Contracts:	The law covering binding agreements between two or more parties. For example, a contract to provide security services for a building.
Warranties:	A special type of promise or statement. For example, a guarantee that a fire extinguisher is effective on a certain type of fire.
Agency:	A very important concept in the security industry. A question of whether one person is acting on behalf of another. For example - a security officer uses excessive force in subduing a suspected shoplifter. If the security officer is liable, is the store also liable because the officer was the store's agent?
Torts:	Torts may be an intentional civil wrong (e.g., assault, battery, wrongful imprisonment, libel or slander), or it may be negligence (e.g., the failure to provide the proper level of security in a dark employee parking lot).

Civil liability has caused increasing concern to the entire business community over the past decade. Damages in court actions in the United States and Canada have skyrocketed and insurance premiums for some types of liability insurance have become prohibitive.

Executives have found it necessary to take measures to defend against these crippling costs by increased security measures and by stringent screening, training and security procedures. The security officer has a strong role to play in protecting business against civil liabilities.

Arrest

It is seldom necessary for the security officer to undertake an arrest, but the occasion does arise from time-to-time and the officer must be aware of what an arrest is and the power of arrest.

1. What is an Arrest

In order for an arrest to take place, it is not necessary that the person be handcuffed, tied up or locked in a room. An arrest can take place with a simple assertion of the security officer's authority.

A court may find that an arrest has taken place if the officer says, "Sit there until the police arrive". It is important that the security officer understands this concept because if the arrest is found to be outside his authority, he or his employer may be found liable even though no force was used to effect the arrest, and even though the person willingly complied.

2. The Powers of Arrest

The powers of arrest are very complex and unfortunately vary from one jurisdiction to the next. The security officer would be well advised to become familiar with the local powers of arrest and ensure a good understanding of them. There are two methods by which a person may be legally arrested:

1. with a warrant
2. without a warrant

Warrants are issued to the police and are executed by them in the course of their duties. Both the police and private individuals have the power to arrest without a warrant under certain circumstances. The police have wide latitude for arrest without a warrant, but the security officer can arrest only under specific circumstances and for certain types of offenses.

The authority to arrest will depend upon:

1. Whether or not the security officer found the person committing the offense; and
2. The seriousness of the offense.

Search

The security officer stops an employee driving out of the plant gate. He asks to look into the employee's lunch bucket which is sitting on the front seat. Does he have authority?

Often it is a condition of employment that employees will submit to a search upon leaving company property. In those circumstances and where the employee voluntarily complies, the security officer has authority.

Searches may be conducted with consent of the party being searched. But where the employee refuses to allow the security officer to look into the lunch bucket (he is withdrawing his consent), then the officer must not force the issue.

He does have a couple of alternatives, however.

1. Where he has reasonable grounds to believe that the employee is in possession of stolen property (not just a mere suspicion), he can call the police and turn the matter over to them.
2. He can report the matter internally and the employee can be disciplined for refusing to submit to the search.
3. Or he can do both of the above.

A Note on Force

The amount of force that a security officer may use will always depend upon the circumstances of the case. The general guideline that is used is — only as much force as is necessary. Several other considerations must be applied to this principle:

1. The force itself must be necessary. The fact that a person is legally arrested does not give the arresting officer authority to mistreat him.
2. The force must suit the circumstances. A security officer does not have authority to shoot a suspect fleeing from a shoplifting.
3. As a general guideline, where force is necessary it should be a restraining type of force — not an attempt to incapacitate the person (unless it is a life-threatening situation).

Evidence

Evidence is the proof which is required to establish the guilt or innocence of the accused. Evidence may be:

1. Real — a physical object, a gun, a piece of stolen property.
2. Documentary — a contract, a bad cheque.

3. Testimony — the oral statement of a witness while under oath.

Evidence must meet certain requirements in order to be admissible in court. For example, a security officer seizes a stolen calculator from an accused, but fails to secure the evidence before it is turned over to the police.

Several months later, the officer is called to testify in court. He is presented with the calculator and is asked if it was the same one that was taken from the accused. He is forced to admit that he cannot be certain. The judge refuses to admit the evidence and the accused goes free.

Any one of the three forms of evidence indicated above may be direct or circumstantial.

Direct Evidence - Evidence which proves the facts in issue directly.

Circumstantial - Evidence which proves the facts in issue indirectly.

A smoking gun does not prove that the person holding it pulled the trigger, but the inference may be drawn and it is therefore circumstantial evidence that is admissible in court.

It is a common misconception that a person cannot be convicted on circumstantial evidence. If the evidence is admissable and the case is strong enough, then it does not matter whether it is circumstantial or direct.

Confessions

Confessions are a special exception to the rule of hearsay (that one person may not repeat the words of another in court). Confessions are admissible as evidence in court only if they are first proven to be voluntary.

There can be no threats, intimidation or promises to the accused which may induce him to make the statement. The police are required to advise the accused of:

1. His right not to make a statement;
2. That the statement will be used against him; and
3. That he has the right to counsel.

There is no similar duty on the private individual, however, and so the security officer need only ensure that the statement was willingly given.

The security officer may receive a confession from an accused in the course of an investigation of an incident. A confession need not be a lengthy statement in writing — it may be a simple oral statement like "I shouldn't have taken it". The officer should ensure that any statements by the accused are noted so that there will be no confusion later in court as to exactly what was said.

If the officer has occasion to interview a suspect, the following steps will help to ensure the admissibility of a confession.

1. Don't make any threats or promises.
2. Ask questions that are direct and pointed. If questions are ambiguous, the suspect will later be able to claim that he did not understand.
3. Give the accused time to explain.

The Burden of Proof

The burden is always on the prosecutor in common law jurisdictions to prove that the accused is guilty 'beyond a reasonable doubt'. The onus is not on the accused to show that he is innocent. This has been referred to as the 'golden thread' that runs through our judicial system. Because of this rule, the security officer must take steps to protect the admissibility of any evidence that is collected.

1. Any real or documentary evidence must be protected from the time that it is obtained. If possible, an identifying mark (for example, initials and the date) should be put on it so that the officer can later identify it in court. (Evidential 'chain of custody'.)

2. Extensive notes should be taken during the inquiry or immediately after — while it is still fresh in your mind. The judge will place a great deal more weight on testimony where your memory can be refreshed from notes. The time that passes from the event to the trial can be several months or even years. The importance of notes cannot be overemphasized.
3. Make sure that your reports are accurate and detailed. The report itself may be entered into evidence and you may be required to explain discrepancies. Make sure that any statements you take from witnesses are also accurate and detailed.
4. Make sure that you are well prepared for the trial. Answer all questions as clearly and directly as possible and don't be afraid to admit that you do not know the answer to a question.

Conclusion

The information in this chapter will help the security officer to understand basic legal concepts which can be used in the day-to-day execution of security duties. It touches on:

- The source of our laws: statutes, the common law and case law.
- The difference between civil law and criminal law.
- Powers of arrest and search and the use of force.
- Evidence, confessions and the burden of proof at criminal trials.

The security officer who understands these basic concepts will be better equipped to ensure that powers and duties provided by law are properly used and are not abused. It will also assist the officer to avoid situations which will expose the employer and the owner of property to liability.

QUIZ
The Legal Aspects of Security

1. A person is arrested only when there is an assertion of _____
(Fill in the blank)

2. A security officer may search an employee where it is a condition of _____
(Fill in the blank)

3. A store can be liable for the actions of its security officer if it can be proven that the officer was their: _____ (Fill in the blank)

4. A person can be convicted on _____ evidence alone.
(Fill in the blank)

5. If a law is not written down and passed by government, we are not affected by it.
☐ T ☐ F

6. The purpose of our legal system is to:
☐ a) set down our obligations to each other
☐ b) set penalties for breaching those obligations
☐ c) Establish procedures to enforce those obligations
☐ d) All of the above

7. The common law is not used in North America today.
☐ T ☐ F

8. You cannot sue someone and press criminal charges. It is double jeopardy.
☐ T ☐ F

9. At criminal trials, the prosecutor must prove the accused guilty:
☐ a. On a balance of probabilities;
☐ b. Beyond a reasonable doubt;
☐ c. By a preponderance of evidence; or
☐ d. Without a shadow of doubt.

10. The police will investigate:
☐ a. civil matters
☐ b. criminal matters
☐ c. whatever they are paid to investigate, or
☐ d. all of the above.

THE PROTECTION OFFICER
AND THE LAW *(AMERICAN)*

LEGAL ASPECTS

Unit VIII, Chapter 1, covers important legal matters that are generic to all Protection Officers. Federal, State and Provincial laws all have significant impact on the application of criminal law in the Security profession. For this reason it was felt prudent to prepare two additional chapters that deal exclusively with American and Canadian Law, which of course is all based upon British Common Law.

The Unit VIII examination process of the Certified Protection Officer (CPO) program is based entirely on Chapter 1 (Legal Aspects), which is necessary knowledge for all Protection Officers. We strongly suggest, however, that each candidate study the two additional chapters; Protection Officer and the Law (American), Protection Officer and the Law (Canadian). At the conclusion of each of these two chapters, CPO candidates will find five true/false and five multiple choice questions. While these questions do not comprise part of the CPO examination process, the reader should be able to answer each question correctly.

This unit includes a number of legal terms. CPO candidates should know the meanings of these terms and how they relate to the role of the Protection Officer.

By Jeff B. Wilt, CPP, CPO

I. INTRODUCTION

The protection officer is in a unique, albeit unenviable, position. The responsibilities and job duties of the protection officer require him or her to perform law enforcement type functions. In many cases, the required uniform of the protection officer closely resembles that of law enforcement officers. If authorized to carry handcuffs, a baton and/or a sidearm, the law enforcement image projected by the protection officer is greatly increased.

The inherent hazard presented by this law enforcement image lies in the possibility that the protection officer may begin to think of him or herself as an accredited law enforcement officer and acts or reacts accordingly. By acting as a law enforcement officer, the protection officer can expose him or herself and the employer or client to both criminal and civil liability.

Personal knowledge of the state statutes and local ordinances concerning the legal authority of protection officers can minimize this liability exposure.

The purpose of this chapter is to provide the protection officer a brief and generic summary of his or her legal authority.

II. LEGAL AUTHORITY OF THE PROTECTION OFFICER

In most states, the protection officer has no more legal authority than any other private citizen. There are two exceptions to this general rule:

A. Accredited law enforcement officers working off-duty (ie; moonlighting) as protection officers retain their police authority. However, they are also still subject to the legal restraints placed on their authority by the U.S. Constitution, state statutes and local ordinances.

B. A few states require that protection officers be "commissioned" or accredited as peace officers by the state. Protection officers in these states are granted full or limited police authority and are also subject to the same legal restrictions placed on this authority by the U.S. Constitution, state statutes and local ordinances.

The vast majority of protection officers obtain their authority from their employer or client. In these cases, the employer or client has designated the protection officer as their legal agent responsible for the security of the employer's or client's property, resources and assets. This agent designation is conveyed either through an employment agreement (proprietary security) or a service contract (contract security service).

In either case, the extent of the protection officer's authority and the methods by which he or she may exercise this authority should be documented as policy directives, standard operating procedures and/or post instructions.

If instructions are issued verbally, the protection officer would be wise to document them in his or her notebook. Include the date and time of issue, and by whom the instructions were issued.

The bottom line regarding the general legal authority of a protection officer is; the protection officer has no more authority than a private citizen. As a result, many of the Constitutional and statutory restrictions that apply to law enforcement officers do not affect the protection officer.

To determine exactly what legal authority you do possess, and what legal restrictions apply to your position, protection officers should refer to the state statutes and local ordinances of their employment location.

III. SEARCH AND SEIZURE

A law enforcement officer with reasonable cause may stop an individual and require him or her to produce identification or, submit to a search without the need of a search warrant.

Without a search warrant, law enforcement officers may make a reasonable search of persons, vehicles and/or property incidental to an arrest.

With a valid search warrant, law enforcement officers may make a more thorough search of vehicles and property as specified by the warrant.

Generally, protection officers do not enjoy this legal authority. Before taking any action that could be considered a search of persons or property, the protection officer must first obtain the consent of the individual(s) involved. Consent can be obtained by several methods among which are:

A. Required by the employer or client - proprietary or contracted employees may be required by their employment agreement, union contract or service contract to submit to a reasonable search of their property by the protection officer.

B. Public notice - signs posted conspicuously at public entrances notifying non-employees that any packages, containers and similar objects are subject to search upon entering and leaving the premises.

C. Tacit approval or submission - the subject does not verbally object to the search and, his or her behavior would lead a reasonable person to believe that they have consented to the search.

However, the subject can withdraw their consent at any time. Employees may prefer to face personnel actions by management rather than submit to a search or allow a search to continue. Non-employees can withdraw their consent with relative impunity from punishment by the employer or client providing they were originally authorized to be on the property.

In both cases, the protection officer should not press the issue by demanding to conduct or continue the search unless the officer has reasonable cause to detain the subject. The protection officer must consider the possibility that consent was denied or withdrawn because the individual feels embarrassed rather than is guilty of a crime. No matter how professionally a search is done, it is a very personal and sometimes offensive action.

The protection officer must consider other alternatives when consent is denied or withdrawn. Among them are; simply letting the subject go on his or her way and reporting the details of the situation to management, or detaining the individual, if sufficient reasonable cause exists, until local law enforcement officers arrive. Upon their arrival, let the police officer(s) conduct the search and accurately document it. Be sure to include the officer's name and ID number.

During the course of a consent search, the protection officer has the right to seize items found such as:

A. Property of the employer or client which the officer is required to protect and, for which the subject has no obvious permission to possess.

B. Evidence of the commission of a crime (ie; company property, burglar tools, controlled substances, etc.).

C. Weapons that could be used to injure the officer, an innocent third party or the subject.

D. Items that could help the subject escape detention.

If no consent exists, the protection officer has no right to conduct a search. Any items found as the result of an illegal search cannot be seized nor entered as evidence in judicial proceedings.

However, any of the previously listed items that are IN PLAIN VIEW may be seized because the seizure is not the result of a search.

All authorized searches and seizures must strictly comply with established procedures developed by the employer or client. Additionally, protection officers should be familiar with state statutes and local ordinances concerning search and seizure by private persons. This will minimize the possibility of criminal or civil actions against the officer and the employer or client.

Familiarity with the local laws will also help assure that the employer's or client's policies and procedures concerning search and seizure are in compliance with the statutes and/or ordinances.

Remember, searches are very personal and can cause great embarrassment even if the subject has committed no crime. Searches should be conducted discretely to minimize; public embarrassment for the subject and adverse public/employee reaction to the officer conducting the search.

Security and the Law

IV. TRESPASS

Both the common law (ie; socially accepted practices over a period of time) and statutory law (ie; written law) recognize the property owner's right to control access to, use of, activity on and protection of their property. As mentioned in Section I, the employer or client designates the protection officer as their agent to protect their property and enforce their guidelines concerning it.

Many protection officers are responsible for property to which the public has access for business or recreation. As a result, it may seem difficult to determine when a trespass occurs.

Generally, one or more of the following must be present for a trespass to occur:

A. The subject does not own or have other legal rights to the property involved.

B. The subject must know this.

C. The subject does not have permission of the property owner or agent (ie; the protection officer) to enter upon or, remain on the property.

D. The property is posted in accordance with local ordinances with signs prohibiting trespass or, fences and/or other barriers are present that would cause a reasonable person to believe they are not to enter the property.

E. The property owner or agent has lawfully requested the subject to leave the property.

F. The subject enters the property and/or refuses to leave after seeing posted notices and/or physical barriers, or receiving a lawful request to leave.

Again, the protection officer should be familiar with state statutes and local ordinances concerning trespass to assure that he or she is acting within the law when dealing with a possible trespass. Generally, the protection officer will not have to arrest a trespasser unless the subject is suspected of or known to have committed other crimes on the property.

In most cases, the subject will leave when advised they are trespassing. In others, the subject may not leave unless the protection officer tells them the local police will be requested to arrest the individual for trespass.

However, if the protection officer must make an arrest, he

or she must know state statutes and local ordinances concerning arrests by private persons.

V. ARREST

Before discussing the aspects of arrest, let's first look over three definitions of crimes:

A. **Felony.** Generally, a crime for which the penalty includes a fine, imprisonment in a Federal or state prison for more than one year or death.

B. **Misdemeanor.** Generally, a crime for which the penalty includes a fine or imprisonment in a county (parish) or local jail for one year or less.

C. **Breach of the Peace.** Generally, a misdemeanor involving conduct that is disruptive to a segment of the public (ie; fighting, causing a disturbance, etc.).

ELEMENTS OF AN ARREST:

A. **Intent.** The person making the arrest must have the intent to deprive the person being arrested of freedom of movement. This does not necessarily mean physical force like using handcuffs. It simply means the subject may not move about of their own free will.

B. **Communication.** The person making the arrest must communicate their intent to the person to be arrested. Additionally, the reason for the arrest must be communicated. This communication must be very clear so the subject does not misunderstand.

C. **Physical action.** In some cases, the protection officer may have to clarify the verbal communication of his or her intent to arrest by a physical action. This action can be as simple as pointing at the subject, or touching the subject's shoulder or arm.

There is an inherent hazard in some contacts a protection officer makes on a daily basis. An officer may be involved in a potential arrest situation but, has determined an arrest is not necessary. The officer's words, tone of voice, physical actions or a combination of the foregoing may cause the subject to believe he or she has been arrested. For this reason, care must be exercised to ensure that the subject understands the verbal or non-verbal communication of the officer.

Despite the fact that the officer did not have the intent to arrest, the subject could believe an arrest was made. This could result in a criminal or civil action against the officer and his or her employer or client for false arrest.

It is the ultimate responsibility of the protection officer to clearly communicate their intent through verbal and

physical communication.

We now have the definitions of certain crimes and the requirements for an arrest. Next, we'll see when and under what circumstances the protection officer may make an arrest. In most states all of the following must be present before a private person (ie; protection officer) can make an arrest:

A. A felony or misdemeanor amounting to a breach of peace must actually have been committed.

B. Felony - The person intending to make the arrest must know the felony has been committed. This does not mean the felony had to occur in the protection officer's presence but, the officer must have more than "reasonable belief" that the felony occurred.

The protection officer requires reasonable belief the person to be arrested actually committed the felony.

C. Misdemeanor, Breach of the Peace - The person intending to make the arrest must have witnessed the misdemeanor.

Additionally, the protection officer must know that the person to be arrested actually committed the misdemeanor.

D. The person making the arrest must release the subject to the custody of an officer of the court (ie; police officer, constable, justice of the peace, etc.) as soon as practical.

To minimize the possibility of criminal or civil actions for false arrest, the protection officer should; refer to the state statutes and local ordinances concerning arrest by a private person and, give some conscious thought to both words and actions when involved in a potential arrest situation.

VI. USE OF FORCE

The most common cause of criminal and civil actions against protection officers and their employers or clients is the officer's use of both physical and/or deadly physical force. Even when force is justified, the officer can expect to be the subject of both internal and police investigations.

Therefore, it is the ultimate responsibility of the protection officer to consider all other alternatives available before resorting to force. The officer must also consider his or her own moral convictions concerning the use of force.

The bottom line is; the protection officer must know *when* force may be used and *how much* force may be used.

A. **When to use force.** Force should be used only as a last resort after the officer has exhausted all of his or her other options. Depending on the circumstances, the officer may not have had a chance to try other alternatives.

Force should be used *only* to protect the officer, an innocent third party or the subject from serious injury or imminent death.

B. **How much force?** The protection officer should use only that amount of force necessary to overcome physical resistance to the performance of his or her lawful duties or, to prevent serious injury or imminent death to the officer, a third party or the subject.

Once the resistance has been overcome or, the threat neutralized, the officer may have an opportunity to try other available alternatives.

As with the preceeding sections, it is to the benefit of the protection officer and his or her employer or client, to know the state statutes and local ordinances concerning the legal use of force.

1 JUDGE ON THE BENCH	9 COURT CLERK
2 WITNESS	10 BALIFF
3 JURY IN THE BOX	11 SPECTATORS AND SEATS
4 STENO	12 CLOCK
5 PROSECUTOR	13 FLAGS
6 DEFENSE ATTORNEY	14 CHALKBOARD
7 DEFENDANT	15 CHAMBERS
8 COUNSEL TABLE	16 JURY ROOM

VII. STATEMENTS

Interviewing witnesses and suspects requires techniques that not everyone can master to the same degree. (Generally, the protection officer will interview witnesses, victims and/or suspects during a preliminary investigation) More thorough interviews may be done later by investigators or law enforcement personnel during the follow-up investigation.

A bad interview during the preliminary investigation can cause information obtained during later interviews to be unusable. The protection officer should know what he or she legally can and cannot do during interviews.

Remember, even though the protection officer as a private citizen is not required to "Mirandize" (ie; give the Miranda Warning) suspects, any statements given by the suspect, victim or witnesses must be voluntary.

The fact that the protection officer has been delegated authority by the employer or client may be sufficient coercion to cause an employee to make an involuntary statement out of fear of losing their job or other punishment if they don't cooperate. The protection must be aware of this possibility.

The officer should make note of any statements made by the suspect prior to the formal interview. If possible, the protection officer should have the person being interviewed sign a declaration to the effect that all statements made are voluntary and not the result of threats or promises.

A second officer should be present to verify that the statements documented are both accurate and voluntary.

If the protection officer uses any kind of coercion or promises of rewards, the statements obtained will be declared inadmissable in court. Additionally, statements gained by such actions may affect the admissability of information obtained later by investigators and/or law enforcement personnel.

Should the subject refuse to speak to the protection officer or, wishes to end a voluntary interview, the officer should note this fact and not press the issue. If the officer insists on continuing the interview process, any statements the subject makes could be considered involuntary and, inadmissable in court.

VIII. CONCLUSION

You have probably noticed at this point that the catch-phrase of this chapter has been, "Know the state statutes and local ordinances of your location of employment." As boring and tedious as it may seem, it's been repeated for a very good reason.

The legal authority of law enforcement officers is well defined and subject to specific Constitutional restrictions. Conversely, the legal authority of the protection officer (ie; private citizen) is not so well defined and varies from state to state and city to city. Additionally, the protection officer is not subject to all the Constitutional restrictions that apply to police powers.

However, just like the law enforcement officer, the protection officer can be subject to criminal and/or civil action for violation or abuse of his or her legal authority. These actions can also affect the officer's employer or client.

For Further Information:

Butterworths (80 Montvale Ave., Stoneham, MA 02180 (617) 438-8464) offers an array of security texts including *Protective Security Law* by Inbau, Aspen and Spiotto and *Prosecuting the Shoplifter: A Loss Prevention Strategy* by James Cleary, Jr.

Gould Publications (199 State Street, Binghamton, NY 13901 (607) 724-3000) specializes in legal texts. Gould has a full line of state criminal codes, complete with annual updates.

Spain & Spain Inc. (4426 Mulberry Ct., Suite J, Pittsburgh, PA 15227 (412) 884-8185) provide seminars on "Civil Law for the Security Manager" as well as other topics. Spain & Spain also publish *The Spain Report*, a security law training newsletter.

QUIZ
Protection Officer & the Law *(American)*

1. Protection Officers generally obtain their legal authority from:
   - ☐ a. Common Law
   - ☐ b. Statutory Law
   - ☐ c. Their employer or client
   - ☐ d. All of the above
   - ☐ e. None of the above

2. In most states, the Protection Officer has the same authority to execute an arrest without a warrant as a Police Officer.
   - ☐ True   ☐ False

3. In the absence of consent for a search, the Protection Officer acting on proper authority, may seize only those items:
   - ☐ a. In plain view
   - ☐ b. Making obvious bulges under the subject's clothing
   - ☐ c. Within the subject's reach but not on his or her person
   - ☐ d. All of the above
   - ☐ e. None of the above

4. Consent for a search, once given, cannot be withdrawn by the consenting party.
   - ☐ True   ☐ False

5. The most common cause of criminal or civil action against Protection Officers is:
   - ☐ a. False arrest
   - ☐ b. Illegal search
   - ☐ c. Use of force
   - ☐ d. Improper interviewing practices
   - ☐ e. All of the above
   - ☐ f. None of the above

6. If a Protection Officer has reasonable grounds to believe an employee has committed a misdemeanor an arrest can be effected.
   - ☐ True   ☐ False

7. The elements required for an arrest are (check one item only):
   - ☐ a. Reasonable cause, communication and action
   - ☐ b. Intent, communication and action
   - ☐ c. Intent, reasonable cause and action
   - ☐ d. All of the above
   - ☐ e. None of the above

8. Statements made to the Protection Officer must be voluntary.
   - ☐ True   ☐ False

9. The Protection Officer should know state statutes and local ordinances concerning the legal authority of a private citizen to (check one item):
   - ☐ a. Make more arrests
   - ☐ b. Impress the employer or client
   - ☐ c. Minimize the possibility of criminal/civil actions
   - ☐ d. All of the above
   - ☐ e. None of the above

10. A Protection Officer could jeopardize the follow-up investigation by forcing a suspect to give an involuntary statement.
    - ☐ True   ☐ False

THE PROTECTION OFFICER AND THE LAW (CANADIAN)

By Rooney H. Hodgins

INTRODUCTION

Protection officers during the course of their duties will exercise powers granted to them by law. Conversely, their authority to take action and the type and extent of action taken is limited by law. Protection officers who do not fully understand the duties and responsibilities imposed by law, expose themselves and their employer/client to possible criminal and civil actions. To be effective, protection officers must be knowledgeable of their legal authority, duties and responsibilities.

The purpose of this chapter is to provide an introduction to the legal authority and limits to that authority found in the Criminal Code of Canada, other statutes and the common law. I encourage all protection officers, once having read this chapter, to continue their research indepth, by going to the source. The subject dealt with in this chapter is complex and constantly changing, each day, reflecting the realty of the world we live in.

AUTHORITY

Protection officers in the main receive their authority, directly or indirectly, as agents of the owner or person in lawful possession of property. The common law and various statutes recognize the right of an owner of property to take whatever steps are considered reasonable to protect and enjoy the use of their property.

Authority to act as an agent for the owner is usually found in whatever contractual arrangements have been agreed upon between the owner and the protection officer. These may be written, verbal or implied. In the best of circumstances, a protection officer will be guided and governed by clear written instructions contained in documents such as directives, standard operating procedures and post orders. If instructions are given verbally, the protection officer should note the details in his/her notebook.

CONSENT

Performing the duties of a protection officer often means inconveniencing people. In the best of circumstances this is done with the consent of those involved. Consent can be obtained by many means:

— the protection officer can ask the subject to cooperate willingly;

— the persons involved may have a contractual arrange-

ment allowing the protection officer to carry out certain procedures, (eg. collective agreements may specify that plant security personnel may carry out searches of persons under certain conditions);

— posted signs can warn visitors entering premises that they may be subjected to certain procedures (eg. a sign at the entrance to a store warning patrons to check their bags or be subject to search); and

— the subject may imply consent by "acquiescent conduct". In other words, their behavior would lead a reasonable person to assume they have consented to certain procedures (eg. a protection officer asks a person to show him/her what is in the bag and the subject does so without protest)

Consent may be withdrawn at any time. For instance, a plant worker may prefer to suffer the consequences of disciplinary action for refusing to be searched, rather than consent to being searched. Protection officers faced with a refusal to cooperate, must consider other alternatives, if they do not have lawful authority to impose their demands. What they might do will depend on the specific circumstances. In this instance they may be wiser to allow the plant worker to go on his/her way and report the details to management.

TRESPASS

The right of an owner of property to control the use of and to protect his/her property, gives protection officers a great deal of authority. Generally speaking the owner or lawful occupier of property may invite who he/she wishes onto their property and may impose conditions on the invitees. These conditions may be verbal, written or implied. For example, a store owner expects that when you enter their store, you are looking to buy something sold in his/her store.

The offence of trespass occurs when a person does not comply with the lawful conditions of the invitation. This is clearest when a person refuses to leave the premises, when ordered by the owner, occupier or his/her agent. For example, an usher asks a patron to leave because the patron has been disturbing the other movie goers by his/her behavior (shouting, throwing popcorn).

The Criminal Code and various provincial statutes deal with trespass. Sections 38 to 42 of the Criminal Code deal with the right of a person to protect his/her property. Section 73 deals with the offence of forcible entry and section 173 with the offence of trespass by night. At least four provinces give the owner, occupier or agent authority to arrest trespassers. In Ontario, for example, a protection officer acting for the owner or occupier of the property, may arrest anyone whom they reasonably believe to be trespassing.

ARREST

"An arrest is a grave imposition on another person's liberty and should only be attempted if other options prove ineffective." (quote from, *This Land is Whose Land*, A legal guide to property protection rights, Ministry of the Attorney General of Ontario).

I couldn't have put it better myself. Besides, arresting people can be hazardous to either party, as well as the risk of criminal or civil action against protection officers who have acted outside the limits of their lawful authority.

An arrest can be deemed to have taken place when a person reasonably believes that they are not free to go on their way without further interference, restraint or public embarrassment. This can become a matter of dispute later in court.

A protection officer, once having made the decision to arrest someone, should do the following:

1. clearly tell the person that they are under arrest;
2. tell them the reason for the arrest;
3. inform them of their right to retain and instruct counsel without delay, (Canadian Charter of Rights and Freedoms, section 10.);
4. touch them to demonstrate physical control. This can be done by tapping their shoulder or by lightly grasping their elbow; and
5. once having physical control of the subject, maintain that control until turning them over to an authorized peace officer (usually the police force having local jurisdiction.)

Although there are several statutes which authorize specified protection officers to arrest without warrant, most often a protection officer will arrest under the authority of section 449 of the Criminal Code, commonly referred to as "Citizen's Arrest". Under section 449, an AUTHORIZED protection officer may arrest anyone he/she FINDS COMMITTING a criminal offence on or in relation to the property he/she is protecting. A protection officer, acting as a private citizen may arrest anyone they find committing an INDICTABLE (serious) offence or someone who they reasonably believe has committed a criminal offence and is being FRESHLY PURSUED by someone who has the lawful authority to arrest the subject.

Protection officers should be aware of the following when using the provisions of section 449:

— if arresting for a criminal offence, as opposed to an indictable offence, the offence must have taken place on or involve the property they are authorized to protect or they must be assisting someone they believe has lawful authority to effect the arrest;
— "finds committing" means they must see the subject commit the offence;
— "dual offences" (theft, assault) are considered to be indictable offences for the purposes of this section; and
— the subject must be turned over to an authorized peace officer as soon as possible.

SEARCH AND SEIZURE

There is a belief held by some, that a protection officer may search someone incidental to an arrest, based on the common law. However, this presumption is not supported by case law. I recommend that protection officers not search persons they have arrested without the consent of the subject.

A protection officer can seize certain items that are IN VIEW, as this does not constitute a search. These items include:

— property which the officer was authorized to protect;
— items related directly to the commission of the offence (evidence);
— items which may be used to injure either the subject or the officer; and
— items which the subject could use to effect an escape.

There are several statutes which give specified protection officers the authority to search persons. Two examples are the Federal Aeronautics Act and Ontario's Public Works Protection Act. Also protection officers can carry out a search pursuant to a search warrant. However this is not often done and is probably best left to the police.

Protection officers carrying out authorized searches should adhere strictly to the procedures laid down by their employer or by the statute authorizing the search. All searches should be carried out with discretion. Even when a person has willingly consented to the search, it is still an invasion of their privacy and emotions can run high. Like arrest, personal searches should only be carried out, when there is no other reasonable option available.

USE OF FORCE

The use of force is always controversial, even when legally authorized. Protection officers must realize that the people who will sit in judgement (the media and public, as well as the courts) on whether they should have used force or whether they used too much force, were not at the occurrence, were not subject to the stresses of the moment and may never have been in a similar situation.

Two rules are paramount when using force:

1. don't, if you can possibly find another alternative; and
2. if you must use force, use as little as possible.

There are several sections of the Criminal Code which deal with the use of force. The following are those which affect protection officers the most:

— **section 25** authorizes protection officers to use as much force as is reasonably necessary to carry out their duties, when acting lawfully;
— **section 26** makes protection officers criminally responsible for the use of excess force; and
— **section 27** justifies the use of reasonable force to prevent the commission of an offence for which the subject could be arrested or that would be likely to cause immediate and serious injury to a person or property.

Other sections of the Criminal Code permit protection officers to defend themselves and others from assault, prevent or stop a breach of the peace or riot and to protect the property under their care.

STATEMENTS

Questioning of suspects and interviewing of witnesses are important aspects of a protection officer's duties. Both require great skill on the part of protection officers. Even skilled investigators find interrogating suspects and interviewing witnesses to be demanding work.

After arresting a subject, the protection officer should keep accurate and complete notes. These notes will be crucial for further investigation and when giving testimony in court. The notes should record any warnings given to the subject and the subject's response.

I would not recommend, except in special circumstances, that the arresting officer question the subject. This is better left to the police. The arresting officer should, however, record anything said by the subject, especially those things said in the heat of the moment (utterances).

Protection officers who do question suspects, should be aware of the protections provided by the Canadian Charter of Rights and Freedom. It seems evident to me that Canadian appeal courts are prepared to rule in some cases that protection officers are "persons in authority". I believe this could be argued successfully in cases where, for instance, an employee might feel their job was at risk, if they don't answer the questions put to them by a company security officer.

Statements provided by a subject must be given voluntarily, without threat or promise of reward. Even if the subject is not under arrest they should be allowed to seek the advice of counsel. In the case of employees, this may mean the presence of a union representative. I recommend that before proceeding with a statement, the subject should sign a caution or warning notice. The wording should be approved by the employer or client's legal counsel. A refusal to sign or give a statement should be recorded by the officer. An example is given here:

I understand that I do not have to make this statement and that I have the right to obtain and instruct counsel. I choose to make this statement voluntarily without fear of threat or offer of reward.

One final word about handling arrested persons or suspects; if at all possible, a second protection officer should be in attendance or near at all times. This officer will act as a corroborating witness should the case to go court.

SPECIAL STATUS

Many protection officers enjoy special status under the law. Railway police possess full police powers within specified distance from railroad property. Security officers who are employees of the Public Service of Canada are designated public officers under the Financial Administration Act. Protection officers are often designated as special constables for the purposes of carrying out some limited legal duty such as parking control or policing duties at a facility, such as on a university campus. Others have special powers granted them by a specific statute, such as the Canada Post Act.

CONCLUSION

As you probably realize by now, a protection officer has more to think of than just catching the bad guys. Indeed, all his/her efforts are wasted if successful prosecutions are not forthcoming. Even worse, an officer and his/her employer/client could face civil/criminal action and/or the resulting bad publicity when a protection officer has overstepped his/her authority or has omitted to perform a duty specified by law or a contract.

QUIZ
Protection Officer & the Law *(Canadian)*

1. Protection Officers who do not fully understand the duties and responsibilities imposed by law, expose themselves and their employer/client to possible criminal and _____ actions.

2. The Protection Officer's _____ to act as the agent on behalf of the owner of property can be derived from written or verbal instructions.

3. An arrest is a grave imposition on another person's _____ and should only be attempted if other options prove ineffective.

4. The consent extended to a Protection Officer to conduct a search of a person that is not under arrest can be withdrawn at any time.
   ☐ True   ☐ False

5. The Protection Officer derives his/her powers to arrest a person without a warrant from:
   ☐ a. Most Federal Statutes
   ☐ b. Most Provincial Statutes
   ☐ c. Canadian Charter of Rights and Freedoms
   ☐ d. Canadian Criminal Code of Canada

6. A visitor to a privately owned facility, becomes disruptive and causes a disturbance, is asked to leave the premises by the Protection Officer in lawful possession of the property. He refuses. This person then becomes a trespasser.
   ☐ True   ☐ False

7. A Protection Officer that has executed a lawful arrest should take all of the following steps except one (mark item out of place):
   ☐ a. Clearly tell the person that they are under arrest.
   ☐ b. Inform the person of his/her rights to retain and instruct counsel without delay.
   ☐ c. Inform the person arrested of the severe consequences of the crime for which the arrest was made.
   ☐ d. Ensure that the subject arrested fully understands the reason for the arrest.

8. When it is necessary to use force, use as much as deemed necessary to immobilize the subject.
   ☐ True   ☐ False

9. Statements provided to the Protection Officer by a subject/suspect are more readily accepted as evidence by a court of law when (mark item out of place):
   ☐ a. The statement was voluntary.
   ☐ b. The statement resulted from a cooperative attitude exhibited by the subject/suspect.
   ☐ c. The statement was in the subject/suspect's own words.
   ☐ d. The statement was witnessed by an independent third party.

10. A collective agreement may provide the necessary consent required for a Protection Officer to conduct a lawful search.
    ☐ True   ☐ False

Unit 9

Health, Fitness, and Exercise Prescription

HEALTH, FITNESS AND EXERCISE PRESCRIPTION

By Florence J. Slomp M.Sc.
and Debbie Y. Minion BA

The lifestyles of the 20th century is one of mechanization, automation and convenience. Although there is an increasing awareness and participation in physical activity, many North American lifestyles still include habits which increase the risk of disease.

Inactivity, poor eating habits, smoking and stressful living are the primary behaviors associated with poor health. People look for special diets and buy gimmicks to attain their dream body — but the truth is, there is no magic formula!

It takes a lot of sweat and maybe even some tears, daily commitment to good eating, sleeping and exercise habits is truly what it is all about. Not a few weeks of fad dieting or the occasional walk to the mailbox, but a change in lifestyle. Good health is not a fad, but an individual responsibility to quality living. Since there are not any hokey broths, good health begins with an appreciation and understanding of what it involves.

Physical activity plays an integral role in the concept of health. Although many factors contribute to the model of health, physical activity appears to play a dominant role by its indirect influence on several other controllable behaviors/factors.

Fitness and health are by no means equivalent, but neither are they mutually exclusive. Imagine the circle in Figure 1 to represent health — a state in which the body is disease-free. Some of these contributing factors are beyond our control, such as age, gender and environment, but there are other factors which are related to behavior.

A common thread can be found through several of these factors — physical activity. If one is physically active, he(she) often attains good eating and sleeping habits. Coping with stress may be eased with physical activity.

Self-image, confidence and satisfaction — mental wellness, are often improved with physical activity. Through its indirect influence on these contributing factors, physical activity becomes a much larger component of the Health Model.

Figure 1 - Health Model

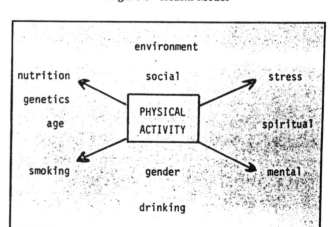

Physical activity is a necessary behavior needed to achieve physical fitness. It can be described as any muscle movements of the body which results in energy expenditure.[2] They are activities which are controllable behaviors including energy spent on the job, household duties and/or recreation. Any combination of these constitutes physical activity.

Exercise is considered to be physical activity, but it has the goal of achieving one or more of the fitness components.[2] Moreover, it is a planned behavior which involves a nature of repetition. Exercise is the means to an end — fitness. The physiological attributes that people strive for or are maintaining is **physical fitness.[2]**

These attributes can be categorized into those involving health or specific skills (i.e., speed, agility and balance). Health-related fitness typically involves the following: cardiovascular, muscular strength and endurance, body composition and flexibility.

People get involved in physical activity for numerous reasons which can be categorized into extrinsic and intrinsic motivations.[1] Employee fitness programs claim that physical activity decreases absenteeism while increasing productivity and morale on the job. In addition, there is a lowering of health costs and general health improvements.

Extrinsic reasons such as these are economically based. Dreams of a lithe, muscular body motivates some people, but it is only one of the many intrinsic or personal reasons for becoming physically active. An improved self-awareness and self-concept as well as the satisfaction of accomplishment are more common motivators. What motivates a person to become physically active varies substantially, but it should be enjoyable.

COMPONENTS OF HEALTH-RELATED FITNESS

Physical fitness means more than bulging muscles or a trim waistline. Becoming fit is a developmental process of the whole person; people begin with their current state of health and lifestyle, and grow from there. It's the emphasis on the physical side of fitness — on body and movement — that leads the way to further personal change and development.

Today, more people participate in physical activity than ever before. They realize the benefits of physical activity and the importance of fitness. However, many of those not presently involved in a fitness program have hesitated to begin because they are uncertain how to get started.

A logical start to any training program is a fitness appraisal. It is a fundamental aspect of human nature to be curious how we compare with others. Physical fitness measurements afford you the opportunity to evaluate your physical status. Most important, they give you a basis for setting personal goals and they enable you to test the effectiveness of your training program. If you want to begin a fitness program, an appraisal will provide you with the basis for developing an exercise program geared to your personal fitness level. If you already participate in a program, a regular fitness appraisal will allow you to evaluate the effects of your exercise program.

What is a Fitness Appraisal?

A fitness appraisal consists of a series of simple measurements which give you an estimate of your overall fitness. These measures are designed to assess your cardio-respiratory fitness, muscular strength and endurance, flexibility and body composition (body fat).

Every fitness appraisal is different. The measures taken depend on your fitness goals and what information you want from the appraisal. The fitness appraiser will incorporate the results of your appraisal into an activity prescription that matches your personal preferences. The result will be a practical action plan to improve your fitness, based on your needs and interests.

What Does a Fitness Appraisal Involve?

A fitness appraisal is a private consultation between you and the fitness appraiser. The appraiser will explain and then demonstrate each test item. You will be allowed to warm-up and then practice before attempting yourself. Since your fitness level can be predicted after a short period of exercise, you will not be required to exercise to exhaustion. In fact, most appraisals are less strenuous than a normal training session.

There is no pressure to excel because you're not in a competitive situation. You can stop whenever you want. After completing all measures, you will receive feedback regarding how you compare with others of the same sex and age, and together with the appraiser will work towards developing an appropriate action plan.

What's in a Fitness Test?

The components of physical fitness: Physical fitness includes several relatively independent components. Through exercise you can exert an influence upon: (see figure 2)

Figure 2

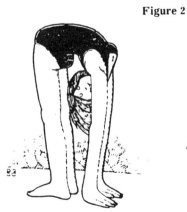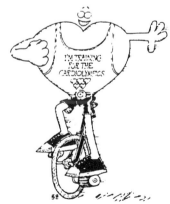

1. **Body Weight and Composition**   2. **Flexibility**   3. **Muscular Strength and Endurance**   4. **Cardio-Respiratory Fitness**

One of the most talked-about health subjects in recent years is that of **cardiovascular fitness.** Enthusiasts can be seen wearing expensive name-brand running gear, pounding the pavement during lunch or wearing fashionable tights and headbands, rushing off to their "aerobics class" after work. Much of the interest in aerobics stems from the association between heart disease, high blood pressure and stroke with a sedentary lifestyle.

An increased fitness level is a result of functional adaptations in the heart, lungs and blood vessels, thus enabling the oxygen-rich blood to be delivered to the muscles with greater efficiency.

Cardiovascular fitness is measured by estimating or directly measuring the maximum amount of oxygen the body utilizes. When working aerobically, oxygen is used. The more oxygen used, the greater the fitness level. Most fitness tests require an individual to walk/run, cycle or step to music while the heart rate is measured.

Maximal oxygen consumption (VO_2 max) refers to the maximal amount of oxygen that can be consumed per minute. As an important measurement of cardiovascular fitness, VO_2 max can be predicted by using a sub-maximal test. The test measures the workload that can be sustained at a given heart rate in a safe range for the subject's age group. Maximal oxygen uptake is then worked out from the test results using a formula. Sub-maximal tests are the rule in general fitness testing because of the safety factor.

Bicycle ergometer test

Hints for Starting a Program

- Get medical clearance first.
- Choose activities that are dynamic and rhythmic (aerobic).
- Choose activities which you enjoy.
- Set aside a specific "workout" time, 3-4 times, spread throughout the week.
- Stick to it!
- Choose activities **that are** affordable and practical.
- If you have been **inactive for** a long time, start easy and gradually **progress.**
- Think '**Positive Lifestyle Change'.**
- Be patient ...**your body** will adapt and show results.
- **Remember** to warm up for several minutes before exercising.
- Gradually increase time, intensity or frequency. Do NOT go "all out".
- Permit your body to cool down gradually after exercising.
- Remember that your fitness program is personal — stick to your goals.
- There are no magic tricks ...it takes work, but it can be a lot of fun too.

Bicycling

Ice skating

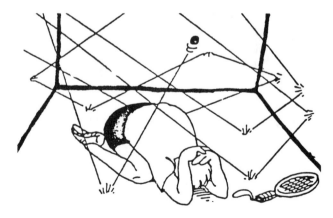

Racquetball

Muscular Strength and Endurance

Muscular strength may be defined as the maximum tension or force a muscle can exert when contracted to its maximum capacity. Muscular **endurance**, on the other hand, relates to the ability of a muscle group to perform repeated contractions against a lighter resistance over a period of time. Most fitness tests will use a grip strength dynamometer to determine muscular strength, and exercises such as timed sit-ups and push-ups in determining muscular endurance.

Improving strength and endurance: A good program of physical conditioning will include exercises to improve the strength and endurance of the large muscle groups of the body (e.g., shoulders, arms, legs).

Special attention should be given to strengthening the muscles of the lower back and stomach to reduce the chances of developing lower back pain. In order to increase strength and endurance, the overload principle of exercise must be adhered to. To produce strength gains, progressively increase the exercise weight. To produce gains in endurance, increase the number of repetitions gradually.

Whether you decide on a specific weight training program or a home calisthenic routine, a number of principles must be followed to obtain results.

- To induce an increase in the functional capacity of the muscle, the system must be overloaded beyond its normal capacity so that adaptations can occur. This overload must be increased progressively through intensity or duration with intensity, probably inducing changes quicker.
- Only the particular systems which are overloaded or stressed are going to obtain this 'training effect'. Using weights to develop the upper body will not make your legs strong. Likewise in aerobic exercise, being a good runner does not mean being able to swim well.

- The higher the fitness level, the harder one must work to achieve improvements. An unfit individual has a lot more ground to cover before reaching his/her ceiling; at first the improvements come quickly, but this rate slows down as fitness improves.
- Depending on whether exercise training is completely stopped or reduced, the resulting improvements will be either completely lost or reduced. Loss of strength appears to be related to the time it took to acquire it. If it took years to build the strength, chances are that it will depreciate slowly over the years.
- Once a certain level/objective has been reached, the frequency or duration may be reduced by approximately one-third, yet maintaining this level of fitness. However, training intensity should be kept up.

Physical fitness measurements will not only help you in evaluating your present condition, but also assist you in setting reasonable goals. Consequently, this information can be used to help you develop a plan for an individualized physical fitness program. Knowledge of your present physical fitness status, as indicated by your test results will assist you in establishing a beginning point in your program. As you progress with your program, you can re-test yourself from time-to-time to see how effective your program has been.

Body Composition

Of the many rituals in today's society, scale-watching is probably the strangest. This curious habit involves clandestine disrobing behind locked doors, stepping carefully onto a raised platform which sets red numbers flashing or dials spinning. Many go through the daily ritual of weighing themselves, presumably to monitor the maintenance of body weight, but few do little other than merely watch their weight; when their weight climbs higher, they watch it climb higher. Indeed, there are even official 'Weight Watching' clubs.

But why all this concern about body weight in the first place? Some 30 years ago, several researchers revealed that

body weight in excess of the recommended height - weight tables was associated with an increased risk of disease. Since then, health scientists have demonstrated that it is over-fatness and not necessarily being overweight which was associated with increased risk of disease.

An individual with a lot of muscle mass may be considered overweight according to height - weight classifications, while body fatness may be low (i.e., weight lifter, football player). So being overweight merely suggests that the body weight is above the recommended weight for that height.

Imagine the body to be made of two components — fat and lean body mass (i.e., blood, organs, tissue, muscle and bone). Over-fatness is a state in which the ratio of fat to lean body mass becomes a medical concern.   The American College of Sports Medicine reports that obesity is associated with in-crease risk of high blood pressure, diabetes, heart disease, stroke, kidney and gall bladder disease, respiratory ailments and abnormal blood lipids.[4] Since it is very difficult to per-manently reverse this state, strong preventive measures should be incorporated into everyone's lifestyle to encourage a healthy weight maintenance program.

The fundamental rule in body composition/weight maintenance is energy balance. Basal metabolic rate refers to the minimal bodily function while awake and resting. This rate, along with the energy required to digest your food, the energy spent at work, leisure and/or in physical activity con-stitutes energy expenditure. An energy balance is achieved when the energy intake (food) equals energy expenditure — no weight is gained.

Individuals who gain weight are in a positive energy balance; it is a result of an increased food intake and/or a decreased energy expenditure. It is apparent that over-fat people suffer from a positive energy balance and in order to lose weight, must undergo a negative energy balance — in-crease physical activity and/or decrease in food intake.

If physical activity was increased by 250 calories per day and 250 calories were trimmed off the food intake, a daily deficit of 500 calories would ensue. This would result in losing one pound per week, since 3500 calories equals one pound (500 x 7 days = 3500 calories).

Weight loss is most effective if it incorporates both an in-crease in the amount of exercise and a decrease in those ex-tra calories in the diet — lifestyle change! A safe and desirable weight loss program is defined by the American College of Sports Medicine[4] as:

— nutritionally sound and has at least a calorie intake of 1200 calories per day (for basal metabolic rate);
— maximizes fat losses (see Folklore of Exercise);
— includes foods acceptable to dieter (habits, taste, cost);
— uses behavior modification techniques;
— has a daily negative calorie balance of 500 - 1000 calories (through diet and exercise);
— uses endurance exercise programs at least 3 days/week; and
— encourages permanent lifestyle behavior.

Although fat is not in vogue, it is an essential component to the body; it protects the vital organs and viscera, is a critical energy reservoir and is found in most neural tissue. Because of the higher levels of the hormone estrogen in females, they usually are about 8 - 10% fatter than males. Both males and females will carry less fat with increased fitness levels.

Although there are several techniques to measure the amount of body fat, the skin-fold technique is probably the most practical. By measuring the thickness of skin folds at various body sites, an estimate can be made as to what percentage of the body weight is actually fat. Skin-fold measurements are based on the rationale that the fat which is deposited under the skin correlates highly with total body fat.

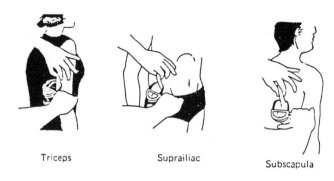

Triceps   Suprailiac   Subscapula

Skinfold sites

Flexibility

Flexibility refers to the range of movement about a joint or series of joints and is specific to each joint. Good flexibility is required to perform various physical movements and ac-tivities with ease. There is also less risk of getting injured if one has good flexibility; however, it does not follow that hyperflexibility is desirable for injury prevention. Females typically have greater flexibility than males; regardless of gender the aging process seems to be associated with some loss of this quality. The actual joint capsule and surrounding musculature present the greatest limitations to flexibility, but excessive fat deposits may also provide a hinderance.

Improving the flexibility of a given joint or series of joints usually involves stretching muscles by slow static stretches, which are held for about ten seconds. Bouncing or jerky stret-ching is not recommended as it actually increases muscle tension and thus makes further stretching action unsafe.

Generally, if a joint bends in one direction (i.e., knee), the best stretching exercise is a static stretch. However, joints with a lot of range (i.e., hip, shoulder) can be stretched by us-ing a slow circular motion; the static technique would be time consuming. Stretching should be performed slowly and smoothly to prevent injury or muscle soreness.

Since the flexibility of a joint capsule seems to be influenc-ed by a warmer temperature, it is suggested that stretching be incorporated into the cool-down period of physical activi-ty; however, it can be incorporated into the warm-up phase as well.

Tips regarding Flexibility Training

— ballistic or jerky movements are potentially hazardous
— should follow a general warm-up (i.e., after a run)
— progress from major to specific joints
— follow progressive overload (increase degree and/or time of stretch)
— train both sides of body

An Exercise Prescription

This section outlines the basic principles and guidelines for designing a personalized program for physical fitness. These guidelines are applicable regardless of your age or present physical condition. Training and conditioning programs should be tailored to the individual.

Nevertheless, the basic principles and guidelines for achieving a desired level of physical fitness are the same for all people. It is agreed that physical conditioning procedures always involve four factors: frequency, intensity, time and type of exercise; or in other words, the F.I.T.T. Principle.

How to Get F.I.T.T.

Frequency: How often should you work out? At least three times a week!

Regular adherence to a vigorous exercise program is necessary if you are to reach and maintain an adequate level of fitness. When you do any activity which is more than you are used to, you will become more fit.

Above average physical fitness will be attained with regular workouts three or four times per week. That improvement in your fitness starts to disappear after 48 hours. That's why you should be active three times per week.

Intensity: How hard should you work out? Use your pulse rate as a workout indicator.

In order to improve cardio-respiratory and muscular fitness, a vigorous overload is necessary. In the normal individual, the rise in heart rate is directly proportional to the cardiovascular stress imposed on the body. For this reason, the exercise heart rate has been used as a simple measure for determining exercise intensity levels.

The heart rate increases in direct proportion to the work load.

In addition to regular daily activity, our hearts and lungs require certain specific amounts of exercise to maintain their optimal level to function. There is a target zone which is unique to each individual. Physical activity within this zone will enable the individual to improve their fitness. The name of the game is finding your own target zone.

Heart Rate Target Zone

Because we are able to count heart rate, but cannot easily determine oxygen consumption, the heart rate target zone is the means used to regulate exercise intensity. Thus, heart rate may be used to determine whether or not you are working hard enough to improve your maximal oxygen consumption.

Exercising both effectively and safely involves keeping your heart rate within the target zone as you perform your activity. The diagram shown describes the principle of the heart rate target zone.

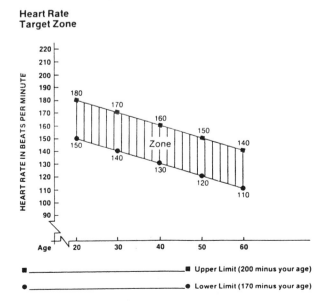

The desired range for heart rate during exercises differs according to age. For each age group, there is a maximal attainable heart rate — that is, the fastest rate at which the heart can beat. Rates are about the same for men and women.

To calculate your own target heart rate, first approximate your maximal attainable heart rate, subtract your age from 220. For example, a 20-year-old has a maximal heart rate of 200. His target zone would be 150 (70%) to 180 (85%) beats per minute. However, a 65-year-old, with an attainable heart rate of 150 beats per minute would have a target zone of 105 (70%) to 135 (85%) beats per minute.

As you exercise, you will need to check that you are achieving your target heart rate. You do this by taking your pulse. Place two fingers on the thumb side of the opposite wrist (palm up). Count heart rate for ten seconds and multiply by six. This is your exercising heart rate. With some practice you will know when you are working in your Target Heart Rate Zone by how you feel and how hard you are breathing.

An alternate method of measuring your heart rate is by placing two fingers on your neck, right below the angle of the jaw (carotid pulse). To take your pulse during exercise, you will probably need to stop for a moment and take the pulse quickly before your heart rate slows down, counting the pulse for 10 seconds.

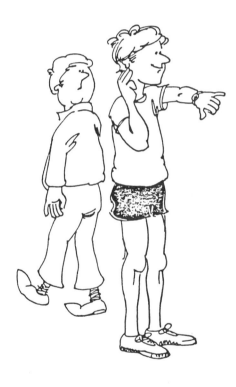

Time: How long should you work out? At least 15 to 20 minutes!

The duration of exercise at 75% of the maximum heart rate must be maintained for at least 15 to 20 minutes in order to achieve an increase in one's level of fitness. This duration is used as a baseline and can be extended as one becomes more fit.

Type of exercise: What should you do for a workout?

For your exercise program, you will need to choose an activity and follow a certain routine during each session. Not all activities will produce cardiovascular fitness. The way in which the cardiovascular system is challenged by the exercise is all-important.

To produce cardiovascular fitness, the activity you choose must involve continuous exercise which increases blood flow from the heart to the working muscles. Thus, the activities which improve cardiovascular fitness are continuous, rhythmic, repetitive, involve motion and are called dynamic.

The key to this improvement is the heart rate. It must be pushed high enough (intensity), you must work at a substantial level of exertion for at least 30 minutes (duration), and you must adhere to this program regularly (frequency). Following these basic principles of training will allow you to structure a fitness program to precisely suit your physical needs.

Because people tend to best maintain their exercise programs by establishing routine, it is important to choose an activity that you will enjoy. As you begin in your exercise program, you may find that even very moderate activity will produce your target heart rate, but as you become more fit increasing amounts of activity will be required before the target rate is achieved.

After six to eight weeks, you should notice measurable improvement and eventually, in three to six months perhaps, you may reach a plateau, signifying that considerable fitness has been achieved. At this point, the principle of 'progressive overload' should be applied, whereby the intensity as well as frequency and duration of the exercise bouts may be modertely increased in order to achieve further increases in your fitness level.

The Exercise Training Pattern

Most workouts for developing physical fitness consist of three essential parts:
1) a warm-up,
2) the conditioning bout, and
3) a cool-down.

All three segments are essential for a sound program.

Warm-up

The Warm-Up

A proper warm-up before each exercise workout is an important habit. A proper warm-up prepares your body for the upcoming workout; the warm-up also being a precaution against unnecessary injuries and muscle soreness. It stimulates the heart and lungs moderately and progressively, as well as increasing the blood flow and muscle temperatures gradually.

A proper warm-up will stretch the muscles and tendons in preparation for more forceful contractions. It also prepares you mentally for the approaching strenuous workout. The time required for warm-up varies with the individual. However, as soon as you begin to sweat (an indicator that the temperature of the deep muscles has increased), you are probably ready for the more intense conditioning workout.

Conditioning bout

The Conditioning Bout

After a sufficient warm-up, you are now ready for the main conditioning segment of your workout. In most workouts, your exercise during this segment should closely approximate an intensity of 75% HR Max., as was explained earlier. Remember, the key is to tailor your program to your personal needs. As your fitness capacity improves over time, it will be possible to modify your workout and increase the total workout accomplished in each session. Always, the duration of the workout should be set so that you feel fully recovered and rested within an hour of its completion. At the start, this duration may be only 20 minutes, but gradually you will become accustomed to 30 or more minutes of vigorous exercise at the intensity level you have established for yourself.

Cool-down

The Cool Down

A cool-down is a tapering-off period after completing the main workout. It is best accomplished by a continuation of the same activity at a lowered intensity. In other words, keep moving. Walking is the most common means of gradually diminishing your intensity level, jogging at a slower tempo is also a common cool-down procedure.

The reason for tapering-off is to allow your muscles to assist in pumping the blood from the extremities back to the heart. If you end a workout abruptly, your heart will continue to send extra blood to the muscles for a few minutes. Since the muscles are no longer contracting and helping to propel the blood back to the central circulation, blood may pool in the muscles.

As a result, there may be insufficient blood for the other organs of the body. In fact, if the brain does not receive enough blood, you may feel dizzy or pass out. Thus, it is wise to keep moving to help your breathing and heart rate return to near normal before you head for a shower. Generally, a five minute recovery period is sufficient under normal conditions. For most people, the heart rate at the end of the cool-down should be below 100.

storage to enable muscles to contract. If a negative energy balance persists for several weeks, these stores will be reduced resulting in a **ratio** change of fat to muscle - body composition.

- **Extra vitamins are needed when exercising a lot** - For those individuals on low-calorie intakes, vitamin supplements may be necessary, but for most individuals the extra vitamins will come in the form of a larger caloric intake. There is also little evidence to suggest a performance improvement with mega dosing of vitamins.
- **Exercise will increase appetite** - Actually, most people see a slight decrease in appetite. This is especially true if a workout precedes a meal, probably due to an elevated internal temperature and circulating hormones.
- **Weight lifting makes women muscle-bound** - It is the male hormone 'testosterone' which enhances the growth of muscle tissue. Very low levels of this hormone enable women to show greater increases in strength before there is a growth in muscle size.
- **Protein supplements are needed to build muscle** - The body needs some protein for building muscle, but expensive supplements are unnecessary. Through a nutritionally sound diet, sufficient energy should be provided for muscular strength and endurance improvements.
- **Massagers and vibrators help get rid of fat** - Gimmicks such as these merely jiggle the fat like a kid playing with his jello. There must be a negative energy balance in order to lose the excess fat. The best way is through a slight caloric reduction and an increase in physical activity.
- **Fat hips can be reduced by doing hip exercises** - Our fat storage bins are genetically determined; some people seem to have more bins around their waists, while others on their thighs. When exercising, the muscles do not select fat from the area with the largest or most bins, but they slowly draw energy from all the sites at a fairly equal rate. Exercising the hips may increase some muscle toneness, but it will NOT turn the fat to muscle.

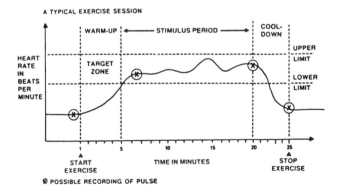

Exercise Training Pattern

FOLKLORE OF EXERCISE

- **No pain, no gain** - For most people, aerobic exercise may be slightly uncomfortable or perhaps during a stretching routine, but it should NOT be painful.
- **Go for the burn** - All this will do is increase muscle soreness the next day. It will NOT improve fitness.
- **Exercise turns fat to muscle** - Although the body is an incredibly adaptable organism, this is one thing it cannot do. The fat on the body is akin to a big storage bin of energy. When exercising, energy is slowly drawn out of

- **Exercising in rubber suits and saunas are a great way to lose weight** -The weight reduction seen here, as well as many fad diets, is a result of water loss. After discontinuation of the diet or exercise, body weight often returns to its previous level as the body rehydrates. Exercising during a state of dehydration is also very dangerous as the body's ability to regulate internal temperature gets distorted. Additionally, heart rate may become elevated to unsafe levels. Behavioral lifestyle changes of slight caloric restriction and increases in energy expenditure is the best method of reducing body fat.
- **Salt tablets are needed when sweating a lot** - Definitely not. After an especially hard workout in a hot room/weather, excessive sweating may result. Our thirst mechanism appears to become distorted, consequently rehydration is inadequate. In fact, it may take several days to replenish lost fluid. The addition of salt tablets on top of this dehydrated state would only make the situation worse. Usually the salt and potassium lost during sweating is replaced by the next meal.

References

1. "Guidelines for the Training and Recognition of Fitness Leaders in Canada", Government of Canada, Fitness and Amateur Sport, 1984.

2. Caspersen, C.J.; Powell, K.E. and G.M. Christenson. "Physical Activity, Exercise, and Physical Fitness: Definitions and Distinctions for Health Related Research." Public Health Reports. 100(2): 126-131, 1985.

3. Getchell, B. "Physical Fitness: A Way of Life" New York: John Wiley and Sons, 1979.

4. Position statement on "Proper and Improper Weight Loss Programs", American College of Sports Medicine.

QUIZ
Health, Fitness & Exercise Prescription

1. Excessive _____ may limit flexibility. (Fill in the blank)

2. Becoming physically active because a company gives extra benefits for such involvement would be a

_____ reason for beginning a program of physical activity. (Fill in the blank)

3. A target _____ _____ _____ is used to monitor aerobic exercise intensity. (Fill in the three blanks)

4. Training _____ cannot be reduced in a maintenance fitness program. (Fill in the blank)

5. Although salt does not have to be replaced in tablet form after heavy sweating, potassium does.

    ☐ T ☐ F

6. Stretching is more beneficial preceeding a workout.

    ☐ T ☐ F

7. The amount of energy it takes your body to break down a chocolate bar is part of your total daily energy expenditure.

    ☐ T ☐ F

8. Body Fat: (check correct answer)

    ☐ a. in excess is associated with an increased probability of getting a fatty liver.

    ☐ b. is usually found in greater quatities on females, due to low levels of estrogen.

    ☐ c. plays an essential role in protecting and insulating vital organs and is a rich storage bin of energy.

    ☐ d. all of the above.

9. When embarking on a program to improve muscular strength and endurance, the following should be considered:

    ☐ a. Special attention should be given to abdominal exercise since it solely prevents the development of low back pain.

    ☐ b. The amount of time spent working out is critical in a maintenance fitness program.

    ☐ c. When using the principle of increased repetitions (endurance), more of the fat will turn to muscle.

    ☐ d. all of the above

    ☐ e. none of the above.

10. A desirable weight loss program includes:

    ☐ a. Encouragement of exercises where considerable sweating takes place.

    ☐ b. Use of behavior modification through appetite suppressant pills.

    ☐ c. Specialized foods that enhance fat loss.

    ☐ d. A negative weekly calorie balance of three to 7,000 calories.

    ☐ e. None of the above.

Unit 10

First Aid for Security Officers
Miscellaneous Items

FIRST AID FOR SECURITY OFFICERS

By Barry D. Panrucker, EMT (A)
Reviewed by Robert Wilson

In all walks of life there is always an attempt made to maintain a balance. In your personal life, you try to balance the good with the bad, the happy with the sad, and the never-ending bank balance with debits and credits. So it is in industry, where the price of a product is dependent upon wages, material cost, production cost, etc.

Businesses are always trying to produce products in the most efficient way to cut down on the overall cost of the product. One area in production costs is Loss Control. Loss control is simply cutting down unnecessary expenses. One large item of cost in this area is employees' health care.

If a company has a poor safety record, their health insurance costs are higher than the 'safety minded' company. They will have an increase in monies paid out in wages, as someone will have to work overtime or as extra people are brought in to cover for someone who is injured on the job.

Whether a person is injured on or off the job, the length of time that the person is off work costs the company directly. The quality of a person's work is enhanced by their overall knowledge of the job. Safety and First-Aid training are as important to production costs, as are material and labor costs.

What is First Aid?

First-Aid may be defined as the temporary care of the sick or injured. This care extends from the time you assume responsibility, to a time when responsibility of the sick or injured person can be transferred to the care of someone with better facilities, and perhaps more advanced knowledge of how to treat the injured person. Temporary care could include the saving of a life, and protecting injuries from becoming worse.

Legal Aspects

There are certain legal aspects that must be considered when rendering first aid to a person who has been involved in an accident. It may be the duty of the Security Officer to apply his first aid knowledge and skills to the best of his ability. If the care follows the training received at a First Aid course, then there should be no fear of legal repercussions. Each province or state has its own set of laws and these should be considered.

The best protection against legal repercussions is to be properly trained and certified, and adhere to those standards when performing first aid. Your organized application of learned first aid skills could mean the difference between life and death.

Accident Assessment

As with any problem presented to us, we must approach a personal injury problem in a systematic and priority-based way. As a security officer, you will be in the best possible position to take control of the situation and guide and direct personnel as required.

The sequence of events through an emergency situation should be as follows:
- Assess the situation, checking for immediate dangers to yourself or the injured person.
- Call, or have someone else call, for emergency help. (i.e.) EMS, Fire, and/or Police, depending on the accident or emergency situation.
- Control the scene. If spectators are present, various jobs could be assigned to them.
- Gain access to the injured person and make sure that their life is not in immediate danger through lack of basic life needs.
- Assess the injuries and treat where possible.
- Ensure transportation is arranged.
- The time of the accident, your finding of the person's injuries and any other pertinent information should be noted, and sent with the injured person to hospital.
- If this is an industrial accident, make sure that all necessary reports are made out, and handed over to the correct company authorities.

The overall examination of an injury situation is usually broken down into two major actions, referred to as the First and Second Action.
- The First Action: this deals with the approach and all immediate life-threatening problems.
- The Second Action: this deals with the treatment of injuries and stabilizing the injured person, making them ready for transport.

First Action

Your initial assessment of an accident scene is to secure personal safety, request immediate emergency assistance from the proper agency and find out generally what happened. Determine how many persons were injured, and gain access to the injured, only if it is safe to do so! If you are able to reach the injured, check their responsiveness and ensure that they are breathing, have a heart beat, and that there is no bleeding that may cause death. Any information that you can transmit to other emergency personnel about the situation will be of great assistance to their response protocols.

Securing the safety of an accident area is very important, mainly because you are the most important person at the scene, and you do not want to get into any situation that is going to cause you harm. Always make certain that whatever caused the injury to the person is not going to do the same to you. In motor vehicle accidents, make sure that some traffic control is organized, and that any source of ignition is eliminated by turning off the ignition switch of the vehicle or vehicles involved.

You must now figure out how many people need assistance, which is called "Triage", meaning "sorting". Triage is usually done without treatment, because if you stop to help the first person, you may jeopardize the life of another injured person.

Some simple life-saving procedures may be applied at this time, but only if they will not take too long. Some examples would be to quickly clear an airway or to stop bleeding.

Keep in mind that if you spend too much time on one person, you may fail to help someone else who has a better chance for survival. One method of sorting the injured is to place them in one of three categories. The first level is the person who appears to be slightly injured and who will survive without immediate attention.

The second level is one who has life-threatening injuries and if given attention has a good chance to survive. In the final category, are those who have a poor chance of surviving or are dead. Unfortunately, you must force yourself to make this cold-hearted decision quickly, or some people may die unnecessarily.

Prior to handling the injured person, you must gain permission. Introduce yourself and ask if you can help them. This simple statement: "I am a security officer, may I help you?" establishes several things.

One, it tells the injured person who is trying to assist them; secondly it establishes a response either positive or negative. If a person gives you a positive response, he may give you permission verbally to help him. If the person does not respond in a coherent manner, you can assume implied consent and carry on with your assistance.

Levels of Consciousness

In a first-aid situation, levels of consciousness can be stated in simple terms. To start off with, is the person awake or does he/she appear to be asleep. If the person is awake, are they alert or drowsy. If the person is asleep, will they respond to a pain stimulus or not.

This now gives us a gradient, from our injured person being wide awake to being unresponsive to pain. The levels of consciousness should be checked frequently to determine if the person's condition appears to be improving, stable or deteriorating.

Once you have gained access to the injured, you must now evaluate their condition. Make certain that their airway is clear, and that they can move air in and out of their lungs. The person must have an uninterrupted supply of air to carry on.

Not only must there be a supply of air to the lungs, but there must be circulation of the blood to carry oxygen (oxygen is extracted from the air) through the body to convert energy and rebuild body cells.

Since it is extremely important to circulate a certain volume of blood, we must make certain that the injured person does not lose any of this blood through holes in the system.

If a person appears unconscious, you must ensure that their airway stays clear. If a person is sitting up, then just maintaining their head in a normal position should allow for a clear airway. If a person is laying on their back, their tongue may relax and drop down and block their airway.

Airway:

As mentioned earlier, your first action for the injured person is to check to ensure they have a potentially clear airway, and are breathing and have a heartbeat. The three: Airway, Breathing, and Circulation are considered the ABC's of First Aid. If the injured person cannot establish any of the ABC's on their own, then you as the rescuer must perform that function for them.

If a person is lying on their back and unconscious, their tongue (which is a muscle) may drop back and block the airway. (see Figure 1)

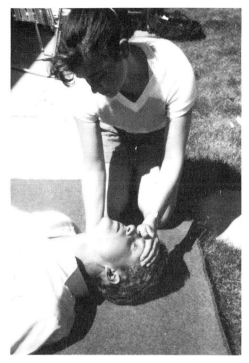

FIGURE 1

If there is no sign of head or neck injury, the head can be tilted back (hyperextended), which lifts the jaw up, pulling the tongue with it and clearing the airway.

If there is a chance that hyperextension may further damage a neck injury, then stabilize the head and simply lift the jaw up at an angle. (See Figure 2) This will clear the airway without moving the neck.

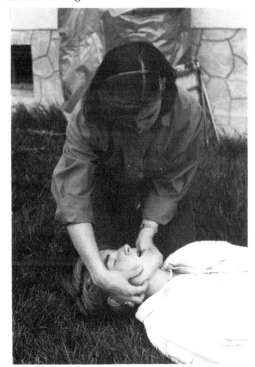

FIGURE 2

You must now check to see if the unconscious person is breathing. This is done by looking to see if the chest is moving up and down, listening and feeling for any air moving in and out of the mouth.

You should have your ear within an inch of the person's mouth and nose in order to determine if there is air movement. Chest movement alone is not good enough to determine if there is air exchange, because the chest will move up and down even if the airway is blocked.

The tongue is the most common obstruction in an unconscious person; a foreign object is the common obstruction in a conscious person. Normally, a cough reflex will produce a large and sudden surge of air, clearing any foreign material from interfering with the airway.

However, sometimes a solid object becomes so lodged that the cough is not strong enough to clear it away. If this occurs, the rescuer must then assist the person by manually creating a cough action. (note Figure 3)

FIGURE 3

This is accomplished by giving four quick abdominal thrusts or, in the case of pregnancy or extreme obesity, chest thrusts which are repeated till the airway becomes clear. (see Figure 4)

FIGURE 4

Another complication that may compromise the airway is vomit. Sometimes during a traumatic situation, stomach contents may be brought up and if a person is unconscious, they may not be able to prevent this material from entering the airway and lungs.

This could be a very serious situation. Immediately clearing the airway of this vomit is a must. This can be accomplished by turning the person's head to the side and scooping with your fingers all the vomitus material from their mouth.

Respiratory System

The respiratory system is the system whereby oxygen is transferred to the blood to maintain the cells. It also removes the unwanted gases such as carbon dioxide from the body.

The system consists of the following:

- mouth
- nose
- pharynx
- larynx
- bronchi
- two lungs
- pulmonary system

FIGURE 5

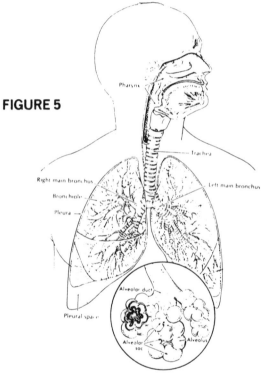

RESPIRATORY SYSTEM

The gases we breathe are about 79% nitrogen, 21% oxygen, some water vapour and other rare gases. The air we breathe out still contains 16% oxygen.

Air drawn into the lungs enters through the nose and mouth and passes down the throat (pharynx), through the voice box (larynx) to enter the windpipe (trachea). The top of the larynx is protected by a flap (epiglottis) which is open for breathing, but shuts when solids or liquids are being swallowed. The passage the air follows is referred to as the airway. Note that the epiglottis does not operate if the casualty is unconscious.

In the chest the trachea divides into two branches, the right and the left bronchus. Each bronchus passes into a lung where it divides into a great number of small tubes (bronchioles) which, after repeated division into smaller and smaller tubes, finally open into numerous minute air-sacs (alveoli). A fine network of blood vessels (capillaries) surround the alveoli through which the exchange of gases takes place.

The respiratory centre which controls respiration is found in the brain at the base of the skull. This centre reacts to various forms of chemical stimulation, the most important of which is an increase of carbon dioxide in the blood.

Normal Respiratory Rates for Persons at Rest:

Age	Normal Rate (in breath/minute)
Newborn	30 to 50
2 years	24 to 32
10 years	20 to 26
Adult	12 to 15

The normal breathing rate is increased if the person has been exercising, has a fever, pneumonia or is in shock.

The Mechanics of Breathing:

The mechanics of breathing are under the automatic control of the brain. The passage of air in and out of the lungs is called respiration.

The act of breathing is like the action of a bellows. The diaphragm that runs across the bottom of the chest cavity completes the enclosure. Breathing in (inspiration or inhalation) is done by the rib muscles contracting, raising the ribs and expanding the chest. The diaphragm also draws downward.

This pulls a vacuum in the lungs (compared to the surrounding air pressure) and air enters the lungs. Breathing out is a passive function and requires no muscular exertion. As the rib muscles and diaphragm relax, the chest contracts and air is expelled from the lungs.

Respiratory Problems:

Due to the extreme importance of the respiratory system, any injury or malfunction is deemed serious. Respiratory problems may range from structural damage such as fractured ribs or holes in the chest walls, to an unsatisfactory atmosphere for breathing or complete stoppage of the muscular action of the chest wall and diaphragm.

Treatment:

If there appears to be fractures of the ribs, then some support should be applied. Padding and bandaging will reduce the pain and enable the injured person to breathe easier.

If holes in the chest wall occur, then the normal airtight seal around the lungs is broken and air may move in and out of this opening (sucking chest wound). This hole must be sealed up immediately, using some occlusive type of bandage.

The atmosphere that we breathe into our lungs must contain sufficient oxygen to support our body functions. If the atmosphere is poor, our bodies will suffocate and eventually die. Ensure that people who are subjected to poor atmospheric conditions are moved to fresh air immediately.

Should respiration ever stop, artificial means of forcing air into the person's lungs must take place immediately. The easiest way to accomplish this is to hyperextend the neck, clearing the airway and simply blowing into the person's mouth and filling up their lungs, simulating their breathing action. (see Figure 6)

The volume of air required is dependent on the size of the person who has stopped breathing. A good rule of thumb is to make the person appear as if they are breathing in a normal fashion. This artificial breathing must continue until other means of inflation are used or the person starts to breathe on their own.

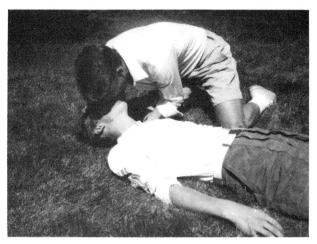

FIGURE 6

The Circulatory System

The circulatory system is the transportation system of the body. It provides a continuous supply of nourishment and oxygen to the cells and disposes of waste products, such as carbon dioxide and water.

The circulatory system is a complex arrangement of tubes called arteries, arterioles, capillaries, venules and veins. Through these tubes, blood is circulated throughout the entire body under pressure from the pumping action of the heart. (see Figure 7)

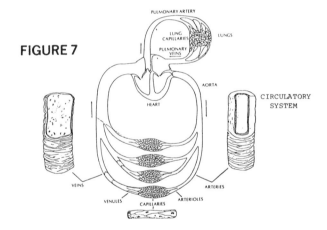

FIGURE 7

The circulatory system is made up of two separate circuits. One provides circulation through the body delivering the nourishment required by the body, and the other is the regeneration of the blood in the lungs.

The normal blood volume in the average body is approximately six litres, with one complete cycle occurring every 60 seconds. The normal heartbeat rate for a body at rest is about 60 beats per minute and will increase depending on the amount of work the body is doing.

Circulatory Problems:

The body depends greatly on a continuous and steady flow of blood. Two major problems encountered by this system are the loss of blood and a malfunction in the pumping system.

Within the blood there are special components that help to plug (clot) small holes that may occur in the normally sealed system. However, if the openings become too large, this normal clotting mechanism does not work and a great deal of blood can be lost in a short period of time.

If there is a problem with the pumping action of the heart itself, then the flow rate of the blood will slow down and the body cells will not receive their required amount of nourishment.

Treatment:

Open wounds are dangerous to the victim because infection can enter the wound and blood can be lost from the wound. If one litre of blood is lost, the injured person will be in shock. Loss of 1½ litres will result in a life-threatening situation.

To stop bleeding, apply direct pressure, elevate and rest the affected body part if possible. By applying direct pressure, blood leakage will slow down and normal clotting should take place. (see Figure 8)

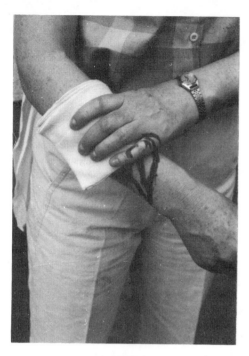

FIGURE 8

If direct pressure does not stop the flow of blood, then applying some pressure on an artery just below (or ahead of) the wound may slow down the bleeding and clotting will take place. (see Figure 9)

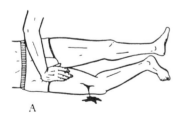

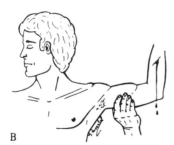

FIGURE 9

If for some reason direct pressure or the alternative pressure point method does not stop the bleeding, then a tourniquet must be applied. (see Figure 10)

This is only done when it is apparent that a life is going to be lost if blood loss is not stopped. A tourniquet should be applied tight enough to stop the flow of blood and left on only until bleeding can be controlled.

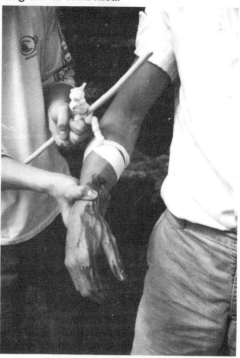

FIGURE 10

Cardiopulmonary Resuscitation (C.P.R.)

As mentioned in earlier sections, the Airway, Breathing and Circulation must always be present in order for a body to survive. If any or all of these are missing, then the rescuer must perform that function for the person.

Normally if the heart stops, breathing will also fail. This means that aritficial breathing and artificial circulation must be performed. This procedure is called Cardiopulmonary Resuscitation or C.P.R.

Once you have deemed the area safe and have gained access to the injured person, you will determine their level of consciousness by asking if they can speak. If the person does not respond, then check to see if they are breathing. (see Figure 11)

FIGURE 11

If they are not breathing, then hyperextend the head by using the chin lift or jaw thrust and recheck for breathing. (see Figure 12)

FIGURE 12

If spontaneous breathing is still absent, you must now breathe for the person by sealing the nose off and blowing into their mouth, ensuring that the chest rises. When initially blowing, two separate breaths should be used to reinflate the lungs. (see Figure 13)

FIGURE 13

The airway must be held open during this time by either the chin lift or jaw thrust method.

Once the Airway and Breathing have been done for this person, you must now ensure that they have Circulation. The most effective way to check the pulse is at the neck area. (see Figure 14)

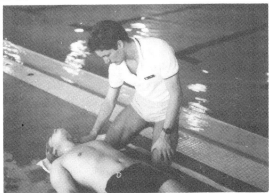

FIGURE 14

On a person with a heartbeat, you can feel a pulse beat in the groove to either side of the Adam's Apple. If there is no pulse, then artificial circulation will be required within four to six minutes of the heart stopping to prevent brain damage.

Artificial circulation is accomplished by squeezing the heart between the breast bone and the spine. The person must be lying on a firm, flat surface.

With your hands locked together and your elbows straight, push down on the person's chest, about 1½ to two inches on a normal size adult, then release the pressure completely without losing contact with the chest. (see Figure 15)

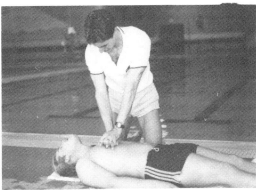

FIGURE 15

To locate the correct hand placement on the chest, place the heel of your hand about two inches up from the lower tip of the breast bone, right in the middle of the breast bone. Compression of the chest should be done just a little faster than one per second or at a rate of 80 per minute.

Artificial breathing must be combined with artificial circulation in order to supply the circulatory blood with oxygen. This is accomplished by interposing two breaths after each 15 compressions.

CPR must be started without delay. Normally, CPR is used to circulate the oxygenated blood to the brain to avoid brain damage. The chances of the heartbeat restarting spontaneously are slim, therefore Advanced Cardiac Life Support must be obtained immediately.

CPR, once started, should be continued until spontaneous circulation starts, you are relieved by qualified personnel such as ambulance staff, you become too tired to continue or the person is pronounced dead by a qualified person (doctor).

Summary of CPR Procedure:

1) Check for response	- Shout loudly, ask the person if they are okay, rub knuckle on breast bone. - This should be done in 10-15 seconds. If the person is unresponsive, then call for help.
2) Check for breathing	- Look, listen and feel for breathing. This should take 3-5 seconds. - If no breathing is detected, then ventilate two times.
3) Check Pulse	- Feel for the pulse at the neck. This should take 5-10 seconds. - If no pulse is felt, then activate the Emergency Medical Service System by designating someone to call for an ambulance.
4) Begin CPR	- Do 15 chest compressions at a rate of 80 per minute. - Do two ventilations - Do four cycles of 15:2 then recheck the pulse. - If no pulse is felt, then continue CPR. - If a pulse is felt, then check breathing, and continue artificial breathing if necessary.

Due to the complexity of the skill in learning CPR, it is recommended that students take a course and be taught by an instructor approved by your local Heart Foundation.

Second Action

Once your First Action is completed, i.e., all immediate life-threatening situations have been attended to, you can deal with all other injuries associated with the trauma.

Monitoring Vital Signs

Vital signs will indicate any change in the person's condition. Some definite indications you should look for are:

BREATHING	breathing or not breathing shallow, deep or laboured fast or slow
PULSE	pulse or no pulse if present, fast or slow weak or strong
SKIN COLOR	normal, pale or flushed
SKIN TEMPERATURE	normal, cool and moist, or hot and dry
EYES	are pupils wide open, appear normal or pinpoint, do they respond to light
LEVEL OF CON-SCIOUSNESS	is the person awake or asleep if awake, is he alert or drowsy if asleep, does he respond to pain or not

Shock:

The body, like any other fuel-burning machine, requires an uninterrupted supply of oxygen to generate energy and preserve life. Shock may be defined as the reduction of the oxygen supply to the body cells — more importantly those cells of the brain — liver and kidneys.

This reduction of oxygen to these vital organs can occur in many different ways: the blood volume (blood carries the oxygen to the cells) is reduced by a bleeding injury or heart attack; the amount of oxygen in the blood is reduced due to a poor supply in the air breathed in; therefore, the blood in the lungs cannot pick up a good supply of oxygen; or, the vessels that contain the blood lose their muscular action and relax, creating a larger than normal container for the existing blood volume, thus slowing down blood flow.

The effects of shock can be immediate or can be delayed by minutes, hours or even days.

Some causes of shock are: bleeding injuries, fractured bones, burns, heart failure, infection, allergic reaction, fright and respiratory problems.

Some significant signs of shock are: shivering, paleness, restlessness, difficulty in breathing, cool and clammy skin. If you can feel a pulse, usually at the neck, it may be weak and rapid. The injured person may feel sick and may vomit. They may also feel thirsty, weak or disoriented.

Shock should be suspected and treated in all types of injuries. The treatment for shock is simple and will not do any harm even if applied when it may not be needed.

If shock is the result of a reduced and insufficient supply of oxygen to the body systems, one treatment is to reduce the amount of activity by the person. The inability to generate heat will be a problem; therefore, it is essential to keep the person warm.

The injuries which may have promoted the shock should be treated as quickly and with as much care as possible. If possible, elevation of the legs will assist in creating a better blood supply to the vital organs. Do not do this if a person has head injuries or other injuries that may be further damaged by this position.

Medical Oxygen should be given if available and you have been trained in its use. Reassure, handle carefully, and transport to medical aid as soon as possible.

Treatment of Wounds:

Direct pressure on the wound is the most effective method of controlling bleeding. If this stops the blood flow long enough, the blood will coagulate usually within 10 minutes. Rest and elevation of the injury also reduces the blood pressure and assists in controlling the bleeding.

When applicable, all wounds should be washed with warm water and soap, a dressing put over the wound, a bulky dressing applied and then a bandage to hold the two dressings in place.

The Body, Its Frame and Associated Injuries

The body has an interior frame called the skeleton. This frame is able to move because of a series of hinged joints and muscles attached to the bones which contract and thus move the bones. (see Figure 16)

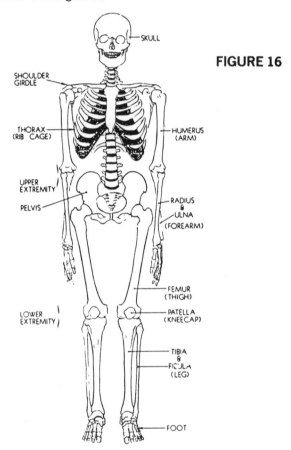

FIGURE 16

If there is an injury to one portion of the body, it may affect a second part of the body. Thus, a first aider must do a systematic assessment of the total body to determine what injuries are present.

Pain can be localized at an injury site or an entire portion of the body can be in pain from the same localized injury. Do your systematic assessment of the entire body starting with the head and working your way down. The most important body functions can be monitored at the head and chest areas.

The Head:

The head contains the brain in a solid bone enclosure. Any blows to the head cause the brain to be jarred (a concussion). Concussions can temporarily impair brain function or if they are severe, cause rupture of blood vessels in the brain and bleeding into the cavity surrounding the brain.

This brain cavity is sealed by several membrane layers to keep infection out of the brain tissues. Any sign of bleeding or clear fluid escaping from the ears is a sign this membrane has ruptured. This is a severe medical emergency and the ear opening should be covered (not plugged) with a sterile dressing to keep infections out.

Concussions are treated by rest **and** treat as for shock. Cuts to the scalp usually look severe because they appear to bleed a lot, but are usually not that deep and can be treated by covering with a sterile dressing and slight pressure to stop the bleeding.

Any concussions to the head can also cause a neck injury. When treating for blows to the head, also treat for neck injuries.

Neck and Back:

The neck is a series of vertebra supported by muscles. Any impact injuries such as those caused in auto accidents can cause the head to whiplash and possibly strain or tear the neck muscles and damage the vertebra in the neck. These vertebra protect the main nervous system that transmits all the nerve signals to and from the rest of the body and are thus very critical.

To treat neck injuries, always suspect the worst injury, a broken vertebra and keep the head from moving. Apply slight traction to the head and a cervical collar if there is one available and transport to the hospital with the neck, head and upper body immobilized on a flat surface such as a backboard (or a door if you need to improvise). (see Figure 17)

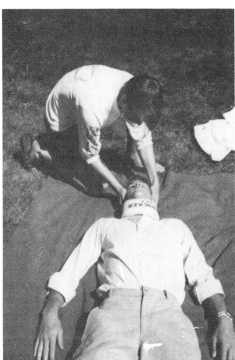

FIGURE 17

If artificial respiration is required and a neck injury is suspected, use the jaw lift method rather than the head tilt to open the airway.

The back (spinal area below the neck) should be checked for any deformities or localized pain. Always check extremities for tingling or numbness as a sign of back injuries. Any spinal injury is extremely serious and great care should be taken in the immobilization and transportation to ensure the spine is protected from further injury.

Mouth and Nose:

The mouth and nose provide an airway and food passage. In an unconscious person, the tongue muscles relax and the tongue may fall back, blocking the airway. The gag reflex also does not work when a person is unconscious.

The mouth may be injured by direct blows or lacerations. A jaw that is broken should be supported by the victim in a comfortable position. Do not bandage the mouth closed as it may impair the airway or block the mouth in the event of vomiting. Check vital signs and monitor for other possible head injuries.

The nose can be broken by a blow, which may cause bleeding from ruptured blood vessels. To stop bleeding from the nose, pinch off the nostril, apply cool cloths and rest in a sitting position. Caution the victim not to blow his nose and to avoid swallowing the blood if possible, as this may cause nausea.

Chest Cavity:

The chest cavity protects the internal organs such as heart, lungs, liver and spleen. The ribs are connected to the breastbone called the sternum in the centre of the chest.

Any hole or puncture in the chest cavity wall may allow air in between the chest wall and lungs. The lung will not inflate when the diaphragm pulls down if there are any punctures in the chest wall.

To treat punctures in the chest wall, cover the puncture with your hand or tape plastic over the hole. Place the injured person tilted toward their injured side to avoid any blood from the injury draining into the good lung. Ensure the airway is maintained and be prepared to do direct artificial respiration. (see Figure 18)

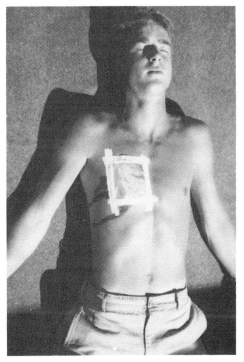

FIGURE 18

Broken or cracked ribs can be taped or supported if the injured person feels more comfortable, otherwise leave unsplinted. Bright red, frothy blood from the mouth will indicate a rib has punctured the lungs. Lay the injured person tilted toward their injured side and transport to medical aid as soon as possible.

Abdomen:

The abdomen encloses the following organs: spleen, liver, pancreas, stomach, gall bladder, intestines, and kidneys.

The abdominal area can be injured by blows which result in ruptured blood vessels in the organs or by wounds which lacerate or expose the organs. If there is bleeding into the body cavity, the area is hard as though the person was stiffening his abdominal muscles.

Treat by lying the injured person on their back with head and shoulders slightly raised with a pillow under their knees and transport them to medical care as soon as possible.

If organs are protruding, apply a sterile dressing or clean towel and secure without undue pressure. If no organs protrude through the wound, apply a dressing and bandage in position. If the injured person is vomiting or coughing, support the abdomen with broad bandages. Give nothing by mouth and remove to a medical facility as quickly as possible.

Pelvic Area:

The pelvic bones form a cradle to support and protect the internal organs such as the lower intestines, the urinary bladder and in females, the reproductive organs. The pelvic bones and hip joint can be injured by a fall or impact injury.

An injury can be determined by pushing inward from the sides of the hips. At the first sign of pain, you should stop pressure on the hips to avoid further cracking of any bone injuries.

The ball and socket joint at the hip may be broken if the leg can be freely rotated along its axis from the foot outward with pain at the hip joint. Any wetness at the crotch indicates a bladder release and may be a sign of internal injuries.

Treat all hip or pelvic injuries by lying the injured person on their back with legs straight or slightly supporting under the knees. Bandage around the hips, knees and ankles for support. (see Figure 9) Transport on a flat surface such as a stretcher to a medical facility.

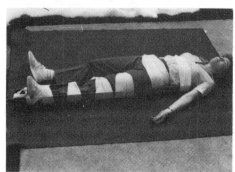

FIGURE 19

Extremities

Collar Bone:

The collar bone supports the shoulder outward and can be broken by a direct blow or shoulder impact. The person will probably support his arm to avoid excess pressure in the break area.

The treatment for a broken collar bone is to place a sling around each shoulder socket and tie them in a figure-8 at the back. This pulls the shoulder back and relieves pressure on the broken collar bone. (see Figure 20)

Upper Arm:

The upper arm may be fractured at any point along the bone. Signs of a fracture are pain and/or deformity at the break site or unnatural movement.

To treat, place the forearm across the body at right angles with the person sitting or standing. (see Figure 21)

FIGURE 20

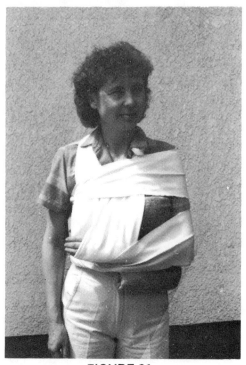

FIGURE 21

Place a small arm sling at the wrist to support the lower arm and allow the weight of the unsupported elbow to apply a natural traction on the upper arm. The arm may need to be stabilized with bandages if the injured person is to be moved.

For dislocation of the shoulder, see the section on dislocations.

Lower Arm:

The lower arm consists of two long bones which may be fractured along the bones at any point. Signs of the fracture may be observed or the injured person may only have pain at the injury site.

Treat by splinting the lower arm in a cardboard or rolled magazine and apply a large arm sling. (see Figure 22) Traction can be applied to relieve pain at the broken bone ends if the break is not located near a joint.

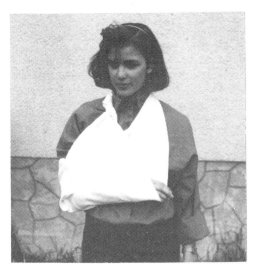

FIGURE 22

Upper Leg:

Considerable violence is required to cause a fracture of the upper leg (the femur bone) in an adult. There may be a loss of large amounts of blood into surrounding tissues and muscle mass.

Elderly persons may break the neck of the femur in a fall. Symptoms resemble those of an upper leg injury or hip injury.

The signs are swelling, extreme pain in hip region, one leg physically shorter than the other, or an open wound from bone fragments. Open wounds should be covered with a sterile dressing to keep out infection.

Treat by stabilizing, immobilize with a long splint, pad between legs, and transport to medical aid on a stretcher. (see Figure 23)

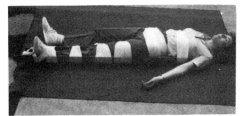

FIGURE 23

Traction (slight pull) on the leg may relieve some pressure on the broken bone ends, but will not overcome any muscle spasms or contractions of the strong thigh muscles. Traction should not be applied for fractures near the joint or for joint injuries.

Lower Leg:

Lower leg fractures are common in impact injuries, ski accidents and falls with one or both bones of the lower leg being cracked or broken. They can be determined by pain, swelling, deformity or discoloration near the pain area and by open wounds from the bone fragments.

Stabilize and support the injured leg and then check for open wounds or bleeding. Splint the leg from the hip to past the ankle or pad between the legs and tie the legs together. (see Figure 24)

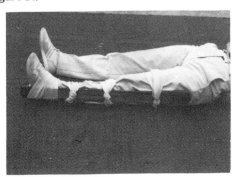

FIGURE 24

Avoid applying any pressure over the injury site. Traction may be applied before and during splinting to align the leg bones and relieve pressure on the broken bone ends. Elevate the injury site to reduce swelling, if possible. (see Figure 25)

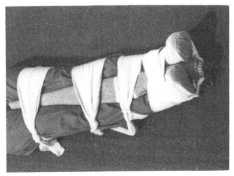

FIGURE 25

Foot and Toes:

The foot can be injured by a fall, by crushing with a heavy object, or by twisting. A broken bone may have the same symptoms as a sprain and both should be treated as a break. Signs are pain, swelling, discoloration or deformity. Immobilize with a towel or pillow and secure for protection. Leave the boot or shoe on as a splint unless it restricts circulation or becomes too painful from swelling. (see Figure 26)

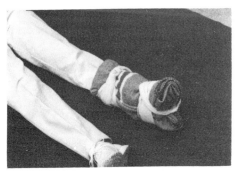

FIGURE 26

Dislocations, Strains and Sprains:

A dislocation occurs when a joint is extended beyond its normal limits and moves out of its socket. Joints are held tightly in their sockets by ligaments. Over-extension of these ligaments is called a sprain. Injuries to either one of these is treated by immobilizing in place with bandages and splints.

Muscles are the power plants of the body system and when damaged require immobilization by splints and bandages along with the application of a cold pack. Injuries to muscles are called strains.

When in doubt as to whether the injury is a sprain, strain or fracture, treat as a fracture and immobilize.

Handling the Injured

Always talk to the injured person and ask them questions. Talking stimulates brain functions and reduces fear. The injured person will begin to think of things other than their injury and the shock levels will be reduced. A response from them gives you an indication of their consciousness, their mood, and allows you to obtain a history of the accident.

Keeping the injured warm, even on warm days, will reduce body heat loss and shock. Blankets, or even your own jacket work well. Ensure you treat the injured in a calm, gentle, reassuring manner.

The usual method of transporting an injured person is on their back with any injured extremity or limb elevated to reduce swelling. Head or back injuries are much more difficult to handle in that there could be a spinal injury.

If an unconscious person lying on their back vomits, the vomit may go into their lungs. These persons should be transported semi-prone, i.e. lying on their side slouched slightly toward their front to keep a clear airway.

Heart attack patients and those with shoulder dislocations usually prefer to be transported in a sitting position leaning back at 45°.

Heat and Cold Injuries

Heat Injuries/Burns:

A person can be burned by heat, radiation or chemicals. Burns damage the skin or tissues which can result in loss of body fluids, cause shock and may lead to infections.

Burns are classified according to depth of tissue damage:
— First Degree: reddening of the skin with minor pain.
— Second Degree: blisters the skin - will be most painful.
— Third Degree: charring of the skin and deeper tissues but not very painful as nerves may also be damaged.

Strong acids or alkalis also burn the skin by their corrosive nature. Electricity will also cause burns, either by the heat produced by short circuit or by passing through the body.

Sunburn can make a person quite ill. If there are blisters or the person develops a fever, transport to medical aid. If they have no other injury, they may be given a salt solution to replace lost body fluids.

Treatment:

The general treatment for burns is to immerse the area in cool water, cover with a clean dressing and keep the dressing damp and cool.

If the victim is on fire, smother any flames or dowse them with water, maintain basic life support, cool any burned areas with clean, cool water and apply sterile dressings to keep the air from the burned area. Extensive burns should be wrapped in a clean sheet. Treat for shock and transport to medical aid.

Some Dont's:

— DO NOT apply ointments or butter to the burned area.
— DO NOT remove pieces of burnt clothing or charred tissue from a burn.
— NEVER apply absorbent cotton or other fibrous material directly to a burn.
— DO NOT break blisters.

Heat Cramps:

Heat cramps are caused by sweating out the chemicals in the muscles. Gentle massage of the cramped muscles and increased intake of salt during meals or salted water will relieve this.

Heat Exhaustion:

Heat exhaustion is caused by a salt and water deficiency resulting from exposure to excessive heat and physical exertion.

The signs are: weak pulse, rapid shallow breathing, generalized weakness, pale clammy skin, profuse perspiration, dizziness, and in some cases, unconsciousness.

The treatment for heat exhaustion is as follows:
— Remove to a cool place.
— Give cool drinks or salted water (½ tsp of salt to one pint water) or (5 ml of salt to one litre of water).
— Do not overcool, treat for shock.
— If patient does not recover quickly, transport to medical aid.

Heat Stroke:

Heat stroke is a result of the collapse of the body's cooling system. The body fails to sweat and the body core overheats. This heat damages the body's nervous system and a coma and death may result if the problem is uncorrected. It is a true emergency.

The signs are:
— Heat stroke occurs quickly.
— hot dry and flushed skin
— initially a full fast pulse that becomes rapid and weak
— deep respirations become progressively more shallow
— muscle twitching or convulsions, or
— progressive unconsciousness leading to death.

Treatment of heat stroke:
— Remove as much clothing as possible.
— Wrap victims in a sheet and soak with water.
— Stabilize airway and monitor vital signs.
— Transport to medical aid with urgency.

Cold Injuries

Frostbite:

When the body tissues are subjected to prolonged cooling, the tissue starts to freeze and crystallize. If the part is not rewarmed promptly, the flow of blood to adjacent tissue is reduced and the chilling spreads. The frozen tissue will appear white and waxy.

The affected part should be rewarmed with a hand or an extremity put in against the warm body (i.e., armpit) before deeper tissues become involved. The white color will disappear and a redness or slight swelling may occur. Do not rub the frostbite or apply snow. This will only increase the chilling effect on the tissues.

Freezing:

Deep freezing is a freezing of the tissue, muscles and nerves and is a much more serious injury. The affected limb will be white and hard to the touch. Do not thaw frozen areas in the field. Medical treatment will be required and the victim will be a stretcher case after the limb has thawed out.

Hypothermia:

Hypothermia is a condition resulting when the body temperature, both internally and on the surface, is reduced below the normal temperature of 37°C (98.7°F) and the body loses more heat than it can produce. Once this has occurred, the person is incapable of producing enough heat to rewarm himself so must receive heat from external sources.

Signs of hypothermia with the associated body core temperatures are:

37 - 35°C   Intense shivering. Ability to perform complex tasks is impaired.

35 - 33°C	Violent shivering. Difficulty talking and some amnesia.
32 - 30°C	Shivering decreases. Some muscle rigidity, jerky movements, may have total amnesia.
29 - 27°C	Victim drifts into a stupor, muscle rigidity, pulse and respiration slow.
27 - 26°C	Unconsciousness occurs, reflexes stop, heartbeat erratic.

Below 26°C Apparent death.

Treatment of hypothermia:

— Prevent further heat loss, cover victim's head.
— Rewarm trunk of victim's body.
— If conscious, give warm drinks and sugar.
— Do not force cold blood from extremities back to the heart. (i.e., forcing rigid limbs to exercise).
— Do not give drugs or alcohol - this further accelerates cooling of the body core.
— Transport to medical aid.

Miscellaneous Health Problems

Epilepsy:

Epilepsy is a disease that results in seizures brought on by uncoordinated brain electrical activity. Epilepsy may cause two forms of seizures.

● A Grand Mal - the involuntary muscular contractions or convulsions may involve parts of the body or the entire body. The convulsion usually ceases on its own within 30 - 90 seconds and the epileptic may have no recollection of the event, but may have known it was coming on.

● A Petit Mal - is characterized by the absence of any overt physical signs. The person may stop talking and go into a trance.

Treatment of epileptic seizures:

— Lay the victim down while supporting the head.
— Remove furniture and objects from around the victim so he will not hurt himself during convulsions.
— Never place your fingers in an epileptic's mouth during a seizure. Maintain an airway during the recovery period.
— Avoid trying to restrain a person during a seizure.
— Reassure victim upon regaining consciousness.

Eye and Ear Injuries:

Eye and ear injuries are usually not life-threatening, but require that infection be kept from the wounds until medical care is available. Do not remove foreign objects from the eye or ear. Bandage to keep out any infection. Both eyes should be covered to avoid the blinking reflex the good eye will cause to the injured eye.

Bites and Stings:

Bites caused by animals or humans are a source of infection and possibly disease. If the wound is bleeding, wash with running water and an antiseptic soap solution. Allow the wound to bleed as some bleeding helps wash the wound. Cover with a sterile dressing and transport to medical aid. If the animal can be caught, a rabies examination may be required.

Stings usually only produce a painful swelling. If a sting causes an allergic reaction and it is not treated promptly, death may result. If breathing difficulties or nausea occur, obtain medical aid at once. Some people with strong allergic reactions carry a case with injectable adrenalin to counter the reaction.

Diabetes

Diabetes is when the pancreas fails to secrete sufficient insulin. Insulin is required to convert the sugar in our blood to usable energy in our bodies. Diabetics may take insulin or other drugs to keep their insulin levels normal, but these may be thrown out of balance by activity levels or food intake.

Insulin Shock is a result of too much insulin or insufficient food eaten. All the sugar in the blood is used up and unconsciousness may result and possibly cause permanent brain damage.

Diabetic Coma is a result of not enough insulin and too much sugar in the blood. The breath may smell of acetone and a coma may result. This is a less serious condition than insulin shock as there will usually not be the associated brain damage.

Get the information from the person while they are still conscious as to whether they have eaten or not and have taken their insulin. If in doubt, give drinks sweetened with sugar while conscious. If unconscious, look for a Medic Alert card or bracelet. Remove to a medical facility as soon as possible.

Poisoning

Poisons may be inhaled, taken by mouth, absorbed or injected.

Inhaled poisons can be fumes from stoves, carbon monoxide from auto exhausts, cleaning agents, hydrogen sulphide or chlorine gas. Remove the person from the source of fumes, being careful not to become a victim yourself. Maintain breathing by artificial respiration if the respiratory system fails. Remove the person to medical aid by the quickest means.

Ingested poisons can be poisonous plants or berries, infected food, household cleaners and solvents, excessive amounts of medicines or hallucinogenic drugs. If you can determine what type of poison was ingested, the Poison Control Centre will advise you whether to induce vomiting or not.

Do not induce vomiting if the poison would re-damage the throat as in the case of acids or alkali agents or be breathed into the lungs and cause further damage.

If you have no access to the Poison Control Centre, then dilute the poison with an 8-oz. glass of water or milk. If instructed to induce vomiting, give syrup of Ipecac or place two fingers in the back of their throat until they vomit.

Absorbed poisons such as pesticides and certain cleaners should be washed off and all contaminated clothing removed. The Poison Control Centre may advise you on any medications or other treatment. Observe closely for signs of shock or respiration trouble.

Angina, Heart Attack and Stroke

Angina:

Angina is an attack of pain in the chest, which often spreads to the left shoulder and arm. It is caused by the arteries in the heart itself becoming too narrow to supply adequate blood to the heart muscle when the heart is working hard. It can be relieved by rest, lasts only a few minutes and recurs periodically.

Nitroglycerine tablets, dissolved under the tongue as prescribed, quickly causes dilation of the blood vessels and reduction of the pain. If nitroglycerine tablets are taken by an angina patient, only two or three are needed. If the pain does not go away, then have the person transported to medical aid.

Heart Attack:

A heart attack is a reduction of the blood supply to the heart muscle, causing damage to the heart and impairing its function.

Signs are:

— chest pain radiating to neck, jaw or left or right arm; may be mild or severe
— pale skin color
— shortness of breath
— sweating
— skin will be cold and clammy
— nausea, possibly vomiting

— anxiety
— feeling of indigestion (or heartburn)
— thirst
— DENIAL (person will not acknowledge they may be having a heart attack).

Treatment:

— Place victim in the most comfortable position - usually sitting up if conscious.
— Loosen clothing around neck and chest.
— Maintain normal body temperature.
— Reassure victim and assist in taking any medications prescribed by a physician.
— Be prepared to give C.P.R.

Stroke

A stroke is the result of a reduction in the supply of blood to a section of the brain due either to blockage or rupture of the artery supplying the area. The signs and symptoms depend upon where the brain has been damaged.

Signs:

— The stroke victim may be unable to talk, or be confused or be unable to express himself by gesture or by writing.
— Breathing may be noisy, almost snoring.
— The pulse may be quite strong, though slow.
— The victim may have one-sided muscle paralysis, or have markedly reduced muscle power on one side of his body.
— One side of his face may not have any muscle tone and will appear to droop.
— On examination, one pupil may be dilated in comparison to the other.
— The victim may have a history of high blood pressure (hypertension), short duration fainting spells or mini-strokes, headaches, periods of dizziness or visual disturbance.

With acknowledgements to:
Norm Ferguson, Canadian Ski Patrol System

Treatment:

Monitor and record vital signs and if possible, a history. Pay particular attention to pupil response. Reassure the victim throughout the examination and treatment.

A stroke victim usually displays very high anxiety levels. They usually know something has happened to them, but are unable to communicate with those around them. Request medical aid and transport the victim to hospital as soon as possible.

Suggested First-Aid Kit
CONTENTS
(1) Condensed First-Aid Manual
(1) Notebook & Pencil
(12) Plastic Bandage Strips
(2) Rolls of Adhesive Tape
(1) Roller Dressing - 2 inch
(6) Guaze Pads - 3 inch
(12) Safety pins
(2) Triangular Bandages
(1) First-Aid Cream
(1) Tweezers
(1) Scissors

COMMUNICABLE DISEASE

It is recommended that all protection officers wear protective gloves whenever there is a possibility of coming into contact with an individual's blood, body fluids, mucous membranes, and sores.

An infectious, or communicable, disease is one that can be transmitted from person to person, or from an infected animal or the environment to a person.

The spread of the disease depends on the ability of the infecting organism to survive outside its source. A source may be an infected person, an animal, an insect, or an inert object.

There are four general routes of transmission. They are: contact, airborne, vehicle, and vector.

Contact Transmission

This is the most common mode. An infected person comes into contact with a non-infected person, and transmits the disease. Contact transmission can be either direct or indirect. Direct transmission involves direct physical contact between two people. Direct transmission also involves droplet contact; the two people do not actually touch, but the infected person through sneezing, coughing or talking, sprays contaminated droplets into the face of the non-infected person. Cold and flu viruses are most commonly spread this way.

Indirect transmission occurs when an infected person spreads the infection to an inanimate object, and a non-infected person comes into contact with that object.

Airborne Transmission

Airborne transmission is much like droplet contact, but it is more pervasive. Droplets that are sneezed, coughed, or sprayed into the air evaporate, but the residue remains in the air for a long period of time. The initial outbreak of "Legionnaire's Disease" was caused by droplets carried and dispersed by an air conditioner.

Vehicle Transmission

With this method of transmission, the infective agent is introduced directly into the body by a "vehicle" or something that carries the infective agent. A person may drink contaminated water, or eat contaminated food. Vehicle transmission also occurs as a result of the injection of contaminated fluids, or contaminated drugs.

Vector Transmission

Vector transmission occurs when an animal provides the route of transmission to a person; an infected mosquito may transmit malaria.

While all routes of transmission are worth noting, the greatest concern to the protection officer in the field is contact transmission.

Identifying Individuals with Infectious Disease

An individual should be handled as infectious, if he or she displays any of the following:
- Medic-Alert tag or identification (will indicate infectious disease)
  - Fever
  - Rash, Open Sores, or Skin Lesions
  - Diarrhea
  - Vomiting
  - Coughing or Sneezing
  - Draining Wounds
  - Profuse Sweating

- Abdominal Pain

These symptoms may indicate a wide range of diseases, many of which are not infectious, but they should alert you to the need to exercise protective measures.

Guidelines for Preventing the Spread of Infectious Disease

- Wash your hands after every incident where you suspect that you may have come into contact with an infected person or object.
- Have disposable gloves and masks available at all times.
- Always wear disposable gloves when searching or handling an individual.
- Always wear disposable gloves when medically assisting an individual or other emergency personnel.
- If your uniform becomes soiled with blood, pus, oral secretions, or mucus, remove it as soon as possible, bag it, and label it, take a hot shower and wash with germicidal soap. Rinse thoroughly. If possible, dispose of the uniform, or wash it for 30 minutes in hot, soapy water and diluted bleach solution, if bleach will not harm your uniform.
- If in doubt, contact your Safety Supervisor and/or company or family doctor.

Guidelines for Cleaning Your Patrol Vehicle

Routine cleaning is recommended, and removal of blood and body fluids should be done as soon as possible. Follow these guidelines:
- Wear disposable gloves during all cleaning and de-contamination procedures.
- Remove any blood, body fluids, or other visible matter.
- Scrub the soiled area with a hospital grade disinfectant-detergent.
- Rinse and let dry.

Recommended Immunizations for Protective Officers

Before you begin active duty, make sure that you are adequately protected against the common communicable diseases.

These include:
- Hepatitis B Vaccination
- Influenza Vaccination (annually)
- DPT, with a Tetanus booster every 10 years
- Polio Immunization
- Rubella Vaccination
- Measles Vaccination
- Mumps Vaccination

Conclusion

We have looked at different types of infectious disease, the various avenues of transmission, and how to protect yourself against infection.

If your employer supplies protective latex gloves, use them. You are primarily responsible for guarding yourself, and possibly your family, against the sometimes harmful effects of these infectious organisms.

DISEASES AND RECOMMENDED PROTECTIVE MEASURES

DISEASE	MODES OF TRANSMISSION	RECOMMENDED PROTECTIVE CLOTHING	RECOMMENDED PROTECTIVE PROCEDURES	RECOMMENDED VEHICLE/EQUIPMENT CLEANING
AIDS	Blood and body fluids Infected needles Blood/blood products	Disposable mask Double utility gloves Eyeglasses/protective eyewear All cuts, lesions, scratches, hangnails, or other open wounds on hands bandaged	Wash hands thoroughly Never perform unprotected CPR	Wash vehicle surfaces with hospital approved germicidal soap, rinse with diluted bleach solution soak and disinfect all non-disposable equipment Immediately clean up any spills of blood or body fluids, disinfect
HEPATITIS B	Blood and body fluids	Disposable gloves All cuts, lesions scratches, hangnails, or other open wounds on hands bandaged	Get Hepatitis B vaccination Have injection of HBIG within two weeks of exposure, and second injection one month later Avoid mouth-to-mouth ventilation if possible	Clean vehicle and non-disposable equipment with a diluted bleach solution Double bag and seal all soiled refuse, dispose of properly
MENINGITIS	Contaminated food/water Direct contact with oral or nasal secretions Droplet spread	Disposable mask	Wash hands thoroughly	Scrub all vehicle parts or surfaces contacted by the patient
HERPETIC WHITLOW		Disposable gloves Bandage open wounds on hands	Wash hands with germicidal soap	Scrub vehicle surfaces and launder clothing
TUBER-CULOSIS	Droplet spread (usually continual) Direct contact with oral or nasal secretions	Disposable mask	Wash hands thoroughly Avoid mouth-to-mouth ventilation (use mechanical devices)	Scrub vehicle surfaces and equipment contaminated by secretions Launder clothing/linens contaminated by secretions in hot soapy water and bleach
INFLUENZA	Droplet spread	Disposable mask	Wash hands thoroughly	Scrub surfaces of vehicle contacted by patient Disinfect all non-disposable equipment used for patient
INFECTIOUS MONO-NUCLEOSIS	Droplet spread	Disposable mask if suctioning	Wash hands thoroughly	Scrub vehicle surfaces contaminated by oral secretions Disinfect all non-disposable equipment used for patient
COMMON CHILDHOOD DISEASES	Droplet spread Oral/nasal secretions Indirect contact (Rubella) Direct contact with skin lesions (Chickenpox)	Disposable mask Disposable gloves (Chickenpox)	Get vaccination if not already immune (Measles/Mumps/Rubella) Avoid touching skin lesions (Chickenpox)	Scrub vehicle surfaces and non-disposable equipment contaminated with secretions or lesions Boil non-disposable equipment

QUIZ
First Aid for Security Officers

1. The temporary care of the sick and injured is a good definition of _____
(Fill in the blank)

2. When you first assess the situation at an accident scene, your first consideration is to ensure that there is no _____ to you or the injured person.
(Fill in the blank)

3. CPR is a life-saving manoeuver that combines artificial breathing and artificial _____
(Fill in the blank)

4. Damage to a muscle is called a _____
(Fill in the blank)

5. If someone is conscious and appears to be injured, you must first obtain their permission in order to help them.
□ T □ F

6. Burns are not considered serious as it is only the skin that is affected.
□ T □ F

7. One significant sign of someone having a heart attack is chest pain.
□ T □ F

8. What is the first thing you should do when you come upon a person that appears to be unconscious?
□ a. Pinch the nose.
□ b. Check for response.
□ c. Tilt the head back.
□ d. Attempt to breathe for the person.

9. What is the appearance of a first degree burn?
□ a. Blistering
□ b. Charred appearance
□ c. Redness
□ d. White appearance

10. A person who has lost a large amount of blood may:
□ a. have severe thirst
□ b. gasp for air
□ c. feel faint
□ d. all of the above.

Unit 11

Use of Force

USE OF FORCE

By Charles T. Thibodeau, M.Ed., CPP, CSS
Christopher A. Hertig, CPP, CPO

Use of Force

The legally and socially acceptable use of force by private protection officers is a key issue in our contemporary - and future - society. As security personnel, we enforce rules, and ensure compliance with them. We are the "preservers of the corporate culture"; management's representative, charged with keeping an orderly, safe, and productive environment, in accordance with the organizational philosophy of our employer. We are the ambassadors of the organization, and serve a substantial public relations role. We enforce rules. We extend ourselves to help others, and assist in making the organization run more smoothly. We must be the "iron fist in the velvet glove".

Obviously, the use of force is something that is unpalatable; yet at times very necessary. We need to decrease the frequency and degree of force used as much as possible, without creating a personal safety hazard. Generally speaking, the more proficient and professional we are, the less that force is needed.

If we find ourselves resorting more and more to the use of force, it is indicative of a systemic failure. Either we are not following instructions, or we are a little short-sighted in our planning, or we have failed to be alert enough to observe imminent danger. When this happens in private security settings, the potential exists for extensive damage, injury to people, and loss of expensive assets. The potential also exists for increased legal liability, and expensive court litigation. Simply put:

"If you have to force it,
you're doing something wrong."
H.H. Thibodeau

Private security, at least ideally, implies a stable, relatively predictable environment, in which an individual, group, or community may pursue its ends without disruption or harm, and without fear of disturbance or injury. This definition necessarily includes personnel safety, fire safety, and emergency medical response, as well as safe and secure streets, homes, commercial businesses, parking areas, and work sites.

To accomplish our society's need to maintain order, we have formed governments based on laws, which express the desires of its citizens. In addition, we rely on physical security, which consists of those counter-measures required to promote a state of well being, to protect life and property, and to avoid or minimize the risks of natural or man-made disasters and crimes. Unfortunately, from time to time, things go wrong, systems break down, and we have no alternative. We have tried verbal persuasion. We have set limits. We have used loud, repeated, verbal commands. We have no time or place to retreat. We can only accomplish the necessary by using force.

The information in this unit of study will deal with this important aspect of the security officer's responsibilities. It is presented as a general educational guideline; specific procedures must be developed and adopted by the officer's employer. It is a starting point. **Each officer is strongly recommended to obtain additional education and training in this important area of a security officer's professional** development.

Use of Force in General

A definition that attempts to describe the reasonable use of force as "an amount of force equal to or just slightly greater than the force used by the aggressor" is sometimes misleading. Use of force is much better defined with respect to the concepts of **belief, reasonableness,** and **necessity.** For instance, you may choose to use pepper spray to disarm a person with a knife. In that case you actually use less force than the aggressor. At the same time, the choice of a less than lethal defensive weapon supports the assertion that the officer's use of force was reasonable.

Use of force is any tactic used to control, disarm, capture, restrain, or otherwise physically manage an aggressive or uncooperative subject. Force is predicated on the security officer's reasonable belief that the choice of weapons, and the amount of force used was necessary, reasonable, and the only alternative.

Each use of force must accomplish a legitimate and lawful purpose. At the same time, each use of force must appear, to a prudent and reasonable person under identical circumstances, to be reasonable and necessary. Reduced to its lowest common denominator in a court of law; the appropriateness of each use of force will be measured by an "objective reasonableness and necessity standard" versus whether the use of force was a "deliberate and wanton infliction of pain."

In use of force litigation, the following motives will most likely not help to acquit the security officer: fear, retaliation, punishment, accident, or loss of control. If the officer claims that the subject was inadvertently injured while in custody, that admission may be viewed in court as an indication of negligence. All force used by private security must be based on the officer's BELIEF that the use of force was the REASONABLE and NECESSARY solution, and that the execution of force was CALCULATED, MEASURED AND DELIBERATE! Failure at any one of these tests and you could be in jail, while the bad guy is out walking around free.

The reasonableness of any force used by a security officer is largely dependent upon the circumstances of the incident. Where the subject presents no threat to the officer, no use of force is permitted. For example, where an arrested person does not resist arrest, any use of force is excessive. Several cases have similarly held that the use of force during interrogation of a suspect is not justified, in the absence of evidence that the suspect attacked the officer. Note: interrogation (or focused interviewing) should never involve the touching of a person.

Justifying the Use of Force

Your primary defense in a charge of excessive use of force will have to do with the question of assault. That is, did the suspect give the officer cause to use force due to the subject's assault of the officer? It is therefore helpful for you to know that the claim of assault consists of four parts: ability, imminent jeopardy, intent, and preclusion. The question that will be asked after the officer's use of force will be:

1. Did the aggressor have the **ability** to harm you?
2. Were you in **imminent jeopardy** of being harmed?
3. Did the aggressor exhibit **intent** to harm you?
4. Were you **precluded** from escape or other defensive/control actions, so that your only way out was to use force?

If the officer cannot answer all of these questions in the affirmative, that officer may have serious trouble justifying his or her use of force.

There are four primary justifications for using force. These justifications consist of the officer's reasonable belief:

1. That harm would come to the officer or to someone else if force was not used.
2. That the actions taken were necessary.
3. That the actions taken were reasonable.
4. That the actions taken conformed with employer policy and training.

It is always better, of course, if force was used under the definition of an assault described above. Using force to defend property may be legally permissible, but it is generally frowned upon by the courts. Courts prefer that property owners utilize legal options, such as civil recovery to gain back property. When using force to protect property it is wise to remember that:

'Property can be replaced, people can't'.

If a security officer is arrested or sued for use of force there are several additional factors which will have an impact on the outcome of that litigation. Courts will consider the following issues:

1. Did the officer act under a reasonable belief?
2. Did the officer have a duty to retreat?
3. Did the officer give the aggressor a request or command to desist?
4. Did the officer follow department policy and procedure?
5. Did the officer follow department training?
6. Did the force used produce the desired results?
7. Did the officer place any third party in jeopardy?
8. Will the truth be relevant?
9. Will the witnesses tell the truth?
10. What or who will the jury believe?
11. What or who will the judge believe?
12. What or who will the public believe?

Force Alternatives Defined

Alternatives to the use of force amount to any method or tactic which can be used to de-escalate incidents, without the use of defensive weapons, gratuitous threats, or aggressive action. This definition necessarily connotes the use of verbal de-escalation, removing persons from the "conflict zone", negotiating conflict resolution,

maintaining a non-combative atmosphere, and calling in public law enforcement. Some of the many alternatives to the use of force which should be attempted before using force are:

I. Take your time - slow down the action. Haste gets people hurt! "Haste makes casualties."

II Awareness - recognize potential threats. Be alert.

III. Evaluate - get all the facts and pieces of evidence that are available. Understand the problem before acting to solve it.

IV. Don't respond in anger! Take a step back. Take a few deep breaths. Take your time.

V. Be an actor - preclude the problem from escalating and erupting - not a reactor.

VI. Maintain a safe distance.

VII. Smile; be as pleasant as appropriate under the circumstances.

VIII. Be polite - show respect to everyone, including the aggressor.

IX. Really care about people! If you do, it is projected in your demeanor.

X. Apply active listening techniques to show interest in what another is saying.

XI. Call for back up before acting, including the police when necessary.

XII. Recruit assistance from persons nearby if necessary.

XIII. Ask perpetrator's friends and relatives to speak to the perpetrator.

XIV. Be slow to speak, slow to anger, fast to listen.

XV. If all else fails, expect to get hit.

XVI. Expect any hit to hurt, brush it off - it is not "The End of the World."

XVII. Engage in tactical retreat when things get hot; back off and get behind cover.

XVIII. Use loud assertive commands - "STOP" and "NO!" "Hit him with your voice".

XIX. Use repeated commands - "DROP THE KNIFE!", "DROP IT". "DROP IT". "DROP IT!", "DO IT NOW!", "NOW", "NOW!".

XX. Continue verbal de-escalation. Be patient for as long as it takes.

Excessive Force Liability

An examination of use of force cases, which resulted in injury and/or liability, shows that these cases commonly involve the following:

* Use (or threat) of any force where subject offers no resistance.

* Negligent use of normally non-lethal force, resulting in death or serious injury.

* Excessive force as an overreaction to subject's resistance to officer commands (continued past point of no resistance).

* Intentional infliction of pain (excessive force), as summary punishment.

* Use of deadly force in situations where it is not permitted.

* Failure to provide medical treatment for injuries from officer's use of force.

* An officer deliberately strikes or inflicts pain upon a subject after the subject is placed in restraints - using force to punish.

*   An officer entices or provokes a subject in reacting aggressively, so as to create cause for using force. *Poor interpersonal skills create crises!*

*   Death of a subject under the officer's control due to positional asphyxia. *Proper restraint techniques, which do not impede breathing, are critical!*

*   Officer mistakenly reacts to a subject with a severe medical problem, such as confusing diabetic shock with alcoholism. *First-aid training and constant monitoring of the subject are necessary for his/her safety and welfare.*

*   Officer is injured by taking a bad position, such as standing directly in front of the subject, too close to the subject, or not using cover.

*   Officer is injured by having the wrong attitude. Carelessness, overconfidence, demeaning tone of voice, cockiness, etc., all cause problems with others.

*   Officer is injured by relaxing too soon. *"It's not over til it's over".*

*   Officer is injured by failing to search suspect - always do a visual search at a minimum!

*   Officer injured by failure to watch suspect hands - see the palms!

Duties that Accompany Use of Force

Private security officers must exhibit restraint and self-control within permissible limits at all times. Public and private protection officers are responsible for responding to the medical needs of subjects against whom force was used. Supervisors and line officers have a duty to intervene when another officer is using excessive force against a subject.

A Formula for Self-Control

Use of force is all about control. Sometimes proactive preventive security plans break down, and force is required to maintain control. The question is: "Who is the person we most earnestly want to control?" Is it the drunk, the jealous spouse, the angry employee? No, it is OURSELF! In order to maintain control of others, we first must find a way to control ourselves when under great pressure. Remembering this formula might help keep everything in perspective, when faced with high-stress, potentially aggressive situations. Carefully examine the following equations:

$$CONTROL = I/E$$
$$I/E + P = E/I$$
$$E/I + T = I/E$$
$$I/E = CONTROL$$

This formula means that control is equal to "I" (intellect) over "E" (emotions). Thus, we are in control when our intellect rules our emotions. When we introduce "P" (problem) to the equation, it may have the effect of turning the equation upside down. Thus, I/E + P = E/I. Emotions then are in control of our Intellect! When we are running on raw emotions, we can get hurt, or we can lose control and hurt someone else. We can use more force than is necessary. We can use excessive force.

However, if you add "T" (training) to the equation, then the tendency is to reverse the negative effects of "P". You then have: E/I + T = I/E. Finally, I/E = Control.

What all of this means is, that by developing a trained response to perceived use of force situations, your emotions can be held in check, and with the intellect in charge, you can more effectively maintain control. That is why verbal de-escalation, if practiced regularly, is an excellent weapon to use in aggressive situations. It can eliminate the use of force in the vast majority of situations. It can also help the officer to get along better with those in the work environment. Resolving conflict amiably is the essence of a protection officer's job. Those who are good at it have long and rewarding careers. Those who do not, get into all sorts of trouble.

"Conflict resolution is the cornerstone of officer survival."

Response to Aggressive Behavior

Dr. Kevin Parsons developed "The Confrontational Continuum", over a decade ago. The "Continuum" serves as a guideline for police officers when specific force applications are appropriate. Since then other entities such as PPCT Management Systems, REB Training International, and Larry Smith Enterprises have developed similar police-types of models. The following outline is not necessarily the model that the private security officer would want to follow, as the officer is generally not armed with a baton or firearm. Also, individual situations can modify the steps used in the application of force. The confrontational continuum outlined below can best be thought of as a general guide. In the final analysis, security officers must always follow the use of force policy established by their employers!

Confrontation Continuum

Step 1. Officer presence is the first step in the continuum. The mere presence of an officer establishes some degree of psychological control. Non-verbal communication can also be employed to control a subject.

Step 2. Initial communications can be thought of as the second step in the use of force. The use of questioning of a subject, as the initial communication, will give the officer an edge. By asking questions, the officer is increasing his/her psychological control over the situation. Persuasion and limit-setting can be part of this step.

Step 3. Commands are the next step. "Heavy control talk" used to direct the subject, such as "Stop", "Back", "Drop it", "Do it now", etc., provides a psychological control factor. Note that there should be short, simple, emphatically verbalized, commands given to a subject who is physically resisting or aggressive. Doing so ensures that the use of force follows a logical, justifiable, continuum. It also dramatically increases the effectiveness of any physical force exerted. Additionally, witnesses to the event will hear the commands, and will be better able to place the use of force in its proper perspective.

Step 4. Soft empty hand control, such as grasping the subject's elbow and wrist, and leading them away (escort hold) may be required to remove the subject from the conflict zone and out of the public eye. WARNING: At this point you must expect to get hit and expect it to hurt. You should not allow yourself to be surprised by a "sucker punch". Whenever you touch an aggressive person, expect an immediate response; an escalation of aggression. You could get stabbed, hit with an object, or shot. You would do best to evaluate the situation carefully before you try to intervene at this stage in the continuum.

Step 5. At this point, if you are not working out regularly and practicing defensive tactics religiously, do not attempt to participate on this level of aggression response. You will not be qualified to respond to required increased levels of aggression. Call for public assistance, and use verbal de-escalation until the police arrive.

Step 6. In extreme cases you will be forced to use a chemical incapacitation device, normally oleoresin capsicum aerosols (pepper spray), on the subject to protect yourself or others, or to obtain compliance with handcuffing or come-alongs. This chemical incapacitation device is considered a less than lethal defensive weapon. Be very careful of weapon retention, and spray-back. Try to avoid bringing a weapon to the confrontation that can be used against you. If you take yourself out of the equation by becoming incapacitated by your own spray, you will be of no use to anyone. Remember, it is required that you administer first-aid to the subject immediately after you have restrained the subject, if you have used this spray.

Step 7. The next level of confrontation escalation is the hard, empty-hand control such as joint manipulation and decentralization. WARNING: Don't attempt this unless you have had documented, professional training. If you have no specialized training, do not attempt to participate in increased aggression escalation. Get lots of help, continue verbal de-escalation, and overwhelm the subject until the police arrive.

Step 8. The next level of escalation is the empty hand impact. Deliver stunning techniques to motor points, and other soft tissue targets. WARNING: Don't attempt this unless you are properly trained and proficient. If you have no specialized training, do not attempt to participate in increased aggression escalation. Get lots of help, keep up the verbal de-escalation, and overwhelm the subject until the police arrive.

Step 9. The next level of escalation is the use of aerosol chemical agents, such as CS and CN gas. These can, if improperly used, cause serious injury. Be careful of weapon retention, spray-back, and the spraying of bystanders inadvertently. Also, remember it is required that you administer first-aid to the subject immediately after you have restrained the subject whenever chemical spray was used.

Step 10. The next level of escalation is the use of intermediate weapons such as batons and other impact weapons, stun-guns, and Tasers. WARNING: Don't attempt this unless you are trained and experienced in the use of batons, and other impact weapons. If you have no specialized training, do not attempt to participate in this level of aggression escalation. Get lots of help, and overwhelm the subject until the police arrive.

Step 11. The next level of escalation is the use of lateral vascular neck restraint, which compresses the carotid arteries in the neck, causing the subject to pass out. Improper use of this hold could cause death. Also included would be impact weapon strikes to joints, which can cause serious bodily injury - and can be considered deadly force. WARNING: Don't even think about this unless you have received specialized training, and there is absolutely no alternative! In addition, don't attempt this level of escalation unless you are trained and experienced in the use of batons and other impact weapons. Also, certain tech-

niques and unusual weapons may be perceived as being brutal by the public. Using them may constitute some inherent liability risk, even if they were used properly.

Step 12. The next level of escalation is the use of deadly force such as firearms, impact weapon strikes to the head or neck, or empty hand blows to the head, neck, throat, etc. There is only one acceptable reason for use of deadly force, and that is the protection of human life. Use of deadly force to protect property will open you up to serious civil law suits and possible criminal prosecution. WARNING: Don't attempt this unless you are trained and experienced in the use of deadly force. Remember that after deadly force is used you have a duty to give first-aid until emergency medical assistance arrives. If you kill someone in the line of duty, even though you were 100% right, expect to be sued. You could even be arrested and go to jail. Expect to go to trial for a civil and criminal proceeding.

Escalation/De-escalation Continuum

To better understand the application of the confrontation continuum, the following escalation/de-escalation continuums have been prepared. If you are a police officer or a member of a highly trained private security contingent, you will be trained to participate in an escalation/de-escalation procedure that will look something like the following:

1.   Officer arrives on the scene, observes the situation, and engages the aggressor immediately. Officer gives verbal commands.

2.   Aggressor escalates aggression, officer escalates force. Officer combines verbal commands with escalation of force.

3.   Aggressor de-escalates aggression, officer de-escalates force and evaluates the situation. Officer combines verbal commands with de-escalation of force.

4.   Officer escalates choice of defensive weapons in response to the aggressor's choice of offensive weapons. If aggressor has a club the officer might choose a fire arm.

5.   This escalation and de-escalation back and forth will continue until the aggressor succumbs to the force of the officer.

6.   The officer must win every round of aggression. If striking the aggressor is required, the officer will use the element of surprise and strike decisively.

7.   The officer will administer first-aid immediately after the subject has been subdued.

8.   The subject will also be debriefed. This means that they should be talked to so that their ego is restored. This can include an interview with the subject for use in assisting him/her, as well as for documentation of the event. Note that the subject may admit to being wrong or may apologize. This should be accepted and noted! A brief statement as to why the subject was restrained and what the violation entailed may be made. This could include the words such as "I had to handcuff you because you were assaulting me", or "I had to search you for your safety and mine". Debriefing is used to set the subject at ease, prevent future problems, and obtain information for the report.

9.   The officer will thoroughly document the entire event. Statements made during debriefing which are admissions or apologies should be recorded. Steps to be taken by the subject during the next crisis situation should

also be included. In many cases a "contract" can be written where the subject agrees not to repeat this behavior in the future. This should be noted in the final report.

If you are a member of the average security contingent, with no training in self defense or the use of weapon, you would want to follow an escalation/de-escalation procedure that looks more like this:

1.   Officer arrives on the scene, observes the situation, and radios for help. Officer chooses a safe distance and location before commencing verbal de-escalation. The communication procedure will commence as soon as the officer has reported the incident, and taken a safe cover.

2.   The officer identifies escape routes, items to use to block aggression if needed, weapons of opportunity that could be used in an emergency, and evaluate each person in the immediate vicinity of the aggressor.

3.   Aggressor escalates aggression, officer backs off, takes cover, keeping a safe distance. Officer combines verbal de-escalation techniques with his move to safety.

4.   Aggressor de-escalates his aggression, officer continues verbal de-escalation techniques. Officer opens up a dialogue and keeps it going.

5.   Officer avoids personal confrontation at all costs except in deadly force situations. If the officer is in the grasp of the aggressor, the officer uses force to break away, give or get space, put something between the officer and the aggressor, and then continues the dialogue at a safer distance.

6.   The officer must ensure that the aggressor is not forcing him into a state of preclusion, where maximum force will be necessary to escape. At the same time, the officer must ensure that the aggressor has a back door or escape route, and is not being backed into a corner. If the aggressor escapes from the area, the security officer will secure the area and the individuals in that area.

7.   The officer must win every round of aggression. If striking the aggressor is required, the officer will use the element of surprise and strike decisively. The only purpose of the escalation of aggression is to break a hold, which the aggressor has put on, and which creates the risk of injury. The officer must break the hold and get to safety. There should be no attempt to force this aggressor into submission, as a trained, armed protection officer would be expected to do.

8.   If a physical confrontation occurs, the officer calls for medical assistance, and renders first-aid until the medics arrive.

Obviously, communication skills are of paramount importance! **This is the essence of defensive tactics; officers dealing with violent, aggressive, persons should become devoted students of interpersonal communication.** In this way, the use of force must be precluded by verbalizing and retreating, where possible.

Officer Safety Issues

There are four individuals or groups who the security officer is concerned with protecting. They are: the security officer himself or herself, the apparent victim, the general public, and the perpetrator. It is important to understand that the order of importance is that the officer comes first on the list. Officer safety is primary, because if the officer is taken out, there may be no hope for the victim or anyone else. However, the officer may be his or her own worst enemy in times of stress, especially if the "body and mind" turns in on itself. That happens when the

"tachy-psyche" effect takes over.

As pointed out above, self-control is the most important factor when engaging in the use of force. It is not unusual, when faced with an aggressor, for the officer to become extremely nervous, tense, and shaky. These signs indicate that the officer is afraid of confrontation. Left unabated, this shaking and fear may escalate into something called the "tachy-psyche" effect. That is when you can really get hurt. "Tachy" means rapid or accelerated. "Psyche" means the mind, functioning as the center of thought, feeling, and behavior, and consciously or unconsciously adjusting and relating the body to its social and physical environment. Some identifying characteristics of this phenomenon are the following:

*Rapid Heart Beat
*Rapid Mental Processing
*Sweating
*Dilated Pupils
*Tunnel Vision Occurs
*Auditory Occlusion Blocks Out Sound
*Numbness and Heaviness Felt in Extremities
*Loss of Dexterity in Fingers, Arms, Legs
*Shortening of Breath
*Everything Goes in Slow Motion
*Loss of Bodily Functions - Stop Breathing, Bladder Release, Pass Out or Paralysis

If this happens to the officer, as the officer approaches an aggressive person, there is no telling what might result. Either the officer will be rendered defenseless, or the officer may respond with excessive force. If you feel this happening, take a tactical retreat until you can regain your composure. Only deep relaxation can counter this condition and alleviate the symptoms. Unfortunately, in most critical incident situations, there isn't enough time to retreat. The only prevention of this condition is training. An officer who is trained to handle critical incident situations, including handling aggressive persons, is not as prone to experience these symptoms.

Optimal Distance

It is possible that while approaching an aggressive subject, you can inadvertently set off an act of aggression, simply by getting too close to the aggressor. That is, if you enter the aggressor's private space, you can make the aggressor so uncomfortable that the aggressor will strike out in anger.

Optimal distance is a term which defines that area, which extends out in all directions from an individual, within which the person feels safe and secure. Invasion of this space will result in a reflex reaction. This space is also known as a person's "comfort zone." Unwelcome invasion of a person's optimal distance could result in escalation of conflict, even if you don't touch the individual. It is important that security officers respect this optimal distance. Our job is to be part of the solution, not part of the problem.

One reason, other than for officer safety, that we recommend communication at 10 feet or more from the subject, is so that you will not inadvertently encroach on the subject's personal space, and set off an aggressive reaction. While this is a great distance, violent persons often have an extended personal zone. They need lots of space!

As for additional safety, the officer must be aware of the different distances that the officer must honor to keep safe, called the "reactionary gap". This gap is the distance between the subject and the officer, within which, if the subject decides to punch, stab, or hit the officer, the officer may, or may not, be able to defend against the attack. The officer should be aware that a reactionary gap of 8 to 10 feet away from the subject will provide a reaction time for the officer to defend against the punch. However, the reactionary gap for using a firearm in defense against the knife is approximately 25 feet.

The reactionary gap to defend against the gun, works in just the opposite way. In fact, the closer to the gun the better to allow disarming techniques, if you are trained in those techniques. Other than in a disarming attempt, reactionary gaps are fairly irrelevant when it comes to guns. Taking shelter and running might work, depending on a number of variables. Let the circumstances be your guide.

Whatever you do, don't rush in and attempt to touch the aggressive subject. If you wish to escort the subject, approach from the side or rear. Even then, unless the aggressor is handcuffed, try to control the subject without bodily contact. Verbal commands and gestures should be employed.

Defanging the Snake

"Defanging the Snake" is a term that is used to mean the elimination of the means of aggression from an aggressive person. It could include the removal of weapons, or the rendering of arms and or legs useless, either by pain, paralysis, breakage, or use of restraints. The fangs of the snake are where the poison, that can hurt us, is located. In our case, the knife blade, the bullet, the club, and the fists, are the "fangs" that can cause us harm, and possibly permanent injury or death.

Another way to defang the snake is to eliminate the fuel of the aggression. Separating warring parties, or removing the combatants from the conflict zone, could have the same effect as pouring water on a fire. Take away the fuel and the fire goes out. Thus, in many cases, if you remove the more aggressive of the two combatants, you can achieve the same effect as taking the weapon away from the aggressor. A word of caution here though. You should only do this with back-up present. Always keep in mind officer safety.

Elements of Aggression

An aggressive situation is usually more complex than a simple case of one person being upset with another. There are usually highly charged emotions driving the aggression. The trick is to attend to the business of assisting, without getting dragged into one side or the other of the controversy. It is important to recognize that aggression has two parts, the fuel of aggression and the means of aggression. The fuel of aggression, consists basically of the emotional side of the confrontation, and may include any number of the following:

*Perceptions/Attitudes
*Belief Systems
*Rebellion
*Mental/Medical Conditions
*Chemical Abuse Problems
*Revenge, Jealousy, Passion
*Feelings of Inadequacy

The means of aggression consists basically of the weapons of the confrontation, and may include any number of the following:

*Hands, Feet, Elbows and Head
*Non-Lethal Weapons (Chemical Sprays)
*Lethal Weapons (Knife, Gun)

*Vehicles
*Weapons of Opportunity (Things laying Around)

Dealing With Aggression

The most dangerous situation you may ever face is a violence-prone situation. Violence-prone situations can easily lead to injury to yourself, or to others. In addition, a lawsuit could result. What can you do in violence-prone situations to reduce the risk of using excessive force? The following are a few ideas on safely managing violence-prone encounters:

1.   **Recognize Your Own Emotions.** In itself, this causes the professional to calm down. In most people, violence is reached in stages - from anxiety, to defensive behavior, to physically acting out violent behavior. Cooling off the escalating violence-prone situation is best done by remaining calm and professional.

2.   **Remember That When A Person Is In A Rage, Options Cannot Be Seen.** As people grow angrier, they fail to realize that they have several options. They usually see their options as FLEEING or FIGHTING. Other options, such as discussing the problem and seeking a solution, may not be considered. Rage takes over cognition. The formula for rage is clearly $C = E/I$.

3.   **Avoid Humiliating Subjects.** Some officers will create problems when speaking to a subject in a sensitive situation. When this happens, the subject will shut down communication, a condition that could become explosive. The best policy is to play it low key. Protect your space, and be ready to execute self-defense plans at the first indication of aggression. Remember that EVERYBODY - even the serene, little old lady - is potentially violent under the proper circumstances. Slowing down the action, respecting the subject's personal space, and using empathic listening skills help to de-escalate.

4.   **If The Encounter Becomes Tough, Get Or Give Space.** As the aggression level escalates, the best relaxant is space. CLEAR THE CONFLICT ZONE! If two people are exchanging heated words, both should take a walk - in opposite directions. Immediate separation of antagonists can prevent a confrontation.   At the same time they both should be "out of sight" and "out of sound" of each other. Get them turned around and as far away from each other as is practical. If possible, use walls to separate the subjects.

5.   **Pro-Active Prevention Works Better Than Reaction.** Officers must be receptive to warning signs of violence, rather than be reactionary. Understand that people who are antagonized by others, may go from calmness to rage in seconds.

6.   **Sharpen Your Observation Skills.** Observing alcohol use, and levels of intoxication, can be obvious warning signs, as can playful pushing and shoving, and loud in-your-face type of communication.   Boyfriend/girlfriend jealousy situations and domestic problems can also become volatile.

Some provocateurs will try to provoke a hostile, angry response from you. This is often done with a reference to your ethnic or racial background, or a derogatory statement about your mother. You must recognize that the name caller is trying to cause you to lose control, permitting escalation of violence to occur.

"When you lose your temper, someone else has control over you."

Remember the formula for control: C = I/E. Remember, WHOEVER LOSES CONTROL - LOSES! Therefore it is in your best interest to identify indicators of aggression which we call "red flags" of aggression. Some of these are:

Weapons Of Opportunity
Disguised Weapons
Weapons in Plain Sight
All Edged Weapons
Perpetrator's Hands
Relatives, Friends, Others In Close Proximity
Subject's Red Face
Subject's Direct Prolonged Eye Contact
Subject's Quick and Deep Breathing
Subject's Head and Shoulders Back
Subject Standing As Tall As Possible
Subject's Hands Pumping
Subject's Finger Pointing
Subject's Moving In and Out of Your Personal Space
Subject's Belligerence, Yelling, Cursing
Subject Pounding Fist on Walls and Tables
Subject's Verbal Threats

Verbal De-Escalation

Verbal de-escalation is just about anything you can say that fits the situation you find at the incident scene. The successful de-escalation will be more a product of your attitude and level of professionalism, than of the actions you take.

At some point you may be surprised by the aggressor, or overwhelmed by more than one aggressor, and you will find yourself in a fight/flee/flow situation. That is, if you can't fight and you can't flee - flow! By "flow" we mean verbal de-escalation. You will have to talk your way out of the predicament. There cannot be a prepared list of canned verbal communication that will fit every situation. You will be more successful drawing on your own words, customized for the particular circumstances. The key to a successful verbal de-escalation is in your level of professionalism with regards to caring, empathy, command of the language, personal sincerity, and candor.

WARNING: When practicing verbal de-escalation, don't let down your guard. Keep in mind officer safety.

Applying Verbal De-Escalation to Aggressive Situations

If you are called to a routine confrontation, where the participants appear to be reasonable and the likelihood of injury to youself or to others is low, then you may wish to follow some of the following de-escalation suggestions:

* Respect subject's dignity.
* Do not shout commands.
* Be careful not to become part of the problem.
* Assume officer safety distance (10 to 15 feet).
* Provide a pleasant greeting such as "How can I help you?".
* Assume a non-combative attitude.
* Use non-threatening questions. Avoid "Why?" questions.
* Slow everything down, take your time. "Calmness is contagious".
* Keep hands and chest high and ready to react.

* Attempt to move subject away from conflict zone.
* Listen intently to subject's words.
* Project empathy with subject's cause.
* Observe subject's hands and body language.
* Conduct a visual frisk, check for observable weapons.
* Look for weapons of opportunity.
* Listen to peripheral persons. They can be witnesses, "cheerleaders", or assailants.
* Keep talking and negotiating a solution.
* Practice officer safety at all times.
* Make the decision to arrest or release.

Procedures for dealing with a violence prone individual differ somewhat from dealing with the average aggressive situation. If the likelihood of injury is certain, or extremely high, then you may wish to follow some of these suggestions:

* Subject's dignity is not the main priority, "defanging the snake" is the priority!
* You will still want to respect the subject's dignity.
* Respect officer safety distance.
* Assume a self-defense attitude.
* Use loud, clear, directive commands for officer safety.
* Keep hands on your choice of weapons, or have weapons drawn.
* Call for back-up before entering the conflict.
* . Give subject directives to reach a solution.
* Keep talking and negotiating a solution.
* Listen intently to subject's words.
* Project empathy with subject's cause.
* Observe his hands and body language.
* When back-up arrives conduct a search for weapons.
* Cuff and search for officer safety.
* Continue dialogue with subject.
* Listen to witnesses, take names, addresses and phone numbers.
* Take notes of what witnesses have said. Use quotes from the witnesses.
* Make the decision to detain, arrest, or release.
* Use deadly force only when a life is threatened, or serious bodily injury is imminent.

Lethal and Less-Than-Lethal Weapons Management

The employment of weapons is often grasped at by protection officers in the wake of a frightening experience. Fear is usually the primary motivator for protection officers asking management if they can be armed. Unfortunately, weapons do not solve the threat problem all by themselves. They are tools that are necessary in certain circumstances. They require increased responsibility and skill to be employed in an acceptable manner. Handcuffing a resistant subject is difficult, and must be done tactfully. Spraying an assailant does not negate the threat, it merely helps to control the person. The officer must still step out of the way of the aggressor and take appropriate follow-up measures. The same is true with impact weapons, and even firearms. Protective body movement out of the danger zone, employment of the weapon, and proper follow-up, must be done for any weapon. In short:

"Weapons are only useful when in the hand of someone proficient at using them, in a situation where they are the appropriate tools to use".

Weapons offer added protection - if properly selected and employed - but they also increase the professional obligations of the protection officer dramatically. Their use involves substantial judgement and skill on the part of the officer. Such judgement and skill only comes after extensive instruction and practice in interpersonal communication, de-escalation, interviewing, unarmed defensive tactics, legal considerations, etc. These are some of the proficiency areas that must be mastered, prior to the effective use of weapons. The following saying helps to put this into perspective:

"You can't use a weapon if you can't use your hands.
You can't use your hands if you can't use your voice.
And you can't use your voice if you can't use your brain."

Whatever weapons are being employed, be they handcuffs, pepper spray, firearms, or impact weapons, the following guidelines will help to maintain that they are handled in a safe, appropriate manner:

1.   Weapons should only be handled by persons who have been trained in how to use them. Training must be refreshed periodically. It must also be thoroughly documented.

2.   Weapons should remain holstered or locked up unless they are to be employed in an actual confrontation, cleaned, or used during formal, supervised training. There must be no showing of weapons to curious persons, and absolutely no playing with weapons.

3.   All weapons should be thoroughly checked by the officer carrying them prior to starting on duty.

4.   The supervisor should check weapons on a regular basis.

5.   A maintenance system should be in place for all weapons to include routine maintenance, as per the manufacturer's instructions, as well as work by armorers or manufacturers when needed.

6.   Weapons should be supplied by the employer. The employer must exercise and retain control over the weapon.

7.   Weapons, ammunition, holsters, etc. should not be modified except by a manufacturer's representative or qualified armorer.

8.   All laws, property owners' wishes, and insurance carrier regulations, on the carrying and use of weapons, must be respected.

Unfortunately, weapons are occasionally "sold" by someone to management without management really assessing them fully. Seemingly impressive demonstration of a weapon's capability, put on by an expert who stages the demonstration, is not the reason to select a weapon for a protective force! Neither is the following of a fad, or the securing of a 'bargain'!

Weapons selection is a serious decision, which must be made only after extensive research. On the other extreme, vacillating on a weapons decision - and not arming security officers when this is needed - raises unacceptable levels of risk to protection forces, and to those they are employed to protect. The following is a list of considerations which managers should review when selecting a weapon/weapons system:

1.   For what specific need was the weapon selected?

2.   How is the weapon most likely to be used (tactical research)?

3.   What was the selection process used for adopting the weapon?

a.   Why was the specific weapon chosen over other weapons?

b.   Who made the decision?

c.   What was the decision making process?
(1)   Independent research studies?
(2)   Medical research?
(3)   Comparative bids?

4.   What type of initial training is required?

5.   Who can provide this training?

6.   What type of refresher training is given?

7.   Who can provide this training?

8.   Can instructor qualifications be clearly demonstrated to the satisfaction of a court?

9.   Is training adequately documented?

10.   Is a continuous tactical review of the weapon's use in place, which shows how it is actually being used?

11.   What training have supervisors had in the use of the weapons?

a.   Initial training?

b.   Periodic training?

c.   Training or education above and beyond what line officers receive?

12.   Are reasonable and enforceable policies, governing the use of the weapons, in effect?

13.   Are weapons carried by, or accessible to, officers who are off-duty?

14.   Is weapon retention addressed?

15.   What is the skill level required for the use of the weapon?

16.   Does the weapon fit in with other weapons used by the organization or other agencies that the organization may interact with during an emergency?

Report Writing in Use of Force Cases

What is involved in writing the report of an incident, where a use of force was necessary and reasonable? It should be enough to just sit down and write, in chronological order, the truthful facts of the case. Unfortunately, in our litigious society, where cash-hungry lawyers and an aggressive media lay in waiting for the next abuse of force case, the officer cannot be carefree. The report must be written, taking into consideration the technical requirements of criminal and civil liability, in both State and Federal court.

Know your audience! You must assume that the paper you are about to write will be in the hands of an opposing attorney, and you will be in front of a judge in the near future. If the use of force required a firearm, pain compliance, a chemical or electronic incapacitation device, baton, kicks, or other physical confrontation, your report must be thorough, concise, and accurate. In addition to all of this, the report must be absolutely true, as you witnessed the truth.

While writing the report, the officer must cover the following:

I.   NECESSITY (What the Perpetrator Did)
A.   Self-Defence
B.   Defense Of Others
C.   To Prevent Escape
II.   REASONABLENESS (What You Did)
A.   Department Policy
B.   Department Training
C.   Supervisor's Instructions

D.   Conscious, Deliberate, Controlled, And Intentional Use of Force
E.   Caused By Aggressiveness Of The Perpetrator
F.   Medical Follow Up - (First Aid)

III.   THE REPORT MUST BE BALANCED AND COORDINATED
A.   The Report Follows A Chronology
B.   The Report Has No Contradictions
C.   Times Stated Match Other Reports and Records
D.   Facts Stated Match Other Reports and Records

Any one of the above components that are lacking in the report will provide an opportunity for the plaintiff's attorney, or the prosecutor, to attack the integrity of the report, and ultimately your testimony could fall apart. You may have performed perfectly, followed all the rules, provided a truthful report, and still lose the case over the fact that you failed to write a proper report.

In reviewing the report, play "devil's advocate" with yourself. Try to anticipate what the lawyers or media might try to make out of what you are about to write. Review your organization's policy before writing it. Leave no gaps in the report to be filled in later. Don't assume anything. Never leave out a fact because you thought everyone would understand the fact without having to write it down. What you may think is common sense may be distorted by the plaintiff's lawyer or prosecutor to appear to the jury or judge as a cover up or a deception.

Keep in mind that the main thrust of the defense lawyer, or the plaintiff's lawyer, is to present their client as the victim in the case, not the perpetrator. They will work hard to accuse you of being the perpetrator and using the "but for" test, they will say, "but for the illegal or negligent acts or omissions of the officer, this poor client would not have sustained the injuries that he did." Be sure that nothing in your report supports the assertion that your acts were illegal or negligent.

Your report should pass the "reasonable person" test. That is, either the jury or the judge, should be able to use your report to get into the scene sufficiently to be able to form a mental picture of what actually took place. From that picture, he or she should be able to determine what he or she would have done under exactly the same circumstances. If the report follows the above guidelines, it should lead that person to the logical conclusion, that the officer acted in a reasonable and necessary fashion.

Conclusion
Ultimately use of force comes down to something to be avoided. Just review all that has been presented here. There are so many traps and pitfalls in this area of a security officer's duties. Careful consideration must be taken before the officer knows about use of force and proper procedure. The better equipped officer will be able to participate successfully, win every round of aggression and escape personal injury and law suits. Personal training is the key to successful aggression de-escalation. The general education provided in this chapter is offered to start the officer's professional development. Every person who puts on the uniform of a security officer, should become an earnest student of the legal and tactical aspects of the Use of Force.

REFERENCES
Fisher, Robert J. and Green, Gion. Introduction to Security, Fifth Edition, Stoneham, MA., Butterworth-Heinemann, 1992, P3.
The American Heritage Dictionary, Second Edition.
Ouellette, Roland. Management of Aggressive Behavior, Powers Lake, WI., Performance Dimensions Publishing, 1993, P8.

RESOURCES
American Society of Law Enforcement Trainers (302/645-4080 or 302/645-4084 fax) sponsors seminars, an annual conference, and publishes THE LAW ENFORCEMENT TRAINER.
Butterworth-Heinemann (800/366-2665 or WWW.bh.com/sec) is the largest publisher of Security texts. USE OF FORCE BY PRIVATE SECURITY PERSONNEL and PRIVATE SECURITY LAW: CASE STUDIES are some of the titles available.
Calibre Press (800/323-0037) is the premier officer survival organization. They provide seminars, books, and videos covering a vast array of officer survival topics.
Crisis Prevention Institute (800/558-8976 or 414/783-5906 fax) is a leader in violence management. CPI provides certification in Nonviolent Crisis Intervention. They have an extensive collection of video-based instructional programs such as "Breaking Up Fights", "The Art of Setting Limits", "Documentation: Your Best Defense", etc.
Performance Dimensions Publishing (800/877-7453) offers consultation, training, videos and books on Officer Survival, Interpersonal Communication, and other pertinent topics.
Professional Training Resources (800/998-9400) is the leading supplier of Security books and videos. Hundreds of titles are available from various publishers on topics ranging from Self-Defense to Civil Liability.
REB Training International (603/446-9393 or 603/446-9394 fax) is a leader in Oleoresin Capsicum Aerosol Training ("pepper spray"). REB also has various training programs for security officers, such as PR-24, and the Management of Aggressive Behavior (MOAB).

QUIZ
Use of Force

1.   Reports written after use of force must have no _____.

2.   Use of force can be defined according to the concepts of _____, reasonableness and _____.

3.   Did the aggressor have the _____to harm you?

4.   Pepper spray is lower on the Use of Force Continuum than mace or tear gas.
☐ T   ☐ F

5.   Security officers may have a legal obligation to use of force under certain state statutes.
☐ T   ☐ F

6.   "Conflict _____is the cornerstone of officer survival".

7.   List five (5) things the officer who is authorized to carry a weapon must bear in mind.
A._____
B._____
C._____
D._____
E._____

8.   Handcuffing a resistant subject is easy.
☐ T   ☐ F

9.   The _____gap is the distance between the subject and the officer, within which the officer may not be able to defend him or herself if the subject decides to attack.

10.   Persons engaged in fighting should be made to sit facing each other in the same room.
☐ T   ☐ F

Unit 12

Public Relations
Police and Security Liaison
Ethics and Professionalism

PUBLIC RELATIONS

By Charles T. Thibodeau, M.Ed., CPP, CSS
Christopher A. Hertig, CPP, CPO
George A. Barnett, CPO

Public Relations consists of a mutual understanding between an organization and its constituent publics.[1] The term *"publics"* is defined as the general community, the people as a whole, or a group of people sharing a common interest.[2] With respect to Private Security, we would define the term "public" as primarily a group of people sharing a common interest relative to our work environment, plus the general public. The actual people we come in contact with changes from work-site to work-site with the exception of that one constant - the general public.[3]

If we are working in entertainment security, where crowd management is the main responsibility, we have a very broad and diverse constituency. If we are working in executive protection, we deal with a much more restricted group of people. However, no matter what the primary responsibility is, and no matter what our primary constituency is, the general public has an interest in how we perform our duties.

For the sake of example, assume we are security at a factory. Our primary constituency would be the employees who work for the company, and any number of vendors, repair persons, and other visitors. However, we cannot forget the general public. The factory is located in a community, and is an integral part of that community. The community has a number of interests including health interests, financial interests, image interests, etc.

Health interests can be in the the form of working conditions within the factory which may make employees from the community sick or injured. There may be toxic smoke belching from the factory reducing air quality in the community. Either of these conditions would be of great concern to those affected by the factory, and would result in very poor public relations.

The financial interest might be in form of a paycheck for employees who live in the community, resale of the products made in the factory to members of the community, or sales of raw materials to the factory by other businesses in the community. This would be a positive impact on the community, and therefore would result in very good public relations.

As for image, if a factory is making bombs for the military, it projects a different image in a community than a factory that is making baby formula or toys for children. The community may become quite disturbed having a bomb factory in their back yard, and they may revolt. Thus, the venture of the business will have either a positive or negative image in the community that reflects directly on public relations.

No matter what the business is involved in, the security officer is many times the 'out front' person for that company, is frequently the first contact that anyone will have with the company, and therefore must pay particular attention to the topic of public relations. Based on the wide variety of responses the general public may have to your company, that first contact could be anything from very friendly to very unfriendly. Therefore, a sincere "How can I help you" must be permanently at the ready when making that first contact. Being a helper, being a pleaser, and being a "Can-Do" problem solver, are the traits of a successful public relations minded security professional.

PUBLIC RELATIONS PLANNING

In maintaining a good public image, the security officer must not only look good, and perform in a reasonable and necessary manner, but the officer must appear truly concerned, speak with a pleasant and polite voice inflection, and show respect. The officer must make the person being served feel like his or her needs are very important, and that they are about to receive superior service. Most importantly, the officer must come to the job equipped with the skills of being capable of delivering what is promised. These things are all part of a well planned public relations program.

To carry out a successful public relations program, the security department cannot do it alone. The entire parent or client organization must be involved. However, the security contingent has no control over the entire company and is not responsible for what the other departments in the company do. Security can only be responsible for their own conduct. In the area of public relations, the security contingent must conduct themselves in a planned and organized fashion, sometimes with blinders on. It would be most unfortunate if the security contingent followed bad examples set by those in other departments.

To accomplish the goal of projecting a positive image, the security contingent must first have a quality program in place. Image is meaningless if it is a false veneer. Once this is done the Ten Rules of Public Relations in Private Security can be applied:

I. The customer is not always right or wrong. Public Relations has little to do with judging others. The key words in Public Relations are "mutual need satisfaction."

While you may disagree with this from a security perspective, the most important thing to remember is to never tell the person with whom you are dealing that they are wrong. It is to the benefit of all concerned that the security officer works toward a position of mutual cooperation and prevent all situations from escalating into a win lose proposition. The person you are dealing with must be skillfully redirected into appropriate behavior, not bullied. This person must, as often as possible, leave a situation feeling that they were well served by the advice and assistance they received from the attending officer. This is not to say that issues of self-defense and defense of others will never be the case for the officer. We mean to say here that you will probably go in the "direction your nose is pointed", so keep things up-beat and positive. The officer must be a part of the solution not a part of the problem!

II.   Know your department's capabilities, as well as other department capabilities.

Successful salespersons always know their product inside and out. They are then in the position to continuously fit the product and service to the needs of the purchaser. A good security officer should be able to do the same. However, it is not good enough for the security officer to just know his or her products and services, the truly successful protection officer will know every other department's products and services as well. This will be a valuable asset in situations where a referral is required to another department. Thus, the successful public relations minded security officer will spend many hours studying the inner workings of the organization he or she is assigned to protect.

III.   Always accentuate the positive.

People don't want to hear negative things; in many cases the negative is obvious and needs no introduction. Emphasize the positive aspects of your service or the situation and you will seldom go wrong. Emphasize the negative and you'll be treated accordingly.

IV.   Image is a valuable asset.

Organizations spend considerable amounts of time and money developing and maintaining a certain image. Single negative events can destroy that image. Chronic unprofessional job behaviors can erode it. The image you project as a representative of the company you work for can, and will, help to mold the company's image. Included in the image building perspective of a security officer are the following ten qualities:[4]

1.   Be dependable
2.   Be courteous
3.   Show interest and concern
4.   Use tact
5.   Be discreet
6.   Respect confidences
7.   Be impartial
8.   Be calm
9.   Be patient
10.   Be helpful

V.   Remember that the most powerful advertising is negative customer service.

Persons who are dissatisfied with an organizations' service tell their friends and associates. Lots of them! This interpersonal message sending is very powerful. You can achieve ten great tasks of service in a day, but one cross word, one failure to satisfy someone, will be the service task remembered far into the future. You cannot afford to fail in the arena of public relations. You may not be successful in every attempt to help, but the person you were trying to serve must be convinced that you did everything possible. If you can achieve this level of success, you have not failed that person.

VI.   Be attentive to the other person's needs.

Each person has his own individual needs. Find out what they are and do what you can to address them. You may feel that this is a bit like soliciting work and you have enough to do already without asking people to, give you more. However, with a little gentle coaxing you can get a reluctant person to express what it is they are really after. Serving those needs will be very well received and a great boost to the public relations record of the department.

VII.   Never "cut someone off cold".

When someone asks for assistance or information and you aren't able to help that person immediately, ask the person to let you get back to him or her after you have researched the problem. Then do so. Ask others for assistance, do the research and solve the problem. Help that person. Remove the following phrases from your vocabulary:

* "No, we do not do that"
* "No, we cannot help you with that"
* "It is not Security's job"

VIII.   When you can help someone, do so.

Whenever possible, help others. If necessary, volunteer to help them. This can make a lasting impression. It can also be a deterrent to crime as it puts would-be criminals on notice that someone is aware of their presence and behavior. Be friendly, don't be afraid to speak with those who seem to be in need. If helping someone won't create other problems, then there is no acceptable reason for not doing so.

IX.   Have something tangible to give the person.

People like to receive things. Even if the tangible item is of little consequence, people seem to be pleased whenever you put something in their hands. Just as the salesman is able to respond to requests for literature on the product he is selling, so must the security officer have brochures, maps, phone books, or even your handwritten instructions. No good salesman would do any less, and neither should you.

X.   Have a "Can-Do" attitude.

The US Navy SEEBEES have a motto: "Can-Do." They say they can do anything given enough time, and the impossible just takes a little longer. What a great motto for your department to follow. Eliminate the words "can't do" as pointed out above, and replace them with the words, "Can Do." Whenever a person comes to you with a request, just say Yes! Then figure out how you will serve that person's needs. Pride yourself in being able to do the impossible when it comes to serving others. This does not eliminate the need for referral of some requests to other departments. However, always try to check back to see if the person received adequate service from your referral.

PROMOTING EFFECTIVE CUSTOMER RELATIONS WITHIN THE SECURITY FORCE

There are a number of steps that security supervisors can take to affect the customer relations capabilities of their subordinates.

1.   To start with, the supervisor's basic personnel management skills should be effective enough to minimize the "malcontent syndrome". Security officers should not be forced to work long hours without relief, get "shafted" out of vacations and days off, or be constantly given less than desirable assignments.

2.   Security supervisors should conduct an inspection and briefing of each shift prior to that shift going on duty, and "on stage". Security supervisors should take this opportunity whether it is done formally in groups, or informally with individual officers. This inspection should include a physical inspection of equipment, officer appearance, and officer demeanor. It should also encompass an evaluation that each officer knows what has happened on previous shifts and what is going on that day in the work site.

3.   Brief each department member on current events within the work site as well as current problems and changes in procedures. This helps to make the protection force members function as ambassadors for the organization. In addition to this daily refresher training, supervisors should make certain that the following work behaviors are adopted by all security force members during periodic staff meetings or other methods of professional development:

*   Have necessary references at the ready. These include staff directories, maps, telephone books, procedures and anything else that the person you serve is likely to inquire about.

*   Be ready and capable of responding to security problems such as fires, bomb threats, disorderly persons, and other critical incidents in a prompt and professional manner. **Developing proficiency in dealing with persons in crisis is a good investment for anyone in security.**

*   Present a professional appearance at all times. Neatness and precision should be obvious attributes of all security officers; easily seen by even the most casual observer. Alertness, openness, and concern must be radiated by posture and behavior.

*   Be prepared to do the job by having the necessary tools for the job. Always have a pen or better yet, two pens - and a small note pad to write down important notes or to give someone directions on. Never come to work without a watch, a small pocket knife, and pocket flashlight. If your job calls for other hardware such as keys, handcuffs, mace, or defensive weapons, be sure they are all in place on the utility belt, and in top operating condition.

*   Two additional pieces of equipment that project the image of security are the officer's ID card and the two-way radio. The ID card should be worn in an obvious location on the front of the uniform. Avoid using a strap around the neck to hold the card for this would place the officer in jeopardy during physical confrontations. Like-wise, the two-way radio should be worn in a holster or fastened to the belt by a belt clip. This leaves the officer's hands free.

*   The officers should be instructed to make personal introductions properly. A smile, a look in the eye, and firm handshake are all important aspects of human relations that security personnel must master. **Security personnel must be salespeople.** As representatives of management, they must sell themselves, the department, and the work site, to everyone who enters the work site.

*   Be especially attentive to the security officer's breath. They should be instructed to never ingest alcohol, garlic, tobacco, onions, or other items which might leave an offensive odor when speaking to someone. Breath mints are a necessary tool for the public relations minded security officer. Making it a rule that no one on the security team be allowed to drink alcoholic beverages 8 hours prior to a shift, and no smoking or tobacco chewing be allowed during the hours of work, will go a far way in ensuring that the officer's breath will be pleasant to be around.

*   Encourage the officers to be "professionally connected". This means that officers should complete certification programs that clearly demonstrate to other members of the parent organization, and customers alike, the officer's professional achievement. Seniority alone is not the answer to this. Neither is employment in a "previous life".

*   Aside from certification programs, the officers should belong to professional organizations for *Security* and *Safety* professionals. There should be professional literature available for officers to read; something which generally comes automatically with membership in professional organizations.

*   In addition to the above suggestions, the officers must be introspective regarding their own world views, their beliefs, fears, suspicions, biases, prejudices, and insecurities in dealing with certain categories of individuals.[5]

*   The International Chiefs' of Police Training Key 94 contains suggestions for improving the one-on-one communications, which would be greatly helpful during attempts to serve the needs of others. The following recommendations are adaptations taken from those suggestions:[6]

*   Officers should always remain polite, respectful, and sensitive to the needs of the person being served. Use empathy, not sympathy, in dealing with people. Remember that you have no more power than that of any other citizen, you are not a police officer (even sworn officers must realize that *power struggles* are unproductive). Remain detached and ignore personal insults. You are only enforcing your employers policies and procedures, they are not your policies and procedures. The insults are actually directed at your employer, not at you.

*   Be businesslike at all times. Treat the person you are interacting with the way you would want to be treated under similar circumstances. Anger, impatience, contempt, dislike, sarcasm, and similar attitudes, have no place in public relations.

*   Treat each contact as a *process*, consisting of several phases, instead of a happening. Slow everything down, and take time to evaluate the environment you are about to enter. Size things up as accurately as possible before making the contact.

*   Remember that although you intend to deliver customer satisfaction with each contact, be it conflict resolution, or simple assistance, it must be resolved within the guidelines of the civil law, criminal law, administrative law, policy, procedure, and ethics. Be sure not to stray outside these parameters.

*   Avoid arguing at all times. Never back the person you are dealing with into a corner. If the situation becomes heated, give or get space, and continue to use verbal de-escalation to defuse the situation.

*   Avoid giving the impression that your presence should be interpreted as a threat. Your demeanor should project your concern and care for the needs of the person you are interacting with. A great opening statement is **"How can I help you?"**

*   Even if the person you come in contact with is being aggressive, avoid physical contact if at all possible. Use verbal de-escalation whenever possible. If

physical contact is necessary, be sure that your physical response is in self-defense, reasonable, and necessary. Most of all, remember that your physical response may be witnessed by the general public and therefore it must look *professional*. It must appear that your are in *control*.

* You are under no obligation to disarm an assailant with a knife or a gun, or to chase down an assailant. Officer safety comes first. Instead of disarming the bad guy, or capturing the bad guy, evacuate the area, create a safety zone and keep your distance until assistance can arrive. This will look a lot more professional to the media, and will keep everyone safe.

HANDLING CUSTOMER COMPLAINTS

While constant practice of the principles of customer relations will preclude most complaints from occurring, there are still times when security officers must play the role of ambassador or diplomat. In some cases they must even act as "referees". A few points to remember about handling complaints are:

1.   Treat all complainers with respect

Every complaint or objection should be handled with respect for the complainant, no matter how absurd it is. Always treat the person with dignity. Never argue. There are no winners in an argument.

2.   Allow the complainant an opportunity to save face

Don't embarrass a person who has been abusive or mistaken. Say, "I can understand if you misunderstood, this policy is confusing" when there is misunderstanding. This rule is integral to conflict resolution, as well as situations where actual physical restraint may be necessary.

3.   Build the ego of the complainant.

Give them credit for their contribution. "You have a good point there, not many people would have thought of that", is a technique that can be applied.

4.   Show genuine courtesy and respect to the complaining party.

Be respectful and considerate to the complainant. Interview the person, and allow for venting of frustrations. Use active listening techniques to demonstrate your concern about the person's irritation and the problem.

SERVICE WHICH CAN MAKE THE DIFFERENCE

Protective service departments must be just that: service departments. Persons who wish to survive in contemporary security/safety environments must be willing and able to take on new responsibilities. In essence:

Security Only Exists For The Services It Can Provide.

Some service options that may be feasible within a security/safety department include those listed below.

Communication:
*Administration of a central operator/voice-mail system
*Whole facility intercom communication systems
*Two way intercom access controls at each perimeter door
*Use of tape dialers with sensitive equipment to enunciate system failures

*Utilization of computerized remote dial up networking for critical system diagnosis
*Emergency call stations in remote parts of the facility tied to the CCTV system
*Two-way intercoms installed near all overhead CCTV cameras

Transportation:
*Employee transport within the work site complex.
*Visitor transport within the work site complex.
*Administering the parking garage.

Risk Analysis:
A risk analysis is an detailed evaluation of identified threats, probability and criticality hypothesis, vulnerability studies, and security surveys of facilities and systems (man-made and natural crisis, critical incident response, sensitive information losses, etc.). By performing a risk analysis, the Security Department is placing itself in a consulting relationship with the parent organization. Risk analyses also help in the *loss control* effort, and pay for themselves many times over. A Risk analysis can be performed for:

*Executives/employees homes.
*Work site offices.
*Satellite facilities.
*New construction/renovation.
*Proposed property acquisitions

Training:
Training and educational services help to integrate the Security Department within the organization and make it more visible. Some options for providing training services include:

*New employee orientation
*Periodic safety/security training
*Nonviolent Crisis Intervention
*Employee college tuition reimbursement programs for security officers
*Security officer cost reimbursement programs for attainment of certifications
*Employee tuition reimbursement for security officer CEU attainment

THE MEDIA; GOOD DREAM - BAD DREAM

With respect to the media, it can be the thing you have been dreaming of, to promote the good work the security department is doing, or to send the message that your security department is not soft on crime, or to help at budget time to make your department look good, or any number of helpful messages. **In today's society, no organization can survive without positive media relations.**

If you save someone's life, intervene in an assault and arrest the bad guy, or drag someone from a burning vehicle at a crash scene just moments before the vehicle blows up, the media wants to know. They will break their necks to get to the scene and start looking for heroes to interview. They will usually arrive with the First Responders because they are out there listening to the emergency scanner frequencies.

On the other side of the ledger, if you mess up, the media can be your worst nightmare. That negative story will hit the media with bigger headlines, more repeat stories and side-bars, than anything positive you can do. The negative story will seem to last forever. From that day on, your security department will be known by that negative story line. Because bad news sells better than good news, the media's motto is that if you can't say something bad, don't say anything at all!

Regardless of the story the media finds when they arrive at the scene, if it is too bland, unexciting or lacks titillation, the media will fill the gap. They are more than willing to create filler-parts to make their stories more appealing to the general public. If you have ever been quoted by the media, you probably found that the words you said during the interview, and the words which were attributed to what you said, don't match exactly. Something has been deleted. Something has been added, and sometimes the entire quote is a fabrication. You then wonder how that can be since you spoke into a tape recorder during the interview!

Now imagine that you have an incident at your place of employment. The media shows up and the first place they stop is at the first person they see. Who would that be on most occasions? You! The security officer. You have a choice. Give them an interview or direct them to the Public Information Officer for your company. You have no other choices! Here are some ideas of what to do:

*Use your very best pubic relations skills as pointed out above.
*Be polite and give the media the number to reach the Public Information Officer (PIO)
*If they press you for a statement, be polite, and continue to refer them to the PIO
*If the PIO is on site, direct them or take them to the PIO.
*If they press you further call in your supervisor, who will repeat the above.
  *   NEVER! NEVER! NEVER! give an interview.
  *   NEVER! say: "No Comment!"
  *   NEVER! be discourteous.

Other problems with the media, that are of a security nature, can be anticipated at the scene of a critical incident. These include:[7]

1.   Access control
2.   Disruption of business operations

Access Control At The Scene Of A Critical Incident

Access control is an absolute priority at the scene of a critical incident. However, access control can set up a power struggle between security and the media. Under most circumstances and for any number of reasons, mainly safety and legal reasons, security must deny access to anyone who is not a public assistance professional; police, medical, or fire professionals. That includes the media.

The media will sometimes utilize devious means to attain a story. They may try to sneak in a back door, or simply walk in when you are not looking. They may even be involved with diverting your attention to allow a reporter to scoot in the front door. They may overwhelm you with numerous reporters attempting access at the same time on the theory that some will get through the lines. Fortunately, in most cases, after meeting a modicum of resistance, the media will back off and revert to other ways of getting the story. Once they have made contact with the PIO, the pressure is usually off the security department.

This "feeding frenzy" of reporters at the critical incident scene relates back to what we pointed out in the beginning of this unit. We told you that the public has a "right-to-know" because they have an interest in what businesses are doing in their community. The media are the keepers of that public right-to-know, and they go after the facts like salmon swimming up stream during spawning season. The key for security is to know where to draw the line on the media. However, you cannot reduce perimeter access control to appease the media. That is why it is so important that the pubic relations department of your company appoints a Public Information Officer to take the pressure off security during critical incidents.

Disruption of Business

Disruption of business operations is another area of concern for security. If the critical incident is of such a nature, like a murder or rape or other crime, the place of business is intact and continues to operate. The valuable security processes must remain intact. Patrols must be maintained, property must be protected, alarms must be responded to, restricted traffic control within the business must be maintained, etc. This is true even if the business is shut down due to a fire, explosion, or accident. That means that there must be a contingency plan to meet the needs of all types of incidence. For that purpose the company has two alternatives:

*Create a Plant Emergency Organization (PEO)
*Call in a Contract Security Contingent

Plant Emergency Organization Control

The Plant Emergency Organization (PEO) is a group of people who work in other departments who are trained to respond to emergencies. Usually a group of a dozen to two dozen individuals, scattered over all shifts, will make up the PEO. During critical incidents, this group stops what they are doing and they report immediately to a pre-determined assignment or location. This immediately expands the private security capabilities, so that both the critical incident, and the critical security procedure, continue to be serviced at the same time.

These trained PEO people, regardless of who they work for, are under the direction of the Security Director. The best candidates for this detail usually are the maintenance workers and facilities workers. However, anyone can be used in the PEO, and they sometimes take volunteers from all departments.

Contract Security Contingent Access Control

Your security department will want to identify a local contract security company to be called in during certain emergency situations. The contract security company will commit to a certain number of emergency staff, each hour, until the required number of personnel can be assembled. Special pricing will be established to ensure immediate response. For instance, during the first hour of the emergency, the contract security company will ensure that at least six security officers will respond. Another six officers will arrive within the next two hours, and the remainder of individuals required will arrive within the next three hours. At that point, three shift contingents will be set up until the emergency is over. Flexibility will be built into the plan, so that the Security Director can control the number of individuals sent by the contract security company.

With these PEO and/or Contract Security people available, they can block all the perimeter doors and set up emergency access control to help control the media. In addition, the security department will have special color coded large tags for everyone to wear during the emergency. If the employees are sent home, everyone who enters the building will have to enter through one door, and receive their special tag at that door. These tags will signify times of access and levels of access and whether or not escort is required. Large brightly colored tags with the word "MEDIA" printed on them, are reserved for use by the media, and these tags should always require escort.

Anyone found without a tag, except public service personnel, should be required to report to the main door and log in or leave the property. If the employees are not sent home, then they should be required to show a badge for access, and should be asked to remain in the building and avoid talking with the media. All employees who are also witnesses to the events surrounding the incident, should be asked to go to a debriefing room set up by security, and they should be asked to give statements of what they have witnessed. Public law enforcement may want to be in that room under certain circumstances. These witnesses should be given special instructions to keep out of the public eye until the issues are resolved. Public disclosure of information vital to the prosecution may destroy the prosecutors case.

The above described security measures are not exclusively set up to control the media. Relatives of injured parties, children, and other innocent parties may be placing themselves in danger by gaining access to an emergency scene under certain circumstances. Your job is to prevent that from happening. However, your primary responsibility is to do your job, while maintaining good public relations, and that means maintaining good relations with the media. The media must be accommodated - they need to do their job. They also must be managed so that they don't jeopardize that asset which is valuable to every organizations image.

1. Encyclopedia Americana, 1995 Edition, Vol. 22, P. 760.
2. American Heritage Dictionary of the English Language, 1973 Edition, p. 1057.
3. See Media section, this unit, below.
4. PSTN (Professional Security Television Network) "Basic Security Officer Training Series, Field Notes".
5. Hess, Karen M. and Wrobleski, Henry M. Introduction to Private Security, Fourth Edition, St. Paul, MN., West Publishing Co., 1996, p. 328.
6. Fay, John J. Encyclopedia of Security Management, Techniques & Technology, Stoneham, MA., Butterworth-Heinemann, 1993, p 592.

FOR MORE INFORMATION

International Association of Health Care Security and Safety has various publications and training/certification programs. The safety certification process is an ideal method of enhancing both image and providing additional services to the parent organization. IAHSS can be contacted at P.O. Box 637, Lombard, IL 60148 (630) 953-0990.

International Foundation for Protection Officers is a non-profit educational organization that sponsors the Certified Protection Officer (CPO), and Certified Security Supervisor (CSS) programs. The Foundation also publishes a newsletter and several short books on various topics. Associate and corporate membership opportunities also exist. IFPO's address is Bellingham Business Park, 4200 Meridian, Suite 200, Bellingham, WA. 98226 (360) 733-1571 or http://www.ifpo.com.

Powerphone, Inc. is a leading company in telephone answering and dispatching. They offer seminars and manuals. Their address is P.O. Box 1911 Madison, CT. 06443-0900 (800)53-Power, chris@powerphone.com or visit http://www.powerphone.com.

Professional Security Television Network (PSTN) produces a wide variety of videos dealing with public relations and related issues. Their address is, 1303 Marsh Lane, Carrolton, TX. 75006 (800) 942-7786 or (214) 417-4302.

"Public Relations" is a course that is offered on campus, and at client locations, by the Special Programs Office, York College of PA, Country Club Road, York, PA 17405-7199 (717) 846-7788, fax (717) 849-1607; bpavlick@ycp.edu or visit http://www.ycp.edu/.

QUIZ
Public Relations

1.   Public Relations consists of _____ understanding between an organization and its constituent publics.

2.   The key words in Public Relations are: "_____ need _____ ".

3.   All of the following should be carried by protection officers except:
A.   Small pocket knife
B.   Duct tape
C.   Two Pens
D.   A watch

4.   "Never _____ someone off _____ ".

5.   Volunteering to help someone is good PR and can be an effective _____ to crime.

6.   The "out front" person for the organization is usually the:
A.   Public Information Officer
B.   Protection Officer
C.   Maintenance Worker
D.   Human Resource Manager

7.   If protection officers are pressed for a statement by a media representative, they can respond "off the record".
☐ T   ☐ F

8.   Each contact with another person should be thought of as a _____ consisting of phases, rather than a happening.

9.   A risk analysis is an informal appraisal of physical security measures.
☐ T   ☐ F

10.   The Security Department must first have a _____ _____ program in place before a public relations effort can be launched.

POLICE AND SECURITY LIAISON

By Johnny May, CPP, CPO

For years the security industry has been negatively stereotyped. A 1971 study, conducted by the Rand Corporation, described the typical private security guard as an aging white male, who was poorly educated and poorly paid. The average age was between 40-55, with little education beyond the ninth grade. The Rand researchers further reported: "The fact is, the average security guard in this country is underscreened, undertrained, undersupervised, and underpaid."

This negative stereotype has followed us into the 21st century. Let's take a look at some recent incidents which have made the media:

* At the Republican National Convention in San Diego, a security guard stole 16 TVs from NBC. The officer, who pleaded guilty, was wanted in another burglary before he was hired.

* Three security guards were arrested at Simon Fraser University in Vancouver, Canada, for selling some computers and athletic clothing.

* The Whitney Museum of Art in New York was involved in a lawsuit because the security guard wrote "I love you Tushee" and "love buns" on a borrowed painting worth more than $1.5 million.

* A female executive of Saks Fifth Avenue is suing the company for $50 million. She was raped in 1994 by a store guard. A pre-employment background check on the guard failed to turn up his 1989 conviction for the sexual assault of an 11 year old girl in Kentucky. The guard is serving 1 1/2 to 4 years in prison.

The sad reality is that yes, these types of incidents sometime occur in our industry, but why don't heroic deeds by security professionals get the media's attention? Chris Hertig refers to private security as "The Invisible Empire" of the criminal justice system, and the security officers are referred to as the "Forgotten Soldiers" of this invisible empire.

In a recent USA Today article (On Guard: Bad Guys Behind the Badge of Honor: All companies are looking for is a warm body in a uniform, September 12, 1996.) Robert McCrie, editor of Security Letter, said "heroic deeds by security officers don't get media play. There are scores, thousands of noble, self-sacrificing security officers, including some who have rescued people from flaming buildings before the fire department arrived," he said.

One example is Brandon Ford of First Security Services, who received the prestigious Brownyard Award in Atlanta, GA, for going above and beyond the call of duty. Ford tackled a man who was shooting a male nurse outside of a hospital in New Haven, CT. Ford who was on duty, likely saved the nurse's life. "I was just doing my job," Ford said. The perception that security officers are merely rent-a-cops, with very little education and training, has greatly hampered the relationship between law

enforcement and private security personnel. In 1976, the Private Security Advisory council, through the U.S. Department of Justice, identified two main factors which contributed to poor relationships between law enforcement and private security: 1) their inability to clarify role definitions and 2) they often practiced stereotyping. The Council cited various areas of conflict and ranked them in order of importance.

1) Lack of mutual respect
2) Lack of communication
3) Lack of cooperation
4) Lack of law enforcement's knowledge of private security
5) Perceived competition
6) Lack of standards
7) Perceived corruption

In the early 1980's, relationships between law enforcement and private security were rated fair to good, at best, by law enforcement executives. Research has confirmed that longstanding obstacles to interaction and cooperation between law enforcement and private security continues to exist.

One step for change is to have both law enforcement and private security personnel understand the differences between the two professions.

Law Enforcement	Private Security
Apprehension/Enforcement	Loss Prevention/Asset Protection
Prosecution	General Services
Reactive	Proactive
Protect a society	Protect an organization

Another way to bridge this gap is to find common ground between the two professions. That common ground for interaction between law enforcement and private security, is crime. The following are several functions which both professions perform:

* Personal Safety - The private sector has a responsibility to ensure the safety of its employees, clients, and anyone else with whom it comes in contact. Local law enforcement is responsible for the safety of the general public.

* Crime Prevention - Both professions have obligation to develop crime prevention programs. Most police departments have acknowledged that it is better to prevent criminal behavior than to combat it after the fact. A large number of metropolitan police departments now maintain a crime prevention unit within the department.

* Order Maintenance - The police are responsible for maintaining public order. In areas maintained by private industry, the job of order maintenance is the responsibility of private security.

Liaison plays an important role in our day to day functions as security professionals. In fact, the (CPP) Certified Protection Professional examination, which is administered by the American Society for Industrial Security, dedicates 5% of the examination to liaison.

According to the Hallcrest Report II, Private Security Trends (1970-2000), private security is America's primary protective resource in terms of spending and employment.

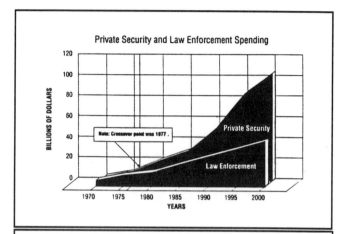

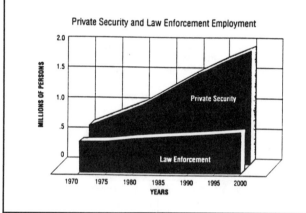

By the year 2000 security officers will outnumber law enforcement officers 3 to 1. Private security currently employes almost 1.5 million people, with annual expenditures of $52 billion. By comparison, roughly 600,000 people work in Federal, State, and local public law enforcement, and expenditures for those services are roughly $30 billion. Among the major findings of the report are:

* The increasing growth of private security, and the limited growth of public law enforcement, are due to 4 main factors:

1)   increasing workplace crime
2)   increasing fear of crime
3)   a decreasing rate of spending for public protection
4)   increasing awareness and use of private security effective protective measures.

* The cost of economic crime in 1990 was estimated at $114 billion. At 2% or more of the gross national product, economic crime is out of control and on the rise.

* Private security personnel are younger and better educated than they used to be. The number of academic security programs has grown significantly, from only 33 certificate and degree programs in the mid 1970's, to 164

such programs in operation currently. Furthermore, employment in private security is projected to grow at 2.3% annually to the year 2000. The U.S. Department of Labor predicts that the national workforce will grow by a little more than half of that projected figure.

Privatization is the trend for the 1990's! For some time, there has been a shift in service industries toward assuming duties once left to government. In 1990 the Mercer Group, an Atlanta, Georgia, based research firm that tracks privatization of services, conducted a survey which revealed that roughly 33% of respondents, comprised of local and municipal governments, special districts, and homeowner associations, contract security services to augment law enforcement.

According to James Mercer, president of the Mercer Group, "the basic reason is that the government can't afford to have a sworn officer with all the fringe benefits that come with that appointment - not when they can hire a security officer for a lot less money".

Private Security and Police in America: The Hallcrest Report, published in 1985 by the National Institute of Justice, Washington, DC, found that law enforcement officials, proprietary security managers, and contract security managers, agreed on the transfer of certain police related activities to private security. Those activities were burglar alarm responses, preliminary investigations, incident reports when victims decline prosecution, certain misdemeanor incident reports, and transporting people taken in citizens arrest. A number of these activities are already being handled by private security in many areas of the United States.

There appears to be a growing potential for contracting private security to perform the following activities:

*Courtroom Security
*Executive Protection
*Parking Lot Security
*Parking Enforcement
*Traffic Control
*Housing Project Patrol
*Special Event Security
*Public Building Security

In Michigan, a large number of shopping malls and hospitals have opted to employ their own security police under what is known as Public Act 330 (see appendix #2). Public Act 330 is regulated by the Michigan State Police, and gives the security officers arrest powers while on duty at their establishment.

Listed below are some general recommendations for improving the working relationship between Police and Security personnel:

*Establish credibility with local law enforcement - Only contact the police: 1) when you have information to exchange; 2) to have someone arrested; or, 3) when there is an immediate danger or need for additional manpower. Knowledge of local codes assists in the arrest process, and helps the security officer testify more effectively in court.

* Establish and/or follow a code of ethics - Security personnel should realize that those individuals who are unethical do not have rewarding careers. They are snubbed by colleagues and superiors, passed over for promotions, and terminated from employment in the more serious cases. The most extreme cases result in revocation of licenses the officer may possess, and/or civil/criminal liability. The International Foundation for Protection Officers Code of Ethics are as follows:

I. Respond to employer's professional needs.
II. Exhibit exemplary conduct.
III. Protect confidential information
IV. Maintain a safe and secure workplace.
V. Dress to create professionalism.
VI. Enforce all rules and regulations
VII. Encourage liaison with police officers
VIII. Develop good rapport within the profession.
IX. Strive to attain professional competence.
X. Encourage high standards of officer ethics.

* Always maintain the highest level of professionalism. In our society we are judged by how we look, what we say, and the manner in which we perform our job (eg. uniforms should be clean, pressed, and properly worn. Written reports should be neat and detailed, use of proper English is recommended, and always be courteous.)

* Increase police knowledge of private security. This can be accomplished through shared training programs or seminars which explain the role of private security to law enforcement personnel. A one hour lecture, at the local police academy by security professionals, is one example. In Michigan, the Detroit Police Department's Crime Prevention Section, and the Detroit Chapter of ASIS cosponsor an annual professional development seminar, entitled "Update", which focuses on current trends and topics, which are of interest to both sectors. One of the primary aspects of the seminar is the cooperation displayed between the two sectors in the development, planning and coordination of the seminar. The law enforcement and security attendees network among themselves to form new relationships, and to share common problems and work out mutual approaches and solutions.

* Support licensing and regulation of security officers as a mechanism to upgrade private security.
* Law enforcement agencies should appoint private security liaison officers within the department for problem resolution, and information exchange with private security personnel.
* Establish Mutual Assistance Agreements between security and law enforcement personnel.
* Develop and/or attend cooperative programs. Beginning in the mid 1980's, cooperative programs between the private and public sectors have emerged at a faster pace than ever before. This creates the opportunity for valuable information exchange, and builds long lasting working relationships. One of the earliest cooperative programs, PRIDE (Pooling Resources in Defense of our Environment), was established in Southfield, Michigan (1981), by Southfield Police Department, to regularly exchange crime-related information, to integrate protective services wherever possible, and to form a better working relationship between the police and private security. Another model cooperative program is the (APPL) Area Police Private Security Liaison. APPL was established in Manhattan, New York (1986), to enhance public/private cooperation in protecting people and property, to exchange information, and to help eliminate the "credibility gap" between police and private security.
* Nurture professional growth and development - Get all the education, certifications and specialized training that you can. One can never learn or know too much. Life is a learning process. Stay abreast of current trends and technologies (see appendix #1 and #3)

The key to maintaining a good working relationship with law enforcement personnel is to maintain a good public perception. Public perception plays a very important part in our day to day operations as security professionals. We must constantly work to improve our image. We must act as professionals if we ever expect to be accepted as such.

Appendix 1

Academic Programs (Colleges which offer degree/courses in Security)

York College of Pennsylvania
Country Club Road
York, PA. 17405-7199
(717) 846-7788

Southern Illinois University
Woody Hall
Carbondale, IL. 62901
(618) 453-5701

Northeastern University
360 Huntington Avenue
Boston, MA. 02115
(617) 437-2200

University of Detroit-Mercy
4001 W. McNichols
Detroit, MI. 48219
(313) 993-1245

John Jay College of Criminal Justice
899-10th Avenue
New York, NY. 10019
(212) 237-8638

Wartburg College
222 Ninth Street, NW
Waverly, IA. 50677
(319) 352-8200

Henry Ford Community College
5101 Evergreen
Dearborn, MI. 48128-1495
(313) 845-9856

Indiana State University
Holmstead Hall, Room 208
Terre Haunte, IN. 47809
(812) 237-2192

Michigan State University
560 Baker Hall
East Lansing, MI. 48824-1118
(517) 355-2192

Missouri Southern State College
3950 Newman Road
Joplin, MO. 64801-1595
(417) 625-9651

Southern Vermont College
Monument Avenue
Bennington, VA. 05201
(802) 442-5427

*Webster University
470 E. Lockwood Avenue
St. Louis, MO. 63119-3194
(314) 968-7000

University of New Haven
300 Orange Avenue
West Haven, CT. 06516
(203) 932-7369

Eastern Kentucky University
253 Stratton
Richmond, KY. 40475
(606) 622-1976

Central Missouri State University
305 Humphrey
Warrensburg, MO. 64093
(816) 543-4616

St. John's University
Grand Central & Utopia Pkwys
Jamaica, NY. 11439
(718) 990-6161

Pennsylvania State University
Fayette Campus, P.O. Box 519
Uniontown, PA. 15401
(412) 430-4232

*City University
919 W. Grady Way
Renton, WA. 98055
(800) 422-4898

*Correspondence Degrees

Appendix 2

MINIMUM TRAINING CURRICULUM FOR PRIVATE SECURITY POLICE
The curriculum herein described is the minimum basic training required for private security guards to which Act 330, PA 1968, as amended, the Private Security Guard Act, is applicable.

SUBJECT	HOURS	EXAMINATION
Regular Training Requirements		
Exemptions from Regular Requirements		
INITIAL ORIENTATION	2	Required
Initial Orientation	1	Required
Professional Responsibility		
Human Relations and Police Liaison	1	Required
LEGAL SECTION OBJECTIVES	38	
Consitutional Law	1	Required
Roots of American Jursiprudence	1	Required
Courts	1	Required
Arrest Procedures	4	Required
Criminal Procedures	9	Required
Admissions and Confessions		
Search and Seizure		
Evidence	2	Required
Criminal Law	10	Required
Juvenile Law	4	Required
Civil Liability	4	Required
Cultural Diversity	4	Optional
SPECIAL CURRICULUM	53	
Firearms Proficiency	24	Required
Pressure Point Control/Defensive Tactics	24	Required
Bloodborne Pathogens/Hepatitis B	1	Required
Risk Management	2	Required
Narcotics and Dangerous Drugs	2	Optional
CRITICAL INCIDENT CURRICULUM	13	
CPR	8	Required
Fire Extinguisher Use	1	Required
Non-Violent Crisis Intervention	2	Required
Emergency Preparedness	2	Required
PATROL OPERATIONS CURRICULUM	14	
Report Writing	8	Required
Crime Scene Investigation and Witness Interview	2	Required
Radio Communication and Civil Disorder	1	Required
Access Control Systems	2	Required
Crime Prevention	1	Required
MAINTENANCE CURRICULUM SECTION	20 (16)	Required

REFERENCES

Cunningham, Strauch and Van Meter, Private Security Trends: 1970-1000. The Hallcrest Report II, Butterworth-Heinemann 1990.

Cunningham, William and Taylor, Todd, The Hallcrest Report: Private Security and Police in America, McLean, VA; Chancellor Press, 1985.

Fay, John J. Encyclopedia of Security Management, Stoneham, MA. Butterworth-Heinemann, 1993

Hertig, Christopher "Liaison with Law Enforcement: Security Officers Should Only Call When," Protection Officer, July-September 1988.

Hertig, Christopher "Who are the Forgotten Soldiers?", Security Management, February 1993.

Nemeth, Charles P. Private Security and the Law. Cincinatti, OH: Anderson Publishing, 1989.

Newborn, Ellen and Jones, Del. "On Guard: Bad Guys behind Badge of Honor: All companies are looking for is a warm body in a uniform," USA Today, September 12, 1996.

Ortmeier P.J. "Adding Class to Security", Security Management, July 1996.

Appendix 3

Professional Certification Programs

(CPO) Certified Protection Officer
(CSS) Certified Security Supervisor
International Foundation for Protection Officers
Bellingham Business Park, 4200 Meridian, Suite 200
Bellingham, WA. 98226
(360) 733-1571

(CST) Certified Security Trainer
ASET Secretariat
Route 2, Box 3644
Berryville, VA. 22611
(703) 955-1129

(CSP) Certified Safety Professional
Board of Certified Safety Professionals
208 Burwash Avenue
Savoy, IL. 61874-9571
(217) 359-9263

(CFE) Certified Fraud Examiner
Association of Certified Fraud Examiners
716 West Avenue
Austin, TX. 78701
(800) 245-3321

(CHPA) Certified Healthcare Protection Administrator
International Association for Healthcare Security and Safety
P.O. Box 637
Lombard, IL.
60148
(708) 953-0990

(CPP) Certified Protection Professional
American Society for Industrial Security
1655 North Fort Meyer Drive, Suite 1200
Arlington, VA. 22209-3198
(703) 522-5800

(PPS) Personal Protection Specialist
Executive Protection Institute
Arcadia Manor, Route 2, Box 3645
Berryville, VA. 22611
(540) 955-1129

(CFSP) Certified Fire Protection Specialist
EMACS
P.O. Box 198
Ashland, MA. 01721
(508) 881-6044

(CDRP) Certified Disaster Recovery Professional
Disaster Recovery Institute
1818 Craig Road, Suite 125
St. Louis, MO. 63146
(314) 434-2272

The IAHS also offers certification programs for security officers. They offer a 40 hour basic Security Officer certification, a 20 hour Supervisory certification, and a 20 hour Safety certification. All 3 programs can be utilized in a self-directed (home study) program.

QUIZ
Police and Security Liaison

1.   A 1971 study conducted by the Rand Corporation described the typical private security personnel as _____, _____ and_____(fill in the blanks)

2.   The common ground for interaction between law enforcement and private security resources is:
A)   Education
B)   Patriotism
C)   Career Development
D)   Crime

3.   In the early 1980's, relationships between law enforcement and private security were rated _____by law enforcement executives.
A)   Fair to good
B)   Excellent
C)   Extremely bad
D)   Very good

4.   Hallcrest Report II found that private security personnel are younger and better educated now, than they used to be.
   ☐ T   ☐ F
5.   Cooperative Programs between the private and public sectors are on the decline.
   ☐ T   ☐ F

6.   Law enforcement expenditures far exceed those of private security.
   ☐ T   ☐ F
7.   Private security and law enforcement both perform the following functions:_____, _____ and _____.
8.   The key to maintaining a good working relationship with law enforcement personnel is to _____ .
9.   By the year 2000, private security personnel are expected to outnumber law enforcement personnel by a ratio of:
A)   2 to 1
B)   3 to 1
C)   4 to 1
D)   5 to 1
10. According to Hallcrest II, American Business losses were estimated at:
A) $114 billion
B) $53 billion
C) $241 billion
D) $16 billion

ETHICS AND PROFESSIONALISM

By Christopher A. Hertig, CPP, CPO

The business realities of contemporary management require that security (asset protection) efforts provide protection for **ALL** of an organization's assets, including people, property, information, and image. Asset protection should incorporate Bottom and Kostanoski's WAECUP Model in order to address these concerns. This Model asserts that losses stem from Waste, Accident, Error, Crime, and Unethical/Unprofessional Practices. Under Unethical/Unprofessional practice are dissemination of confidential information, lying to clients, discrimination, profanity in public, poor relations with law enforcement and other security organizations, and slovenly dress. Most of this loss relates to negative public/client image. Additionally, within organizations that are stricken by a serious scandal, there are legal costs, increased personnel turnover, and lowered efficiency by a demoralized workforce.

An additional concern regarding ethics and professionalism is the role that protection officers play for the public at large. As protection officers increase in number and take on an increasing array of functions which place them in contact with the public; it becomes readily apparent that there is an acute need for higher standards of professionalism. Consider the following trends:

* A steady increase in the number of security personnel, particularly in the contract service sector.

* More contact with the public-contemporary protection officers is more commonly found in shopping centers, office buildings, and parks, than in the warehouses and industrial facilities guarded by their predecessors.

* Gradual - yet often unrecognized - assumption of duties formerly performed by public entities, such as maintaining order at special events, transporting prisoners, and responding to alarms (privatization).

Obviously, the role played by security officers is changing! When one looks at future trends (see PRIVATE SECURITY TRENDS: 1970-2000 by Cunningham, Strauchs and Van Meter, Butterworth-Heinemann) it becomes apparent that:

The greatest issue in *public* safety is *private* security.

From a personal perspective, officers should realize that those individuals who are unethical and unprofessional do not have rewarding careers. They are snubbed by colleagues and superiors, passed over for promotion, and terminated from employment in the more serious cases. The most extreme cases result in revocation of licenses that the officer may possess, and civil and criminal liability.

Those who make the wrong choices do not last.

Protection officers must be equipped with the decision-making skills and professional knowledge to make the right choices. For too long words like "professional" have been used indiscriminately without a complete examination of their meaning. Understanding what the terms represent is a necessary step towards adopting and implementing professional behavior!

Key Terms and Concepts

Ethics: the study of good and bad conduct within a profession. Ethics deals with the examination of moral philosophy combined with the duties and obligations within a certain profession. Ethical behavior results when the correct ethical decisions have been made and carried out. The International Foundation for Protection Officers Code of Ethics is:

I.	Respond to employer's professional needs.
II.	Exhibit exemplary conduct.
III.	Protect confidential information.
IV.	Maintain a safe and secure workplace.
V.	Dress to create professionalism.
VI.	Enforce all lawful rules and regulations.
VII.	Encourage liaison with public officers.
VIII.	Develop good rapport within the profession.
IX.	Strive to attain professional competence.
X.	Encourage high standards of officer ethics.

Duty: a professional obligation to do a certain thing. Protection officers have a duty to protect the lives and property of employees, conduct professional investigations, maintain order and assist visitors/employees/customers. Duties may be established by statute, custom, or contract.

Professionals think in terms of their duties and obligations, *not* their authority!

Professional: One who practices a profession. One who has special knowledge and skill which results from advanced training and education. Often an apprenticeship is required, such as the experience qualifications necessary for professional certification (Certified Protection Officer, Certified Security Supervisor, Certified Protection Professional etc.). Professions have professional codes of ethics, and professional organizations which members belong to. A professional is loyal to his or her chosen profession. A true professional has the following:

1. Education relating to the profession.
2. Training for the tasks and duties that must be performed.
3. Experience within the profession.
4. A *commitment* to the profession marked by continuously striving for excellence.

The acronym **"PROFESSIONAL"** outlines the attributes of a professional:

P	-	precise, exact, detailed
R	-	responsive to clients and the public
O	-	objective in thought; free of prejudice and preconceived notions
F	-	factual in all reporting processes; honest

E   -   ethical
S   -   sincere about doing the best job possible
S   -   striving for perfection by trying to constantly improve one's job performance
I   -   informed about events and trends within one's profession
O   -   observant of people and the work environment
N   -   neat and orderly in dress and work
A   -   accommodating and helpful to others
L   -   loyal to one's employer, clients and profession

DEPORTMENT: How one carries oneself. Bearing. Outward manifestation of attitude and image. A few things to bear in mind about deportment are:

* Dress should be neat, precise and conservative.
* Shoes should match belt.
* No purses for women.
* Socks should always match the pants and cover the calf.
* Conservative ties, properly tied; silk is a good choice of material.
* Jewelry worn judiciously!
* "Less is more" with makeup and cologne.
* Uniforms should be worn uniformly. All officers should have the same placement of insignia and equipment.

The acronym **"DEPORTMENT"** provides additional insight into the meaning - and practical application - of the term:

D   -   dress as a representative of your employer and/or client.
E   -   efficient in performing both routine and emergency job duties.
P   -   precision. Ironed shirts, neatly combed hair, all buttons, zippers, and pins properly secured.
O   -   organized on the job.
R   -   responsive to customers, clients, visitors, and community members; approachable.
T   -   talk as a professional does, using proper English.
M   -   manners - respect for others - exhibited at all times.
E   -   edit and review interviews and notes before concluding these segments of an investigation.
N   -   nurture professional growth and development at all times. Strive to learn!
T   -   timely. Being on time is essential. "Fashionably late" is out of style in professional settings.

Manners: Manners are simply accepted means of conducting oneself in public. Politeness. They consist of *consideration* and *respect* for others. They are *social graces*. A few basic tenets of proper manners are:

* Allow people to talk and express their views; DO NOT INTERRUPT - not only is this good manners, it is effective interviewing - and the truly professional protection officer makes every conversation an interview.
* Be respectful of people's input. *Compliment rather than criticize.*
* Praise others when appropriate. **Be genuine in doing this.**
* Stand up to greet people entering the room - especially a women, client or VIP. This is a show of respect and consideration. It is an opportunity to create a personal bond that no true professional can afford to pass up.

Ethical Decision Making
Protection officers must be equipped with the ability

to make *professional judgements.* They need to be proficient at decision making as it applies to ethics. Basic **decision making** consists of **problem solving.** Problem solving consists of the following steps:

1. Problem identification. There should be a descriptive definition of the problem. Inadequate problem definition often results in poor decisions being made.
2. Determination if a decision needs to be made immediately or if it can wait.
3. Research among the various options that are available - *many poor decisions stem from a failure to fully explore all of the options.* Professional knowledge of law, technology and organizational structure/chain of command is important in understanding all of the options.
4. Choosing an option. Pick that one which seems best.
5. Implementing the decision. Put it into effect.
6. Evaluating the decision and following it up. This means seeing how it works and reporting/documenting it. Keeping superiors informed is always important! Soliciting feedback from them is essential.

A practical, 'real world' method of dealing with ethical dilemmas can make use of simple, easy to remember acronyms. Once the problem has been identified, the ethical dilemma can be managed by use of the **PORT** acronym:

P   -   problem - define and describe it. If possible write a sentence or two describing it.
O   -   options - what are they? Be sure to list all of them.
R   -   responsibilities to employers, family, the public, the profession, etc.
T   -   time; the test of - "How will I feel about my decision in 20 years?"

Ethical decision making must be real. It must exist in everyday work situations. Using the PORT acronym can help to maintain ethical conduct by protection professionals.

WHY UNETHICAL BEHAVIOR OCCURS
It is important to understand why unethical and unprofessional behavior occurs so that it can be prevented. Some of the more common causes of ethical lapses are:

* Protection officers - or any other person in a position of trust - must possess good character. As past behavior is the most reliable indicator of future behavior, it is necessary to do a check of prior employment. There can be no substitute for screening!
* Taking the 'path of least resistance'. This is human nature. Unfortunately, doing what is easy does not always solve the problem. Taking a 'short cut' usually means *problem avoidance* where the person confronting the dilemma just hopes the problem will either go away or solve itself. It won't! Avoiding the problem almost always causes the problem to become larger and more damaging over time.
* Conflict with full-time and part-time employment. The practice of 'moonlighting', with its inherent division of loyalties between the full and part-time employers, can create a breeding ground for unethical conduct.
* Fatigue. People often make the wrong choices simply because they are tired. Fatigue and stress impede good decision making. This can set up a vicious cycle where poor decisions are made and more stress is the result!
* "Traditionalism" and a resistance to change. Just because protection officers haven't been trained in first-aid and CPR doesn't mean that the practice should continue! Just because protection officers have not had a full and complete orientation to the organization they are protecting, does not mean that this should remain as standard practice. A pertinent example of "Traditionalism" is the practice of

handcuffing.   Handcuffs are rarely double-locked. Not doing so can cause the cuffs to cinch tightly on the subject's wrist which may result in permanent nerve damage.   Another example is traffic control.   Many organizations do not train their officers to direct and control traffic, in spite of the fact that this is a key safety issue, not to mention a crucial juncture in public relations!

REFERENCES

Black, H.C. (1990).   BLACK'S LAW DICTIONARY.   St. Paul, MN.

Fulton, R. (1993). "How to Stay on the Team" in Nowicki, E. (Ed.) TOTAL SURVIVAL.   Powers Lake, WI: Performance Dimensions Publishing.

Hertig, C.A. (1993). PROTECTION OFFICER GUIDEBOOK.   Bellingham, WA; International Foundation for Protection Officers.

Hoffman, T.W. (1996).   DUTIES AND RESPONSIBILITIES FOR NEW YORK STATE SECURITY OFFICERS. Flushing, NY: Looseleaf Law Publications.

Merriam, G. & C. Co. (1972). WEBSTER'S SEVENTH NEW COLLEGIATE DICTIONARY.   Springfield, MA: G & C Merriam.

Minion, R.R. (1992). PROTECTION OFFICER TRAINING MANUAL. Stoneham, MA: Butterworth-Heinemann.

Pollock, J.M. (1994).   ETHICS IN CRIME AND JUSTICE: DILEMMAS AND DECISIONS.   Belmont, CA: Wadsworth.

Tasks Force on Private Security (1976). REPORT OF THE TASK FORCE ON PRIVATE SECURITY. Washington, DC: Law Enforcement Assistance Administration.

Trautman, N.E. (1993).   "Dealing with Attitude Anger, Lust and Greed" in Nowicki, E. (Ed.) TOTAL SURVIVAL. Power Lake, WI: Performance Dimensions.

Walters, R.W. (1984). EXECUTIVE GUIDE TO BEHAVIORAL SCIENCES TERMINOLOGY, Mahwah, NJ: Roy J. Walters and Associates.

FOR MORE INFORMATION

INTERNATIONAL FOUNDATION FOR PROTECTION OFFICERS (360)733-1571 or http://www.ifpo.com publishes ETHICAL DECISION MAKING as well as a newsletter entitled PROTECTION NEWS.   The Foundation web site is also tied in with other sources, providing an extensive array of current security information.

NATIONAL INSTITUTE OF ETHICS (407)399-0322 sponsors workshops on ethics and related aspects of professionalism throughout North America.

QUIZ
Ethics and Professionalism

1.   List three reasons why ethics and professionalism are important to the employer, public, and individual officer.
A)_____
B)_____
C)_____

2.   Complete the acronym "PROFESSIONAL".
P_____
R_____
O_____
F_____
E_____
S_____
S_____
I_____
O_____
N_____
A_____
L_____

3.   List five steps that can be taken to enhance one's professional development.
A._____
B._____
C._____
D._____
E._____

4.   List three methods by which the protection officer can dress to create professionalism.
A._____
B._____
C._____

5.   When looking at the increasing role of private security personnel in contemporary society, it becomes apparent that the biggest issue in _____safety is _____security.

6.   List three reasons for unethical conduct.
A._____
B._____
C._____

7.   List three common errors in decision-making.
A._____
B._____
C._____

8.   Professionals think in terms of their _____and _____rather than their authority.

9.   A true professional has the following:
A._____relating to the profession.
B._____for the tasks and duties that must be performed.
C._____within the profession.
D.A_____to the _____and continuous striving for excellence.

10.   Fill in the blanks of the PORT Model of ethical decision making. List a question that needs to be addressed in each of the letters of the acronym.
P_____
O_____
R_____
T_____

APPENDIX

BASIC KEY CONTROL
FOR ALL LEVELS OF SECURITY

By Cecelia Sharp

Prior to setting up a Masterkey system:

1) Consult all levels of management and the different operations within the organization.
2) Review the blueprints (if applicable) or draft plans of the area or buildings.
3) Determine future requirements or operations expansion.
4) Define the level of protection or security required.
(see Basic Key Control Chart below)

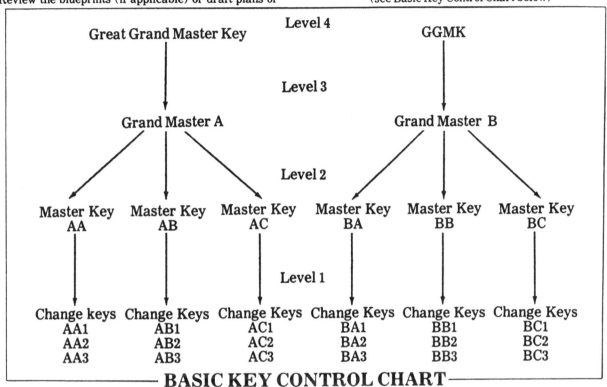

— BASIC KEY CONTROL CHART —

PATROL PREPARATION

Equipment (Foot Patrols)
- Flashlight
- Hand-held Radio
- Pen - Notebook
- Whistle (if required)
- S.O. ID
- Keys
- Access Cards, Combinations

Equipment (Mobile Patrols)
- All Previous (Foot Patrol)
- First Aid Kit
- Fire Extinguishers
- Auxiliary Lights - Flares
- Radio Communications
- Flashers - Spot Lights
- Camera

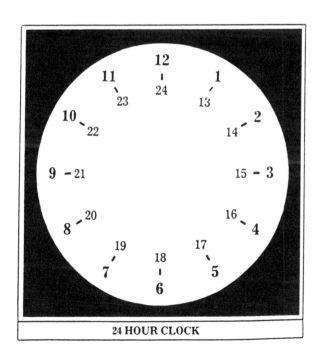

24 HOUR CLOCK

RADIO TEN CODES

The use of hand-held, portable radios, radio telephones and other forms of mobile communications are often an integral part of the protection officer's role. While codes and related messages may vary, the following is a generally acceptable guide for security personnel. The purpose of coded radio messages is to enhance and improve confidentiality.

10-3	Repeat
10-4	O.K. - Will Comply
10-5	Stand By
10-6	Busy - Will call
10-7	Out of service (location - time)
10-8	In Service
10-10	Continuing Patrol
10-11	Returning to Office
10-12	Will telephone
10-20	Your location please
10-30	Ready for Assignment
10-70	Message for all cars
Mayday	Emergency

PHONETIC ALPHABET

As in the case of Radio codes, the phonetic alphabet is not always identical in all security organizations. It is essential that all members of a particular department are conversant with the letters and accompanying words that are utilized. The following list is a generally used and accepted method of attaining greater clarity in transmitting messages by radio or telephone.

PHONETIC ALPHABET

A	Alfa	N	November
B	Bravo	O	Oscar
C	Charlie	P	Papa
D	Delta	Q	Quebec
E	Echo	R	Romeo
F	Foxtrot	S	Sierra
G	Golf	T	Tango
H	Hotel	U	Uniform
I	India	V	Victor
J	Juliet	W	Whiskey
K	Kilo	X	X-ray
L	Lima	Y	Yankee
M	Mike	Z	Zulu

INDEX

Also from Butterworth-Heinemann

The Art of Successful Security Management by Dennis R. Dalton
1997   312pp   hc   0-7506-9729-6

Encyclopedia of Security Management: Techniques and Terminology Edited by John J. Fay
1993   450pp   pb   0-7506-9660-5

The Executive Protection Professional's Manual by Philip T. Holder and Donna Lea Hawley
1997   168pp   pb   0-7506-9868-3

Guard Force Management by Lucien G. Canton
1995   144pp   hc   0-7506-9299-5

Handbook of Loss Prevention and Crime Prevention, Third Edition Edited by Lawrence J. Fennelly
1995   640pp   hc   0-7506-9703-2

Instructor Development Training: A Guide for Security and Law Enforcement
by Sandi J. Davies and Ronald R. Minion
1995   192pp   hc   0-7506-9632-X

Security Consulting, Second Edition by Charles A. Sennewald
1995   192pp   pb   0-7506-9643-5

The Ultimate Security Survey by James L. Schaub and Ken D. Biery, Jr.
1994   256pp   pb(with 3.5" disk)   0-7506-9577-3

Workplace Violence by Sandra L. Heskett
1996   210pp   hc   0-7506-9671-0

Detailed information on these and all other BH-Security titles may be found in the BH-Security catalog(Item #800). To request a copy, call 1-800-366-2665. You can also visit our web site at: http://www.bh.com

These books are available from all good bookstores or in case of difficulty call: 1-800-366-2665 in the U.S. or +44-1865-310366 in Europe.

E-Mail Mailing List
An e-mail mailing list giving information on latest releases, special promotions/offers and other news relating to BH-Security titles is available. To subscribe, send an e-mail message to majordomo@world.std.com. Include in message body (not in subject line) subscribe bh-security